Annotated Bibliographies of
Old and Middle English Literature

VOLUME IV

OLD ENGLISH PROSE OF SECULAR LEARNING

The annotations of this volume cover the prose proverbs, dialogues, and romances, the computistical texts and Byrhtferth's *Enchiridion*, as well as the magico-medical literature and associated texts (including the prognostics and the lapidary). The summaries of the scholarship which accompany the annotations highlight the opportunities for further research in this field. The summaries also draw attention to changing attitudes on the part of scholars to the Anglo-Saxon past. Particular attention is given in this volume to publications which appeared before 1970, since *Old English Newsletter* has carried annual reviews of scholarship from 1967 onwards. The *terminus ad quem* is 1989; two items of later date which are of particular interest are also included. The compilers are conscious that interdisciplinary research, rather than a narrowly text-based approach, is appropriate to the study of the corpus, and have included information on studies which assist in the contextualization of the secular prose literature.

Annotated Bibliographies of
Old and Middle English Literature

General Editor: T. L. Burton

Editorial Assistants:
Sabina Flanagan and Rosemary Greentree

Annotated Bibliographies of
Old and Middle English Literature

VOLUME IV

OLD ENGLISH PROSE OF
SECULAR LEARNING

STEPHANIE HOLLIS

AND

MICHAEL WRIGHT

with the assistance of
Gwynneth M.D. Mills and Adrienne Pedder

D. S. BREWER

First published 1992 by D. S. Brewer, Cambridge

D. S. Brewer is an imprint of Boydell & Brewer Ltd
PO Box 9, Woodbridge, Suffolk IP12 3DF, UK
and of Boydell & Brewer Inc.
PO Box 41026, Rochester, NY 14604, USA

ISBN   0 85991 343 0

British Library Cataloguing-in-Publication Data
A catalogue record for this book is available from the British Library

Library of Congress Cataloging-in-Publication Data applied for

The paper used in this publication meets the minimum requirements
of American National Standard for Information Sciences –
Permanence of Paper for Printed Library Materials, ANSI Z39.48–1984

Typeset in LaTeX at the University of Adelaide

Printed in Great Britain by
St Edmundsbury Press Ltd, Bury St Edmunds, Suffolk

IN MEMORY OF
TERENCE GEORGE WRIGHT
1918–1991

The study is so attractive that I feared anticipation from the 'inevitable German'; and my apprehensions were in part realized.

Frederick Tupper, Jr., 1895 [**276**]

I can hardly blame myself for not having known of the existence of the articles: in this age of multitudinous periodicals nothing is more difficult than to make sure that one has covered the field of search.

Montague Rhodes James, 1929 [**157**]

Contents

GENERAL EDITOR'S PREFACE

The last two decades have seen an explosion in the production of annotated bibliographies in the humanities, motivated in part by the sheer impossibility of keeping up with the mass of critical literature produced since the fifties. They fill a need, felt by students and teachers at all levels, for reliable, concise, yet detailed guides to what has been written. Medieval English literature has been no exception to this general trend, with annotated bibliographies of many of the major authors and areas appearing in the last twenty years, or being now in preparation.

The primary aim of the current series of some two dozen volumes (of which this is the first to be published) is to produce an annotated bibliography for every area of medieval English literary studies for which such a tool is not already in existence or in preparation. One of the major benefits of the series will thus be to focus attention not only on those of the more popular areas not covered in other bibliographies, but also on those hitherto marginalized. The individual volumes will contribute to our knowledge of our cultural heritage by showing, through a summary and evaluation of all known writings on the area in question, why that area is worthy of closer study, what sorts of interest it has already provoked, and what are the most fruitful directions for future research in it.

One of the distinguishing features of this series is the chronological arrangement of items, as opposed to the alphabetical arrangement more commonly adopted. Chronological arrangement facilitates the reading of annotations in the same order as the publication of the items annotated, and thus gives readers at one sitting a sense of the development of scholarship in the field. At the same time, the convenience of alphabetical arrangement is retained through the index of authors, which allows readers to locate with ease all items written by a particular scholar.

Each bibliography in the series is concentrated on a relatively small, reasonably self-contained area, defined on generic lines. This concentration leads to a second distinguishing feature of the series: the fullness and detail both of the annotations themselves and of the introductory sections. With the aim of letting the original authors speak for themselves the authors of the bibliographies keep their annotations as neutral as can reasonably be hoped; in the introductory sections, however, they offer critical analyses of the works annotated, drawing attention to the major trends in scholarship, showing which approaches have been most influential, which are exhausted, and which are most in need of further development.

This major undertaking is the work of an international team of scholars. Much of the work is being undertaken in Australia and New Zealand, and contributors from these countries will doubtless derive some satisfaction

ix

from the propriety with which antipodean scholarship is helping to reclaim some of the forgotten areas of medieval literary studies; but there are substantial contributions also from Canada, Japan, the United Kingdom, and the United States.

The editorial work for the series has been supported since 1991 by grants from the Australian Research Council, allocated by the University of Adelaide, to both of which bodies grateful acknowledgement is here made. Thanks are due also to several individuals at the University of Adelaide: to Sabina Flanagan and Rosemary Greentree, the editorial assistants for the series; to Marea Albanese, Ninette Ellis, and Elizabeth Lee of the Barr Smith Library; and to Andrew Cheel and Christian Legg (presently) and Andrew Trevorrow (formerly) of the Information Technology Division. I wish finally to thank Richard Barber of Boydell & Brewer for the tact and patience with which he has dealt with the inevitable problems arising from the launching of a new series.

T.L. BURTON

ACKNOWLEDGEMENTS

It is fitting that we should acknowledge first our debt of gratitude to Inter-loan librarians in both hemispheres, without whose assistance this project could never have been completed. Our particular thanks are due to the staff of the University of Auckland Library, and especially to Christine Woods and Shelley Taylor, whose efficiency and forbearance are much appreciated. We also wish to thank the British Library and the University of London Library for making available their facilities and for assistance received while we were in England.

Above all we are indebted to Gwynneth Mills and Adrienne Pedder, for their help with the compilation of annotations; their enthusiasm and interest, as well as their hard work, have been of invaluable assistance. Few University teachers can have done so little to deserve such a gener-ous and practically useful return of bread cast upon the waters; to them, and for them, our heartfelt thanks. We are grateful, too, to Shirley Peder-sen, for compiling a bibliography of Byrhtferth scholarship, to Greg Mor-gan, for his meticulous work on the prose dialogues, and to Daphne Lalor; their contribution to the early stages of the project is acknowledged with thanks. Our thanks are also due to John Mills, for translations of Greek and to Christine Richardson-Hay, for her generous and painstaking assis-tance with proof-reading. We also wish to take this opportunity to thank our colleagues, Roger Nicholson and Claudia Marquis, for their support and encouragement over the past years, and the University of Auckland for financial assistance received.

We are substantially indebted to the work of previous scholars, and ac-knowledge a particular debt to the annual bibliographies of *Anglo-Saxon England* and *Old English Newsletter*, to *Year's Work in English Studies*, to *Dissertation Abstracts* and *Dissertation Abstracts International*, to *In-dex of Theses* and to the following bibliographies: Wilfrid Bonser, *An Anglo-Saxon and Celtic Bibliography (450–1087)*, 2 vols. (Oxford: Black-well, 1957); Stanley B. Greenfield and Fred C. Robinson, *A Bibliography of Publications on Old English Literature to the End of 1972* (Toronto: U of Toronto P, 1980); Claudia Kren, *Medieval Science and Technology: A Selected, Annotated Bibliography* (New York: Garland, 1985); Phillip Pulsiano, *An Annotated Bibliography of North American Doctoral Disser-tations in Old English Language and Literature*, Medieval Texts and Stud-ies 3 (East Lansing, MI: Colleagues, 1988). We also acknowledge our indebtedness to two other indispensable works, N.R. Ker, *A Catalogue of Manuscripts Containing Anglo-Saxon* (Oxford: Clarendon, 1957), and Roberta Frank and Angus Cameron, eds., *A Plan for the Dictionary of Old English* (Toronto: U of Toronto P, 1973).

ABBREVIATIONS

A–G	*OE Dicts*, added apothegms
Ad	OE *Adrian and Ritheus*
Alex	OE *Letter of Alexander*
ASC	*Anglo-Saxon Chronicle*
ASE	*Anglo-Saxon England*
BT	Bosworth and Toller, *An Anglo-Saxon Dictionary*
ByrM	Byrhtferth's *Manual*
CorpÉpErfLeyd	Corpus, Épinal, Erfurt and Leyden glossaries
DA	*Dissertation Abstracts*
DAI	*Dissertation Abstracts International*
DNR	Bede's *De Natura Rerum*
DP	*Durham Proverbs*
DR	*Durham Ritual*
DT	Bede's *De Temporibus*
DTR	Bede's *De Temporum Ratione*
EETS	Early English Text Society
FC	Frank and Cameron, *A Plan for the Dictionary of Old English*
Herb	Old English *Herbarium Apuleii* (enlarged)
HomCath	Ælfric's *Catholic Homilies*
Ker	N.R. Ker, *A Catalogue of Manuscripts Containing Anglo-Saxon*
Lac	*Lacnunga*
Lb	*Leechbook*
*Lb*1&2	Bald's *Leechbook*
Lap	OE *Lapidary*
MED	*Middle English Dictionary*
MedQuad	OE *Medicina de Quadrupedibus*
MGH	*Monumenta Germaniae Historica*
ODEP	*Oxford Dictionary of English Proverbs*
OE ApT	OE *Apollonius of Tyre*
OE Dicts	OE *Dicts of Cato*
OEN	*Old English Newsletter*
OFr	Omont Fragment (recipes)
PD	*Peri Didaxeon*
PL	*Patrologia Latina*
RA, RB, RC	Redactions A, B, C of *Historia Apollonii* (as defined by Riese, 1871, 1893)
SA	Note on St Augustine, *OE Dicts*
SS	OE *Solomon and Saturn* (prose dialogue, unless otherwise stated)
Suppl.	N.R. Ker, 'A Supplement to *Catalogue of Manuscripts Containing Anglo-Saxon*,' *ASE* 5 (1976): 121–31
Wond	OE *Wonders of the East*

GENERAL INTRODUCTION

SELECTION OF OLD ENGLISH TEXTS

This volume of annotations covers scholarship relating to the OE writings which are classified as follows by Frank and Cameron's *Plan for the Dictionary of Old English*.[1] The grouping of texts in the five sections of annotations, however, differs in some respects from FC (*Apollonius*, for instance, has been linked in this volume with *Letter of Alexander* and *Wonders of the East*, and the 'Magico-medical' section covers FC's 'Medical Texts,' and 'Folklore' as well as the *Lapidary*).

Prose Romance, Vision Literature:
    Apollonius of Tyre   FC B.4.1

Proverbs: FC B.7
    Dicts of Cato
    Faustina, Royal and Rawlinson Proverbs
Glosses: *Durham Proverbs*   FC C.25

Prose Dialogues: FC B.5
    Solomon and Saturn
    Adrian and Ritheus
Alfredian and Other Translations: *Elucidarium*   FC B.9.9

Computus (includes Byrhtferth's *Manual*)   FC B.20

Medical Texts: FC B.21
    Herbarium Apuleii, Medicina de Quadrupedibus
    Plant Names
    (Bald's) Leechbook
    Lacnunga
    On the Human Foetus
    Recipes
Not Classified: *Peri Didaxeon*

Other Scientific Texts: FC B.22
    Alexander's Letter to Aristotle

---

[1] Roberta Frank and Angus Cameron, eds., *A Plan for the Dictionary of Old English* (Toronto: U of Toronto P, 1973). 'FC,' which is employed throughout both as an abbreviated reference to this volume and to designate the classification system of the Toronto Dictionary Project, is treated as a grammatical plural; it should be noted, however, that the classified list of texts, 25–306, bears the authorship of A. Cameron.

    Wonders of the East
    Lapidary
Folklore   FC B.23
    Prose Charms and Charm Headings
    Tables of Lucky and Unlucky Days
    Prognostics
    Prohibition against Blood-letting
Glosses: *Prognostics*   FC C.16

    This volume thus covers complete text groups as defined by FC, with one exception, i.e., the omission of the *Vision of Leofric*, a generically unique work, which FC group with *Apollonius*. We have also included the *Elucidarium*, as it does not sit very comfortably with the 'Alfredian and Other Translations' to which FC assign it and is sometimes associated with the prose dialogues in the scholarship annotated. *Peri Didaxeon*, omitted by FC, is included here; medical historians have generally associated it with the OE corpus, and, since the appearance of *A Plan for the Dictionary of Old English*, the claim that it is linguistically OE has gained a fair degree of acceptance. Glosses (FC classification C and D), as well as the miscellaneous jottings classified as 'Notes and Commonplaces' (FC B.24), some of which are related to the prose dialogues, clearly have significant bearing on the study of Anglo-Saxon learning and education, but they fall within the scope of one of the later volumes of this series. We have, however, included two interlinear glosses in the coverage of this volume, the *Durham Proverbs*, the most substantial of the Latin–OE collections of proverbs, and glosses to prognostic texts in Tiberius A.iii, which are closely related to OE prognostic texts in the same manuscripts. A few publications dealing with miscellaneous notes and other glosses which are closely related to study of the texts covered by this volume are included in the annotations.

    Any classification of texts is bound to cut across other well-established groupings; the selection of texts, for instance, separates *Letter of Alexander* and *Wonders of the East* from the Life of Saint Christopher, with which they are linked in a number of studies because all three prose pieces are preserved in the same manuscript as *Beowulf*. Central to most classifications of the OE corpus is the distinction between prose and metre; as the introductions to the annotations observe, the adoption of metrical form in OE writings (or, in some cases, perhaps—short proverbs, for instance—modern scholars' construction of the text as metrical) does not necessarily signify a qualitative difference, and it seems a pity that some of the OE compositions classified as prose—particularly the proverbs, dialogues and folklore—have not been more fully drawn into the discussion of wisdom literature (the relative neglect of the secular prose texts is demonstrated by the fact that 'wisdom literature' tends to be synonymous with wisdom 'poetry'). Included in the compositions classified by FC as 'Poetry' are twelve 'Metrical Charms' (FC A.43.1–12), which include five extracts from

Lacnunga and one from the *Leechbook*. Recent scholarship rightly questions the methodology of study which is reflected in FC's classification, but because commentary on these six extracts is inextricably embedded in studies of OE poetry, they have been excluded from the coverage of this volume in order to ease the task of the editor of the Annotated Bibliography of Old English Poems of Wisdom and Learning. For the convenience of users of this volume, some publications on charms whose titles do not clearly indicate that they are exclusively devoted to metrical charms are briefly annotated to that effect.

Even leaving aside the fact that the *Elucidarium* may have more in common with 'Alfredian and Other Prose' than it has with the texts listed above, the description of this group of texts as 'Prose of Secular Learning' is certainly open to question, but the category is a long-established one, and a more convenient identifying title could not be found. With the exception of the *Elucidarium*, these texts are, at any rate, recognizably distinct from the homiletic, devotional and hagiographic works which constitute the bulk of surviving OE prose. Whether and in what sense these texts are 'secular' is one of the issues raised by the scholarship annotated and touched upon in the summary introductions; 'heterodox' might, conceivably, be more accurate to describe some of them. Whether they were the creation of a learned, literary culture, and to what extent they derive from Latin sources, are moot points; debate over the part played by popular, pagan and Teutonic influences, which figured in earlier studies, continues, in a variety of different forms, and then, as now, there are many who regard learning in the late OE period as having been in a state of extreme decline. (Whether or not the perception of Anglo-Saxon culture on the eve of the Norman Conquest as 'decadent' represents anything more than an *a priori* assumption concerning the relationship of military and cultural superiority, is an open question, but it appears, at any rate, to reflect the belief that culture is synonymous with the use of Latin, rather than the creation of a prose that is written in 'such a Tongue as the people understandeth.'[2]) Some of the texts covered by this volume are, indisputably, relatively close translations of Latin works, although, interestingly, an exact Latin source has, in most cases, not yet been found. Much more interesting, however, is the fact that the editor of *Durham Proverbs* (Arngart, **28**) argues that the Latin proverbs are translated from OE—more interesting because the historical dominance of source studies has, inevitably, given the impression that OE secular prose is highly derivative. Very likely, the impression is somewhat exaggerated, particularly as earlier editors (Förster, **311**, **312**, **315**, **316**, **317**, **318**, **319** and **321**, for instance) were by no means as careful as Cross and Hill, **55**, in distinguishing between Latin sources and Latin analogues.

---

[2] *Book of Common Prayer*, Articles, 24.

Generally, the texts covered by this volume are regarded as the products, or, in some cases, the by-products, of monastic education. The view that the magico-medical literature reflects the pastoral involvement of monastic centres (see Flint, **575, 97**) has not yet been much pursued; nor, despite the fact that some of Ælfric's didactic works were written for devout laymen, has the possibility been fully examined, in any of the specialist articles annotated, that some of the secular prose was translated for, or at least read by, literate members of the laity, although there are occasional suggestions that the monastic orders' monopoly of literacy was not complete (see, e.g., Grattan and Singer, **326**, Rubin, **562**).[3] The secular prose is commonly associated with the Benedictine Reform movement; most manuscript copies of secular prose, however, date from the mid-11th century or later, and in some cases the original translations are dated to the Age of Alfred (see Sisam, **193**) or, more recently, to the 8th or early 9th centuries (see Bately, **564**). Some early scholars speculated, in view of Bede's references to the curriculum taught at the school established by Theodore,[4] that the Latin texts on which some of the vernacular prose is based were brought to England by Theodore's mission (e.g., Cockayne, **297**) or early pilgrims to Rome (e.g., Goldberg, **12**), and recent scholarship has, in some cases, found confirmation of this (e.g., Kitson, **285**). It is also suggested that Latin works compiled in England and transmitted to the continent by Anglo-Saxon missionaries may have played a part in the development of the Latin textual tradition (see esp. Talbot, **369**, Kortekaas, **152**; cf. Sisam, **193**). The innovative nature of the insular textual tradition might, conceivably, help to explain why OE translations that derive from popular classical works (such as *OE Dicts, Apollonius, Letter of Alexander* and the Herbarium) are not an exact translation of any of the surviving Latin copies.

COVERAGE OF SCHOLARSHIP

Study of the OE works covered by this volume of annotations is intimately bound up with study of the Latin textual traditions to which they are related. Study of the OE magico-medical literature has tended to be topic-based rather than text-based, and has, very properly, always drawn on the published research of specialists in medicine, botany, social history, archaeology, palaeopathology, folklore, anthropology and other fields. Increasingly, contemporary literary scholars incline towards the study of texts in their social and historical context, and are perhaps even more conscious than their predecessors of the value of research that takes into account the research of specialists in other disciplines—palaeographers, Anglo-Latinists and art historians, to name only the most obvious. This

---

[3] An important study by C. Patrick Wormald, 'The Uses of Literacy in Anglo-Saxon England and its Neighbours,' *Transactions of the Royal Historical Society* 5th ser. 27 (1977): 95–114, argues that aristocratic men were resistant to literacy and that a vernacular literature does not itself imply a *wide* reading public.

[4] *History*, 4.2, 5.3.

Annotated Bibliography of Old English Prose of Secular Learning is, inevitably, text-based and primarily concerned with publications in the field of Old English literature. Coverage of scholarship pertaining to the magicomedical material, however, is not confined to publications in the field of Old English literary studies, and some studies which make no specific reference to OE texts but which have evident bearing on the study of them (chiefly studies of manuscripts and the visual arts) are included in other sections. Annotations of Byrhtferth scholarship include publications concerning his connections with the Latin manuscript, Oxford, St John's College 17, and Latin works attributed to him.

We have endeavoured, in the first instance, to include all specialist publications prior to 1989 which are centrally devoted to the OE texts listed above.[5] Most of these are listed in Greenfield and Robinson's *Bibliography of Publications on Old English Literature to the End of 1972* (1980),[6] and the classified bibliographies published annually in *Anglo-Saxon England* (1972–) and *Old English Newsletter* (1967–). (Some bibliographies of Old English literature which pre-date Greenfield and Robinson have been consulted, and so have annual bibliographies other than *ASE* and *OEN*, but they have yielded very little in the way of specialist publications centrally devoted to the OE texts which does not appear in these three sources.) The recently published Quinn *Manual*, 1990, has also been consulted.[7] For the identification of relevant North American dissertations we have relied on the *Annotated Bibliography* of Pulsiano, 1988.[8] We have also drawn on the bibliographies of specialist studies and editions of the OE texts. For the magico-medical section, we have drawn extensively on Bonser's *Anglo-Saxon and Celtic Bibliography*, 1957,[9] which lists many of the non-literary publications cited by earlier scholars, and we have made selective use of the *Annotated Bibliography* of Kren, 1985.[10] A few publications encountered while scanning the non-literary sections of the bibliographies in *ASE* and *OEN* for prospective titles have also been annotated. The coverage of literary scholarship in which the OE texts figure only marginally, and of significantly related publications which make little or no reference to OE texts, is necessarily selective; the compilers have generally endeavoured to reflect the emphases and interests of past and present specialists in the

---

[5] Two publications of a later date, too seminal to omit, are included: Riedinger, **156**, and Flint, **575**.

[6] Stanley B. Greenfield and Fred C. Robinson, *A Bibliography of Publications on Old English Literature to the End of 1972* (Toronto: U of Toronto P, 1980).

[7] Karen J. Quinn and Kenneth P. Quinn, *A Manual of Old English Prose* (New York: Garland, 1990).

[8] Phillip Pulsiano, *An Annotated Bibliography of North American Doctoral Dissertations in Old English Language and Literature*, Medieval Texts and Studies 3 (East Lansing, MI: Colleagues, 1988).

[9] Wilfrid Bonser, *An Anglo-Saxon and Celtic Bibliography (450–1087)*, 2 vols. (Oxford: Blackwell, 1957).

[10] Claudia Kren, *Medieval Science and Technology: A Selected, Annotated Bibliography* (New York: Garland, 1985).

field, but have occasionally incorporated annotations of publications which they regard as likely to be of interest to users of this volume.

The summary introductions to the annotations in this volume outline some of the most recent developments in the study of the OE texts covered. In the past two decades, however, *Anglo-Saxon England* and *Old English Newsletter* have made it possible to keep abreast of publications in all fields of study of the Anglo-Saxon period, and, in addition to annual bibliographies, *Old English Newsletter* carries regular reviews of literary scholarship, reports on research in progress, and much other useful information. For this reason, we have been more inclusive in our coverage of publications which appeared prior to 1972. Less recent publications are, moreover, less likely to be held in the local libraries of many scholars, and the annotations are particularly designed to assist those whose situation is similar to that of the editors. That is, they aim to assist scholars who rely on the interloan service and travel to major centres for filling gaps in the holdings of their local libraries to determine whether or not a publication is, for their purposes, worth pursuing. Judgements of relevance and intrinsic value have no rightful place in the annotations, and are, in any case, highly individual matters; but one who has laboured long in the field of past scholarship may perhaps be permitted to observe that although there were giants on the earth in those days, past scholars also contributed their fair share of publications which do not seem to merit either the time or the money that was expended in acquiring them. In particular, a number of the background studies included in the annotations headed 'General and Miscellaneous Magico-Medical' have a place in the history of scholarship but are not regarded by most late 20th century researchers in the area as important enough to cite.

Literary histories and surveys have been excluded from coverage. Language studies are included only if they are exclusively devoted to one of the OE texts; vocabulary studies are included only if they have been identified as relevant by the authors of specialist publications.[11] Metrical charms, as mentioned above, do not, as such, fall within the scope of this volume, but some items encountered in bibliographies whose exclusive concern with metrical charms is not evident from the title are included for the purposes of clarification (e.g., 'Ein Zauberspruch,' 'A Woman's Charm'). Reviews are annotated only if they make a significant contribution to the study of a text. Other indications of limitations in the coverage of scholarship are included in the introductions in order to remind readers of, or alert them to, the existence of other dimensions to the study of the texts.

---

[11] Matsuji Tajima, *Old and Middle English Language Studies: A Classified Bibliography, 1923–85*, Library and Information Sources in Linguistics 13 (Amsterdam: Benjamins, 1988), is useful but incomplete.

SOME NOTES ON THE ORGANIZATION
AND USE OF THIS VOLUME

Textual References and Identification of Texts

In the first four sections, passages of a text under discussion are identified in terms of the most recently published edition (unless there is a particular reason for retaining the form of reference employed by an author whose work is annotated), except in the case of computistical texts, which are identified by their FC classification. Thus, for *OE Dicts* the edition cited is Cox, **9**; for *Durham Proverbs*, Arngart, **29**; for *Solomon and Saturn* and *Adrian and Ritheus*, Cross and Hill, **55**; for Byrhtferth's *Enchiridion*, Crawford, **212**; for *Apollonius*, Goolden, **101**; for *Letter of Alexander* and *Wonders of the East*, Rypins, **165**. Square brackets indicate that the reference has been supplied by the annotator.

Identification of most of the texts covered in the magico-medical section, whole or in part, is problematic. Charms, prose and metrical, are identified by scholars according to the editorial numbering of either Storms, **325**, or Grendon, **314**, whose classifications, though based on different principles, have some confusing superficial resemblances. For passages of *Lb* and *Lac*, some scholars cite the volume and page number of Cockayne's edition (**297, 298**); others employ his editorial section numbering of the two works, or, for *Lac*, the more cumbersome editorial numbering of Grattan and Singer, **326**. The 90 or so passages of *Lb* and *Lac* which were anthologized as 'charms' by Storms or Grendon may, alternatively, be identified in terms of one or the other of these two editions. Other, shorter texts—chiefly prose charms, prognostics and recipes—have no established descriptive titles, and are normally identified only by volume and page number in Cockayne's three-volume edition of the magico-medical corpus (except for a few texts which were not printed by him). Further, citations of the magico-medical literature in a number of publications are either incompletely or wholly undocumented.

To have standardized references would have introduced further possibilities for error, and would have contributed little to readers' immediate recognition of the text under discussion (references to the Grattan and Singer edition of *Lacnunga*, and Leonhardi's edition of *Lacnunga* and the *Leechbook* (**310**), however, have been silently excised). An attempt has been made to indicate derivation from *Lacnunga* or the *Leechbook* when an author employs Storms or Grendon numbering for extracts from these works, and, for prose charms, FC classification has normally been supplied in square brackets. Prognostics, recipes and other short texts are also identified in the annotations by their FC classification. For the charms, a concordance to the editions of Cockayne, Grendon and Storms has been included to assist the reader (at pp. 251–6). The detailed annotations of Cockayne's three-volume edition (**400, 297, 298**) are also intended to assist in the identification of texts referred to by authors, and it is hoped that readers who do not have a copy of FC at hand will find the information they are likely to need by referring to the descriptions of the 'Folklore' texts which introduce the annotations.

Where practicable, references for undocumented citations are supplied in square brackets, but as a number of magico-medical texts contain similar material and vocabulary, we have been disinclined to hazard textual references in such cases. Many publications in the field of magico-medical literature, moreover, range widely over the corpus; our practice has been to include references to texts which are discussed at length by an author, and to indicate by some means or other that the range of reference exceeds the scope of a brief annotation.

Organization of Annotations in the Magico-medical Section

Because scholarship pertaining to magico-medical literature has been topic-based rather than text-based, often tending to range widely over the three volumes of material edited by Cockayne, there is no entirely satisfactory means of organizing the annotations—a single series of chronologically ordered annotations, for instance, would have been more convenient for a user of this volume wanting to look up a specific article whose publication date was known, but would have seemed unhelpful to readers wishing to scan annotations of publications dealing with a particular text. The four-fold division of the annotations is a compromise solution. Publications relating to the *Lapidary*, which is not a regular member of the magico-medical corpus, are kept distinct. Annotations centrally and exclusively devoted to the Herbarium, *Medicina de Quadrupedibus*, the OE plant names which appear in a Latin manuscript of the same work, and/or *Peri Didaxeon*, are distinguished from those which are centrally and exclusively concerned with one or more of the remaining magico-medical texts. All other publications in the field are annotated under the heading 'General and Miscellaneous Magico-medical Literature'; this last section thus includes articles which refer to the *Leechbook* and/or *Lacnunga* as well as to the Herbarium complex, histories of medicine, 'background' studies, works dealing only with metrical charms, editions of texts listed under 'Medicine' by Greenfield and Robinson, 1980, or by Bonser, 1957, but not normally regarded as OE magico-medical texts, etc. *Users of this volume wishing to locate all of the annotations which refer to a particular text should, therefore, always scan the annotations under 'General and Miscellaneous Magico-medical Literature.'* Some guidance to entries in the 'General and Miscellaneous' section which have significant bearing on individual texts is offered in the introductions to the two major sections of annotations.

Manuscript Descriptions and Dating

Description of the manuscripts and their principle OE contents usually appears at the beginning of the introductions; occasionally, it has proved more convenient to incorporate the information into the description of minor texts or into a later sub-section of an introduction. Manuscript description generally follows Ker's *Catalogue*,[12] indicating any major disagreements or additions encountered in the scholarship annotated. Manuscript description derived from Ker is necessarily abridged, but endeavours to include any information which does or might have significance for codicological study. Conventions of dating follow Ker. In the lists of manuscripts at the head of the introductions, dates enclosed in brackets immediately after the Ker *Catalogue* number indicate that Ker's dating of the relevant article(s) differs from his dating of the manuscript as a whole; otherwise Ker's dating appears, without brackets, after the article number.

Summaries of Scholarship

The introductions to each section of annotations outline the major findings of specialist publications. The emphases of the introductions are intended to reflect those of scholars in the field; matters such as the extent of the text, identification of sources and analogues, the Latin manuscript tradition, date and provenance of the manuscript and the original translation, manuscript relations, the style of the OE translation and its relationship to Latin sources, thus figure prominently.

A summary overview of the study of individual texts generally appears in the final subsection of the introductions (the chief exception is 'Recipe Collections,' where the summary is incorporated in the preliminary remarks on the three principle groups of texts); general observations on the study of the magico-medical corpus are included in the surveys of scholarship pertaining to the *Leechbook, Lacnunga* and the Herbarium. In drawing attention to the limitations of our knowledge to date, avenues that have not been explored and research that waits to be done, we by no means intend to derogate the achievements of existing scholarship; we intend, rather, to suggest some of the many opportunities that have been made possible by the primarily text-based and textual work of earlier scholars and the rich implications of the most recent scholarship. With a few notable exceptions, for instance, we have not found many studies of the texts covered by this volume which consider their manuscript context; whether such study holds the key to, say, the motives underlying the translation of *Apollonius*, or the milieu of the prognostics, may be open to doubt (see, e.g., Archibald, **151**), but it seems likely that codicological study has much to contribute to our understanding of individual texts and the period as a whole.

Above all, we have not encountered much recent or extended study of the secular prose works as cultural documents. Yet the themes and issues which recur in earlier scholarship are strikingly close to many of the preoccupations of the varieties of cultural study to which many Departments of English are currently tending. The interaction of Romano-Christianity and

---

[12]N.R. Ker, *A Catalogue of Manuscripts Containing Anglo-Saxon* (Oxford: Clarendon, 1957).

pagan culture which is reflected in the secular prose, for instance, is redolent with implications for the creation of culture in early medieval Western Europe, the development of heterodoxy and the nature of popular religion. And although *Apollonius*, *Letter of Alexander* and *Wonders of the East* were regarded by earlier scholars as historically significant precursors of the literary tastes to which later medieval romance catered, questions of cultural continuity and discontinuity have scarcely been canvassed in relation to the secular prose in the last twenty years (but see Riedinger, **156**). There is, surprisingly, not even a comparative examination of OE and ME versions of *Disticha Catonis* which aims to discover whether there are historically significant differences in the rendering of what was a staple text of elementary education throughout the Middle Ages and beyond. It is surprising, too, that the rise of Women's Studies as a University discipline has impacted so little on study of the magico-medical literature, although the published papers of Deegan, **559**, and Meaney, **573**, are an excellent beginning. But despite the fact that early Anglo-Saxon monastic women's enthusiasm in the pursuit of learning is well known, and despite the fact that early medical historians often quoted Tacitus's assertion that Germanic women tended the wounds of the warriors (see, e.g., Berdoe, **437**, Payne, **449**),[13] it is widely assumed that Anglo-Saxon women played no part in healing (although hagiography and manuscript ownership suggest otherwise);[14] as to whether monastic women participated in any way in late Anglo-Saxon education, however decadent it may have been, the question does not yet seem to have been posed.[15]

The relative slowness with which study of the secular prose writings has responded to contemporary preoccupations is perhaps a consequence of their relative neglect (despite its intrinsic interest and historical significance, for instance, secular prose is less well represented in undergraduate Primers and Readers than it was in the first half of this century). The relative neglect of much of the secular prose corpus is, at least in part, attributable to the view that it consists of little more than debased translations of Latin compilations. It is suggested above that study of OE secular prose texts—particularly study of the prognostics—whose aim is not the successful identification of the nearest exact source, but the concerted examination of the implications of the substantive differences between OE translations and their established sources, might find reason to challenge this view.

Finally, the editors hope that this volume will help in some small way to encourage the further development of studies of the history of Anglo-Saxon scholarship, particularly studies which enquire into the assumptions, whether implicit or explicit, that have shaped the methodology of earlier

---

[13] *Germania*, ch. 7.

[14] See further p. 236.

[15] See Christine Fell, et al., *Women in Anglo-Saxon England and the Impact of 1066*, Paperback edn. (Oxford: Blackwell, 1986) 109–28.

scholarship—as, for instance, the conviction that the OE magico-medical literature was compiled and copied by monks who invariably drew on Latin sources, and who, together with lay society as a whole, shared the orthodox Christian mind-set which, it appears, is exemplified in the writings of Ælfric and Bede (see, e.g., Talbot, **524**, and Jolly, **395**). There seems, in short, to be a vital connection between the belief that early medieval culture was entirely the creation of monastic scholars and commitment to the cultural dominance of an orthodox church, which makes possible such certain affirmations as: 'I find nothing of the tension between pagan and Christian values which strikes Greenfield so forcibly. I think that, by the tenth century, people knew exactly where Ingeld fitted in the scheme of things.'[16] One who inclines to the view that the conversion of Europe consisted to a high degree of the conversion of the teachings of Christ to the service of the world, who has never been entirely sure what the scheme of things is, let alone how anything fits into it, respectfully suggests that there may be as much to be gained from reading medieval writings from this point of view as from reading them with the fixed eye of faith, while acknowledging that a predilection for discovery of the survival of pagan customs, the existence of popular culture, heterodox and syncretistic religious beliefs, and the prevalence of a rather more fluid and open world view than that which, we are led to believe, occupied the mind of the Venerable Bede, itself invites deconstruction.

STEPHANIE HOLLIS

---

[16] Angus Cameron, 'The Boundaries of Old English Literature,' *The Anglo-Saxons: Synthesis and Achievement*, ed. J. Douglas Woods and David A.E. Pelteret (Waterloo, Ont.: Wilfrid Laurier UP, 1985) 27–36, at 35.

I

Proverbs

DICTS OF CATO

MANUSCRIPTS

FC B.7.1

Cambridge, Trinity College R.9.17, ff. 45r–8v   T
Ker 89, arts. 2, 3*   s. xi/xii

London, British Library, Cotton Julius A.ii, ff. 141r–4v   J
Ker 159, art. 4   s. xii med.

London, British Library, Cotton Vespasian D.xiv, ff. 7r–11v   V
Ker 209, art. 3   s. xii med.

Junius Transcript:
Bodleian, Junius 45, ff. 4r–8r   JJ

* As Cox, 9, 30, points out, Ker incorrectly states that art. 3 (SA) concludes with the apothegms drawn from *OE Deuteronomy*; they are in V.

MANUSCRIPTS: CONTENTS, DESCRIPTION, DATE AND PROVENANCE (following Ker and Cox)

OE Dicts is preserved in three, slightly different, versions. Editorial dating differs somewhat from Ker's (see further p. 18 below, 'Language, Date and Provenance').

T is dated s. xi/xii by Ker. It also contains Ælfric's *Grammar* in an abbreviated form. Ker describes the hand of this manuscript as 'a rather pointed, backward-sloping hand, becoming rounder latterly.' Cox, 9, states that the initial *N*, and the *A* which introduces the homiletic section (tabled as a separate item by Ker), are in red, and that individual apothegms usually begin with majuscules in the text hand, and are touched with red. He also adds that T 'has been corrected by a hand probably contemporary with the original and in no way distinct from it'; most of the corrections are an attempt to restore conventional (earlier) spellings to words which have begun to show phonological change (30). Cox dates T to the late 11th century (34).

J contains the shortest version of *OE Dicts*. It also contains one of the prose dialogues (*Ad*), and a Miscellaneous Note,[1] as well as a metrical prayer. There is a Junius transcript of J (Junius 45); Ker observes that the transcript is 'valuable because, as a result of the Cottonian fire, some

---

[1] 'Miscellaneous Notes' is used throughout as a synonym for the texts classified as FC B.24, 'Notes and Commonplaces.'

of the text on ff. 140–1 and 143–4 [the beginning and end of *OE Dicts*] cannot now be read.' Ker dates J to the mid-12th century, and describes the hand as 'fair-sized' and 'neat.' Cox is of the opinion that the hand is somewhat conservative for such a late date, and perhaps belongs instead to the late 11th century. He considers that corrections to J may be in the original hand, and adds the information that 'each initial begins what the scribe conceives to be a new apothegm'(31); initials are in red, blue, green or a yellow which Ker calls 'brown.'

V is described by Ker as a collection of theological pieces, mostly from Ælfric's *Catholic Homilies*; it also contains the *OE Elucidarium*, as well as some Miscellaneous Notes and prognostics. Like J, V is dated s. xii med. by Ker, who deduces that it may have been in female ownership in s. xii ex. *OE Dicts* would appear, from Ker's description, to be in the main hand. The script is of the 'prickly' kind used at Canterbury and Rochester; there are no indications in Ker of the provenance of T or J. Cox, who understands Ker to have dated the 'prickly' hand to the first half of the 12th century, observes that the sermon of Archbishop d'Escures in V strengthens the connection with Rochester and Canterbury, and gives a *terminus a quo* of 1108. He adds that apothegms 'begin with a majuscule in the text hand, touched with red or with a red initial.' Cox also adds that 'corrections to V are in at least two hands.' The first is skilled and indistinguishable from the text hand, and corrects the copyist's mistakes; the second hand ('rather messy') changes rather than improves the text (34).

V has also been studied by Förster, **94**, and Handley, **96**, both of whom argue for a Canterbury provenance (see further pp. 23–4 below, 'Study of *OE Dicts*'); Richards, **95**, favours Rochester, and assigns the manuscript to the second quarter of the 12th century.

MANUSCRIPT AND TEXTUAL RELATIONSHIPS; EXTENT OF THE TEXT

The textual relationship is clearly set out by Cox, **9**. T contains 81 apothegms, and is followed by a homiletic piece (termed 'SA' by Cox) that claims the authority of St Augustine. SA is distinguished from the apothegms by its red initial capital, and Ker tables SA as a separate item; all editors of T, however, accept it as integral (and Ker observes that it is connected in subject with apothegm 81). V contains the same 81 apothegms; it lacks SA but contains additional gnomic material at the beginning (termed 'A' by Cox), and at the end ('C–G'), and within the body of the text after 45 ('B'). J ends incompletely with 78 and omits 13, 55 and 66.

There is a consensus of opinion among editors that all the extant manuscripts are copies, at least one remove from the original. Schleich, **10**, clarifying Nehab's handling of the relationship of the manuscripts (3), argued that T and J derived independently from the same exemplar, and that V belonged to a different manuscript group. Brunner, **8**, argued that V was more directly descended than T and J. Cox represents all three versions as having been independently derived from a common exemplar. He concludes that T best represents the original; in his view, V is markedly innovative and J is corrupt.

EDITIONS; TRANSLATIONS

A few apothegms from each manuscript were transcribed by Wanley for the purposes of identification.[2] Müller, **1**, who, in 1835, was the first to edit *OE Dicts*, printed T and V, collated with J. Kemble, **52**, who printed J some ten years later, appears to have found it less legible than Grundtvig, who made the transcript used by Müller.[3] V was printed without apparatus by Warner, **4**, and was used as a copy-text by Brunner, **8**. T was used as the copy-text by Nehab, **3**, and by Cox, **7** and **9**; Cox conflates with T the gnomes that are found only in V (A–G), which he regards as later interpolations.

Müller's misapprehension that *OE Dicts* was part of Ælfric's *Grammar* (v) was dispelled by Nehab. Nehab's edition was attacked on all fronts and at excessive length by Schleich, **10**. Cox's description of Schleich's review as 'a good scholarly discussion of the *Dicts*' (1, n. 1) is difficult to endorse. Cox's edition, which appeared in *Anglia* in 1972, is by far the most scholarly edition of *OE Dicts* to have appeared, and also offers a reconstructed Latin text. Although Cox's conclusions concerning manuscript relations and dating differ from those of Nehab and Brunner (whose dissertation represents the only full-length study of V), he does not directly address the arguments of either; somewhat fuller critical and textual apparatus is found in Cox's dissertation, **7**, on which his published edition is based.

In addition to the editions listed above, *OE Dicts* is among the texts printed by Sievers, **5**; the text is heavily emended in order to demonstrate the validity of his theories concerning the metrical nature of OE works which are generally regarded as prose. Cockayne, **2**, prints SA only. A translation of J is included in Brunner's edition and in Kemble, **52**. As Larsen, **68**, explains, a few copies of the earlier bound page proofs of Kemble's work survive; the bound page proofs contain the text of *OE Dicts* (220–5), but the translation appears only in the edition. There is a more recent translation by Swanton, 1975.[4]

---

[2] Humphrey Wanley, *Librorum Veterum Septentrionalium, qui in Angliae bibliothecis extant ... Catalogus Historico-Criticus*, vol. 2 of *Linguarum Veterum Septentrionalium Thesaurus*, by George Hickes (Oxford: Oxford UP, 1705; Hildesheim, NY: Olms, 1970). Wanley transcribed distichs 2–4 and 84 of T (167), distich 2 of J (183) and distichs 1–2 and 86 of V (202).

[3] Wülcker, **13**, 501, incorrectly states that Kemble's edition was also based on V.

[4] Michael Swanton, *Anglo-Saxon Prose* (London: Dent, 1975). Swanton translates *OE Dicts* under the title 'A Collection of Proverbs,' 174–9.

LANGUAGE; DATE AND PROVENANCE OF THE TEXT AND ITS ORIGINAL

Cox, **9**, states that all three manuscripts employ, for the most part, the spelling conventions of an 11th century West-Saxon *koine*. But non-West-Saxon forms occur at the same point in at least two manuscripts often enough to suggest that the dialect of the common exemplar, probably the original, was not West-Saxon. Cox does not find it possible to determine on linguistic grounds whether the common exemplar was Kentish or Mercian; he is disinclined to attach particular significance to the fact that pre-12th century English manuscripts of the Latin *Disticha Catonis* are associated with Kent. He concludes that composition of *OE Dicts* was probably begun between the mid-10th and the mid-11th century. This beginning may have included only apothegms 1–76, or even only 1–67, and may not have included 7: '1–81, however, were established as the text of the Dicts by the end of the eleventh century when T was made' (34).

Cox, then, dates all three manuscripts earlier than Ker, since he appears to favour a late 11th century date for T as well as J, and assigns V to the early 12th century. Cox draws no explicit conclusions concerning the relative dating of the three versions, but clearly states that T, which he considers to be most directly descended from the original, is the earliest version. He also states that T shows little sign of inflexional decay; J (which he considers the most corrupt version) shows some signs of decay, and V shows a great deal. Nehab, **3**, on the basis of his comparative study of the language, dated T, J, and V, respectively, to the early, mid-, and late 12th century (cf. Förster, **14**). Both editors of T, then, are in agreement that T is the earliest version; see also Brunner, **8**.

Nehab speculated, chiefly on the basis of stylistic and syntactic similarities with the *OE Deuteronomy*, and also because of the manuscript association of *OE Dicts* and Ælfric's *Grammar*, that Ælfric might have been the translator of *OE Dicts*. Goldberg, **12**, who favoured a mid-10th century origin for *OE Dicts*, associated the translation with Æthelwold's Winchester school. Cox agrees with Ker on the likelihood that V is of Canterbury or Rochester origin, but offers no suggestions concerning the provenance of T or J, or the place of the original translation (cf. Cox, **7**).

THE LATIN *DISTICHA CATONIS*

The derivation of *OE Dicts* from *Disticha Catonis* was evident to early Anglo-Saxonists, at least as early as Kemble, **52**. Studies of the development of *Disticha Catonis* conclude that the verses of *Disticha Catonis* accumulated gradually, and were finally set into four books of hexameter couplets by an unknown person in the 4th century. They were first attributed to Cato 'the Censor' (234–149 BC) *c.* 375 AD, presumably because of his reputation for wisdom and virtuous conduct. Plutarch's account of how carefully Cato taught his son may also have had significant bearing, since the *Disticha Catonis* are in the form of admonitions to a young man (this feature is not reproduced in *OE Dicts*).

The textual history of *Disticha Catonis* was studied by Boas, 1952.[5] Boas's edition provides the basis for Cox's reconstruction of the Latin text underlying *OE Dicts*: Cox uses Boas's basic text, but makes frequent changes in favour of his late Vulgate readings (see further pp. 21–2 below, 'Relationship to the *Disticha Catonis*').

The influential educational role of *Disticha Catonis* in the Middle Ages has been studied by Hazelton, **19**, who draws attention to the importance of pedagogic commentaries for an understanding of the conversion of its pagan ethics to Christian educational purposes. Hazelton focuses on the 13th and 14th centuries; although he makes no specific mention of *OE Dicts*, his study significantly illuminates the role of *Disticha Catonis* in earlier centuries. Hazelton explains that *Disticha Catonis* held an important place in the elementary education system from the 4th century onwards. It figured in the curriculum of Roman schools, and is quoted by continental writers from the 5th century onwards. By the 9th century, when Remigius of Auxerre (d. 908) wrote his commentary, *Disticha Catonis* had become the standard first reader in the Christian schools of Western Europe.[6] The fact that Alcuin draws upon it (in *Praecepta vivendi*, ch. 62) possibly suggests that it was already in use in early Carolingian schools.[7] There may have been an 11th century movement to dislodge *Disticha Catonis* from the elementary curriculum (it has been suggested that the appearance of home-grown proverb collections reflects opposition to the use of non-Christian teaching material)[8] but its position remained secure, and the most fully developed commentaries were produced in the 13th and 14th centuries.

ENGLISH MANUSCRIPTS OF THE LATIN *DISTICHA CATONIS* AND ENGLISH VERSIONS

Cox, **9**, lists three pre-Conquest manuscripts which contain the Latin *Disticha Catonis*; he considers that *OE Dicts* is not a translation of any of these versions. He also mentions the late West-Saxon discontinuous gloss found in another manuscript, which has 'no relation whatsoever' to *OE*

---

[5] Marcus Boas, *Disticha Catonis recensuit et apparatu critico instruxit Marcus Boas. Opus post Marci Boas mortem edendum curavit Henricus Johannes Botschuyver* (Amsterdam: North Holland, 1952).

[6] Lapidge, **20**, 131, n. 34, draws attention to the need for a complete edition of the commentary of Remigius; Boas, 1952, and others cited by Lapidge, print only excerpts.

[7] *Praecepta vivendi* is not a translation of the *Disticha Catonis*, but an independent poem composed by Alcuin in the late 8th century; it was, however, inspired by the *Disticha Catonis*, and contains a number of references to that work. Alcuin of York (who spent much of his life at the court of Charlemagne) is sometimes said to be the first Englishman to show knowledge of *Disticha Catonis*. His knowledge and treatment of *Disticha Catonis* is the subject of a separate study by Boas. See Marcus Boas, *Alcuin und Cato* (Leiden: Brill, 1937).

[8] See Ernst Voigt, 'Über die ältesten Sprichwörtsammlungen des deutsches Mittelalters,' *Zeitschrift für deutsches Alterthum* 30 (1886): 260–1.

Dicts (3), as well as a book-list reference to a gloss of Cato; it would, he believes, be rash to assume that this refers to *OE Dicts*. A fourth Latin manuscript is added by Lapidge, **20**. For other evidence of Anglo-Saxon knowledge of *Disticha Catonis*, see pp. 22–3 below, 'Study of *OE Dicts*.'[9]

Manuscripts

Cambridge, Gonville and Caius College 144, ff. 74v–7r
London, British Library, Cotton Vespasian D.vi, ff. 73v–6v
Cambridge, Trinity College 0.2.31, ff. 34r–40v
Cambridge, University Library Gg.5.35, ff. 407v–12r

Ker, 1964, dates Gonville and Caius College 144 to the late 9th century and the Vespasian and Trinity manuscripts to the mid-10th century.[10] The Latin version not mentioned by Cox, Cambridge, University Library Gg.5.35, is dated mid-11th century by Lapidge, **20**. Trinity is from Christ Church, Canterbury; the other three manuscripts belonged to St Augustine's. The date and provenance of Gonville and Caius 144 are disputed (Lapidge, **20**, 131, n. 36); it was once suspected that it originated on the continent, but a 10th century English origin is also entertained.[11] Lapidge states that this manuscript contains excerpts from Remigius's commentary on *Disticha Catonis*. Vespasian is incomplete, and has neither OE nor Latin glosses.

OE Glosses (FC C.55.1, 2)

A discontinuous gloss in West-Saxon of 113 words (late 11th century) is contained in Oxford, Bodleian Library, Rawlinson G.57, ff. 1r–5v (Ker, 350; s. xi ex.(?)).[12] The first 34 distichs are missing. Lapidge, **20**, 130, n. 32, thinks it uncertain that the Latin in Rawlinson was written in England, and considers that the interlinear gloss derives directly from the commentary of Remigius (131, n. 34). There are also two OE 11th century glosses

---

[9] Ogilvy, **141**, 109, who gives an incomplete list of Anglo-Saxon manuscripts containing *Disticha Catonis*, mentions, as a doubtful possibility, that Archbishop Wulfstan (in *Gerefa*) may have been familiar with Cato's distichs. Ogilvy's work has been superseded by that of Helmut Gneuss; see particularly his indispensable supplement to Ker, 'A Preliminary List of Manuscripts Written or Owned in England up to 1100,' *Anglo-Saxon England* 9 (1981 for 1980): 1–60.

[10] See N.R. Ker, *Medieval Libraries of Great Britain: A List of Surviving Books*, Royal Historical Society Guides and Handbooks 3, 2nd edn. (London: Royal Historical Society, 1964) 41, xxxii.

[11] Gneuss, 1981, 11, dates Gonville and Caius 144 's. ix/x,' and enters the continental origin as doubtful. The manuscript is not listed by Jennifer Morrish, 'Dated and Datable Manuscripts Copied in England during the Ninth Century: A Preliminary List,' *Mediaeval Studies* 50 (1988): 512–38. F.A. Rella, 'Continental Manuscripts Acquired for English Centres in the Tenth and Early Eleventh Centuries: A Preliminary Checklist,' *Anglia* 98 (1980): 110, does list it, but does not list Rawlinson G.57.

[12] The interlinear gloss has been edited by Max Förster and A.S. Napier, 'Englische Cato- und Ilias-Glossen des 12.Jahrhunderts,' *Archiv für das Studium der neueren Sprachen und Literaturen* 117 (1906): 17–28.

to the text of *Disticha Catonis* in the Trinity manuscript listed above (one scratched).[13]

Book-list

A list of books belonging to Athelstan which mentions a *Glossam super Catonem* is added on f. 55v of a manuscript owned by St Augustine's, Canterbury, in the Middle Ages, British Library, Cotton Domitian i. Athelstan has been identified with King Athelstan and Ealdorman Athelstan the 'Half-King.' Lapidge, 1985, the most recent editor of the book-list,[14] considers that the subject matter of the list 'indicates rather that an otherwise unknown schoolmaster or grammarian was the owner of the books' (51). He dates the book-list 'perhaps to the second half of the tenth century' (50); the *c.* 1000 dating of Lapidge, **20**, is closer to Ker (s. x/xi). Various speculations on the nature of the book owned by Athelstan have been entertained; Lapidge presumes that it was the commentary of Remigius because a partial copy of his commentary is found in Gonville and Caius 144.

ME Versions

Owing to the widespread familiarity with *Disticha Catonis* occasioned by its use in elementary instruction, it is echoed in a number of ME proverb collections. One of these is the *Proverbs of Alfred* (13th century, but thought to date originally from *c.* 1150); Arngart, **18**, who argues that *Proverbs of Alfred* shows no knowledge of OE literature, and that its Catonian distichs go back to the Latin, tables correspondences between *Proverbs of Alfred* and *OE Dicts*. A bibliographical description of ME proverb collections is found in Wells, 1916.[15]

RELATIONSHIP TO THE *DISTICHA CATONIS* AND OTHER SOURCES

Cox, **9**, like Nehab, **3**, shows that apothegms 1–76 (excluding 7) are a loose rendering of excerpts from *Disticha Catonis*. But, although Nehab found Latin equivalents for many of the individual apothegms, he did not attempt an overview of their relation to the Latin textual tradition. Cox shows that the original of *OE Dicts* must have incorporated commentary on the text,

---

[13] The glosses are described by Herbert Dean Meritt, *Old English Glosses: A Collection* (New York: Modern Language Association of America, 1945; New York: Kraus, 1971) no. 13.

[14] All the surviving book-lists are edited by Michael Lapidge, 'Surviving Booklists from Anglo-Saxon England,' *Learning and Literature in Anglo-Saxon England: Studies Presented to Peter Clemoes on the Occasion of his Sixty-fifth Birthday*, ed. Michael Lapidge and Helmut Gneuss (Cambridge: Cambridge UP, 1985) 33–90; Athelstan's book-list at 500–2.

[15] John Edwin Wells, *A Manual of the Writings in Middle English, 1050–1400* (New Haven: Yale UP, 1916) 374–85. It is generally held that, although Alfred may have compiled a collection of useful quotations, he is unlikely to have had any direct connection with *Proverbs of Alfred*.

and he also concludes that the Vulgate tradition of *Disticha Catonis*, rather than the Carolingian version upon which modern editions are based, lies behind *OE Dicts*; variants first recorded in 13th century manuscripts are often closest to the OE. Cox considers that these resemblances may stem from commentary influencing *OE Dicts* and later affecting the Latin itself, or they may simply represent parallel developments (36–7).

Recorded sources have been found for only a few of the OE apothegms which are not based on *Disticha Catonis*. Förster pointed out that 77a and 80 are adapted from the Alfredian translation of Boethius's *Consolatio* (and Cox thinks that 77b also resembles the OE translation of Boethius). Cox summarizes the situation by stating that there is no known source for SA, 7, 78, 79, and 81, although Matt. 20.26–7 or Luke 9.48 may lie behind 78, as Nehab suggested (study of Cox's notes, however, reveals that some of his attributions are tentative). Nehab thought that A derived from the prose Preface to Bk. 1 of *Disticha Catonis*; Cox thinks it is as likely to derive from a monostich. B is perhaps a marginal comment on 45 that was copied into the text by a later scribe. Nehab identified *OE Deuteronomy* as the source of F and G; Cox does not agree that E also derived from *OE Deuteronomy*, and thinks C–E may have come from oral tradition.

Michael W. Twomey entered information on the sources of *OE Dicts* into the Manchester Database in 1989.[16] The material is in substantial agreement with Cox: minor corrections are made, *OE Deuteronomy* is accepted as a possible source of E, and no source for B is entered.

STUDY OF *OE Dicts*; CONTEXTS AND BACKGROUNDS

There appears to have been no specialist study of *OE Dicts* since the publication of Cox's edition in 1972. Although there has been considerable interest in Anglo-Saxon education in the last decade or so, there still appears to be no extended study of the educational role of *Disticha Catonis* in the OE period; nor is there any study of the *OE Dicts* which relates it to the use of *Disticha Catonis* as an elementary instructional text. *Disticha Catonis* is among five works on the Anglo-Saxon curriculum briefly discussed by Lapidge, **20**; his account of the study and transmission of glosses and Latin manuscripts is of valuable assistance, but *OE Dicts* lie outside his scope. Hazelton's study (**19**), as has already been mentioned, is specifically directed to the 13th and 14th centuries. The OE period figures only briefly in the historical surveys of Goldberg, **12**, and Chase, **16**.

Familiarity with *Disticha Catonis* in the OE period is established by Cox, who states that *OE Dicts* does not derive from any of the three

---

[16] Michael W. Twomey, 'The Sources of the Anonymous Old English Distichs of Cato,' *Fontes Anglo-Saxonici, A Database Register of Written Sources used by Authors in Anglo-Saxon England*, ed. D.G. Scragg and M. Lapidge (University of Manchester), 19 entries: nos C.B.7.1.0001–19. *OE Deuteronomy* is edited by S.J. Crawford, *The Old English Version of the Heptateuch, Ælfric's Treatise on the Old and New Testament*. EETS 160 (London: Oxford UP, 1922) 333–76.

extant Anglo-Saxon copies of *Disticha Catonis*, and that it is unrelated to the late 11th century West-Saxon gloss (see p. 20 above, 'OE Glosses'). Bullough, **230**, in an essay on Anglo-Saxon educational movements, observes that Byrhtferth is the first to refer to Cato's distichs in a vernacular context. The *Durham Proverbs* might also testify to the currency of *OE Dicts* in the late OE period. Arngart, **28**, 10, 16, following *ODEP*, **35**, gave the source of *DP* 1 as *OE Dicts* 23. (See further pp. 37–8 below, 'Relationship of *DP* to *OE Dicts*.') Cox, **9**, 40, however, disagrees that *DP* 1 originates with *OE Dicts*; he concludes that the translator of *OE Dicts* has a tendency to add short maxims of popular origin, and thinks it likely that 'geðyld bið middes eades,' in *OE Dicts* 23, is one of these additions. Cox examines rhetorical patterning in *OE Dicts*, but does not raise the possibility of connections between the nature of the OE translation and the use of *Disticha Catonis* in elementary education.

Superficially at least, the information Cox assembles seems to suggest that elementary education in England mirrored the continental developments outlined by Hazelton, **19**, since there is one copy of *Disticha Catonis* extant which Ker dates late 9th century and evidence of more widespread currency in the 10th and 11th centuries (to which can be added the lost version incorporating commentary on *Disticha Catonis* that Cox postulates as the source for *OE Dicts*). The possibility exists—at least in theory—that *Disticha Catonis* was brought in by continental clergy during the reign of Alfred. That most English manuscripts of *Disticha Catonis* prior to the 12th century are associated with Kent is, as Cox remarks, 'a fact of uncertain significance' (33), but, given Canterbury's continental links in the reign of Alfred, it is certainly suggestive. On the other hand, a number of the studies which are annotated in the present work suggest that Theodore's Canterbury school may have played a significant role in the transmission of Latin texts, and Cox, **7**, ventured the suggestion that the *Disticha Catonis* was introduced into England by Theodore and Hadrian (see also Goldberg, **12**). It would seem that some Latin texts underwent distinctive developments in England, which were then transmitted to the continent by Anglo-Saxons (particularly missionaries); see, e.g., Kortekaas, **152**, Talbot, **369**. Perhaps this may explain why Cox finds that *OE Dicts* are often closest to variants first found in 13th century manuscripts. In sum, conditions seem to be ripe, both for a study of the transmission of *Disticha Catonis* to England, and for an investigation of the milieu, both intellectual and geographical, in which *OE Dicts* took shape. (The possibility that Ælfric was the translator of *OE Dicts*, originating with Müller, **1**, and reflected in the work of Nehab and Goldberg, was entertained with increasing scepticism in the first half of this century, and has been silently abandoned.)

For the study of *OE Dicts*, Handley's work on Vespasian D.xiv (V) is of considerable significance (**96**). V was of particular interest to Förster, who, as well as publishing a full description of its contents, edited a number of

texts from it, and on several occasions, before the appearance of Warner's
edition, he announced his intention of bringing out an edition of *OE Dicts*
(**62, 14, 15** and **5**). Förster, **89**, was at first inclined to associate V with
one of the great centres of learning such as Winchester, but later (in a note
on the *Elucidarium*, **91**) he advanced the view that V was a preacher's
commonplace-book, designed for an audience of uneducated religious. Handley thinks it likely that V originated at Canterbury, and that it was probably copied there after the 1067 fire; she regards V as a teaching manual for
young monks. The existence of V, she points out, 'demonstrates that there
was in the South-East in the twelfth century, a monastic scriptorium capable of preparing and copying with understanding a body of Anglo-Saxon
material' (250). Further consideration of the manuscript contents of T and
V might conceivably throw light on *OE Dicts* and its role in Anglo-Saxon
education, and on the continuing use of Anglo-Saxon for educational purposes in the post-Conquest period. Arngart, **44**, argued that the pedagogic
use of Latin–English proverb collections is confirmed by their appearance
in manuscripts containing Ælfric's *Grammar*, and the fact that T contains
a copy of Ælfric's *Grammar* was regarded by Goldberg, **12**, as evidence of
the role of *OE Dicts* in elementary instruction.

Whereas Goldberg regarded translation of *Disticha Catonis* as symptomatic of a decline in the knowledge of Latin in the late Anglo-Saxon period, Arngart's work suggests that vernacular translations of proverbs are
pedagogic exercises reflecting efforts to acquire knowledge of Latin. Cox, **7**,
and Brunner, **8**, however, though conscious of the educational role of *Disticha Catonis*, regard Anglo-Saxon fondness for proverbial wisdom as the
motivating impulse behind the translation (see also Nehab, **3**), and Brunner discerns a distinctly secular cast of mind in the accretions. Anderson,
17, assumed that the translation was made for the purpose of educating
the laity at large.

As a pagan work employed as an elementary text in Christian education, *Disticha Catonis* was significantly instrumental in the formation of
culture. Hazelton observes that its impact went far beyond its intrinsic
value, in part because, being the first full-length text a student read, it
had considerable impact on the young. In the context of the commentaries,
he observes, *Disticha Catonis* reveals itself as a compendium of the root
ideas of medieval man: 'Cato, with the help of the assiduous schoolmasters, had fixed for him the ethical coordinates of his world' (173). In the
light of this, *OE Dicts* is a rich source of information with central bearing on the Christian–pagan debate, whose potential has yet to be realized.
Förster, **14**, in identifying the Alfredian *Consolatio* as the source of two
of the OE distichs, speculated that Anglo-Saxon translation of the *Consolatio* and *Disticha Catonis* represented a tendency to gravitate towards
Latin works that had originated in a society more pagan than Christian.
Hazelton argues that the pedagogic commentaries in which *Disticha Catonis* became enmeshed were, by intention, a check upon the assimilation of

a pagan ethic, although he recognizes that whether *Disticha Catonis* was read according to the pagan letter or the Christian spirit was ultimately an individual matter. Although *OE Dicts* is usually described as a 'free' translation, commitment to the establishment of the sources of OE texts is generally apt to minimize awareness of substantive departures from the Latin; Cox, **9**, does, however, observe that in some cases *OE Dicts* 'makes quite different sense from any extant Latin version' (37), and he regards the addition of short popular proverbs as characteristic of the OE translator (see also Brunner, **8**). Hazelton's approach suggests that an enquiry into the philosophical orientation of *OE Dicts*, pursued through a study of its substantive departures from the Latin, is likely to prove fruitful. Arngart, **18**, who tables comparisons between *OE Dicts* and the proverbs derived from *Disticha Catonis* in *Proverbs of Alfred*, observes that comparative study of translations of *Disticha Catonis* is 'instructive,' but is concerned only to define the extent of verbal correspondence with the Latin.

According to Hazelton, the retention of *Disticha Catonis* as a teaching text in the 9th century was assisted by its concordance with the sapiential books of scripture, which were drawn into relationship with *Disticha Catonis* through the commentaries. Like the OE prose dialogues, *OE Dicts* has rarely been considered in relation to the OE wisdom 'poetry,' and it would be interesting to know whether use of *Disticha Catonis* in elementary teaching helped to transmit the familiarity with the sapiential books that some scholars believe is reflected in the OE wisdom 'poetry.' Given that *Disticha Catonis* was essentially a teaching text, however, it is striking that one of the ways in which *OE Dicts* diverges from the Latin is that the apothegms are not presented as admonitions to a young man, but open with an exhortation to the self-motivated pursuit of wisdom: 'Mann sceal þurh his modes snoternysse hine sylfne geglengen to wisre lare.'

DICTS OF CATO: ANNOTATIONS

SEE ALSO Förster, **24**; Arngart, **28**; Skeat, **31**; Smith, **35**; Whiting, **41**; Newman, **48**; Kemble, **52**; Förster, **62**; Förster **94**

Greenfield and Robinson also refer to the following:

Mynors, R.A.B. *Durham Cathedral Manuscripts to the End of the Twelfth Century*. Oxford: Oxford UP, 1939.
Greenfield and Robinson's reason for cross-listing no. 22 of Mynors's work under *Distichs of Cato* could not be ascertained; it may be in some way connected with the fact that the *DP* manuscript, said to have originated at Canterbury, is no. 21 in this manuscript catalogue.

EDITIONS

1 **Müller, Ludvig.** *Collectanea Anglo-Saxonica, maximam partem nunc primum edita et vocabulario illustrata*. Copenhagen: Wahl, 1835.

   Prints T (including SA), and V, as 'Proverbia Anglosaxonica,' 28–48; collates J from transcripts by Grundtvig. No apparatus.

2 **Cockayne, Thomas Oswald.** *The Shrine. A Collection of Occasional Papers on Dry Subjects*. London: Williams and Norgate, 1864–70.

   Prints SA from T, 162.

3 **Nehab, Julius.** *Der altenglische Cato. Eine Übertragung und Bearbeitung der* 'Disticha Catonis.' Diss. U Göttingen, 1879. Berlin: Unger, 1879.

   Prints T (including SA); collates J and V from Müller, **1**, and transcripts by Schleich, 46–54. Regularized text. Textual variants, 54–60.

   Introduction discusses the Germanic fondness for proverbs and compares *OE Dicts* with *Exeter* and *Cotton* gnomes. Manuscript description, 6–14; language (concludes that T, J, and V are, respectively, early, mid- and late 12th century; favours a Winchester provenance), 15–41; manuscript relationship (T and J are more directly related to one another than to V), 42–5. In his discussion of the sources, 61–71, Nehab concludes that apothegms 1–76 are loose translations of *Disticha Catonis*, and all but eight follow the sequence of the original; he identifies *OE Deuteronomy*, 17.15; 18.11–12; 16.19 [ed. Crawford, 1922] as the source of E, F and G respectively, and suggests that 78 is derived from Matt. 20.26–7 or Luke 9.48, and that A is from the prose preface to Bk. 1 of *Disticha Catonis*. At 71–4, Nehab argues that there are stylistic and syntactical similarities between *OE Dicts* and *OE Deuteronomy* and conjectures that both works were translated by the same person, possibly Ælfric, whose *Grammar* is preserved with T. [For reviews see Schleich, **10**; Cosijn, **11**.]

4 **Warner, Rubie D-N.** *Early English Homilies from the Twelfth Century MS.*
   Vesp. D. XIV. EETS 152. London: Kegan Paul, 1917. New York: Kraus,
   1971.

   Prints V, as 'The Old English Cato,' 3–7, with marginal summaries. Minimal apparatus; the projected second volume, which was to have contained
   a description of the manuscript, did not appear.

   Also prints, as separate items, the two parts of *OE Elucidarium* [FC B.9.9],
   140–5; both items entitled 'The Old English Honorius.'

   Also prints two prognostics, from Vespasian D.xiv [FC B.23.3.5]: 'Weather
   Prophecies,' 66; and a brontology, *Emb ƿunre*, 91.

5 **Sievers, Eduard.** *Metrische Studien IV. Die altschwedischen Upplandslagh*
   nebst Proben formverwandter germanischer Sagdichtung. Abhandlungen
   der kgl. Sächsischen Gesellschaft der Wissenschaften, Philologisch-historische
   Klasse 35. Leipzig: Teubner, 1918–9.

   Text, 601–15, entitled 'Die Sprüche Catos und Verwandten.' Based on
   Müller's edition of T (**1**); collates J and V from transcripts by Förster.
   Sievers's text, very heavily emended to support his theory that *OE Dicts*
   were written in *ljóðahattr* verse but without alliteration, is not a reliable
   guide to what is contained in the manuscripts.

6 **Wyatt, Alfred J.** *An Anglo-Saxon Reader*. Cambridge: Cambridge UP,
   1919.

   Text of *SS*, 45–6; Notes, 221. Extracts from *OE Dicts* (12 apothegms);
   text, 46–7; Notes, 221–2. Both entitled '*Solomon and Saturn.*'

   At 221, Wyatt explains: 'These apothegms are allowed to shelter under the
   wing of *Solomon and Saturn* rather than make of them a separate extract—
   a convenience partly justified by Kemble's inclusion of them in his *Salomon*
   and Saturn [**52**] on the ground of a certain degree of kinship.'

7 **Cox, Robert S., Jr.** 'The Old English Dicts of Cato and Others.' Diss.
   Indiana U, 1965. Dir. Rowland Collins. [*DA* 26 (1965): 6694.]

   Near-diplomatic edition of T, conflated with A–G from V, 77–175; apparatus
   (at foot of page) records variants from J and V and Latin parallels; includes
   explanatory notes. Appendices, 176–89, table information concerning the
   relationship of the three versions, distinction between ð and ƿ, forms of *beon*
   and *mann*, personal and demonstrative pronouns, and accented forms in T.

   Chapters on manuscript description, 4–24, language, 25–35, and sources,
   36–51, are effectively summarized by Cox, 9; the dissertation differs in concluding that the use of Kentish spellings in all three manuscripts and the
   attribution to Kent of both T and V (on palaeographic grounds), makes
   likely a Kentish origin and line of descent (25). The manuscripts have
   a complicated history; Cox (70–1) rejects the stemma of Nehab, **3**, and

Schleich, **10**. 'Medieval Reputation of the *Disticha Catonis*,' 52–69, gives a fuller account of the transmission and popularity of the work than Cox, **9**. Cox thinks it probable that the *Disticha Catonis* was introduced into England by Theodore and Hadrian, and attributes the OE translation to a native Anglo-Saxon taste for proverbs and sententious sayings: 'Those who read no Latin still wished to read the wisdom of the fabled Cato' (62). Survey of previous scholarship, 69–75.

8 Brunner, Ingrid Arvide. 'The Anglo-Saxon Translation of the Distichs of Cato: A Critical Edition.' Diss. Columbia U, 1965. [*DA* 26 (1965): 3296–97.]

Critical edition of V, 95–108; textual variants from J and V, 111–30. Also prints SA from T, 109–10. Notes, 131–212, include translation, Latin sources, textual and editorial commentary. Appendices, 213–17, table information on capitalization and foliation.

Ch. 1, 'History of the Latin Text,' 1–40, includes discussion of the popularity and function of proverbs in the Anglo-Saxon period and relation of *OE Dicts* to the Latin; the final distichs, which are not derived from *Disticha Catonis*, contain 'advice applicable to public life or statesmanship rather than private morals, and this might possibly be an indication of the personal interests of the translator' (40). Ch. 2 'The Manuscripts of the Anglo-Saxon Version,' 41–52. Ch. 3, 'Orthography and Inflections in the Manuscripts,' 53–70, concludes that V is the latest, transitional to ME, and T is the oldest. Ch. 4, 'The Relationship of the Manuscripts,' 71–86, argues that T and J have a common original and that V is more directly descended; it has the most felicitous wording where the three differ, and 'may represent the complete text as far as the additional distichs are concerned' (84). Ch. 5, 'Previous Editions of the Anglo-Saxon Version,' 87–94.

9 Cox, R.S. 'The Old English Dicts of Cato.' *Anglia* 90 (1972): 1–42.

Prints T (including SA); conflated with A–G from V, 5–16; reconstructed Latin source (based on Boas, 1952) printed parallel. 'Textual notes and commentary,' 17–29, gives variants from V and J (including contemporary corrections to the text), and brief remarks on sources.

Cox sketches the development of *Disticha Catonis* and its place in medieval education, and explains that *OE Dicts* are not related to extant Anglo-Saxon copies of *Disticha Catonis*, or to the late WS gloss [FC C.55.2]. Manuscript description, 29–32, dates J to late 11th century and V to first half of the 12th century. 'Origin,' 32–4, concludes that the dialect of the exemplar was either Kentish or Mercian, and that composition was begun between the mid-10th and mid-11th century and complete by the end of the 11th century when T was made. 'Relationship of the Manuscripts,' 34–6, concludes that T shows less innovation than V, and J is corrupt. Examination of sources, 36–8, explains that the common exemplar of TJV was a text of *Disticha Catonis* (Vulgate, not Carolingian) which incorporated commentary: 'Recorded sources have been found for only a few of the Dicts which are not based on the *Disticha*' (38). 'Translator's Method,' 39–40, remarks on the translator's 'tendency to accompany an apothegm with a short maxim of popular origin' (40). 'Rhetorical Patterns,' 40–2, briefly considers some examples of larger syntactical patterns; the apothegms are as formal as OE gnomic verse, but the patterns are quite different.

COMMENTARY

10 **Schleich, Gustav.** Rev. of *Der altenglische Cato: Eine Übertragung und Bearbeitung der* 'Disticha Catonis,' by Julius Nehab [3]. *Anglia* 3 (1880): 383–96.

Schleich's attack on Nehab, **3**, is comprehensive and minutely detailed; corrections to the text, and criticism of various editorial procedures, etc., 383–8. The most substantial charge is that Nehab made use of Schleich's transcriptions without consulting either Schleich or the manuscripts, and therefore mistook Schleich's symbols for scribal notations. Schleich is least disparaging of Nehab's examination of language and does not actively dispute his dating. On 388–92, Schleich takes issue with Nehab's explanation of the manuscript relationship; in essentials, he is in agreement with Nehab, concluding that T and J do not derive from one another but from a common exemplar; V belongs to a different manuscript group. He thinks it possible that a single copyist, rather than a single translator, could account for the linguistic similarities between *OE Dicts* and *OE Deuteronomy*.

11 **Cosijn, P.** 'Anglo-Saxonica: *Disticha Catonis*, ed. Dr. J. Nehab.' *Tijdschrift voor Nederlandsche Tall- en Letterkunde* 1 (1881): 143–58.

Cosijn's review, at 150–8, of Nehab, **3**, offsets the criticisms of Schleich, **10**; there is a textual discussion of some 30 of the distichs.

12 **Goldberg, Max O.** 'Die Catonischen Distichen während des Mittelalters in der englischen und französischen Literatur. 1. Theil. Der englische Cato.' Diss. U Leipzig, 1883. Leipzig: Joachim, 1883.

'Der angelsächsische Cato,' 7–11. Wisdom was eagerly sought in Britain from the earliest times, and Goldberg suggests that *Disticha Catonis* was among the books imported by Benedict Biscop. The earliest reference to the work is the *Glossa super Catonem* in Athelstan's book-list, which Goldberg dates early 9th century [*sic*], but he considers that vernacular translation is symptomatic of a decline in the knowledge of Latin, and thus doubts that OE translations of Cato (as opposed to glosses) would have been made before 950, that is, the era which saw the establishment of Æthelwold's Winchester school. Goldberg dates the original of *OE Dicts* to the second half of the 10th century (10). In reviewing previous scholarship, Goldberg opines that

Ælfric may not have been responsible for *OE Dicts*, but, because translation of the distichs was a means of instructing the young, Müller, **1**, was not fundamentally wrong to connect them with Ælfric's Grammar. Manuscript relationships, as expounded by Nehab, **3**, are summarized. The OE version is a free paraphrase; the compiler seems to have made two passes over the Latin work and some OE proverbs have no parallel in the original. There are resemblances between *Proverbs of Alfred* and *OE Dicts*, but *Proverbs of Alfred* derives from the Latin, not the OE translation. The sentiments expressed in the gnomic-didactic poem, *Precepts*, are so widely shared that it would be otiose to connect them closely with the *Disticha Catonis*.

13 Wülcker, Richard. *Grundriss zur Geschichte der angelsächsischen Litteratur.* Leipzig: Veit, 1885.

Annotated Bibliography, 500–3; summarizes Nehab, **3**, treatment of sources only, and Schleich, **10**.

14 Förster, Max. 'Kleine Mitteilungen: Zum altenglischen Boethius.' *Archiv für das Studium der neueren Sprachen und Literaturen* 106 (1901): 342–3.

Förster shows that *OE Dicts*, 77a and 80, derive from the Alfredian translation of Boethius' *Consolatio*, 32.1 and 27.2, respectively (ed. Sedgefield, 1899). Förster finds this vernacular combination of Cato and Boethius significant, because both these works fall only marginally within the Christian era, and he suggests that the two translations belonged to the same milieu. He notes that T is the oldest version of *OE Dicts*; second half of the 11th century, not 12th century as Nehab (**3**) and Schleich (**10**) think (342, n. 1). [This article is listed in FC as an edition of *OE Dicts*; Förster prints, from Nehab, **3**, only the apothegms for which he gives a source.]

15 Skutsch, Franz. 'Dicta Catonis.' *Paulys Real-Encyclopädie der classischen Altertumswissenschaft.* Vol. 5. Stuttgart: Metzler, 1905. 358–70. 33 vols. 1893–1972.

Description of the Latin work; bibliography of editions of vernacular translations, 368, provided by Förster. Skutsch refers to Förster's forthcoming three-volume edition of OE and ME versions of *Disticha Catonis*.

16 Chase, Wayland Johnson. *The Distichs of Cato: A Famous Medieval Textbook.* U of Wisconsin Studies in the Social Sciences and History 7. Madison: n.p., 1922.

Latin text (based on Baehrens, 1881) with MnE trans. 'Introduction,' 1–11, outlines briefly the composition and development of *Disticha Catonis* and its importance throughout the ages as a first reader and textbook on morals: 'From an examination of its career as a textbook we find that the seventh century monastery schools in Ireland made use of it and that it is in the eighth, ninth, tenth and eleventh century school-book lists of both the British Isles and the Continent' (8). Chase observes *Disticha Catonis*'s influence on literature and popular proverbs (8–11), and remarks that many literary works of parental and ethical instruction, from the time of Columban through that of Alfred the Great and much later, are largely outgrowths of *Disticha Catonis*. [No specific reference to *OE Dicts*.]

17 Anderson, George K. *The Literature of the Anglo-Saxons.* Princeton: Princeton UP, 1949. New York: Russell, 1962. Rev. edn. 1966.

Ch. 11, 'Secular Didactic Writing in OE Prose,' 370–4, explains that, just as a distinction between secular and religious didactic poetry can be made, *SS* and *OE Dicts* are moralistic without being dogmatic. *SS* 'needs no further attention here beyond the statement that it represents a perennial kind of instruction-piece' (370). *OE Dicts* are 'another instance of the careful compiling by enthusiastic churchmen and teachers of such worldly wisdom as could be found in their academic and spiritual traditions, and the making accessible of that wisdom to their native English flocks' (371), although there is more than a trace of classical paganism in them.

On *OE ApT* and *Wond*, ch. 12, 'Prose Fiction of the Old English Period,' 375–83, observes that the presence of foreign importations suggests 'that story-telling for its own sake was returning ... we have reached the point of transition ... to the beginnings of the romance' (375). The mere outline of the story of Apollonius illustrates the difference between prose romance and heroic epic: 'Can anyone imagine Beowulf as falling in love, let alone blushing when that love was revealed to him?' (377). *Alex* and *Wond* 'probably owe their origin to the same scholarly interest of the time in the exotic' (379–80).

Ch. 13, 'Scientific Writings in the OE period,' 384–402. 'The Anglo-Saxon scholar could be eminently practical.... Yet even in this scientific and quasi-scientific literature one must make generous allowance for the incredible as well as the superstitious' (384). Anderson briefly surveys *ByrM*, *Herb*, *MedQuad* ('far more committed to folklore than to practical medicine,' 388), *Lb* (whose prescriptions 'bring us closer to the realization that the Anglo-Saxons were as other men than do all the pages of their Christian prose and poetry together,' 391), *PD* and miscellaneous treatises ('what is generally annoying ... is their total lack of order or method or design,' 395).

18 Arngart, O. 'The Distichs of Cato and the Proverbs of Alfred.' *Kungl. Humanistiska Vetenskapssamfundets i Lund, Årsberättelse* (1951–2): 95–118.

Arngart surveys the tradition of ascribing sententious sayings to Alfred, which cannot be traced back beyond the 12th century. *Proverbs of Alfred* shows no knowledge of any OE writings and the chief classical influence is *Disticha Catonis*. At 104–18, Arngart sets out the chief agreements between *Proverbs of Alfred* and *Disticha Catonis*, citing parallels with *OE Dicts* (nine in all) and a late 14th century ME translation of *Disticha Catonis* (Vernon MS, ed. Furnivall, 1901). 'As observed by Goldberg [**12**, 10–11], the author of the *Proverbs of Alfred* did not use the OE paraphrase but the *Distichs* themselves, yet a study of the approach of the different translators and paraphrasers to their text is instructive' (104). Commentary on *OE Dicts* is limited to occasional observations on the fidelity or freedom of the translation.

19 Hazelton, Richard. 'The Christianization of "Cato": The *Disticha Catonis* in the Light of Late Mediaeval Commentaries.' *Mediaeval Studies* 19 (1957): 157–73.

The focus of Hazelton's article is the 13th and 14th centuries, when the commentaries were fully developed. Pedagogues, accessible to us in the glosses and commentaries that accompany classical texts in many manuscripts, are the key to the survival of pagan books and the eminence some attained. *Disticha Catonis* is 'a distillation (from the modern point of view, an adulteration) of many of the ideas and sentiments found in Augustan and Silver Latin literature' (162). Hazelton considers the question of whether widespread use of Cato in the schools indicates uncritical assimilation of a pagan ethic, and argues that 'Cato was converted into a Christian moralist' (163); examination of the glosses shows how this may have come about. What made this conversion possible was the concord between Cato and the sapiential books of the scriptures—their worldly practical precepts were obviously equivalent. Cato was a type of the wise man; commentaries reveal how thoroughly *Disticha Catonis* was expounded, and it was read according to the spirit. The eminence of *Disticha Catonis* goes beyond its intrinsic worth—because it was valued for its 'utility' and because of its impact on the young. It was the first full-length literary piece the student read, and in the context of the commentaries it 'reveals itself as a compendium of the root ideas' of medieval man: 'Cato, with the help of the assiduous schoolmasters, had fixed for him the ethical co-ordinates of his world' (173). As the commentaries reveal that assimilation of *Disticha Catonis* was not uncritical, it is unlikely that the effect of study was to inculcate the medieval world with ancient morality; but 'whether the individual responded to the letter of the pagan text or to the spirit of the Christian interpretation depended ultimately, one must suppose, on individual temperament' (173). [No specific mention of *OE Dicts*.]

20 Lapidge, Michael. 'The Study of Latin Texts in Late Anglo-Saxon England: (1) The Evidence of Latin Glosses.' *Latin and the Vernacular Languages in Early Medieval Britain.* Studies in the Early History of Britain. Ed. Nicholas Brooks. Leicester: Leicester UP, 1982. 99–140.

Disticha Catonis is one of five works on the Anglo-Saxon syllabus discussed by Lapidge (102–5), who argues that, although manuscripts of Christian-Latin works were not necessarily used as classbooks, they alone enable us to estimate the way in which Latin culture was absorbed by the Anglo-Saxons. Glosses to Cambridge, University Library, Gg.5.35, and Trinity

College O.2.31 are independent of one another and appear to have been present in the exemplars. Remigius's commentary was evidently known in the late Anglo-Saxon period (it appears in a St Augustine's book-list, *c.* 1000, and is partially preserved in Gonville and Caius College 144/194, ff. 74v–5v, which may be of English origin (131, n. 36)); the glosses in these two manuscripts are not influenced by Remigius, but it is doubtful whether they preserve a record of a classroom exposition. Rawlinson G.57, whose interlinear glosses do appear to derive from Remigius, was not certainly written in England (130, n. 34). *OE Dicts* is referred to only in passing.

DURHAM AND OTHER PROVERBS

MANUSCRIPTS

DURHAM PROVERBS

Durham, Cathedral Library, B.III.32, ff. 43v–5v   D   FC C.25
Ker 107A (s. xi¹), art. 3   s. xi med.

FAUSTINA, ROYAL AND RAWLINSON PROVERBS

London, British Library, Cotton Faustina A.x, f. 100v   F   FC B.7.2*
Ker 154A (s. xi²), arts. 2, 3   s. xi ex., s. xii²

London, British Library, Royal 2 B.v, f. 6   R   FC B.7.3*
Ker 249 (s. x med., xi), art. b   s. xi med.

Oxford, Bodleian, Rawlinson C. 641, f. 13v   Ra   FC B.7.4
Ker 348, art. b   s. xii/xiii

*Includes two metrical proverbs (FC A.35).

MANUSCRIPTS: DESCRIPTION, CONTENTS, DATE AND PROVENANCE (following Ker)

Durham

The sole copy of *Durham Proverbs* is added in mid-11th century script on some originally blank leaves between a hymnal and a collection of canticles. The manuscript consists of two parts, which were bound together at an early date. *DP* are found in Part A; Part B contains a copy of Ælfric's *Grammar*, preceded by a preface, but without the glossary which usually accompanies the *Grammar*. The manuscript is said to have been given to Durham Cathedral in the early 18th century; it is probably of Canterbury origin.

Faustina

Part A of F also contains Ælfric's *Grammar* (with glossary). A group of three Latin–English proverbs and a bilingual proverbial saying have been added in the blank spaces at the end of the last quire. Ker dates the proverb group s. xi ex., and the proverbial saying s. xii². Part B contains an OE translation of the Rule of St Benedict and an account of King Edgar's revival of monasticism, together with some Latin and OE charms and recipes (Cockayne, **298**, 3: 292). The two parts have probably been together since the 12th century, and art. 1 of Part A was written probably in the same scriptorium as Hatton 115 (Ker, 332).

Royal

The group of three Latin–English proverbs in R are among the additions in OE (mostly prayers, together with a note of Friday fasts) made at the beginning and end of the manuscript; its principle contents are 'a continuous interlinear gloss to a Latin psalter and canticles of the Roman version.' The additions are in various hands; Ker dates the proverbs s. xi med. The psalter was perhaps written at Winchester, but the manuscript was at Christ Church, Canterbury, in s. xi and later.

Rawlinson

The two proverbs in Ra are the only trilingual items in an anonymous collection of French–Latin proverbs; Ker dates these proverbs s. xii/xiii. Elsewhere in the manuscript, OE appears only in occasional glosses to the text that Liebermann called 'Instituta Cnuti,' dated s. xii², perhaps of Kentish provenance.

All four proverb collections, then, are later additions to their respective manuscripts, but it is worth noticing a difference in presentation. The small groups in R and F are jottings in blank spaces and include an isolated maxim recorded among scribbles and pen trials. *DP*, however, although badly written, seems to have a different status; Arngart, **28**, notes that the first letters or capitals of the Latin lines are frequently missing, and the capitals that do occur are mostly later additions and are not always certain to be correct. This description strongly suggests that *DP* was intended to have illuminated capitals; Ker reports that the first letter of each hymn and canticle in this manuscript is in red, green, or blue, with a little decoration.

DESCRIPTION OF THE TEXTS, COVERAGE

DP, the earliest known collection of vernacular proverbs, consists of 46 Latin–OE proverbs; each Latin proverb is followed by its OE equivalent. A number of the proverbs in the Durham collection have been described as metrical. FC list *DP* under 'Glosses.'

There is also a cluster of four Latin–English proverbs in Royal 2 B.v (R) and a cluster of three in Faustina A.x (F). On the same leaf of Faustina A.x is a bilingual proverbial saying, overlooked by editors, but transcribed by Ker, and included with the Faustina group in FC's classification ('Ad traeam dixit pereant tot buffo magistri. þa tadda cƿ to þar éiþa Forwurþa swa fola maistres.') None of the four proverbs in R is unique; two of them also occur in F, and the remaining two are essentially the same as *DP* 37 and 39. The two proverbs which R and F have in common were defined by editors (see **25, 27**) as metrical types. FC, reflecting the historical significance attached to the identification of metrical-alliterative patterns in OE texts, classify the two proverbs common to F and R as 'Poetry' (A.35). FC also include two English proverbs which are found (as trilingual glosses) in a Latin–French collection in Rawlinson C. 641. Förster, **24**, described these proverbs as early ME (13th century).

In FC's schema, then, the category 'prose proverbs' covers only *OE Dicts*, two proverbs in R (which are also in *DP*), two in F (one of them being the bilingual proverbial saying), and two dubiously OE proverbs in Rawlinson C. 641. Metrical discriminations, however, obscure the fact that R, F and *DP* are significantly connected as proverb *collections*.

The best-known and oldest datable OE proverb is the 'Proverb from Winfrid's Time,' which appears in an anonymous letter found among the Boniface correspondence, (Vienna, Nationalbibliothek Lat. 751, ff. 34v–5r), dated 757×786 (FC A.16), and edited by Dobbie, **27**, 57. The letter, seemingly intending to urge an ecclesiastical dignitary not to desist from the course of action he has chosen, contains the passage 'memento saxonicum uerbum. oft daedlata dome foreldit sigisitha gahuem suuyltit thi ana.'[1] The proverb is regarded as too firmly associated with the metrical corpus for inclusion here.

Foremost among the proverbs that do not have an established place in the poetic corpus are two which occur in the *ASC*, and one found in the Alfredian translation of *Regula Pastoralis*. Two publications on these proverbs (Klaeber, **30**, Taylor, **38**), which are listed by Greenfield and Robinson under 'Durham and Miscellaneous Proverbs,' are included in the annotations for the sake of completeness. Recently come to light, and thus not classified by FC, is a proverb (or maxim) which appears among Latin scribbles and OE pen trials in a blank space in Leningrad, Public Library, Lat.O.v.XVI.I, f. 15r, following a Latin grammatical text in Anglo-Saxon minuscule. This manuscript, overlooked by Ker in his *Catalogue*, is included in Ker, *Suppl.*, 415, (he dates the proverb s. x[1]). It reads 'a scæl gelæred smið swa he gelicost mæg be bisne wyrcan but he bet cunne.' Blockley, **45**, who draws attention to it, identifies it as verse. Trahern, **46**, identifies a hitherto unnoticed proverb, which he describes as metrical, but the article is of undoubted interest for the study of OE proverbs, and, as the proverb appears in a prose context and may derive from a Latin source, there seems good reason to include it among the annotations.

EDITIONS; DATE AND LANGUAGE OF THE TEXTS

DP was not edited until 1956, when Arngart brought out a separate edition of the bilingual text (**28**); this was followed, in 1981, by a revised edition, which appeared in *Speculum* (**29**). There are no other editions. Only the 1956 edition contains a glossary and a facsimile of the opening page of the proverbs. The notes to the 1981 edition offer translations for most of the proverbs, as well as additional sources and analogues. The brief introduction to the revised edition raises topics not dealt with in the earlier publication; in particular, it considers the question of the age of the

---

[1] E.G. Stanley, 'The Oldest English Poetry Now Extant,' *Poetica* (Tokyo) (1974), who seems to have been the last to study the proverb, observes that it sums up an ideal of heroic fellowship, applied surprisingly, but not incongruously, to missionary endeavour.

proverbs. Like *ODEP*, **35**, Arngart places *DP* midway between the traditional wisdom of the *Exeter* and *Cotton* gnomes (*Maxims* I and II) and later ME proverb collections. Arngart's suggested date is second quarter of the 11th century, and he concludes that *DP* are late West-Saxon with only a few distinctly non-West-Saxon forms.

The most readily available edition of the Royal and Faustina proverbs is that of Dobbie, **27**, who edits the two metrical proverbs they have in common and gives the text of the prose proverbs in the apparatus (the text of the bilingual proverbial saying in Faustina, however, is printed only by Ker, 154A.) Dobbie found no indications for dating the Faustina and Royal proverbs, other than that provided by the script. The two English proverbs in Rawlinson were printed by Förster, **24**, from Stengel, **23**; given that Förster had no hesitation in describing them as early ME, their acceptance as OE by FC is rather surprising.

RELATIONSHIP OF OE AND LATIN IN *DP*; RELATION OF *DP* TO *OE Dicts* AND OTHER PROVERB COLLECTIONS; PURPOSE OF THE PROVERB COLLECTIONS

Arngart, **28** and **44**, argues that the Latin of *DP* is a translation of the OE (and in many cases an erroneous or infelicitous translation), and relates *DP* to the practice of translating vernacular proverbs as a means of acquiring a working knowledge of Latin, to which Singer, **34**, refers in his study of continental proverb collections. In other words, Arngart regards *DP* as a school exercise, having the same function as *OE Dicts*, but reversing the direction of the translation. Arngart, **44**, finds confirmation for his view in the fact that *DP* 1 echoes one of the distichs of Cato (but Cox, **9**, disagrees). Arngart's argument that the Latin is a translation of the OE provides a persuasive explanation of its unusual degree of corruption, but he offers no comment on the fact that the Latin version of each proverb precedes its OE equivalent (so also Faustina and Royal). Arngart's view of *DP* is accepted by both Storms, **37**, and Whiting, **39**.

Wülcker, **22**, observing that the Faustina and Royal proverbs have two items in common, speculated that they derived from a common store of proverbs. Arngart, **29**, noting that two of the Royal proverbs also occur in *DP*, points out that *DP*, even if it is not 'the very fountainhead' of the Royal and Faustina proverbs (290), seems to have been much copied, and furnishes us with an example of the kind of proverb collection that others drew upon. He further strengthened the case for the status of the proverb collections as pedagogic exercises by pointing to the fact that both the Faustina manuscript and the *DP* manuscript contain copies of Ælfric's *Grammar*. (For the differing manuscript presentation of *DP* and the minor groups, see p. 35 above, 'Manuscripts'.)

A somewhat different view of the function of proverb collections was put forward in the 1948 edition of *The Oxford Dictionary of English Proverbs*,

35 (*ODEP* anticipates Arngart in regarding *DP* as a means of instruction in Latin, but seems to assume that the pedagogic method consisted of translation *from* Latin). The editors of *ODEP* advanced the view that the main reason for the proverb collections was the growing interest in the art of rhetoric, and remarked that proverb collections were employed, in rhetorical practice, to round off anecdotes and point the moral, and were particularly useful to medieval secretaries, who drew on them for the *exordium* which was a conventional feature of letter writing. As the rhetorical uses to which proverbs were put is reflected, in later medieval proverb collections, in the grouping of proverbs according to topic, Arngart's identification of some thematic clusters in *DP* is of considerable interest.[2]

ANALOGUES: RELATION TO OE LITERATURE AND ME PROVERB COLLECTIONS

Biblical and classical analogues to *DP*, as well as continental and ON parallels, are offered in Arngart's editions as well as in his supporting publications (**28, 29, 36** and **43**). He also notes some substantive parallels with other OE writings (chiefly an echo of *The Wanderer*, first noted in *ODEP*), as well as the employment of the *sceal-* and the *byþ-* formulas, which link them with the *Exeter* and *Cotton* gnomes. Zupitza, **21**, pointed out that one of the metrical proverbs in both R and F ('hat acolað hwit asolað') is comparable with *Riming Poem*, 67; Dobbie, **27**, cxi–cxii, hazards the view that the proverb is an imitation of the poem.

It is generally held that few OE proverbs reappear in ME (see Taylor, **38**, Whiting, **39**). Arngart, **28**, points out that the *cwæþ-* formula of *DP* links them with two 13th century collections, the *Proverbs of Hendyng* and the *Proverbs of Alfred*; but *DP* has no other point of contact with *Proverbs of Alfred*, and only two proverbs in *DP* resemble *Proverbs of Hendyng*. ME and continental parallels to the prose proverb in the Faustina group are cited by Jente, **33** (somewhat puzzlingly, since he argues that the same proverb entered Germany from Asia). Ker, 154A, in printing the bilingual proverbial saying in Faustina, refers to 'similar Latin and French proverbs.' He also notes that the first of the Rawlinson proverbs ('Si stille suge fret þere grunninde mete') occurs in a 13th century manuscript, Digby 53, f. 53; Förster pointed out that the second ('On dai bringd þet al ier ne mai') is also found in Douce 52, f. 13 (15th century).

The two major reference works for the study of proverbs are Singer's three-volume work on continental proverb collections (**34**) and Whiting's Dictionary, **41**, which gives fuller coverage to OE literature than *ODEP*, and supersedes Skeat, **31**, for all practical purposes.

---

[2] For two studies which, in different ways, find unity in the gnomic poetry, see Nigel F. Barley, 'Structure in the Cotton Gnomes,' *Neuphilologische Mitteilungen* 78 (1977): 244–9; R. MacGregor Dawson, 'The Structure of the Old English Gnomic Poems,' *JEGP* 61 (1962): 14–22.

STUDY OF *DP* AND OTHER OE PROVERBS

The *DP* manuscript was omitted from Wanley's *Catalogue*. Attention was first drawn to *DP* by a short note in the second edition of the *Oxford Dictionary of English Proverbs* (1948); it would appear from this note that the editors owed their knowledge of *DP* to Wormald, who had examined the manuscript in 1935,[3] and that a facsimile of *DP* was sent to Förster in the hope that he would prepare an edition of the proverbs.

Most of the lines of thought touched upon in *ODEP*, **35**, have been taken up and developed by Arngart. The omission of *DP* from Wanley's *Catalogue*, and the absence of an edition until 1956, doubtless helps to explain the fact that *DP* is a relatively neglected text, figuring in the history of proverbial sayings, but rarely entering the discourse of OE literary studies. In particular, it is surprising it has not been drawn into the orbit of wisdom 'poetry,' since, if Arngart is right about the direction of translation, *DP* is in origin a collection of vernacular proverbs, and might therefore be fruitfully studied in relation to the *Exeter* and *Cotton* gnomes. Barley, **42**, in a methodological study which aims to define the structural characteristics of proverbs and maxims, links them with the charms;[4] cf. Newman, **48**.

Underlying much of the commentary on all the texts covered by this Annotated Bibliography is a difference of opinion concerning the creation of culture, a dichotomy between those who regard 'the people' as the richly innovative possessors of a native wisdom, and those for whom popular culture is nothing but the debasement of classical learning. Whereas Skeat, **31**, agreed with Kemble, **52**, that OE writings were 'reproducing in English the wisdom of the Latins rather than recording the deep but humorous philosophy of our own people' (vi), Williams, **32**, on the other hand, inferred from her study of gnomic literature the nature of Teutonic life and thought. Although Arngart cites classical and biblical parallels for *DP*, he also states that they 'furnish insights into contemporary folklore and social life' (**29**, 290). The editors of *ODEP*, for their part, took the view that popular and learned culture interacted in the creation of proverbs. The practical common sense of 'the ordinary man' took formulaic shape, and in the course of time entered the literature and assumed the characteristics of a proverb, they postulated: but 'as education became more general,

---

[3] See F. Wormald, 'Two-Anglo Saxon Miniatures Compared,' *British Museum Quarterly* 9 (1934–5): 113–15. Wormald confirms the Canterbury connections of the Durham manuscript by examining the iconographic resemblance between f. 56v of this manuscript and Tiberius A.iii, f. 2v (a Canterbury connection had been previously mooted in view of the Kentish character of some of the glosses to the Durham manuscript). The Durham manuscript was also described by R.A.B. Mynors, *Durham Cathedral Manuscripts to the End of the Twelfth Century* (Oxford: Oxford UP, 1939) no. 21.

[4] Morton Bloomfield, 'Understanding Old English Poetry,' *Annuale Mediaevale* 8 (1967): 5–25, in a seminal essay calling attention to the neglect of wisdom literature, also linked proverbs with charms; both, he said, are ways to understand the world, to make it more predictable and control it.

the sayings or *sententiae* of the wise men were incorporated in books and gradually penetrated downwards until they were adopted as proverbs by the people.... In both cases there is a process of gradual penetration of the spoken word from above to below and below to above, with literature as a kind of eternally moving wheel on which proverbs were caught up, and from which they were thrown off again' (viii). Perhaps, finally, *DP* are a manifestation of the cultural dynamic described by *ODEP*, but against the background of debate concerning the formation of culture—as much alive in the late 20th century as in the late 19th—Arngart's claim concerning the priority of the OE proverbs in the Durham collection appears to have a good deal of potential for development.

DURHAM AND OTHER PROVERBS: ANNOTATIONS

SEE ALSO Roeder, **269**
Greenfield and Robinson also refer to Dietrich, **299**

EDITIONS

21 Zupitza, Julius. 'Lateinisch-englische Sprueche.' *Anglia* 1 (1878): 285–6.

Prints three proverbs from Faustina A.x, Latin and OE. The textual notes analyse the last two proverbs as verse; Zupitza compares the second of these with *Riming Poem*, line 67, and states that, in the first [i.e., prose] proverb, *he cyð* represents a negative.

22 Wülcker, R.P. 'Aus englischen Bibliotheken.' *Anglia* 2 (1879): 354–87.

Edits, at 373–4, four proverbs from Royal 2 B.v, Latin–English text. Wülcker points out that two of the proverbs are the same as two proverbs in Faustina A.x, and suggests that both groups may have derived from a common store of proverbs.

23 Stengel, E. 'Die beiden Sammlungen altfranzösischer Sprichwörter in der Oxforder Handschrift Rawlinson C 641.' *Zeitschrift für französische Sprache und Literatur* 21 (1899): 1–21.

Prints in full the Latin–French proverb collection from ff. 13v–18, and the two OE proverbs found there, 3.

24 Förster, Max. 'Frühmittelenglische Sprichwörter.' *Englische Studien* 31 (1902): 1–20.

Prints, from Stengel, **23**, two English–Latin–French proverbs in Rawlinson C 641, at 16, which Förster describes as 13th century. He notes that the second of these ('On dai bringd, thet al ier ne mai') is also found in Douce MS 52, f. 13r (15th century). In his introduction to this collection of proverbs from various sources (1–4), Förster remarks on the paucity of folk proverbs in OE, and cites examples from the *Exeter* and *Cotton* gnomes and *OE Dicts* (part of 6, 81, 18, 62, and the whole of B, D and C).

25 Holthausen, F. 'Kleinere altenglische Dichtungen.' *Anglia* 41 (1917): 400–4.

Prints, at 400–1, the two metrical Latin–OE proverbs from Faustina A.x, and draws attention to their similarity to the two metrical proverbs in Royal 2 B.v.

26 Krapp, George Philip, and Arthur Garfield Kennedy. *An Anglo-Saxon Reader*. New York: Holt, 1929.

Prints proverbs from Faustina A.x, 138.

27 Dobbie, Elliott van Kirk. *The Anglo-Saxon Minor Poems*. Anglo-Saxon Poetic Records 6. New York: Columbia UP, 1942.

Edits the metrical proverbs from Faustina A.x, with variants from Royal 2 B.v, Latin–English, 109. Textual Notes, 201. Description of manuscript and textual relationship, cx–cxii, gives the text of the prose proverbs from F (cxi, n. 2) and from R (cxi, n. 4). The editor does not consider that the text of F is 'noticeably superior' to R. The first metrical proverb may be an imitation of *Riming Poem*, line 67. The proverbs are of interest in 'illustrating the informal use of the alliterative line.'

28 Arngart, O. *The Durham Proverbs: An Eleventh Century Collection of Anglo-Saxon Proverbs Edited from Durham Cathedral MS. B.III.32*. Lunds Universitets Årsskrift, N.F. Avd. 1, Bd. 52, Nr. 2. Lund: Gleerup, 1956.

Critical edition of Latin–English text, 10–15. Notes, 16–18. Glossary, 19–22. Facsimile of f. 43v, 24.

Introduction, 3–9, contains brief observations on the manuscript, the text's relations with OE literature (including the Faustina and Royal proverbs, and *OE Dicts*), the character of its humour, its links with *Proverbs of Alfred* and *Proverbs of Hendyng*, the corrupt nature of the Latin text (which Arngart argues is translated from the OE), alliteration and metre. From an examination of the language, Arngart concludes that it is late WS with a few non-WS forms. [For reviews see Storms, **37**.]

29 Arngart, Olof. 'The Durham Proverbs.' *Speculum* 56 (1981): 288–300.

Revised edition of the Latin–English text in Arngart, **28**, at 291–5. Notes, including translation (also revised), 295–300. No glossary.

In the preliminary remarks (288–90), Arngart concludes that most *DP* maxims are 'intermediate in time between the early, or "pre-Ælfredian," gnomic sentences, such as the *Cotton* or *Exeter* gnomes, and the Middle English collections' (289). He observes that the appearance of *DP* 37 and 39 in Royal 2 B.v has bearing on the dating, and suggests that *DP* represents the kind of common store of proverbs from which the Faustina and Royal proverbs derive. Arngart discerns no overall organizing principle in *DP*, but identifies some small thematic groups. He lists OE words and meanings not elsewhere evidenced, and remarks that the text illustrates various OE idioms and 'furnishes insights into contemporary folklore and social life' (290). His suggested date is second quarter of the 11th century.

COMMENTARY

30 Klaeber, Fr. 'An Old English Proverb.' *JEGP* 5 (1905): 529.

The remark concerning Ælfric's treachery in *ASC*(CDE), 1003 ('Ðonne se heretoga wacað, þonne bið eall se here swiðe gehindred'), appears to be marked as a quotation in E, and the phrase introducing it ('swa hit gecweðen is') seems to point to its proverbial nature (cf. 1130, 'oc man seið to biworde, hæge sitteð þa aceres dæleth'). Plummer, 2: 183, compared it with a similar saying in an Alcuin letter (Haddan and Stubbs, 3: 535). How far it can be claimed as an OE proverb in the strict sense is uncertain, but Alfred's 'rather free and pointed' rendering of a passage in *Cura Pastoralis*, Bk. 2, ch. 7 ('sua eac bið se here eal idel, ðonne he on oðer folc winnan sceal, gif se heretoga dwolað'), 'seems suggestive of proverbial wisdom.'

31 Skeat, W.W. *Early English Proverbs, Chiefly of the Thirteenth and Four-teenth Centuries.* Oxford: Clarendon, 1910.

In the introductory remarks to his compendium, Skeat states that OE writings were 'reproducing in English the wisdom of the Latins rather than recording the deep but humorous philosophy of our own people' (v). Not one of the *OE Dicts* has a familiar ring, and the proverbs in *ASC*, 1003 and 1130, are not recorded elsewhere. Only three of the proverbs in his collection appear in the 10th century, and two of these (Skeat 3, 26) are homiletic translations (of Eccl. 3.30 and Augustine respectively); Skeat 158, 'Ase fele thedes, ase fele thewes' (*Proverbs of Hendying*, stanza 4) contains the same idea as *Gnomes 1*, line 17, 'efenfela bega þeoda and þeawa,' and is found in most European languages.

32 Williams, Blanche Colton. *Gnomic Poetry in Anglo-Saxon.* New York: Columbia UP, 1914.

Williams's purpose is to locate the significance of the gnomic reflections which occur so often in early Anglo-Saxon literature, trace their gradual decadence as the Anglo-Saxon period declines, bring together the most prominent examples, and from them draw inferences regarding Teutonic life and thought. Williams concludes that distinctions between proverbs and gnomes fall short in practice (6–8); Bede's Death Song and the 'Proverb from Winfrid's Time' are of interest because of their early form, definite dating and the fact that they 'chanced to be lifted out of popular currency to an abiding place in literature' (70).

33 Jente, Richard. 'German Proverbs from the Orient.' *PMLA* 48 (1933): 17–37.

'Der Apfel fällt nicht weit vom Stamme,' commonly included in 17th century German proverb collections, is one of four proverbs still in common use in Europe which, Jente argues, are of Asiatic origin (26–30). Jente notes that the proverb was known in OE [FC B.7.2] and in early ME (*Owl and the Nightingale*, 135–8); there is also a later form, 'Trendle the appel neuere so fer, he couthes fro what tree he cam' [cf. Whiting, **39**, A169; Bozon, *Contes*, *c.* 1400]. Later Spanish and English ignorance of this proverb shows that it is not of French origin; East European knowledge of it points to the direction of its entry into Europe, and its Asiatic origin is proved by its appearance in Tamil. 'The fact that there existed already several common European proverbs, similar in content and form to this foreign one, made its acceptance easy' (30).

34 Singer, Samuel. *Sprichwörter des Mittelalters.* Bern: Lang, 1944–7. 3 vols.

Itemizes the proverbs occurring in major pre-14th century collections and examines their derivation; copious citation of analogues. The collections are mostly continental, but English proverbs figure occasionally throughout, and *Proverbs of Hendyng* is examined in detail. Vol. 1 (up to the 12th century) includes detailed examination of some Eddic lays, *Salomo und Marcolf*, Notker, Egbert von Lüttich's *Fecunda Ratis* and Nirvadus of Gent's *Ysengrimus*. Index of Proverbs, 179–87; Bibliography, 190–8.

35 Smith, William George, and Janet E. Heseltine. *The Oxford Dictionary of English Proverbs.* 2nd edn. revised by Sir Paul Harvey. Oxford: Clarendon, 1948. [1st edn. 1935. 3rd edn. 1970.]

'Note on the *Durham Proverbs*,' xxviii [omitted in 3rd edn.], observes that they 'are of interest both as illustrations of the freakish humour so often expressed in the gargoyles and grotesques of medieval sculpture and illumination, and as surprisingly early examples of the "quoth the" type of proverb.' Förster (private communication) has pointed out that *DP* 1 derives from *Distichs of Cato*. The Latin is unusually corrupt even for medieval Latin, and the collection seems to lend support to Wülcker's suggestion (**22**) that there was a common source of proverbs from which the surviving fragmentary collections derive. The editors note that *DP* shares material with the Royal proverbs and that Sisam (private communication) has identified an echo of *DP* 23 in *The Wanderer*, 68. The Introduction also remarks on *DP*, explaining their presence in the manuscript in terms of their usefulness to the medieval teacher: 'He had to teach Latin grammar to the novices, and what method of teaching could be better than making them familiar with the sayings of everyday life? We know that this system was practised, for at the end of Ælfric's Grammar, dating from the tenth century, there are Latin colloquies, with the Anglo-Saxon written between the lines, describing the daily tasks of life in a monastery' (ix).

36 Arngart, O. 'A Note on the Durham Proverbs.' *English Studies* 37 (1956): 259.

DP 28 is paralleled by *Hávamál* 145. This proverb, not noticed by Singer, **34**, and possibly unknown on the continent, may have been one of the sayings introduced by the Vikings into English from ON.

37 Storms, G. Rev. of *The Durham Proverbs: An Eleventh Century Collection of Anglo-Saxon Proverbs from Durham Cathedral MS. B.III.32*, ed. O. Arngart [**28**]. *English Studies* 37 (1956): 266–7.

Storms offers alternative translations to Arngart, **28**, for *DP* 5, 15, 33, 34, together with a Nederlandish analogue for 46.

38 Taylor, Archer. ' "He that will not when he may; when he will shall have nay." ' *Studies in Old English Literature in Honor of Arthur G. Brodeur.* Ed. Stanley B. Greenfield. Eugene: U of Oregon, 1963. 155–61.

The proverb in *Be Gecyrrednesse*, which Skeat, **31**, incorrectly states to be a translation from Augustine, has a parallel in *Regula Pastoralis*, 3, 12. The Alfredian translation and *Be Gecyrrednesse* make specific reference to tardiness; it is thus unlikely that ME and later versions can be traced back to the OE versions. The proverb employs a pattern already known in classical Latin and possibly in classical Greek (although Singer, **34**, traces a number of continental versions of this proverb back to *Regula Pastoralis*, John of Salisbury's *Policraticus*, line 1159, attributes it to Basil). Taylor argues that there was no continuing tradition of the proverb from OE into ME; but he attributes its appearance in the ME *Disticha Catonis* (where it occurs instead of a literal translation), and in one manuscript of *Proverbs of Hendyng*, to the fact that the proverb 'enjoyed considerable popularity in England and could be readily absorbed by such miscellaneous didactic collections' (158). Although the proverb is used by Alfred with reference to conversion, it is used in Henryson's *Robene and Makyne* 'with reference to neglected opportunity in sexual affairs' (158), and Taylor is inclined to think that it originated in the latter context.

39 Whiting, Bartlett Jere. 'A Collection of Proverbs in BM Additional MS. 37075.' *Franciplegius: Medieval and Linguistic Studies in Honor of Francis Peabody Magoun, Jr.* Ed. Jess B. Bessinger, Jr., and Robert P. Creed. New York: New York UP, 1965. 274–89.

Whiting describes *DP* as the earliest of the medieval proverb collections, which were regarded as useful for learning Latin and the 'inculcation of common sense,' and a convenient source of rhetorical devices (274). He also observes that, of the Anglo-Saxon sayings, not all seem popular, and few turn up in ME (276, n. 3).

40 Robinson, Fred C. 'Notes and Emendations to Old English Poetic Texts.'
Neuphilologische Mitteilungen 67 (1966): 356–64.

At 363–4, Robinson observes that Arngart, **28**, translates *DP* 44 'It is far
from well, said he who heard wailing in hell.' But as *BT* does not support
Arngart's 'artful rendering of *wide*,' Robinson would translate: 'It is not
well afar.... ' Cf. the wailing in hell in *Christ and Satan*, lines 332, 337–9.

41 Whiting, Bartlett Jere (with Helen Westcott Whiting). *Proverbs,
Sentences and Proverbial Phrases From English Writings Mainly Before
1500*. Cambridge, MA: Belknap–Harvard UP, 1968.

Covers a wide variety of OE prose and metrical texts, including *DP*. The
proverbs are alphabetized by key words, occurrences according to chronological order. There is an index of key words and proper names.

42 Barley, Nigel. 'A Structural Approach to the Proverb and Maxim with
Special Reference to the Anglo-Saxon Corpus.' *Proverbium* 20 (1972): 737–
50.

Barley argues that 'the concept "structural description" familiar to lin-
guists' (749) offers the appropriate methodology for study (particularly
cross-cultural study) of proverbs. Consideration of the Anglo-Saxon corpus, 744–9, includes brief classificatory remarks on *DP* 7, 8, 6, 17, 29, 31,
27, 13, 28, 44, 10, 45, 11. *DP* contains true proverbs and maxims, whereas
the status of the *Exeter* and *Cotton* Gnomes is unclear; but all three confirm
the thesis that 'relevance restrictions are to be treated as irregularities from
the point of view of a full description whereas the formal processes involved
in proverb use are less culture-based' (744). Like the proverbs, OE magical
formulas (Cockayne, **400**, 1: 391, **297**, 2: 385) show the paradigmatic use of
events as a source of structure.

43 Arngart, O. 'Further Notes on the Durham Proverbs.' *English Studies* 58
(1977): 101–4.

Addenda to Arngart, **28**; textual obscurities in, and further analogues for,
DP 2, 5, 6, 7, 15, 19, 20, 33, 36, 42.

44 Arngart, O. 'Durham Proverbs 17, 30, and 42.' *Notes and Queries* NS 29
(1982): 199–201.

Arngart reconsiders some of his translations in Arngart, **29**: *breostum* in
DP 17 may be a rare locative; *hame* in *DP* 30 is likely to be used in a
homiletic sense (cf. *The Seafarer*, 103–24); we may come closer to the exact
significance of *DP* 42 by rendering *fægror* as 'more evenly, more on a level.'
This meaning also occurs in the corresponding continental maxim (Singer,
34, 1: 156). Arngart defines these three proverbs as metrical types. The

proverbs in *DP* have continental, ON, classical and biblical parallels; most seem to be later than the earliest attested specimens, and the metrical irregularity of some is consistent with comparative lateness. 'On the continent too, schools relied on these renderings of vernacular proverbs for the instruction of Latin' (201); see Whiting, **39**, xii, and Singer, **34**, 2: 5. 'It may be more than a coincidence that the Durham collection starts with a snatch of that well-known work [*Distichs of Cato*], summoning up patience in the face of the task to be attempted' (201). Arngart also considers it suggestive that two collections of Latin–English proverbs (*DP* and Faustina) occur in manuscripts containing copies of Ælfric's *Grammar*.

45 Blockley, Mary. 'Addenda and Corrigenda to N.R. Ker's "A Supplement to 'Catalogue of Manuscripts Containing Anglo-Saxon.'"' *Notes and Queries* NS 29 (1982): 1–3.

Blockley notes a number of scribbles, etc., which she or others define as metrical. Among these is *DP* 2, which 'alliterates, though it does not scan, as verse' (1). She also comments on the 'maxim' in Ker, 415 [not listed FC]; 'like *Maxims I and II*, the lines are verse' (2). The maxim reads:

A scæl gelæred smið   swa he gelicost mæg
be bisne wyrcan,   butan he bet cunne.

46 Trahern, Joseph B., Jr. 'An Old English Metrical Proverb in the Junius 121 *De Descensu Christi*.' *Anglia* 100 (1982): 419–21.

Although secular metrical proverbs occur not infrequently in the OE corpus, they are rare in sermons. In 'De Descensu Christi ad Inferos' [FC B.3.2.28], 47–51, Christ's words (from John 18.23), are followed by a metrical proverb, 'Se ðe on oðres mid unrihte geræsð / se his agen þurh þaet oft forlyseð,' which derives from a fable of Phaedrus (ed. Perry, 1975, 196); Caxton's *Aesop*, 1, 5, has, hitherto, been regarded as the earliest English version of this proverb. As the homilist's use of the proverb is out of keeping with its meaning in the fable, he may have known the proverb outside the context of the fable (the earliest Anglo–Latin version is preserved in Rawlinson G.57 and G.111); alternatively, his version may represent a misreading of the Latin or a deliberate reworking.

47 Arngart, O. '*Durham Proverb* 23, and Other Notes on *Durham Proverbs*.' *Notes and Queries* NS 30 (1983): 291–2.

The similarities that have been shown to exist between some proverbs in OE collections and OE literature have been differently interpreted; whereas *ODEP*, **35**, 'seems to presume the existence of the proverbs in question before what are usually taken to be very old Anglo-Saxon poems' (291),

Dobbie, **27**, supposes that one of the Faustina proverbs may be an imitation of the *Riming Poem*. Arngart suggests that the variants and inter-relations of the texts and proverbs could repay further study, but the purpose of this note is to further clarify the Latin of *DP* 23 ('One should be neither quickly afraid nor promptly smiling'). Arngart also comments on the literal meaning of *DP* 17. It 'is truistic, and can be assumed with a great deal of certainty to conceal a more sophisticated thought' (292); the literal meaning 'provides no ready explanation' for the use of the dative plural *breostum*.

48 Newman, D.M. 'Gnomic Elements in Old English Poetry, with Special Reference to *Maximus* [*sic*] I and II and *Beowulf*.' M.Phil. diss. U of Manchester, 1988.

Not sighted. According to *Index of Theses*, the work includes comparison of *Maxims* I and II with *OE Dicts* and *DP*, in order to establish that *Maxims* I and II are not random lists of proverbs but gnomic poems.

II

Dialogues

SOLOMON AND SATURN AND ADRIAN AND RITHEUS

MANUSCRIPTS

SOLOMON AND SATURN   FC B.5.1

London, British Library, Cotton Vitellius A.xv, ff. 86v–93v V
Ker 215, art. 2 s. xii med.

ADRIAN AND RITHEUS   FC B.5.2

London, British Library, Cotton Julius A.ii, ff. 137v–40 J
Ker 159, art. 2 s. xii med.

Junius Transcripts of J:
Oxford, Bodleian, Junius 45   JJ
Oxford, Bodleian, Junius 61

MANUSCRIPTS: DESCRIPTION, CONTENTS, DATE
AND PROVENANCE (following Ker)

Solomon and Saturn

SS is preserved in a single manuscript, dated mid-12th century by Ker, which is now generally known as the Southwick Codex. It is bound with the Nowell (or *Beowulf*) Codex (which is dated s. x/xi by Ker). *SS* is preceded in the manuscript by a translation of the *Soliloquies* and the OE *Gospel of Nichodemus*, and followed by a few lines of a homily on St Quintin. According to the table of contents drawn up for Cotton, there was once an OE fragment of the Legend of St Thomas between the *Soliloquies* and the *Gospel of Nichodemus*, but there is no sign of it now. A late 13th century inscription identifies it as having been owned by Southwick Priory, Hampshire. Ker states that the angular, pointed script has a more irregular character from f. 60 on, but there is no change of hand. Ker reports archaic features of the script, which probably derived from an exemplar s. ix/x or s. x; these would seem, from his description, to be confined to the *Soliloquies*. Cross and Hill, **55**, add that the pages containing *SS* are badly discoloured and have deteriorated at the edges, and also state: 'The hand, where it is legible, is clear, and corrections appear to have been made by the same hand' (14).

Förster, **180**, discerned two different hands where Ker sees a change of style in the same hand, and dated the manuscript to the first quarter of the

12th century; he thought it probable that the manuscript was written at Southwick Priory. More recently, the Southwick Codex has figured in the controversy over the dating of *Beowulf*, to which Kiernan, **206**, has given rise (see further p. 119 below). There is a full description of the Southwick Codex by Torkar, 1986,[1] who argues against the view that a Legend of St Thomas was lost from between the *Soliloquies* and the *Gospel of Nichodemus* after the manuscript came into the possession of Cotton. Torkar casts doubts on Kiernan's conclusion that the scribe responsible for the Southwick Codex copied it in two separate parts at different stages of his life; he takes a more favourable view of Förster's description of the manuscript than Kiernan does, but argues against the view that the manuscript originated at Southwick Priory.

Adrian and Ritheus

The single manuscript in which *Ad* is preserved is also dated mid-12th century by Ker (as Cross and Hill explain, the manuscript is a fragment of only nine folios, bound with a larger manuscript under the same title). The manuscript also contains a copy of *OE Dicts* and a metrical prayer. *Ad* is immediately followed by a Note on the two thieves, etc. (FC B.24.12.1), which has been regarded by some as a continuation of the prose dialogue (see further pp. 53–4 below, 'Extent of the Text'). Ker reports damage by fire; Cross and Hill state that the folios have deteriorated at the edges, particularly at the top, where legibility of the text is affected, but that the hand itself is clear. There are no orthographic corrections to *Ad*. For further manuscript description, see above, pp. 15–16.

Ker mentions that, owing to the deterioration of J, the transcript in Junius 45 is of value; Cross and Hill also draw attention to the existence of the Junius 61 transcript. Both transcripts of *Ad* include the Note, but it is headed 'Appendix.' Both *Ad* and the Note have been cancelled in Junius 45; only the Note is crossed through in Junius 61.

EDITIONS AND TRANSLATIONS

Kemble, **52**, and Etmüller, **54**, printed both *SS* and *Ad*, as do Cross and Hill, **55**, whose edition supersedes all others. Cross and Hill are the first to edit the text of *SS* from the manuscript since it was first edited by Thorpe, **49**, in 1834; Kemble, Etmüller, Ebeling, **51**, and Klipstein, **53**, all reprinted Thorpe's diplomatic text. *Ad* was first published by Wright, **50**, whose transcript was reproduced by Etmüller.

Cross and Hill have 'attempted to produce a readable and accurate text, but one which is as nearly diplomatic as possible in view of the comparative lack of knowledge about permissible scribal variations in the

---

[1] Roland Torkar, 'Cotton Vitellius A. xv (pt. I) and the *Legend of St Thomas*,' *English Studies* 67 (1986): 290–303.

eleventh/twelfth century' (18). Stanley, in reviewing the edition,[2] praised its accuracy, but thought that more might have been made of the difficulty encountered in reading the manuscripts. The extensive section-by-section commentary of Cross and Hill includes a translation of both dialogues. *SS* and *Ad* were also translated by Kemble, who included them (together with *OE Dicts*) among the texts that accompany his essay on dialogue literature; as Larsen, **68**, explains, a number of texts, including *SS* and *Ad*, are lacking in the bound proofs of Kemble's edition, of which a few copies survive.

EXTENT OF THE TEXT OF *Ad*

Ad 48 is followed, on f. 140v, by a passage which opens with a statement on the two thieves and catalogues the measurements of Noah's Ark, St Peter's Church, Solomon's temple and the world. It then gives the number of veins and bones in the human body and the days in the year. The passage is tabled by Ker as a separate item (art. 3), and classified by FC under 'Notes and Commonplaces' (FC B.24.12.1). Förster, **62**, printed the passage, and argued that, even though it does not retain the dialogue form, it should be considered as part of the text of *Ad*. The last answer of *SS* (*SS* 59), he pointed out, is similarly extended by a direct statement, and this extension, like the passage on f. 140v of J, contains the number of veins and bones in the human body and the number of days in a year. Utley, **74**, was inclined to accept Förster's argument. Editors, however, including Cross and Hill, have not accepted this passage as part of the text; Cross and Hill point out that their view of the limits of the text was shared by Ker and by Wanley,[3] as well as by Junius (see p. 52 above, 'Manuscripts'). Cross and Hill reject Förster's suggestion on the grounds that *Ad* (unlike *SS*) holds rigidly to the question-and-answer format. They also point to the manuscript presentation: a blank space at the bottom of the page, roughly equal to two lines of text, follows the last answer of *Ad*, and the Note begins on the next folio, with a large capital for the first word. They observe, too, that, unbeknown to Förster, Napier, **56**, had already printed the Note on f. 140v of J, together with a number of passages similar in character, drawn from several different manuscripts, and they suggest that, if Förster had known of the miscellaneous Notes printed by Napier, 'he might have concluded that such unconnected additions are not unparalleled in Anglo-Saxon manuscripts' (16). Subsequent acquaintance with Napier's publication did not, in fact, cause Förster to revise his opinions (see Förster, **89**), and it is worth noting that editorial treatment of such accretions differs; the OE apothegms derived from *Disticha Catonis*, for instance, are followed, in one manuscript,

---

[2] E. G. Stanley, rev. of *The Prose* Solomon and Saturn *and* Adrian and Ritheus, ed. James E. Cross and Thomas D. Hill [**55**], 'McMaster Old English Studies and Texts,' *Notes and Queries* (1984): 433–4. Stanley also regretted the absence of manuscript accents in the printed text.

[3] Wanley transcribed, for the purposes of identification, the introduction to *Ad*, *Ad* 1, and *Ad* 48 (183).

by a quasi-homiletic passage which is not dissimilar in character to the Notes printed by Napier, and which is distinguished from the apothegms by its manuscript presentation, but it is, nevertheless, accepted as an integral part of the text by editors of *OE Dicts* (for 'Miscellaneous Notes,' see further pp. 60–1 below.)

LANGUAGE AND DATE

The language of *SS* and *Ad* still awaits study; Cross and Hill, **55**, explain that, in view of the present state of knowledge of 11th and 12th century orthographical conventions, they have not attempted to draw any conclusions about the language of the texts, but linguistic studies 'are cited where necessary in the textual notes, and the glossary, which is inclusive and contains cross-references to various forms, is intended to aid any future study of the language of the manuscripts' (18). Of the Southwick Codex, they remark that Ker's mid-12th century dating 'is approximately supported by certain features of language and/or orthography' (14). Noting that Ker dates J to the mid-12th century, whereas Cox, **9**, dates it late 11th century, they remark: 'Features of the language and/or orthography are of that period known loosely as "transitional," whose present limits would cover both those dates' (15).

THE RELATIONSHIP OF *Ad* AND *SS*

SS has 59 questions and answers; *Ad* has 48. The textual connection between *SS* and *Ad* was recognized by Kemble, **52**, who observed that certain questions and answers in *SS* were clearer if read against *Ad*. Kemble estimated that the two works had one-third of their material in common, and concluded: 'It is not unreasonable to believe that both are fragmentary portions of one original' (179). Utley, **74**, 56, stated that *Ad* and *SS* have 20 questions and answers in common. Cross and Hill, **55**, state that 17 questions correspond in content, but that in each case there are differences in phrasing. Eight of the shared questions and answers are from *Joca Monachorum* lists. From their study of the relationship of *SS* and *Ad*, Cross and Hill concluded that both works 'were composed independently of each other, although drawing on some common sources, no doubt at different removes' (12).

ANALOGUES AND SOURCES; THE *JOCA MONACHORUM* LISTS

Kemble, **52**, recognized that *SS* and *Ad* were members of a complex tradition of dialogue literature pervasive throughout Europe, and he printed many medieval Latin and vernacular European examples. The relationship between *Ad* and *SS* was given a more specific consideration by Förster, **62**, who also demonstrated that two of the dialogues printed by Kemble, *Adrian et Epictus* and the pseudo-Bede *Collectanea et Flores*, share material with them. The underlying textual tradition was examined by Suchier, whose work was drawn upon by Utley, **74**; Suchier's conclusions are clearly explained and fully applied by Cross and Hill, **55**.

Suchier, 1955, demonstrated that there were two basic question-and-answer lists, the *Joca Monachorum* group and the *Adrian and Epictetus group*; *SS* and *Ad* 'belong to the circle' of the *Joca Monachorum* group.[4] The *Joca Monachorum* lists were in circulation at least as early as the 7th century, and have links with certain Greek, Slavonic and oriental collections. The *Joca Monachorum* lists (all of which are in Latin) are paralleled by lists in Greek, and the Latin lists may owe their origin to Greek series, although immediate contact is impossible to demonstrate. The *Joca Monachorum* Latin lists are thought by Suchier to have influenced certain questions in the *Adrian and Epictetus* lists, and the vernacular lists printed by Suchier, 1910,[5] all of which are later in date than *SS* and *Ad*, also take over questions from *Joca Monachorum*.

Cross and Hill conclude that there is no single source for either of the OE question-and-answer lists, but that, of the 59 questions in *SS*, 24 are found in extant *Joca Monachorum* lists, and of the 48 questions in *Ad*, 20 are paralleled. It follows, then, that 35 questions in *SS* and 20 in *Ad* do *not* derive from *Joca Monachorum* lists. As Cross and Hill state that *SS* and *Ad* have 17 questions in common, and eight of these are from *Joca Monachorum* lists, there must also be nine questions in common which were derived from other sources.

The editors explain that they have speculated about the questions that have no parallels in *Joca Monachorum* lists, 'partly to suggest that the OE lists or exemplars were individually or collectively augmented, but also to indicate certain cultural contacts' (8). A number of questions appear to get information from Irish texts or traditions (as represented, for instance, by a Hiberno-Latin catechism, *Prebiarum de multorium exemplaribus Collectanea Bedae*). Not all of the questions without analogues are necessarily unique Anglo-Saxon additions, but *Ad* 26–7, 45–8, may be Anglo-Saxon additions from scriptural or patristic reading. Some additions may derive from earlier Anglo-Saxon texts (e.g., the exemplar of Vercelli Homily xix; a gloss on the metrical *De Virginitate*).

Concerning the nine questions which *SS* and *Ad* have in common which do not derive from *Joca Monachorum*, Cross and Hill state that one has parallels in Hiberno-Latin catechisms. Five have parallels in the ME *Questiones bytwene the Maister of Oxenford and his Clerke*, and are probably

---

[4] Walther Suchier, ed., *Das mittellateinische Gespräch Adrian und Epictitus nebst verwandten Texten (Joca Monachorum)* (Tübingen: Niemeyer, 1955) 92.

[5] Walther Suchier, ed., *L'Enfant Sage (Das Gespräch des Kaisers Hadrian mit dem klugen Kinde Epitus)*, Gesellschaft für romanische Literatur 24 (Dresden: Niemeyer, 1910). See also Lloyd William Daly and Walther Suchier, eds., *Altercatio Hadriani Augusti et Epicteti Philosophi*, Studies in Language and Literature 24.1–2 (Urbana: Illinois UP, 1939). The Daly–Suchier monograph includes a useful survey of the origins and varieties of question-and-answer dialogue.

from the same lost Latin original. One has a parallel in *Alfræð Íslenzk*, and probably derives from the same missing *Joca Monachorum* list as the Icelandic work. In sum, the present writer has failed to achieve numerical concordance.[6] The commentary to Cross and Hill's edition is a masterpiece of erudition, but one could wish that the editors had given a more specifically detailed summary of their findings in the Introduction, or, better still, that they had summarized in tabular form the literary relationships that they have identified.

Most studies of the sources and analogues of the prose dialogues which pre-date Cross and Hill have been incorporated into their edition. Foremost among the previous publications on *SS* and *Ad* are two excellent articles by Utley, **73** and **74**, which examine, respectively, the names of the cities where the sun rises and sets (*SS* 26–7, *Ad* 29–30), and the tree called Chy (*SS* 18). Although the latter article focuses on Chy, it also offers an overview of the structure of *SS* and makes comparative reference to *Ad*. The documentation includes annotated bibliographies of some of the more arcane areas of scholarship which have bearing on the prose dialogues, such as rabbinical texts and cuneiform writings.

There is also a cluster of articles by Förster, **64**, Evans, **76**, and Cross, **78**, which make some reference to *SS* 9 (Whitbread, **81**, adds nothing to the study of the prose *SS*). Of these three, Förster's treatment of the theme of the constituent elements of Adam is the fullest; but he was primarily concerned to classify occurrences, and his study has been largely superseded by Tristram, **80**. See also Creed, **67**, Hill, **83**, and Henel, **222**. For names of the wives of Noah and his sons see Bouterwek, **59**, and Utley, **69**. For studies of other themes, see pp. 60–1 below, 'Miscellaneous Notes.'

Pictorial Analogues

Henderson, **75**, in a reply to Schapiro, **71**, confirms that *SS* 36 is the earliest known literary identification of Cain's weapon as a jaw-bone (see Emerson, **63**), and (without claiming direct relationship) he relates the appearance of this motif in *SS* to an illustrated manuscript of Ælfric's *Pentateuch*. See also Raw, **82**, on *SS* 1.

NAMES OF THE INTERLOCUTORS; RELATION TO THE POETICAL *SOLOMON AND SATURN*

None of the lists of the *Joca Monachorum* type have named protagonists. Cross and Hill point out that the relative independence with which *SS* and *Ad* developed is confirmed by the different names they give to the protagonists. They consider that the most likely originals of the names of

---

[6] See Cross and Hill, **55**, 11. Attempts to resolve the discrepancy by studying the commentary have proved unsuccessful. The problem is compounded by the fact that, where the OE coincides with *Maister of Oxenford*, one question in *SS* coincides with two in *Ad* (*Ad* 1 and 2 parallels *SS* 16). The writer trusts that she has not overlooked an obvious explanation.

the speakers of *Ad* are Adrian and Epictetus (that is, although *Ad* does not derive from the *Adrian and Epictetus* lists, it has taken the name of its speakers from them). The names Solomon and Saturn may have been taken over from the metrical series, or they may derive from a common ancestor. Cross and Hill do not think that this question can be resolved either way, but observe that, as Solomon's opponent is called Saturn only in the English dialogues, this may suggest some form of connection between the OE prose *SS* and the OE dialogue poem that is known by the same title. However, as Cross and Hill explain, the prose *SS* and the poetic *SS* are connected only through the names of the protagonists; the poetic *SS*, whose protagonists are, respectively, a Christian and a pagan, is generically different from the prose *SS*, combative rather than catechistical, and does not appear to have derived from *Joca Monachorum* lists.

Kemble's discursive essay on the Solomon and Saturn dialogues (**52**) is concerned with the history of the legend, and has oblique bearing on the prose *SS* only in so far as the names of the protagonists are a particular concern of his. Kemble's essay is of historical interest; Menner's edition of the poetic *SS* (**70**), which is still regarded as definitive, rejects much of Kemble's argument concerning the names of the disputants and the history of the legend.

The Prose Solomon and Saturn Paternoster Dialogue

Between the two dialogues which make up the poetic *SS* (FC A.13), usually termed *SSI* and *SSII*, there is a prose section; Menner, **70**, 8–12, argued that the prose section was a separate work, and he relegated it to the Appendix of his edition of the poetic dialogues. There are, then, two prose Solomon and Saturn dialogues as well as two poetic ones. Like the poetic dialogue *SSI*, the prose section concerns the paternoster, but Menner considered that it was more mechanically catechistical than the poetic dialogues, as well as more fanciful: 'The petty personifications of the poem are comparatively restrained beside the absurd exaggerations and colourful allegorical analysis of the prose. The Pater Noster of the prose is itself a gigantic creature, while only the letters of the Pater Noster are personified in Poem I' (9).

Notwithstanding Menner's analysis of the text, the interpolated prose dialogue is not generally thought of as having an existence independent of the poetic dialogues. Utley, 1972,[7] for instance, states that the prose section 'connects the originally separate Poems I and II' (737), and it has no separate FC classification. For this reason, commentary on the prose section is not easily disentangled from commentary on the poetic dialogues, and it has not seemed appropriate to include annotations on the prose paternoster

---

[7] Francis Lee Utley, 'Dialogues, Debates, and Catechisms,' *A Manual of the Writings in Middle English, 1050–1500*, ed. J. Burke Severs and Albert E. Hartung, 8 vols. to date (New Haven: Connecticut Academy of Arts and Sciences, 1967–), vol. 3, ed. Albert E. Hartung (1972) 669–745, 829–902.

dialogue in this volume. For a recent restatement of the textual integrity of the paternoster prose dialogue, and a study of it as a 'transformation combat,' see Hill, 1988.[8] The text has also been edited separately by Cilluffo, 1980.[9]

MEDIEVAL VERSIONS; *QUESTIONES BY-TWENE THE MAISTER OF OXENFORD AND HIS CLERKE*

The *Maister of Oxenford*, a prose dialogue between pupil and master (more correctly, a catechism) is closely related to *SS* (and contains five questions and answers which *SS* has in common with *Ad*). It is preserved in two late medieval manuscripts, Lansdowne 762 (late 15th or early 16th century), and Harley 1304 (15th century).[10] Kemble, **52**, who included the Lansdowne version of the *Maister* in his anthology of dialogue literature, described it as 'a virtually verbatim translation' of *SS* (216); the Harley version is considered by later commentators to be somewhat closer to *SS*. Förster (**89**, 87, n. 8) suggested that the two ME texts derived independently from the original of *SS*. Cross and Hill (**55**, 11–12, 21, n. 35), are inclined to agree that Harley was translated from the same Latin original as *SS*, but think it probable that Lansdowne is a copy of Harley or its exemplar. Utley, **74**, expressed the opinion that the *Maister* might, in some cases, better represent the original than *SS*; this article contains some extended comparison of *SS* and the *Maister*, but the relationship does not appear to have been studied in depth.

STUDY OF *SS* AND *Ad*

By and large, Cross and Hill's edition represents the sum of what is known to date about the two prose dialogues; its most significant contribution (over and above its scholarly presentation of the text) lies in its wide-ranging identification of analogues and its explication of the underlying Latin textual tradition. It does not, however, supersede Utley, **74**, whose suggestive account of the structure of *SS* finds no echo in the Cross and Hill edition, and Tristram's study of the *homo octipartitus* theme (**80**) appears to have been overlooked. Some of the gaps in the sum total of our knowledge have already been mentioned above.

Proportionately, the material derived from *Joca Monachorum* lists does not seem very great. Cross and Hill may well be right in assuming that

---

[8] Thomas D. Hill, 'The Devil's Forms and the Pater Noster's Powers: "The Prose Solomon and Saturn *Pater Noster* Dialogue" and the Motif of the Transformation Combat,' *Studies in Philology* 85 (1988): 164–76.

[9] Gilda Cilluffo, 'Il dialogo in prosa Salomone e Saturno del ms. CCCC 422,' *Annali, Istituto Universitario Orientale de Napoli, Filologia germanica* 23 (1980): 121–46.

[10] The Harley version has been edited by Carl Horstmann, 'Questiones By-Twene the Maister of Oxenford and His Clerke,' *Englische Studien* 8 (1885): 284–7. The Lansdowne version was edited by Richard P. Wülcker, *Altenglisches Lesebuch* (Halle a. S.: Niemeyer, 1874–80) 2: 191 ff., 303 ff.

the *Joca Monachorum* lists constitute the nucleus from which *SS* and *Ad* grew, and that their compilers supplemented material drawn from these lists from a wide variety of other sources; perhaps, however, a tabular summary of the diverse literary relationships that they have pointed out might ultimately assist in the identification of single, underlying sources, comparable in significance to the *Joca Monachorum* lists. Nor is the amount of material shared by *SS* and *Ad* very considerable, even though the two dialogues have generally been closely linked. Further study of the material that the two works have in common (particularly the exchanges that do not derive from *Joca Monachorum* lists), might further advance our knowledge of their origins and transmission; but perhaps, too, much could be gained from an attempt to establish the ways in which *SS* and *Ad* differ, both in their selection and handling of material and in their general style. Some distinctions are made by Cross and Hill, who remark, for instance, that *SS* is more diffuse than *Ad*. Just as a substantive comparison of the OE and ME versions of *Disticha Catonis* might illuminate the cultural continuities and discontinuities of the two periods, so too a study of the relationship of *SS* and *Maister of Oxenford* might achieve more than the simple clarification of manuscript relationships.

As is to be expected, Cross and Hill are at pains to emphasize that they have identified analogues rather than sources (see Cross, **78**), but intimate that *SS* and *Ad* derive, at least in part, from Irish traditions. Tristram, **86**, on the other hand, in her study of the Ages of the World theme, finds only evidence of English influence on Irish writings, despite the fact that 'it has been quite popular in certain academic circles to postulate an Irish influence for many Anglo-Saxon features, which (to the modern mind) may seem somewhat odd.'[11] The nature of contacts between Ireland and England are well known, but there is perhaps a good deal more to be discovered concerning the echoes of rabbinical and cuneiform writings; Cook, **60**, and **61**, who argued that early Anglo-Saxons had first-hand contact with Judaism (see also Wiessmann, **202**), provoked a sharp rebuttal from Hart, 1892.[12]

Cross and Hill urge that *SS* and *Ad* afford valuable insight into medieval habits of mind. This being so, it seems particularly unfortunate that the prose form of these two dialogues should have precluded them from consideration of some of the critically innovative studies of OE wisdom 'poetry' which are beginning to appear.[13] The prose dialogues may be less inherently interesting than the 'poetic' dialogues. But metrical form in OE literature is not necessarily the mark of qualitative difference, nor are the prose *SS* and *Ad*, based on a body of material which 'fills the silences of scripture,' as Cross and Hill put it (5), markedly less 'secular' than the

---

[11] Abstract of Tristram, **86**, *English and American Studies in German* (1983): 31–2.

[12] J.M. Hart, 'Judaism in Early England,' *Modern Language Notes* 7 (1892): 53–6.

[13] See especially Elaine Tuttle Hansen, *The Solomon Complex: Reading Wisdom in Old English Poetry* (Toronto: U of Toronto P, 1988).

paternoster dialogues of the metrical series; they deserve a place in the history of Anglo-Saxon enquiry into the nature of Life, the Universe and Everything. Their catechistical form may be 'mechanical,' but it is perhaps no less redolent with epistemological significance than the *débat*. Bisher, **87** (not sighted), appears to combine inquiry into the epistemology of *SS* with investigation into the significance of its heterodox elements.

Cross and Hill provide a general indication of the intellectual milieu of *SS* and *Ad* when they relate them to Ælfric's remarks on the circulation of erroneous writings;[14] Tristram, **80**, also refers to these remarks, in her study of the *homo octipartitus*. She explains that heterodox literature continued to be copied in the late OE period despite the efforts of reformers like Dunstan and Æthelwald. What is striking about *SS* and *Ad*, however, is the lateness of the copies, particularly as Tristram would seem to be implying that a more widespread orthodoxy prevailed in monasteries after the Conquest. The catechistical form inevitably suggests pedagogic instruction; the appearance in J of a copy (a corrupt copy) of *OE Dicts* also points towards the schoolroom. The prospect of a religious house, in the mid-12th century, or even the late 11th, employing Anglo-Saxon as the vehicle for instruction in traditional Anglo-Saxon heterodoxy is an intriguing possibility, and one can only hope that future study of the language and the manuscripts of *Ad* and *SS* will find it possible to identify their provenance. Perhaps, though, in view of the fact that Flint, 1977, concludes that the compilation of questions and answers in Honorius's *Elucidarium* was intended to encourage Anglo-Saxon monks to undertake pastoral care by providing them with ready-made answers to questions they were likely to encounter, *SS* and *Ad* may represent a convenient compendium of answers to problematic questions put by the laity (see further p. 80 below).

MISCELLANEOUS NOTES ('Notes and Commonplaces')

The prose pieces that FC classify as 'Notes and Commonplaces' (FC B.24), are not, as such, covered by this volume of annotations, but some of the items that fall within the classification FC B.24.10–24.26 are related in subject matter to *SS* and *Ad*. Among these is the short passage that follows *Ad* 48 (FC B.24.12.1), whose relationship to the poem is disputed (see further pp. 53–4 above, 'Extent of the Text of *Ad*').

Most of the Miscellaneous Notes whose relation to *SS* and *Ad* has been noticed were printed by Napier, **56**. Förster, **58**, studied those that deal with the ages of the world (FC B.24.25.3, 4); see also Tristram, **86**. Hall, **88**, examines the Notes on the age of Christ and the Virgin (FC B.24.16, 17), and Sauer, **84**, also includes some Miscellaneous Notes in his analysis of the '72 peoples' theme. As Hall demonstrates, the Miscellaneous Notes are

---

[14] Benjamin Thorpe, ed. and tr., *The Homilies of the Anglo-Saxon Church. The First Part, Containing the Sermones Catholici, or Homilies of Ælfric*, 2 vols. (London: Aelfric Society, 1844–6) 1: 2.

also of interest in their own right, for treatments of the same 'conventional' theme can in fact differ significantly; the Miscellaneous Notes on the age of Christ and the Virgin, in testifying to the existence of a multiplicity of apocryphal traditions are, simultaneously, evidence of the absence of a single, authoritative tradition.

The miscellaneous nature of these collections of Notes makes them extremely difficult to classify; and it may be helpful, if ungracious, to remark that FC's attempt to classify them according to their constituent topics is incomplete and likely to mislead. The composite Note in Tiberius A.iii, f. 43, for instance, printed by Napier, **56**, 2, includes a short passage on Rebecca and the wives of the prophets which does not figure in FC's classification. Study of the Miscellaneous Notes and their relationship to the prose dialogues is more likely to be advanced by consideration of the various collections in their totality.

A few correspondences between the Miscellaneous Notes and the prose dialogues were pointed out by Napier, **56**, and Förster, **58** and **66**; their findings have been incorporated into the commentary of Cross and Hill, who have identified some additional correspondences; they do not invariably take account of all of the extant versions of a particular theme (as Hall, **88**, observes). Study of Cross and Hill's commentary suggests that the correspondences with Miscellaneous Notes tend to occur in clusters (e.g., *SS* 10–17 and *Ad* 1–2), and that the Miscellaneous Notes and the prose dialogues are not much indebted to the *Joca Monachorum* lists for the material they have in common.

The Miscellaneous Notes themselves are largely unsourced and their interrelationships have been little studied. Napier could be said to have implicitly recognized the Miscellaneous Notes as a distinctive genre by the act of assembling a substantial number of them for publication; they appear to represent the same impulse towards the accumulation of arcane 'facts' as the prose dialogues. Some of the Miscellaneous Notes printed by Napier, such as the 'Note on the Gold brought to Solomon' (FC B.24.15), begin with a question, but rapidly abandon the question-and-answer form, and it is tempting to suppose that these were originally miniature dialogues whose questions have been suppressed for the purposes of economy. Such a development was, in fact, assumed by Förster, when he argued that the Note on f. 140v of J should be regarded as an integral part of *Ad*, but the possibility that the Miscellaneous Notes represent a development towards, rather than away from, the question-and-answer form cannot be outruled. The purpose of the Miscellaneous Notes—whether pedagogic or aids to the composition of sermons, for instance—does not appear to have been determined. Trahern, **77**, may have bearing on this matter.

SOLOMON & SATURN; ADRIAN & RITHEUS: ANNOTATIONS

SEE ALSO Wyatt, 6; Anderson, 17; Förster, 89; Henel, 222

EDITIONS

49 **Thorpe, Benjamin.** *Analecta Anglo-Saxonica. A Selection, in Prose and Verse, from Anglo-Saxon Authors of Various Ages; with a Glossary.* London: Arch, 1834. 2nd edn. London: Smith, 1846.

Near-diplomatic text of *SS*, 95–100 (2nd edn., 110–15). Note on the text, viii–ix. No apparatus.

50 **Wright, Thomas.** 'Adrian and Ritheus.' *Altdeutsche Blätter.* Vol. 2. Ed. Moriz Haupt and Heinrich Hoffmann. Leipzig: Brockhaus, 1840. 2 vols. Repr. as 1 vol. Hildesheim: Olms, 1978.

Prints *Ad*, 189–93. No apparatus.

51 **Ebeling, Friedrich W.** *Angelsächsisches Lesebuch.* Leipzig: Romberg, 1847.

Text of *SS*, 40–5; based on Thorpe, 49. Notes, 40.

52 **Kemble, John M.** *The Dialogue of Salomon and Saturnus, with an Historical Introduction.* Aelfric Society Publications 8, 13, 14. London: Aelfric Society, 1845–8. New York: AMS, 1974.

Text of *SS*, from Thorpe, 49, 178–93, with translation facing. Explanatory notes, 192–7, include some biblical sources.

Prints *Ad*, 198–207, with translation facing. Explanatory Notes, 206–11, include some analogues.

The prefatory remarks observe of *SS*: 'It is solemn and serious but more wide-ranging on biblical matters and physical science' (179). The details of its questions and answers are more clear if read in comparison with *Ad*. *Ad* differs from *SS* in little more than the names of the speakers. As nearly one third is common to the two 'it is not unreasonable to believe that both are fragmentary portions of one original' (199). Also prints a Latin *Adrian and Epictus*, from Arundel 351, 212–16, and *Master of Oxford*, from Lansdowne 762, 216–20, the latter described as 'a verbatim translation of one of the preceding dialogues' (216). Appendix, 221–326, contains 'compositions similar to those published': *Proverbs of Alfred, Proverbs of Hendyng, St. Serf and the Devil, Demaundes Joyous, Der Phaffe Amis,* and *Bedæ Collectanea et Flores.* [See also Larsen, **68**.]

Kemble traces the history of the legend of Salomon and Saturn, observing that the dialogues in this tradition are coarsely humorous and become a vehicle for satire at the Renaissance. Only the OE dialogues are of a serious nature: 'Monstrous as the absurdities found in them are we may be well assured that the authors were quite unconscious of their existence. That which is with us either blasphemy or nonsense, was with them religious wonder and knowledge; they loved mystery and mysticism even more' (2). Kemble holds that German pagan tradition underlies the verbal combat; and argues that Marcolfus, who is usually Salomon's antagonist, despite his Teutonic-sounding name, is a later substitution for Saturn, who was regarded as a pagan god, and whose name is preserved only in the OE dialogues. 'I want to restore Saturn or Marcolfus *the God* to his place in the pagan Pantheon of our ancestors. The ludicrous or hateful character which in Marcolfus gradually replaces the solemn and grave dignity of Saturnus confirms my view: Christianity never succeeded in rooting out the ancient creed, it only changed many of its objects' (6–7). [Prose and poetic *SS* dialogues are not distinguished by Kemble; specific reference is to the poetic dialogues only.]

Also prints *OE Dicts* from J, as 'Anglo-Saxon Apothegms,' 258–69. Silently regularized; translation facing; some omissions owing to illegible MS. Kemble notes the existence of T and the probability that there are other copies, and states that *OE Dicts* is 'a free paraphrase of the well-known distichs of Cato' (257). [See also Larsen, **68**.]

53 Klipstein, Louis F. *Analecta Anglo-Saxonica. Selections, in Prose and Verse, from the Anglo-Saxon Literature.* Vol. 1. New York: Putnam, 1849. 2 vols.

Text of *SS*, 187–94; based directly or indirectly on Thorpe, **49**. Notes, 343.

54 Ettmüllerus, Ludovicus. *Engla and Seaxna Scôpas and Bôceras: Anglosax-onum pöetae atque scriptores prosaici.* Bibliothek der gesammten deutsch-en national-literatur 28. Quedlinburgh: Bassius; London: Williams, 1850. Amsterdam: Rodopi, 1966.

Text of *SS*, 6–9, 26–7, 32, 41, 50, 55–6 only, from Thorpe, **49**; with textual notes, 42–3.

Prints *Ad*, from Wright, **50**, 39–42.

Praefatio, vii–xxiv (in Latin), introduces this anthology of texts.

55 Cross, James E., and Thomas D. Hill. *The Prose* Solomon and Saturn *and* Adrian and Ritheus. MacMaster Old English Studies and Texts 1. Toronto: Toronto UP, 1982.

Near-diplomatic text: *SS*, 25–34; *Ad*, 35–40. Commentary for each question and answer is divided into three sections: a MnE translation; parallels within other extant dialogues (Latin and vernacular) and/or other relevant illustrations; the reason for, and explanation of, the OE question and answer (sometimes, also, a discussion of relevant parallels and/or points of interest), 59–160. Glossaries, 163–85. Bibliography, briefly annotated, 43–58.

Introduction, 3–7, characterizes the texts; their content 'reveals aspects of the medieval imagination which may illuminate obscurities in the major literature and certainly accustoms a modern reader to medieval attitudes' (3). 'Relationships and Genre,' 7–13, explains that there is no single source for either text: the OE lists 'belong to the circle of' the *Joca Monachorum* group. The editors have speculated about the questions that have no parallels, 'partly to suggest that the Old English lists or exemplars were individually or collectively augmented, but also to indicate certain cultural contacts' (8). A number of questions appear to get information from Irish texts or traditions (as represented, e.g., by a Hiberno-Latin catechism, *Prebiarum de multorium exemplaribus* and *Collectanea Bedae*). Some additions may derive from earlier Anglo-Saxon texts (e.g., the exemplar of Vercelli Homily xix, a gloss on the metrical *De Virginitate*). Seventeen questions in *SS* and *Ad* correspond in content. Both lists 'were composed independently of each other, although drawing on some common sources, no doubt at different removes' (12). None of the lists of the *Joca Monachorum* type have named protagonists. The most likely originals of the names of the speakers of *Ad* are Adrian and Epictetus; whether the names Solomon and Saturn came by derivation from the poetical series or from a common ancestor 'is a matter for conjecture alone' (12). Description of manuscripts and transcripts, together with survey of previous editions and a note on the extent of *Ad*, 14–23. The editors have not attempted to draw conclusions about the language of the texts, but lexical comments are included in the Commentary, and the Glossary, inclusive and containing cross-references to various forms, 'is intended to aid any future study of the language of the manuscripts' (18). [For reviews see Russom, **85**.]

MISCELLANEOUS NOTES

56 Napier, A. 'Altenglische Kleinigkeiten.' *Anglia* 11 (1889): 1–10.

Prints Miscellaneous Notes (items within FC B.24.10–B.24.26), as follows: (1) Tiberius A.iii, ff. 43–4 (which Napier compares with Kemble, 182 [*SS*]); (2) Tiberius A.iii, f. 73; (3) Vespasian D.vi, f. 69v (already printed by Wright and Halliwell, *Reliquiae Antiquae*, 2: 283, and in the same hand as the Kentish hymns which precede it and the Kentish psalms which follow); (4) Julius A.ii, f. 140v, also in Junius 61 [FC B.24.12.1, which Förster, **62**, argued was the continuation to *Ad*]; (5) Titus D.xxvii, f. 55v; (6) Caligula A.xv, f. 139v; (7) Caligula A.xv, f. 140v; (8) Harley 3271, f. 90; (9) Harley 3271, f. 92v; (10) Harley 3271, f. 128v. [For FC classification, see pp. 60–1 above, 'Miscellaneous Notes.']

Includes two computistical texts: 'Three Fridays for Fasting,' from Tiberius A.iii, f. 44 [FC B.20.11.1], 3; 'On Moon and Tide,' from Titus D.xxvii, f. 55 [FC B.20.8], 6.

57 **Birch, W. de G.** *Liber Vitæ: Register and Martyrology of New Minster and Hyde Abbey, Winchester.* Hampshire Record Society. London: Simpkin, 1892.

Prints Miscellaneous Notes: 'On the Age of the Virgin,' from Stowe 944 [FC B.24.16.2], and from Titus D.xxvii [FC B.24.16.1], 83; 'The Six Ages of the World,' from Stowe 944 [FC B.24.25.4], 81–3. Birch considers that the entry in Stowe 944 has been seriously tampered with in order to bring the date down to the year 1031 (82, n. 1).

58 **Förster, Max.** 'Die Weltzeitalter bei den Angelsachsen.' *Neusprachliche Studien. Festgabe Karl Luick zu seinem 60. Geburtstage.* [Ed. F. Wild.] Die Neueren Sprachen 6. Marburg: Elwert, 1925. 183–203.

Prints Miscellaneous Notes: 'The Six Ages of the World,' from Stowe 944 [FC B.24.25.4], 191–2, from Arundel 60 and Cotton Caligula A.xv [FC B.24.25.3], 192–3; 'The Age of the World,' from Vespasian D.vi [FC B.24. 26.1], 195–7, from Harley 3271 [FC B.24.26.3], 197–8, and from Vespasian D.xiv [FC B.24.26.2], 199.

Förster compares classical and Christian Ages of the World, and distinguishes three types of the sixfold (specifically Christian) division known to the Anglo-Saxons. (1) Augustine-Bede type: Adam-Noah-Abraham-David-Babylonian Exile-Christ-End. Represented by: Ælfric *HomCath*, 2: 58; pseudo-Wulfstan (ed. Napier, 1883, 311/24); *ByrM* (ed. Crawford, **212**, 244–7); cf. Bede, *De temporum ratione*, ch. 66. (2) Nennius type: Adam-Noah-Abraham-Moses-David-Christ-End. Represented by: Stowe 944, ff. 81–3 [FC B.24.25.4]; Caligula A.xv, f. 139v and Arundel 60, f. 149r [FC B.24.25.3]. (3) Æthelweard type: the same as (2), but the fourth age is bounded by Solomon's temple instead of David. Represented by: (a) Vespasian D.vi, f. 69v [FC B.24.26.1], and *SS*; (b) Harley 3271, f. 128v [FC B.24.26.3]. These, especially (a), agree so closely with Æthelweard's Chronicle that there must be direct or indirect borrowing. Warner, **4**, 139–40 [FC B.3.4.57] (cf. *PL* 172: 854, and an Icelandic text), recognizes a sevenfold division, created by the addition to (3) of an Age bounded by the Babylonian Exile.

COMMENTARY

59 **Bouterwek, K.W.** *Caedmon's des Angelsachsen biblische Dichtungen.* Vol. 1. 2nd edn. Gütersloh: Bertelsmann, 1849. 2 vols.

At cxiii–cxiv Bouterwek compares the names of the wives of Noah's sons in *SS*[21] with those in *Genesis A* ('Percoba, Olla, Olliua and Olliuani');

Olliuani or Ollibana, perhaps also Olliva, derive from Ezek. 23, where two women, Oholâh and Ohilabâh, stand for the kingdoms of Israel and Juda. An 'Oholibamâh' is mentioned in Gen 36.2, which the Vulgate renders as 'Oolibama.'

60 Cook, Albert S. 'The Name Caedmon.' *PMLA* 6 (1891): 9–28.

In discussing whether or not there was sufficient knowledge of the Oriental tongues to enable an Oriental name to be conferred on the Whitby poet, Cook includes as evidence 'links connecting the prose dialogue of *SS* with the Genesis attributed to Caedmon' (22), which takes the form of a quotation from Bouterwek, **59**.

61 Cook, Albert S. 'Old English Literature and Jewish Learning.' *Modern Language Notes* 6 (1891): 142–53.

Further to Cook, **60**. Late Jewish influence has been recognized in Anglo-Saxon literature (e.g., Kemble, **52**, Bouterwek, **59**), thus raising the question of the channels by which Rabbinical learning became accessible. Cook quotes liberally from Graetz, *Geschichte der Juden*, Vol. 5, and concludes that 7th century intercourse between England and France made it possible for ecclesiastics and others to associate with Jews who possessed some biblical and Talmudic learning, and persecuted Jews from France and Spain may have sought refuge in England in the 7th century. The traditions of the English church, under the sway of Gregory's humanitarian attitude to the Jews, would have been favourable to their reception. 'The impulse received from the Arabs, and which resulted in the creation of the Neohebraic poetry, must in some measure have communicated itself to the Jews of Western Europe as late as towards the middle of the seventh century' (151). Connections between OE and Neohebraic poetry are adduced. 'It may not seem too bold to assert that the beginnings of English literature have a traceable connection with the establishment of Mohammedanism' (152).

62 Förster, Max. 'Zu Adrian und Ritheus.' *Englische Studien* 23 (1897): 431–6.

Förster collates Kemble, **52**, with J, and gives a comparative table, which shows that *Ad* and *SS* have a good deal of material in common with two other dialogues in Kemble, *Adrian et Epictus* and pseudo-Bede *Collectanea et Flores*. Förster also prints Julius A.ii, f. 140v [FC B.24.12.1], at 433–4, and suggests that it should be regarded as part of the *Ad* text; it includes the number of bones, veins and days of the year, to which *SS*[59] also refers.

Förster mentions that *OE Dicts* are preserved in J (434), and that he intends to bring out a critical edition of this work.

63 Emerson, Oliver F. 'Legends of Cain, Especially in Old and Middle English.' *PMLA* 21 (1906): 831–929.

Examination of the origins of the jaw-bone as Cain's murder weapon mentions *SS*[36] at 853: 'In English the earliest reference so far found occurs in the parallels to the Salomon and Saturn dialogue' (Kemble, **52**, 186). 'The Giants and Gods of the Heathen,' 905–16, observes that *SS* alludes covertly to the same idea as OE *Metres of Boethius* (Grein, 3, 2, 46); 'Salomon reminds Saturn of his connection with an evil race which strove against God.' The writer 'no doubt had in mind the common medieval interpretation of the war of the giants with Jove which connected them with the giants of *Genesis*, probably with Nimrod and the tower of Babel. In that case, the work which they did not accomplish was very likely the tower itself, though possibly the rebellion in general' (906).

64 Förster, Max. 'Adams Erschaffung und Namengebung.' *Archiv für Religionswissenschaft* 11 (1907–8): 477–529.

Förster distinguishes five groups of texts that deal with the origins of Adam's name and substances of his composition; only in *Durham Ritual*, *SS* and *Maister of Oxenford* (group E) is the verbal resemblance close. Förster concludes that *SS*[9] must derive from the Latin of the *Durham Ritual*, and cites two Latin parallels which, he believes, must have ultimately derived from the same source as *Durham Ritual* (493–7). [See also Cross, **78**, Evans, **76**.]

65 Merrill, Elizabeth. *The Dialogue in English Literature.* Yale Studies in English 42. New York: Holt, 1911. New York: Franklin, 1970.

In ch. 2.1, 'The Dialogue in the Middle Ages,' 10–30, Merrill distinguishes two forms of medieval European dialogue, the catechism-exposition, and the contention-poem or *débat*, which grew out of native tendencies that readily combined with the influence of Prudentius and others. In England, even more than elsewhere, these two forms overlapped, as did the religious and secular matters with which they deal. The Alfredian translations of the *Consolation*, *Soliloquies* and *Dialogues*, entering the literature at a time when the dialogue form was still comparatively undeveloped, were also influential. Like the first part of the poetic *SS*, the prose *SS* and *Ad* tend towards catechism and expository dialogue. 'These dialogues present a strange conglomeration of medieval lore, mingling Biblical statements ... with the dimly comprehended phenomena of the world of that day' (20–1). The *Elucidarium* of Honorius ['Resurrection' fragment] 'affords one of the best examples of a purely theological catechism' (21).

66 Förster, Max. 'Kleinere mittelenglische Texte.' *Anglia* 42 (1918): 145–224.

At 209–17, Förster makes some observations on medieval question and response literature, and asserts that *SS* and *Ad* have similarities with a number of other OE pieces, all of which must derive from the same Latin original. These are: Tiberius A.iii, f. 44r [FC B.24.10.2]; Caligula A.xv, f. 131v (Cockayne, **298**, 3: 228), f. 139v [FC B.24.11]; Titus D.xxvii, f. 55v [FC B.24.16.1];

Bodley 343, f. 154v [FC B.24.16.3]. He notes that the number of human veins and bones and their relation to the number of days, found in *SS*[59], and in the lines he regards as the conclusion to *Ad* [FC B.24.12.1], is also found in Rawlinson F32, f. 205 (*c.* 1470); cf. Gen. 1.27. The apocryphal NT, Förster observes, is also a source for material in the dialogues. [See also Napier, **56.**]

67 **Creed, J.M.** 'The Heavenly Man.' *Journal of Theological Studies* 26 (1925): 113–36.

Creed reviews the Gnostic and allied documents in which the myth of the Heavenly Man, from whom the human race and sometimes the present world is derived; he considers the possible sources of the idea in oriental (particularly Iranian) speculation, and discusses its possible relations to the Son of Man in later Jewish and early Christian thought. [No specific reference to *SS.*]

68 **Larsen, Henning.** 'Kemble's *Salomon and Saturn.*' *Modern Philology* 26 (1928–9): 445–50.

Larsen distinguishes the 1848 Aelfric Society edition of Kemble, **52,** from an earlier version (*Proofs*), for which BM Catalogue conjectures 'London? 1845?' *Dictionary of National Biography*, 30: 369 ff., confuses these. A detailed external comparison of *Edition* and *Proofs* is followed by a comparison of contents: (1) The *Proofs* contain much illustrative material omitted from the *Edition*. (2) The *Edition* adds the texts of *SS* (prose and poetic), *Ad*, *Master of Oxford* and *Adrian and Epictus*, as well as translation of *OE Dicts* and two other texts. (3) The *Edition* shows a careful revision of many passages as to content, diction and typography and adds discussion of 'The Traditional Character of Marcolfus.' The exact date of *Proofs* cannot be fixed, but the task was begun in 1833: 'Everything speaks of an edition abandoned in the making and of page proof, not fully revised, bound for the convenience of a few until the real edition should appear' (450).

69 **Utley, Frances Lee.** 'The One Hundred and Three Names of Noah's Wife.' *Speculum* 16 (1941): 426–52.

An alphabetical list of all known names for the wives of Noah and his three sons is followed by an outline of their development; reasons for the numerousness of the names for Noah's wife are found in the aetiological tendency, magicians' need for names to conjure with and the ill repute of Noah's wife. *SS* and *Genesis A* (possibly influenced by Byzantine dialogue-books), together with certain Irish sources which may have been used by English writers, are the most interesting attempts in the West to supply the wants of the Bible. *SS*[19–21] offers a less trustworthy version of a tradition also found in Comestor's 12th century expanded Bible, mingled with the tradition represented by *Maister of Oxenford*, for Shem's wife is omitted and

Comestor's name for Ham's wife, Cathaflua, has become Catafluuia, and is applied to Japhet (447, 440, n. 19).

70 **Menner, Robert J.** *The Poetical Dialogues of Solomon and Saturn.* New York: Modern Language Association of America, 1941. New York: Kraus, 1973.

Menner's definitive edition of the two poetical *SS* dialogues also prints the associated prose (paternoster) dialogue as an Appendix, 168–71. The prose dialogues do not fall within the scope of this edition; Menner remarks that 'the great popularity of the Solomonic dialogue attached the names of Solomon and Saturn to the dialogues of a catechistic type' (56). 'The Legend of Solomon' is examined at 21–35. Contrary to Kemble, **52**, Menner thinks it impossible to determine whether Marcolf was substituted for Saturn or Saturn for Marcolf, and observes: 'Kemble's whole discussion of Saturn is obscured by his adoption (120–130) of Grimm's view, now rejected, that Saturn-Sætern was a Germanic god' (33, n. 5).

71 **Schapiro, M.** 'Cain's Jaw-bone that did the first murder.' *Art Bulletin* 24 (1942): 210–11.

Schapiro suggests that the identification of Cain's weapon as a jaw-bone is due to the association of OE *cinbān* ('jaw bone') with *Cāin bana* ('Cain slayer'). He finds evidence for this in 'the vernacular linguistic context' of the story of Cain, citing *SS*[36] and *Beowulf*, lines 1261–2, where Cain is described as the *ecg-bana* of Abel. *SS*, dated 9th century [*sic*], is the earliest literary reference to Cain's jaw-bone, pre-dating the representations of this weapon in the carvings of Cain on 10th century Irish stone crosses. [See Henderson, **75**.]

72 **Menner, Robert J.** 'Two Old English Words.' *Modern Language Notes* 59 (1944): 106–12.

Treats (*ge*)*strynd* in its several occurrences in the prose and poetic corpora, and *gullisc* in the prose section of the poetic *SS*, 111–12. [Cross-listing by Greenfield and Robinson appears mistaken.]

73 **Utley, Francis Lee.** 'Jaiaca, the City of Sunrise.' *Names* 5 (1957): 208–21.

Utley considers the 'pretty problem' posed by the name of the city where the sun rises (*SS*[26] and *Ad*[29]). For the name of the city where the sun sets, *SS*[27] has 'Garita' and *Ad*[30] has 'Janita,' and Utley concludes that the dialogues 'reflect the idea of a planiform earth, with the sun setting in the ocean beyond Cadiz or "Garita" ' (211). But Jaiaca is not so easy to identify. Possible 'real places' are: India, River Ganges, Cathay, Java, Japan, River Jaxartes, and River Jaec; the latter is perhaps 'the best candidate from the point of view of spelling' (216), although most of the notices are too late for the 12th century. There are also three 'fabulous' possibilities. (1) Strabo refers to a people called Coniaci who lived in Spain and in the East;

loss of *con-*, and a confused tradition, 'might have suggested that the world was properly bounded by a balanced set of names' (217), so that Jaiaca originated to be later juxtaposed to the classical Garita. (2) Lore concerning Alexander's discovery of the Eastern Pillars: 'Though all this lore about the Eastern Pillars provides us with no name to correspond to our Old English Jaiaca, there is ample evidence that Gades or Garita had its eastern counterpart, also complete with pillars. To such a legend as this may have been attached any one of the names we have put forward' (220). (3) 'Aiaia, where Dawn has her dwelling,' in the *Odyssey*. Utley regards Aiaia as 'an excellent candidate' (220), and also favours the Eastern Pillars, as well as Jaec, which Marco Polo called Jaiac.

74 Utley, Francis Lee. 'The Prose *Salomon and Saturn* and the Tree Called Chy.' *Mediaeval Studies* 19 (1957): 55–78.

Utley draws on studies of cuneiform, rabbinical and pseudepigraphical writings, in order to shed light on the hidden truths expounded in *SS*. He explores first the entire sequence, defining structural groupings and their relationships, before turning to *SS*[18], which gives 'Sem' as the name of the tree from which Noah's ark was made. *Maister of Oxenford* gives the tree's name as 'Chy,' and it is 'a distinct possibility and an interesting one' (77) that *Maister of Oxenford* preserves a better reading of the original than does *SS*. The tree called 'Chy' (*Chi-Rho*) equates Christ and the trees of Eden and Calvary; it is 'a tree which is a central link both in the Chain of Being and what we may call the Chain of History' (67). 'Sem,' in *SS*, might have been eye-skip from the sons of Noah, or a scribal substitution for an earlier misreading of 'Chy' as 'Cham'; or the Tree of Sem might have been coined on the Tree of Jesse. But Utley's preferred explanation is that Shem's connection with the cross legend caused his name to become identified with the wood of the ark and the cross. As many of the relevant typological developments are 12th century or later, Utley turns to the *Dream of the Rood*, which demonstrates that 'the Cross, Christ, sinning man and Tree of Paradise were all eternally present and figuratively joined, though not yet surely joined in the West to Seth's Tree of Mercy and literal Chain of History. The seeds were there, they must grow, and their final issue into a tree called Chy and the four corners of Noah's Ark was merely the recurrent miracle of poetry' (78).

75 Henderson, George. 'Cain's Jaw-Bone.' *Journal of the Warburg and Courtauld Institutes* 24 (1962): 108–14.

Disposes of the argument of Schapiro, **71**. Not only has he misdated *SS*, but his linguistic argument is invalid: *cinbāna* and *Cāin bana* are not homonyms, and *Cāin bana* (which does not occur in the passages Schapiro cited) is not a subjective genitive in OE. But it remains true that *SS*[36] is the earliest literary identification of Cain's weapon as a jaw-bone, because Cain's weapon on the 10th century Irish crosses is actually a coulter. The earliest visual representation is also English (Ælfric's *Pentateuch*, Cotton Claudius B.iv, f. 8v.) Henderson argues that Cain's jaw-bone does not derive from an exegetical transference of Samson's weapon but by pictorial borrowing: the Ælfric illustration is of the same type as the illustration of Samson slaughtering Philistines in the 9th century Paris Homilies and on an 11th century Augsburg door. It is possible that the Ælfric illustrator used a Samson model because the illustration of Cain was lacking in his exemplar; but the Irish crosses show that there existed illustrations in which Cain's coulter looks like a jaw-bone, and Henderson prefers the explanation that Cain's weapon in the Ælfric illustrator's exemplar looked so like a jaw-bone that he modified his original to bring it into line with the standard type of Samson illustration.

76 Evans, J.M. 'Microcosmic Adam.' *Medium Ævum* 35 (1966): 38–42.

Evans identifies *Liber Enoch*, 3.8 as the ultimate source of both *SS*[9] and *Durham Ritual* [*Surtees Society* 140: 192]; they list the same eight ingredients of Adam, but in a different order. Evans believes that *DR* must depend on *SS*: '*anhela frigida* is clearly the result of misreading the OE *æðung geseald* as *æðung geceald*, [and] ... Latin *sudor* for the element derived from dew can only be explained by the ambiguity of OE *swāt*' (39). In the Anglo-Saxon versions, some component ingredients of Adam have undergone modification in the course of transmission, and the human endowments derived from them have changed; ME versions (*Cursor Mundi*, lines 539–46, EETS 57, and *The Wheatley MS.*, EETS 155) are more faithful to the *Liber Enoch*, and Ralegh's *History of the World* (Bk. 1, ch. 2, sect. 5) reproduces the original list almost exactly: 'The only possible conclusion seems to be that better texts of *The Secrets of Enoch*, or of an intermediary source containing the *Enoch* list, gradually became available in England after the tenth century' (42).

77 Trahern, Joseph B. 'The *Ioca Monachorum* and the Old English *Pharaoh*.' *English Language Notes* 7 (1970–1): 165–8.

It is generally agreed that the Exeter dialogue poem on Pharaoh is of the genre exemplified by the prose *SS* and *Ad*, but a question and answer on this subject have not to date been found in any dialogues of this kind. Trahern finds a parallel for *Pharaoh* in an 8th century manuscript of *Ioca Monachorum* (ed. Suchier, 1955, 111). It thus appears that the subject matter of *Pharaoh* has a place in the *Ioca Monachorum* tradition, but it does not follow that *Ioca Monachorum* is its immediate source, because *Pharaoh* is of the 'Saga me' type exemplified in *SS* and *Ad*, and though this introductory formula occurs in the *Ioca Monachorum* tradition, it does not appear in the source manuscript.

78 Cross, J.E. 'The Literate Anglo-Saxon—on Sources and Disseminations.' *Proceedings of the British Academy* 58 (1972): 67–100. Also published separately: British Academy, Gollancz Memorial Lecture. London: Oxford UP, 1972.

Evans, **76**, and Förster, **64**, illustrate the invalidity of deducing direct relationships between texts that deal with a common theme (discussed at 8–9). Evans's suggestion that the Latin of the 10th century *Durham Ritual* depended on the 12th century *SS* is demonstrably incorrect, and Förster's conclusion that *SS* derived from the Latin of *Durham Ritual* is doubtful. *Durham Ritual*'s putative misreading of *SS*[9], on which Evans's argument chiefly rests (*geseald* as *geceald*), involves a unique form of the adjective *ceald*, and *s* and *c* are dissimilar in the *SS* script; equally important, there are other examples of this theme in pre-10th century texts. To the examples assembled by Förster, Cross adds one from the *Catéchèses celtiques*, but would not attempt to draw conclusions: 'For, in the case of this common theme, examples of which are surely lost or as yet unprinted, one may well ask against Förster, why a man with an exemplar before him should vary the order of the items. I suspect also that the Solomon scribe saw "breath" alone as in, but not necessarily in, the *Catéchèses celtiques*' (9).

79 Frank, Roberta. 'Some Uses of *Paronomasia* in Old English Scriptural Verse.' *Speculum* 47 (1972): 207–26.

In demonstrating that (pseudo)etymological word-play is an aspect of OE poetic imagination, Frank instances *SS*[3]. Christian champions fought with words as weapons, and Solomon wins this round because he has shown Saturn how Christian learning can fathom the secret significance of things: 'Not only has he managed to recapture the sounds of *heofan* in this etymological explanation, but he has approximated in Old English the newest and most deliberately Christian of the several Latin etymologies for *caelum*' (207). Kemble, **52**, 193, recognized word-play in *SS*, and observed that it was worthy of Isidore, but this form of etymology first appears in Cassiodorus and Bede.

80 Tristram, Hildegard L.C. 'Der "homo octipartitus" in der irischen und altenglischen Literatur.' *Zeitschrift für Celtische Philologie* 34 (1975): 119–53.

Tristram explains how the *homo octipartitus* theme in insular texts was assimilated to dialogue literature and further developed, particularly by its association with the etymology of Adam's name. From a comparison of the structure, formulation and textual relations of versions in OE (*SS*[9] and *Durham Ritual*) and in medieval Irish (including 'Evernew Tongue'), she concludes that the OE and Irish are independently derived from a continental Latin version. Close textual comparison of *SS* and *Durham Ritual* (at 132–3) suggests that *SS* is further from the Latin original than *Durham*

Ritual; two continental manuscripts which are based on versions partly English and partly Irish are further removed from the original. Heterodox material such as this was preserved by reformed monasteries in the late OE period, but writers like Ælfric made no use of it (in treating the creation of Man, he refers only to scriptural texts), and there is no continuity of the OE tradition of the *homo octipartitus* theme; ME and later versions derive from continental texts introduced with the Conquest. [See also Förster, **64**, Evans, **76**, Cross, **78**.]

81 Whitbread, L. 'Adam's Pound of Flesh: A Note on Old English Verse *Solomon and Saturn* (II), 336–339.' *Neophilologus* 59 (1975): 622–6.

Whitbread proposes *eahta pundum* for MS *of niehtes wunde* in the poetic *SS* 2, 336–9, and links it to the tradition specifying the constituent substances of Adam as weights or pounds (in *SS*[9]). He illustrates this tradition by printing *Liber Enoch*, 30.8, the three passages cited by Cross, **78**, and *Maister of Oxenford* (see Förster, **64**).

82 Raw, Barbara. 'The Probable Derivation of most of the Illustrations in Junius 11 from an Illustrated Old Saxon *Genesis*.' *Anglo-Saxon England* 5 (1976): 133–48.

God on the winds at creation in *SS*[1] is mentioned in the discussion of illustrations in Utrecht Psalter and Junius 11 ('Caedmon Manuscript'), at 143; like the illustrations, *SS*[1] alludes to Psalm 103.3.

83 Hill, Thomas D. '*VIII Genitus Homo* as a Nomen Sacrum in a Twelfth-Century Anglo-Latin Fever Charm.' *Notes and Queries* NS 30 (1983): 487–8.

The Latin fever charm in Cambridge, Queens' College 7, f. 142v (Storms 64), which invokes the power of the 70 names of God (72 is a more conventional number), lists only about 50 such names, including 'VIII genitus homo.' Hill suggests that this is an allusion to the myth of the creation of Adam from eight *pondera*, ultimately derived from *The Secrets of Enoch* and widely diffused in medieval Latin and vernacular texts (e.g., *Durham Ritual* and *SS*); this usage confirms Adam as one of the names of Christ. The prayer provides information about the currency of Enochian matter, and about the thought world of the compilers of such prayers. Most of the names are from pre-existing lists, but 'eight-born man' as a name for God appears to be an original addition or drawn from an unconventional source; thus, 'the author's attitude seems much more "magical" than "religious," in that he seems to have believed that the hidden name of God is more powerful than a more conventional one precisely because it is hidden, strange, and new' (488).

84 Sauer, Hans. 'Die 72 Völker und Sprachen der Welt: ein mittelalterlicher Topos in der englischen Literatur.' *Anglia* 101 (1983): 29–48.

Sauer classifies, and examines the derivation of, OE and ME versions of the 72 peoples motif, which arises from the building of the Tower of Babel, is

associated with the descendants of Noah, and is typologically related both
to the 72 sent out to preach (Luke 10.1–20) and to the number of books of
the Bible. Sauer relates *SS*[14] and *SS*[59] (and *Maister of Oxenford*) to
Tiberius A.iii, f. 43v [FC B.24.10.2]; Caligula A.xv, f. 139v [FC B.24.11];
Lord's Prayer II, 20. He also treats the appearance of the motif in the
Alfredian *Consolatio*, Ælfric (*HomCath* and *Interrogationes Sigewulfi*), the
'Heavenly Letter,' and some anonymous homilies. CCCC 448 (first half 11th
century, Winchester) is included in the table of comparisons (48).

85 **Russom, Geoffrey.** Rev. of *The Prose* Solomon and Saturn *and* Adrian and
Ritheus, ed. James E. Cross and Thomas D. Hill [55]. *Speculum* 59 (1984):
388–90.

Russom observes that Cross and Hill, **55**, 'prefer to emphasise religious concepts, even in a few cases where the text provides no justification for doing
so' (389). The OE questions which correspond to Latin 'Quid est gravis-
simum terre?' have as their answer 'hlafordes yrre' (*Ad*[32]) and 'mannes
synna and hys hlafordes yrre' (*SS*[48]), whereas the analogues have 'ira
regis.' Cross and Hill (at 115) consider that reference to God's anger is
implicit in *Ad*'s rendering of 'rex,' and unambiguous in *SS*'s addition. But
syn[n] (see *BT*) often refers to offences against secular laws or earthly rulers,
and 'the Lord' usually appears as *dryhten* (e.g., *Ad* 3, 4). Russom regards it
as significant that the OE questions ask about life in *this* world (*on eorðan*):
'In this world, surely, an Old English malefactor would have found it hardest
to endure the wrath of a secular *hlaford*' (390).

86 **Tristram, Hildegard L.C.** *Sex aetates mundi: Die Weltzeitalter bei den Angelsachsen und den Iren. Untersuchungen und Texte.* Anglistische Forschungen 165. Heidelberg: Winter, 1985.

The study of the Ages of the World theme in Part 1 classifies insular variants
(7th–12th centuries) of the three major patterns: Eusebian (which most frequently recurs in early chronological writings), Augustinian (developed by
Isidore), and Bedean (which employs Vulgate numbers and adds a seventh
and eighth age, and prevails in exegetic and poetic writing throughout the
period studied). Tristram finds no evidence of Irish influence on English
writings; rather, the Bedean pattern influenced Irish thinking from the 8th
century onwards, and, by the 11th century, had become the most widely
used pattern, even in chronological writings. Table of relationships, 36–
49. English prose texts (Latin and OE, listed 31–2) include *SS*; three of
the Miscellaneous Notes on 'The Six Ages of the World' [FC B.24.25.2–4];
the Miscellaneous Notes on 'The Age of the World' [FC B.24.26.1–3], two
of which (Vespasian D.vi and Harley 3271) are related to Æthelweard's
Chronicle; and *ByrM* (ed. Crawford, **212**, 208–10, 234–42), whose relation
to Bede's schema is discussed at 89–93. Part 2 edits Ælfric's OE *De sex
aetatibus huius seculi* and an anonymous Irish text; illustrative texts appended include Latin fragments from Nero A.ii, Vespasian B.vi, Regius 2
B.v, Tiberius C.i, and St John's College Oxford 17.

87 Bisher, E. Franklin. 'Heterogenous Religious Expression in the Old English "Solomon and Saturn" Dialogues.' *DAI* 49 (1988): 1136A. [Diss. SUNY, Buffalo, 1988.]

Dissertation not sighted. According to *DAI*, Bisher's exploration of the function of dialogic utterance includes an investigation into the relevance of Bakhtinian theory to the roles of the two interlocutors in the prose *SS*; the introduction reviews the classical and medieval literary history of Solomon, and Bisher concludes that 'the heterogenous quality of the Solomon and Saturn dialogues allows diverse Christian religious expression while simultaneously exhibiting a secular, and at times, pagan spirit.'

88 Hall, Thomas N. 'The Ages of Christ and Mary in the Hyde Register and in Old English Literature.' *Notes and Queries* NS 35 (1988): 4–11.

A miscellaneous entry in the Hyde Abbey Register, Stowe 944, on the age of Christ [FC B.24.16.2] and the age of the Virgin [FC B.24.17] is examined. 'This series of seemingly meticulous calculations appended to a commonplace enumeration of the ages of the world [FC B.24.25.4] contains evidence for as many as five distinct ages of Christ, some of which are unattested elsewhere' (5). The paragraph on the age of Mary appears in four other Anglo-Saxon manuscripts [FC B.24.16.1, B.23.16.3, B.24.10.2, B.24.11]; Hill notes (8, n. 10) that Cross and Hill, **55**, cite all but one of these (Caligula A.xv, f. 139r) in their commentary on *SS* 17. These four manuscripts are all contemporary with or post-date the Hyde Register entry, and thus suggest its place in a particular line of transmission. Hall deduces that the note was copied first in the Hyde Register or in Titus D.xxvii [FC B.24.16.1]; in either case this tradition seems to be connected with Winchester. The figure of 63 years adduced as the length of Mary's life is peculiarly English (rather than insular). 'The collection of ages noted in the Hyde Register—for Mary and for Christ—reflects something of the confusion arising from a bit of popular lore whose myriad versions were never fully reconciled' (9). 'Very few of these numbers appear to have gained authority, while others seem purely arbitrary, and caution against assumptions that many items of numerical lore in Old English literature are but "commonplace" or "conventional" ' (11).

ELUCIDARIUM

MANUSCRIPT

London, British Library, Cotton Vespasian D.xiv,   V   FC B.9.9
    ff. 159–63v, 163v–5
Ker 209 (s. xii med.)
        art. 48 *De Peccato*
        art. 49 'Resurrection' Dialogue

MANUSCRIPT DESCRIPTION, DATE AND PROVENANCE
(following Ker and Förster)

V, which Ker dates mid-12th century and assigns to Rochester or Canterbury, also contains a copy of *OE Dicts*. Ker identifies three different hands,
but intimates that the first two are sometimes difficult to tell apart. He
says nothing to suggest that *De Peccato* is in the second, rather than the
main, hand.[1] The 'Resurrection' dialogue, however, is in the third hand,
and is among the entries which seem to have been added in originally blank
pages; part of the homily which immediately follows it is written in the
same hand. Förster, **89**, described this hand as 'thin' and 'old-fashioned
looking' (89). He also commented on the scribe's use of insular and caroline
g; Ker states that the use of these two forms of *g* is also characteristic of
the second hand.

Förster, **89**, accepted the early 12th century dating of V suggested by
Napier, 1890;[2] Förster, **91**, dated it *c*. 1125. In his extended examination
of the language of the 'Resurrection' dialogue, **89**, he inclined to the view
that the manuscript originated from the Wessex district, perhaps somewhere near the Mercian border, and he suggested that a study of the whole
codex might make it possible to ascribe it to one of the great centres of ecclesiastical learning such as Winchester. In his later publication on *De Peccato*
(**91**), however, he emphasized its Canterbury connections, and suggested
that V was a preacher's commonplace-book, designed for an audience that
included uneducated monks and lay brothers. Ker assigns the manuscript
to either Canterbury (endorsed by Handley, **96**) or Rochester, for which
Richards, **95**, argues; Richards dates the manuscript second quarter of the

---

[1] Förster, **89**, 94, identifies only a main hand and the hand which added the 'Resurrection' dialogue. Utley, 1972, 741, states that both of the OE dialogues are in a hand
different from the rest of the manuscript.

[2] A.S. Napier, 'Some Points of English Orthography in the Twelfth Century,' *Academy*
37 (1890): 134.

12th century. (For further manuscript description, see 'Manuscripts,' *Dicts of Cato*, p. 16 above.)

TEXT DESCRIPTION; EDITIONS

As *OE Elucidarium* is among the latest of the texts which are accepted as linguistically OE, it consorts somewhat uneasily with the prose translations dating from the reign of Alfred with which FC classify it.[3] The doctrinal character of *OE Elucidarium* also sets it apart from most of the works covered by this volume of annotations, but the text is occasionally mentioned in connection with *SS* and *Ad* as one of the forms of dialogue represented in OE, and is for that reason included here.

OE Elucidarium consists of two short pieces, written in different hands. They have the form of a question-and-answer dialogue, but the interlocutors are not named. The first piece concerns the nature of sin and the contrasting earthly fortunes of good and evil men; the second concerns the resurrection, Christ's appearances to the disciples and Mary Magdalene, and his ascension. Both pieces are included in Warner's *EETS* edition of V (4). Förster, 89, prints the 'Resurrection' dialogue only (OE and Latin); the 'Resurrection' dialogue was also included in a primer edited by Zupitza and Schipper, 90. The two dialogues have no conventionally established titles; '*De Peccato*' is a shortened form of Wanley's title (202).

THE LATIN *ELUCIDARIUM*

Förster, 91, identified the source of *De Peccato* as Bk. 2, chs. 1–6 of the *Elucidarium sive Dialogus de summa totius christianae theologiae* (*PL* 172: 1133 ff.), and the source of the 'Resurrection' dialogue as Bk. 1, chs. 23–5 of the same work (89, 91). The Latin *Elucidarium* is a prose work comprising three books; the first deals with the problems concerning human knowledge of the divinity, the second with the problem of evil and the third with paradise, purgatory and hell. The interlocutors are identified as *Magister* and *Discipulus*. It was edited in 1954 by Lefèvre, who gives an account of its manuscript development, which needs, however, to be read in the light of Flint's more recent work.[4]

The Latin *Elucidarium* has been variously dated, and the ascription to Honorius has not invariably been accepted; Lefèvre accepted the authorship of Honorius, and assigned the work to the early 12th century. Flint, however, in a series of articles on the life and works of Honorius, places his

---

[3] In addition to the translations associated with Alfred, FC's category 'Alfredian and Other Translations' includes two other pieces found in V, a translation of Alcuin's *De Virtutibus et Vitiis* (not unique to this manuscript) and a homiletic fragment on the teachings of Augustine.

[4] Yves Lefèvre, *L'Elucidarium et les lucidaires*, Bibliothèque des Écoles françaises d'Athènes et de Rome 180 (Paris: Boccard, 1954). In addition to the studies by Flint mentioned below, see also 'The Original Text of the *Elucidarium* of Honorius Augustodunensis from the Twelfth-Century English Manuscripts,' *Scriptorium* 18 (1964): 91–4, for corrections to Lefèvre's text.

authorship of the *Elucidarium* beyond doubt, and dates the first of the three recensions in or shortly before 1100.[5] She also establishes that the work was written in England. The real identity of Honorius remains uncertain, but Flint concludes that he may have been a canon of Lotharingian sympathies at Hereford and that he became a monk at Worcester. He left England for the continent about the time of Anselm's last exile (1103); works in which English material appears to have been used fall into a period which stretches from approximately 1098 to 1100.

The *Elucidarium* was much copied. According to Lefèvre, it survives in some 60 manuscripts. Flint, 1977, who gives a handlist of 12th century manuscripts of the works of Honorius (119–27), states that there are 41 12th century manuscripts of the Latin *Elucidarium*. It was translated or adapted into many West European languages; Mertens, 1968, suggested that translation into German took place earlier than was hitherto supposed.[6] There is a ME translation, dated late 14th or early 15th century (edited by Schmitt, **92**), which comprises the first and part of the second book of the Latin and incorporates additions which are said to be of a Wycliffite cast, and a short, early 16th century version translated from the French by Andrew Chertsey, which was printed by Wynkyn de Worde. For a bibliographical description of the three English versions of the *Elucidarium*, and two ME versions which are in the same tradition, see Utley, 1972, 741–4.

STUDY OF *OE Elucidarium*; LANGUAGE AND RELATIONSHIP TO THE LATIN

Förster appears to be the only scholar to have published on *OE Elucidarium*; a dissertation by Schlemilch, **93**, said to contain an exhaustive study of the language and orthography, tables a few features of the 'Resurrection' dialogue.

---

[5]For study of the sources and purpose of the *Elucidarium/Elucidarius*, see Flint, **97**. V.I.J. Flint, 'The Career of Honorius Augustodunensis: Some Fresh Evidence,' *Revue Bénédictine* 82 (1972): 63–86, argues that 'his associations with England must be widened to include Worcester and his connections with southern Germany must give place to those with Lambech, in Austria' (80), and suggests identification with 'Heinricus' (named as a donor in a Göttweig book-list which contains a high proportion of works by him). 'The Chronology of the Works of Honorius Augustodunensis,' *Revue Bénédictine* 82 (1972): 215–42, examines earlier scholars' dating of the corpus, including works clearly associated with England (*Elucidarius, Sigillum, Speculum Ecclesiae, Offendiculum, Gemma Animae* and *Imago Mundi*); there is some discussion of the dating of the three recensions of the *Elucidarius* and its relation to the works and teachings of Anselm. 'The Place and Purpose of the Works of Honorius Augustodunensis,' *Revue Bénédictine* 87 (1977): 97–127, argues that 'serving the Benedictine Order, in its pursuit of influence in the reformed church' was not just the motivating force of the *Elucidarius* (see Flint, **97**) but 'the focus of Honorius's whole productive life' (97). As his works, not devised for the furtherance of monastic meditation or even for purely monastic instruction, were copied by the Benedictines and also by their rivals and critics, 'the place and purpose of Honorius may be not merely more definable but also more sinister than we have supposed' (118).

[6]Volker Mertens, 'Ein Lucidarius-Fragment des 12. Jahrhunderts,' *Zeitschrift für deutsches Altertum und deutsche Literatur* 97 (1968): 117–26.

Förster, **89**, accepted that the Latin *Elucidarium* was composed in the late 11th century (perhaps before 1092) and that it was written by Honorius in the south of Germany. As Förster was aware, remarkably rapid transmission would have had to occur to enable a late 11th century German work to be translated into English in the early 12th century. In his examination of the 'Resurrection' dialogue, he entertained the possibility that the OE text was taken from the source used by Honorius. Whereas, on the one hand, the diphthongs and inflexions were consistent with a 10th or 11th century original, the vowels of the unaccented syllables clearly favoured a 12th century date, and in the solution Förster proposed to these contrary indications, he leaned towards the view that the OE derived directly from the Latin *Elucidarium*: 'Perhaps the difficulty is best met by the assumption that the OE translation was made by an old man at the turn of the eleventh century' (101).

The 'Resurrection' dialogue was primarily of interest to Förster from a linguistic point of view: 'Whether copied from a tenth or eleventh-century original, or not, the text, such as it stands in the manuscript, exhibits very uniformly the advanced state of the English language of the twelfth century, unfortunately somewhat disguised under a traditional three centuries old orthography, from which, however, the scribe has emancipated himself sufficiently often to give us some glimpses of the real English then spoken' (92–3). Some years later, however, in a note on *De Peccato* (**91**), Förster shifted his attention to the intellectual milieu of the translation. Having discovered, from the *Speculum ecclesiae* of Honorius (*PL* 172: 183 ff.), that the author had preached to 'fratres Cantuariensis ecclesiae' (which Förster interpreted as Christ Church),[7] he abandoned the speculation that the OE translator(s) drew on the same source as the Latin *Elucidarium*. In this later article, Förster linked *OE Elucidarium* with another item in V, *Sermo in festis Sancte Marie uirginis*, which, he argued, derived from a work written by Anselm. *De Peccato* and the *Sermo*, he concluded, are not only of interest because they are among the few English texts that can confidently be dated to the early 12th century, but because they are the earliest English texts to reflect the influence of the scholastic thought of Anselm of Canterbury. Förster, **91**, further linked V with the works of Honorius by identifying a passage of *Speculum ecclesiae* as the source of a homiletic piece on the ages of the world [FC B.3.4.57].

The *Sermo in festis Sancte Marie uirginis* was subsequently identified as a translation of a Latin sermon of Ralph d'Escures (Bishop of Rochester, 1108–14, Archbishop of Canterbury, 1114–22).[8] More importantly, Flint,

---

[7] Förster, **91**, 313, n. 2, disagreed with Johann Nepomuk Kelle, who took the phrase to mean the canons of Canterbury Cathedral: 'Untersuchungen über das *Speculum ecclesiae* des Honorius und die *Libri deflorationum* des Abtes Werner,' *Sitzungsberichte der Kaiserlichen Akademie der Wissenschaften* (Vienna) 145 (1902): 41. Bibliographical information on studies of Honorius appears in the documentation of Flint, **97**; see also fn. 5 above.

[8] See Ker 209, art. 44; the *Sermo* is preserved among authentic works of Anselm.

in a series of articles on the life and works of Honorius, indispensable to the study of the *OE Elucidarium*, has shown that the Latin *Elucidarium* was written in England *c.* 1100. (As the *OE Elucidarium* lies outside the scope of her research, only the article which is centrally concerned with Honorius's *Elucidarium* is included in the annotations.) Flint, **97**, concludes from her examination of the sources of the *Elucidarium* that Honorius made use of sources employed by the compilers of the *Glossa ordinaria*, and that he drew on the writings, as well as the otherwise unrecorded teachings, of Anselm. Flint's work seems to suggest, in a variety of ways, that Honorius was closely connected with Anselm, presumably a disciple of his; but whereas links between the work of Honorius and Anselm are regarded by Förster, **91**, and Handley, **96**, as confirming the Canterbury origins of V, Flint, 1972, argues that Honorius's connections lie with the diocese of Worcester, and points out that, while he evidently visited Canterbury, early copying of his work does not suggest that his work was influential there: 'no important early manuscript can be assigned with certainty to Canterbury' (76).

Whereas Förster, **91**, considered that the *OE Elucidarium* was historically significant as one of the first attempts to transmit the scholastic thought of Anselm in the vernacular, one of Flint's most significant findings is that the purpose of the *Elucidarium* (and the motivating force of Honorius's career) was to encourage the participation of Benedictine monks in pastoral work. The *Elucidarium* of Honorius is not a harbinger of the 12th century Renaissance but a crude simplification of the thought of Anselm designed to provide 'profoundly unintellectual' Anglo-Saxon monks (184) with ready-made answers to the questions they would encounter, and the extensive copying of Honorius's work, abroad as well as in England, not only by Benedictines but by houses of canons and Cistercians, leads her to suspect that pastoral reform was achieved at the expense of the intellectual achievement of the monasteries (Flint, 1977). In the light of this, it is tempting to speculate that *SS* and *Ad* were intended for lay instruction as much as for instruction in the monasteries; if that is so, the problem facing Anglo-Saxon monks was not merely how to frame roughly orthodox answers, but how to bring about a change in the nature of the questions.

Like Flint's findings on the life and works of Honorius, Ker's mid-12th century dating of V renders the speed with which the Latin *Elucidarium* found its way into English less remarkable than it appeared to Förster; conversely, however, Ker's mid-12th century dating makes more striking the retention of the OE inflexion system and diphthongs in the interpolated 'Resurrection' dialogue which prompted Förster to assign it to the earliest date consistent with derivation from the Latin *Elucidarium*. Whether the language of *De Peccato* differs significantly from that of the 'Resurrection' dialogue is one of the many questions that Förster did not answer.

Although Förster considered that his parallel printing of the OE and Migne's text of the Latin *Elucidarium* was sufficient to establish that the OE was a close translation of Honorius' work, a casual glance suggests that the OE version is a selective rendering of the source; unless, of course, Förster was correct in his initial speculation that the OE and the Latin derive from a common source (the table of sources provided in Flint, **97**, shows that only two of the nine chapters of the *Elucidarium* covered by the OE translation derive from Anselm's writings). Utley remarked some time ago (1972) that 'all three English versions need close comparison with the improved text of Lefèvre and with one another' (742).[9] There is, clearly, plenty of scope for a new scholarly edition of *OE Elucidarium*.

[9] See fn. 4 above.

ELUCIDARIUM: ANNOTATIONS

SEE ALSO Warner, 4; Merrill, 65

EDITIONS

89 Förster, Max Th. W. 'Two Notes on Old English Dialogue Literature.' *An English Miscellany presented to Dr. Furnivall in honour of his seventy-fifth birthday.* [No ed.] Oxford: Clarendon, 1901. 86–106.

Prints parallel, 90–2, the 'Resurrection' fragment of *OE Elucidarium*, and excerpts from the Latin *Elucidarium* (*PL* 172) [i.e., Bk. 1, chs. 23–5, wrongly described as Bk. 1, chs. 21–2; see Förster, **91**].

Note (a) draws attention to the fact that the item he prints, added to Vespasian D.xiv in a hand found nowhere else, is a remarkably early (and close) translation of the late 11th century *Elucidarium* of Honorius. Förster admits the possibility that the OE translator of this extract may have used the same source as Honorius (89), and observes that the absence of any Scandinavian or French element is remarkable; but the 12th century character of the work, despite its traditional orthography, is almost invariably brought out in the vowels of unaccented syllables. From an extended study of the language, 93–101, he concludes: 'The pretty correct use of the OE. diphthongs and the fair preservation of the OE. inflectional system seem to point to an eleventh-century original, while the probable date of the Latin source (but see p. 89) does not allow us to go very far back. Perhaps the difficulty is best met by the assumption that the OE. translation was made by an old man at the turn of the eleventh century' (101). Förster suggests that the manuscript may have been written somewhere near the Mercian frontier, and that study of the whole codex might reveal that it originated at one of the great centres of ecclesiastical learning such as Winchester. Introductory observations on the Teutonic fondness for dialogue form are included, 86–8.

Note (b) offers two ME (15th century) analogues to *SS* and *Ad*, which illustrate the point that collections of biblical questions and answers were read and translated throughout the medieval period. A passage in Ashmole 59, written by Shirley, parallels *SS* 15 and *Ad* 28. Two sentences on the number of teeth, bones and veins in the human body in Rawlinson, F.35, f. 205, are the same as two sentences found at the end of *SS* and *Ad* which, as Förster, **62**, argued, originally must have formed part of the dialogues, although as they stand in the manuscript now only the answer has been retained. At 105, Förster prints 'the two fifteenth-century collections of biblical sayings most closely agreeing with our ME. couplets'; both collections are found in German manuscripts.

90 **Zupitza, Julius, and J. Schipper.** *Alt- und mittelenglische Übungsbuch mit einem Wörterbuch.* 14th edn. Rev. Albert Eichler. Wien: Braumüller, 1931.

Not sighted. According to Utley, 1972, 899, the 'Resurrection' fragment of *OE Elucidarium* is printed at 84.

COMMENTARY

91 **Förster, Max.** 'Altenglische Predigtquellen. I.' *Archiv für das Studium der neueren Sprachen und Literaturen* 116 (1906): 301–14.

In a note on *OE Elucidarium*, 312–14, Förster states that the 'Resurrection' fragment is a translation of the *Elucidarium* of Honorius Bk. 1, chs. 23–5, not 21–2 [see Förster, **89**] and that the source of *De Peccato* is Bk. 2, chs. 1–6, of the same work. He prints the first question and answer of *De Peccato*, OE and Latin, in order to demonstrate that this fragment is, similarly, a close translation of the Latin. Förster suggests that the whole of Vespasian D.xiv, including both OE excerpts from the *Elucidarium* of Honorius, served as a preaching commonplace-book. Transmission of this southern German work during its author's lifetime is explained by *Speculum ecclesiae* (*PL* 172: 138 ff.), where Honorius states that he had preached to *fratres Cantuariensis ecclesiae.* Förster takes this to refer to Christ Church, and observes that Endres, *Historische-politische Blätter* 130 (1902): 160, suggests that Honorius was born in Britain. The manuscript also contains *Sermo in festis s. Mariae Virginis*, which Förster regards as a translation of an Anselm homily (310–12); this work and the *OE Elucidarium* are important because they are among the few English texts that can be dated with certainty to the early 12th century, and because they are the first English texts to reflect the Scholastic thought of which Anselm was a leading exponent.

92 **Schmitt, Friedrich.** *Die mittelenglische Version des Elucidariums des Honorius Augustodunensis.* Diss. U Würzburg. Burghausen a. S.: Trinkl, 1909.

Not sighted. According to Utley, 1972, 899, Schmitt describes the language of *OE Elucidarium* as 'Oxforder Gelehrtensprache' (xxiv); authorship and date are discussed at viii.

93 **Schlemilch, Willy.** *Beiträge zur Sprache und Orthographie spätaltengl. Sprachdenkmäler der Übergangszeit (1000–1150).* Studien zur englischen Philologie 34. Halle a. S.: Niemeyer, 1914. Tübingen: Niemeyer, 1973.

Utley, 1972, 899, who states that *OE Elucidarium* 'is one of the basic texts studied exhaustively' by Schlemilch, is misleading; the monograph-length study draws examples from over 70 texts. Schlemilch identifies the passage edited by Förster, **89**, as early 12th century (xiii), and cites it among the examples of *beo* for the preposition and particle *be*, a peculiarity of the southeast (7); *ch* for OE *c*, an Anglo-Norman feature (48); lengthening of intervocalic consonants (65). *U* instead of *y*, which becomes more frequent from the mid 12th century, occurs sporadically in Vespasian D.xiv; *OE Elucidarium* has *caðð* (14). Texts covered include *PD* (second half of the 12th century), which figures much more prominently.

94 Förster, Max. 'Der Inhalt der altenglischen Handschrift Vespasianus D. XIV.' *Englische Studien* 54 (1920): 46–68.

The bibliographical description of manuscript contents identifies sources for some items. Nothing is added to the study of *OE Dicts* (48); the description of *OE Elucidarium* (63) summarizes the conclusions of Förster, **89** and **91**. Latin analogues (found in two 12th century German manuscripts) are cited for the canonical hours brontology, for which Förster, **311**, was unable to find a parallel (63). He identifies the source of a homiletic piece on the ages of the world [FC B.3.4.57] as Honorius's *Speculum ecclesiae* (*PL* 172: 854 f.), and outlines the three versions of the ages of the world found in OE (as in Förster, **58**), at 60–3. There is further commentary on the *Sermo in festis s. Mariae uirginis* [see Förster, **91**], at 58–60. Overall conclusions concerning the manuscript (66–8) echo Förster, **91**. Most of the texts, including *OE Dicts* and the first *OE Elucidarium* dialogue [*De Peccato*], are, linguistically, southern English (mid- or eastern, not western).

95 Richards, Mary P. 'On the Date and Provenance of MS Cotton Vespasian D. XIV ff. 4–169.' *Manuscripta* 17 (1973): 31–5.

Richards argues that the homiletic pieces on ff. 4–169 [excluding the additions in two different hands on ff. 67, 75 and 103?], were copied at Rochester in the second quarter of the 12th century. Linguistic features—retention of *i*-mutation of *a* before nasal consonants at the early stage (*æ* instead of *e*), the fact that the only purely Kentish features are two forms of *beon/wesan*, the exclusive use of *beo* for the preposition *be*, weak declension of strong nouns and preservation of final *n*—support a Southern/Southeastern provenance and a date before 1150. The script is 'rather compressed and casual like the variation of the Christ Church style written at Rochester' (34), and the manuscript differs from the two major OE manuscripts copied at Rochester in the first quarter of the 12th century in its use of the Caroline *g* and less marked splitting of ascenders and minims. As the manuscript includes a translation of part of a sermon by d'Escures, the orthography probably represents the Rochester style in its decline, rather than Rochester influence on an outlying area.

96 Handley, Rima. 'British Museum MS. Cotton Vespasian D. xiv.' *Notes and Queries* NS 21 (1974): 243–50.

Handley concludes that Vespasian D.xiv 'may have been intended as a teaching manual for young religious' (247), and argues that the original compilation, of which this volume 'is only a slightly modified copy' (250), came from Canterbury and that it was copied there after the fire that occurred in the time of Lanfranc. 'Its existence demonstrates that there was in the South-East in the twelfth century, a monastic scriptorium capable of preparing and copying with understanding a body of Anglo-Saxon material' (250). The rendering of religious material in the vernacular at Christ Church after the Conquest probably owed its inspiration to Anselm; examples of related activity include the glosses to Prosper's *Epigrammata* and *Disticha Catonis* in Trinity O.2.31, and *Herb* in Vitellius C.iii. As Ker, arts. 48 to 52 [includes *OE Elucidarium*], are not in the main hand, they may not have been in the exemplar, but they confirm the organization of the whole. Handley also mentions *OE Elucidarium* as a text that associates the volume with Canterbury. It is thought that Honorius spent some of his early years at Canterbury because two of his works greet the monks at Christ Church, and because his *Elucidarium* (1092×1106) is so reliant on Anselm's work (249, n. 48), and the two passages may have been excerpted on account of a local interest. 'Both pieces are considerably simplified by the translator, in a way consistent with the simplifying treatment of other sources throughout the volume' (246–7).

97 Flint, Valerie I.J. 'The "Elucidarius" of Honorius Augustodunensis and Reform in Late Eleventh Century England.' *Revue Bénédictine* 85 (1975): 178–98.

The contents and manner of composition of the *Elucidarius* are examined (179–83). Bk. 1 draws on sources 'and, more especially, selections from sources, which were clearly available to, and used by, compilers of the *Glossa Ordinaria*,' and thus 'shows that Honorius was at this point involved in that intense exegetical activity which absorbed the best of scholarly effort in the late eleventh century' (180). He sometimes seems to report Anselm's spoken word (Bk. 3 uses 'a very early, and perhaps spoken, version of St Anselm's sermon *De Beatitudine*'); when he reflects the spirit but not the text of Anselm he may be relying on memory or on Anselm's teachings, and marginal references to Anselm which cannot be traced may indicate use of Anselm's teaching. Of Anselm's written works, Honorius makes most use of *Cur Deus Homo* and the *Monologion*. Although aware of the criticisms of *Cur Deus Homo* in the *Sententiae Divinae Paginae*, he prefers Anselm's views on 'some questions of striking importance' (182); but Anselm's thought is crudely simplified. Paradoxically, Honorius 'displays the greatest mental acumen in the understanding and collecting of his material, at the same time firmly repressing any encouragement this material may have offered to its readers to think' (183). Explanation of the character of the *Elucidarius* is found in the 11th century movement for the reform of the clergy (183–9); it is a convenient, comprehensive collection of easily-understood answers to questions that pastoral reformers were bound to meet, designed to encourage Anglo-Saxon monks ('defensive, eccentric,

inward-looking and profoundly unintellectual,' 184) to take up 'the task of
serving and renewing the pastorate' (188). Extensive copying and speedy
vernacular translation of the *Elucidarius* shows that the needs it served
'were not in all their aspects exclusive to England' (179). Table of sources,
including references to authorities in manuscript margins, at 190–8.

III

Romance

APOLLONIUS OF TYRE

MANUSCRIPT

Cambridge, Corpus Christi College 201, pp. 131–45   C   FC B.4.1
Ker 49B, art. 53 s. xi med.

MANUSCRIPT DESCRIPTION, CONTENTS AND DATE
(following Ker)

OE ApT is preserved in a single copy in CCCC 201; the manuscript consists of two distinct parts, bound together in the 16th century. *OE ApT* is in Part B, which chiefly contains homilies and law codes attributed to Wulfstan, Archbishop of York and Bishop of Worcester (d. 1023). *OE ApT* is written in the same clear, round script as most other items in the manuscript (pp. 8–145), which Ker dates mid-11th century. According to Ker, at least one quire is missing between pp. 141–2: 'More than half the text is lost between these points, which correspond respectively to f. 210v/19 and f. 221v/5 of the Latin text in Bodleian, MS. Laud misc. 247.' The handwriting has no distinguishing marks which might associate it with any particular school or area. Wanley and James[1] ascribed the manuscript to Worcester, but this ascription, as Goolden, **101**, pointed out, rests on the nature of the contents (see further p. 90 below, 'Manuscript Provenance and Purpose.')

Goolden's manuscript description adds that periods and small capitals are used frequently. There are only two large capitals; a large *A* marks the beginning of the text, and a large *H* begins a new paragraph on p. 140; with this exception, there are no paragraph breaks.

LANGUAGE; DATE AND PROVENANCE OF THE ORIGINAL TRANSLATION

Raith, **100**, and Goolden, **101**, whose editions of *OE ApT* coincided with the appearance of Ker's *Catalogue*, independently concluded that the text is the work of an Essex scribe who introduced dialect forms into a late West-Saxon exemplar, and that the translation was originally made in the first half of the 11th century in the south of England. As Goolden put it: 'There is nothing in the language and orthography which would contradict the hypothesis that the work was composed at about the same time as the

---

[1] Montague Rhodes James, *A Descriptive Catalogue of the Manuscripts in the Library of Corpus Christi College, Cambridge*, 2 vols. (Cambridge: Cambridge UP, 1909–12) 1: 485–91.

Wulfstan material of the same manuscript' (xxxiv). Both editors observe
that scribal errors confirm that the text is a copy; Goolden remarks that
'the good state of the text suggests not many transcriptions' (xxxiv).

Prior to the appearance of the editions of Raith and Goolden, the language had been extensively studied, in 1899, by Märkisch, **122**, who described the text as West-Saxon, not earlier than the second half of the 11th
century; Raith criticizes Märkisch, particularly for his failure to distinguish
between the scribe and the exemplar. More recently, the language of *OE
ApT* has been studied by Simpson, **150**, who gives particular attention
to the classical West-Saxon aspects of the text; from a study of the style
and word order of phrases and clauses, she concludes that at least two
translators were responsible for the translation, but draws no conclusions
concerning the identity of the translators, or the place of translation, beyond the fact that it originated in the south of England.

MANUSCRIPT PROVENANCE AND PURPOSE

Goolden recognized that, although the scribe had introduced Essex forms,
it did not automatically follow that he was working in his own homeland,
and Gneuss, in a review of Goolden, mentioned some texts with the same
linguistic features which cannot have been of Essex origin (particularly,
the Worcester Chronicle and the Winchester Psalter).[2] More recently,
Whitbread, **137**, has argued that the material was originally assembled
at Worcester during or not long after Archbishop Wulfstan's death in 1023,
but that it was copied at Canterbury in the time of Lanfranc after the 1067
fire. The manuscript, he concludes, is 'a repository for the safe preservation
of the religious culture of an earlier generation' (110). Superficially, then,
the appearance of *OE ApT* in this manuscript is anomalous (see further
pp. 99–100 below, 'Study of *OE ApT*').

THE LATIN *HISTORIA APOLLONII REGIS TYRI*; ORIGINS AND TEXTUAL HISTORY

Rohde's study of the Apollonius story (**124**), which appeared in 1914, argued that it was of Greek origin, presumably written in the period to which
other Greek romances belong, and that it derived from Asia Minor in the
3rd century. In his view, new elements were added to the Greek romance of
Apollonius in the course of its transmission; some of the accretions reflect
the culture and beliefs of late Latin society, others are specifically Christian
in character.

The textual tradition was first studied by Riese. In his first edition
of the *Historia*, which appeared in 1871, Riese made use of the readings

---

[2] *Anglia* 78 (1960): 364–6.

implied by *OE ApT*.[3] His second edition, published in 1893,[4] was based
on the discovery of many more Latin manuscripts (well over 50), which
enabled him to distinguish two separate recensions (RA and RB), independently derived from the original Latin version. He concluded that two
manuscripts in Class A (listed below) best preserve the original version,
but that Class B manuscripts suffer less from interpolation and in some
cases offer more convincing alternatives. Riese's Class C includes all of the
remaining manuscripts. Some Class C manuscripts show closer affinities
with Class A than with Class B; in others the position is reversed. Most
Class C manuscripts, however, are indiscriminately connected with both of
the better texts, and all are seriously corrupt throughout.

Riese's work was elucidated and developed by Klebs, **121**; his examination of the textual tradition had more direct bearing on *OE ApT*, and his
study of the Apollonius story (which rejects Rohde's arguments in favour
of a Greek original) was more wide-ranging than Riese's. The textual tradition of the *Historia* has been more recently studied by Kortekaas, **152**,
who re-edited the A and B recensions in 1984. Kortekaas concludes that
the original was written in Syria, late in the 2nd or early in the 3rd century. Since the appearance of Riese's second edition, the number of known
manuscripts of the *Historia* has more than doubled. Kortekaas's study of
the textual tradition clearly supersedes Riese's, but leaves intact the essential configurations of his analysis, which are set out below. Other editions
have appeared since Kortekaas's, notably Schmeling, 1988.[5] Archibald,
1991 (see Archibald, **151**), who prints a text and translation, examines origins, but the Latin textual tradition does not concern her.

Manuscript Classes

Class A (closest to the Latin original)

Florence, Bibl. Med. Laurenziana, plut. LXVI 40.   9th or 10th century
    (Incomplete)

Paris, Bibl. Nat. lat. 4955.   14th century

Class B (independently derived from the Latin original; fewer interpolations)

Leiden, Üniversiteitbibl. Vossianus lat. 13.F.   10th century

Oxford, Magdalen College 50.   11th century

Class C

Class C includes the family group ('the English group') to which *OE ApT*
is most nearly related, consisting of the following three manuscripts:

---

[3] A. Riese, *Historia Apollonii Regis Tyri* (Leipzig: Teubner, 1871). An edition of the
Latin *Historia*, based on *OE ApT* and six Latin manuscripts, which include Laud 247,
regarded by Riese as the nearest-source manuscript for *OE ApT*.

[4] A. Riese, *Historia Apollonii Regis Tyri*, 2nd edn. (Leipzig: Teubner, 1893; Stuttgart:
Teubner, 1973). Parallel edition of the two recensions of the Latin *Historia*, based on
Laurent. 40 (RA) and Paris 6485 (RB), the latter unknown to Riese, 1871.

[5] Gareth Schmeling, ed., *Historia Apollonii Regis Tyri* (Leipzig: Teubner, 1988), edits
all three versions.

Cambridge, Corpus Christi College 318.   12th century.
Cambridge, Corpus Christi College 451.   12th–13th centuries.
Oxford, Bodleian, Laud Misc. 247.   12th century.

For a complete list of manuscripts, including lost manuscripts, see
Kortekaas, 15–22, 413–24. Goolden, xv–vi, gives an incomplete list of the
English manuscripts in Class C.

LATIN RECONSTRUCTIONS OF THE OE SOURCE

Well over 50 extant medieval copies of the *Historia* were known to earlier
scholars, but a Latin version to which the OE corresponds exactly has not
been found. Thorpe, **98**, and Leo, **103**, assumed that ch. 153 of *Gesta
Romanorum* represented the source of *OE ApT*; Riese's work revealed that
the OE translation was not directly related to this 14th century abridgement. The intention of Riese, 1871 and 1893, was not to identify the source
of the OE, but to determine the manuscripts which best preserved the original Latin version. He intimated, however, that *OE ApT* derived from a
Class C version, possibly Laud 247. Mommsen, **114**, suggested that the
Tergensee Fragment represented the Latin exemplar of the OE translator,
and Meyer, **115**, argued in favour of Vienna 226, but their work is regarded
by Goolden, **101**, and Raith, **100**, as having been superseded by Zupitza,
117, whose conclusions were confirmed by Klebs, **121**.

Goolden understood Zupitza to have demonstrated that, although
CCCC 318 was the nearest source manuscript for *OE ApT*, there were
a number of points at which *OE ApT* was closer to other manuscripts.
Raith puts the matter somewhat differently (and is possibly closer to the
drift of Zupitza's argument); he explains that the source of *OE ApT* is represented by a family of three manuscripts ('the English group'; see above):
it is closest to CCCC 318 and Laud 247, but it cannot derive from their
common original. Raith and Goolden, then, differ in their conception of *OE
ApT*'s relationship to the extant manuscripts, and this difference underlies
their reconstructions of the Latin source of *OE ApT*. Raith's edition of *OE
ApT* includes his reconstruction of the archetype of 'the English group.'
The reconstruction was also separately printed (Raith, **100**). Goolden's reconstructed Latin text is based on CCCC 318; wherever *OE ApT* diverges
from CCCC 318 and Goolden was able to find 'a precise equivalent' in the
20 or so versions he consulted, he conflated the reading with his base text
(Goolden drew on most of the English manuscripts known to him, together
with some continental versions). Reviewers of Goolden (especially Gradon,
138) expressed doubts concerning the soundness of this procedure.

A reconstructed Latin source had been attempted earlier by Märkisch,
122. Märkisch is among those who appear (perhaps understandably) to
have failed to notice that Riese had concluded that *OE ApT* derived from
a Class C manuscript; Märkisch used Magdalen 50 as a basis, conflating it

with readings from other manuscripts, but Magdalen 50, as Raith pointed out, is a Class B manuscript.

TRANSMISSION OF THE APOLLONIUS STORY; ENGLISH VERSIONS

Vernacular translations and adaptations of the *Historia* are numerous; *OE ApT* has historical significance as the earliest surviving vernacular version. Early scholars, however, did not attempt to explain how and when it was transmitted to England. Nor do studies of the manuscript development of the *Historia* appear to have established the position occupied by English redactions; the fact that a substantial number of Class C manuscripts are of English provenance might conceivably suggest that English redactors played a significant or distinctive role in the manuscript development. Recently, Kortekaas, **152**, has speculated that the *Historia* was brought to England by early pilgrims to Rome, and transmitted to France by Anglo-Saxon missionaries.

Most commentaries on the Apollonius story remark on its widespread and enduring currency. Goolden, **101**, for instance, writes that 'its place is unique as the one story designed primarily for amusement and plea- sure that continued to be read and rehandled in Old, Middle and Modern English' (xiii). He points out that the early popularity of the story is indi- cated by Fortunatus's 6th century reference (*MGH*, AA 6.1); *Apollonius* is also quoted by a 7th century grammarian and is listed in *Gesta Abbatum Fontanellensium* among the books owned by Wando, who became abbot in 742. For a full and up-to-date account of knowledge of the Apollonius story prior to the earliest manuscripts (9th century), see Kortekaas, **152**.

Early studies of the vernacular versions of the Apollonius story include Klebs, **121**, Singer, **119**, and Smyth, **120**. The OE translation is, in- evitably, overshadowed by Shakespeare's *Pericles*, as well as by Gower's treatment of the story in *Confessio Amantis*; notwithstanding its chronolog- ical priority, *OE ApT* receives only passing mention in these three studies. Goolden lists English versions up to 1738 (whence Kobayashi, **102**). Raith, **100**, gives a fuller account of vernacular versions, and includes an edition of the 14th century ME metrical fragment (*c.* 250 lines) in Bodleian, Douce 216.[6] See also Goepp, **132**, and Olsen, **154**. A few doctoral dissertations also undertake comparative examination of the vernacular versions of the Apollonius story: see Pettengill, **123**, Lawrence, **143**, Archibald, **151**. Full bibliographical description of vernacular versions of the Apollonius story, up to 1609, is included in the published version of Archibald's dissertation.

---

[6] The narrator claims that its author was 'vicary, y understonde, at Wymborne Myn- ster.' J.O. Halliwell, ed., *A New Boke About Shakespeare and Stratford-on-Avon* (Lon- don: privately printed, 1850); Smyth, **120**, 49–55, Raith, **100**, 67–84. Description of this work is often confused. The text Halliwell printed was from Douce 216, as Raith showed, and there is, therefore, only one fragment.

There is also a reference to an English version of the Apollonius story in the *c.* 1175 catalogue of the Benedictine Abbey at Burton-on-Trent (British Library, Add. 23,944, f. 157). Attention was first drawn to this by Omont, 1892.[7] Wilson, 1952, saw no reason to connect this entry with *OE ApT*, and speculated that the work referred to may have been a more complete translation.[8]

There appears to be an earlier book-list reference which has not been noticed by Apollonius scholars. Included among the book-lists edited by Lapidge, 1985, is Oxford, Bodleian Tanner 3, ff. 189v–90r, added on blank folios 'probably in the late eleventh century,' which includes 'Apollonius.' It is 'principally a list of books intended for use in the classroom.' Lapidge assigns it, tentatively, to Worcester (69–73).

According to Smyth, **120**, all vernacular translations from the 14th century onwards derive from the popular 14th century abridgement, *Gesta Romanorum*, ch. 153, which was edited by Oesterley, 1872.[9]

EDITIONS AND TRANSLATIONS

OE ApT was first edited in 1834 by Thorpe, **98**; neither his edition, nor the edition by Zupitza, **99**, which was brought out posthumously by Napier, has an apparatus. There are two scholarly editions. Goolden's edition was published two years later than Raith's, but as publication of Goolden's edition was delayed it makes no reference to Raith's work. The two editions are complementary. Goolden's edition is well tuned to undergraduate readers. Raith has a much more elaborate critical and textual apparatus; his account of the Latin manuscripts is more comprehensive (and less lucid) than Goolden's, but his notes on the text are relatively brief, and there is no glossary. Both editors include a Latin text which, in their opinion, approximates as closely as possible to the original from which the OE translator was working (see further p. 92 above, 'Latin Reconstructions').

The full text of *OE ApT* also appears in Kobayashi, **102**. Kobayashi's intention is to present a text suitable for beginners. The text is normalized according to principles set forth by Magoun;[10] the norm adopted by the editor is 'a version of Early West Saxon, which corresponds roughly to the spellings in the readily available dictionaries by Henry Sweet, J.R. Clark Hall, and F. Holthausen' (40). Anglo-Saxonists since Thorpe, **98**, have evidently regarded *OE ApT* as a suitable text for readers acquiring familiarity with the language; extracts, often quite substantial ones, are included in a

---

[7] H. Omont, 'Anciens Catalogues des Bibliothèques anglaises,' *Zentralblatt für Bibliothekwesen* 9 (1892): 207–22.

[8] R.M. Wilson, *The Lost Literature of Medieval England* (London: Methuen, 1952) 81–2. But in *Early Middle English Literature*, 3rd edn. (London: Methuen, 1968) 21, Wilson states that the catalogue may refer to *OE ApT*.

[9] H. Oesterley, ed., *Gesta Romanorum* (Berlin: Weidmann, 1872). (A collection of 181 stories first published at Cologne.) Also ed. Singer, **119**, 68–105.

[10] See F.P. Magoun, 'A Brief Plea for a Normalization of Old English Poetic Texts,' *Langues modernes* 45 (1951): 63–9.

number of elementary anthologies (see **103–113**). Kobayashi's list of these is almost complete.

Thorpe, **98**, also carried a translation of the OE; as Thorpe believed that a large part of *OE ApT* had been deliberately destroyed by 'a gloomy monk,' he supplemented his translation with material drawn from ch. 153 of Swan's 1824 translation of the *Gesta Romanorum*,[11] which he took to be the source of *OE ApT*. More recently, *OE ApT* has been translated in full by Swanton, 1975, 158–73.

STYLE AND CHARACTER OF THE TRANSLATION.

Substantive omissions aside, *OE ApT* is generally agreed to be a close translation of a corrupt Latin text. Märkisch, **122**, Raith, **100**, and Goolden, **101**, made close verbal comparisons of the OE and Latin texts, pointing out omissions, abbreviations, additions and instances of periphrasis, as well as mistranslations and attempts to make sense of a corrupt original; detailed verbal comparison can also be found in other studies, particularly in the dissertations of Laubenthal, **144**, and Simpson, **150**. Thorpe, the first editor of *OE ApT*, described it as 'a model of English prose,' and its prose style has generally been much praised: even Raith, the least admiring of commentators, concedes that the translator is worthy to rank with Ælfric. Goolden's praise was qualified, too: he was appreciative of its lucid and idiomatic style, but was conscious of its inferiority to the Latin: 'All these deviations make a substantial addition to the many errors bequeathed by the source, and together they give the appearance of carelessness and obscurity where all was once clarity and coherence' (xxiii). Whereas Goolden finds its diffuseness a fault, Laubenthal considers that the expansions were appropriate to the courtly setting of the narrative. She attributes the smooth idiomatic style and expert use of dialogue to the influence of oral prose; Goolden, on the other hand, considers it a substantial enhancement of the OE translator's achievement that he can have had no native models. So too does Hamilton, **142**, the most enthusiastic admirer of *OE ApT*'s prose style. He considers that *OE ApT*, *qua* prose, compares favourably with Ælfric's *Lives of Saints*, and concludes: 'It is remarkable that an Anglo-Saxon translator working with material for which, as far as we know, there was no native prose tradition and only remote correspondences in its heritage of verse, could manage a prose style as light, easy, and idiomatic, as witty, breathless and intricate as this' (192). See also Bodden, **153**.

LINGUISTIC STUDIES

The OE translator's handling of Latin constructions is of linguistic significance; his handling of participle constructions has been studied by Chase,

---

[11] Charles Swan, tr., *Gesta Romanorum*, 2 vols. (London, 1824); rev. and corr. by Wynnard Hooper, 1 vol. (London: Bell, 1877), Tale 153, 259–99.

118, Wedel, **147**, and Hemling, **129**; Mochizuki, **149** (in Japanese), examines the location of adverbial prepositional phrases. *OE ApT* is commonly included among the texts analysed in linguistic studies; this volume covers only linguistic studies devoted solely to *OE ApT*. Disagreement exists concerning the extent to which the OE translator attempted to reproduce Latin constructions. Taking his cue from Hemling and Chase, Goolden affirms that 'Latin constructions are carefully avoided' (xxiii). Raith, for his part, concludes that the translator was not avoiding the Latin constructions but attempting to render their general meaning; Brodeur, **136**, points out a striking instance of the retention of a Latin construction. The most recent linguistic study of *OE ApT* (particularly its syntax and morphology) has been carried out by Simpson, **150**.

THE *YFEL WIF* CRUX

The reply of Apollonius to the heroine's question in ch. 20 is generally regarded as obscure: 'Mid þam þ þæt mæden geseah Apollonium, þa cwæð heo: Lareow, hwi gæst ðu ana? Apollonius cwæð: Hlæfdige, næs git yfel wif, nim ðas gewrita ðe þin fæder þe sænde and ræd.' Attempts have been made to resolve this crux by reference to the Latin manuscripts; resolution has not been aided by the fact that none of the early scholars who tackled this crux referred to the manuscript group that Riese, 1893, identified as being closest to the OE translator's source. The conclusion to be drawn seems to be that the OE translator's source was corrupt but that, particularly as we do not know the precise reading he had in front of him, reference to the Latin manuscripts does not remove the problems presented by the OE text.

Pottle, **131**, summarizes earlier attempts to resolve the *yfel wif* crux. See Riedinger, **156**, for the most recent comment; her conclusions are based on an examination of the translator's overall attitudes to women.

ANGLICIZATION, CULTURAL ADAPTATION

Although Goolden, **101**, was qualified in his praise of the translator's prose style, he was full of admiration for the way in which he had succeeded in adapting and naturalizing his sophisticated source to an Anglo-Saxon setting. This aspect of the translation is examined in detail by Laubenthal, **144**, who argues that the translator 'seems deliberately and subtly to have Anglicized to suit the taste of his countrymen' (342; like Donner, **145**, she regards the toning-down of the incest motif as an accommodation to Anglo-Saxon attitudes). More impressive than the handling of externals, in Goolden's view, was 'the extent to which the story's psychological content is translated into idiomatic Old English.' Greek life and literature, he pointed out, was highly sophisticated, whereas 'the Anglo-Saxon world had no such tradition of life and letters, and yet here, in a light, lucid style, the settled standards of a highly civilized community seem nearly at home' (xxvi). For Goolden, then, as for Hamilton, the prose style of *OE ApT* is an index of civilized qualities: 'Its very facility of expression shows an advanced sensitivity to delicate aspects of personal relationships.... Its pages introduce us more than any other Old English document to ordinary human nature, and the people we see are not after all very different from ourselves' (xxvii).

SUBSTANTIVE OMISSIONS

The OE translator's substantive departures from the *Historia* do not appear to have been comprehensively studied; the dissertation of Goepp, **133**, however, has not been sighted, and as Goepp, **132**, examines the narrative structure and composition of the *Historia*, with comparative remarks on *OE ApT*, it is possible that the omissions are studied there. Additions are few—Goolden, **101**, xx, describes the epilogue as the only point at which the translator 'purposefully' departed from his source. Most conspicuously, *OE ApT* lacks the *Historia*'s account of the trials of Apollonius's wife, Arcestrate, and their daughter, Thasia. The *Historia* relates the birth of Thasia during a sea voyage; Arcestrate seemingly dies and is cast overboard, and subsequently becomes a servant in the temple of Diana. Thasia, entrusted to a jealous foster mother, is carried off by pirates and sold to a brothel, where she contrives to preserve her virginity; she is finally sent to console Apollonius, who has come in search of her. He repulses her when she attempts to console him with songs and riddles, but her narration of her life story results in their mutual recognition. There are numerous other omissions; the only substantial one is the scene in which Arcestrate goes to bed, sick with love, and her doctors are at a loss for a diagnosis.

The absence of the lovesickness scene is variously interpreted. Goepp, **132**, observed the deliberately unsensational handling of the incest motif, but suggested that the omission of this scene may have been an oversight. Donner, **145**, who appears to assume that *OE ApT* was for general, not monastic, reading argued that the handling of both these episodes revealed that the translator 'reacts prudishly to both love and lust' (95), and speculated that, in this respect, *OE ApT* may have been representative of early Anglo-Saxon literary taste (his findings are significantly qualified by Riedinger, **156**). Laubenthal, **144**, claims that the scene was omitted because it conflicts with the characterization of the princess as a young innocent.

Thorpe, **98**, believed that the story of Arcestrate and Thasia had been torn from the English manuscript because it was considered unsuitable for monastic readers; Raith and Goolden (who give scant attention to the substantive departures) are in agreement with him in so far as they speak of pages missing from the manuscript in the second half of *OE ApT*. Kobayashi, **102**, **148**, on the other hand, argues that the story of Arcestrate and Thasia has not been lost—in Kobayashi's opinion, much of this

story is adequately summarized in the recollections of the central characters at the conclusion of the narrative, and the remainder—'the brothel
scene'—was deliberately expurgated by the translator (or perhaps by the
copyist) because of its offensive nature. As Kobayashi appears to be aware
that Ker reported that there was at least a quire missing from *OE ApT*, it
is surprising that an examination of the manuscript was not undertaken.

HISTORICAL SIGNIFICANCE; GENRE

Both Raith, **100**, and Goolden, **101**, foreground the place of *OE ApT* in
literary history; Goolden regarded it as representative of a shift in literary
taste, although, as Goepp, **132**, observed, *OE ApT* is a unique survival
of vernacular prose fiction. Raith held that *OE ApT* was important, not
because of its intrinsic qualities, but because it represents the first attempt
to write a prose romance. Goolden went much further: 'In his awareness of
the emotional relationship of characters the translator has done more than
give us our first English romance. It would not be too much to say that
he has introduced to English literature centuries before its time the first
English novel' (xxvi).

Opinions differ as to whether the Norman Conquest fortuitously instilled
new life into a decaying society or whether, on the contrary, it cut off in
its prime the development of a unique and sophisticated English culture.
Laubenthal, **144**, like Goolden, embraces the latter view: she regards *OE
ApT* as one of the signs of widening cultural horizons in the late Anglo-
Saxon period, and compares it with the development of 18th century pre-
romanticism. She concludes that: 'The late tenth and eleventh centuries,
then, were not the last flicker of a declining culture but a period of vigorous
creative power, especially in prose' (345). Raith, on the other hand, asserted
that *OE ApT* did not demonstrate that the Norman Conquest had nipped
the flowering of English prose romance in the bud, because prose romance
was destined to develop from metrical narrative.

Goolden considered that *OE ApT* revealed that 'the break in taste between our pre-Conquest ancestors and ourselves was evidently not so radical
as the bulk of the surviving records would lead us to suppose' (xxv). He
found continuity between the OE and ME periods, not only in the courtly
moral tone and 'touch of humour that anticipates Chaucer' (xxv), but also
in the unexpected and delicate handling of love at court. In particular
he considered that *OE ApT* showed that the Anglo-Saxon and later medieval period shared an interest in the strange and marvellous, 'a demand
for escape entertainment, a taste for the imaginative world of fantasy, ex-
citement, and sensationalism' (xxv). Treneer, **128**, also regards *OE ApT*
as representative of a shift from the conceptual modes of epic to those of
romance. Riedinger, **156**, demonstrates that *OE ApT* reflects a movement
towards the creation of a female ideal which became stereotypical in later
medieval romance.

Gradon, **138**, felt that Goolden's critique of *OE ApT* rested upon an over-estimation of the discontinuity between the Old and Middle English periods, and pointed to the Alexander translations and *Beowulf*, as well as the Cambridge Songs, to illustrate her point that there was not so much a 'radical break in taste' as a gradual development from the 10th century onward. Raith argued that, in terms of literary taste, *OE ApT*'s connections lay with hagiography rather than the Alexander translations; in this, he echoes Baker, **126**. Archibald, **151**, argues against the generic classifications of earlier commentators; she also rejects the view that it was read as historical fact (see Stanley, **140**).

STUDY OF *OE ApT* AND ITS CONTEXTS.

It will be evident from the foregoing that study of *OE ApT* has been more than averagely dominated by sources and analogues, and that most commentary on the text has been devoted to establishing its relationship to its source and evaluating the quality of its prose style. The emphases are inevitable given that the work is a translation, but there is perhaps a case to be made that studies of *OE ApT*, particularly those which seek to evaluate the nature and quality of the OE translation by close verbal comparison, are insufficiently mindful of the fact that the Latin text from which the OE translator was working has not been precisely identified. Goolden, **101**, for instance, who was comparing *OE ApT* with a Latin text that he had reconstructed from the OE, concluded, not surprisingly, that 'everything in the Old English answers to something in the Latin' (xxi); the possibility that there never existed a Latin text which corresponded precisely to *OE ApT* does not appear to have been considered. Though much work has been done on the Latin textual tradition, study of its English manifestations has barely begun; McGowan, **155**, however, plans to undertake an in-depth study of the insular manuscript tradition, 9th–11th centuries. Unlike the prose dialogues and *OE Dicts*, study of *OE ApT*, attracted by analogues in the work of major literary figures, has advanced across period boundaries, although the ME metrical fragment has been virtually ignored.

OE ApT has long been regarded as an important index of literary taste and cultural developments, with attention tending to concentrate on sex and ethnicity, opinion remaining divided on the larger implications. A recent article by Riedinger, **156**, draws together most of the preoccupations of *OE ApT* study in arguing that the translator's re-shaping of his sources produces, in Arcestrate, an embryonic romance heroine adapted to the tastes of an English audience. Like Donner, **145**, Riedinger could be accused of not having questioned whether the attitudes of society at large can be deduced from a single work of fiction.

The inclusion of *OE ApT* in a manuscript containing homilies and law codes attributed to Wulfstan, which are written in the same hand, remains unexplained. Kobayashi's suggestion (**102**, 43, n. 12), that *OE ApT* was one of the 'erroneous' English translations admired by the unlearned but deplored by Ælfric (*HomCath*, 1: 2), raises more questions than it answers. The possibility that the manuscript was destined for a lay audience cannot perhaps be outruled, but Whitbread's study of the composition of the manuscript confirms the monastic setting that some commentators have, not unnaturally, assumed for *OE ApT* (**137**). Whitbread, in arguing that the manuscript is a Canterbury copy of material assembled at Worcester in the lifetime of Archbishop Wulfstan, explained the inclusion of *OE ApT* by pointing to the English translation in the catalogue of the Benedictine Abbey of Burton-on-Trent as evidence that the Apollonius story was considered suitable for monastic reading. There is no way of knowing whether that version, or the version owned by Abbot Wando in the 7th century, bore any generic relationship to *OE ApT*, but Kortekaas's study of transmission (**152**) leaves no doubt that, at least from the 9th century onward, the *Historia* was much copied in the monasteries. Archibald, **151**, argued that it was read as an exemplary story of 'The Man Tried by Fate'; the point is less strongly urged in Archibald, 1991 (and, indeed, if it was the moral power of the story that appealed to monastic audiences, it is curious that the good men did not simply extract the *moralité* but, instead, repeatedly copied, and translated, the *Historia* in its entirety). Archibald, 1991, inclines instead towards the view that the story's overt moral signification authorized the indulgence of literary tastes of a more secular kind (positively transgressive, even, given the incest theme).

To the Worcester connections of the Apollonius story in England that Kortekaas adduces may be added the late 11th century book-list in Bodleian, Tanner 3 (see p. 94 above, 'Transmission of the Apollonius Story') and an allusion in *Imago Mundi*, 3.25,[12] by the Worcester-based Honorius (see p. 78 above, 'The Latin *Elucidarium*'). Despite this, and despite the continuity of the script of CCCC 201, it may yet be that *OE ApT* is a Canterbury addition; for whereas a Canterbury provenance seems plausible in the light of the comparison between *OE ApT* and the Cambridge Songs which Gradon draws, **138**, it is extremely difficult to associate pagan-classical romance with the hard-line puritanism of Archbishop Wulfstan.

Although monastic sensibilities have been called upon to explain omissions from the narrative, there has been no corresponding attempt to explain its psychological sensitivity and civilized sophistication in terms of monastic literary tastes; Raith, in drawing a connection between *OE ApT* and hagiography, offers a profitable line of investigation. Monastic familiarity with late classical novels such as Apollonius must have played a significant part in the cultural shift which, reflected in secular and devotional literature alike, separates the world of romance from the heroic age. More information on the milieu of the translation would undoubtedly aid our understanding of *OE ApT* and its historical significance.

---

[12] This, and other medieval and Renaissance allusions, are listed by Elizabeth Archibald, *Apollonius of Tyre: Medieval and Renaissance Themes and Variations* (Woodbridge: Brewer–Boydell, 1991) 217–33.

APOLLONIUS OF TYRE: ANNOTATIONS

SEE ALSO Anderson, **17**; Hahn, **203**

EDITIONS: COMPLETE

98 **Thorpe, Benjamin.** *The Anglo-Saxon Version of the Story of Apollonius of Tyre.* London: Arch, 1834.

Text, 1–28; translation, 29–83 (interpolates ch. 153 of *Gesta Romanorum*). Glossary, 85–92. No apparatus.

Preface, iii–iv, explains that, as we probably owe the loss of a large portion of this interesting work to 'the destroying hand of a gloomy monk ... on account of some passages that might by a devotee be deemed unfit reading for the inmates of a cloister,' the chasm thereby created has been filled in Thorpe's translation with material drawn from Swan's English version of *Gesta Romanorum* (1824).

99 **Zupitza, Julius.** 'Die altenglische Bearbeitung der Erzählung von *Apollonius von Tyrus.*' *Archiv für das Studium der neueren Sprachen und Literaturen* 97 (1896): 17–34.

Critical edition, 18–34; no apparatus.

Napier's introductory note, 17–18, explains that the text has been collated with the Latin version that Zupitza, **117**, identified as closest to the OE, CCCC 318.

100 **Raith, Josef.** *Die alt- und mittelenglischen Apollonius-Bruchstücke, mit dem Text der* Historia Apollonii *nach der englischen Handschriften gruppe.* Studien und Texte zur englischen Philologie, 3. München: Hueber, 1956.

Critical edition, with brief textual notes, 52–66. Latin text, based on CCCC 318, collated with 'the English group,' 85–132. Also edits a ME metrical version (Bodleian, Douce 216), 67–84.

Introduction examines: manuscript contents, 4–8; language (late WS with Essex forms, second half of the 11th century), 8–37; sources, 37–40; character of the translation, 40–51. Discussion of textual relationships, 85–91.

Raith describes the translator's method as 'hwilum word be worde, hwilum andgit of andgiete,' and considers that he was not so much avoiding Latin constructions as attempting to render their general meaning. Raith details omissions, abbreviations, expansions and misunderstandings (including attempts to make sense of a corrupt original). In his view, the translator is worthy of a place beside Ælfric, but the significance of *OE ApT* lies in its status as the first attempt to write a prose romance, not its inherent qualities. Laud 247 and Paris lat. 8503 contain Latin versions of both the Alexander and Apollonius legends, but, in terms of literary taste, Raith would link *OE ApT* with hagiography (especially *Blickling Homilies*, translations of the Life of Andreas and *De vitis patrum*); he notes the appearance of a Life of Thecla in CCCC 318. Raith disagrees that *OE ApT* presaged a flowering of prose romance that was nipped in the bud by the Conquest; the development of prose romance lay through verse romance, and *OE ApT* is a remarkable achievement, but not a trail-blazing one.

101 **Goolden, Peter.** *The Old English* Apollonius of Tyre. Oxford English Monographs 6. Oxford: Oxford UP, 1958.

Critical edition, collated with Thorpe, **98**, and Zupitza, **99**, 2–43. Partially normalized. Reconstructed Latin source, on facing pages, based on CCCC 318, with collations from 21 manuscripts (chiefly English) and three printed texts. Commentary, 44–62; Glossary, 63–75.

Introduction, ix–xxxiv, examines: history of the story, ix–xiii; the Latin text, xiv–xx; the OE translation, xx–xxvii, language (late WS with Essex forms, mid-11th century), xxvii–xxxii; manuscript, xxxii–xxxiv.

Goolden's view of the OE translation, xx–xxvii, is that the addition of a short epilogue is the only purposeful departure. The weakness of the OE version is only apparent when it is considered as a translation of the Latin; it has an 'appearance of carelessness and obscurity where all was once clarity and coherence' (xxiii). Yet its style is its best feature. 'Some of the more delicate nuances have been missed, but the straightforward narrative has been well reproduced in a pleasing Old English idiom' (xxiii). *OE ApT* shows that the OE period shared with the ME period a taste for the imaginative world of fantasy and courtliness. Even more impressive than the Anglicization of the externals of the classical world is 'the extent to which the story's purely psychological content is translated into idiomatic Old English' (xxvi). Unlike the Greeks, Anglo-Saxons had no sophisticated tradition of life and letters, yet in *OE ApT*, 'the settled standards of a highly civilized community seem nearly at home' (xxvi). In his awareness of emotional relationships, the translator has introduced the first English novel centuries before its time. [For reviews see Brodeur, **136**; Gneuss, 1960; Gradon, **138**; Schramm, **139**; Stanley, **140**.]

102 **Kobayashi, Eichi.** 'The Old English *Apollonius of Tyre*.' *Annual Reports: Division of Languages, International Christian University* 3 (1978): 33–84.

Normalized text (early WS), 45–66. Glossary, 67–84. No apparatus.

Introduction, 33–44, contains a brief summary of the origins of the story, its popularity through the ages, and some remarks on *OE ApT*'s relationship to the Latin versions. Kobayashi describes *OE ApT* as two fragments; the first of these is 'a charming love-story complete in itself' (37); the second fragment is 'rather remotely related functionally' (38). Kobayashi lists six 'themes' in the Latin version which are said to have been lost from *OE ApT*, and states that three of these are sufficiently reproduced in the recollections of Apollonius, Arcestrate and Thasia before the temple of Diana: thus, what has really been 'lost' is the three 'themes' which, roughly speaking, make up the brothel sequences: 'It may be conjectured that the Old English translator had quietly expurgated entirely these brothel sequences which might have been too unpleasant for him to translate' (39). [See also Kobayashi, 148.]

EDITIONS: PARTIAL

103 **Leo, Heinrich.** *Altsächsische und Angelsächsische Sprachproben.* Halle: Anton, 1838.

Prints an extract from Thorpe, **98** [chs. 13–21], at 32–9, with explanatory notes.

Concerning 30/30–1, Leo holds that 'næs git yfel wif' was an interpolation by the OE translator; his interpretation of the phrase is 'Noch war keine Herrin ein schlechtes Weib' (38).

104 **Müller, Th.** *Angelsächsisches Lesebuch.* 1855.

Not sighted; according to Wülcker, **13**, 504, prints an excerpt, 56–62.

105 **Thorpe, Benjamin.** *Analecta Anglo-Saxonica. A Selection, in Prose and Verse, from Anglo-Saxon Authors of Various Ages; with a Glossary.* 2nd rev. edn. London: Smith, 1846.

Prints an extract, 108–9 [chs. 25–7]. Composite Glossary, 191–303.

Preface, viii, states that *OE ApT* is based on a tale in *Gesta Romanorum*, and is 'a model of English prose.'

106 **Cook, Albert S.** *A First Book in Old English.* London: Ginn, 1894.

Abridged and normalized text [omits chs. 1-11, 50], with notes, 164–88.

107 **Wyatt, Alfred J.** *An Anglo-Saxon Reader.* Cambridge: Cambridge UP, 1919.

Prints an extract [chs. 9–22], 28–38; Notes, 215–18.

108 **Brook, George Leslie.** *An Introduction to Old English.* Manchester: Manchester UP, 1955.

Prints an extract, with explanatory notes [chs. 15–17], 102–4.

109 Moore, Samuel, and Thomas A. Knott. *The Elements of Old English.*
10th edn. rev. by James R. Hulbert. Ann Arbor: Wahr, 1955.

According to Kobayashi, **102**, prints an extract, 60 ff.; could not be verified,
possibly an error for 1st edn., 1919 (not sighted).

110 Kaiser, Rolf. *Medieval English: An Old and Middle English Anthology.*
3rd rev. edn. Berlin: Kaiser, 1958.

Prints an extract [chs. 11–51], 162–6.

111 Fowler, R. *Old English Prose and Verse.* London: Routledge, 1966.

Prints an extract [chs. 15–21], 29–33.

112 Kishimura, Y. *Adventures in Old English.* Rev. edn. Tokyo, 1970.

Not sighted; according to Kobayashi, **102**, prints an extract, 35–45.

113 Marckwardt, Albert H., and James L. Rosier. *Old English Language
and Literature.* New York: Norton, 1972.

Prints discontinuous extracts, in chs. 15–25; each excerpt is accompanied
by glossary and structural notes. Non-normalized text, with vowel length
indications.

COMMENTARY

114 Mommsen, Tycho. *Pericles, Prince of Tyre. A Novel by George Wilkins
printed in 1608 and founded upon Shakespeare's play.* Oldenburg, 1857.

Not sighted; according to Zupitza, **117**, Mommsen suggests (xviii ff.) that
OE ApT may be more closely related to the Tergensee Fragment [Bay-
erische Staatsbibliothek, Clm 19148] than to *Gesta Romanorum,* ch. 153
(cf. Thorpe, **98**).

115 Meyer, W. 'Über den lateinischen Text der Geschichte des *Apollonius von
Tyrus.*' *Sitzungsberichte der philosophisch-philologischen und historische
Classe der K. Bayerischen Akademie* 2 (1872): 1–28.

Meyer collates excerpts from *OE ApT* with Vienna Hofbibl. 226 (12th century) which appears to have been unknown to Riese, 1871, but which, in
Meyer's view, is closer to the OE than Laud Misc. 247 (17–21).

116 Zupitza, Julius. 'Verbesserungen und Erklaerungen.' *Anglia* 1 (1878):
463–83.

Nine emendations and textual notes to Thorpe, **98**, at 463–7, in the light
of the Latin versions. [See Pottle, **131**, for the 'yfel wif' crux.]

117 Zupitza, Julius. 'Welcher Text liegt der altenglischen Bearbeitung der Erzählung von *Apollonius von Tyrus* zu Grunde?' *Romanische Forschungen* 3 (1887): 268–79.

Zupitza reviews earlier attempts to identify the source of *OE ApT*, and disagrees with Mommsen, **114**, and with Riese, 1871, who considered that Laud 247 was the closest surviving version. The source of *OE ApT* belonged to the same manuscript group as Laud 247, CCCC 318 and CCCC 451, and comparison shows that it is most closely related to CCCC 318.

118 Chase, Frank H. 'The Absolute Participle in the Old English *Apollonius*.' *Modern Language Notes* 8 (1893): 486–9.

In *OE ApT* (Thorpe, **98**), five cases of the dative absolute are present. Four of them are used to render an ablative absolute, and one is used for an ablative of quality. There is also one instance of the 'crude' or uninflected form translating an absolute ablative. In the Latin (ed. Riese), 44 ablatives absolute occur. Only six are rendered by an ablative construction in the OE, two of these by the formula 'gode fultumiendum.' Of the remainder, 16 are translated by a subordinate clause, 10 by a co-ordinate clause, 11 by a prepositional phrase, and one by an adverb.

119 Singer, S. *Apollonius: Üntersuchungen über das Fortleben des antiken Romans in späteren Zeiten.* Halle a. S.: Niemeyer, 1895.

National provenance is the organizing principle of Singer's survey of versions of the Apollonius story. *OE ApT* receives notice at 220–1; brief remarks on Zupitza, **117**.

120 Smyth, Albert H. *Shakespeare's Pericles and Apollonius of Tyre. A Study in Comparative Literature.* Philadelphia: MacCalla, 1898. New York: AMS, 1972.

Smyth purports to give 'a complete historical sketch of the romance, to compare its more important narratives with particular reference to its final shape in Shakespeare, and to indicate its relations to the Vilkina saga, the poem of King Orendel, the *chanson* of Jourdain de Blaivies, the Solomon-Markolf cycle, and the *Anetheia and Habrokornes* of Xenophon of Ephesus' (5–6). Notice of *OE ApT* consists of a short bibliography and the following remark: 'Before the Norman conquest brought the chivalry and romance of southern Europe into England, some unknown but not unskillful hand, as if presaging the time when the new ideas of courtliness and chivalry should embody themselves in the romantic forms of the Elizabethan age, had translated this universal favourite' (48).

121 Klebs, Elimar. *Die Erzählung von Apollonius aus Tyrus. Eine geschichtliche Untersuchung über ihre lateinische Ürform und ihre späteren Bearbeitungen.* Berlin: Reimer, 1899.

The relationship between the Latin manuscripts (listed 529–60) is analysed in detail, 18–178. *OE ApT* figures in the examination of 'Die Redaktion RC,' 125–54, where Klebs's comparisons confirm Zupitza's identification of CCCC 318 (**117**) as the version closest to the OE (138–55). Klebs's survey of vernacular versions of the Apollonius story, 228–93, merely notes that the *OE ApT* is of historical interest as the earliest vernacular version (para. 459).

122 Märkisch, Robert. *Die altenglische Bearbeitung der Erzählung von Apollonius von Tyrus. Grammatik und Lateinischer Text.* Palaestra 6. Berlin: Mayer, 1899. New York: Johnson, 1970.

Märkisch analyses phonology and accidence, 1–17, and syntax, 17–36, and concludes that the language is WS, not earlier than second half of the 11th century. At 37–51, he prints his reconstruction of the Latin version he believes to have underlain *OE ApT*, based on Magdalen 50 (ed. Riese), collated with Thorpe, **98**, Zupitza, **99**, and other manuscripts. His comparison of the OE and Latin, 51–62, deals with the following topics: abbreviations; expansions; misunderstandings and errors; the literalness of the translation; and its distinctive characteristics.

123 Pettengill, Ray Waldron. 'The *Apollonius von Tyrland* of Heinrich von Neustadt: A Study of the Sources.' Diss. Harvard U, 1910.

Not sighted. According to Pulsiano, 1988, 804, *OE ApT* is mentioned.

124 Rohde, Erwin. *Der griechische Roman und seine Vorläufer.* 3rd edn., with a forward by Karl Kerényi. Leipzig: Schmid, 1914. Hildesheim, NY: Olms, 1974.

Listed Goolden, **101**; *OE ApT* does not fall within the scope of Rohde's argument that the *Historia* is basically a pagan-Greek *Romandichtung*, with some obvious Christian-Latin additions (440–53).

125 Emerson, Oliver F. 'Notes on Old English.' *Modern Language Notes* 38 (1923): 269–72.

Emerson's purpose is to demonstrate that comparison with the Latin assists in the reading of certain sentences (18/11–13; 20/11–13; 22/12–14; 34/10–13). Emerson considers that 'Hlæfdige, næs git yfel wif' (30/31) renders 'Domina, nondum mulier et mala' (Magdalen 50, ed. Riese). 'Nondum mulier et mala' is, he suggests, a parenthetical narrator's remark, interpolated by a monk or cleric who opposed *mulier*, meaning 'married woman' to *domina* (here meaning 'unmarried princess'), and signified his disapprobation of the married state by the addition of *et mala*. [See Pottle, **131**.]

126 Baker, Ernest A. *The History of the English Novel. Vol 1: The Age of Romance from the Beginnings to the Renaissance.* New York: Barnes, 1924. London: Witherby, 1950. 11 vols.

In ch. 2, 'Anglo-Saxon Fiction,' Baker advances the view that popular ha-giographies in the Middle Ages contained situations and incidents parallel to the romances. *OE ApT* is discussed at 56–60. The incest motive, prominent in the well-known story of Holy Dymphna (*c.* 600), is the starting point of *OE ApT*, 'the only piece extant in Old English that can be called a regular prose romance' (57). The story 'teemed with thrilling adventures, bizarre situations and sentimentality in its frankest shapes' (57) and the style of *OE ApT*, though heightened to suit the romanticism of the narrative, owes a good deal to the Latin.

Baker translates several passages from *Wond*, 60–1; the OE rendering is 'a very amusing romance of travel anticipating Mandeville' (60).

127 Hibbard, L.A. *Medieval Romance in England: A Study of the Sources and Analogues of the Non-cyclic Metrical Romances*. Oxford: Oxford UP, 1926.

'Romances of Love and Adventure,' 164–9, gives a brief bibliographical sketch of versions of the Apollonius story in medieval Latin, English, French and German. *OE ApT* 'has a special interest in presaging, before the Nor-man Conquest, the introduction into England of the spirit of romance' (165, n. 2).

128 Treneer, Anne. *The Sea in English Literature, from Beowulf to Donne*. Liverpool: Liverpool UP, 1926.

Whereas the old heathen spirit persists in *Blickling Homilies*, 17, *OE ApT* (discussed 42–4) represents the high degree to which southern-derived ro-mance had penetrated England, even before the Conquest, whose effect was 'to make definite a change which affected not only the nature of stories but the forms of words and ways of measuring them' (44). The storm is vigor-ously described 'but differs in essence from the storms in OE poetry.' The gulf between *Beowulf* and *OE ApT* is marked by the episode in which Apol-lonius stands naked on the shore and cries to the sea: 'The effect is pitiful rather than heroic. For the equal combat between man and sea, which gives tone to *Beowulf*, has been substituted robbery and violence, with the sea as spoiler and man as victim' (43).

129 Hemling, Emily M. 'The Absolute Participle in the *Apollonius of Tyre*.' *Modern Language Notes* 45 (1930): 175–8.

Out of the 80 participles in the Latin, only six are allowed to remain in the OE. This studious avoidance of participial construction confirms the findings of M. Callaway (Diss. Johns Hopkins U, 1889), who studied only authors considered classic; the renderings of the participle correspond to those pointed out by Callaway, although there is a variation in the compar-ative frequency of certain constructions. Callaway believed OE writing was adversely affected by heavy use in translation of the finite verb, but Hemling feels that in *OE ApT* the opposite is true. The independent statements of the OE version lend vigour to the directness of the narrative (e.g., 'Ða stod he nacod on ðæm strande and beheold ða sæ' [16/25-6] for 'stans in litore nudus intuens mare tranquillum').

130 Chapman, Coolidge Otis. 'Beowulf and Apollonius of Tyre.' *Modern Language Notes* 46 (1931): 439-43.

Chapman discerns 'striking parallels' (439) between Beowulf's arrival at Heorot and Apollonius's arrival at the court of Arcestrates. Both are seafarers, and are met by a messenger who goes ahead to make an announcement to the king, who extends a cordial welcome. In both, a courtier, jealous of the king's favour to a stranger, attempts to stir up a quarrel. In both, the lady of the household enters the banqueting hall, then goes about the guests, finally speaking discreetly to the stranger. Chapman suggests that the *Beowulf* poet may have seen a Latin translation of the romance. [See Ogilvy, **141**.]

131 Pottle, Frederick A. 'Næs gīt yfel wīf in the Old English Apollonius.' *JEGP* 30 (1931): 21-5.

Zupitza, **116**, who disposed of the comments on 'næs git yfel wif' by Thorpe, **98**, and Leo, **103**, by pointing out that it does have a Latin original, considered that the translator was following 'nondum mulier mala' (i.e., a Magdalen version in which *et* was omitted), and suggested that *næs* represented *ne ealles*; hence, 'Herrin, die du noch keineswegs ein schlechtes weib bist.' Pottle disagrees, because such usage is rare and poetical. His own translation is 'Lady, there never was a wicked woman'; it does not make sense in context, but Pottle does not think that fact would have troubled the OE translator. The hypothesis of Emerson, **125**, is shown to be untenable by Riese's 2nd revised edition; by collating a greater number of Latin manuscripts, Riese, 1893, showed that the better tradition is preserved in the family represented by the Laurentian and Paris manuscripts. Pottle believes that the reading: 'Domina, es nondum mulier et male habes' must underlie the passage, and cannot be a clerical interpolation—at least, not for the reason Emerson assigned. In Pottle's view, the Latin signifies Apollonius's disapproval of the invitation implicit in the princess's question ('so young and yet so knowing'). The OE translator was unable to make sense of the passage because he did not have the fuller version of the Paris manuscript to help him.

132 Goepp, Philip H., II. 'The Narrative Material of *Apollonius of Tyre*.' *ELH* 5 (1938): 150-72.

Goepp defines 15 narrative motifs in the *Historia* and concludes that, with few exceptions, they were not the invention of the Latin author; it is a literary version of a traditional story or stories, almost certainly related to the group that forms the Constance cycle. The OE translation (discussed 170-2) consists of a self-contained episode, aesthetically the best part of the Apollonius story, and its faults (notably poverty of vocabulary) are those of the original. Although the treatment of the incest motif appears deliberately unsensational, the omission of the description of the daughter's lovesickness may be an oversight. The king's statement that she is busy studying is more likely to represent deliberate irony than a misunderstanding of the explanation that she is ill from studying. The translation is on the whole accurate and stylistically adequate, and it would be interesting to know if this unique survival of vernacular prose fiction was typical of its kind.

133 **Goepp, Philip H., II.** 'The Old English *Apollonius of Tyre.*' Diss. Johns Hopkins U, 1938.

Not sighted. Listed Pulsiano, 1988, 805; not included in *DA*, 1938–40.

134 **Förster, Max.** *Der Flussname Themse und seine Sippe: Studien zur Anglisierung keltischer Eigennamen und zur Lautchronologie des Altbritischen.* Sitzungsberichte der Bayerischen Akademie der Wissenschaften, Philosophisch-historischen Abteilung 1. München: Beck, 1941.

No reference to *OE ApT* could be located in the index. Gradon, **138**, observes that, although there is much to interest the philologist in this mighty work, it can hardly be considered sufficiently central to the study of *OE ApT* to warrant inclusion in the bibliography of Goolden, **101**.

135 **Raith, J.** *Historia Apollonii Regis Tyri. Text der englischen Handschriftengruppe.* München: Teubner, 1956.

Edits the Latin *Historia* from CCCC 318, with emendations from 'the English group,' as in Raith, **100**. Preface, iii–xviii, discusses manuscript relationships and the putative Greek original.

136 **Brodeur, Arthur G.** Rev. of *The Old English* Apollonius of Tyre, by Peter Goolden [**101**]. *Comparative Literature* 11 (1959): 182–3.

As Goolden, **101**, xxiii, observes, *cwicsuslene hus* is a felicitous translation for *Tartaream domum*; but the term occurs as a poetic appellation for hell in OE religious poetry and is thus not original to the translator. Goolden has not noticed that there are some examples of exceptional word order which are indicative of a late date (e.g., 36/23) and, despite Goolden's claim that *OE ApT* avoids Latin constructions, there is a striking retention of the Latin construction at 42/3.

137 **Whitbread, L.** 'MS. C.C.C.C. 201: A Note on its Character and Provenance.' *Philological Quarterly* 38 (1959): 106–12.

Whitbread argues that, although the material in CCCC 201 was originally assembled at Worcester during Archbishop Wulfstan's life, or not long after his death in 1023, the manuscript itself was copied at Canterbury under Lanfranc after the fire of 1067, when the monks made strenuous efforts to replace their books; it is 'a repository for the safe preservation of the religious culture of an earlier generation' (110). *OE ApT* is mentioned as an exception to Whitbread's thesis that the unity of the first two parts of the manuscript derives from their association with the activities of Wulfstan; he points to a lost English version listed in a 12th century catalogue of the library of the Burton-on-Trent Benedictine abbey as evidence that the Apollonius story was considered suitable monastic reading (109, n. 9).

138 Gradon, Pamela. Rev. of *The Old English* Apollonius of Tyre, by Peter Goolden [**101**]. *Medium Ævum* 29 (1960): 33–6.

Contra Goolden, **101**, Gradon holds that the Conquest effected no radical break in taste. Rather, there was an evolution from the beginning of the 10th century; *Beowulf*, *Alex*, *St Eustace* and *The Seven Sleepers* are evidence of a developing taste for marvels, and if the *Cambridge Songs* (esp. 'verna feminæ suspiria') really are mid-11th century, *OE ApT*'s interest in romantic love is not uniquely early (36). Gradon is also critical of Goolden's editorial procedures; she considers that he has not perceived the limits of a reconstructed Latin text, and that the effect of his partial normalization (presumably to a statistical norm) is the loss of valuable philological information.

139 Schramm, O.K. Rev. of *The Old English* Apollonius of Tyre, by Peter Goolden [**101**]. *Review of English Studies* 12 (1960): 194–5.

Lists 12 *hapax legomena* not noted by Goolden, **101**.

140 Stanley, E.G. Rev. of *The Old English* Apollonius of Tyre, by Peter Goolden [**101**]. *Modern Language Review* 55 (1960): 428.

Stanley questions Goolden's assumption that *OE ApT* evinces a taste for fantasy; like the OT account of Jonah and the legend of Offa's queen, the Apollonius story may have been regarded as historical truth by Anglo-Saxons. In view of the absence of the Symphosius riddles in the OE version, Stanley wonders whether riddles did have a special appeal for Anglo-Saxon audiences; the taste of the audience of CCCC 201 might not have been the same as those who sniggered at the obscenities of the Exeter Riddles.

141 Ogilvy, J.D.A. *Books Known to the English, 597–1066.* Cambridge, MA: Medieval Academy of America, 1967.

Ogilvy points out that the difficulty with the parallels Chapman, **130**, draws between *Apollonius* and *Beowulf* is that they rest upon the ungracious courtier tradition and on customs (such as that of the lady of the house greeting the guests at a banquet) which are common to many ancient peoples (74).

142 Hamilton, David Bailey. 'Studies in Anglo-Saxon Literary Styles.' Diss. U of Virginia, 1968. [*DAI* 29 (1969): 3972A–73A.]

Hamilton regards *OE ApT* and Ælfric's *Lives of Saints* as representative of the best narrative prose of the period, and ch. 4, 'Apollonius and Late

Anglo-Saxon Narrative Prose,' 147–92, compares them throughout. The style of *OE ApT* 'is basically a prose rhythm influenced by the associative rhythm of speech' (150), unencumbered by patterns of metre or sound that would detract from the essential prose process of predication; but it has two 'decorated' styles, 'one creating a kind of celebrational reverie based on a heightened rhythm of free-prose, the other euphemistically heightening word-play and puns' (192). The decorated passages (the harp-playing scene, the lovers' reunion, and the conclusion) coincide with narrative climaxes. Hamilton sees a connection between the style of *OE ApT* and its narrative mode: *OE ApT* is linear, continuous and compulsively forward-moving, never alluding to analogous incidents. It thus stands in contrast with *Lives of Saints*, which employ a uniformly heightened style, and break down into a series of units whose function is more discursive-meditative than narrative. Hamilton considers that Goepp, **133**, 170, has over-stressed the didacticism of *OE ApT*, because 'its clever manipulation of language makes a witty if half whimsical appeal to our intelligence' (192). He concludes that the prose style of *OE ApT* 'can tolerate and finally control more variety, discontinuity, and even paradox than any verse, or verse-inclined style is able to do.... It is remarkable, surely, that an Anglo-Saxon translator working with material for which, as far as we know, there was no native prose tradition and only remote correspondences in its heritage of verse could manage a prose style as light, easy, and idiomatic, as witty, breathless, and intricate as this' (192).

143 **Lawrence, Harold Whitney.** ' "To Sing a Song that Old Was Sung": *Pericles* and *Apollonius of Tyre*, the Play and the Tradition.' *DAI* 31 (1971): 6062A–63A. [Diss. Texas Christian U, 1970. Dir. Marjorie Lewis.]

Dissertation not sighted. According to *DAI*, *OE ApT* is included in discussion of the story tradition.

144 **Laubenthal, Sanders Anne.** 'The Net of Words: Translations and Critical Interpretations of Old English Poetry and Prose.' Diss. U of Alabama, 1970. [*DAI* 31 (1971): 5410-A.]

Ch. 10, 'Aspects of Old English Prose,' includes a discussion of the relation of *OE ApT* to the Latin, 333–46. Expansion gives the English a more idiomatic and leisured quality, which is entirely suitable to the nature of the story; the narrative becomes both more courtly and more charged with feeling and action. The smooth idiomatic style, and the expert use of dialogue, are likely to reflect oral prose. The translator 'seems deliberately and subtly to have Anglicized to suit the taste of his countrymen' (342). Examples of this are: the expurgation of the incest passage; the substitution of 'to þam he beseah' for Apollonius's prostration at the fisherman's feet (ch. 12); *sarlice* for *profusis lacrimis*; and the striking of the top for the massaging of the king (ch. 13), whereby 'the king's sense of rejuvenation becomes purely psychological, due to watching sports of the young' (343).

Apollonius's entertainment at the feast (ch. 16) also becomes suggestive of scopic performance; *plegode* perhaps means that he performed a sword-dance, and the bringing forth of beautiful things, which must come from his mind, may mean that he recited poetry or a prose story or gave a display of oratory. The lovesickness scene is omitted because it would have spoiled the characterization of the princess as a young innocent. 'The late tenth and eleventh centuries, then, were not the last flicker of a declining culture but a period of vigorous creative power, especially in prose' (345).

145 Donner, Morton. 'Prudery in Old English Fiction.' *Comitatus* 3 (1972): 91–6.

The absence of sexuality in the surviving OE corpus is natural considering its predominantly clerical authorship. More unexpected is the underlying prudery of translations of romantic fiction from Latin. There is nothing prurient in the Latin of *Wond*. Two brief passages in the *Epistola* (ed. Rypins, **165**) have been modified or omitted (91/19–21, cf. 32/20–33/5; 94/14–15, cf. 41/1–4). A description of wild men who capture water nymphs in order to kill them is omitted in the OE (see 99/3–9), but this has less value as evidence of prudery since it occurs as part of a substantial section of the narrative, almost 100 lines of Latin, which is lacking in the OE translation. In *OE ApT*, Antiochus's rape of his daughter has been toned down; the handling of Arcestrate's love and courtship shows that the author 'reacts prudishly to both love and lust, to sexuality whether in thought or deed' (95). Donner notes that the survival of texts was 'a chancy matter,' but concludes: 'Prudery in Old English fiction may well reflect the influence of general standards of Anglo-Saxon literary taste' (96). [See also Riedinger, **156**.]

146 Pickford, T.E. '*Apollonius of Tyre* as Greek Myth and Christian Mystery.' *Neophilologus* 59 (1975): 599–609.

Pickford argues that the Apollonius story 'while revealing its origins in Greek myth, is nevertheless capable of a fully Christian meaning, and that this fact, if not alone at least primarily, made it a subject fit for translation and constant retelling throughout the early and late Middle Ages, and indeed, into our own time' (607). [No specific reference to *OE ApT*.]

147 Wedel, Alfred R. 'Participial Construction in High German and West Saxon of the Eleventh and Twelfth Centuries: Latin and Germanic Differences.' *JEGP* 77 (1978): 383–97.

Wedel examines the functions of present and past participles in Latin and vernacular texts, with particular reference to the OHG translation of the *Physiologus*, and *OE ApT*. The investigation supports the author's view of the late OHG appositive as a syntactical unit expressed only by strong adjectival endings, and shows that late WS had already developed its Anglo-Saxon characteristics, which are different from late OHG syntax. The syntactic functions of the Anglo-Saxon participle came into existence before the old participle ending -*nd* was replaced by the all-purpose ending -*ing*. The non-Germanic co-ordinate and relative present participles had already been adopted into the English language. German, like English, did adopt the adverbial use of the present participle when denoting manner, but did not adopt, to the same extent as English, the other adverbial uses of the participle.

148 **Kobayashi, Eichi.** 'On the "Lost" Portions in the Old English *Apollonius of Tyre.' Explorations in Linguistics: Papers in Honor of Kazuko Inoue.* Ed. George Bedell, Eichi Kobayashi and Masatake Muraki. Tokyo: Kenkyusha, 1979. 244-50.

The author reiterates the claim that only the brothel sequence is actually missing, and that it has been deliberately expurgated by either the translator or copyist (see Kobayashi, **102**); the 'yfel wif' addition (30/31) is the work of a Christian monk, and other passages that a monk or his readers might have found unpleasant have been expurgated. 'The fact that the manuscript has no indication of a break in the story and that the whole story is written in the same hand may help us further to conjecture that there is no lost quire of parchment' (249).

149 **Mochizuki, Ikuko.** ['Location of Adverbial Prepositional Phrases in *Apollonius of Tyre.'*] *Essays and Studies* (Tokyo Women's Christian University) 33 (1983): 51-69.

Not sighted; in Japanese.

150 **Simpson, Dale Wilson.** 'Word Order and Style in the Old English *Apollonius of Tyre.'* Diss. North Texas State U, 1983. [*DAI* 44 (1984): 2468A.]

Ch. 1, 1-28, describes the manuscript and the Apollonius story, and surveys scholarship on *OE ApT* and on OE syntax and style. Ch. 2, 29-157, illustrates *OE ApT*'s general conformity to the word order of late WS, by analysis of phrases and clauses. Ch. 3, 158-249, compares the OE and Latin texts in Goolden, **101**, and offers reasons for the OE additions, omissions, paraphrases and mistranslations. Simpson considers that, after 140 (ed. Goolden) there are differences in word order and the morphology of several words and, in ch. 4, 250-88, she advances the theory that at least two translators were responsible for *OE ApT*, but concludes that their identities, and the identity of the southern scriptorium where the translation was made, lie beyond the limits of the knowable.

151 **Archibald, Elizabeth Frances.** '*Apollonius of Tyre* in the Middle Ages and the Renaissance.' Diss. Yale U, 1984. [*DAI* 46 (1985): 697A.]

Ch. 1 of this literary history of the Apollonius story up to 1609 surveys vernacular versions, 17-61; it 'may have appealed to Anglo-Saxons because of its similarity to their popular poetic theme of wandering exile and to their

epic saints lives (it has been compared to the *Andreas*), but it is striking
that absolutely no attempt is made to Christianize it' (20–1). Chapters on
plot structure, 62–107, literary origins and sources, 108–60, and the incest
theme in medieval literature, 161–87, make no reference to *OE ApT*. Discussion of the genre of the story, 188–239, as perceived by the Middle Ages
and Renaissance, includes consideration of reasons for its stability and popularity. Archibald considers that characterization of *OE ApT* as a 'romance'
or 'the first vernacular novel' is unhistorical (209); arguments drawn from
manuscript context are 'a two-edged weapon' (210) because the story is preserved in a wide variety of contexts. Archibald also rejects the view that
early adaptors and audiences regarded the story as historical, and argues
that, although the story was not generally read as an explicitly Christian
exemplum (cf. Pickford, **146**), it was widely regarded as an exemplary study
of 'The Man Tried By Fate'; the OE translator's introduction stresses its
moral content (211). Appendices list pre-1609 versions, 245–47, medieval
allusions to Apollonius, 248–57, and manuscripts consulted, 258. The dissertation, revised and re-organized, has now been published, together with
text of the *Historia* (as in Kortekaas, **152**), translation facing: Elizabeth
Archibald, *Apollonius of Tyre: Medieval and Renaissance Themes and Variations* (Woodbridge: Brewer–Boydell, 1991).

152 Kortekaas, G.A.A. *Historia Apollonii Regis Tyri*. Medievalia Groningana
3. Groningen: Bouma, 1984.

Parallel edition of the *Historia* (RA and RB). Kortekaas surmises that the
two recensions, circulating in Northern France in the late 8th or early 9th
century, were perhaps introduced from (Southern?) England (96, 132, *et
passim*). He suggests (264–5, n. 736) that the *Historia* may have been
among the books brought from Rome by Benedict Biscop and others, and
that, subsequently, the text 'in its religious interpretation' was brought to
the continent by Anglo-Saxon or Irish monks. The earliest manuscript of
RA (Montecassino, 9th century) is preserved with a copy of a hymn to
St Patrick, attributed to Abbot Cellanus, who was in correspondence with
Aldhelm (discussed 24, 27–9); a better text of this hymn, dated 8th/9th
centuries, circulated in England. The oldest known text of the hymn is
from Worcester (discussed 173, n. 3), and Kortekaas regards it as significant
that later Apollonius manuscripts, including *OE ApT*, have Worcester connections (cf. Whitbread, **137**); 'perhaps these later data allow us to infer
an earlier familiarity' (265). Kortekaas also points to Anglo-Saxon missionary contact with the Werden on Ruhr monastery, to which are assigned the
fragments of the *Historia* containing illustrations that Ring, 1888, 65, characterized as 'figurae anglosaxonica ratione adumbratae' (discussed 180, n.
156).

153 Bodden, Mary Catherine. 'Anglo-Saxon Self-Consciousness in Language.'
English Studies 68 (1987): 24–39.

Part 1 deals with 'Language Difficulties in Anglo-Saxon Translation Techniques,' 26–32; Part 2 discusses 'The Effect of Cultural Differences upon Translation Techniques,' 32–9. *OE ApT* is briefly mentioned as 'one of the instances in which the translator's awareness of the resources of his language produces a better version than the source' (38). Its word-play constitutes 'self-consciousness of the most creative sort' (39), and when the king dismisses the three suitors (ed. Goolden, **101**, 32, 34) 'we get just a whiff of that wonderfully light self-complacent humour that reached its refinement in the Shakespearean jester' (39).

154 **Olsen, Alexandra Hennessey.** 'Literary Artistry and the Oral-Formulaic Tradition: The Case of Gower's *Appolinus of Tyre.*' *Comparative Research on Oral Traditions*. Ed. John Miles Foley. Columbus OH, 1987. 493–509.

Olsen argues that Gower's handling of the storm scene in *Confessio Amantis*, Bk. 8, demonstrates neither realism nor the simple translation of a Latin source, but the use of an OE poetic type-scene of the Sea Voyage. By extended comparison, she shows that 'Gower has departed from his Latin source in order to depict the voyages in terms of the Old English type-scene, a departure not found in the Old English prose, which translates the Latin with greater fidelity than does Gower' (501).

155 **McGowan, Joseph.** 'Royal Titles in the Old English *Apollonius.*' *Studia Neophilologica* 61 (1989): 3–6.

Raith, **100**, emended *geong* to *cyng* in Stanguilio's greeting, 'Hlaford geong Apolloni' (ed. Goolden, **101**, 12/25–7). Elsewhere, Apollonius is commonly addressed as *cyngc*, but never as *geong*; emendation to *cyngc* realigns the OE translation with the Latin original (Recension C has *domine rex*, whereas Recensions A and B have only *domine*) and is supported by 'Hlaford cyngc,' 10/12 (where all recensions have *domine rex*). McGowan also agrees with Raith (and Thorpe, **98**), that the half-line erasure in the *incipit*, for which Goolden, 2/2, offers *tiriscan*, should be filled by *tiriscan ealdormen*, not only 'the better to fill the erasure in the MS ... but to balance *historia apollonii regis tyri*, the title of the romance which derives from the *incipit* to the Latin MSS' (5).

156 **Riedinger, Anita R.** 'The Englishing of Arcestrate: Women in *Apollonius of Tyre.*' *New Readings on Women in Old English Literature*. Ed. Helen Damico and Alexandra Hennessey Olsen. Bloomington: Indiana UP, 1990. 292–306.

Riedinger compares *OE ApT* with Goolden's reconstructed Latin source, in order to determine 'what kind of woman was acceptable to an Old English audience in the last years before the Conquest. The question is an important one, because Arcestrate represents a "new" type of heroine, one very unlike her Old English predecessors, yet one who was to be as long-lived as the genre of romance itself' (293). Concerning Donner, **145**, Riedinger (304,

n. 15) observes that he uses Goolden's base text (**101**) rather than his conflated text; the conflated text reveals that one of the passages Donner instances (28/21–2) is not an emendation. Although Donner finds that the translator prefers not to mention the word 'love,' Riedinger finds it mentioned five times in the early stages of the 'love story' alone. Concerning the 'yfel wif' crux, Riedinger remarks: 'For this translator, in particular, just the change from "maiden" to "woman" is sufficient to justify the adjective "bad"' (305, n. 18). Riedinger argues that the translator is very consistent in his translation of words for women. *Fæmne* means only 'virgin' in this text; *wif* means not only 'wife' but also 'a woman who is not a virgin.'

ALEXANDER'S LETTER TO ARISTOTLE AND WONDERS OF THE EAST

MANUSCRIPTS

ALEXANDER   FC B.22.1

London, British Library, Cotton Vitellius A.xv,   V
  ff. 107–31v
Ker 216, art. 3   s. x/xi

WONDERS   FC B.22.2

London, British Library, Cotton Vitellius A.xv,
  ff. 98v–106v
Ker 216, art. 2   s. x/xi

London, British Library, Cotton Tiberius B.v, Vol. 1,   T
  ff. 78v–87v
Ker 193, art. b   s. xi¹

DESCRIPTION OF THE TEXTS

The sole remaining copy of *Alex* is preserved, together with one of the versions of *Wond*, in the same manuscript as *Beowulf*. *Wond* in T is fuller than in V, and is accompanied by a Latin text; the Latin is in 36 unnumbered sections, each followed by its OE version (V lacks sections 5 and 34–6). The OE and Latin versions of *Wond*, however, are not intimately related. A number of different types of fictional writings attached to the figure of Alexander circulated in the West in the early Middle Ages, and are thought to have derived ultimately from a single Greek prototype. *Alex* is based on the *Epistola Alexandri* (a chronicle of Alexander's campaign in the form of a letter to his tutor, Aristotle). *Wond* derives from the equally apocryphal Letter of Pharasmanes to the Emperor Hadrian. Alexander figures only marginally in this work, which concentrates more on the monstrous races in India than on military exploits. In the process of translation into OE, the Letter of Pharasmanes lost its epistolary structure and became more or less a *catalogue raisonnée* of Eastern wonders. Both copies of *Wond* are accompanied by a series of coloured drawings (chiefly depicting monsters and other fabulous creatures), too noticeably dissimilar to have been copied from a common source; T is a *de luxe* copy.

117

MANUSCRIPTS: DESCRIPTION, CONTENTS, DATE, PROVENANCE AND PURPOSE (following Ker, et al.)

Vitellius A.xv

V, the *Beowulf* (or Nowell) Codex, is bound with the Southwick Codex (whose contents include *SS*). The manuscript was damaged in the Cotton Library fire, and leaves are mounted separately. It contains both *Alex* and a copy of *Wond*; for the illustrations accompanying *Wond* in V, and its relationship to T, see below.

Ker, as is well known, dates the *Beowulf* Codex s. x/xi, and states that there are two hands, contemporary with one another, but dissimilar in character. The first hand, responsible for *Alex*, *Wond*, a prose Life of St Christopher and part of *Beowulf* (ff. 94–175v/3), is influenced by Caroline minuscule, and is smaller, more pointed and delicate than the second hand, a late type of square Anglo-Saxon minuscule, responsible for the remainder of *Beowulf* and for *Judith*; arts. 1–4 are 'inseparable,' but *Judith* was not always in its present position, and must originally have come before the three prose texts or have been shifted to the end from some other position 'before the worm got to work' on the concluding folios of *Beowulf*.

Ker also explains that 'a former foliation, followed by Zupitza and by Klaeber, is sometimes 3 and sometimes 2 behind that now in use' (282); see Rypins, **181**, who also pointed out that, in the earliest binding, the leaves containing *Alex* were misbound (ff. 110–17 occupied the position that should have been held by ff. 118–25).

The first full description of the manuscript was published by Förster, **180**, in 1919; like Sisam, **177**, three years earlier, Förster recognized that the Southwick Codex was distinct from the *Beowulf* manuscript with which it was bound, and of a later date. At the time Förster wrote, *Beowulf* was generally dated about or a little before 1000. But Wülcker, **13**, 505, had asserted that *Alex* and *Wond* could not be earlier than the mid-11th century, and this dating was adopted by early literary historians and also by Knappe, **163**, who studied the language of *Wond* at some length in his 1906 edition. Förster himself had accepted a 12th century date for *Wond* in his discussion of its sources (**173**).

In his 1919 study of the manuscript, however, Förster, **180**, pointed out that, as *Wond* and *Alex* are written in the same script as *Beowulf*, they must have been copied at the same date; literary historians had, therefore, been incorrect in claiming that oriental subject matter was not introduced into England until after the Conquest. This point had already been made three years earlier, by Sisam, **177**. The same point was repeated, in 1920, by Rypins, **181**, who, not having read Förster, **180**, claimed in his 1924 edition of *Alex* and *Wond*, **165**, that only Sisam, of the many who had examined the manuscript, had called attention to the fact that there were only two hands (xi–xii); actually, as Kiernan, **208**, points out, 'Madden had already confidently sorted out the scribal hands, text by text, some hundred years earlier' (129), but the terms of his will had prevented the publication of his discovery.[1] Förster, Sisam and Rypins, then, all accepted a *c.* 1000 date for *Alex* and *Wond*, the dating of *Beowulf* being regarded by them as too secure to admit of the possibility that *Beowulf* might have been copied in the mid-11th century or later.

With the publication of Kiernan, **206**, the dating of the *Beowulf* Codex became a contentious issue.[2] Kiernan sought to establish that the poem was composed in the reign of Cnut and that the manuscript evidence fitted admirably with this while that of the language did not disagree. Palaeographers did, however. Dumville, **209**, re-examined the script at length; a salient point made by him is that the first hand is more 'modern' than the second. Dumville also points out that Ker's dating was a compromise, meeting the need for a conventional formulation that would allow for the conjunction of two such discrepant styles. Dumville concludes that the proper conventional dating for the manuscript is (depending on the system employed) '*saec.* xi in.' or '*saec.* xi $\frac{1}{4}$,' but that 'this should not blind us to the apparent necessity of dating the book *very* early in the eleventh century' (63). Simultaneously, Gerritsen, **210**, published an exhaustive description of the manuscript, and affirmed that it was designed as an integral codex. Here the matter does not rest.[3] A full description of the manuscript was also included in Malone's facsimile (**158**), which dates it two decades either side of *c.* 1000.

From the ill-matched style of the scripts, and the poor quality of the illustrations to *Wond*, Sisam, **193**, concluded that the manuscript could not have been produced as a presentation copy for a patron, whether ecclesiastical or lay; for much the same reasons, Dumville suggests that the manuscript was produced in a minor scriptorium. Malone, pursuing the implications of Sisam, and deducing that *Judith* was added about the time of Nowell, regarded interest in the marvellous as the *rationale* underlying the gathering together of *Beowulf* and the three prose pieces (see also Taylor, **196**). Pickles, **167**, considered that V contained material now lost, and expressed doubts concerning theories of a single principle of composition.

---

[1] Sisam, **177**, pointed out that W.J. Sedgefield, ed., *Beowulf* (Manchester: Manchester UP, 1910) xiv, had noted that the first scribe also wrote the texts immediately preceding *Beowulf*, but had not realized the significance of this.

[2] This full-length study was foreshadowed by Kevin S. Kiernan, 'The Eleventh Century Origin of *Beowulf* and the *Beowulf* Manuscript,' *The Dating of Beowulf*, ed. Colin Chase (Toronto: U of Toronto P, 1981) 9–21. Although this collection of papers, both for and against the 11th century dating, is central to the study of *Beowulf*, the almost complete absence of reference to *Alex* and *Wond* outrules inclusion in the annotations. Among those in disagreement with Kiernan is Richard W. Clement, 'Codicological Consideration in the *Beowulf* Manuscript,' *Proceedings of the Illinois Medieval Association*, ed. Roberta Bux Bosse et al. (Macomb, IL: Western Illinois UP, 1984) 13–27. See also Torkar, 1986, who outlines some of the issues and publications involved in the controversy.

[3] Johan Gerritsen, *'Have With You to Lexington!' The Beowulf Manuscript and Beowulf* (Dordrecht: Foris, 1989), has not been sighted.

For ME glosses on f. 102v of *Alex* see Leake, 1962.[4] Full bibliographical information on manuscript studies, generally focused on *Beowulf*, can be found in the most recent major studies.

Tiberius B.v

T is a handsomely written miscellany, which contains *inter alia* Cicero, Aratea, and the Periegesis of Priscian. Apart from *Wond*, the only OE texts are a translation of Bede's *De temporibus*, and a list of popes, emperors, bishops and English kings (which appears to date from the time of Archbishop Sigeric, 989–95); there are also two short scribal notes. The OE of *Wond* is in the same hand as the Latin, in a small round neat script which Ker dates second quarter of the 11th century. He dates the manuscript s. xi[1], and assigns it to 'some important centre, perhaps Winchester.' It was at Battle Abbey in the 12th century, where annals and documents were added (Nero D.ii, ff. 238–41). The order of the volume differed in the 16th or 17th centuries; the Nero folios occupied first place and were immediately followed by *Wond*. There are descriptions of the manuscript in the two facsimiles, James, **157**, and McGurk, **159**; the latter dates the manuscript *c.* 1050 and assigns it to Christ Church, Canterbury. T is lavishly illustrated; James speculated that it may have been descended from the illustrated Cosmography that Bishop Ceolfrith gave Aldfrith of Northumbria in exchange for some lands in the 7th century and/or the volume which Archbishop Koaena of York mentions in a letter to Lull as having writing and pictures and being hard to copy.

ILLUSTRATIONS, DESCRIPTION, DATE AND PROVENANCE; RELATIONSHIP OF V, T AND BODLEY 614

Wond in V and T is accompanied by illustrations of fabulous people, monsters, animals and plant and architectural motifs. T is closely related to a sequence of 39 coloured drawings in Bodley 614; Bodley was copied either directly from T or from its exemplar, *c.* 1120–40. According to Temple, 1976,[5] the pictorial cycle was probably based ultimately on an illustrated Latin version of the Greek prototype; the illustrations in V do not derive from the original on which T depends, but follow a different tradition.

V contains 29 rather rough and incompetent framed and unframed drawings, placed in the text-column, and executed in brown ink and coloured in blue, ochre, shades of brown, and yellow. There is one large composition on two-thirds of a page (f. 101v) illustrating the accompanying story of the gold-digging ants and the gold-seekers (described by Temple, 52). T has 38 outstandingly fine framed drawings illustrating each section of the Latin

---

[4] Jane Acomb Leake, 'Middle English Glosses in the Beowulf-Codex,' *Modern Language Quarterly* 23 (1962): 229–32.

[5] Elżbieta Temple, *Anglo-Saxon Manuscripts 900–1066*, Vol. 2 of *A Survey of Manuscripts Illuminated in the British Isles*, ed. J.J.G. Alexander (London: Miller, 1976), 5 vols. to date, 1975–.

text and its OE translation, usually two to a page, which are firmly and vividly drawn in sepia and red inks on coloured backgrounds and painted in pale ochre, orange, greenish-grey, brown and blue with white in the highlights. There is one full-page composition, showing the magician Mambres at the mouth of Hell (f. 87). All three parts of the volume are illustrated, and were probably executed by one artist; there is, in addition, a Macrobian zone map, and a fine Mappa Mundi (described by Temple, 87). James, **157**, who collates and compares the representations in all three manuscripts, describes T as 'magnificent' and Bodley as 'handsome but tame compared to T.'

Art historians' deductions concerning dating and provenance of illustrations sometimes differ slightly from those of palaeographers.[6] Temple gives the date of V as late 10th century, and says that 'the drawings, in firm outline, are vaguely reminiscent of manuscripts of the Æthelstan period and, in the highly formalized vegetation, resemble the first group of illustrations in the "Caedmon" Genesis.' She dates T second quarter of the 11th century, and considers that stylistic considerations favour connection with Winchester, but that the calendar illustrations (in the first part of the manuscript) show links with Canterbury.

The illustrations of all three manuscripts are reproduced by James, **157**; for the illustrations in V, see Malone, **158**, and for T, see McGurk, **159**, whose comparative study of the illustrations supersedes James. Friedman, **207**, considers that the *Mirabilia* group of manuscripts testify to 'an intense Anglo-Saxon interest in wonders and marvels and help to elucidate the aesthetic milieu of the poem *Beowulf*' (319). He compares the attitudes to the monstrous in V, T and Bodley 614, and suggests that T may have been influenced by *Liber Monstrorum* (not accompanied by illustrations), which, it has been suggested, was known to the *Beowulf* poet (see p. 125 below, 'Anglo-Saxon Knowledge of Alexander Legends').[7] Friedman, **207**, **205**, includes a number of black-and-white reproductions. See also Druce, **183**, and Wittkower, **190**.

Illustrated medieval Alexander literature was catalogued by Ross, **195**. Art historians' interest in the illustrations to *Wond*, especially those in T, makes it impractical to attempt to annotate commentary on the pictorial cycles unless it has figured in bibliographies of textual studies.

EDITIONS AND TRANSLATIONS

Cockayne, **160**, the first editor of the text, printed *Alex* from V and the OE and Latin text of *Wond* from T, with variants from V. Baskervill, **162**,

---

[6] Other studies of the illustrations commonly cited are: Otto Pächt and J.J.G. Alexander, *Illuminated Manuscripts in the Bodleian Library, Oxford*, 3 vols. (Oxford: Clarendon, 1966–73), vol. 3 (1973); C.M. Kauffmann, *Romanesque Manuscripts 1066–1190* (London: Miller, 1975), vol. 3 of *A Survey of Manuscripts Illuminated in the British Isles*, ed. J.J.G. Alexander, 5 vols. to date, 1975–.

[7] See Leslie Whitbread, 'The *Liber Monstrorum* and *Beowulf*,' *Mediaeval Studies* 36 (1974): 434–71, at 452.

who printed *Alex* only, without apparatus, did not consult the manuscript (emendations were suggested by Rypins, **178**, Bradley, **179**, and Klaeber, **172**). The two versions of *Wond* were edited by Knappe, **163**, who printed parallel the OE from V and T and the Latin from T. Rypins, **165**, whose near-diplomatic edition was based on his dissertation, **164** (not sighted), printed *Alex* and *Wond* from V, and the Latin of *Wond* from T. Although his edition reproduces the lineation of the manuscript, it reverses the order in which the texts appear. Both Cockayne and Rypins included a Latin analogue for *Alex*. Cockayne's transcription was not very accurate; nor, in the opinion of Rypins, was Holder's collation of both manuscripts (**170**, **171**). Emendations to Rypins were offered by Gordon, **185**, Swaen, **189**, Burchfield, **191**, Davis, **192** and Malone, **194**.

Rypins's 1924 EETS edition is, unfortunately, the only published edition available. It was out of touch with the most recent scholarship on the Latin textual tradition from the moment that it appeared; subsequent study of the two manuscripts has left it far behind, and its handling of the language is, in contemporary terms, methodologically unsound. There are four dissertation editions of *Wond*. Garrad's critical edition of V (**166**, not sighted) appears to concentrate on phonology and illustrations. Pickles, **167**, also a critical edition of V, with parallel printing of the Latin from T and a Picard translation, is lucid and informative on the textual tradition and compilation of the manuscript; both dissertations contain material whose continued non-publication is to be regretted. Knock's massive polychrome study of the textual tradition (**169**) is best approached through McGurk, **159**, and should not be attempted by the faint-hearted. Gibb, **168** (not sighted), also foregrounding the textual tradition, appears to be the only dissertation editor to consider the OE translations as literary documents.

Alex has been translated into MnE by Davidson and Campbell, **198**, and into Japanese by Haga, **201**. A MnE translation of *Wond* is included in Gibb's dissertation.

LANGUAGE, DATE AND PROVENANCE OF THE ORIGINAL

Knappe, **163** (who accepted the mid-11th century dating for *Alex* and *Wond* proposed by Wülcker, **13**, and dated the Life of Christopher to the 11th century), compared the language of *Wond* in V and T, and concluded that an Anglian original has been rendered into late WS, with more Anglian forms being allowed to remain standing in V. Braun, **174** (not sighted), rejected the possibility of an Anglian origin, and located Alexander on the Kentish border. Rypins, **182**, argued that the first scribe of V was more accurate than the second, and preserved the dialect forms of his exemplar (Hulbert, **187**, disagreed). Rypins was therefore in agreement with Knappe that the Anglian element was present in the exemplar of *Wond* as well as in the exemplar of *Alex* (whereas the Life of Christopher's exemplar was pure WS); he drew no conclusions concerning manuscript provenance. Rypins emphasized the lexicographical value of both texts; both in his edition, and in an early article which summarizes the substance of the examination of language in his edition (**165**), he gives a list of lexically significant items. Two other early dissertation studies of language are referred to by Pickles, 167 (Heschl, **175A**, and Garrad, **166**).

Sisam, **193**, in 1962, argued that the originals of *Wond* and *Alex* were of an early date (the period beginning with the reign of Alfred and ending with Æthelstan), and of Mercian provenance. Pickles is in guarded agreement. Sisam's early dating of the original translation has been called into question; see DiMarco, **200**, and, as an indication of the doubts that surround linguistic identification of Mercian provenance, see Bately, **564**. See also Reynolds, **193A**.

SOURCES

Owing to the great popularity of Alexander legends in the Middle Ages, the textual tradition is highly complicated, and much remains obscure. The explanatory catalogue of Cary, 1956,[8] though in some respects obsolete, remains a useful aid to the identification of some of the various recensions and permutations referred to by textual scholars.

Alexander

In his examination of the origins and development of the *Epistola Alexandri*, Rypins, **165** (drawing on earlier German scholarship), observed that there was no study of the relationship of the 60 Latin manuscripts known to him (listed, xxxiv–xxxv). It is still generally accepted that most fabulous accounts of Alexander in the West ultimately derive from pseudo-Callisthenes, probably an Alexandrian production of the 3rd century, which was translated into Latin, *c.* 340, by Julius Valerius; a 9th century abridgement of the Julius Valerius translation, known as the (*Zacher*) *Epitome*, became the most popular source of the Alexander legend. The *Epistola Alexandri* on which the OE is based derived either from pseudo-Callisthenes or from the somewhat fuller version of Julius Valerius, and circulated as an independent, self-contained work. The earliest surviving manuscripts of the *Epistola Alexandri* date from the 9th century (and only a few others pre-date *Alex*), but it is widely held that the *Epistola* came into existence not later than the 7th century.

The Latin version used by the OE translator of *Alex* has still not been identified, and the attempt is regarded by Pickles, **167**, as fruitless. It was certainly not the version represented by Nero D.viii, which Cockayne, **160**, printed in his edition of *Alex*, nor was it that of CCC Oxford 82, which Rypins printed, as Rypins himself was aware. Hamilton, **186**, had earlier suggested that one of the three 9th century manuscripts (Leiden, Vossianus lat. Q.20) should be accepted as the nearest source.

---

[8] George Cary, *The Medieval Alexander*, ed. D.J.A. Ross (Cambridge: Cambridge UP, 1956).

A critical edition of the *Epistola* was undertaken by Boer, 1953, based on 28 of the 67 manuscripts known to him, which 28 manuscripts he divided into four groups (his handling of the textual tradition is brief).[9] DiMarco, **200**, suggested that the OE translator's exemplar combined features of two of Boer's family groups.

Wonders

Identification of the Letter of Pharasmanes as the textual tradition to which *Wond* belongs was impeded by the fact that scholars in the area had only limited access to one another's publications. Early attempts to identify the source of *Wond* were made by Knappe, **163**, and by Förster, **173**, who presented evidence that the source of *Wond* was ultimately Greek. Knappe tabled correspondences with the *Epistola*, a number of classical writers, and *De monstris et beluis*. Rypins, in his 1924 edition, echoed Knappe in stating that *Wond* was ultimately derived from the *Epistola* and many other classical sources. In 1928, Pfister, **188**, pointed out that the Anglo-Saxon versions were not unique as Rypins (as well as Cockayne and Knappe) had supposed, but a version of the Letter of Pharasmanes (or Fermes) in which impersonal narrative had replaced the epistolary form. One version of this, *Fermes*, had been printed by Omont, 1913.[10] Omont, for his part, had believed that the text he printed was unique, but the following year Faral, **176**, demonstrated the incorrectness of this by printing two analogues, (*Epistola*) *Premonis* and *Otia* (the latter included in the work of a 13th century English writer, Gervase of Tilbury).

James, **157**, whose facsimile of the text appeared in 1929, had seen Omont, 1913, and realized that the source of the OE was a Letter of Pharasmanes which had lost its epistolary structure. James had also discovered that there was a version of the Letter of Pharasmanes by Gervase of Tilbury, but the work of Faral, which anticipated this discovery, and the work of Pfister, came to his attention only as the facsimile was going to print; he was thus unable to take account of their findings in the main body of his work.

Relationship of the V and T texts of Wond: *Relation to the Latin* Mirabilia *in* T

Rypins, **165**, considered that the two OE texts had derived independently from a common archetype (see above for the independence of the pictorial cycles). Gordon, **185**, disagreed. Although Rypins did not know of the existence of the Letter of Pharasmanes, he was certain that V was not a translation of the Latin in T. He also doubted whether the OE in T

---

[9] W. Walther Boer, ed., *Epistola Alexandri ad Aristotelem*, Beiträge zur klassischen Philologie 50 (The Hague: Excelsior, 1953; Meisenhem am Glanz: Hain, 1973). Over 100 full or fragmentary copies, 9th–15th centuries, were known to D.J.A. Ross, 'A Check-List of MSS of Three Alexander Texts,' *Scriptorium* 10 (1956): 127–32.

[10] H. Omont, 'Lettre à L'Empereur Adrien sur les merveilles de l'Asie,' *Bibliothèque de l'École des Chartes* 74 (1913): 507–15.

was a translation of the Latin it accompanies; Sisam, **193**, considered that the OE in T had been added after the Latin text and illustrations were complete. Pfister, **188**, studied the textual history of the Letter of Pharasmanes, showing that it had assumed a number of different forms; he was unable to determine conclusively whether the OE translations were based on the Latin in T or a version closer to other extant versions of the Letter. James, however, assumed that the OE versions were closely related, and offered a reconstructed source based on T and Bodley 614.

More recent textual studies (the dissertations of Pickles, **167**, Gibb, **168**, and Archibald, **169**; see also McGurk, **159**) are particularly concerned with the relationship between *Wond* and the Latin analogues which were unknown to Rypins; other works have been added to the three to which Faral, **176**, drew attention, including a French (Picard) translation, whose significance for the reconstruction of the text of *Wond* was first recognized by Pickles.

ME AND OTHER VERNACULAR VERSIONS

The *Epistola*, though much copied, was not the source most frequently drawn on, and the only full ME translation is found in Worcester Cathedral F.172, ff. 138r–46v (mid-15th century), edited by DiMarco and Perelman, **200**, who list other ME versions influenced by the *Epistola*.

ANGLO-SAXON KNOWLEDGE OF ALEXANDER LEGENDS; *LIBER MONSTRORUM*

Familiarity with Alexander legends in England dating from the reign of Alfred, a concomitant of Sisam's early dating of the originals of *Alex* and *Wond*, had already been argued by Hamilton, **186**; the evidence, chiefly references to Alexander in Orosius and a letter from Alcuin to Charlemagne, is reassessed by Pickles, **167**. Cf. Förster, **180**, who associated transmission of the material with the Benedictine Reform.

Study of the *Liber Monstrorum*, particularly the establishment of its date and provenance, is widely regarded as likely to cast light on the compilation of the *Beowulf* Codex and the works it contains. The *Liber Monstrorum* (prefaced with an address by the anonymous author to an eminent person who commissioned the work) mentions the *Epistola* several times, is closely related to the *Mirabilia*, and refers to Beowulf's uncle, Hygelac; the view that it is a 7th/8th century English work, possibly by Aldhelm, has long been entertained but is not universally accepted (see Pickles, Gibb, **168**, and Archibald, **169**).[11]

There has been a good deal of comparative study of the medieval European vernacular literature of Alexander as, for instance, in the publications of the Groningen University Alexander Project, which include Aerts,

---

[11] See Whitbread, 1974; Michael Lapidge, ' "Beowulf", Aldhelm, the "Liber Monstrorum" and Wessex,' *Studi Medievali* 3rd ser. 23 (1982): 151–92.

1978.[12] This volume is well spoken of as a history of the Alexander legend, but does not appear to contain any discussion of the OE. Comparative references to *Alex* and *Wond* in studies devoted to the Alexander material in ME occasionally register in bibliographies of OE literature (see Hahn, **203**), but it is likely that some comparative discussion has been overlooked.

STUDY OF THE TEXTS AND CONTEXTS

Alex and *Wond* have not been widely studied as literary texts. For *Alex* and *Wond*, as for *OE ApT*, no exact source can be identified, despite the fact that the Latin textual tradition to which *Alex* belongs is relatively well represented by surviving manuscripts, and despite the fact that *Wond* in T is accompanied by a Latin text. Whereas Goolden's readily accessible reconstructed Latin source for *OE ApT* (however assailable in principle) has encouraged comparison of *OE ApT* and the Latin *Historia* (**101**), there is no single text either of the *Epistola* or of the Letter to Pharasmanes that has established status as a closely approximate source, and versions of the Letter to Pharasmanes (apart from the Latin of T) are not very accessible. A replacement for Rypins's edition of the texts, now outdated in most respects and a penance to use, is badly needed; a new edition able to clarify the OE texts' relationship to the Latin textual tradition would undoubtedly do much to encourage literary study of *Alex* and *Wond*. Four dissertations, three of them editions of *Wond* (see pp. 121–2 above, 'Editions and Translations') account for most of the original research undertaken since the appearance of Sisam, **193**, in 1953.

Alex is held to be a much freer translation than *Wond* (none of the three translators is thought to have been very good at Latin); it is not a full translation of the *Epistola*, and a substantial part of the conclusion is lacking. Sisam, **193**, Butturff, **197** (cf. Wiessmann, **202**), and Donner, **155**, variously interpret the substantive departures as deliberate omissions by the translator; DiMarco, **200**, opined that the conclusion was missing in the translator's exemplar. Detailed verbal comparisons of *Wond* and its Latin analogues are included in the dissertation editions of *Wond*.

The lack of established Latin texts against which the OE versions can be evaluated has likewise inhibited exploration of their cultural significance, although Sisam, **177**, drew attention long ago to their importance in the history of literary taste by showing that the dating of the first scribal hand of *Beowulf* carried with it the implication that interest in the marvellous and exotic, generally associated with the 12th century development of a 'romance mode,' was already current in the late OE period (see also Gradon, **138**). Friedman, **207**, however, has advanced understanding of Anglo-Saxon interest in the marvellous by a comparative examination of

---

[12] W.J. Aerts, Jos. M.M. Hermans, and Elizabeth Visser, eds., *Alexander the Great in the Middle Ages: Ten Studies in the Last Days of Alexander in Literary and Historical Writing*, Mediaevalia Groningana 1 (Nijmegen: Alfa, 1978).

the representation of monsters in the manuscript illustrations of V, T and Bodley 614; the comparisons he draws with *Beowulf* are of particular interest, in view of the fact that interest in the marvellous has sometimes been claimed as the motivating impulse behind the appearance of *Alex* and *Wond* (and Life of Christopher) in the same manuscript as the epic poem. Friedman suggests that the visual arts have generally received insufficient attention from literary historians of the Anglo-Saxon period, and urges that 'by studying contemporary visual images.... we can find those relationships that explain and illuminate the broader tradition, the deeper texture, and the wider significance of a culture whose achievements have not yet had their final description' (338–9). Not all readers of *Beowulf* would agree with him that the 'ethnocentric and rhetorical fear and distaste' which he discerns, to varying degrees, in the illustrations of all three manuscripts, also characterize the *Beowulf* poet's attitude to the Grendel family, but his study unquestionably validates his claim for the value of inter-disciplinary study.

Temple's observations on the style of the illustrations to *Wond* in the *Beowulf* Codex (see above) perhaps suggest, in view of the uncertainty still surrounding its provenance, that palaeographers might also find it useful to extend their consideration of the visual elements in V. Recent study of the *Beowulf* Codex does not appear to have called into question Sisam's conclusion that, whereas T has the appearance of a presentation copy, V was intended for the use of a monastic community. Whether it follows that the translations of the Alexander material in V (not to mention *Beowulf*, and not forgetting the Life of Christopher, or *Judith*) are adequately explained by the hypothesis that a monastery with a small scriptorium was indulging its interest in monsters is another matter—but if so, the precise nature of its interest in what were, from an orthodox point of view, the aberrant forms of creation, becomes crucially important. The contents of T suggest that, at Christ Church (or possibly Winchester), translation of *Wond* was part of the cultivation of classical learning and cosmological knowledge. Friedman finds surprising the appearance of 'three luxurious Anglo-Saxon programmes of secular illustration' which have 'no utilitarian reasons for their existence and treat pagan subject matter without the justification of didactic intent' (319). Discussions of the monstrous in *Wond* are found in Gibb, **168**, Wittkower, **190**, Wiessmann, **202**, Friedman, **205** and **207**, and Campbell, **210A**. Campbell, who takes issue with Gibb, and concludes with chapters on Columbus and Raleigh, makes explicit the highly topical connection with later European colonial encounters which is implicit in Friedman.

ALEXANDER'S LETTER; WONDERS OF THE EAST: ANNOTATIONS

SEE ALSO Anderson, **17**; Baker, **126**; Donner, **145**; Jordan, **447**

FACSIMILES

157 James, Montague Rhodes. *Marvels of the East: A Full Reproduction of the Three Known Copies.* Roxburghe Club Publications 191. Oxford: Roxburghe Club, 1929.

Monochrome facsimile, 36–51, of: V, ff. 98v–106v; T, ff. 78v–87v; Bodley 614, ff. 36–51.

The Preface speculates that T had 'an ancient and royal pedigree.' Bodley is an indirect copy of T; V copies another model. The Introduction gives a brief account of the three manuscripts (their contents and history), 1–8; the sources and date of the Latin text in T, 9–11. *Wond* is derived from, but not identical to, Fermes's Letter to Hadrian, 4th/5th century, probably of Greek origin, also drawn on by Gervase of Tilbury in *Otia Imperialia*. There follows a discussion of the Kalendar in Bodley, 12–14; a Latin text, constructed from T and Bodley, 15–24; notes on the text, especially origins of mythological themes, 24–32. In 'Epistola Premonis, etc.,' 33–40, James explains that Faral, **176**, came to his attention after his introduction had been typeset; James thinks that T and the *Epistola Premonis* of the burnt Strassburg manuscript printed by Faral (reprinted by James, 37–40) may have a common ancestor from which T is more directly descended. Other issues raised by Faral, including the relationship of Fermes and *De Monstris et Belluis* are discussed; parallels between Fermes and Gervase are tabled at 41–50. Description of the illustrations, 51–62. James identifies a total of 50 visual topics in the three manuscripts and compares representations. The archetype of Bodley, 'handsome but tame' compared to the 'magnificent' T, was probably the parent or sister of T.

158 Malone, Kemp. *The Nowell Codex. British Museum Cotton Vitellius A. XV Second Manuscript.* Early English Manuscripts in Facsimile 12. Copenhagen: Rosenkilde, 1963.

Facsimile of V, ff. 94–209. Contains a full description of the Nowell codex: foliations, 12–14; gatherings, 14–16; format, 16–17; transcripts, 17; comparison of the hands of the two scribes, 17–20; capital letters, 20–5; abbreviations, 25–6; accent marks, 26–9; points, 29–32; readings, 32–114 (*Wond*, 35–9, *Alex*, 39–49). Brief description of the texts, 114–17; the illustrations to *Wond*, 117–19; origins and history of the manuscript, 119. Malone observes that the two hands 'differ markedly, though both belong to the insular tradition and to the period A.D. 980–1020' (17). In his remarks on the origins of the manuscript, Malone, who considers that *Judith* was added in Nowell's time or a little earlier, follows Sisam, **193**, in regarding the compiler as a man interested in wonders.

159 McGurk, P., D.N. Dumville, M.R. Godden and Ann Knock. *An Eleventh Century Anglo-Saxon Illustrated Miscellany. British Library Cotton Tiberius B. V Part 1. Together with Leaves from British Library Cotton Nero D. II*. Early English Manuscripts in Facsimile 21. Copenhagen: Rosenkilde, 1983.

Monochrome facsimile of T; 18 plates include colour reproductions, illustrations from V and Bodley 614.

Introduction includes description of contents of the manuscript, 15–24; manuscript history, 25–7; palaeography and illumination, 28–39. In 'Marvels of the East,' 88–103, Knock examines the textual relations of T, 88–95. She discusses the manuscript tradition with particular reference to the validity of Pitra's text of *Fermes* (Paris, 1884) as a witness to early versions of the text, 89–90, and the light it casts on cruces, 90–1. Knock rejects the suggestion that *Mirabilia* was an English composition (cf. Sisam, **193**), analyses the misplaced material, 91–2, and argues that Bodley 614 is directly descended from T, corrected on the basis of the OE or the illustrations, 92–5. Textual differences between T and V are tabled. McGurk's examination of pictorial relationships, 96–103, argues that V differs from T and Bodley 614 in its iconography and in its placing of illustrations (descriptive table of comparison, 99–103; plates IV–VIII). V and T suggest two cycles of illustrations, which are unlikely to have been English inventions; T's model may have been an illustrated book of the Rheims school. Conclusion, 107–9, by McGurk. It is difficult to determine at what stage in the transmission of the Latin text the OE version was added; also unclear is the relationship of the OE text in T and V, and the purpose of T (like *ByrM*, it presents 'a not very clearly defined section of knowledge,' 109). There are no certain palaeographical or art-historical pointers to T's place of origin, around the second quarter of the 11th century, but internal evidence points to Christ Church, Canterbury.

EDITIONS

160 Cockayne, T. Osvaldvs. *Narrativncvlæ Anglice Conscriptæ*. London: Smith, 1861.

Prints *Alex* from V, 1–33. Also prints *Epistola Alexandri*, 51–62, from Cotton Nero D.viii, collated with Royal MSS 13 A.i, 15 C.vi, 12 C.iv, 13 A.v.

Prints *Wond* from T, with variants from V, 33–9. Also prints *Mirabilia* from T, 62–6.

Editorial Notes (in Latin): *Alex*, 67–76; *Wond*, 76–80.

161 Baskervill, William Malone. *The Anglo-Saxon Version of the 'Epistola Alexandri ad Aristotelem'*. Diss. U Leipzig. Halle: Karras, 1881.

Not sighted.

162 Baskervill, William Malone. 'Epistola Alexandri ad Aristotelem. MS. Cott. Vitellius, A.XV.' *Anglia* 4 (1881): 139–67.

Prints *Alex*; based on Wülcker's collation of V with Cockayne, **160**. Text only.

163 Knappe, Fritz. *Das angelsächsische Prosastück Die Wunder des Ostens: Uberlieferung, Quellen, Sprache und Text nach beiden Handschriften*. Diss. U Greifswald. Berlin: Bernstein, 1906.

Prints parallel V and T, and the Latin from T, 43–64.

Introduction examines: manuscript contents, 5–9; relationship of the three versions, 9–12; sources, 12–20; language, 21–42.

Knappe shows that the OE of T is not a close translation of the Latin; V and T are not directly related. The examination of sources concludes that the author of the original of the Latin in T was well acquainted with *Epistola Alexandri*, and that a large part agrees verbally with the 6th century *De Monstris et Belluis*; parallels with a number of other works are tabled. The comparative examination of the language of V and T concludes that an Anglian original has been rendered into late WS, with more Anglian forms being allowed to remain standing in V; Knappe endorses Wülcker's mid-11th century dating (**13**, 505).

164 Rypins, Stanley I. 'Three Anglo-Saxon Prose Tracts of MS. Cotton Vitellius A. XV with Their Sources and a Study of Their Characteristics.' Diss. Harvard U, 1918. 2 vols.

Not sighted. According to Pulsiano, 1988, 764, not all of the material contained in the dissertation appears in Rypins, **165**.

165 Rypins, Stanley. *Three Old English Prose Texts in MS. Cotton Vitellius A xv*. EETS 161. London: Oxford UP, 1924.

Prints *Alex*, 1–50; near-diplomatic edition of V, collated with Baskervill, **162**, Cockayne, **160**, Holder, **170** and **171**. Also prints *Epistola Alexandri*, from CCC Oxford 82, with variants from other manuscripts, 79–100.

Prints *Wond*, 51–67; near-diplomatic edition of V, collated with Knappe, **163**, Cockayne, **160**, Holder, **170** and **171**. Also prints *De Rebus in Oriente*

Mirabilibus, from T, with variants from Knappe, **163**, Cockayne, **160**, 101–7. (Also edits *Life of St Christopher*, OE and Latin.) Facsimile of f. 125r, frontispiece.

Introduction, vii–l; Notes, 111–14; Glossarial index, 115–48.

Description of the manuscript includes analysis of foliation, together with examination of the script and the orthography. Rypins points out that all three prose texts in V are in the hand of the first *Beowulf* scribe, and must therefore be of the same date. The first scribe, he argues, is more accurate than the second, and preserves the dialect forms of his exemplar (unlike Braun, **174**, Rypins considers that the Anglian element was present in the exemplar for *Wond* and *Alex*, whereas *Life of Christopher*'s exemplar was pure WS). Rypins gives a brief survey of the origins of the *Epistola*, lists extant versions, and explains that he prints CCC Oxford 82 (the unique representative of the intermediate stage between the Julius Valerius translation and the *Epitome*) 'because its text is superior to that of other MSS., and illustrates the Anglo-Saxon version as adequately as any known variant' (xxxvii). He discusses the relation of V and T; they are independently derived from a common source and it is questionable whether *Wond* in T is based on the Latin there. The source is a compilation of fabulous classical material, which makes use of the *Epistola*. [For reviews see Gordon, **185**.]

166 **Garrad, B.L.** 'The Wonders of the East: The Anglo-Saxon Prose Translation from Cotton MS Vitellius A XV, Collated with the Text of Cotton MS Tiberius B V vol. 1.' Diss. U of London, 1925.

Not sighted. Cited Knock, **159**, 89. According to Pickles, **167**, who gives the title as 'An Edition of the Wonders of the East from the Cotton Manuscript Vitellius A XV Collated with Tiberius B V,' Garrad analyses grammar and phonology at length; he detects, in the illustrations, the influence of continental schools during the Ottonian Renaissance, and finds that the hand in T is almost identical with an 11th century copy of the Gospels in Pembroke College, Cambridge (James, *Catalogue*, 1905, no. 302).

167 **Pickles, John Drayton.** 'Studies in the Prose Texts of the Beowulf Manuscript.' Diss. Cambridge U, 1971.

Parallel edition of *Wond* from V (emended from T); Latin from T (emended from Bodley 614); Picard translation from Brussels, Royal Library, 14562, ff. 5v–6v, 61–82. Variants (OE from T and Latin from Bodley) in apparatus. Notes, 83–7.

Introduction, 34–56, details manuscripts and editions, 34, 38–9; examines the Latin Paradoxographic tradition, 35–40, textual and pictorial relationships of T, V and Bodley 614, 41–7, character of the translation, 47–51, language, 51–2, illustrations and script, 52–3, dating and provenance, 53–5. Ch. 1, 'The Manuscript,' 1–14, describes V (following Malone, **158**), its history, and scholarship since 1815. Ch. 2, 'The Life of Saint Christopher,'

15–33. Ch. 4, 'The Letter of Alexander,' 88–119, surveys transmission, editions of the *Epistola* and *Alex*, 88–107, character and style of the translation, particularly omissions, additions and word-pairing, 108–12; origins of the translation, 112–17. Ch. 5, 'The Prose Texts and Old English Lexicography,' 120–9, tables corrections to dictionaries (including *BT*) and Rypins, **165**; remarks on the diction. Ch. 6, 'Theories Concerning the Compilation of the Manuscript, and Conclusion,' 130–41, favours Sisam, **193**; a single principle of compilation is outruled and V may have contained material now lost. *Alex* is certainly Mercian, *Wond* may be; close dating is impossible, a 9th century origin is preferred. Appendix A, Corrections to Rypins, **165**. Appendix B, *The Liber Monstrorum*, 145–52, surveys scholarship, its origins and links with *Beowulf* and *Mirabilia*. Copyright notice could be construed to prohibit more detailed annotation.

168 Gibb, Paul Allen. '*Wonders of the East*: A Critical Edition and Commentary.' *DAI* 38 (1977): 2107A–8A. [Diss. Duke U, 1977. Dir. Holger Olof Nygard.]

Dissertation not sighted. According to *DAI*, Gibb edits OE and Latin texts (with emendations on the basis of previously unknown evidence); includes translation, explanatory notes, and glossary, together with closely related texts, largely from the continent, which descend from the same ancestral *Letter of Farasmenes*. Attention is given to the textual history and development of the Letter, early Christian and medieval attitudes towards monsters and the extent to which medieval audiences gave credence to the information on geography and natural history offered by the text; Gibb argues that the ancestral text was highly structured, written as literature, not as science or entertainment.

169 Knock, Ann Elizabeth. 'Wonders of the East: A Synoptic Edition of The Letter of Pharasmanes and the Old English and Old Picard Translations.' Diss. U of London, 1982.

Synoptic text, 390–515, presented in interlinear form, with colour coding of individual texts; employs manuscript-based section divisions. Appendices, 873–1040, list variant readings within a version. Section-by-section Commentary, 517–872, considers evidence for the wording of the ancestral text, the Classical and Medieval analogues, and discusses points of interest. Includes glossaries for the vernacular texts.

Section 1, 19–358, examines the textual tradition of the Letter of Pharasmanes ('*Mirabilia* and the OE *Wonders*,' 57–164); date of composition in Greek, attribution to Pharasmanes, the attempt at verisimilitude and the relationship to itinerary literature, date of translation into Latin and subsequent development of two groups. *Mirabilia* is shown to have been influenced by the accompanying picture cycles. The major variation between the OE texts is traced to retranslation following an accident to an antecedent manuscript. Phonological studies of both vernacular versions are presented.

The use made by *Liber Monstrorum* and *Historia de Preliis* of material from the Letter is examined, and the hypothesis of Aldhelm's authorship of the *Liber Monstrorum* is reconsidered.

COMMENTARY

170 **Holder, Alfred.** 'Collationen zu angelsächsischen Werken. II. *Epistola Alexandri ad Aristotelem.*' *Anglia* 1 (1878): 507–12.

Collates Cockayne, **160**, with V.

171 **Holder, Alfred.** 'Collationen zu angelsächsischen Werken. I. *De rebus in oriente mirabilibus.*' *Anglia* 1 (1878): 331–7.

Collates Cockayne, **160**, with V and T.

172 **Klaeber, Fr.** 'Notes on Old English Prose Texts.' *Modern Language Notes* 18 (1903): 241–7.

Three emendations to Baskervill, **162**, at 246–7. 'As Cockayne's edition of the Old English text, together with the Latin version, cannot be consulted here, the remarks on lines 584 f. and 758 ff. [ed. Baskervill, **162**] have merely the value of guesses' (247).

173 **Förster, Max.** 'Zur altenglischen Mirabilien-Version.' *Archiv für das Studium der neueren Sprachen und Literaturen* 117 (1906): 367–70.

Förster observes that *Wond* combines Alexander material with accounts of fabulous monsters. He would relate it, not to the Alexander legend, but to the collections of anecdotes concerning natural, geographical and historical marvels that were characteristic of the late Grecian era (the so-called 'Paradoxographen'). The OE works betray their ultimately Greek origin by reckoning distances in 'stadien,' as well as in the term 'cenocephali,' and the countries mentioned were within the Greek cultural orbit. In this article, Förster (cf. **180**) accepts that *Wond* in V is 12th century, T mid-11th century, and states that both are clearly a translation of the Latin in T.

174 **Braun, Adolf.** *Lautlehre der angelsächsischen Version der 'Epistola Alexandri ad Aristotelem'.* Diss. U Würzburg, 1911. Borna-Leipzig: Noske, 1911.

Not sighted. According to Rypins, **165**, locates *Alex* on the Kentish border and rejects the possibility of an Anglian original.

175 **Bright, James W.** 'An Idiom of the Comparative in Anglo-Saxon.' *Modern Language Notes* 27 (1912): 181–3.

Bright argues that the construction that earlier scholars regarded as an anacoluthic comparative with *ponne*, which chiefly occurs in biblical translations, represents 'subordination of idiom to a reverential transference of the exact word' (181), although its use in *Beowulf*, lines 69–70, is difficult to explain. In his view, both prose examples of the construction can be eliminated; the sole example of *swiþe* followed by *ponne*, in *Alex* [ed. Rypins, **165**, 26/9–10] probably arises from scribal error (*swiþe* for *swiþor*).

175A Heschl, Sigmund. 'Beiträge zur Untersuchung der altenglischen Epistola Alexandri ad Aristotelem.' Diss. U Graz, 1913.

Not sighted. According to Pickles, **167**, the dissertation (handwritten), is independent of Braun, **174**, and anticipates Sisam's conclusions (**193**) concerning the Anglian origin of *Alex*.

176 Faral, Edmond. 'Une source latine de l'Histoire d'Alexander *La lettre sur les merveilles de l'Inde*.' *Romania* 43 (1914): 199–215, 353–70.

At 199–215, Faral prints parallel three texts which he identifies as versions of the Letter of Fermes: (1) 'Fermes divo Adriano Salutem,' from Paris, Bibliothèque Nationale nouv. acq. lat. 1065 (10th/11th century); reprinted from H. Omont, *Bibliothèque de l'École des chartes* 74 (1913): 507–15, who was unaware that there were related versions; (2) 'Epistola Premonis Regis ad Trajanum Imperatorem,' from Strassburg, C.iv.15 (8th/9th century), burnt, ed. Graff, *Diutiska* (1829), 2: 192 ff; (3) Gervase of Tilbury, *Otia Imperialia*, ed. Leibniz, *Scriptores rerum brunsvicensium*, 1: 984 ff. At 353–6, Faral prints extracts from the Latin of *Wond* in T (from Cockayne, **160**); argues that *De Monstris et Belluis* borrows from the Letter to Fermes and that the texts are ultimately of Greek origin; describes the Letter.

177 Sisam, Kenneth. 'The "Beowulf" Manuscript.' *Modern Language Review* 11 (1916): 335–7.

Sisam aims to dispel 'the intolerable confusion in the dating of the prose pieces preceding *Beowulf*' (336), variously dated 11th or 12th century. The two hands of the first codex of Vitellius A.xv are mid-12th century hands; the two hands of the *Beowulf* codex are usually dated *c*. 1000, 'with good reason' (335). Literary history must be brought into line with this date. The appearance of Oriental themes in English literature has been placed at the very end of the OE period. But the three prose pieces are undoubtedly 'in a manuscript which is certainly not an autograph, and which seems to represent originals carrying back well into the tenth century. It would appear, then, that the introduction of these Oriental themes belongs to the great period of Continental influence which began with the tenth century, and not to the later period of Norman influence' (337). To date only *Judith* has been drawn into the discussion of the language of the scribes of *Beowulf*. 'But here, in the first hand, are prose texts of four times the bulk of *Judith*, free to some extent from the circumstances which make poetical texts so confusing in forms, and probably themselves due to more than one author. The detailed comparison of one with another, and of all with *Beowulf*, cannot fail to throw light on the characteristics of the first scribe, and on the explanation of the more obscure dialect forms in *Beowulf'* (337). Sisam instances genitive plurals in *-o* ('rare in careful WS texts,' 337), which occur both in *Beowulf*, first hand, and in *Alex*.

178 **Rypins, Stanley I.** 'Notes on *Epistola Alexandri ad Aristotelem*.' *Modern Language Notes* 32 (1917): 94–5.

Emendations to Baskervill, **162** (further to Klaeber, **172**).

179 **Bradley, Henry, and K. Sisam.** 'Textual Notes on the Old English "Epistola Alexandri." ' *Modern Language Review* 14 (1919): 202–5.

Emendations to Baskervill, **162**.

180 **Förster, Max.** *Die Beowulf-Handschrift*. Berichte über die Verhandlungen der Sächsischen Akademie der Wissenschaften zu Leipzig, Philologisch-historische Klasse 71. Leipzig: Teubner, 1919.

Förster examines all of Vitellius A.xv [i.e., Southwick Codex and *Beowulf* Codex]; foliation, 4–10; folding, 10–23; script, 23–36; date of the script, 36–53; provenance, 54–7; manuscript history, 57–66; contents, 66–89. He identifies two distinct manuscripts, both written in two different hands. He dates the first of these second quarter of the 12th century, and suggests that it was written at St Mary's in Southwick. He accepts a *c*. 1000 date for the two hands of the *Beowulf* Codex, and [not having seen Sisam, **177**] points out (at 44–6) that, because *Alex*, *Wond* and *Life of Christopher* are in the same hand, they cannot be of a late date. Förster draws the conclusion that, despite the claims of literary historians, oriental themes must have been introduced before the Conquest; he relates this evidence of unusually early familiarity with late Greek material (via Latin) to the Benedictine Reform.

181 **Rypins, Stanley I.** 'The "*Beowulf*" Codex.' *Modern Philology* 17 (1920): 541–7.

Rypins first explains the origins of divergent editorial foliation. Three leaves ignored in the earliest numbering of the manuscript were included in later foliations; one of these leaves was subsequently removed to Royal 13, D.i. Further, Cockayne, **160**, and Baskervill, **162**, took account of the fact that, in the earliest binding, ff. 110–17 occupied the position that should have been held by ff. 118–25. The latest binder has restored these folios to their proper position. The important fact that the three prose texts are all the work of the first hand in *Beowulf* has been noted only by Sisam, **177**; possibly because the scribe's hand 'varies from page to page so that, to the unaccustomed eye, it may often seem to be the work of more than one writer' (546). Rypins considers that the identity of the scribe of the first three works is implied by Wanley's *Catalogue*, and argues that shared peculiarities in the formation of certain letters (*k*, *s*, *æg* ligature, *y*, and capital *M*) are critical for identification. In addition, there are indications that the three prose pieces and *Beowulf* (in which the scribe breaks off) once formed a book by themselves. The implication is that since *Beowulf* 'is accepted by all authorities as a work of about 1000' (547), the three prose texts, variously dated, must be strictly contemporary with it. [According to Greenfield and Robinson, 195, revised version in *Colophon* 10 (1932), [9]–[12].]

182 Rypins, Stanley I. 'A Contribution to the Study of the Beowulf Codex.' *PMLA* 36 (1921): 167–85.

Rypins argues that the first scribe of *Beowulf* (who was also responsible for the three prose texts) gives conclusive evidence of his accuracy, and that the second gives equally certain proof of his unreliability. [Substantially reproduced in Rypins, **165**.]

183 Druce, G.C. 'An Account of the Μυρμηκολέων or Ant-Lion.' *Antiquaries Journal* 3 (1923): 347–64.

Druce examines the development of the ant-lion (mentioned in the Greek text of Job 4.11) in the west (derived from Gregory's *Moralia*), and the (unidentifiable) dog-like Ethiopian/Indian ant, found in literature of the east, which is described by Herodotus, Nearchus, Megasthenes, Strabo and Pliny, appears in Alexander's Romance, and also figures in western Bestiaries; the illustrations of the ant-lion accompanying *Wond* in T (where there are two illustrations, which follow the text carefully) and in V (where all events are combined into one picture) are reproduced and described at 356–7. 'While the east conceived the ant-lion as a composite animal and blessed it as such, Gregory and those who followed him adopted the view that the ant-lion was simply "the lion among ants," that is, a large ant which preyed upon the smaller' (362).

184 Rypins, Stanley I. 'The Old English *Epistola Alexandri ad Aristotelem*.' *Modern Language Notes* 38 (1923): 216–20.

Rypins draws attention to linguistic peculiarities of *Alex*. The WS is frequently interspersed with Anglian forms; the preposition *in* is found side by side with *on* throughout the text; there are six examples of the -*o* gen. pl. Rypins postulates an Anglian original for *Alex*, drawing support from the fact that Knappe, **163**, attributed *Wond* to an Anglian source. Braun, **174**, who claims that the Anglian forms in *Alex* were introduced by the scribe, fails to take account of the fact that the same scribe copied *Life of Christopher*. Presumably the original of *Life of Christopher* was in WS 'of a very pure type' (219), and thus lent no encouragement to the introduction of Anglian orthography by the copyist. As evidence of the lexicographical importance of *Alex*, Rypins appends 'a lengthy list of words chosen from the text, which for their spelling, their meaning or their rarity deserve special attention' (220). [Substantially reproduced in Rypins, **165**.]

185 **Gordon, E.V.** Rev. of *Three Old English Prose Texts in MS. Cotton Vitellius A xv*, by Stanley Rypins [**165**]. *Year's Work in English Studies* 5 (1924): 67–72.

Gordon argues that it is unlikely that the relative accuracy of the two scribes can ever be determined by examination of the *Beowulf* manuscript alone, and offers some emendations to Rypins, **165**, chiefly based on collation with the Latin. Gordon is also critical of the reliability of the apparatus and the absence of a textual history of *Wond*; he offers, without supporting argument, a stemmatic representation which shows T to be more directly descended than V from a common original. 'There is also reason to suppose that the exemplar of the Vespasian text contained parallel versions in Latin and English, as does the Tiberius manuscript' (71).

186 **Hamilton, George L.** 'Quelques notes sur l'histoire de la légende d'Alexandre le Grand en Angleterre au moyen âge.' *Mélanges de philologie et d'histoire offerts à M. Antoine Thomas*. Paris: Champion, 1927. 195–202.

Hamilton regards *Alex* as confirmation that there was considerable interest in the Alexander romance in the Anglo-Saxon period. Alexander material is first found in vernacular form in the Alfredian translation of Orosius; it appears in the letters of Alcuin and Charlemagne, and the legendary material in 'Parva recapitulatio de eodem Alexandro et de suis' is treated exclusively in manuscripts of English provenance. Hamilton considers that Leyden, Vossianus Latinus Q.20 (9th century) is sufficiently closely related to *Alex* to be regarded as its prototype (198).

187 **Hulbert, James R.** 'The Accuracy of the B-Scribe of "Beowulf."' *PMLA* 43 (1928): 1196–9.

Rypins's case for the greater accuracy of the second scribe (**165** and **182**) is based on an irrelevant examination of *eo* and *io* spellings, and must be abandoned. 'It may well be that A preserves the "linguistic colour" of his texts, but that fact does not prove much concerning a particular detail such as the treatment of *eo* and *io* and some other spellings which were perhaps not in accord with certain scribal habits of his' (1197).

188 **Pfister, Friedrich.** 'Auf den Spuren Alexanders des Grossen in der älteren englischen Literatur.' *Germanisch-romanische Monatsschrift* 16 (1928): 81–6.

Pfister draws attention to the fact that the Latin version of *Wond* in T is not unique, as Cockayne, **160**, and Rypins, **165**, thought, because Faral, **176**, has shown that there are three related texts. Knowledge of these three texts may shed light on the corrupt Latin text of T, and opens the way to study of their relationship. Pfister raises the question of whether the OE

translators based their work on the Latin of T, or whether they referred
to a version closer to one of the other Latin versions. He considers that
a *Mirabilia* text once circulated in the form of a Letter of Alexander, and
that it was known to Albertus Magnus (*De animalibus*, 26.16, ed. Stadler).
There are three references to Alexander in T, two of which occur in the
Strassburg manuscript: the explanation would seem to be that what was
originally a Letter reporting Alexander's observations was turned into an
impersonal narrative (as in T and in Gervase of Tilbury); or into a Letter to
Trajan (in the Strassburg manuscript); or into a Letter to Hadrian (in the
Paris manuscript). [For the Strassburg and Paris manuscripts, see Faral,
176.]

189 Swaen, A.E.H. 'Is *seo hiow* = "Fortune" a Ghost-word?' *Englische Studien*
71 (1936–7): 153–4.

Rypins, **165**, cites *hio*, 'fortune,' in his list of words that are of special
interest, and *BT*, for *hiw, hiow,* 'fortune,' gives *Alex* as the only example.
Swaen argues that there is no reason for this addition to the Anglo-Saxon
copia verborum. *Hiw*, 'appearance,' which appears in Rypins's glossary,
gives very good sense in connection with *wyrd* (10/18–11/3); i.e., 'the aspect
of things,' 'the (favourable) appearance of things.'

190 Wittkower, Rudolf. 'Marvels of the East: A Study in the History of
Monsters.' *Journal of the Warburg and Courtauld Institutes* 5 (1942): 159–
97.

This study of the survival and transmission of ethnographical monsters argues that the Greeks (drawing primarily on Indian epics) gave visual form to
primeval conceptions which, despite greater knowledge of the East, lived on
in pseudo-scientific dress into the 18th century; it includes discussion (166–
71) of the assimilation of the monstrous races to a Christian world view
(with particular reference to Augustine's *De Civitate Dei*, 16.8, Isidore's
Etymologiae, 11.3, and Hrabanus Maurus's *De universo*, 7.7), and of the
pictorial tradition (171–82). The illustrations of T evidently derive from a
different source from the text, because classical monsters are represented
even where the Latin text describes an 'Eastern' monster (e.g., the centaur,
f. 82v). In T the specimen of the race with long ears (f. 83v) has snakelike
ears wound round his arms, whereas the text says that these people 'have
ears like winnowing fans.' V, f. 104r, shows the man with fan-like ears.
These two different pictorial types have their origins in different translations by Greek authors from the Sanskrit; Skylax (6th century BC) speaks
of ears like a winnowing fan, whereas Ktesias (4th century BC) says that
their ears cover their arms as far as the elbows. 'As the Latin authors
[Isidore and Solinus] are in this case general and vague, it must be assumed
that a pictorial formula based on Ktesias's text had been evolved in Greece'
(173). Includes reproductions of T, f. 83v and V, 104r.

191 Burchfield, R.W. 'A Source of Scribal Error in Early Middle English Manuscripts.' *Medium Ævum* 22 (1953): 10–17.

At 14, Burchfield quotes Gordon, **185**, 68, on the misreading of MS *gehuntiaþ* (f. 105v/7) as *tohuntiaþ* by Rypins, **165**, 65, line 7, owing to the fact that *g* is missing and what is left resembles a *t*; there is no reason to assume that *tohuntian* ever existed. [No further reference to *Wond*.]

192 Davis, Norman. ' "Hippopotamus" in Old English.' *Review of English Studies* NS 4 (1953): 141–2.

Rypins, **165**, and earlier editors have not commented on the apparent rendering of Latin *hyppotami* by OE 'mere' in *Alex* (ed. Rypins, 15/20; cf. 84), or on the OE translator's 'unexpectedly precise knowledge of the sex of the hippopotamuses' (141). But the manuscript quite clearly reads 'nicra' not 'mera,' a reading which is consistent with the sequel (16/9–13).

193 Sisam, Kenneth. 'The Compilation of the Beowulf Manuscript.' *Studies in the History of Old English Literature*. Oxford: Clarendon, 1953. 2nd edn. 1962. 65–96.

Sisam argues that, in differing degrees, *Wond* (discussed at 72–83), *Alex* (discussed at 83–93) and *Beowulf*, preserve forms which point to a Mercian dialect, and that they form the core of a compilation, unified by an interest in monsters, which was made no earlier than the mid-10th century, somewhere in Mercia where West-Saxon influences were strong, perhaps at London; the ill-matched hands, poor capitals and 'childish draughtsmanship' of the illustrations to *Wond* are evidence that the codex was not intended as a presentation copy. Consideration of the Latin text of *Wond* and of the relationship of T, V, and Bodley 614, lead to the conclusion that the *Mirabilia* was probably compiled in England in the 8th century and that the illustrations were associated with the Latin text before the translation was made; Sisam assigns the original translation to the period beginning with Alfred and ending with Athelstan, and considers that V is 'the better witness' (83), because T's language has been modernized and the text has sometimes been corrected by reference to the accompanying Latin. The shaky Latin, uncouth translation and martial bias of *Alex* 'accords well with the period of King Alfred's wars' (88). All the texts of the *Beowulf* manuscript have a different textual history, and although *Wond*, *Alex* and *Beowulf* are all 'fairly old,' there is no evidence to support 'the hypothesis that they, or any two of them, make an old nucleus for the collection' (94); *Alex* and *Beowulf* may perhaps have been together for a generation or two.

193A Reynolds, Robert L. 'Note on "Beowulf's" Date and Economic-Social History.' *Studi in onore di Armando Sapori*. Vol. 1. Milan: Istituto editoriale cisalpino, 1957. 175–8. 2 vols.

The argument that the poem was composed in the late 9th century at the earliest, and more probably, at some time in the 10th, is supported by

similarities with monsters in the *Mirabilia*, of which there are adjacent illustrations in T. Grendel is 'drawn directly, formed as to body and characteristic behaviour, from the description of the monster called *Hostis*' (176);
the *Draca* is 'reasonably close' to the *Draco*. Both *Beowulf* and *Wond*,
dated late 9th century by Sisam, **193**, take over the latter name unchanged.
Beowulf translates *Hostis* as *Feond*, and also calls the dragon a *wyrm*: 'This
rather indicates that *Beowulf* was more modern in authorship than the Old
English texts in the *Mirabilia*, but it is not a conclusive indication' (177).

194 Malone, Kemp. 'Readings from Folios 94 to 131 MS. Cotton Vitellius
A XV.' *Studies in Medieval Literature in Honor of Professor Albert Croll
Baugh*. Ed. MacEdward Leach. Philadelphia: Pennsylvania UP, 1961. 255–
71.

Collates Rypins, **165**, with the manuscript: *Wond*, 259–64; *Alex*, 264–70.

195 Ross, D.J.A. *Alexander Historiatus. A Guide to Medieval Illustrated Alexander Literature*. Warburg Institute Surveys 1. London: The Warburg
Institute, U of London, 1963.

The work aims to list briefly the illustrated manuscripts and early printed
editions of all European literary materials connected with Alexander produced in antiquity and during the Middle Ages (Index of Manuscripts, 125–
8). Systematic arrangement is intended to assist understanding of relationships. There is a brief, basic bibliography of each work. 'The Letter of
Pharasmanes to Hadrian,' 33–4, lists the picture cycles in V, T, and Bodley 614, together with an early 14th century French version, Brussels Royal
14561–4, ff. 5v–6v. Behind the various corrupt forms of the written names
(Fermes, etc.) lies Pharasmanes, a real contemporary of Adrian, to whom
the letter was attributed by its original concoctor. The various monsters
contained in this text entered the Alexander tradition through the first interpolated redaction of the *Historia de Preliis*. The Letter of Pharasmanes is
also of some possible importance to the iconographic history of the Alexander romance as it is fully illustrated in the three manuscripts. The picture
cycles in V, T and Bodley may possibly have had some influence on the
illustration of *Historia de Preliis* and its derivatives.

196 Taylor, Paul Beecham, and Peter H. Salus. 'The Compilation of Cotton Vitellius A XV.' *Neuphilologische Mitteilungen* 69 (1968): 199–204.

The authors speculate that the Southwick and Nowell manuscripts were
brought together in the time of Nowell because a connection between the
fragmentary Passions was assumed, and argue, against Sisam, **193**, that
wonders (particularly wonders in other lands) are the unifying theme of the
Nowell manuscript, not monsters inimical to man.

197 Butturff, Douglas R. 'Style as a Clue to Meaning: A Note on the Old
English Translation of the *Epistola Alexandri ad Aristotelem*.' *English Language Notes* 8 (1970): 81–6.

Butturff argues that the OE translator intended to provide an *exemplum* of
superbia by consistently exposing the egotism of Alexander, who is eventually humbled by the eventual fate of all mortals. The translator shows
Alexander consistently placing his own personal needs before the needs of
his men and his animals; he substitutes the first person possessive pronoun wherever possible; reflexive pronouns are regularly used, with intensive force. The translator has not neglected the conclusion, but has abridged
and altered it to accentuate Alexander's egotism; the OE is more focused
on Alexander and his reaction to death. He does not write to Aristotle for
consolation but because he wants his life to serve as an *exemplum*; thus, his
last words are ironic, and the audience would have understood him as an
exemplum of the fate of those who put their hopes in the earthly city.

198 **Davidson, Donald, and A.P. Campbell.** 'The Letter of Alexander the
Great to Aristotle: The Old English Version turned into Modern English.'
Humanities Association Bulletin 23 (1972): 3–16.

MnE translation of *Alex*, based on Rypins, **165**, checked against Malone,
158, 6–16. The translators consider that, of the three prose pieces in the
codex, *Alex* 'most resembles *Beowulf* because it involves a hero, his travels and his amazing encounters' (4), and instance other points of contact.
Sources and transmission are outlined (5); the fact that no surviving version
of the Epitome of Julius Valerius corresponds faithfully to the OE 'argues for
both the popularity of this marvellous work and for the conclusion that the
letter was deliberately extracted from "pseudo-Callisthenes" or from Julius
Valerius, to circulate as a separate work' (5). [Followed by Pierre Kunstmann's edition of the medieval French version from a Picard manuscript in
Brussels, Bibliothèque Royale de Belgique, 14561–4, described as previously
unpublished, 17–34.]

199 **Berg, Beverly Joan Brown.** 'Tales of Alexander and the East: Wonders
and Wise Men.' *DAI* 33 (1973): 6889A. [Diss. Stanford U, 1973.]

Dissertation not sighted. According to *DAI*, Berg's study deals with Alexander legends written in the period from his death to the 5th century (*Alexander Romance*, Alexander's *Letter to Aristotle*, *On the Races of India and
the Brahmans*, *Collatio*). Described by Pulsiano, 1988, 765, as useful background material for OE.

200 **DiMarco, Vincent, and Leslie Perelman.** *The Middle English 'Letter
of Alexander to Aristotle'*. *Costerus* NS 13. Amsterdam: Rodopi, 1978.

'The *Epistola* in Old English,' 24–7, connects Anglo-Saxon interest in the
Alexander romance with the interest in exotic geography that occasions
the accounts of the travels of Ohthere and Wulfstan. Sisam's arguments
in favour of an early dating of the original—during or shortly after the
reign of Alfred (**193**)—are rejected; insufficiency in Latin may show itself
at any time, and the military bias 'could merely represent the individual

prejudices of the translator' (26). Moreover, the omissions of many fabulous elements towards the end of the work may merely suggest that the corresponding passages were lacking in the translator's Latin source. Boer, 1973, xxix, connects *Alex* with his third family of Latin manuscripts; but the passages omitted by the OE translator are present in Boer's third family of manuscripts (which include the manuscript that Hamilton, **186**, regards as the prototype), whereas they are omitted in the second family group. The authors therefore postulate as a source a manuscript of family three which had been contaminated by a manuscript of the second family.

201 Haga, Shienori. ['Letter of Alexander the Great to Aristotle: A Translation and Notes.'] *Bulletin of Akita College of Economy* 21 (1978): 20–47; 22 (1979): 85–108.

Translates *Alex* into Japanese.

202 Wiessmann, Chaim Bell. 'Giants and Giantism: Jewish Sources of the MS Cotton Vitellius A XV.' *DAI* 39 (1978): 2911A. [Diss. Purdue U, 1978. Dir. Thomas Ohlgren.]

Dissertation not sighted. According to *DAI*, the author argues that uniquely Jewish sources, which provide the connecting link between the rabbinical doctrine of *yetzer-ha-ra*, 'evil inclination,' and the giant descendants of Cain, influenced the compilation of the *Beowulf* codex, and that its underlying principle of design is to be found in every man's fight against the internal and external monster of pride.

203 Hahn, Thomas. 'The Middle English *Letter of Alexander to Aristotle*: Introduction, Text, Sources and Commentary.' *Mediaeval Studies* 41 (1979): 106–60.

Mentions *Alex* only in passing: like *Wond*, *OE ApT* and (perhaps) the *Life of Christopher*, it 'satisfied a growing taste for marvels and romances among the Anglo-Saxons' (108).

204 Cilluffo, Gilda. '*Mirabilia ags.*: il *Vasa Mortis* nel *Salomone e Saturno*.' *Annali, Istituto Universitario Orientale di Napoli, Filologia germanica* 24 (1981): 211–26.

This study of the broad cultural horizon shown by the description of *Vasa Mortis* in the poetic *SS*, lines 244–72 (ed. Menner, **70**), gives particular attention to the relationship of the *Vasa* to the *Monstrum nocturnum* of the *Liber Monstrorum* and Virgil's Fama. Pagan curiosity for knowledge acquired through travel, evinced by Saturn in the poetic dialogue (lines 176–92), also inspires Alexander in *Alex* (ed. Rypins, 1/13–18). None of the monsters in *Alex* approaches *Vasa Mortis* (e.g., 22/14–19); the griffin in the T version of *Wond* (ed. Knappe, **163**, 63) is closer (215–17).

205 Friedman, John Block. *The Monstrous Races in Medieval Art and Thought*. Cambridge, MA: Harvard UP, 1981.

A study of 'the medieval attitudes toward the fabulous races and the way in which Western Christian thinkers came to terms with the questions these beings posed about the nature of humanity' (3). Ch. 7, 'Exotic Peoples in Manuscript Illustration,' 131–62, argues that 'the Plinian races in art mirror the decline of the moralizing impulse found in late medieval culture' (131). The approach of travel literature differs somewhat in that it takes as its subject not the races themselves but their relationship to Westerners. In the illustrated Alexander manuscripts these relationships are antagonistic, and in the Anglo-Saxon manuscripts, 'this Alexander material, with its stress on the horrific, overshadows the more innocuous traditional Plinian races' (144). An important characteristic of the Anglo-Saxon Wonders texts and their illustrations is that 'the races are seen in some sort of relationship to the viewer, rather than in the isolation of an empty frame' (144). Typically, the monstrous races are crowded into a landscape, and associated with mountains (e.g., Tiberius B.v, ff. 80r, 81v), which 'had moral connotations for medieval Westerners' (146). *Liber Monstrorum*, the earliest work to give a markedly and consistently hostile treatment of the monstrous races, 'sheds considerable light upon this aspect of the Anglo-Saxon *Mirabilia* texts' (149). In both Vitellius and Tiberius the 'uneasy relationship of creature to frame suggests that the monstrous men are leaving the borders confining them to the static page and beginning to occupy landscapes; they cannot be contained in isolation as they were in the miniatures presenting the moralists' point of view' (154). Black-and-white illustrations include Tiberius B.v, ff. 83v, 86r, 80, 81v, 82r; Vitellius C.iii, ff. 104r, 102v. Alexander literature figures throughout; related chapters include: ch. 1, 'The Plinian Races,' 5–25; ch. 5, 'Cain's Kin,' 87–107; ch. 6, 'Signs of God's Will,' 88–130; ch. 9, 'The Human Status of the Monstrous Races,' 178–96.

206 Kiernan, Kevin S. *Beowulf and the Beowulf Manuscript.* New Brunswick, NJ: Rutgers UP, 1981.

Kiernan seeks to establish that *Beowulf* was composed in the reign of Cnut, primarily on the basis of manuscript evidence. Ch. 2, 'The History and Construction of the Composite Codex,' examines the origins of the multiple foliations (71–110), and argues that the different views of Förster, **180**, and Ker, concerning the number of scribes responsible for the Southwick Codex (discussed at 110–19) can be resolved by concluding that 'the scribe copied the *Nicodemus* fragment, *The Debate of Solomon and Saturn*, and the *St Quintin fragment*, for one codex as a young man, and that he copied the *Soliloquia* for another codex as an older man, after his script became more established and uniform' (113). Kiernan, who agrees with Malone, **158**, that *Judith* is a late addition to the codex, then argues (133–50) that 'the *Beowulf* MS was originally copied as a separate book, and that only later did it become the fourth item in a prose anthology' (169). In Kiernan's view, Malone was wrong in claiming that the first two folios of *Beowulf* belonged to the last gathering of *Alex*, and the prose texts and the poem are distinguished by different styles of capitals and fundamentally different gatherings. He further supports his view by the argument that *Beowulf* was carefully copied and proofread (by the second scribe), whereas the prose texts were very carelessly copied; *Alex*, unlike *Wond*, has been corrected by the scribe as well as by a later proof-reader, 'a medieval spelling reformer, who went through ... rather fecklessly modernizing archaic spellings' (144).

207 Friedman, John Block. 'The Marvels-of-the-East Tradition in Anglo-Saxon Art.' *Sources of Anglo-Saxon Culture*. Ed. Paul E. Szarmach and Virginia Darrow Oggins. Studies in Medieval Culture 20. Kalamazoo, MI: Medieval Institute, 1986. 319–41.

Friedman considers that V, T and Bodley 614 testify 'to an intense Anglo-Saxon interest in wonders and monsters and help to elucidate the aesthetic milieu of the poem *Beowulf*' (319). His purpose is to distinguish among the differing responses to the monstrous races on the part of the artists of the *Mirabilia* group and to suggest a literary source for the responses of the painter of T. Although the *Mirabilia*-text's non-judgemental recording (its 'catalogue raisonnée') might have been expected to give rise to impersonal illustration, 'in varying degrees, these three artists take an attitude towards monsters—one of ethnocentric and rhetorical fear and distaste—which is very similar to that shown in *Beowulf* towards the Grendel family' (322). The figures of V are the 'most emotionally neutral of the group' (322), and there is little suggestion of interaction between men and monsters. In T and Bodley 614, illustrations of crags and mountains indicate the essential savagery and incivility of the monstrous races. Friedman suggests that the attitudes of the T painter were affected by *Liber Monstrorum*, which 'describes unusual races of men in terms of a natural animosity between men and monsters much like that which we find in *Beowulf*' (323), and its style of rhetoric plays on the idea of monstrosity, identifying it with Asianisms, excess violence and disorder. There is no surviving illustrated version of *Liber Monstrorum*, but Friedman postulates the existence of an illustrated version of Continental origin reflecting the attitudes of the text, which may have been known to the T painter at Winchester or Canterbury. Eighteen black-and-white plates.

208 Kiernan, Kevin S. 'Madden, Thorkelin, and MS Vitellius/Vespasian A XV.' *The Library*. 6th ser. 8 (1986): 127–32.

Madden's journal, bequeathed to the Bodleian on condition that it remain unopened until 1920, shows that he was the first to recognize that only two scribes copied the entire Nowell Codex. His description incorporates the first expert palaeographical analysis of this codex. Because Madden's journal remained unknown, Rypins, **165**, could still say, as late as 1924 (xi–xii), that, except for Sisam (**177**) no one, of the many who had examined the manuscript, had called attention to the fact that there were only two hands: 'In fact, Madden had confidently sorted out the matter of the scribal hands, text by text, some hundred years earlier' (130). Discussion of Madden's account of the condition of the manuscript and the handwriting, at 127–30.

209 **Dumville, David N.** 'Beowulf come lately: Some Notes on the Paleography of the Nowell Codex.' *Archiv für das Studium der neueren Sprachen und Literaturen* 225 (1988): 49–63.

Dumville examines the palaeographical evidence and considers Ker's conventions of dating. The scribes wrote two distinct styles of Insular minuscule; this, and the fact that neither scribe was a master penman and no other work of theirs survives, suggests that the *Beowulf*-manuscript was written in a minor scriptorium. The problem for Ker was that he had to assign a date, expressed in conventional formulation—to find a time-range that would allow for the conjunction of two such discrepant styles: 'If the work of Scribe A and Scribe B had been found in complete independence of one another, Hand A would have been dated "s. XI in." or "s. XI^1", while Hand B would probably have been dated "s. X ex." ' (55). Ker therefore compromises, recognizing that the manuscript was created in a period of transition in scribal practice, and not wishing to narrow that period too closely or arbitrarily. 'Square minuscule is likely to have been in use for only a very few years after A.D. 1000. The few manuscripts, like that containing *Beowulf*, which display contemporaneous writing in these two successive styles of Insular minuscule must therefore have been written very early in the eleventh century.... The proper conventional dating for the *Beowulf*-manuscript is (depending on the system employed) "*saec. xi in.*" or "*saec.* xi $\frac{1}{4}$," but this should not blind us to the apparent necessity of dating the book *very* early in the eleventh century' (63).

210 **Gerritsen, Johan.** 'British Library MS Cotton Vitellius A.xv—A Supplementary Description.' *English Studies* 69 (1988): 293–302.

This primarily codicological description of the Nowell codex, its condition, binding and make-up, concludes that there is every reason to think that Nowell was designed as an integral codex.

210A **Campbell, Mary B.** *The Witness and the Other World: Exotic European Travel Writing, 400-1600.* Ithaca: Cornell UP, 1988.

Ch. 2, 'The Fabulous East: "Wonder Books" and Grotesque Facts,' 47–86, a study of the *Mirabilia* which treats it as 'an apparent paradox: a transparent, denotative piece of exposition which is nevertheless organized symbolically and which can be best understood if we expand the term *grotesque* to include images of the actual' (57), draws its specific textual and pictorial examples from *Wond.* Campbell, who describes the 'Wonder Books' as 'the most extreme and exquisite projections of European cultural fantasy' and argues that 'the fear and loathing here influentially implicit became explicit—and murderous—when opportunity arose' (8), takes issue with Gibb, **168**: 'Some of the same features that provoke a perception of *Wonders* as grotesque provoke the allegorical reading of it, but neither provides a real escape from the ethical problem of the work's factuality, nor does the remote allegorical *hypnoia* cancel out the appeal of its grotesque surface' (79).

IV

Byrhtferth of Ramsey

and Computus

BYRHTFERTH OF RAMSEY

EXPLANATORY NOTE

ByrM, written in alternating OE and Latin, naturally falls within the sphere of both OE and Anglo-Latin studies, and, in recent decades, a number of works, mostly in Latin, have been attributed to Byrhtferth. The annotations, divided into three section, cover: *ByrM*; the scientific compendium which contains two items thought to have originally formed part of *ByrM* and now believed to have been compiled by Byrhtferth (J); and the Byrhtferth canon. Studies devoted to works attributed to Byrhtferth, whether Latin or OE, are included only if they discuss his authorship; studies of J are included only if they have specific bearing on its connection with Byrhtferth.

MANUSCRIPTS

MANUAL (*ENCH(E)IRIDION*) AND ST JOHN'S COLLEGE 17

Oxford, Bodleian, Ashmole 328, pp. 1–247	A	
Ker 288, art. 1. s. xi med.		FC B.20.20.1
art. 2, 'Iohannes ait,' pp. 247–51		FC B.3.4.38
art. 3, 'Ammonitio Amici,' pp. 251–8		FC B.3.4.39
Cambridge, University Library, Kk.5.32, f. 60v		FC B.20.20.2
Ker 26 s. xi/xii		
Oxford, St John's College 17 + London,		
British Library, Cotton Nero C.vii, ff. 80–4	J	
Ker 360 s. xii in.		

MANUSCRIPTS, DESCRIPTION AND DATE; TEXTUAL RELATIONSHIP OF J TO *ByrM*

Ashmole 328

The OE and Latin work attributed to Byrhtferth, variously known as his *Manual, Handboc, Gerim* or *Ench(e)iridion*, is found only in Ashmole 328 (A). *Ench(e)iridion* is currently the term most frequently used. *ByrM*, Henel, **270**, explained, is not simply a computus but a commentary on a computus. Sometimes regarded as the script of Byrhtferth's lectures to his

149

Ramsey pupils (Byrhtferth is named at Crawford, **212**, 94, and Ramsey at 14), *ByrM* contains a short rhetorical and grammatical treatise and an explanation of a variety of other matters such as weights and measures and number symbolism, as well as instruction in the fundamental elements of arithmetic and astronomy necessary for an understanding of the determination of the year and the establishment of the calendar, and is illustrated by diagrams.

Crawford dated *ByrM* 1011; Ker dates A mid-11th century and states that the contents of pp. 1–54 are disarranged, owing probably to the misplacing of the third quire in the scribe's exemplar, and single leaves are missing after pp. 156 and 168. The seventh leaf of the first quire is a fragment paged 12 *bis*, 12 *ter*, which contains on the recto a piece of a diagram resembling the diagram in J, f. 7v, and Harley 3667, f. 8v. It is written in a neat, but in detail ill-formed, round hand; titles in Latin are in red rustic capitals, titles in OE are usually in the script and hand of the text, and initials are green or red.

Oxford, St John's College 17

J has a long history of association with Byrhtferth. Since the appearance of Van de Vyver, **239**, in 1935, it has been held that J is a copy of a collection of materials assembled by Byrhtferth, although conceptions of the nature of the materials in the exemplar of J, and its relation to *ByrM*, have differed.

J contains two items, not in A, which, early this century, were claimed to have originally formed part of *ByrM*:

> Diagram of 'the physical and physiological fours,' or 'the four fours,' J, f. 7v. Inscribed 'byrhtferð monachus ramesiensis,' and said to be (Singer, **235**) an inexact copy of a diagram once illustrating *ByrM*, of which only a fragment remains in A, at p. 12.

Proemium/Preface/Epilogue/*Epilogus*, J, ff. 12r–13v.

> An item, in Latin, appearing under the rubric 'Proemium Brihtferthi Ramesiensis Cenobii Monachi super Bedam De Temporibus,' which begins 'Spiraculo,' formerly associated with the commentaries on Bede attributed to Byrhtferth. Edited by Forsey, **238**, as 'Byrhtferth's Preface,' it was claimed by Henel, **241**, as the Epilogue to *ByrM*. Some contemporary scholars, following Van de Vyver, **239**, regard the Proemium as the preface to computistica in J, and refer to it as *Epilogus*.

The chief contents of J are a practical computus, Bede's *De Temporibus*, *De Temporum Ratione* and *De Natura Rerum* (with marginal commentaries very different from those attributed to Byrhtferth in the 16th century), and a version of *Computus Helperici*. *Computus Helperici*, as well as two tracts on astronomy contained in J, are attributed to Abbo of Fleury, who spent two years at Ramsey during the lifetime of Byrhtferth (Van de Vyver, 239). J also contains some medical material (see Singer, 236); this, like the manuscript as a whole, is in Latin, but includes an OE charm heading (FC B.24.16). There are also some OE glosses and marginalia, which include names of the months (FC B.24.4) and names of the days of the week (FC B.24.3), edited by Gough, 532.

Ker states that the OE is perhaps all in a hand which occurs throughout the manuscript in Latin marginalia and interlineations and in places in the text, and which wrote the Thorney annals up to the year 1111; the OE hand is contemporary with the main hand of the manuscript, part of which appears to have been written in 1110. The manuscript belonged to Thorney Abbey soon after it was written. (See also Ker, 240.)

There has been a certain amount of disagreement concerning the date and provenance of the manuscript. Van De Vyver, 239, concluded that J was a late 11th century manuscript originating from Thorney. Hart, 242, argues that J was written at Ramsey up until 1081 and transferred to Thorney in the period 1081×1092. But Lapidge, 246, asserts that the marginalia of scribe B give no reason to believe that J was written anywhere but at Thorney, or earlier than 1110. Lapidge's 1110–11 dating of J thus confirms the dating that Singer, 236, deduced from a calculation on f. 3v (cf. Wallis, 247). The same deduction was made by Coxe, 1852,[1] who gave a full description of the manuscript; Ker's is very brief and (in accordance with his customary practice), he does not table the Latin contents. There is a full table of J's contents in Baker, 245, 125–6. Most studies of J (see further below) contain some description of the manuscript and its contents.

EDITIONS OF *ByrM*: EXTENT OF THE TEXT, EXCERPTS

The earliest editor, Kluge, 211, printed only the OE sections from A; he also omitted the diagrams, rubrics and glosses. The Latin and OE text of A was edited (with translation) by Crawford for EETS in 1929 (212); the edition carried facsimiles of 16 of the diagrams in A. The second volume envisaged by Crawford, which was to have contained an introduction and glossary, did not eventuate (but see Crawford's dissertation, 213, not sighted). Crawford's edition also included a facsimile of J, f. 7v, the diagram of the 'physical and physiological fours,' whose recognition as a copy of the figure missing from A, p. 12, the Singers had done much to ensure (235, 237; Singer, 235, carried facsimiles of A, pp. 10–12.).

Crawford also included, in an appendix to his edition, the Latin item at J, f. 12v, which had already been edited by Forsey, 238, at the instigation of Crawford, as 'Byrhtferth's Preface.' (Forsey did not, however, advance any conclusions concerning the work to which the Preface had

---

[1] Henry O. Coxe, *Catalogus codicum MSS. qui in collegiis aulisque Oxoniensibus hodie adservantur, etc.* (Oxford: Oxford UP, 1852), Pt. 2 (Collegii S. Johannis Baptistae XVII) 5–8.

been attached, and Crawford printed it without comment; see Crawford, **249**.) Subsequently, Henel, **241**, argued the case for its identification as the Epilogue of *ByrM* (taking his cue from the Proemium's peroration, 'Post huius denique epilogii descriptionem libet articulum flectere ad totius libri recapitulationem.... '), and suggested that it had originally occurred after the passage on the Ages of the World derived from Bede's *De Temporum Ratione* (at Crawford, 238/30).

The passage on the Ages of the World is followed in A by two homiletic pieces. The first of these, concerning the Last Judgement and the eight capital sins, begins: 'Johannes ait: *Post mille annos soluetur Satanas*'; the second, once attributed to Wulfstan, is entitled 'Ammonitio Amici.' In Crawford's edition, the first of the homiletic pieces forms the conclusion to *ByrM*, and the second is printed as an appendix, a procedure which Henel found inconsistent. Henel suggested that the two homiletic pieces constituted a later, alternative ending, and he tentatively attributed them to Byrhtferth's authorship (cf. Lucas, **228**). The two homiletic pieces are separately tabled both by Ker (who states that they are both in the main hand) and by FC (B.3.4.38–9.) Ker notes that the two pieces are also found together in Ker, 69 (CCCC 421).

The combined work of Ker, **224**, and Henel, **270**, established that Crawford had not recognized that the manuscript was incorrectly quired, and that his edition should be read thus: 2/1–30/9; 44/28–56/29; 30/9–44/27; 56/30–end. Reviewers commented unfavourably on the text and translation of Crawford's edition. Henel, who published a number of emendations to Crawford's edition in the course of his articles on Byrhtferth and OE computus (**214**, **225**, **270**), attributed many of its shortcomings to Crawford's lack of familiarity with Byrhtferth's subject matter, and, adding 43 previously unpublished corrections to those which he and other scholars had put forward in the decade since the edition's first appearance, observed: 'Nor is it pretended that all the errors of text and translation are now rectified' (Henel, **225**). In 1966, Crawford's edition was reissued by EETS,[2] with a list of errata by Ker. A new edition of *ByrM*, jointly edited by Lapidge and Baker, is among the new editions of works attributed to Byrhtferth which are projected by Lapidge, **262**.

Fragmentary Notes

Whether the notes on computus in Cambridge Kk.5.32, f. 60v, and Caligula A.xv, Part B, ff. 142v–3, are textual variants of *ByrM*, or works distinct from it, is a matter on which opinions have differed. Henel, **214**, regarded the note on division in Cambridge Kk.5.32, as well as notes at Caligula A.xv, f. 142v, as excerpts copied from *ByrM*, although Forsey, **238**, had regarded the latter as an earlier, self-contained piece by Byrhtferth. FC

---

[2] The reprint is said to have been based on the text of Crawford's doctoral thesis, **213**.

give the Cambridge fragment as a textual variant of A (FC B.20.20.2), but
list a note on concurrents and ferial regulars in Caligula A.xv (Ker 139B,
art. 2) as separate computus items (FC B.20.3.1, B.20.4); these pieces were
printed by Henel, **270**, 53–4. Crawford, **212**, 36–7, printed a note on epacts
which occurs in Caligula A.xv as an appendix to Ælfric's translation of *De
Temporibus*, which he thought was possibly Byrhtferth's own composition
(Ker 139B, art. 3); this is separately listed by FC as B.20.2.3, but cross-
referenced to *ByrM*. These items are included in (or correspond to) the
'two notes and perhaps the following fragment'[3] at Caligula A.xv, Part
B, ff. 142v–3, which Baker, **259**, adds to the Byrhtferth canon. Henel,
241, considered that the Manual had not circulated widely: 'Apart from
A, there are extant only some fragmentary excerpts in J, Mss Cambridge
University Library Kk.5.32, Cotton Caligula A.xv, and, possibly, Cotton
Tiberius C.i [Henel, **270**, 1]. The Diagram in J is one such fragment and, I
think, the *Epilogue* is another' (302). The note on division in Cambridge,
University Library Kk.5.32, is described by Ker as written in a blank space
of a manuscript partly in a hand of s. xi[1] (ff. 49–60) and partly in a hand
of s. xi/xii (ff. 61–72).

MS J: ITS RELATIONSHIP TO BYRHTFERTH (AND THE COMMENTARIES ATTRIBUTED TO HIM)

J has long been associated with Byrhtferth, but the precise nature of its
relationship has been problematic. The most recent thinking on J is that
it is a copy of a species of commonplace book that Byrhtferth assembled,
and used as the basis of Bks. 1–3 of *ByrM*.

The Singers' argument regarding the diagram in J, f. 7v—that it is a
copy of the figure referred to on A, p. 12, of which a fragment is still visible,
and that the diagram in J must have been inexactly copied from *ByrM* because it does not fully conform to Byrhtferth's explanation of 'the physical
and physiological fours' (**235**, **237**)—does not to appear ever to have been
disputed. (Lapidge, **246**, who argues that the two scribes of J 'were following an exemplar very closely and were attempting accurately to reproduce
the exact *mise-en-page* of that exemplar' (349), does not discuss this diagram.) For connections between diagrams in J and other manuscripts,
including *ByrM*, see Singer, **237**, Ker, **240**, Hart, **231**.

The item at J, f. 12v ('Proemium'), was once connected with the commentaries (*Glossae*) on Bede which scholars from the 16th century onwards
ascribed to Byrhtferth; many, including the Singers, **235**, accepted the
Proemium as confirmation of Byrhtferth's authorship of the commentaries

---

[3] Which this writer understands to mean Ker, 139B, arts. 1, 2 and 3; hence, Baker
presumably means FC B.1.9.4, B.20.3.1, and perhaps B.20.2.3, though it is possible that
what is meant is FC B.20.3.1, B.20.2.3 and perhaps B.1.9.4, matters being complicated
by the fact that Ker 139B, arts. 1 and 4 (ff. 144–53v) are duplicated items, described by
Ker as part of the OE rendering of Bede's *De Temporibus*, the second of them bearing
the 17th century (?) title 'Ædthelardus de Compoto.'

that Herwagen (in 1563) had published under his name,[4] and the Proemium was presumed to be the Preface to commentaries on Bede written by Byrhtferth. Forsey, **238**, who edited and translated the Proemium (in 1928) as 'Byrhtferth's Preface' was essentially concerned to argue that Byrhtferth was not the author of the commentaries on Bede that Herwagen had ascribed to him. For Forsey, as for Henel later, the question of the Proemium's relationship to the commentaries attributed to Byrhtferth was complicated by the fact that the 14th/15th century *Catalogus Scriptorum Ecclesiae* of 'Boston of Bury' states: *'Birdferthus* monachus Ramesiae floruit A.C.... et scripsit Super librum Bedae de temporibus, lib. 1. Pr. Spiraculo. 82,'[5] since *Spiraculo* is the opening word of the Proemium.

Forsey speculated that a misunderstanding of the nature of the Proemium on the part of the 16th century antiquarian, Leland, was the ultimate source of the attribution of the commentaries to Byrhtferth. The Singers, **235**, had observed that a manuscript described in Leland's *Collectanea* resembled J,[6] but Forsey hesitated to identify J as the manuscript that Leland had seen because the Singers had drawn attention to minor discrepancies between J and Leland's description. Subsequent scholarship (from Van der Vyver onward) has affirmed the identity of these two manuscripts (see particularly Ker, **240**), and Baker, **263**, confirms Forsey's speculation. Forsey, however, was troubled by the fact that Tanner (1674–1735) had stated, on the authority of 'Boston,' that there was once a commentary on Bede's *De Temporibus* in the library of Bury which began 'Spiraculo uitae humanum genus.'[7] Forsey therefore concluded instead that there was a lost commentary by Byrhtferth which began 'Spiraculo uitae humanum genus,' which had become confused with the commentaries attributed to him by Herwagen, and that the appearance of the word 'Spiraculo' at the beginning of the Proemium was merely coincidence.

Van de Vyver, **239**, in his seminal study, identified the lost exemplar of J as a collection of computistical writings by Bede, Abbo and Helpericus assembled by Byrhtferth, to which Byrhtferth attached his own preface. Henel, **241**, in arguing that the Proemium was the Epilogue to *ByrM*, took issue with this aspect of Van de Vyver's work. The so-called Preface, he said, mentions only *De Temporibus*, whereas J has all three of Bede's famous scientific treatises: 'One must add that J does not follow

---

[4] John Herwagen, ed., *Opera Bedae Venerabilis ... omnia in octo tomos distincta,* 8 vols. in 4 (Basel: Herwagen, 1563) 2: 1–173. The glosses were reprinted in *PL* 90: 188–518.

[5] *Catalogus Scriptorum Ecclesiae,* in the Preface of Thomas Tanner, *Bibliotheca Britannico-Hibernica, sive de Scriptoribus, qui in Anglia, Scotia, et Hibernia ad Saeculi xvii Initium Floruerunt* (London: Bowyer, 1748; Tucson: Audax, 1963) xvii–xliii. Baker, **263**, states that the catalogue is actually the work of a 14th century monk, Henry of Kirkstede; Boston is the name of one of the scribes involved in copying it.

[6] *Joannis Lelandi Antiquarii de Rebus Britannicis Collectanea,* ed. Thomas Hearne, 2nd edn., 6 vols. (London: Richardson, 1770) 4: 97.

[7] See fn. 5.

the order which is announced at the end of the "preface." Instead of the expected order: preface, *DTR*, Abbo, Helpericus, we find *DT*, *DNR*, *DTR*, and Helperic's *Computus* on fols. 58v–135v, the "preface" on fols. 12v–13r, and fragments from Abbo's writings dispersed over the first forty fols. Thus, if one wished to adhere to Van de Vyver's view, it would be necessary to assume that in J the "preface" had become detached from the corpus of writings which it was meant to introduce, that Abbo's tracts were placed before instead of after Bede, and that the latter's *DT* and *DNR* were added to the corpus which Byrhtferth had gathered. At any rate it is clear that J is not simply a copy of X [the codex that Byrhtferth prepared]. There must certainly have been a rearrangement, and very probably also additions and omissions' (296–7).

Henel, writing during the war, was unable to gain access to J, but he postulated that the exemplar of J had originally contained computistical material assembled by Byrhtferth *and also* his Manual, of which only the diagram and Epilogue had been copied into J. The work of Van de Vyver and Henel led Hart, **231**, **242**, to demonstrate that the exemplar of J was the source of *ByrM*, and a similar view is elaborated by Baker, **245**, who demonstrates that *ByrM*, Bks. 1–3, is a commentary on materials assembled in the lost exemplar of J (note Lucas, **228**, on Bk. 4). In the course of these developments, Henel's view of the Proemium seems to have been abandoned in favour of the view that it is the introduction to the materials in J. It is now generally referred to as the *Epilogus*; Baker, **263**, 69, 'an *Epilogus* (Byrhtferth's word for "preface").' Lapidge, **246**, for instance, who rejects the argument of Hart, **242**, that J was written at Ramsey up until 1081 and transferred to Thorney sometime before 1092, observes: 'In this *Epilogus* Byrhtferth introduces the materials that make up the bulk of the manuscript—the practical computus, Bede's writings and that of Helperic—which suggests that it was Byrhtferth himself who assembled them' (350). Lapidge, in the same article, suggests 993 as the date for Byrhtferth's compilation of the exemplar of J and argues that J is a very exact copy of its exemplar. He also suggests that an early 12th century Winchcombe manuscript, Tiberius E.iv, is 'very possibly another copy of Byrhtferth's lost commonplace-book' (359).

Singer, the first 20th century scholar to recognize J's important place in intellectual and scientific history, described it as 'a scientific encyclopaedia, perhaps the earliest work of its kind since the classical period' (**235**, 51). Although attention is now focused on the computistic contents of J, it was the five folios of medical material which struck Singer as being, relative to their time, of a superior quality. This collection of material was printed by Singer (including the OE charm heading [FC B.23.1.16]), together with an introductory essay on J's place in the history of medical science (see also Singer, **237**, and Cameron, **551**).

An edition of J in its entirety, which the Singers hoped to bring out, has still not appeared, but the recent revival of interest in its precise connection

with *ByrM*, and, beyond that, the light it sheds on the cultural and intellectual history of the late Anglo-Saxon period, is reason for expecting that
the manuscript in its entirety will be made more widely accessible in the
near future (Lapidge, **262**, draws attention to the need for a facsimile of the
whole of J). The diagram of 'the four fours,' reproduced in Crawford, **212**,
had been reproduced and described by the Singers, who observed that the
same set of relationships was represented, in a simpler form, in the diagram
at J, f. 39v, which derives from Isidore, and 'the four fours' diagram, with
accompanying illustration, described in much the same terms, continued to
figure in almost all of Charles Singer's many publications on Anglo-Saxon
medical literature. A reduced facsimile of the Proemium, and the diagram
at the end of it, was included in Forsey, **238**. There is an impressive body of
scholarship devoted to the scientific works in J, especially those attributed
to Abbo (most of it lies outside the scope of this Annotated Bibliography,
but see McGurk, **243**), and some of the texts have been separately edited.[8]
J is the subject of a recent dissertation by Wallis, **247**.

BYRHTFERTH'S CANON

From the 16th century onwards Byrhtferth was credited with commentaries
on Bede's *De Temporibus* and *De Natura Rerum* (varying in number, but
usually said to be four),[9] together with two lost works, *De Institutione
Monachorum* and *De Principiis Mathematicis*, and a Life of Dunstan whose
author calls himself 'B.' The attributions began to lose ground from 1874
onwards, when Stubbs rejected (on stylistic grounds) Byrhtferth's authorship of the Life of Dunstan,[10] first attributed to him by Mabillon.[11] In
1896, Classen, **248**, who had available to him only the OE sections of
ByrM edited by Kluge, argued on a variety of grounds against Byrhtferth's
authorship of the commentaries published under his name in Herwagen's
1563 edition of Bede; Classen recognized, however, that the pivotal issue
was the reliability of the early modern scholars who gave currency to the
attributions, and his low opinion of their testimony appears, in the light of
subsequent scholarship, to have been justified. Forsey, **238**, in 1928, and

---

[8] See, e.g., David N. Dumville, 'Motes and Beams: Two Insular Computistical
Manuscripts,' *Peritia* 2 (1983): 248–56; Ron B. Thomson, 'Two Astronomical Trac-
tates of Abbo of Fleury,' *The Light of Nature: Essays in the History and Philosophy of
Science Presented to A.C. Crombie*, ed. J.D. North and J.J. Roche (Dordrecht: Nijhoff,
1985) 113–33.

[9] See fn. 4 for Herwagen's edition. Jones, **223**, explained that *De Natura Rerum*
and *De Temporibus* were each accompanied by several extensive commentaries, one of
which was ascribed without explanation to Byrhtferth of Ramsey. Two chapters of *DT*
with commentaries were printed by Herwagen as separate works, hence the ascription to
Byrhtferth of four commentaries on Bede.

[10] William Stubbs, ed., *Memorials of Saint Dunstan, Archbishop of Canterbury*, Rolls
Series (London: HMSO, 1874; [New York]: Kraus, 1965) xviii–xxii.

[11] Luc d'Archery and Jean Mabillon, eds., *Acta Sanctorum Ordinis S. Benedicti in
Saeculorum Classes Distributa*, 2nd edn., 9 vols. (Venice: Coleti, 1733–38), 7 (saec. 5)
639–40. Not in the first edition.

Henel, **241**, in 1943, continued investigation into the origin and transmission of the attribution of the commentaries on Bede. Crawford's editorial work on the full Latin and OE text of *ByrM*, by affording familiarity with the Latinity of Byrhtferth, provided both Forsey and Henel with an additional basis on which to argue for the exclusion of the commentaries from the canon.

Although Forsey's enquiry into the part that the Proemium might have played in an erroneous attribution did not perhaps advance matters very far, resulting, finally, in his addition of a lost commentary to the 'ghost canon' of Byrhtferth, he mounted a strong case on the argument that Byrhtferth could not have written the commentaries that Herwagen attributed to him because they were altogether more polished and sophisticated than *ByrM*. Steele, **221**, rejected this argument, on the grounds that it was unreasonable to expect Byrhtferth to have written his commentaries in the 'turgid metaphorical style' of his *Manual* (351). Byrhtferth's authorship of the Herwagen commentaries was disposed of by Jones, **251**, in 1938, who showed that they had been assembled a century before Byrhtferth flourished. Jones's argument was regarded as definitive, although the attribution continued to be repeated for some decades in non-specialist works. But Henel pursued the enquiry into the reliability of the attributions because Jones had 'unfortunately revived Leland's old conjecture that Byrhtferth's four books of Bede are identical with the material in J' (300).

In 1982 Baker, **263**, reopened the question of the origins and transmission of 16th century attributions to Byrhtferth, clarifying the work of Classen, Forsey and Henel, and a full bibliography of early attributions can be found in this article. Baker traces the origins of the attributions of the two lost works; his demonstration that Bale's attribution to Byrhtferth of *De Institutione Monachorum* arose from his misinterpretation of his own notes bears out Baker's belief that the 'lost' work on mathematics that Bale (1495–1563) ascribed to Byrhtferth probably arose from a similar kind of confusion. Baker also shows that Bale played a crucial role in the attribution of the commentaries on Bede to Byrhtferth. Jones had concluded that Herwagen had not based his attribution to Byrhtferth on the authority of a manuscript which has since been lost, but attached Byrhtferth's name to the commentaries that he published merely because he had read in Bale's *Scriptorum Illustrium* that Byrhtferth had written commentaries on Bede.[12] Baker argues that Bale, in his turn, was misled both by the late medieval *Catalogus Scriptorum Ecclesiae* of 'Boston of Bury' and by Leland (*c.* 1503–52). Leland, having seen J and described its Proemium/*Epilogus* in his *Collectanea*, attributed to Byrhtferth a commentary on Bede's *De Natura Rerum* in his *De Scriptoribus*,[13] and it was the latter work that

---

[12] John Bale, *Scriptorum Illustriũ maioris Brytanniae, quam nunc Angliam & Scotiam vocant: Catalogus*, 2 vols. (Basel: Oporinus, 1557–9) 1: 138. (The 1548 edition contains no discussion of Byrhtferth.)

[13] John Leland, *Commentarii de Scriptoribus Britannicis*, ed. Anthony Hall, 2 vols. in

Bale had read. In fact, Baker points out, there are marginal glosses to the fragmentarily preserved copy of Bede's *De Natura Rerum* in J, and he considers that evidence of style and subject suggests that Byrhtferth wrote some of these, but he does not think that Leland could have recognized such indications of authorship: 'Thus, unless there was an attribution to Byrhtferth in the missing section he examined, Leland's own attribution was little more than a guess' (72).

The origins of the entry in the 14th/15th century *Catalogus Scriptorum Ecclesiae*, which gave Forsey and Henel more trouble than the Renaissance attributions, appear to be less easily accounted for ('*Birdferthus* monachus Ramesiae floruit A.C.... et scripsit Super librum Bedae de temporibus, lib. 1. Pr. Spiraculo. 82'); Baker identifies this as a reference to the Proemium/*Epilogus* as it appears in J and presumes that 'Bury of Boston' was describing a lost Bury St Edmunds manuscript. The conclusion to be drawn, perhaps, is that whereas Henel, **241**, thought that the paucity of excerpts from *ByrM* bore out the view that it was 'little suited for wider circulation' (302), at least some of the contents of Byrhtferth's Latin commonplace-book were preserved at Bury as well as at Winchcombe (see Lapidge, **246**).

As Renaissance attributions have been rejected, a number of new attributions have arisen to take their place. No longer the acknowledged author of the *Vita s. Dunstani*, Byrhtferth has now emerged as the author of two Latin Lives as well as the compiler of J. His hand has been discerned in six chronicles, both vernacular and Latin, and he is a strong candidate for authorship of other works, including three poems. The wave of new attributions began to surface in 1974. In this year Clemoes, **253**, advanced Byrhtferth's authorship of the anonymous parts of the *OE Hexateuch* as well as *Pseudo-Ecgbert's Penitential*, and suggested that other works might be attributable to Byrhtferth. The following year, Lapidge, **254**, attributed to him the Life of Ecgwine, and re-attributed to him the Life of Oswald (both works in Cotton Nero E.i, vol. 1) which Crawford, **249**, had assigned to Byrhtferth in 1929; in 1981, Lapidge, **261**, concluded that Byrhtferth was the author of the early sections of *Historia Regum*. The same conclusion was independently arrived at by Hart, **260**, **265**, who also connected the B version of the *Anglo-Saxon Chronicle* with Byrhtferth and found evidence of his authorship of the chronicle poem on King Edgar (**264**). In 1983, Hart, **266**, assigned to him the early sections of the *Worcester Chronicle*, and no longer saw any obstacle to accepting that Byrhtferth had been personally responsible for the *East-Anglian Chronicle* (cf. **260**); Hart also attributes to Byrhtferth the precursors to the C and D versions of *ASC* and the OE metrical *Menologium* (**260**, **264**). In the following year, Lapidge, **246**, hesitated to assign the Ramsey Calendar poem to Byrhtferth on the

---

1 (Oxford: Oxford UP, 1709) 1: 171. For the *Collectanea*, see fn. 6.

grounds that 'Byrhtferth was a scholar of impressively wide learning and literary enterprise but was not, as far as we know, a Latin poet'(357).

Not all of these attributions have been accepted. Crawford's 1929 attribution of the Life of Oswald was doubtfully received by Robinson, **250**, and Millinger, 1979, observing, in a footnote, that the attribution had returned to currency, expressed the opinion that Robinson's case had not been answered.[14] Baker, **256, 259**, who took up the suggestion of Clemoes, **253**, that there was need for a close linguistic study to determine the vernacular canon of Byrhtferth, rejected Clemoes's attribution of the *Hexateuch* and *Pseudo-Ecgbert's Penitential*. Some of the minor texts that Baker, **259**, added to the OE canon had been accepted as Byrhtferth's by earlier scholars, but were not regarded as distinct from the *Manual*. Crawford's edition assumes his authorship of the first, if not the second, of the two homiletic pieces in A which occur after the point at which, in Henel's view, the Epilogue originally appeared (that is, FC B.3.8.38, 39; see pp. 151–2 above, 'Editions of *ByrM*'); Henel inclined to the opinion that they represented a later, alternative ending to the *Manual* that had been authorized by Byrhtferth, and that the second of the two pieces, at very least, was the work of Byrhtferth himself (cf. Lucas, **228**). Jost, **252**, rejecting them from the Wulfstan canon, to which Wanley had ascribed them, also gave reasons for believing that the two homilies were integral to the *Manual* which Byrhtferth composed. For the two short notes and fragmentary paragraph in Caligula A.xv, Part B, ff. 142v–3, accepted as Byrhtferth's by Baker, see pp. 152–3 above, 'Fragmentary Notes.' Baker also finds evidence that Byrhtferth was the glossator of *ByrM*; Lapidge, **262**, like Baker, **259, 263**, accepts Byrhtferth's authorship of Latin glosses in J; Lapidge, **258**, also suggests that Byrhtferth was responsible for OE glosses in the manuscript containing the Lives of Ecgwine and Oswald. Smith, **217**, has not been sighted.

SURVEY OF SCHOLARSHIP

Commentary on Byrhtferth has been dominated since the Renaissance not by the one work which is undoubtedly his, but by the works that he might or might not have written, and the most visible recent development, already indicated above, has been the extension of his canon, in what could be regarded as a concerted attempt to endow him, on the basis of quantity of output, with the distinguished literary reputation that few have ever claimed for him on the basis of the quality of his *Manual* alone. As Lapidge,

---

[14] Susan P. Millinger, 'Liturgical Devotion in the *Vita Oswaldi*,' *Saints, Scholars and Heroes: Studies in Medieval Culture in Honour of Charles W. Jones*, ed. Margot H. King and Wesley M. Stevens, Hill Monastic Manuscript Library, 2 vols. (Collegeville, MN: St John's Abbey and the University, 1979) 2: 253–4, n. 3. Further, Hart's view of the *East-Anglian Chronicle* is not shared by Michael Lapidge and David Dumville, eds., *The Annals of St. Neots with Vita Prima Sancti Neoti*, The Anglo-Saxon Chronicle: A Collaborative Edition 17 (Woodbridge: Brewer–Boydell, 1985) lxiv.

262, observed in his 1981 survey of Byrhtferth scholarship, recent studies of Byrhtferth's canon have enlarged it to the point where 'he may eventually emerge as one of the most prolific authors of the late Anglo-Saxon period' (60). It is perhaps worth recalling that one of the chief grounds on which early 20th century scholars rejected Byrhtferth's authorship of commentaries on Bede was that his Latin was 'incomparably inferior' (Forsey, **238**) and that Henel, **241**, affirmed: 'The final result of our investigation is that in all likelihood Byrhtferth never wrote more than one work, the *Manual*. That is really as one would expect to find. The *Manual* bears ample evidence that its author found literary composition hard. He compiled it as a service to his students, to meet the need of a computistical textbook in the vernacular' (302).

The recent attributions and ascriptions, although often backed by evidence of Ramsey provenance or some form of association with Ramsey, depend on the observed occurrence of isolated features of a style, whether Latin or OE, which is held to be unmistakably characteristic of Byrhtferth. *Year's Work in English Studies* 61 (1980), in reviewing Baker, **259**, expressed doubts concerning the lexical and stylistic criteria, and a question that has still to be considered is one that also has bearing on the established canon of Wulfstan (another commonplace-book compiler whose claims to attention depend on the extensiveness of his literary activities). Wulfstan's authentic works were distinguished (chiefly by Jost, **252**) from a large body of material which they closely resemble—now ascribed to Wulfstan imitators—on the basis of what is still alleged to be Wulfstan's unmistakably characteristic style: what is not clear is whether a handful of linguistic and stylistic features that draw attention to themselves as unmistakably characteristic are also uniquely the possession of a single individual. Matters would seem to have been further complicated by Hart's decision to attribute to Byrhtferth Latin works that are not written in the 'hermeneutic' style (**266**). Troubling, too, is the self-sustaining nature of some of the attributions, particularly noticeable in Hart, **260** and **264**, where the case rests on acceptance of Hart's argument for Byrhtferth's authorship of the OE verse *Menologium*, said to be presented in a forthcoming article (**264**, 298), which still does not seem to have appeared. Perhaps the writings attributed to Byrhtferth should be regarded, rather, as the work of Byrhtferth imitators (see Lapidge, **254**, and Hart, **260**), or, better still, as the work of a particular school or circle, since, as Robinson, **250**, intimated when, very early on, he raised questions concerning stylistic criteria of authorship, it may not have been Byrhtferth's style that was the focus of imitation.

For Lapidge, the extension of the Byrhtferth canon is inseparably related to Byrhtferth's intellectual stature and the establishment of him as a significant figure in the cultural and intellectual history of the Anglo-Saxon period. Hart, responsible for most of the chronicle attributions to Byrhtferth, presented him in 1982 (**265**) as 'our only English historian of substance, apart from Bede, for the whole of the Anglo-Saxon period.' Hart, **231**, on the other hand, described Byrhtferth, in his 1972 examination of *ByrM*, as a pedestrian teacher in a monastery never of the first intellectual rank, and concluded: 'After studying Byrhtferth's writings, it becomes apparent that he had no claim to remembrance as a mathematician and very little as a man of science, and that only the uninformed can continue to speak of Bede and Byrhtferth in the same breath' (105). Stenton, 1943, described Byrhtferth as 'the most eminent man of science produced by the English Church since the death of Bede.'[15] Crawford, **212, 249**, evidently thought well of Byrhtferth, and the projected second volume of his edition would doubtless have lodged in the tradition of Byrhtferth scholarship a literary evaluation of *ByrM* as well as an account of its relation to the intellectual heritage of Bede, which figures substantially in the notes to his edition. But although Byrhtferth has always had an assured place in the history of Anglo-Saxon education during the Benedictine Reform period, Hart's evaluation of the intellectual calibre of *ByrM* itself was shared by some earlier writers. Singer, who made some mention of Byrhtferth (particularly the diagram of 'the four fours') in most of his surveys of medical history, described *ByrM* as 'the first attempt at a cosmic philosophy in English' and conceded that its scheme of the world 'though it seems to us fantastic, was at least coherent' (**326**, 93), but from a strictly modern scientific point of view, Byrhtferth epitomized the nadir of the human intellect, 'the sophisticated childishness, the inane learning, and the humourless edificatory imbecility of the men of the Dark Age' (**219**, 285). Byrhtferth is viewed less darkly, but still dimly, by Bullough, **230**, in his study of education in the OE period; Bullough was also less impressed with the intellectual stature of Byrhtferth's teacher than Lapidge, **262**, who describes Abbo as 'one of the most learned men in the Europe of his day' (59). Gatch, **232**, in his survey of scholarship pertaining to OE prose, concluded that Byrhtferth 'will always be ... valued for what his work indicates about the qualities of a rather more ordinary side of late Anglo-Saxon culture and for the contrast he provides with his greater contemporaries' (237).

As a bilingual writer on a wide variety of branches of knowledge, Byrhtferth would seem to provide excellent opportunities for interdisciplinary studies, but it is hard to avoid the impression of a sharp disjunction between the man who wrote the *Manual*, in which Anglo-Saxonists have been hard pressed to find enduring value, and the man who is being advanced by Anglo-Latinists as a leading intellectual light; and Singer, who regarded J as representative of early 12th century scientific knowledge and one of the more intellectually respectable productions of its era ('absurd and childish as it is, [it] marks a real advance on what had gone before,' **236**, 160), would surely have been disconcerted to discover that Byrhtferth was responsible for the compilation of J's exemplar. Although Hart, **242**, and Baker, **245**, have demonstrated that *ByrM* is based on the exemplar of J, Byrhtferth

---

[15] F.M. Stenton, *Anglo-Saxon England* (Oxford: Clarendon, 1943) 390.

would seem not to have incorporated the superior medical knowledge that J contains. The Singers, **237**, did discern one passage of *ByrM* (the passage accompanying the diagram copied in J) which, they believed, showed remarkably early Salernitan influence (cf. Talbot, **369**); Cameron, **390**, 150, however, observes that everything of medical interest in *ByrM* derives from Bede's *De Temporum Ratione*, ch. 35, and that there is no need to suppose that he even knew the sources from which Bede drew his information; he holds that the medical folios in J are a later addition.

The specific nature of Byrhtferth's intellectual contribution and historical significance is still in the process of discovery. One definition of his historical significance is advanced by Lapidge, **262**, when he concludes that 'before any overall assessment of the Anglo-Saxon school curriculum can be made, the Latin writings of Byrhtferth will require scholarly attention' (61). Perhaps extended examination of his intellectual contribution is to be found in scholarship dealing with the scientific material in J; Evans, **244**, for instance, in her study of the abacus, offers positive testimony to the contribution of Byrhtferth. Some consideration of Byrhtferth's place in intellectual history was offered by Keller, **216**. Henel, **270**, is still the classical study of *ByrM* as a commentary on computus; some technicalities are also explained in Henel, **225**, and Henel, **222**, includes comparison of the cosmological teachings of Ælfric and Byrhtferth. *ByrM* and the computus tradition has also been studied by Lucas, **288**. Murphy, **229**, studies Byrhtferth's relation to the rhetorical tradition. Lutz, **233**, offers a sympathetic view of Byrhtferth as a teacher on the basis of her reading of *ByrM*; she makes the point that we cannot judge his capacities as a teacher, or his intellectual stature, from an elementary instruction book, but her argument is weakened by its dependence on the now discredited claim that Byrhtferth was the author of a Latin work on mathematics. An admiring view of *ByrM* is presented by Berry, **234**, who discerns in its structure a reflection of the mystery of the creation which is the subject of Byrhtferth's teaching.

BYRHTFERTH OF RAMSEY: ANNOTATIONS

PART I: BYRIITFERTH'S MANUAL

SEE ALSO Anderson, **17**; Förster, **58**; Tristram, **86**; McGurk, **159**; Henel, **270**; Tupper, **276**; Enkvist, **279**; Cockayne, **298**; Henel, **323**; Grattan and Singer, **326**; Singer, **470**; Talbot, **524**; Cameron, **551**

EDITIONS

211 Kluge, Friedrich. 'Angelsächsische Excerpte aus Byrhtferth's Handboc oder Enchiridion.' *Anglia* 8 (1885): 298–337.

Prints the OE portions only of A (also omits diagrams, rubrics, glosses, etc.). No apparatus: the textual study foreshadowed here, which was to have appeared in *Anglia* 9, did not eventuate.

212 Crawford, S.J. *Byrhtferth's Manual (AD 1011).* EETS 177. London: Oxford UP, 1929. Repr., with list of errata by Neil R. Ker, 1966.

Edits the OE and Latin text from pp. 1–251 of A, with translation facing, at 2–250. Also prints 'Proemium Brihtferthi,' from J, f. 12v (Appendix I, 244–6); 'Ammonitio Amici' from pp. 251–8 of A (Appendix II, 247–50); and a note on epacts from Caligula A.xv, f. 143, at 36–7, which Crawford attributes to Byrhtferth [FC B.3.4.39; FC B.20.2.3]. Notes to the text, chiefly sources, at foot of page. Seventeen plates, including the 'four fours' diagram from J, f. 7v. The projected Vol. 2, which was to have contained the Introduction, etc., did not appear. [For reviews see Steele, **221**.]

213 Crawford, S.J. 'A Critical Edition of the *Handboc* or *Enchiridion* of Byrhtferth.' Diss. Oxford U, 1930.

Not sighted.

214 Henel, Heinrich. 'Ein Bruchstück aus Byrhtferþs *Handbuch*.' *Anglia* 61 (1937): 122–5.

Prints Cambridge, University Library Kk.5.32, f. 60v [FC B.20.20.2], consisting of a fragment of about 20 lines (on division, etc.), corresponding to *ByrM*, 188/23–190/14; 190/21–5; 190/28–192/7; 192/10–16. Textual variants from Crawford, **212**. Henel remarks that, as this manuscript is later and less reliable than A, it is chiefly of interest in illuminating contemporary lack of circulation of Byrhtferth's work, since, with the diagram in J, two fragments in Caligula A.xv and one in Tiberius C.i, it brings the total of known excerpts to four (see Henel, **270**, 1, 52). A note on the text explains,

and gives the correct form for, three material errors (presumed to be Byrhtferth's) shared by both manuscripts, which Crawford passed over.

COMMENTARY

215 **Keller, Wolfgang.** 'Zur Literatur und Sprache von Worcester im X. und
XI. Jahrhundert. I: Literarische Bestrebungen in Worcester bis zum Tode
des Erzbischofs Oswald (992).' Diss. U Strassburg, 1897.

Incorporated in Keller, **216**.

216 **Keller, Wolfgang.** *Die Litterarischen Bestrebungen von Worcester in ags
Zeit*. Quellen und Forschungen zur sprach- und culturgeschichte der germanischer Völker 84. Strassburg: Trübner, 1900.

Examines the literary endeavour of Worcester Cathedral and the general
cultural development of the Anglo-Saxon period, especially 10th and 11th
centuries; discussion of Abbo at Ramsey and *ByrM*, 16–17.

217 **Smith, Frank Clifton.** 'Die Sprache der Handboc Byrhtferths und des
Brieffragmentes eines unbekannten Verfassers. Ein Beitrag zur Lautlehre
des Spätags.' Diss. U Leipzig, 1905.

Not sighted.

218 **Crawford, Samuel J.** 'The Source of a Passage in Byrhtferð's *Handboc*
(A.D. 1011).' *Modern Language Review* 19 (1924): 335.

Notes that a passage printed by Kluge, **211**, 325, for which Toller suggests
Isa. 6 as a source, appears to be somewhat reminiscent of the beginning of
Paradise Lost. The whole passage is a rather loose translation of a portion
of Aldhelm's *De Laudibus Virginum* (*PL* 89: 239). The passage (in OE)
begins with a reference to 'castilades nymphas, þæt synt dunylfa.'

219 **Singer, Charles.** 'The Dark Age of Science.' *The Realist* 2 (1929): 281–95.

Some observations on Byrhtferth, who is representative of 'the sophisticated
childishness, the inane learning, and the humourless edificatory imbecility of
the men of the Dark Age' (285), serve to demonstrate the superior defining
characteristics of modern scientific thinkers. Computus had a prominent
place in Dark Age study because temporal cycles offered the only certainty
in an insecure world. 'To men of the Dark Age there was no real distinction between physical events, mental abstractions, and moral truths' (288).
Modern scientific man uses analogy purely as an exploratory tool. Medieval
man 'started with the idea that the universe was built on a systematic plan
or pattern' of which he had an inkling; 'therefore the investigation of the
rest of the pattern, on an analogical basis, should yield results similar to the
pattern already known' (288–9). Whereas men like Byrhtferth were engaged

in 'fitting missing pieces into a known pattern,' the infinity of the universe conceived by modern thought is 'a boundless ocean on which man of science now embarks' (295).

220 **Crawford, S.J.** 'Beowulfiana.' *Review of English Studies* 7 (1931): 448–50.

A note on *Beowulf*, line 600, refers to Crawford, **212**, 132/32, to support the meaning 'feasts' for 'sendaþ' (450).

221 **Steele, R.** Rev. of *Byrhtferth's Manual (AD 1011)*, ed. S.J. Crawford [**212**]. *Modern Language Review* 26 (1931): 351–2.

Steele thinks it probable that *ByrM* is the *De institutione monachorum* that Bale ascribed to Byrhtferth, and does not accept the argument of Forsey, **238**, who denies Byrhtferth's authorship of commentaries on Bede 'apparently because the notes on the *De rerum natura* of Bede are not written in the turgid metaphorical style of his fine writing. Why should we expect them to be? I must protest against the superseded fashion of treating manuscript ascriptions as *prima facie* proof of their own falsity' (351). As a pupil of Abbo, Byrhtferth would have been a strict adherent of the Rule, and this explains his condemnation of clerks who do not wish to retain their phylacteries (Crawford, 40). 'On the whole it must be said that Byrhtferth is a very poor computist, he does not always understand what he is writing about, e.g., the *saltus lunae*, and he does not touch upon any of the questions about which the writers of his time were interested, such as the date of the Nativity or of the Crucifixion. How much the St John's figure owes to him must remain an open question.... Anglo-Saxon does not distinguish between spring or high and neap or low tides; it is evidently not a language suitable for scientific works' (352). [Steele incorrectly describes Herwagen's 1563 edition as the work of Pamelius; see Jones, **223**, 84.]

222 **Henel, Heinrich.** 'Planetenglaube in Ælfrics Zeit.' *Anglia* 58 (1934): 292–317.

Henel enquires whether astrological lore, including belief in planetary in-fluences, sometimes attributed to Arab influence, was cultivated in the late OE period, or whether references to it merely reflect patristic tradition. Of the six references Henel lists—Bede's *DTR*, chs. 3 and 8, *Poenitentiale Pseudo-Ecgberti*, 2.23, Ælfric's Epiphany Homily, *Interrogationes Sigewulfi* 21, *ByrM* (Crawford, **212**, 130)—the first four are nothing but mechanical repetition of commonplaces. Henel examines the significance of *gescead*, as used by Ælfric (on whom discussion focuses) and by Byrhtferth (cited at 301–2), and compares their teachings on the planets. Byrhtferth (discussion at 305–6) is less cautious than Ælfric; he enumerates the names of the planets (Crawford, 4/5; 4/24 f.), and writes at length on their movements (Crawford, 128/6–130/4), and on pagan planetary beliefs, in a passage based on *DTR*, ch. 8, which Ælfric's translation omits (Crawford, 130/5–130/30). There fol-lows (at 313–17) a discussion of the microcosm-macrocosm relationship, as reflected in the 'Mythos von "Adams Erschaffung" ' (see Förster, **64**), which includes reference to the prose SS and Byrhtferth (J diagram and Crawford, 86). 'Der Adamsmythos war im alten England bekannt, Ælfric hat einen Splitter davon aufgenommen, seine Elementenlehre bezieht er nicht (oder nich nur) von Beda, er bringt sie in Zusammenhang mit dem Namen Adams, das Gleiche tut Byrhtferð, und Alcuin wie Byrhtferð überliefern eine vom Adamsmythos berührte Planetendeutung.... durch eben solche Texte der Laienastrologie der Planetenglaube auch schon vor dem arabischen Einfluss nach England gebracht worden war' (316–7). The article also includes general consideration of OE lunar prognostics.

223 Jones, Charles Williams. 'Polemius Silvius, Bede, and the Names of the Months.' *Speculum* 9 (1934): 50–6.

In copying the names of the months from Polemius in *DTR*, chs. 11–14, Bede shifted the Hebrew names forward one month, altering their relation to the Roman months. This change makes it possible to establish that most lists of foreign names of the months that were compiled after Bede were taken from his *DTR*, not from *Laterculus*. The names of the months in *ByrM* are from *DTR*. Crawford, **212**, hesitated to assign the correct source because Giles's garbled edition of *DTR* led him to believe that there were discrepancies between Byrhtferth's list of the 'Greek' (i.e., Macedonian) months and those in *DTR*.

224 Ker, Neil R. 'Two Notes on MS. Ashmole 328 (*Byrhtferth's Manual*).' *Medium Ævum* 4 (1935): 16–19.

What Crawford, **212**, took to be substantial lacunae in the manuscript at pp. 26 and 40 are the consequence of dislocation; if Crawford, 30/9–44/27, is read after 56/29, confusion and repetition disappear. In addition to the loss of a leaf after p. 156, which Crawford recognized, the loss of a leaf after p. 168 may be inferred from the composition and ruling of the eleventh gathering, which has six leaves instead of the normal eight. Since the ruling of the first and last leaves is not proper for outside leaves, Ker thinks it probable that the original outer bifolion is missing, particularly as the sense of the last lines of the text on p. 168 seems incomplete and the table on p. 169 contains only three of the five lists of *lunar termini* for Lent, Easter, the Rogation days, Pentecost and Septuagesima in each year of the cycle of 19/14 years.

225 Henel, Heinrich. 'Notes on Byrhtferth's *Manual*.' *JEGP* 41 (1942): 427–43.

Henel, remarking that Crawford, **212**, suffers from the editor's insufficient familiarity with the subjects treated by Byrhtferth, presents 43 emendations, corrections and notes, many of which explain technical points in the computistical subject matter of Byrhtferth. Particular attention is given to Crawford, 88/3: 'Agusti' for MS 'Septembris' is erroneous.

226 Whitbread, Leslie. 'Byrhtferth's Hexameters.' *Notes and Queries* 193 (1948): 476.

Identifies the source of the Latin hexameter couplet which appears at Crawford, **212**, 134, and, with an OE rendering, at the top of a diagram (facing p. 150), as Arator's *De Actibus Apostolorum* (*PL* 68: 115 ff.), which was popular with OE writers from the time of Bede. The OE lines, especially if 'gyfe' is read as a monosyllable, can be scanned as hexameters, although the arrangement of feet is different in the Latin. This attempt at hexameters, remarked on by Stubbs, 1874, xx, but not by Crawford, deserves notice, if only because it is without parallel in the period.

227 Tucker, Susie I. 'The Anglo-Saxon Poet Considers the Heavens.' *Neophilologus* 41 (1957): 270–5.

Tucker shows that, just as the *Anglo-Saxon Chronicle* regards heavenly bodies as portents and also describes them 'in a scientific spirit, for their own sake' (270), so, too, the OE poets differ in their depiction of the relationship, or lack of it, that exists between Nature and human affairs. *ByrM* (Crawford, **212**, 132) is quoted as an example of the attribution of portentous significance to comets.

228 Lucas, Robert Anthony. 'Prolegomena to Byrhtferth's *Manual*.' *DAI* 31 (1971): 6559A. [Diss. U of Illinois, Urbana-Champaign, 1970.]

Dissertation not sighted. According to *DAI*, the first three chapters deal, respectively, with the relationship of the study of time-reckoning to the early theoretical studies of the quadrivium; the roles of teachers and the pedagogical methods employed in late Roman and early medieval schools; education in the Carolingian period and the role of the capitularies of Charlemagne in the study of time-reckoning. The writer then examines the relationship of *Computus Graecorum et Latinorum* to *ByrM*, together with the methods employed in the teaching and testing of the computus, and argues (in ch. 5) that *ByrM*, in the manner of *Computus Graecorum et Latinorum*, is a unified work based on the study of computus. The first three parts can be placed in the quadrivial study of astronomy, and appear to be the result of a series of lectures given at a specific time each year (probably Lent) to an audience of oblates, monks and priests to prepare them for examinations on the dating of Easter; the fourth part belongs with the quadrivial study of arithmetic and differs from the other three in style, technique, audience and palaeography, and appears originally to have been an independent treatise by Byrhtferth which has been incorporated into *ByrM*, either by a scribe or Byrhtferth himself.

229 Murphy, James J. 'The Rhetorical Lore of the *Boceras* in Byrhtferth's *Manual.*' *Philological Essays: Studies in Old and Middle English Language and Literature, in Honour of Herbert Dean Meritt.* Ed. James L. Rosier. The Hague: Mouton, 1970. 111–24.

Murphy discusses Crawford, **212**, 170/17ff., in the light of the two separate traditions (grammatical and rhetorical) underlying the use of medieval 'figurae.' Having compared the 'Barbarismus' of Donatus to the pseudo-Ciceronian 'Rhetorica ad Herennium'; Bede's 'De arte metrica' to Donatus 'Ars minor III'; and the rhetorical devices in Byrhtferth to those in Bede's 'De schematibus et tropis,' Murphy concludes that *ByrM* inserted a translation of the first part of Bede's 'De schematibus et tropis,' which represents the first English rendering of these devices. It would be a misnomer to term them rhetorical devices, as Bede is in the grammatical tradition which goes back to the 4th century Donatus. However, Byrhtferth apparently had access to some later rhetorical source, or a gloss on Bede, because his use of the OE 'hiw' = Latin 'color' indicates some source of the late 10th or early 11th century. [See Gatch, **232**.]

230 Bullough, D.A. 'The Educational Tradition in England from Alfred to Ælfric: Teaching *Utriusque Linguae.*' *La scuola nell'occidente latino dell'alto medioevo.* Settimane di studio del centro italiano di studi sull'alto medioevo 19 (1972): 453–94. Report of discussion (in Italian), 547–54.

Byrhtferth occupies 484–7 in a survey of Alfred's initiation of a teaching tradition that Ælfric enlarged and maintained. From the work of Byrhtferth can be reconstructed the type of 'scientific' texts that Abbo brought to Ramsey, which, along with his Fleury manuscripts, 'show the undoubted limitations of his abilities and of the teaching tradition that he initiated' (485). *ByrM* lacks distinction of content, and its importance derives from the fact that it made available in the vernacular Bede's writings on the principles of time-reckoning. It is not clear how far Byrhtferth had to create new words for this purpose, Bullough says (for Ælfric had partly anticipated him), but the range of the English language as a medium was now greatly extended. Byrhtferth is the first to refer to *Disticha Catonis* in an English context (Crawford, **212**, 132).

231 Hart, Cyril. 'Byrhtferth and his Manual.' *Medium Ævum* 41 (1972): 95–109.

Hart tests the validity of the view that Byrhtferth was second only to Bede in the history of Anglo-Saxon science (see especially Crawford, **249**, 100). The first part of *ByrM* was aimed at the instruction of unlettered clerks, but by the end of the second part Byrhtferth had dealt with as much of the computus as his clerks were capable of absorbing, and the third and fourth parts were directed at a more sophisticated audience, the older scholars of the monastery. An examination of the format of the manual, its transmission and sources, the place of symbolism and allegory in Byrhtferth's thinking, and the diagrams in *ByrM*, and J (ff. 7v, 13v, 39v), together with three in Tiberius C.i, which may once have formed part of *ByrM*, leads Hart to the conclusion that Byrhtferth's chief contribution was the development of the allegorical diagram as a tool of pedagogy. English monasteries in the 10th and 11th centuries lacked the intellectual ferment that characterized their continental counterparts, and any scientific expertise that Byrhtferth may once have possessed would have atrophied. 'The more one studies his writings, the more apparent it becomes that Byrhtferth had no claim whatever to remembrance as a mathematician and very little as a man of science ... and in the light of present-day knowledge of his canon, only the uninformed can continue to speak of Bede and Byrhtferth in the same breath' (105). Appendix, 108–9, tables correspondences between *ByrM* and J, as evidence that *ByrM* drew substantially on J's exemplar. Hart accepts the argument of Henel, **241**, that the J 'Proemium' originally formed the epilogue of *ByrM* and suggests (100) that a diagram in J, f. 39v, is the *recapitulatio* referred to by this epilogue.

232 Gatch, Milton McC. 'Beginnings Continued: A Decade of Studies of Old English Prose.' *Anglo-Saxon England* 5 (1976): 225–43.

Gatch disagrees with the argument of Murphy, **229**, that Byrhtferth may have had access to a more properly rhetorical source or gloss because his term *hiw* for *figura* may have been related to the use of the Latin *color* in later rhetorical treatises; he cites evidence that meanings of *hiw* included 'shape' as well as 'colour' (236, n. 4). Murphy's article, together with those of Hart, **231**, and Clemoes, **253**, 'open the way to the full study of Byrhtferth which will be needed in the coming years' (237). The additions to the canon proposed by Clemoes and by Lapidge, **254**, seem likely to establish Byrhtferth as a major author. In Gatch's view, Byrhtferth 'was conscientious, pedantic and fussy, as was Ælfric in entirely different ways, but as a stylist and scholar he will always be a star of far less magnitude than Ælfric and Wulfstan, ... valued for what his work indicates about the qualities of a rather more ordinary side of late Anglo-Saxon culture and for the contrast he provides with his greater contemporaries—a contrast which, I believe, adds to their lustre' (237).

233 Lutz, Cora E. *Schoolmasters of the Tenth Century*. Hamden, CT: Archon, 1977.

Ch. 5, 'Byrhtferth of Ramsey,' 53–62. A brief description of *ByrM* is followed by some observations on the insights it offers into Byrhtferth as a teacher. Images of radiance appear throughout, but some unusual images appear when he considers his own mission as a teacher. He 'reveals himself consistently as a sympathetic teacher, ever alert and sensitive to his hearers' (57), and especially toward young boys. He appears to have regarded the reluctance of some of his pupils as a challenge, but makes clear to them their responsibilities for learning. In expounding the 'mysteries'

he employed very simple pedagogical methods; every familiar device for
enlisting and holding the attention of the hearer is used. Lutz considers
that we cannot fairly judge his stature as a teacher from *ByrM*. Its effect
depended on oral delivery, and it may not be truly representative of his
own knowledge of mathematics, because Byrhtferth apologizes for the elementary nature of the mathematical teaching he perforce provides, and two
works by him have not survived (*De principiis mathematicis* and *De institutione monachorum*). Lutz speculates that Byrhtferth must have trained
some of his students to such proficiency that they were able to succeed him
as master of the Ramsey school; perhaps his successor was Oswald, the
nephew of Bishop Oswald, who spent some time studying at Fleury. Ch.
4, 'St. Abbo of Fleury,' 41–52, refers in passing to Byrhtferth's testimony
(Crawford, **212**, 232) 'to his teacher's skill in the art of teaching and his
fund of information in arithmetic' (48).

234 Berry, Reginald. ' "Ealle þing [*recte* þing] wundorlice gesceapen": The
Structure of the *Computus* in Byrhtferth's Manual.' *Revue de L'Université
d'Ottawa* 52 (1982): 130–41.

Berry argues that *ByrM* represents the structural application of the basic
principle of medieval rhetoric as defined by Murphy, **229**; that is, the relation of the subject of the discourse to the method of presentation. 'The
relation exists through the sacred "mystery" that all things in nature are
purposefully related in the fact of Creation' (132). Byrhtferth's awareness of
the necessity for informing structure is seen in the house-building figure in
Part 3. Behind man's mental mode is the archetypal plan of God's order in
the creation, and Byrhtferth is engaged in demonstrating this divine coherence to his students. Berry regards *ByrM* as more than a simple textbook;
a table of the structure of Part 1 (at 136–7) demonstrates its symmetry.
'The house that Byrhtferth built cannot be called aesthetically grand, yet
in its representation of the principles of correlation and number, it succeeds
in revealing the grandeur of God's creation' (141).

PART II: MS J, ITS RELATION TO BYRHTFERTH

235 Singer, Charles, and Dorothea Singer. 'A Restoration: Byrhtferð of
Ramsey's Diagram of the Physical and Physiological Fours.' *Bodleian Quarterly Record* 2 (1917–9): 47–51.

The Singers announce that the diagram in J, f. 7v, is a copy of the 'sequens
figura' promised on p. 12 of A, of which there are still traces on p. 13. The
Singers consider that J is an inexact copy of the diagram now missing from
ByrM, because J's diagram does not completely conform to Byrhtferth's
explanation in the text. They point out the similar terms in which J ascribes
to Byrhtferth the diagram and the item at f. 12v ('Proemium'), which they

identify with the commentary on Bede that 16th century scholars attributed to Byrhtferth. The diagram illustrates 'the mediaeval attempt to found on *analogy* in the structure of different parts of the universe that sense of oneness and solidarity sought by modern schools of thought through the conception of *growth* and *development*' (51). The authors conclude that a manuscript described in Leland's *Collectanea* was similar to J, but not identical.

236 **Singer, Charles.** 'A Review of the Medical Literature of the Dark Ages with a New Text of about 1110.' *Proceedings of the Royal Society of Medicine* 10 (1917): 107–60.

A survey of 'Medical Science in the Dark Ages' (which refers briefly to *Lb*, *Herb* and *ByrM*), 107–17, locates J as one of the Anglo-Saxon medical works that show the influence of Salernitan literature. Salernitan literature, though Dark Age, preserved the memory of ancient learning, and was therefore superior to Anglo-Saxon vernacular literature and the extra-Salernitan Latin which pre-dates the era of Arabian influence; hence, the treatment of the theoretical aspect of medicine in J, 'absurd and childish as it is, marks a real advance on what had gone before and is at least superior to the futile list of remedies contained in the works of pseudo-Apuleius and Sextus Placitus on which the vernacular medicine so largely draws' (160). Singer dates J, on internal evidence, to 1110–12, and discusses it as a scientific encyclopedia which reveals the range and nature of early 12th century knowledge (117–27); there is some discussion of Byrhtferth's diagram of the 'four fours,' and Singer points out that the relationship is more simply represented in the diagram on f. 39v, which is of 9th century origin. The text of the medical section of J (ff. 1–2, 175–7) is printed at 128–49, and followed by a partial translation and commentary (149–60). Includes text of OE 'charm to stop nose-bleeding' at 139 [FC B.23.1.16], 'a type common enough in Anglo-Saxon literature' (155).

237 **Singer, Charles, and Dorothea Singer.** 'An Unrecognized Anglo-Saxon Medical Text.' *Annals of Medical History* 3 (1921): 136–49.

ByrM may be an earlier reflection of Salernitan influence than J and *PD*. The Latin text of an OE–Latin passage [ed. Crawford, **212**, 10–12], once accompanied by a diagram, preserved in J (**235**), also occurs in Treves MS 40, f. 30r, a late 10th century manuscript, containing much OHG magic (146, n. 16); it derives from 'Isagoge Sorani Ephesii' (ed. Torinus, 1528), which is perhaps the earliest surviving Salernitan medical textbook (136–41). Glosses to the *ByrM* passage (perhaps in the same hand as the manuscript) include *nomina id est grece onomata*, 'part of a much wider attempt to adjust the special Greek names of the winds to the cardinal points' (141). J's diagram of the 'Physical and Physiological Fours' (reproduced, with Latin key and simplified English version) is elucidated (142–8). The central circle, identical to Julius A.vi, 10v (147, n. 22), represents 'the division of

time of the Anglo-Saxon sundial' (comparative diagram of 'the Teutonic sundial' [cf. Tupper, **276**] at 147); the inexplicable bar above it includes an unintelligible Irish ogham. The diagram is thus a specifically Anglo-Saxon development of a scheme outlined by Isidore; its importance, taken together with *ByrM*'s explanatory text, is that it gives 'insight into the [ultimately Greek] theories on which the minds of the early English *physici* were working' (148). It 'exhibits to perfection the fundamental doctrine of the *interrelation of macrocosm and microcosm*' (148), the innermost part 'representing the prototype of man, Adam,' the outermost part suggesting 'Him in whose image man was made' (149). Bibliography of 16th–19th century publications mentioning Byrhtferth (138, n. 10).

238 Forsey, George Frank. 'Byrhtferth's *Preface.*' *Speculum* 3 (1928): 505–22.

Prints, with translation, J, ff. 12v–13r, at 516–22; includes photographic reproduction. Introduction, 505–16, traces the history of the attribution to Byrhtferth of commentaries on Bede, and outrules Byrhtferth's authorship of the commentaries printed under his name by Herwagen, 1563. Forsey strengthens Byrhtferth's connection with J, and agrees with the Singers, **235**, that the manuscript described by Leland in his *Collectanea* (ed. Hearne, 1715, 4: 97) must have been closely similar to J, if not J itself. Forsey considers that Leland's confusion concerning the contents of J was the ultimate source of the ascription of the commentaries to Byrhtferth. But to postulate that these were ascribed to Byrhtferth solely through confusion arising from the Preface leaves unexplained the words 'uitae humanum genus,' quoted by Boston of Bury as the opening of Byrhtferth's commentary on Bede. Forsey therefore postulates a lost work by Byrhtferth which began 'Spiraculo uitae humanum genus,' and suggests that it was this that become confused with the commentaries ascribed to him by Herwagen. On the basis of the language and style of the Latin Preface, Forsey confirms Classen's rejection of Byrhtferth's authorship of the Herwagen commentaries (**248**). Particularly characteristic of Byrhtferth is the close similarity of his vocabulary to Aldhelm's prose *De Virginitate*, and Forsey lists verbal parallels. 'If we turn to the commentaries on Bede, not only do we find Latin of an entirely different type, exhibiting little trace of these peculiarities of vocabulary and much nearer to the classical model, but also a range of ideas and subject matter quite alien to the pedestrian Byrhtferth' (515).

239 Van de Vyver, A. 'Les œuvres inédites d'Abbon de Fleury.' *Revue Bénédictine* 47 (1935): 125–69.

In the course of a study devoted to the literary activities of Abbo (at 140–50), Van de Vyver identifies the *Dicta Abbonis* and the *Expositiones Heririci* which are referred to at the end of the 'Proemium' in J as, respectively: two short tracts on astronomy composed by Abbo in 978 which appear in J, ff. 37v–9r; and Abbo's edition of the *Computus* of Helpericus, also dated 978, which appears in J, ff. 58v–135v, and which, Van de Vyver thinks,

Abbo may have brought with him when he came to teach at Ramsey where Byrhtferth was a pupil. Van de Vyver deduces: that J (which he identifies as a late 11th century manuscript originating from Thorney) derives from a codex that Byrhtferth assembled; that Byrhtferth intended this codex as a corpus of works on the computus; and that in this codex he placed his own preface ('Proemium') at the head of computistical writings by Bede, Abbo and Helpericus.

240 Ker, N.R. 'Membra Disiecta.' *British Museum Quarterly* 12 (1937-8): 130-5.

At 131-2, Ker identifies J (dated 1109-10 on the basis of ff. 3v and 30), as a manuscript owned in the 16th century by Robert Talbot and lent to Leland (*Collectanea*, 1770, 4: 97). J was subsequently borrowed from St John's by Cotton, who returned it only at Laud's urgent entreaty. Cotton Nero C.vii, ff. 80-4, contains the Thorney annals for 961-1421, missing from J; 'it is difficult not to relate Cotton's temporary possession of the manuscript to the fact that five leaves have been torn out between ff. 143 and 144 and now form part of the Cotton collection' (131). Local notices and later additions (which include an addition to the calendar at 29 December in the hand of Ordericus Vitalis, who stayed near Thorney, *c.* 1115) make it probable that J was written at Thorney shortly after 1109-10, and transferred to Oxford in the later middle ages. At 132, Ker points out that Cotton Tiberius C.i, ff. 2-42, and Harley 3667 (fragments of a scientific manuscript written at Peterborough, *c.* 1122) have much in common with J: notably, a wheel calendar (Tiberius, f. 9; J, f. 34); a copy of Byrhtferth's diagram not noticed by Singer, **235** (Harley, f. 8); and an astrological treatise ascribed to Abbo, not noticed by Van de Vyver, **239** (Harley, f. 8v).

241 Henel, Heinrich. 'Byrhtferth's *Preface*: The Epilogue of his *Manual*?' *Speculum* 18 (1943): 288-302.

Henel argues that J, ff. 12v-13r ('Proemium'), is the lost Epilogue to *ByrM* (cf. Forsey **238**) but does not consider that the diagram on f. 13r is the 'recapitulatio' to which f. 12 refers. Henel acknowledges the difficulties presented by 'hunc perspicuum.' His case depends on the demonstration of internal connections and the argument that a formal peroration that eulogizes Bede is a fitting conclusion to *ByrM*. Henel argues that the 'Proemium' cannot have been the preface to a computistical compilation by Byrhtferth contained in the exemplar of J, (contrary to Van de Vyver, **239**), because J does not follow the arrangement postulated in ff. 12v-13r. Henel hazards that J is a copy of a manuscript that originally contained *ByrM* and works by Abbo, and that the copyist has substituted Bede's treatises for most of *ByrM*, retaining only the diagram at f. 7v and the Epilogue. After examining the process by which antiquarians attributed to Byrhtferth a four-book commentary on Bede, Henel concludes that both of Boston of Bury's entries refer to the same work, i.e., *ByrM* (in four books), and that either

Boston only ever saw the Epilogue, or he knew *ByrM* and the Epilogue in one manuscript and the Epilogue in another. Henel raises the question of why the 'Proemium' in J (which he would place at Crawford, **212**, 383/30, after the survey of the Ages of the World taken from Bede's *DTR*) was omitted from the Ashmole copy of *ByrM* if it is the true ending of that work. He suggests that the two homilies with which *ByrM* concludes in the extant copy may have replaced the Epilogue in the course of transmission, but leans more to the view that Byrhtferth authorized two editions with different perorations, because the style and subject matter of a passage in 'Ammonitio Amici,' which is unique to Ashmole (Crawford, 248/8–16), suggest Byrhtferth's authorship.

242 Hart, Cyril. 'The Ramsey *Computus.*' *English Historical Review* 85 (1970): 29–44.

Hart's demonstration that much of J and *ByrM* make use of the same computistical material and have a common source includes a table of comparative data. A comparison of the hands for the Latin annals in J shows that the annals as far as 1081 are the work of Ramsey monks, and subsequent entries from 1092 onwards were made at Thorney Abbey. It appears therefore that J was written at Ramsey up until 1081 and transferred to Thorney in the period 1081×1092, possibly at the request of Abbot Gunter of Thorney. The likely sources of the Ramsey Annals are discussed (35–8). Appendix, 38–44, collates the *Annales Ramesiensis* in J, ff. 139r–43v, with Nero C.vii, ff. 80r–4v.

243 McGurk, P. 'Computus Helperici: Its Transmission in England in the Eleventh and Twelfth Centuries.' *Medium Ævum* 43 (1974): 1–5.

McGurk classifies some 11th and 12th century English manuscripts of Computus Helperici. The first of the three groups he identifies (pre-Conquest in origin) includes J [referred to by McGurk as '17'], and four other manuscripts (two of which are associated, by Van de Vyver, **239**, with Abbo of Fleury). This group (which has some variants in common that are not found in otherwise related continental manuscripts) 'was clearly that used by Byrhtferth in his Manual when quoting or translating from Helpericus, and Hart's view of the connection between Byrhtferth's text and that of St. John's Oxford MS. 17 [**242**] receives some confirmation' (2).

244 Evans, Gillian R. 'Schools and Scholars: the Study of the Abacus in English Schools *c.* 980–*c.* 1150.' *English Historical Review* 94 (1979): 71–89.

In the course of this study, Evans notes that Byrhtferth may have been principally responsible for Ramsey's continued interest in the abacus, long after the departure of Abbo, who undoubtedly introduced knowledge of it to England. Byrhtferth's influence is clear in J, 'where a work of his own, with much derived from Abbo and from the work of later abacists, contributes to a full and varied collection of material on mathematical topics' (73). On 81–5 of the Appendix, Evans describes several works on the abacus in J.

245 **Baker, Peter S.** 'Byrhtferth's *"Enchiridion"* and the Computus in Oxford, St. John's College 17.' *Anglo-Saxon England* 10 (1982 for 1981): 123–42.

After defining 'computus' in terms of its historical development and outlining the scholarship which culminated in Hart's identification of the lost exemplar of J as the source for *ByrM* (**242**), Baker examines each of the first three books in turn, in order to demonstrate that each is keyed to a particular section of the J computus, which it summarizes or explicates (the fourth is omitted from consideration because it has little to do with computus). 'The organizational principle of the *Enchiridion* is simply to follow the order of the J computus. It does so, it is true, by fits and starts, for Byrhtferth was all too easily distracted by matters not related to the computus, but the pattern is plain enough; bk I covers J 13v–14r, bk II covers 14v–21v and bk III covers 22r–34r' (141). The computus and other works in J are the source for most of *ByrM*: even when Crawford's notes (**212**) show that Byrhtferth used works not in this manuscript, the same material is sometimes found to have been copied into its margins. 'The J corpus is important to the student of Byrhtferth in the same way that the Ælfric and Wulfstan commonplace books are important; all help us to appreciate how these authors selected and arranged their sources and thus give us valuable insight into the intellectual life of late Anglo-Saxon England' (141–2). Abbreviated table of contents of J, 125–6.

246 **Lapidge, Michael.** 'A Tenth-Century Metrical Calendar from Ramsey.' *Revue Bénédictine* 94 (1984): 326–69.

Lapidge prints, 363–5, the Latin hexameter calendar which is inserted into an Abbonian calendar in J, and argues that it took shape at Ramsey in the late 10th century (the metrical calendar, he shows, ultimately originated from York, was transmitted to Fleury, and brought back into England, perhaps through the agency of Abbo). The metrical calendar is quoted in two works that Lapidge, **254** and **261**, attributes to Byrhtferth (*Vita S. Oswaldi* and *Historia Regum*), but he concludes that the question of authorship has to be left open because, although Byrhtferth was 'a scholar of impressively wide learning and literary enterprise' (357) he was not, as far as we know, a Latin poet. Further grounds for attributing the metrical calendar to Byrhtferth are suggested by Lapidge's account of J (348–52). Lapidge accepts the arguments of Baker, **245**; he regards the *Epilogus* as the introduction to the computistical materials that make up the bulk of J, and argues that J is a very close copy of material originally compiled by Byrhtferth (perhaps in 993). *Contra* Hart, **242**, the marginalia of scribe B give no reason to believe that J was written anywhere but at Thorney, or earlier than 1110 (Lapidge dates it 1110–11). Lapidge also prints the metrical calendar from an early 12th century Winchcombe manuscript, Tiberius E.iv, which is 'very possibly another copy of Byrhtferth's lost commonplace-book' (359.)

247 Wallis, Faith Elena. 'MS Oxford St. John's College 17: A Mediaeval Manuscript in its Context.' *DAI* 46 (1986): 2782A. [Diss. U of Toronto, 1985. Dirs. L.E. Boyle and O. Lewry.]

Dissertation not sighted. According to *DAI*, J is the focus of a study which seeks to define the genre of *computus* manuscripts; Wallis concludes that the *computus* has as its core a group of computistical texts, around which are added analogous texts from other disciplines, and that the core can either be varied or added to extensively to form an encyclopedia. The writer considers that J was written at Thorney Abbey, *c*. 1102–10, and that its closest cognates are Tiberius C.i, Harley 3667 (the Peterborough Abbey *computus*) and *ByrM*; some attention is given to the historical and symbolic factors that could have contributed to the creation of the manuscript. [Cf. Hart, **242**, and Lapidge, **246**.]

PART III: OTHER WORKS ATTRIBUTED TO BYRHTFERTH

248 Classen, Karl M. *Über das Leben und die Schriften Byrhtferðs, eines angelsächsischen Gelehrten und Schriftstellers um das Jahr 1000.* Diss. U Leipzig. Dresden: Teubner, 1896.

Classen argues that the commentaries attributed to Byrhtferth were written for a non-English audience by an author who had himself little interest in England, and concludes that they were erroneously attributed to him by Renaissance scholars.

249 Crawford, Samuel J. 'Byrhtferth of Ramsey and the Anonymous Life of St. Oswald.' *Speculum Religionis: Being Essays and Studies in Religion and Literature... Presented... to Claude G. Montefiore.* Ed. F.C. Burkitt. Oxford: Clarendon, 1929. 99–111.

Crawford draws attention to the fact that Byrhtferth, probably born about 960, was a monk at Oswald's most famous foundation, and must have been well acquainted with Oswald (d. 992); *ByrM*, written in 1011, mentions the saint with deepest reverence. The author of *Vita S. Oswaldi* was obviously a Ramsey monk, intimately acquainted with Dunstan, Oswald, Eadnoth and Abbo, and schooled in the Fleury tradition. He was writing while Ælfric was still Archbishop of Canterbury, and before Abbo's death in 1004. Place and date thus favour identification. So, too, do parallels between the style and vocabulary of the Life and Byrhtferth's authenticated works (*ByrM* and the J 'Proemium'), and the attribution is strengthened by the fact that these parallels point to an author who had considerable knowledge of science and the liberal arts. Crawford (at 100–1) agrees with the arguments against Byrhtferth's authorship of the commentaries on Bede advanced by Classen, **248**, and Forsey, **238**.

250 Robinson, J. Armitage. 'Byrhtferth and the Life of St Oswald.' *Journal of Theological Studies* 31 (1929–30): 35–42.

Robinson examines some of the verbal parallels adduced by Crawford, **249**, as evidence of Byrhtferth's authorship of the Life of Oswald, with particular reference to the 'immense influence' of Aldhelm on 10th century writers, and concludes: 'The abundance of coincidences in phrase and material to which he [Crawford] has pointed must not lead us to forget that among the pupils of Abbo of Ramsey there may have been contemporaries of Byrhtferth who had the same training in the older literature as himself, one of whom might have had no less capacity of commemorating the virtues and achievements of the saintly founder' (40). Stylistic criteria of authorship 'must take account of other elements than vocabulary and phraseology. It is in the construction of sentences and the use of connecting participles that surer tests are to be found' (41). Robinson states that he has counted 40 instances of loose construction involving the relative pronoun *qui* in the Life of Oswald, whereas 'in the Latin portions of the *Manual* and in the *Preface* of Byrhtferth to Bede's *de temporibus* I have not found a single instance of strained or ambiguous use of the relative pronoun' (41). Robinson also points out some stylistic peculiarities of the Life (the inversion of *quo in* and the frequent use of the passive infinitive instead of the active), and instances some repeated phrases used by the hagiographer.

251 Jones, Charles W. 'The Byrhtferth Glosses.' *Medium Ævum* 7 (1938): 81–97.

Jones shows that the attribution to Byrhtferth of *Glossae* on Bede's *DTR* and *DNR* originated with Herwagen (1563), and cannot be regarded as authoritative. Jones thinks it probable that Herwagen's edition came from manuscript(s) of Bede containing glosses after each chapter, which Herwagen attributed to Byrhtferth (*Glossae De Temporum Ratione: auctore Brideferto Ramesiensi*) because, Jones argues, he had read in Bale's *Scriptorum Illustrium* that Byrhtferth had written commentaries on the two works he found glossed. Jones emphasizes that there are, in actuality, only two glosses attributed to Byrhtferth in Herwagen's edition; chs. 1 and 4 of *DTR* are published as separate works, accompanied by Noviomagus's *Scholia* and the *Glossae* that Herwagen attributed to Byrhtferth. This led later writers to believe that Herwagen corroborates Bale's claim that Byrhtferth wrote four commentaries on Bede. Examination of the *Glossae* shows that it is impossible to determine final authorship from style or content, but Jones deduces that the material already existed in 850, and the commentaries were actually compilations by several writers who worked at Auxerre in the late 9th and early 10th centuries. He demonstrates that, in *ByrM*, epithets are used for almost every proper name, but rarely occur in the *Glossae*.

252 Jost, Karl. *Wulfstanstudien.* Swiss Studies in English 23. Bern: Francke, 1950.

In the course of determining that the two homiletic pieces in A should be excluded from the Wulfstan canon (Crawford, **212**, 240–2, 246–50), Jost, at 240–5, argues that these pieces, the first more certainly than the second, appear to have been integral to *ByrM*. He remarks particularly on the links between the numerological exposition of the first piece and *ByrM*, and observes that the second seems to be directed to the 'Weltgeistlichen,' the same people to whom Byrhtferth taught the computus. [See also Henel, **241**, and Baker, **259**.]

253 Clemoes, Peter. 'The Composition of the Old English Text.' *The Old English Illustrated Hexateuch: British Museum Cotton Claudius B. iv.* Ed. C.R. Dodwell and Peter Clemoes. Early English Manuscripts in Facsimile 18. Copenhagen: Rosenkilde, 1974. 42–53.

Having defined the contribution of the compiler of the Hexateuch, Clemoes (at 50–3) points out that the Frankish reckoning of twelve pence to a shilling is attested in pre-Conquest England only in late 10th century Ely; the only OE documents to use this reckoning are the Hexateuch, *ByrM* and *Poenitentiale Pseudo-Ecgberti*, and Clemoes argues, with supporting examples, that *ByrM* and the compiler's contribution to the Hexateuch 'share quite substantial positive features of language' and 'show no major disagreement' (50). Clemoes also instances stylistic similarities between *ByrM* and the penitential, and identifies pedagogic techniques common to the three works. He concludes that 'the present evidence justifies the conclusion that the anonymous parts of the Hexateuch probably were by the same author and that quite probably the penitential was too' (52). Clemoes suggests that there is need for a systematic and wide-ranging study of other texts, beginning with the *Confessionale Pseudo-Ecgberti* and *Ordo Confessionis* (see Spindler, 1934, 124, 168), in order to determine Byrhtferth's vernacular canon; such a study, undertaken in conjunction with a study of the sources of Byrhtferth's already recognized writings, 'could lead to the writing of the first adequate account of Byrhtferth as a man of learning and science in the late Anglo-Saxon period' (53).

254 Lapidge, Michael. 'The Hermeneutic Style in Tenth-Century Anglo-Latin Literature.' *Anglo-Saxon England* 4 (1975): 67–111.

Lapidge defines 'hermeneutic' as 'a style whose most striking feature is the ostentatious parade of unusual, often very arcane and apparently learned vocabulary' (67), and argues that 'the energy and thoroughness of its application in England were unique' (73), because the study of difficult and hermeneutic texts was a traditional feature of the English curriculum since the days of Aldhelm, who, together with Abbo, was the most important of the 'difficult' writers studied in the 10th century. Byrhtferth is discussed at 90–5. Although *ByrM* is didactic in intention 'there is some discernible predilection for hermeneutic vocabulary' (90). Some verbal parallels between *Vita S. Ecgwine* and *Vita S. Oswaldi*, attributed to Byrhtferth by

Crawford, **249**, which are 'more striking when one considers how unusual the appearance of scientific material (such as the names of the four *climata*) is in a saint's life' (93), persuade Lapidge that Byrhtferth was the author of both Lives (see further Lapidge, **255**, **257** and **258**). These two Lives show the same predilection for hermeneutic vocabulary as *ByrM*; Lapidge lists grecisms (some of which also appear in *ByrM*), rare adverbs and adjectival and nominal neologisms. The 11th century poem of 'Osuualdus' (printed, 106–7) 'suggests that there were more authors at Ramsey cultivating the hermeneutic style than Byrhtferth' (95).

255 Lapidge, Michael. 'The Medieval Hagiography of St Ecgwine.' *Vale of Evesham Historical Society Research Papers* 6 (1977): 77–93.

Lapidge considers the migrations of the Life of St Ecgwine, from Byrhtferth to Dominic of Evesham, and then to later redactors, one of them discernibly embroiled on the side of King Henry against Anselm, *c.* 1100. [See further Lapidge, **257** and **258**.]

256 Baker, Peter Stuart. 'Studies in the Old English Canon of Byrhtferth of Ramsey.' *DAI* 41 (1981): 3569A–70A. [Diss. Yale U, 1978.]

Dissertation not sighted. It would appear from *DAI* that the conclusions reached concerning Byrhtferth's OE canon are summarized in Baker, **259**, and that the examination of the relationship of *ByrM* to J is summarized in Baker, **259**, but that the dissertation differs from Baker, **259**, in regarding the computistical notes in Caligula A.xv as fragments of an OE computistical work compiled by Byrhtferth. In addition, the dissertation contains a section on the use of pedagogic devices in *ByrM*, which concludes that Byrhtferth was a good teacher, despite the evident deficiencies of his scholarly work, as well as an examination of some texts which share rare words with *ByrM*, chiefly glosses to Latin works associated with Canterbury and Winchester, which, Baker concludes, are unlikely to be by Byrhtferth, although there is evidence that Byrhtferth adopted 'glossing words' from these or similar texts into his own work; the abstract also intimates that some consideration is given to the influence of the Latin hermeneutic style on Byrhtferth's OE prose.

257 Lapidge, Michael. 'Dominic of Evesham "Vita S. Ecgwini Episcopi et Confessoris." ' *Analecta Bollandiana* 96 (1978): 65–104.

In the introduction to his edition of Dominic's *Vita S. Ecgwini* (text at 77–104), Lapidge refers to 'the perverse penchant for numerology' and 'bizarre vocabulary' of Byrhtferth's version of this Life (66; see further Lapidge, **254**), and explains (at 71–2) that the hermeneutic style was not acceptable to Norman taste; *Vita S. Ecgwini* is one of several Lives which were revised in the post-Conquest period. 'Furthermore, Byrhtferth's work was marked by many personal idiosyncrasies.... It must also be admitted that Byrhtferth was not a very accomplished writer, and he often loses the thread of his narrative in long and tedious digressions, or in an irrelevant mass of detail. Dominic was clearly aware of the deficiencies of the earlier work' (71).

258 Lapidge, Michael. 'Byrhtferth and the *Vita S. Ecgwini.*' *Mediaeval Studies* 41 (1979): 331–53.

Lapidge argues that *Vita S. Ecgwini* was written by Byrhtferth, perhaps at the request of Abbot Ælfweard of Evesham, *c.* 1000. The *Vita S. Ecgwini* is collocated in Nero E.i with the *Vita S. Oswaldi*, which Crawford, **249**, attributed to Byrhtferth; Lapidge assembles evidence, in the form of parallel passages, stylistic idiosyncrasies, common vocabulary and common solecisms, the predilection for numerology, the citation of identical excerpts and doctrines, which suggests 'almost incontestably' (341) that the author of these two Lives was the author of *ByrM* and the *Epilogus*. Lapidge points out that two hexameters are quoted from Arator in *Vita S. Ecgwini* which appear twice in *ByrM*; they are correctly quoted at Crawford, **212**, 150, and described as 'oratio patris Byrhtferði.' *Vita S. Ecgwini* introduces them as 'exordium meae orationis' and misquotes in exactly the same way as *ByrM*, Crawford, 134. Lapidge also notes that the Evesham monastery for which *Vita S. Ecgwini* was written was, like Ramsey, a dependency of Worcester and that Ælfweard had been a monk at Ramsey. At 343–50, he examines *Vita S. Ecgwini* in detail; at 353–3, he argues that the Latin and OE glosses accompanying this Life were written by Byrhtferth, and suggests that the glosses accompanying *Vita S. Oswaldi* in Nero E.i may also prove to be his.

259 Baker, Peter S. 'The Old English Canon of Byrhtferth of Ramsey.' *Speculum* 55 (1980): 22–37.

Baker reassesses the attribution of OE works to Byrhtferth and suggests the addition of several minor texts to the canon. He examines the distribution of *forðam (ðe)* in *ByrM* as compared with that of the *Hexateuch* and Penitential of pseudo-Ecgbert, attributed to Byrhtferth by Clemoes, **253**: he also examines the use of words meaning 'God' and words used for 'to name'; modal auxiliary verbs; use of *eac* and *eac swylce; forþam* and *þy; soðlice* and *witodlice; winter* and *gear*; placement of modal auxiliaries in subordinated clauses. On the basis of this, and other differences in style and vocabulary, Baker rejects Byrhtferth's authorship of the *Hexateuch* and Penitential of pseudo-Ecgbert, advanced by Clemoes, **253**, and accepts as integral to *ByrM* the two homiletic pieces with which it ends in A. The second of these ('Ammonitio amici') is less closely related to the subject matter of *ByrM* but manuscript presentation supports the view that it constitutes Byrhtferth's epilogue to the whole work (cf. Henel, **241**). Baker also finds stylistic evidence to support Byrhtferth's authorship of many, or perhaps most, of the OE and Latin glosses to *ByrM*; rare words that he has identified as typical of Byrhtferth are used, and there are significant verbal parallels between glosses and parts of the work. Finally, Baker offers stylistic support for Byrhtferth's authorship of the note on computus in

Caligula A.xv, ff. 142v–3. The fragmentary paragraph and table of lunar regulars that follows it, as well as the passage printed by Crawford, **212**, 36, are likely to be by Byrhtferth, as they closely parallel passages in *ByrM*, and Baker finds some stylistic evidence to support this likelihood. [See also Henel **270**.]

260 Hart, Cyril. 'The East Anglian Chronicle.' *Journal of Medieval History* 7 (1981): 249–82.

Hart examines the sources of the Annals of St Neots ('*East Anglian Chronicle*'), and argues that it was composed by a Ramsey monk, shortly after Abbo's visit. At 279–80, Hart instances stylistic similarities between the *East Anglian Chronicle* and the *Northumbrian Chronicle* (see Hart, **265**, and Lapidge, **261**); but as the absence of the style and vocabulary characteristic of hermeneutic texts tells decisively against Byrhtferth's authorship, Hart concludes that the *East Anglian Chronicle* was written by one of Byrhtferth's fellow monks, writing perhaps under his tutelage: 'Germanus and Oswald are both known to have had literary ability ... and the community could well have numbered others capable of producing a chronicle in simple straightforward Latin' (280). The chronicle's inclusion of entries concerning the computist Dionysius, Priscian, and Arator 'can all be explained as a result of Byrhtferth's teachings at Ramsey' (276). Other indications of the chronicle's Ramsey origin include its special interest in the family of St Helena, because she figures prominently in the OE verse *Menologium*, which Hart also regards as a Ramsey composition (276).

261 Lapidge, Michael. 'Byrhtferth of Ramsey and the Early Sections of the *Historia Regum* Attributed to Symeon of Durham.' *Anglo-Saxon England* 10 (1982 for 1981): 97–122.

Lapidge examines the first five sections of *Historia Regum*, the two Lives he attributes to Byrhtferth (**254**, **257** and **258**), the Latin sections of *ByrM*, and the *Epilogus* (J 'Proemium'), with regard to their Latinity, habits of mind and use of sources. Lapidge compares words, phrases, topics, glosses and sources and finds that 'similarities of vocabulary, phrasing, mental predilection and common sources between the works in question are best explained by supposing that the *Historia Regum* author was Byrhtferth of Ramsey' (118).

262 Lapidge, Michael. 'The Present State of Anglo-Latin Studies.' *Insular Latin Studies: Papers on Latin Texts and Manuscripts of the British Isles: 550–1066*. Pontifical Institute of Mediaeval Studies, Papers in Mediaeval Studies 1. Ed. Michael W. Herren. Toronto: Pontifical Institute of Mediaeval Studies, 1981. 45–82.

At 59–62, Lapidge advances the view that Ramsey (together with Winchester and Christ Church, Canterbury) contributed most to Anglo-Latin literature. The writings of Byrhtferth are one of a number of signs of the

influence of Abbo of Fleury, who was among the most learned men in Europe
of his day. Recent studies of Byrhtferth's canon (Hart, **260**, Baker, **259**, and
Lapidge, **254, 257, 258** and **261**) have enlarged it 'to the point where he
may eventually emerge as one of the most prolific authors of the late Anglo-
Saxon period' (60). 'Byrhtferth writes Latin in an absolutely unmistakable
way, and the imprint of his authorship can be recognized wherever it occurs'
(61). Study of Byrhtferth's Latin works, together with *ByrM* and J, will
make possible an accurate estimate of the contents of the library at Ramsey
in the late 10th and early 11th century; Lapidge instances some authors
quoted in works attributed to Byrhtferth. 'Before any overall assessment
of the Anglo-Saxon school curriculum can be made, the Latin writings of
Byrhtferth will require scholarly attention' (62).

263 Baker, Peter S. 'Byrhtferth of Ramsey and the Renaissance Scholars.'
Anglo-Saxon Scholarship: The First Three Centuries. Ed. Carl T. Berkhout
and Milton McC. Gatch. Boston: Hall, 1982. 69–77.

Building on the conclusion of Jones, **223**, that Herwagen (1563) attributed
commentaries on Bede to Byrhtferth because he had read in Bale's *Scriptorum Illustrium* that Byrhtferth had written commentaries on *De Natura
Rerum* and *De Temporibus*, Baker explores the reasons for Bale's attribution of four works to *Bridferthus Ramesiensis*. Bale's account of Byrhtferth was chiefly derived from Leland, whose *De Scriptoribus* attributed
to Byrhtferth a commentary on Bede's *De Natura Rerum* in J, which Leland had earlier described in his *Collectanea*. Bale's notebooks show that
he also used two works that he erroneously ascribed to 'Boston of Bury.'
From these he derived Byrhtferth's purported authorship of '*In Bedam De
Temporibus*' (which probably refers to Byrhtferth's *Epilogus*) and of *De Institutione Monachorum* (Bale recorded his debt to 'Boston of Bury's' *De
Prima Monachorum Institutione* as *Ex Institutione Monachorum*, and later
took this note to refer to a work by Byrhtferth). Baker considers it likely
that Bale's attribution of *De Principiis Mathematicis* rested on a similar
kind of confusion: 'What is most surprising, however, is the way in which
later, even modern, scholars accepted unquestioningly this network of error
by Renaissance writers. ... It is our very dependence on these tools, the
fruits of past scholarship, that makes us liable to perpetuate the errors of
our illustrious Renaissance forebears' (73–4).

264 Hart, Cyril. 'The B Text of the *Anglo-Saxon Chronicle*.' *Journal of Medieval History* 8 (1982): 241–99.

Works ascribed to Byrhtferth (particularly the OE verse *Menologium*, which
Hart assumes to be his) are compared at 262–5 with the poem on King Edgar
in the B text of the *Anglo-Saxon Chronicle*; shared words and phrases persuade Hart that there is a connection between Byrhtferth and the Edgar
poem. Hart examines at length the B text's relationship to other manuscripts of the Chronicle, arguing that it was written at Ramsey, probably

977–8, at the instigation of Oswald, who wished Ramsey to become the fore-most centre for the cultivation of the new learning; he also finds reason to believe that the early annals of the B text were translated and transcribed into the exemplar of J in about 993. Hart concludes, primarily on the basis of 'ceas him oðer leoht' in the Edgar poem, a phrase that has 'computis-tical and eschatological undertones which are characteristic of Byrhtferth's thought' (295), that Byrhtferth was the author of the B text, which, in Hart's opinion, is an autograph copy. Hart's attribution is also influenced by the fact that Byrhtferth is credited with the *Vita S. Oswaldi*, and he himself attributes to him the Northumbrian Chronicle (Hart, **265**), the pre-cursors to the C and D texts and to the Worcester Chronicle (Hart, **266**), as well as the *Menologium*, which introduces the C text.

265 Hart, Cyril. 'Byrhtferth's Northumbrian Chronicle.' *English Historical Review* 97 (1982): 558–82.

Hart's case for the attribution to Byrhtferth of the first five sections of *Historia Regum* ('Northumbrian Chronicle'), anticipated by Lapidge, **261**, rests in the first instance on historical considerations. Hart also adduces the chronicle's stylistic similarities with *ByrM* and the Lives of Oswald and Ecgwine (see Lapidge, **254**, **257** and **258**); he argues, too, that the chronicle has quotations in common with these three works, and that it manifests a similar interest in numerology, computistical matters and coronations. From an examination of the written sources available to Byrhtferth for the com-position of the Northumbrian Chronicle, together with its date and purpose, Hart concludes that there were two recensions, both completed at Ramsey, 987–1001. Unlike the East Anglian Chronicle, which Hart believes to have been written at Ramsey, 987–92, 'the Northumbrian Chronicle betrays the mind of a pedagogue' (579). Hart suggests that it was written for the Ram-sey novitiate, and that it represents 'an attempt by Byrhtferth to bring for the first time to a Southern audience some knowledge of the history of the North, based on primary materials hitherto unused, and perhaps unknown, in the South' (579).

266 Hart, Cyril. 'The Early Section of the *Worcester Chronicle*.' *Journal of Medieval History* 9 (1983): 251–315.

Hart argues that the Latin chronicle attributed to Florence of Worcester, down to the end of the reign of Æthelred the Unready, was compiled at Ramsey Abbey during the last two decades of his reign, and he explores the repercussions of this on the transmission of the vernacular texts of the *Anglo-Saxon Chronicle*. At 258–65, Hart compares the *Worcester Chronicle* (up to the end of annal 1017) with the writings of Byrhtferth; he instances some shared attitudes and motifs, including echoes of Byrhtferth's exposi-tion of the three cardinal and four subsidiary virtues, and concludes that the phraseology of the *Worcester Chronicle* 'is sufficiently close to the style employed in the Ramsey scriptorium in Byrhtferth's day to suggest that

the *WCl* author was working in a similar *milieu'* (261). Hart acknowledges
that stylistic evidence is not in itself sufficient to identify Byrhtferth as the
author of the *Worcester Chronicle*, and argues at length that the chronicle
has strong historical links with Ramsey and that its many sources (which include the *Vita S. Oswaldi*, as well as the B text of the *Anglo-Saxon Chronicle*
and the *Northumbrian Chronicle*, which Hart, **264** and **265**, attributes to
Byrhtferth) are most likely to have been available at Ramsey. Like the *East-
Anglian Chronicle*, the *Worcester Chronicle* is not 'hermeneutic' in style;
Hart (at 238) now inclines to the opinion that Byrhtferth may have varied
his style according to subject matter and audience, and the *East-Anglian
Chronicle* may, therefore, also be attributable to Byrhtferth.

COMPUTUS

MANUSCRIPTS

PRINCIPAL MANUSCRIPTS

FC B.20

Sigla in bold type identify groups defined by Henel.

London, British Library, Harley 3271, ff. 91r–2v
Ker 239, arts. 10–11(c), 11(e)–12   s. xi[1]

Art. 10, *De Diebus fesstis*[1] (Prose Menologium) [FC B.20.18]; **A**
art. 11(a) Epacts [FC B.20.2.7]; (b) Rules for Finding Movable
Feasts [FC B.20.1.6]; (c) Concurrents [FC B.20.3.2]; (e) Number
and Names of the Seasons (*De solae*) [FC B.20.15]; (f) Number
of Weeks, etc., in the Year [FC B.20.13.1]; (g) Length of Shadow
('of wegferendra manna dægmæl') [FC B.20.12.1]; (h) Number of
Weeks, etc., in the Year [FC B.20.13.1];[2] (i) Length of Summer
and Winter [FC B.20.16].

Art. 12, Rules for Finding Movable Feasts (as in art. 11(b), but **B**
in a different hand) [FC B.20.1.6].

Cambridge, Corpus Christi College 422, pp. 28–43, 46–9
Ker 70B, arts. b–d, e–h   s. xi med.

Art. b, Epacts [FC B.20.2.1]; art. c, Number of Days in the Month **C**
[FC B.20.14]; Length of Day and Night [FC B.20.17]; Length of
Shadow [FC B.20.12.1]; Names of Months [FC B.24.4; 'Notes and
Commonplaces']; art. d, Rules for Finding Movable Feasts [FC
B.20.1.1].

Art. e, Rules for Finding Movable Feasts [FC B.20.1.1]; Ember- **G**
fasts [FC B.20.10]; Epacts [FC B.20.2.1]; Concurrents: Rules for
Finding the Age of the Moon [FC B.20.6]; art. f, Three Fri-
days for Fasting [FC B.20.11.1]; art. g, *De diebus festis* (Prose
Menologium) [FC B.20.18]; art. h, Number of Weeks, etc., in the
Year [FC B.20.13.1].

---

[1] Ker, and Henel, **270**, *fesstis*; FC '*festis*.'

[2] As Henel, **270**, 67, points out, in arts. f and h (both classified as FC B.20.13.1,
'Number of Weeks, etc., in the Year'), the same item is copied by the same hand in a
slightly different form.

London, British Library, Cotton Titus D.xxvii, ff. 25v, 54v–6v
Ker 202, arts. e, g, h, j   1023–35, s. xi[1]

Art. e, Number of Weeks, etc., in the Year [FC B.20.13.2]; art. g,   **D**
Rule for Calculating Septuagesima, Lent and Easter [FC B.20.1.3];
art. h, Concurrents and Epacts [FC B.20.2.4]; art. j, Moon and
Tide [FC B.20.8].

London, British Library, Cotton Vitellius E.xviii, ff. 9, 13
Ker 224, arts. b–c, e–f   s. xi med.

Art. b, Rules for Finding Movable Feasts [FC B.20.1.5]; art.   **E**
c, Rules for Finding the Age of the Moon [FC B.20.6]; art. e,
Epacts [FC B.20.2.6]; art. f, Rules for Finding Movable Feasts
[FC B.20.1.5].

London, British Library, Cotton Caligula A.xv, Part A, ff. 126v,
     ff. 127v, 130v, 131v
Ker 139A, arts. b–c, f, g, j–o   s. xi[2].

Art. b, Duration of Moonshine [FC B.20.9]; art. c, *De bissexto*   **F**
[FC B.20.5]; art. f, Calculation of Advent [FC B.20.1.2]; art. g,
Dates of Easter Sunday [FC B.20.1.2]; art. j, Rule for Finding
Septuagesima, Lent and Easter [FC B.20.1.2]; art. k, Concurrents
and Epacts [FC B.20.2.2]; art. l, Rule for Finding Septuagesima
[FC B.20.1.2]; art. m, Epacts [FC B.20.2.2]; art. n, Age of the
Moon [FC B.20.6]; art. o, Three Fridays for Fasting [FC B.20.11.2].

London, British Library, Cotton Caligula A.xv, Part B,
     ff. 142v–3v
Ker 139B, arts. 2, 3   s. xi[2]

Art. 2, Concurrents [FC B.20.3.1]; Ferial Regulars [FC B.20.4];
art. 3, Epacts [FC B.20.2.3].

SINGLE ITEMS

London, British Library, Cotton Tiberius A.iii, f. 44
Ker 186, art. 8c   s. xi med.
Three Fridays for Fasting (*De ieiunio*)   FC B.20.11.1

London, British Library, Cotton Tiberius A.iii, f. 179
Ker 187, art. 1   s. x ex.
Length of Shadow ('Horologium')   FC B.20.12.2

London, British Library, Cotton Vitellius C.viii, f. 25
Ker 221 (s. xi[1]), arts. 4, 5
Art. 4, Rules for Finding Movable Feasts   FC B.20.1.4
art. 5, Epacts   FC B.20.2.5

London, British Library, Royal 2 A.xx, f. 44
Ker 248, art. d   s. x[1]
Moonrise   FC B.20.7

London, British Library, Royal 2 B.v, f. 196v
Ker 249 (s. x med., xi), art. f   s. xi[1]
Three Fridays for Fasting   FC B.20.11.3

Oxford, Bodleian, Laud Misc. 482, f. 27v
Ker 343, art. 6   s. xi med.
Ember-fasts   FC B.20.10

Brussels, Bibliothèque Royale, 8558–63, f. 153v
Ker 10C, art. 2f   s. xi[1]
Ember-fasts   FC B.20.10

London, British Library, Galba A.ii or A.iii [burnt]
Ker 156
Quaedam de computo ecclesiastico   FC B.20.19

MANUSCRIPTS; EDITIONS

The computus texts chiefly consist of calculations pertaining to the liturgical calendar, but also include pure observation of phenomena (e.g., Moon
and Tide, and the Horologium, which FC entitle 'On the Length of Shadow'),
as well as numerical data of the kind that figure in the prose dialogues and
in miscellaneous Notes (such as the number and names of the seasons).
The bulk of the computus texts are found, generally in small clusters, in
six manuscripts, two of which are bound together (Caligula A.xv, Parts A
and B). In Harley 3271, the notes on computus appear among entries in
the blank space at the end of the last quire of Ælfric's *Grammar*, in hands
nearly contemporary with it. In CCCC 422, computistical notes and tables
are preserved in a preliminary quire with a calendar of Sherbourne use. Titus D.xxvii (described by Birch, **274**), contains Ælfric's *De temporibus* and
many short pieces in Latin and OE; notes on computus are in two different
hands (arts. e, g and h are 1023–35; art. j is one of the early additions in
blank spaces, s. xi[1]). In Vitellius E.xviii, the computus notes are among a
number of OE items in the same hand as the interlinear gloss to a psalter.
Miscellaneous OE entries in Caligula A.xv, Part A, are all in the same
hand; in Part B, the two computus texts are preserved with extracts from
Ælfric's *De temporibus*, and are in the same hand as the earliest of these
extracts (s. xi[2]). For further manuscript description, see 'Prognostics,' pp.
259–60. Six other manuscripts, and a single leaf of Tiberius A.iii, each
contain one or two items (the OE notes on computus in one of the two Galba
manuscripts destroyed by fire are known only from Wanley's description).
Most of the computus material was edited by Henel, **270**. The remaining
texts can be found in Cockayne, **298** (FC B.20.9, B.20.11.2, B.20.12.2),
Napier, **56**, Förster, **321**, Crawford, **212**, Wormald, **271**, and Henel, **214**.
Other computus texts printed by Cockayne, and those printed by Hampson,
272, Roeder, **269**, and Holthausen, **267**, were re-edited by Henel.

COVERAGE

A number of the miscellaneous notes classified as 'Notes and Common-places' by FC are of related interest, particularly: Names of Week Days (FC B.24.3); Names of Months (FC B.24.4 and C.88); Names of Winds (FC B.24.5); Names of Numbers (FC B.24.7). Names of Months (appear-ing in liturgical calendars, four of them edited by Wormald, **271**, and one by Wilson, **268**) are linked with those found in the poetic Menologium (FC A.14), and with the list of Anglo-Saxon names of the months given by Bede, *De Temporum Ratione*, ch. 15. Bede's list has always been of interest to comparative philologists, and Names of Months and Names of Week Days inevitably figure in broad-ranging studies devoted to Germanic culture and religion (particularly those of 19th century German scholars), a few of which are annotated in this volume (e.g., Grimm, **430**, Fischer, **436**, Kemble, **429**). 'Notes and Commonplaces,' as well as glosses (although they are valuable indices of scientific and secular study in the Anglo-Saxon period) are not, as such, within the scope of this volume of annotations, but a few early articles on the Names of Months, associated with the study of computus in bibliographies consulted, are included. A recent study of pa-gan practices in the works of Bede and contemporary writings by Meaney, 1985, includes a translation and discussion of 'Months of the English' in *De Temporum Ratione*, ch. 15 (2–8).[3]

Ælfric's *De Temporibus Anni*, translated from Bede, is clearly rele-vant to Anglo-Saxon study of computus, and it appears in four of the manuscripts containing OE computus texts. For the purposes of this series of annotations, however, it is regarded as falling within the orbit of Ælfric scholarship (FC B.20.21/B.1.9.4).

MANUSCRIPT RELATIONSHIP

Henel concluded that the seven groups contained in the five principle manu-scripts that he studied (see list of manuscripts above) had a common source (X); he discerned three distinct recensions, and (appropriately) expressed the relationship in a formula: 'X = (AC + B) + (DE + F) + G.'

STUDY OF COMPUTUS, TIME-KEEPING

Henel, **270**, remains the only study devoted to OE computus, and has au-thoritative status (see also Henel, **225**, Wallis, **247**, Lucas, **228**). Henel explained and defined the various types of computus texts, but he does not set out to make his subject comprehensible or interesting. Henel also tabled a number of correspondences with *ByrM*, but he was not generally disposed to attribute the computus fragments to Byrhtferth's authorship. The computus texts he chiefly associated with Byrhtferth were: a note on Epacts attached to Ælfric's *De Temporibus Anni* in Caligula A.xv, Part B,

---

[3] Audrey L. Meaney, 'Bede and Anglo-Saxon Paganism,' *Parergon* NS 3 (1985): 1–29.

attributed to Byrhtferth and printed by Crawford, **212** [FC B.20.2.3]; and a
note on Concurrents and Ferial Regulars, also found in Caligula A.xv, Part
B [FC B.20.3.1, B.20.4], which corresponds closely with *ByrM*. For these,
and a note on division classified with *ByrM*, see pp. 152–3, 'Fragmentary
Notes.'

Individual computus texts are by no means easy to identify in Henel's
edition, even with the invaluable assistance of FC; the classification of computus in the Quinn *Manual*, 1990,[4] which identifies items by their opening
line and includes a key to the manuscripts, is somewhat easier to work with,
but is less reliable than FC. There are some differences between the subdivisions adopted by Henel for the purposes of discussion and those of FC;
in particular, Henel distinguishes between Rules for Finding Five Movable
Feasts and Calculation of Advent, whereas FC classify both types of text
under 'Rules for Finding Movable Feasts.' There may also be actual, as
well as formal, differences in the classification of Epacts and Concurrents.

Tupper, **276**, surveys timekeeping in the OE period in a more elementary fashion than Henel. Hampson, **272**, covers the history of the liturgical
calendar, as well as seasonal festivals and many related matters. As many
of the calculations are lunar based, they impinge occasionally on the study
of lunar prognostics (see Henel, **323**, Förster, **321**). Technical, specialist
studies of computus in the European middle ages cast light on OE computus texts, even if they do not make specific reference to them; Kren, 1985, is
of great assistance in locating such studies.[5] Among the most recent studies
on timekeeping in European middle ages is Borst, 1988.[6] Griffiths, 1991,
has not been sighted.[7] Harrison (see **280**, **281**) has published extensively
on the Anglo-Saxon lunisolar calendar; some of his work, including **280**, is
incorporated in a full-length study of the repercussions of the lunisolar calendar on Anglo-Saxon historical writing (Harrison, 1976).[8] Stevens, 1985,
provides a useful introduction to Bede's computistical and scientific work.[9]

---

[4] Karen J. Quinn and Kenneth P. Quinn, *A Manual of Old English Prose* (New York:
Garland, 1990).

[5] Claudia Kren, *Medieval Science and Technology: A Selected, Annotated Bibliography*
(New York: Garland, 1985).

[6] Arno Borst, 'Computus: Zeit und Zahl im Mittelalter,' *Deutsches Archiv für Er-
forschung des Mittelalters* 44 (1988): 1–88.

[7] Bill Griffiths, ed., *Anglo-Saxon Times: Study of the Early Calendar* (London:
AMRA, 1991).

[8] Kenneth Harrison, *The Framework of Anglo-Saxon History to A.D. 900* (Cambridge: Cambridge UP, 1976). The period 200–800 is covered by his 'Lunisolar Calendars: Their Accuracy and Some Types of Usage,' *Saints, Scholars and Heroes: Studies
in Medieval Culture in Honour of Charles W. Jones*, ed. Margot H. King and Wesley M.
Stevens, Hill Monastic Manuscript Library, 2 vols. (Collegeville, MN: St John's Abbey
and University, 1979) 2: 65–78.

[9] Wesley M. Stevens, *Bede's Scientific Achievement*, Jarrow Lecture (Jarrow: St
Paul's Church, 1985).

COMPUTUS: ANNOTATIONS

SEE ALSO Napier, **56**; Crawford, **212**; Henel, **214**; Cockayne, **298**; Förster, **321**; Henel, **323**; Gough, **532**

EDITIONS

267 Holthausen, F. 'Anglo-Saxonica.' *Anglia* 11 (1889): 170–4.

Prints without comment 'On Moonrise,' from Royal 2 A.xx, f. 44r [FC B.20.7], 173.

268 Wilson, H.A. *The Missal of Robert of Jumièges.* Henry Bradshaw Society 11. London: Henry Bradshaw Society, 1896.

Prints a calendar from Rouen, Bibliothèque Municipale, Y.6, including 'Names of Months' [FC B.24.4], at 9–20.

269 Roeder, Fritz. *Der altenglische Regius-Psalter: eine interlinearversion in Hs. Royal 2.B.5 des Brit. Mus.* Studien zur englischen Philologie 18. Halle: Niemeyer, 1904.

Prints, in description of contents of Royal 2 B.v, 'Three Days for Fasting,' from f. 196v [FC B.20.11.3], xii.

Roeder also transcribes, at xii, the proverbs on f. 6, which he describes as two Latin *Sprichwörter* with OE translation [FC B.7.3].

270 Henel, Heinrich. *Studien zum altenglischen Computus.* Beiträge zur englischen Philologie 26. Leipzig: Tauchnitz, 1934.

Prints most of the extant computistical texts, with explanatory comment and identification of manuscript relationships, in 'Altenglische Texte im Gerīm,' 36–70, classifying them as follows. (1) Rules for Finding Five Movable Feasts [FC B.20.1], 38–47; (2) Calculation of Advent [FC B.20.1.2], 47–8; (3) Epacts and Concurrents [FC B.20.2, 3, B.20.3.2], 48–51; (4) Ferial Regulars, Concurrents, Lunar Regulars, and Epacts [FC B.20.3, 4], 51–4; Rules for Finding the Age of the Moon [FC B.20.6], 54–5; (6) Moonrise [FC B.20.7], 56–8; (7) Horlogium [FC B.20.12.1], 59–60; (8) The Four Ember-fasts [FC B.20.10], 61–2; The Three Fridays for Fasting [FC B.20.11.1], 64–5; Reckoning of the Year [FC B.20.13, 15], 65–8. Henel includes some examination of parallels with *ByrM*; at 54, he regards the note on Concurrents [FC B.20.3.1, cf. Crawford, **212**, 50/29 ff.; 52/8 ff.] as excerpts from *ByrM*, not, as Classen, **248**, suggested, early works of Byrhtferth. Conclusion, 66–70, summarizes the relationships of the seven groups of computistical texts found in the five principal manuscripts containing the texts, which are: Harley 3271 (*c.* 1032), Titus D.xxvii (1034–57), CCCC 422 (*c.* 1066), Vitellius E.xviii (*c.* 1060), Caligula A.xv (*c.* 1083).

'Begriff des Computus,' 1–4. 'Byrhtferð's Handbuch: ein Kommentar des *gerīm*,' 5–35, analyses the contents of the four parts of *ByrM*, including comparison with OE *gerīm* and examination of the types of OE *gerīm*; argues that *ByrM*, especially its first and third parts, is not a computus but a commentary on a computus, the archetype of which may have originated about 970. Henel considers that there is a close relation between Titus D.xxvii, Arundel 60 and CCCC 422 and a still closer connection between the *gerīm* of the Leofric Missal and that of Tiberius B.v. 'Ein Prosa-Menologium,' 71–91, contains an edition of the text [FC B.20.18, entitled *De Diebus Festis*], and an examination of its relationship with the metrical Menologium [FC A.14]; includes comparison with liturgical calendars and *ByrM* (Crawford, 8ff.). Index of Manuscripts, 92–5.

271 Wormald, Francis. *English Kalendars before A.D. 1100.* Vol. 1, Texts. Henry Bradshaw Society 72. London: Henry Bradshaw Society, 1934. Woodbridge: Brewer–Boydell, 1991.

Prints a calendar from CCCC 422, pp. 29–40, including (in the form of rubrics) three computistical texts: 'Length of Shadow' [FC B.20.12.1]; 'Number of Days in the Month' [FC B.20.14]; 'Length of Day and Night' [FC B.20.17 and C.88], 183–95. Also prints four calendars containing 'Names of Months' [FC B.24.4], 128–39, 156–67, 184–95, 254–65. The proposed second volume did not appear.

COMMENTARY

272 Hampson, R.T. *Medii Ævi Kalendarium.* 2 vols. in 1. London: Causton, 1841.

Subtitled: 'Dates, charters, and customs of the Ages, with kalendars from the tenth to the fifteenth century and an alphabetical digest of obsolete names of days forming a glossary of the dates of the middle ages, with tables and other aids for ascertaining dates.' The purpose of the work is to determine the age of medieval chronological terms and elucidate obscurities; still a useful aid to study of computistical material. A treasure-hoard of antiquarian and folklore material; draws heavily on *Hickes Thesaurus.* Cites some OE lunar prognostics, which are held to have their origin in moon worship [FC B.23.3.3], 133–4, 373–4.

Vol. 1. Bk. 1, 'Charters and Dates,' 1–51, relates particularly to medieval chronological confusions; Bk. 2, 'Popular Customs and Superstitions connected with Dates,' 52–388, introductory remarks on the distribution of the four seasons, followed by discussion of the festivals, ecclesiastical and pagan, celebrated in each season. Bk. 3, 'Ancient Kalendars,' 389–483, edits and describes calendars from: Galba A.xviii (with variants from Tiberius B.v and Julius A.vi), 397–420; Vitellius E.xviii [cf. FC B.20.1.5, B.20.2.6], 421–33; Titus D.xxvii (includes table of epacts, concurrents, etc. for 978–1097 [cf. FC B.20.1.3, B.20.2.4, B.20.8, B.20.13.2]), 435–46; and from three Harley manuscripts of later date. Index, 483–5; Additions and Corrections, 486–92.

Vol. 2. Bk. 4, Glossary (editorial notes on the calendar), 1–416; Perpetual lunar calendar, including golden numbers and epacts, 417–23; Additions and Corrections to Vols. 1 and 2, 424–30.

273 Fowler, James. 'On Medieval Representations of the Months and Seasons.' *Archaeologia* 44 (1873): 137–224.

Fowler tables illustrations of occupations of the months (and zodiac signs where appropriate) in the calendars in Tiberius B.v and Julius A.vi, 137–9, the Runic Calendars and Staffordshire Clogg Almanacs, 140–3, on two Norman fonts, 144–6, and the Norman porch of St Margaret's, Yorkshire, which contains 'the signs and symbols of the thirteen months of the Anglo-Saxon embolismic year,' 146–9, and later representations in English and continental churches, 149–82; comparative tables of medieval and classical representations at 190–7. Fowler argues, 182–9, that 'every particle of ancient ecclesiastical architecture had a mystic or symbolic import' (182); e.g., the zodiac's frequent appearance on doorways is connected with the idea of Christ as Sun of Righteousness and Door of his Church. Notes, 198–224, chiefly concerned with agricultural practices and pastimes, occasionally make connections with OE names of months and seasons. Line drawings of later medieval representations.

274 Birch, Walter de Gray. 'On Two Anglo-Saxon Manuscripts in the British Museum.' *Transactions of the Royal Society of Literature* 2nd ser. 11 (1878): 463–512.

Descriptive catalogue of the contents of Titus D.xxvi, 466–94, and D.xxvii, 495–511. Some items are quoted in full, with incidental commentary, including: a recipe [FC B.21.5.7] (484); Number of Weeks in the Year [FC B.20.13.2] (505–6); Rules for Finding Movable Feasts [FC B.20.1.3] (507); Alphabet Divination [FC B.23.3.4] (508–9). Birch suggests that this last item might be a description of a set of illustrations that had been prepared for an alphabet of illuminated initial letters.

Birch deduces that the two manuscripts were originally one, the work of a single scribe, and the property of an ecclesiastic. He identifies the owner as Abbot Ælfwine of Newminster, on the basis of a prayer in Titus D.xxvi, f. 61, and a calendar in Titus D.xxvii, ff. 3–8 (printed at 496–500), which contains entries relating to the deaths of five members of the family of 'Aelfwinus' and indicates his promotion from monk to abbot. This calendar also mentions Wulfthrytha and Heahfleda, abbesses of St Mary at Winchester. In both manuscripts some masculine forms are overlaid with feminine ones; Birch suggests that the codex may have fallen into the hands of one of these two women after the date of its production for Ælfwine in the early years of the 11th century (492–4, 500–2). The contents of this volume 'are of their kind the most typical that are now in existence of a class of man who represents the learned man of 850 years ago' (511). Of this class, Birch's commentary conveys no very high opinion, but he hopes for the publication of the manuscripts, 'which may be not inaptly styled the Religious and Scientific Commonplace books of Ælfwine the Abbot of Newminster' (512).

275 Skeat, Walter W. 'Anglo-Saxon Names of the Months.' *Notes and Queries* 7th ser. 7 (1889): 301.

Explanatory notes on names of the months [*DTR*, ch. 15]. February, *Sol-mōnath* = 'mud month'; March, *Hreda* = 'fierce month' (*contra BT*); April is 'Easter month'; May, *Thrīmylce*, signifies that the cows might be milked thrice a day. *Lītha* is the definite form of *lĭthe*, 'mild,' so that June and July are the mild, or warm, months; August is 'weed-month'; September is 'holy month' (a great time for sacrifices to idols in heathen days); November is 'sacrifice-month' (also refers to heathen sacrifices). Skeat finds no certain explanation for October, *Winter-fylleth*, but hazards 'storm felling,' i.e., the time of year when a storm or colder weather causes the leaves to fall from the trees.

276 Tupper, Frederick, Jr. 'Anglo-Saxon Dæg-Mæl.' *PMLA* 10 (1895): 111–241.

In Ch. 1, 'The Anglo-Saxon Day,' 117–87, Tupper argues that natural and artificial day began at sunrise and that the evidence for unequal hours is conclusive, 117–28; he presents a 'scientific study' of the data given in connection with the Horologium in Tiberius A.iii, f. 176 (Cockayne, **298**, 3: 218), 122–6; cites descriptions of the divisions of day and night (including Cockayne, **298**, 3: 242), 126–8; describes Anglo-Saxon horologies, and lists three sundials with OE inscriptions, 128–32 (Kirkdale inscription at 130); and considers the length of Sunday, 132–5. Examination of the canonical hours, 135–87, includes a survey of previous scholarship and ME comparisons. Ch. 2, 'The Rubrics to the Anglo-Saxon Gospels,' 187–241, presents the rubrics in calendar form and traces, by comparative study of other liturgies, the connection between text and date from the early days of the church until the present time. Feasts and fasts discussed are: Midwinter, Yule, *On Cylda mæsse-dæg*, Eighth Mass-day to Midwinter, 12th day, Septuagesima and Sexagesima (Titus D.xxvii, IV; and Caligula A.xv, f. 126, Cockayne, **298**, 3: 227), *To Caput Jejunii on Wodnes-dæg*, Friday in the 'Cys-wucan,' *Halgan Dæg*, Lent, *Myd-fæstene*, Sunday of the 5th week in Lent, St Gregory's Mass-day, Thursday before Easter, *Langa Frige-dæg*, Easter Even,

Easter Day, *Ofer Eastron be þære rode*, Gang-days, Ascension, Pentecost, Ember Days, Midsummer, St Michael's Mass-day, All Saints' Mass, Advent, *On Sætern-dæg to Æw-fæstene ær Middan-wintra, To Cyric-halgungum*. Refers throughout to *ByrM* and Ælfric's *De Temporibus* [FC B.20.21], but there are a few citations of Computus texts.

277 Nilsson, Martin P. *Primitive Time-Reckoning. A Study in the Origins and First Development of the Art of Counting Time among the Primitive and Early Culture Peoples.* Skrifter Utgivna av Humanistiska Vetenskapssamfundet i Lund. Acta Societatis Humaniorum Litterarum Lundensis 1. Lund: Gleerup, 1920.

Ch. 11, 'Popular months of the European Peoples,' 282–310. Nilsson discusses Anglo-Saxon names of the months (Bede, *DTR*, ch. 15) at 292–5, and concludes that Anglo-Saxon months present the 'usual characteristics in the nomenclature, and in the fluctuation of names' (294). Bede's further statements concerning the Anglo-Saxon year are important and have been much disputed; here alone we have an account of a heathen Germanic lunisolar year. Tacitus (ch. 11) said the Germans observed the lunar months; the question is whether they also named the months and arrived at a fixed series, whereby the empirical intercalation of a month would arise of itself. Nilsson argues against the view that the Anglo-Saxon names are nothing more than native terms for Julian months. He finds difficulty, however, in Bede's statement that the beginning of the year was December 25th, and concludes that Bede 'erroneously substituted the ecclesiastical beginning of the year at the Christmas festival, and that the cause of his error was the fact that at this time the heathen Anglo-Saxons celebrated a Feast of the Mothers, which corresponded to the Scandinavian Yule festival celebrated at the same time of the year; whereas in reality the Anglo-Saxons, like most peoples, had no defined beginning of the year' (297). Bede's account is, nevertheless, a trustworthy indication of 'the probability that the heathen Anglo-Saxons had arrived at a fixed series of months with empirical intercalation in the summer. But even if this was so, the case is isolated, and does not advance our knowledge of the form of the year among other Germanic peoples' (297).

278 Schumacher, Karl-Heinz. *Die deutschen Monatsnamen.* Deutsches Werden 13. Greifswald: Bamberg, 1937.

At 31–45, the names of the months of the year in Bede's *DTR* are comparatively considered and regarded as a guide to the feasts and days of Germanic life; Schumacher argues that the year began with winter (October), not January as Bede claims. Also discusses conflict between the Roman and the Anglo-Saxon lunar calendar.

279 Enkvist, Nils Erik. *The Seasons of the Year: Chapters on a Motif from Beowulf to the Shepherd's Calendar.* Scientiarum Fennica. Commentationes Humanarum Litterarum 23.4. Helsingfors: Centraltryckeriet, 1957.

Ch. 4, 'The Place of the Seasons in Some Medieval Traditions,' 38–55, states that 'the basic principles of the computus stayed remarkably constant throughout the Middle Ages.... It makes comparatively little difference, as far as the main principles are concerned, which medieval handbook we turn to. All of them, including Bede and Hrabanus Maurus, or, in English, Ælfric and Byrhtferth, expound much the same basic doctrines' (40). *ByrM* (which Enkvist regards as expressly intended for the lower orders unfamiliar with Latin) is described at 41–5; in his discussion of Byrhtferth's handling of the 'Physical and Physiological Fours,' Enkvist remarks: 'In brief, the seasons become part of a well-reasoned cosmological, scientific, philosophical and religious theory which bore witness to the great unity of God's universe. A writer who thought about spring was immediately reminded of all the other things that were hot and moist like spring, or that occupied corresponding places in the great scheme' (42). Enkvist also discusses the growing importance of the four seasons in computistic tradition, cosmology, astronomy, astrology, medicine and philosophy during the Middle Ages.

280 **Harrison, Kenneth.** 'The Primitive Anglo-Saxon Calendar.' *Antiquity* 47 (1973): 284–7.

'The type of luni-solar calendar employed by the Anglo-Saxons, before the arrival of Christianity and the Julian calendar, is examined in as much detail as present knowledge allows. It was able to furnish a reliable sequence of years, running from midwinter to midwinter, for historical purposes practically in step with the Julian reckoning' (284). Realization that 12-month and 13-month years could be balanced into a cycle did not come *directly* from the Easter calculations of the Christian church; perhaps the Anglo-Saxons arrived at the notion of the cycle themselves (286), for recent work on megalithic sites shows that astronomical progress was not confined to the Near East or to developed civilizations. Bede does not make it clear whether a 19-year or an 8-year cycle was employed; inscriptions and literary sources of the period, including Cockayne, **298**, shed no light on this question, but perhaps future archaeological finds will. [Refers to Bede, *DTR* ch. 15.]

281 **Harrison, Kenneth.** 'A Twelfth Century Example of the Anglo-Saxon Calendar.' *Yorkshire Archaeological Journal* 52 (1980): 172.

A York porch carving, second half of the 12th century, at the Church of St Mary, originally from the Lazar house of St Nicholas, is a unique illustration; signs of the zodiac alternate with symbols of the Anglo-Saxon calendar, which is of lunisolar form and requires intercalation from time to time by a thirteenth month, *Thrilidi*, here represented by a man scything. We owe our knowledge of this calendar to Bede's *DTR*. Links with the past were strong in the 12th century, but the Julian calendar must have dominated at York by then.

V

Magico-Medical

Literature

MAGICO-MEDICAL LITERATURE

EXPLANATORY NOTE

Annotations are divided into four groups:

1. *Lapidary*. Annotations are divided into works which have specific reference to *Lap*, and titles suggesting but not providing reference to the OE text, some of which are of contextual interest ('Background or Redundant Items,' pp. 209–10).

2. *Leechbook*, *Lacnunga*, Recipes, Prose Charms and Headings, Prognostics, Alphabet Divination, Tables of Lucky and Unlucky Days, Prohibition against Bloodletting and 'On the Human Foetus.'

3. Publications that refer centrally and exclusively to one or more of the following: *OE Herbarium*, *Medicina de Quadrupedibus*, *Peri Didaxeon*, 'Plant Names' (in Bodley 130), and the *De Beta* recipes.

4. 'General and Miscellaneous Magico-Medical.' Annotations include studies referring to texts in groups (2) and (3), e.g., historical surveys ranging over the OE corpus, and studies which make no specific reference to the OE texts covered in this section (FC B.21, 'Medical Texts,' FC B.23, 'Folklore,' FC C.16, the interlinear glosses to prognostic texts in Tiberius A.iii, and the *Lapidary*).

Studies devoted to 'Metrical Charms,' FC A.43, which include five extracts from *Lac* and one from *Lb*, are not, as such, included in this volume of annotations, but a few are included in 'General and Miscellaneous Magico-Medical' (pp. 341–83), for the purposes of clarification.

Textual references have not been standardized. A concordance to charms in the editions of Cockayne (**400**, **297**, **298**), Grendon (**314**) and Storms (**325**) appears at pp. 250–6. Reference to the entries for these editions may help to identify texts referred to in the annotations to scholarly publications.

Further details of coverage and use of this Annotated Bibliography can be found in the 'General Introduction,' pp. 1–11.

LAPIDARY

MANUSCRIPT

London, British Library, Cotton Tiberius A.iii, ff. 101v–2r   FC B.22.3
Ker 186, art. 23   s. xi med.

MANUSCRIPT DESCRIPTION, DATE AND PROVENANCE; LANGUAGE

The contents of the manuscript in which *Lap* appears include an interlinear gloss to Ælfric's *Colloquy*, the translation of *De Temporibus*, some prognostics, computus texts and prose charms (as well as homilies and prayers), a continuous interlinear gloss to the Rule of St Benedict, and a unique copy of *Monasteriales Indicia*. Ker distinguishes three OE hands; *Lap* is in the same hand as the *Monasteriales Indicia* and interlinear glosses to prognostic texts. Kitson, **285**, describes the hand as 'clearly legible,' and states that the introductory sentence of *Lap* is in red. So too are the capitals; the *A*s are outlined in black. Evans and Serjeantson, **284**, observed that the initials were evidently added after the completion of the texts, as they stand strikingly far from the rest of the word. Evans and Serjeantson considered that two capitals had been omitted, but Kitson, **285**, holds that the capitals introduce sections, not sentences. Kitson is in agreement with earlier scholars,[1] who concluded that the manuscript is of mid-11th century, south-eastern origin, and that the language of *Lap* is WS standard with a sprinkling of Kenticisms. Ker considers that the manuscript is almost certainly one described in a medieval catalogue of Christ Church.

DESCRIPTION OF THE TEXT; EDITIONS, TRANSLATIONS AND FACSIMILE

The text consists of what purports to be a list of the 12 stones named in the Apocalypse, followed by an account of some other marvellous stones. Wanley, 198, described the text as two items, but all its editors have accepted it as a single work which constitutes the earliest surviving vernacular lapidary. Kitson, **285**, states that the manuscript presentation of the text confirms its unitary nature. *Lap*'s list contains two stones which do not appear in Rev. 21.10–20 (*onichinus* and *carbunculus*), and the numerical ordering is somewhat different. The tenth stone is evidently missing, and there is a consensus of opinion that *Lap* is a corrupt copy, at least one remove from the original. The hiatus is marked by an asterisk. Garrett, **283**,

---

[1] These include F. Kluge, 'Zur Geschichte der Zeichensprache. Angelsächsische *Indicia Monasterialia*,' *Internationale Zeitschrift für allgemeine Sprachwissenschaft* 2 (1885): 116–37, at 130–1; H. Logeman, ed., *The Rule of S. Benet*, EETS 90 (London: Trübner, 1888).

took this to be the scribe's own sign, but Kitson argues that it was inserted by an early reader. Evans and Serjeantson, **284**, considered that the name of the penultimate stone had also been omitted in the account of marvellous stones and supplied *acates*, claiming that the passage was a confused version of Pliny (132). Kitson, however, argues that this passage is based on a misunderstanding of Solinus, and that the compiler took *insicilia* to be the name of a stone (see also von Fleischhacker, **282**, and Zettersten, **289**).

Kitson's near-diplomatic edition, with translation, is the most scholarly treatment of the text, and represents the only extended study of *Lap* to have appeared. The text was first printed in 1890 by von Fleischhacker. A critical edition was included in Evans and Serjeantson's EETS edition of medieval lapidaries, and also in Garrett's study of precious stones in OE literature (**283**). Evans and Serjeantson's edition is accompanied by a translation. Turner, **286**, the first modern scholar to bring *Lap* before a non-specialist public, paraphrased the first half of the text only; Wanley's description was not perhaps the sole cause of Turner's misapprehension concerning the nature of the text. A translation also appears in Meaney's study of Anglo-Saxon amulets (**548**); she does not accept all of Kitson's textual arguments. A facsimile of f. 102r (reduced) is included by Evans and Serjeantson.

SOURCES; DATE AND PLACE OF COMPOSITION

Kitson, **285**, argues that *Lap* does not derive from Bede or Isidore, as von Fleischhacker, **282**, and Evans and Serjeantson, **284**, supposed; nor does it make direct use of Pliny's *Natural History*. Garrett, **283**, thought that the list of stones purporting to derive from the Apocalypse had been influenced by other biblical lists, but he anticipated Kitson in deducing that the source for the first half was a gloss underlying the *CorpÉpErfLeyd* glosses. Von Fleischhacker included Augustine and Solinus among the possible sources for the second half of *Lap*, and Zettersten, **289**, taking his cue from von Fleischhacker, argued that *mocritum* was a corruption of a reference to Democritum in Solinus, but Kitson explains in detail the nature of the derivation and process of composition. He concludes from examination of the *CorpÉpErfLeyd* glosses that the first half of *Lap* was based on a set of Latin glosses, compiled (probably in Kent, *c.* 680) to explain the gems of the Apocalypse. Early in the gloss-list's Latin transmission, two items were lost and *onichinus* and *carbunculus* were acquired; the missing tenth gem was probably **crisolitus*. The account of marvellous stones, based on passages of Solinus's *Collectanea Rerum Memorabilium*[2] and Augustine's *De Civitate Dei*, was added when the glosses were translated, *c.* 1000, or at least between 950 and 1050. Kitson considers that the Kentish associations

---

[2] *C. Ivlii Solini: Collectanea Rerum Memoriabilium*, ed. Th. Mommsen (Berlin: Weidmann, 1895).

of the manuscript 'may, but need not,' reflect the place where the translation was made (54).

STUDY OF *Lap*

Lapidary History

Lap is the earliest known vernacular lapidary; as a historical land-mark, however, it tends to be eclipsed by the long Latin lapidary poem written in the late 11th century by Marbod, Bishop of Rennes, which represents a new, secular type of lapidary, and which formed the basis for most medieval vernacular and Latin lapidaries.[3] Kitson, **285**, gives an extended account of the European and native lapidary traditions to which *Lap* belongs. He regards all previous surveys of lapidary writings between late antiquity and the late 11th century as inaccurate and/or unsatisfactory. In particular, he considers that lapidary historians have given insufficient attention to Apocalypse commentaries (see also Kitson, **293** and Kitson, 1984, in 'Background or Redundant Items,' p. 210). Kitson's documentation includes a briefly annotated bibliography of lapidary scholarship; few of the works he cites, including historical surveys of the lapidary, mention the OE text. The extensive bibliography of Meier, **291**, is also a valuable source of background studies and comparative material.

Kitson notes, as a limitation on the study of lapidary traditions, that many lapidary texts remain unedited, and states that lists of 11th and 12th century manuscripts containing lapidaries, chiefly unpublished, appear in Steinschneider, 1897,[4] and Thorndike, 1960.[5] There are, in addition, many Latin and vernacular lapidary manuscripts containing medical material which are listed by Riddle, **290**.

The Influence of Theodore

One aspect of Kitson's work which is of particular significance is his suggestion that a recension of the Latin Damigeron may have been known to the *Lap* author. Earlier lapidary historians consider that Marbod was the first to make use of the Latin Damigeron, but Kitson finds reason to believe that it came to England in the years following the arrival of Theodore and Hadrian (see **285**, **293**). Kitson is thus one of a number of researchers who, in the last decade or so, have pointed towards Theodore's Canterbury school as a significant underlying influence on the intellectual history of the Anglo-Saxon period as a whole.

---

[3] Marbod's poem and three minor lapidary compositions (one in verse) have been edited, with translation, by John M. Riddle, who argues, from the poem's association with herbals and medical manuscripts, that it was considered a guide to the medical use of stones: *Marbode of Rennes' De lapidibus Considered as a Medical Treatise*, Sudhoffs Archiv: Zeitschrift für Wissenschaftsgeschichte 20 (Wiesbaden: Steiner, 1977).

[4] M. Steinschneider, 'Lapidarien: ein culturgeschichtlicher Versuch,' *Semitic Studies in Memory of Rev Dr Alexander Kohut*, ed. George Alexander Kohut (Berlin: Calvary, 1897) 42–72.

[5] L. Thorndike, 'De Lapidibus,' *Ambix* 8 (1960): 6–23.

Stone and Gem Lore; Terminology

Garrett locates *Lap* within the context of Anglo-Saxon interest in precious stones, but it would be possible to draw a much more illuminating account of the cultural significance of jewels and stones in the Anglo-Saxon period from the occurrences in OE and Latin literature that he catalogues. Both he and Kitson take the view that OE stone and gem lore is mostly of learned, rather than popular, origin, Kitson regarding lapidaries as highly arcane.

Terminology figures prominently in Garrett's investigation. It also receives attention from Kitson, **285**, 25–31, who explains that the naming of stones of the Apocalypse 'was a conceptual novelty for which Anglo-Saxon students needed some explanation' (28), and that the group of glosses in *CorpÉpErfLeyd* with which he connects *Lap* are designed to meet that need. Kitson, **285**, 29, n. 9, also points out that Garrett's chapter on 'Precious Stones in the Glosses' (**283**, 46–57) does not include the Latin–Latin portions of the 10th century Harley Glossary.

Purpose and Character of the Work; Connections with Magico-medicine

Kitson has definitively placed *Lap* within the Christian-classical intellectual tradition, but is not concerned to define its broader historical implications. However, he does remark, suggestively, that 'it may be part of the secret of the huge success of Marbod's poem that he was the first to write for a reading public familiar enough imaginatively with [the Apocalypse commentaries'] basic stock of gems to have grown imaginatively curious for wider lapidary lore' (**285**, 31). Viewed against the background of Europe's intellectual heritage, *Lap* readily assumes the aspect of a characteristic product of the Dark Ages, whose intellectual decadence Charles Singer (e.g., **483**) repeatedly deplored (a corrupt copy, for specialist circulation, of a work substantially derived from Latin sources imperfectly understood). But the addition of an account of exotic stones with marvellous properties to a list of the stones of the Apocalypse is a phenomenon that seems to call for interpretation, whether as embryonic humanism, monastic *curiositas*, or an appetite for exotic marvels which, like *ApT*, *Alex*, and *Wond*, points to the emergence of the literary tastes to which the later medieval romance catered (see, e.g., Gradon, **138**).

Most commentators have remarked that, relative to later ages, Anglo-Saxon stone-lore is not markedly magical. Emphases differ: Evans, who considers that *Lap* reflects the survival of the more scientific strands of the classical tradition, is somewhat misleading when she says that *mocritum* is the only stone to which it attributes magical properties (**284, 288**). The last stone, for which she and Serjeantson supply *acates* and which Kitson takes to be *insicilia*, is said to be efficacious against 'æghwylcum attre [7] duste'; if there was a substance to be found in the Persian Empire which grew when the moon waxed and shrank when it waned, it cannot have been a stone; that everything which comes into contact with diamond is rendered worse ('forcuðra'), and that a stone may burn with a fire that cannot be extinguished by either water or wind, are propositions open to serious rational doubt. Kitson remarked that both the compiler of *Lap* and the glossator on whose work he drew 'tended toward the picturesque rather than the scientific,' although he notes that *Lap* makes some distinction between 'jewels' and 'stones' (**285**, 54).

The connection of lapidaries with medicine, which Riddle identifies as a largely 11th century development, can be discerned in *Lap*. Kitson, on the other hand, states: 'Precious stones pertain to the least reputable parts of medicine, for obvious reasons. Some figured nevertheless in the mainly botanical work of standard Greek medical writers such as Galen, Dioscorides and Oribasius. Hellenistic lapidaries take for granted the medical efficacy of jewels. So do some medical compendia, setting forth vegetable, animal and mineral medicaments on a level in successive books' (11). This tradition is examined by Thorndike, **487**, chs. 25–6. Kitson thinks it probable that the Latin Damigeron, the source of much later medieval gem lore, was used as a text for the study of medicine at Theodore's school.

Attribution of curative properties to stones is also to be found in the OE medical literature, particularly in *Lb*, which Evans, **288**, and Meaney, **548**, both mention in connection with *Lap*. Evans discusses *gagates* in *Lb*2.66, and mentions the pebbles taken from the maw of young swallows in *Lb*3.1; Meaney's chapter on mineral amulets includes discussion of *Lb*2.66, and the 'white stone,' whose properties the Patriarch of Jerusalem ordered to be made known to King Alfred (*Lb*2.64; see also Meaney, **382**, Wright, **294**). The most recent discussion of *gagates* in *Lb*2.66 is Kitson, **570**. There is some discussion of the curative use of stones in Payne, **449**, 115, Grattan and Singer, **326**, 25–31, Talbot, **524**, 11–12. According to Riddle, the dissertation of Fühner, 1902,[6] represents the only attempt to understand the specifically medical aspect of medieval stone lore.

In the last decade or so, some scholars have called for a re-evaluation of the 'superstitious' element in early medical literature (see Sanborn, **424**, Riddle, **530** and **557**, Voigts, **543**, Cameron, **565**); the sympathetically receptive attitude to magico-medical literature also has 19th and early 20th century exponents. Fernie, 1907, who identifies himself as a medical practitioner and pronounces that merely writing about precious stones has done him good, is thus of interest for the history of scholarship (see 'Background or Redundant Items,' p. 209).

---

[6]Herman Fühner, *Lithotherapie; Historische Studien über die medizinische Verwendung der Edelsteine*, diss., U Berlin (Berlin: Calvary, 1902).

LAPIDARY: ANNOTATIONS

SEE ALSO Meaney, 548

EDITIONS

282 **Von Fleischhacker, Robert.** 'Ein altenglischer Lapidar.' *Zeitschrift für deutsches Alterthum und deutsche Litteratur* 34 (1890): 229–35.

Text of *Lap*, with notes, 229–35. The notes substantiate von Fleischhacker's belief that the work derives from Bede and shows the influence of Pliny and Solinus; he also cites parallels with Dioscorides, Isidore, Augustine, *Orphei Lithica* and Marbod. He concludes that the text is not an original because of the omission of two stones and the misunderstanding of *þemocritum* (MS *þe mocritum*); the omission of the name 'achates' and the erroneous 'seleten' and 'stircites' are perhaps also attributable to the copyist (234–5).

283 **Garrett, Robert Max.** *Precious Stones in Old English Literature.* Münchner Beiträge zur Romanischen und Englischen Philologie 47. Leipzig: Böhme, 1909.

Critical edition of *Lap*, 35–6, with notes, 36–40. Bibliography, ix–xiv. The introductory remarks, 31–5, conclude that the first half of *Lap* is not an incomplete list of the stones in the Apocalypse, but is a compromise form of at least two of three biblical lists, though it is impossible to say which. Garrett states that he is unable to find a source for the second part, but deduces that the first half of *Lap* had the same source as the *CorpÉpErfLeyd* glosses. He describes the language as late WS with Kentish traces.

'Introduction,' 1–6, concludes that OE lore of precious stones shows few indications of popular origins; its sources are chiefly biblical, and treatment follows Pliny, Solinus and Isidore, with occasional references to the writings of the Fathers. In 'Precious Stones in the Latin Literature of the Old English Period,' 7–31, Garrett discusses 32 references in Aldhelm, Bede, Alcuin, Boniface and Tatwine; he also examines 'Precious Stones in the Glosses,' 46–57. In 'Precious Stones Called by Name in the Old English Literature,' 57–79, he concludes that, in the poetry, precious stones are named only twice, but there are many kennings with precious stones as their subject. They are signs of wealth and power, but are also spoken of as transitory, vain and weak. Only in the Boethius translation are they looked on as dangerous; otherwise 'precious stones are portrayed with charming naïveté as objects of beauty and of legitimate pleasure' (70). In the prose there is a wider range of application, which defies classification, but here too precious stones are symbolic, and also appear in similes. 'Conclusion,' 89–90, asserts that the veneration of stones was not confined to the laity, and was prompted, not by costliness, but by peculiarities of size, location, colour or marking. *Contra* Payne, **449**, 115, Garrett finds no grounds for inferring that oriental ideas regarding the specific powers of engraved gems worn in rings, and carried as amulets, had found a home in England. He discusses some collective terms for gems in OE. There is a list of stones in Anglo-Latin texts, 89–90, and in OE texts, 90–1; most words (22 in all) retain their Latin form, and six retain the Greek form.

284 Evans, Joan, and Mary S. Serjeantson. *English Medieval Lapidaries.* EETS 190. London: Oxford UP, 1933.

Critical edition of *Lap* (collated with von Fleischhacker, **282**), with translation facing, 13–15. Composite glossary covers *Lap* and six 15th and 16th century lapidaries also printed, 198–205; the stones mentioned in the texts are listed, together with a comparative table of occurrences, 188–97. Facsimile of f. 102r (reduced), frontispiece.

Brief manuscript description; the language is described as 'late West Saxon, with few divergencies from the normal' (1). At 13, *Lap* is said to have been 'derived from Isidore and Bede with a few additions from Pliny' and parallels are cited in the notes, 131–2. The editors also observe that *Lap* 'serves to show how early an interest in the lore of precious stones was felt in this country' (13), and that it lacks the interest in magical properties that characterizes later lapidaries.

285 Kitson, Peter. 'Lapidary Traditions in Anglo-Saxon England: part I, the background; the Old English Lapidary.' *Anglo-Saxon England* 7 (1978): 9–60.

Near-diplomatic edition, with translation, 32–3. Brief examination of manuscript presentation and language, 31, 34; the sprinkling of Kenticisms is general throughout the manuscript and likely to reflect its Kentish provenance. Annotated bibliography in the footnotes.

Kitson examines the three main streams of lapidary knowledge current in the early Middle Ages, 9–25: classical encyclopaedists; exegesis; and the medical tradition, particularly the recensions of the Latin Damigeron (also examined in Appendix, 55–60), which is likely to have come to England in the wake of Theodore, and might have influenced *Lap* [see further Kitson, **293**]. He also examines terminology and lapidary traditions in Anglo-Saxon England, with particular reference to the glosses, 25–31. Close examination of the *CorpÉpErfLeyd* glosses demonstrates that they and the first half of *Lap* were based on a set of Latin glosses compiled in England (*c.* 680) to explain the gems of the Apocalypse; the first authority drawn on was Epiphanius, but most of the information came from Pliny. Early in the gloss-list's Latin transmission, two items were lost and two new ones (*onichinus* and *carbunculus*) were acquired; the missing tenth gem was probably **crisolitus*. The knowledge of Greek in the glossator's milieu (implied by knowledge of Epiphanius) indicates that the gloss-list was composed in Kent. The second half of *Lap* was based on passages in Augustine's *De Civitate Dei* (21, 4–5) and Solinus's *Collectanea Rerum Memorabilium*. It was added when the glosses were translated (950×1050), possibly in Kent. Neither the glossator nor the translator was well-versed in Latin, and the work of both had only specialist circulation.

COMMENTARY

286 **Turner, Sharon.** *History of the Anglo-Saxons.* 6th edn. Vol. 3. London: Longman, 1836. 3 vols.

In a survey of the material luxuries of the Anglo-Saxon world, Turner supports the statement that 'The Anglo-Saxons seem to have been acquainted with the precious stones' (56) with a condensed translation of the first half of *Lap* (the rubric which refers to the Apocalypse is omitted). The gifts of frankincense, pepper, cinnamon, storax, costus and cozombri exchanged among members of the Boniface circle are also mentioned.

287 **Dieter, F.** 'Altenglisch Healstan.' *Anglia* 18 (1896): 291–2.

Crustula, which, like *colliridam* (from Gk), is glossed *halstan* or *healstan* (*ErfCorp* glosses and elsewhere) does not stand for 'crystal,' but is the plural of Latin *crustulum*, a diminutive of *crustum*. [*Lap*, 'cristallem,' does not appear to have been noticed.]

288 **Evans, Joan.** *Magical Jewels of the Middle Ages and Renaissance, particularly in England.* Oxford: Clarendon, 1922.

Evans gives a full account of the lapidaries of Hellenistic Alexandria and from Marbod onwards, but offers little on the intervening period: 'From the time of Isidore of Seville till the eleventh century there appears to be a break in the chain of Western lapidaries' (31). In ch. 4, 'Western Medieval Lapidaries,' 51–3, she observes that the dawn of vernacular literature in the West shows the tradition of the classical lapidary still surviving in a form derived from the sources least contaminated by superstition: OE scientific treatises of the 11th century draw their knowledge almost exclusively from Pliny, Solinus and Isidore, and consequently include little that is magical in character. In her view, *Lap* attributes magical properties only to *mocritum*; *Lb* (Cockayne, **297**, 2: 306, 209) attributes magical and medical properties to swallow stone and the 'white stone.' The first, second, fourth and sixth virtues of agate (Cockayne, **297**, 2: 297) are not those of later medieval convention, and may represent 'an ancient English traditional belief' (53). On 72, *Lap* (wrongly described as 'B.M. Cott. Tit. D.iii, fol. 98v') is instanced as a treatise concerned with the symbolism of the stones of the Apocalypse.

289 Zettersten, A. 'The Source of **mocritum* in Old English.' *Studia Neophilologica* 41 (1969): 375–7.

Zettersten quotes a passage from Solinus's *Collectanea Rerum Memorabilium* in which *cathotices* is described (ed. Mommsen, 1895, 45–6), in order to show that *mocritum* in *Lap* is a corruption of *Democritum*, and concludes that 'items XX and XXI of the OE text belong together and deal with only one stone' (376).

290 Riddle, John M. 'Lithotherapy in the Middle Ages: Lapidaries Considered as Medical Texts.' *Pharmacy in History* 12 (1970): 39–50.

Riddle states that the connection between lapidaries and medicine was principally a late 11th century development, and observes that information on the presumed medicinal virtues of stones is often buried among other kinds of lore about stones. He lists many medieval Latin and vernacular lapidaries containing medical material, and compares the information given on *smaragdus* in order to demonstrate that they were an everchanging, popular mode of medieval medical and scientific expression.

291 Meier, Christel. *Gemma Spiritalis: Methode und Gebrauch der Edelsteinallegorese vom frühen Christentum bis ins 18 Jahrhundert.* Münstersche Mittelalter-Schriften 34.1. Vol. 1. Munich: Fink, 1977. [Projected 2nd vol. had not appeared at time of writing.]

Vol. 1 of Meier's study of the allegorical use of precious stones by Christian writers up to the 18th century contains full and detailed treatment of patristic writings. No index; *Lap* is listed in the extensive bibliography, 523–42, but no discussion of it could be located. The 'Table of Contents' for the projected Vol. 2 includes ch. 4, 'Die Traditione der Edelsteinallegorese in Texten vom Beda Venerabilis bis zum Ende des 18. Jahrhunderts.'

292 Howe, Nicholas Phillies. *The Latin Encyclopedia Tradition and Old English Poetry.* *DAI* 40 (1979): 241A. [Diss. Yale U, 1978.]

Dissertation not sighted. Pulsiano, 1988, 334, lists *Lap* among the texts referred to by Howe in the course of his argument that Latin encyclopaedias, through their use of catalogue, served as models of formal structure for a limited number of OE poems. Howe's book length study names *Lap* in the introduction but does not discuss it. See Nicholas Howe, *The Old English Catalogue Poems*, Anglistica 23 (Copenhagen: Rosenkilde, 1985).

293 Kitson, Peter. 'Lapidary Traditions in Anglo-Saxon England: part II, Bede's *Explanatio Apocalypsis* and related works.' *Anglo-Saxon England* 12 (1983): 73–123.

This detailed examination of Apocalypse commentaries, with particular reference to Bede (which also deals with a Hiberno-Latin tract used by Bede, and a *c.* 1000 poem, *Cives celestis patrie*, which is closely dependent on

Bede), contains no examination of writings in OE but includes two addenda to Kitson, **285**. It no longer holds true that there is no trace of use of the Latin Damigeron before Marbod, because Kitson, 1984, shows that description of four marvellous stones in the 10th century Irish Apocryphon, *In Tenga Bithnua*, implies that the Latin Damigeron entered Ireland by word of mouth before the 10th century; this enhances the possibility that material from Damigeron was known to the *Lap* author (74, n. 3). The priority of Zettersten, **289**, on *mocritum*, is acknowledged (73, n. 1).

293A Corsi Mercatanti, Gloria. 'Perchè lo zaffiro è detto " ... *sunnan gelic*"?' *Schede medievali* 14–15 (1988): 64–8.

The 'sapphirus' of the ancient world did not correspond to the modern sapphire, but perhaps to lapis lazuli, and was customarily described as being like the sea or the cloudless sky. Corsi Mercatanti accepts Kitson's hypothesis (**285**) that 'sunnan gelic' is the result of a deficiency in the exemplar of *Lap*. She rejects Kitson's explanation that the expected word 'sæ' was partially illegible and misinterpreted. Instead, the word was completely illegible, and the scribe filled the lacuna by recourse to a text of the type of *De Duodecim Lapidibus*, in which 'sapphirus' is likened to 'crisolitus' in its emission of 'fulgor.' The reference to the sun was confirmed for the scribe by the clause which follows: 'on him sta[n]dað swilce gildene steorran.'

BACKGROUND OR REDUNDANT ITEMS

The following prospective-seeming items appear in the bibliographies of the works annotated above, but contain no reference to *Lap* or to OE literature.

King, C.W. *The Natural History, Ancient and Modern, of Precious Stones and Gems, and of the Precious Metals*. London: Bell; Cambridge: Deighton, 1865.

A general encyclopedia.

Fernie, W.T. *Precious Stones: for Curative Wear; and other Remedial Uses: likewise The Nobler Metals*. Bristol: Wright; London: Simpkin, 1907.

An anecdotal compendium; no specific textual reference. The author's purpose is 'to vindicate on sound, and even scientific, grounds the confidence reposed by our forefathers in Precious Stones for remedial uses, whether by outward wear, or by other such means as were inspired by nature and gleaned by simple experience' (4).

Studer, Paul, and Joan Evans. *Anglo-Norman Lapidaries*. Librairie de la Société de France et de la Société des Anciens Textes Français. Paris: Champion, 1924.

Exclusively concerned with AN lapidaries (particularly their sources); classifies them as mineralogical, symbolic or astrological.

Holmes, Urban T. 'Medieval Gem Stones.' *Speculum* 9 (1934): 195–204.

An examination of 14th and 15th century jewel inventories.

Byrne, E.H. 'Some Medieval Gems and Relative Values.' *Speculum* 10 (1935): 177–87.

Post-13th century Genoese mercantile dealings.

Basier, L. *The Lapidaire Chrétien: Its Composition, Its Influences, Its Sources.* Diss. U of Washington, 1936. New York: Catholic UP, 1936.

Not sighted; regarded as highly erroneous by Kitson, **285**.

Closs, A. 'Die Steinbücher in kulturhistorischer Überschau.' *Graz Landesmuseum Joanneum Mineralogisches Mitteilungsblatt* 8 (1958): 1–34.

Ranges over Europe, Islam and the orient and contains very little on the Latin west in the first millennium; no apparent reference to *Lap*.

Harden, Arthur Robert. 'The Carbuncle in Medieval Literature.' *Romance Notes* 2 (1960): 58–62.

The carbuncle as ornament and source of illumination in the *chansons de geste*.

Terpening, Ronnie H. 'The Lapidary of *L'Intelligenza*: Its Literary Background.' *Neophilologus* 60 (1976): 75–88.

Sketches the development of the lapidary genre with particular reference to the diamond appearing in the 13th century Italian poem.

Kitson, Peter. 'The Jewels and the Bird Hiruath of the "Ever-New Tongue." ' *Ériu* 35 (1984): 113–36.

Continues the investigation into insular knowledge of Damigeron, a significant underlying issue in Kitson, **285**.

LEECHBOOK

MANUSCRIPT

London, British Library, Royal 12 D.xvii, ff. 1–58v (*Lb*1),   FC B.21.2.1
    ff. 58v–109 (*Lb*2), 109–17v (*Lb*3)
Ker 264, arts. 1–3   s. x. med.

DESCRIPTION AND DEFINITION OF THE TEXT

Lb, which is preserved in a single manuscript (R), consists of three books of recipes. In each book, the recipes are organized into numbered chapters (88, 66 and 76 respectively) and preceded by a numbered table of contents. The descriptions in the table of contents make it possible to gauge the contents of missing chapters; the chief hiatus occurs between the now incomplete chs. 54 and 64 of *Lb*2 (Ker considers that one quire is probably missing at this point). In *Lb*3, chs. 73–4 are misnumbered in the text as 72 and 73 (with which the manuscript ends); 72, called in the contents 'Wiþ attre drenc ⁊ smiring,' is omitted. Ker suggests that it was perhaps supplied by a later hand in the margin of f. 127v, but the passage there has been treated with a reagent and is mostly illegible (Cockayne, **297**, 2: 360, transcribed a few words).

Relation of Lb1&2 to Lb3

Wright, **294**, in the introduction to the facsimile of R, established beyond doubt that *Lb*1&2 originally ended with the Latin colophon of Bald and Cild, and that *Lb*3 had existed as a separate work before it was copied into R. Wright discussed the colophon at the end of *Lb*2 at some length, and also adduced manuscript presentation as evidence that the scribe of R was copying two separate works. He also pointed out that the remedies of *Lb*3, in a less orderly way than those of *Lb*1&2, begin with the head and work downward, and that this further confirms its status as an originally independent work. Storms, **325**, 12–16, had affirmed the independence of *Lb*3, but also argued that *Lb*1 and *Lb*2 were originally independent.

Writers prior to Wright tended to describe all three books as 'Bald's Leechbook' (*Lb* is used in the annotations when the author does not distinguish between *Lb*1&2 and the three-volume work). Recognition of a difference in character had been current, however, from the time of Cockayne, who thought that *Lb*3 was probably of the same age as *Lb*1&2 and by the same hand, but remarked that it included more prayers for the sick.

211

Singer, in his revision of Cockayne, **327**, found a considerable number of 'folk practices' sprinkled throughout both *Lb*3 and *Lb*1, which appear in *Lb*2 only towards the end, and he, as well as Cockayne, considered that *Lb*2 was distinguished by the fact that it was recognizably derived from classical writings. Recent scholars, especially Meaney, **393**, and Cameron, **390**, have further differentiated *Lb*1&2, with which they are primarily concerned, from *Lb*3. Meaney, who does not think that the compiler of *Lb*1&2 would have left the material of *Lb*3 undigested if it had come within his ken, finds only five recipes shared by *Lb*3 and *Lb*1&2, and considers it unlikely that *Lb*3 originated at the same centre as *Lb*1&2. Cameron, too, regards *Lb*3 as a separate recipe collection, whose sources were different from, and more various than, those of *Lb*1&2.

EDITIONS, FACSIMILES AND TRANSLATIONS

A facsimile of the whole of R was published by Wright, **294**, in 1955; there is a facsimile of f. 55v in Cockayne. The three books were edited by Cockayne in 1867, as Vol. 2 of *Leechdoms, Wortcunning and Starcraft*, **297**, accompanied by a deliberately archaic translation and a discursive introduction; they were edited also by Leonhardi, **310**. Both Cockayne and Leonhardi print the Harley recipe collection to cover the missing quire in *Lb*2 (see further pp. 232–3, 'Leechbook-related Recipes,' FC B.21.2.4). It was generally thought, by the closing decades of the 19th century, that a new scholarly edition was needed to replace Cockayne, and Leonhardi's edition, which appeared in 1905, was not thought to fulfil that need; nor did Singer's revised edition of Cockayne's three-volume work, which, as it left Cockayne's text and translation unaltered, while stripping it of its introductions, indexes and glossaries, represented an increase in the portability of the text at the expense of a diminution in its usefulness. No attempt has been made to search out all of the numerous collations, emendations, improvements and philological arguments to which the editions of Cockayne and Leonhardi gave rise (see esp. Schlutter, **455**). *Lb*3 was edited and translated as a dissertation in 1984 by Olds, **331**. A new edition of *Lb* is being prepared by Voigts and Bierbaumer (announced Voigts, **385**).

The 'charms' in *Lb* (reflecting the predominant interest in the magical elements of Anglo-Saxon magico-medical literature in the first half of the 20th century) were separately printed by Grendon, **314**, in 1909, and later by Storms, **325**, in 1948; Grendon's collection was reissued in 1930. Both anthologies, especially Storms's, provide extensive commentary on, and translation of, individual charms taken from *Lb* (as well as from *Lac* and other manuscripts); among the passages excerpted from *Lb* is a metrical charm, 'For the Water-Elf Disease' (Grendon B5, Storms 5), which has been established as part of the poetic corpus. Grendon and Storms were essentially concerned to assemble and interpret the material, rather than to provide a scholarly text, and a substantial body of emendations was proposed by reviewers (see esp. Magoun, **353** and **363**, who includes valuable commentary on the anthologized excerpts). For a concordance to the editions of Cockayne, Grendon, and Storms, see below, pp. 250–6.

MANUSCRIPT DESCRIPTION; DATE, PROVENANCE AND LATER MEDIEVAL OWNERSHIP

The manuscript was fully described by Wright, **294**, in the introduction to his facsimile. Wright also gives a bibliographical account of earlier manuscript descriptions; there are also brief manuscript descriptions in Cockayne, **297**, and Leonhardi, **310**. Wright shows that Cockayne's interpretation of manuscript marks is erroneous. Ker is in agreement with Wright when he says that Latin marginalia (e.g., f. 125v) and frequent 'nota' signs throughout show that the manuscript was read in s. xii/xiii. (See also Voigts, **385, 543**.) Ker also comments on another sign of continuing use, a recipe 'Wiþ þa blacan blegene' (Cockayne 2: 128), which is added on f. 49 in a poor hand, s. xi. Ker, who dates the manuscript mid-10th century, describes the script as a decorative and practised Anglo-Saxon minuscule; the manuscript has black initials, ornamented like those of the *Exeter Book*.

Ker also states that the script is identical to that of the 925–55 annals in the Parker Chronicle, and concludes that R was written in the same scriptorium, presumably Winchester. In this, he agrees with the findings of Wright, who dated R to the 950s and established a strong connection with Winchester, not only through the identity with the Parker script but also by drawing on the evidence of the Tollemache Orosius and Cotton Otho B.xi (both containing works associated with Alfred and his circle). Cockayne speculated that R was the work referred to in an early medieval Glastonbury Catalogue; Wright thought Rochester ownership more likely. Ker observes that manuscripts called 'Medicinale anglicum' (the title given to R, in a hand perhaps s. xiii) are listed in the medieval catalogues of Glastonbury and Rochester, 'but there is no evidence that this is either of them.'

DATE AND PROVENANCE OF THE ORIGINAL; CIRCUMSTANCES OF PRODUCTION

All readers of *Lb* since Cockayne, **297**, have noticed the report of medical ingredients and medical knowledge communicated to Alfred by the Patriarch of Jerusalem (*Lb*2.64), and the report has been generally accepted as authentic, especially as Stevenson's edition of Asser's Life of Alfred drew attention to the confirmation it offered.[1] Wright, **294**, suggested that pilgrims to the Holy Land were the intermediaries. Wright was not prepared to go as far as Cockayne in claiming *Lb*1&2 as a copy of prescriptions in the Alfred Commonplace-book mentioned by Asser, but like Cockayne he

---

[1] W.H. Stevenson, ed., *Asser's Life of King Alfred* (Oxford: Clarendon, 1904).

referred the origins of *Lb* to the revival of learning inspired by Alfred. R, he pointed out, is evidently a copy of an earlier work, and Quirk's brief note on the language, appended to Wright's introduction, confirmed that the language was 'consistent with West Saxon dialect and scribal practice of about 950 A.D., with some forms ... possibly suggesting an archetype of perhaps fifty years earlier.' The association with Winchester and Alfred has been more fully explored by Meaney, **375, 382**. She is more confident of the Winchester provenance than Wright was, and is more inclined to refer the origins of *Lb* to the Winchester scriptorium, which she regards as the instrument of Alfred's revival of learning, rather than to Alfred personally.

LANGUAGE, VOCABULARY, GLOSSES

Quirk's brief note in Wright's facsimile, together with Schmitt, **341** (not sighted), appear to have been the chief studies of the language of *Lb* prior to the appearance of Bierbaumer's three-volume lexicographical study of the OE botanical vocabulary, which includes a volume devoted to *Lb*, **374** (based on Leonhardi's edition), and represents an important first step to the preparation of a reliable text. Meaney, writing before its appearance, expressed the hope that it would cast light on the separate origins of *Lb3*. (See further pp. 325–6, 'Plant Names.') The medical terminology of *Lb* has been studied by Curtis, **359**; for other studies of its medical terminology, see esp. Lambert, **502**, Bonser, **510**, and Stuart, **536**.

SURVEY OF SCHOLARSHIP; SOURCES; RELATION TO OTHER OE RECIPE COLLECTIONS; MAGICAL ELEMENTS

Until the late 1970s, extended discussion of *Lb* was chiefly to be found in historical surveys of the whole OE medical corpus, particularly those of Payne, **449**, Rohde, **473**, and Rubin, **531**. *Lb* also figures in the many historical surveys of Singer, whose publications span the 1920s to the 1960s. Very little of the commentary on Anglo-Saxon medicine prior to the 1970s is text-based; publications in this area have generally been topic-based. Bonser, **517**, in particular, casts light on the nature and prevalence of particular diseases and medical practices, but his method of accumulating without comment illustrations drawn from textual and non-textual sources, both Anglo-Saxon and Celtic, OE as well as Latin, is not designed to advance understanding of specific texts; on the contrary, the effect is to deny that the texts have a distinctive integrity.

In the second half of the 19th century, all the material brought together in Cockayne's three-volume edition, including *Lb*, was quarried for apposite examples by antiquarians, philologists and folklorists (both scholarly and amateur) as well as by botanists, physicians and veterinarians with an interest in the past, and the practice continued throughout much of the 20th century, attention to the OE medical literature also reflecting the emergence of anthropology as a discipline. The anthologies of Grendon, **314**, and Storms, **325**, which drew substantially on *Lb* and *Lac*, conveniently brought together most of the passages which, in the century following the appearance of Cockayne's edition, were drawn into the discussion of elvish lore, arcane rituals, Germanic and Celtic religious beliefs, culturally universal customs and the intuitive knowledge of the race, or, alternatively, the specific constitution of the primitive or medieval mind and the severe handicap under which it laboured in the absence of rational thought and scientific system.

Wright, **294**, summing up *Lb* scholarship to date in 1955, observed the foregrounding of the magic elements of *Lb* that Grendon and Storms had achieved by excerpting 'the charms,' and called for an integrated study of *Lb*, which, he believed, would restore magical elements to the relatively insignificant position that they hold in the work as a whole. Wright applauded Thorndike, **487**, for having given *Lb* its due place in the history of science. But Payne, **449**, whose pioneering study of Anglo-Saxon medicine appeared in 1904, had made it clear that *Lb* was to be regarded as a more respectably 'rational' work than *Lac*; in his opinion *Lb* (leaving aside its charms) compared very favourably with *Peri Didaxeon*. Singer recognized a distinction between *Lb* and *Lac* in so far as he regarded *Lac* as the most superstitious of the Anglo-Saxon medical texts (see, e.g., Grattan and Singer, **326**, 7). As discussion of *Lac* provided Singer with ample opportunity for deploring the debased standard of indigenous Anglo-Saxon culture—of which, in his view, *Lac* was representatively typical—his publications on Anglo-Saxon medical literature, more numerous than varied, devote very little attention to *Lb*. Bonser, **517**, although making a more concerted effort to find evidence of efficacious cures and rational practices in Anglo-Saxon literature, did not conceal the fact that he was not overwhelmed by the quantity of the evidence.

A turning point in the study of Anglo-Saxon medical literature in general, and *Lb* in particular, was initiated in 1965 by Talbot, **369**, in an article which chiefly deals with the sources of *Lb*2. Payne, although the most appreciative historian of Anglo-Saxon medicine until quite recently, considered that the medical knowledge contained in the 12th century *Peri Didaxeon* was superior to that of English works before the Conquest. He attributed this superiority to the transmission to England, through the Normans, of the influence of the renowned medical school of Salerno, which flourished in the 11th century (whether its enlightenment was due to Arab influence or the better preservation of the classical tradition was debated; see Singer, **236**; cf. Sigerist, **474**).[2] Payne was following Löweneck, the editor of *PD*, **406**, who had identified, as its primary source, a work attributed to the 11th century Salernitan writer, Petrocellus. Talbot, however, demonstrated that *Lb*2 made use of the same sources as *PD* (only one of Talbot's examples is taken from *Lb*1); the reason for this, Talbot showed, was that the

---

[2] Riddle, **530**, by contrast, doubts that the post-Salernitan era of medicine was, in practice, superior.

Practica, which Löweneck, **406**, believed to have been written by Petrocellus, had been falsely attributed to him in a late manuscript, and was in fact a compilation of classical medical writings, and was already in circulation in the 9th century. Talbot thus disposed of Payne's belief, promulgated by Singer and Bonser, that *PD* represented a more advanced and enlightened form of medical knowledge than was available to the Anglo-Saxons; for an important exception, whose implications seem never to have been pursued, see Singer, **237**.

That *Lb*, especially *Lb*1&2, contained material ultimately derived from classical medical writings was recognized by Cockayne, **297**, who described *Lb* as a combination of Greek, German and Celtic material. (Cockayne had in mind that Theodore brought knowledge of Greek to England in the 7th century; Cameron, **551**, considers that Greek medical writings were transmitted through Latin and that there is no reason to believe that medical writings were read in Greek by the Anglo-Saxons.) Cockayne's edition of *Lb* indicated parallels with Greek medical writings in the apparatus; in particular, he discerned that *Lb*2 derived substantially from Alexander of Tralles, a point emphasized by Storms in his edition of the charms, **325**. Singer, in a survey of the history of medicine from classical times to the 12th century which had been well-honed by repetition by the time it appeared as the introduction to his revision of Cockayne's edition, **327** (see Singer, **326, 470, 486, 496, 516**), delivered the opinion that *Lb* had Latin sources comparable to, but not the same as, the OE Herbarium.

Talbot, **524**, writing for a more general audience, developed the line of approach adopted in his earlier study, being concerned to demonstrate the intellectual respectability of Anglo-Saxon medical literature (the OE Herbarium as well as *Lb*) by summing up and adding to the store of classical writings known to have been available in England before the Conquest, in order to dispel the impression that the magical charms and superstitious practices of *Lac* were representative of Anglo-Saxon medicine. Quoting from Singer, **326**, he concluded: '*Lacnunga* may show "the final pathological disintegration of the great system of Greek medical thought," but it does not show that Anglo-Saxon scholars were involved in it' (23).

Lb has thus replaced *Lac* as the text representative of Anglo-Saxon medical literature, with a concomitant shift from the folklorist identification of pagan religious beliefs and magical practices to the scholarly identification of Latin sources and the establishment of the predominately rational (or at least practically efficacious) character of Anglo-Saxon medicine. Cameron, **551**, refined, increased and gave specific definition to, Talbot's outline of Latin sources available to Anglo-Saxon writers. He refers to *Lb*1&2, as well as the writings of Bede, Byrhtferth's Manual, and two 11th/12th century Latin medical collections, Oxford, St John's College 17 and the Canterbury Classbook; following Talbot, he considers the possibility that the *Practica* may have been a compilation originally made in England (**551**, 149, n. 46). In this article Cameron still echoed, though faintly, the low opinion of the intrinsic value of Anglo-Saxon medical knowledge that Singer had held, and with which Rubin, **531**, in a historical survey written after the appearance of Talbot's work, was not in fundamental disagreement. Cameron, having demonstrated the extent to which Anglo-Saxon medical knowledge derived from classical writings, concluded: 'Like all ancient medicine it was largely useless in curing the sick ... it was based on an entirely erroneous theory of the four humours .... If English medicine had a national character, it was that perhaps less emphasis was placed on bleeding and more on diet and medicine, though even in that it was seldom acting to the patient's advantage' (152).

Cameron, **390**, however, in his study of the sources of *Lb*1&2, also examined its handling of Latin sources. He gave particular attention to the work's selective adaptation of the material in response to contemporary English conditions, and observed: 'One gets the impression that he [the compiler] was a practising physician who was familiar with the ailments he wrote about and that he was drawing on personal experience when choosing treatments, which he took care to present in a way designed to be most useful to other physicians' (170). Cameron concluded that *Lb*1&2's approach to medicine was predominately rational; relative to its time, he pointed out, it contains very few charms. Like Payne, as well as Cockayne (a surprisingly sympathetic commentator), Cameron, **390**, pointed out that even the most highly regarded medical works of the classical era compromise with the irrational; Alexander of Tralles, for instance, on the authority of Galen, stated that, all else failing, a charm was permissible, as it cannot do harm and may do good. Bald's Leechbook, Cameron concluded, 'is a precious social and cultural, as well as medical, document, and deserves close study in all its aspects' (178).

Cameron, **565**, which draws primarily on *Lb*1&2 for its examples, offers a far-reaching rehabilitation of the Anglo-Saxon medical corpus. In this article, Cameron makes explicit his move towards identification with the humanely receptive stance of the pioneer of Anglo-Saxon medical history: 'I will close by quoting Payne's kindly advice again: "the only way to understand these old writers is to try to put ourselves as far as possible in their place, and conceive how nature and science presented itself to the eyes of the early teacher and learner in the tenth and eleventh centuries .... That they tried to understand them at all is proof of their wisdom, not of their folly" ' (215).

The rehabilitation of OE medical literature proposed by Cameron, **565**, was, in the broadest general terms, anticipated by Sanborn, **424**, in an article entitled 'Anglo-Saxon Medical Practices and the *Peri Didaxeon*.' In adducing a handful of examples of rational and efficacious treatment to be found in OE medical literature, Sanborn echoes the methodology which was, with varying degrees of willingness to be persuaded, adopted by the medical historians, Payne, Singer, Bonser and Rubin, and her examples are much the same (as, for instance, the observation that the honey, beer and vinegar which figure in the cures have antiseptic properties). But Sanborn's investigation was placed within a polemical framework in which, explicitly opposing the denigratory stance of Bonser, **517**, and Grattan and Singer, **326**, she called for a more radically holistic approach; although herbal remedies fell into disesteem with the emergence of multi-national drug companies, she observed, more recent advances in medical science 'are actually creating new respect for centuries old plant medicine' and 'many accepted notions concerning medicine must be drastically altered in favour of those of the ancients' (9).

Sanborn, in turn, echoes the line of approach which underlies the more technical research of Riddle, who, however, is centrally concerned with the links between modern medicine and the ancient world (see **557**), and she acknowledges a debt to Voigts, whose research on the OE Herbarium, published from the late 1970s onwards, has produced new evidence that the OE medical books are the repositories, not of arcane lore, but of empirical knowledge, and were made use of in medical practice (see esp. **543**). Cameron, **565**, is also concerned to establish the rational and efficacious nature of OE remedies, but his study, which particularly takes issue with Storms, **325**, and Nöth, **377**, marks an important methodological advance, both in demonstrating that 'magical' elements of OE cures are the interpretive constructs of their readers, and in pointing out that modern healing, in its own way (like modern disease, and surely ancient disease as well) involves psychic as well as somatic factors.

Jolly, for her part, in a study of charms with particular reference to *Lb*3.61–8, also follows Wright in considering that the decontextualized printing of passages from the medical literature in anthologies of charms gives an undue, and distorting, prominence to 'magical elements,' but the context in which she wishes to locate them is the orthodox Christian world view of Ælfric, which, she believes, typifies late Anglo-Saxon society as a whole (**395**). See further pp. 226–7, 'Lacnunga.'

The relation of *Lb*1&2 to other vernacular recipe collections, especially the collections preserved in the Omont Fragment and the Nowell transcript of Otho B.xi, is examined by Cameron, **390**. This relationship is examined more comprehensively and in greater detail by Meaney, **393**, who casts light on the development and transmission of *Lb*1&2 by studying its relations with the minor recipe collections as well as with *Lac* and *Lb*3. She considers that *Lb*1&2, resulting from an Alfredian compilation, is 'the most comprehensive and best organized of all the OE medical compilations.' (See further pp. 230–4, 'Recipe Collections.') *Lb*1&2 would also seem to be related to the OE Herbarium, but this relationship, Meaney intimates, is particularly elusive, because the version known to the compilers of *Lb*1&2 and other recipe collections appears to have differed from that of Vitellius C.iii; some correspondences between the OE Herbarium, *Lb* and *Lac* are tabled by de Vriend, **401**.

LACNUNGA

MANUSCRIPT

London, British Library, Harley 585, ff. 130–93   FC B.21.3
Ker 231, art. 2   s. x/xi, xi¹
(Includes the Lorica, Latin–OE gloss, ff. 152r–7r/1, FC C.22)

MANUSCRIPT DESCRIPTION, DATE

Lac immediately follows one of the surviving versions of the OE Herbarium Complex; these two medical works are the sole contents of the manuscript. Ker describes *Herb* and most of *Lac* as written in 'a rather rough and debased square Anglo-Saxon minuscule.' The Latin is not distinguished in the script, except at ff. 191–3. Initials are in black or red; there is some crude zoomorphic ornamentation (f. 130r). According to Ker, the manuscript originally ended at f. 179/10; the rest (to f. 193) is an addition, which he dates s. xi¹. These additional folios are printed by Cockayne, **298** (at 3: 58/19–80), and by Grattan and Singer, **326** (entries CLIII–CXCIV). The top of f. 193r is torn away; the recipes on the lower part in French and Latin, added in s. xii/ xiii, are printed by Grattan and Singer in the apparatus, 204 (the Latin–French recipes are not printed by Cockayne). A leaf or more is missing after f. 188.

Opinions concerning the date of H have differed and continue to do so (see further p. 315, 'Herbarium Complex'). Grattan and Singer, 208–9, noted in 1952 that Wanley assigned it to the 10th century, Cockayne to the 11th (mid- or second half), and Leonhardi, **310**, to the late 11th century. British Museum experts consulted by Grattan and Singer (Drs Wright and Flower) dated it respectively to the 10th century and 'quite early eleventh century'; unlike Ker, they considered that the entire manuscript was of the same date, but distinguished a separate hand at ff. 190–3. The script appears to be problematic; Wright and Flower concluded that ff. 130–90v were all in one hand but with considerable variations. Leonhardi, **310**, 158, considered that these folios were the work of one man using many quills; Meaney, **393**, is inclined to the view that there is only one hand, but agrees that f. 179r onwards was written later. Grattan and Singer, in their description of the manuscript, stated 'the possibility cannot be ruled out that *Lacnunga* ... originally began a quite separate volume' (207). They found numerous scribal errors, probably attributable to the last scribe, and observed two serious omissions, which they took to be evidence that the manuscript was a copy.

EDITIONS; THE LORICA (OF GILDAS)

Lac was printed, with translation, in Vol. 3 of Cockayne's *Leechdoms* (**298**); 'Lacnunga' is Cockayne's title for the work. It was subsequently edited in 1905, together with *Lb*, by Leonhardi, **310**. Leonhardi omitted five metrical charms from *Lac*, because they had already been edited by Wülcker.[1] Grattan and Singer's edition, with translation, is the most recent (1952). Unlike *Lb* and the OE Herbarium, *Lac* has no table of contents or numbered chapters. Cockayne's editorial sections (118 in all) were taken over by Leonhardi. Grattan and Singer, **326**, rejected Cockayne's divisions on the grounds that they bear no relation to divisions of the subject-matter. The section divisions of Grattan and Singer, then, do not correspond with Cockayne's, and they employed Roman numerals, combined with alphabetic sigla identifying the strata of compilation to which they assigned each entry; to assist cross-referencing, the margins carried both folio numbers and page references to Cockayne's edition (OE medical literature is seriously afflicted by the proliferation of discrepant and cumbersome classifications of the material). Grattan and Singer also supplied editorial chapter headings.

The editions of Cockayne and Leonhardi omit from the main body of the text the Latin text and OE interlinear gloss of the so-called Lorica of Gildas (ff. 152–7r/2), which is classified as FC C.22. (Cockayne also omits some Latin prayers and an OE heading which precedes the Lorica, most of which is entitled 'Fragment of Lost Apocrypha as Charm' by Grattan and Singer; see entries LXVIc–LXVIIc. These entries were included by Leonhardi, chs. 33–4.) Cockayne printed, in the introduction to Vol. 1 of *Leechdoms* (**400**), only the OE gloss from *Lac*, together with the Latin and OE gloss of the Lorica from Cambridge, University Library, Ll.1.10. (The interlinear gloss in this manuscript, known as the *Book of Cerne*, or the 'Prayer Book of Æðelwald,' is classified as FC C.83). The *Book of Cerne* gloss is of an earlier date than that in *Lac*. Cockayne offered the glossed versions of the Lorica as evidence, along with the Colloquium of Ælfric Bata, that 'the Saxons, in their way, tried to learn languages' (1: lvii–lxxv); his account of the surviving Latin manuscripts of the Lorica was incomplete. Leonhardi, **310**, also printed separately the *Book of Cerne* version (together with a description of the six known Latin versions); he compared the two OE interlinear glosses and studied the language of the *Lac* glosses in detail (see also Leonhardi, **450**). By the time Singer came to revise Cockayne's *Leechdoms*, the Grattan and Singer edition of *Lac* had appeared; Singer had also brought out an edition of one of the oldest Latin texts of the Lorica, Harley 2965 (*Book of Nunnaminster*) together with a study of its vocabulary (**466, 516**). Singer omitted Cockayne's three 'Introductions' in his revisions of the edition (**327**); observing that there had been much scholarly publication on the Lorica since Cockayne wrote,[2] he remarked:

---

[1] Richard P. Wülcker, ed., *Bibliothek der angelsächsischen Poesie I* (Kassel: Wigand, 1883).

[2] More recent studies of Irish loricas, superseding Singer, include K. Hughes, 'Some

'It would be unfair to inflict the *Lorica of Gildas* on the reader' (xxxix);
the Grattan and Singer edition of *Lac* is thus the only one to contain H's
Latin and OE text of the Lorica. The Lorica of Gildas in *Lac* is connected
with the metrical 'Journey Charm' in CCCC 41 by Hill, **547**, and Amies,
550.

Charms from *Lac* as well as from *Lb*, including the five metrical charms
which are classified as 'Poetry,' were included in the anthologies of Grendon, **314**, and Storms, **325** (for a concordance to the editions, see below,
pp. 250–6). Both anthologies have facing translations and an introductory
survey; Storms also provides a commentary on each of the charms.

LANGUAGE, VOCABULARY

Grattan and Singer, **326**, concluded from their study of the phonology that
the WS text contained traces of Anglian and two types of South-Eastern
dialect, late Kentish and 'Sächsische Patois.' In the body of the text, few of
the Anglian forms are specifically Northumbrian; the Lorica alone (which
Grattan and Singer assigned to the third and last substantial stratum of
composition) contains a very few forms common to Northumbrian and late
Kentish. They agreed with Leonhardi, **310**, that 'the first version of the
whole *Lacnunga*' [i.e., the substantially complete version] was Northern
and considered that the Late Kentish forms were introduced either before
or soon after the text 'acquired WS dress' (212). They found it impossible
to determine whether the language of the first transliteration into WS already contained traces of 'Sächsische Patois' or whether these were due to
a later scribe. Grattan and Singer also noted the presence of some transitional forms, 'more like ME than AS' (226). *Lac* is covered in Vol. 2 of
Bierbaumer's lexicographical study of OE botanical terms (based on Grattan and Singer's edition), **416**. Grattan and Singer drew on a vocabulary
study by Fazakerly, **356**.

COMPOSITION, TRANSMISSION AND SOURCES; MILIEU

Storms, **325**, in the introduction to his anthology of charms, observed a
number of parallel passages in *Lb* and *Lac* which ultimately derived from
Greek medical writers, particularly Alexander of Tralles. He concluded
that both works had originally derived independently from translations
from the Greek made in the north of England before the reign of Alfred
(i.e., the age of Bede, when the learning brought by Theodore was still re-
membered). Storms was centrally concerned to distinguish Germanic pagan
from Christian-classical elements in the charms. He organized the charms
in his collection according to the degree to which they showed outward
conformity with Christian-classical influences (for magic 'did not die out
when Woden and his Valhalla vanished into the dust, it merely changed

---

Aspects of Irish Influence on Early English Private Prayer,' *Studia Celtica* 5 (1970):
48–61.

its outward appearance and lived on as before'). Lower numbers in Storms identify charms of 'true Germanic origin, free from classical or Christian elements. Then follow those that show incidental foreign influence, and finally those that were borrowed from non-Germanic sources or were made up on the model of the original charms' (129). *Lac* was the single major source for the charms Storms printed (Grendon, **314**, drew more or less equally on *Lb* and *Lac*, and classified the charms according to function/type). Like earlier scholars (see above, pp. 215–18, 'Leechbook'), Storms placed *Lb* and *Lac* in a contrastive relationship: 'The majority of the prescriptions of the Leechbook are taken from Latin or Greek sources. It is different with the Lacnunga. Although many passages are translated and copied from classical authors, a great many seem to be of Germanic origin and several charms are certainly so. Christian influence is at least as strong as in the Leechbook' (24).

From the time of Cockayne, if not earlier, opinion had been divided on whether English popular folklore substantially preserved ancient Germanic beliefs and customs, or, conversely, whether it was, by and large, merely debased classical learning. Storms argued against the latter view (held, particularly, by Singer, **496**): 'I do not mean by this that we must begin by assuming Anglo-Saxon origin, but I do mean that we must not begin by assuming classical origin,' and he pointed out that correspondences between beliefs evidenced in Anglo-Saxon and classical writings did not outrule the possibility that such beliefs had existed among the Anglo-Saxons before the arrival of Christianity: 'Greek, Roman and Germanic magic goes back to one Indo-European source, and though we may succeed in establishing the existence of an Anglo-Saxon tradition, this tradition need not differ from that of Italy and Greece' (121). It was generally agreed, even among those who leaned towards the position that the learned men of Greece and Rome were the only true begetters of culture in the pre-Scholastic world— and whose general opinion of the populace at large was that, throughout the ages, its contribution had not amounted to much more than the transmission of misunderstood fragments of classical learning—that survivals of Germanic paganism were to be found in *Lac*. The history of medicine which introduced Grattan and Singer's edition of *Lac* reiterated the formula which Singer employed in his surveys of medical knowledge in the Anglo-Saxon period (**470, 486, 496, 516**): 'Native Teutonic magic is distinguishable from imported Mediterranean elements by four characteristic views of disease causation. These are: (1) the *flying venoms*; (2) the *evil nines*; (3) the *worm* as cause of disease; and (4) the power of elves and especially of the *elf-shot*. The association of these four elements is widely distributed, for it is found among the Northern peoples and in the Indian Vedas. When several of these doctrines are associated in a passage of English origin the material may safely be regarded as having been brought to this country either by Anglo-Saxons or by Norsemen' (52). A number of scholars, particularly Wright, **294**, Talbot **369**, and Cameron, **565**, regard Storms (and

Grendon) as having significantly distorted the nature of Anglo-Saxon medical knowledge and practice. It may not now be held in Storms's favour that he both popularized and gave intellectual respectability to the study of magical elements in the OE recipe collections (other major scholars who pursued the same line of approach include Bonser, **517**, and Magoun, **357** and **505**), but, for better or for worse, it is undoubtedly true that Grendon and Storms broadened the range of study of the magical elements beyond the identification of *flying venoms, evil nines, 'worm'* (*wyrm*) and *elf-shot*, which, from the time of Cockayne, defined the parameters of most discussions of the non-classical elements of the Leechdoms.

Grattan and Singer's historical survey confidently identified three main strata in *Lac*, thereby imposing the rational system and orderly method which is generally held to be conspicuously lacking in the work itself: (a) classical pagan (especially marked in the first 18 sections); (b) Teutonic pagan; (c) emotional Christian piety. The editors outlined a hypothetical process of compilation with a degree of circumstantiality that is rarely encountered in textual studies. A collection of recipes, on the head-to-toe plan, was put together in the 9th century from the leechcraft exemplified in the Herbarium, perhaps by a monastic *medicus*. A second leech added especially sections LXXIV–LXXXIII and CLXIX–CLXXII. 'He collected charms, incantations and rituals that were used by his brother leeches and by the people themselves .... He had had some monastic training, probably in one of the smaller Western houses where local superstitions were more influential, but he did not dwell in a monastery and had only a vestigial knowledge of Latin' (21). It is unlikely that this 'almost pagan' compiler was a professional leech; he probably held 'some office equivalent to that of bailiff to a monastic estate' (22). The third compiler was an inmate of a small monastery in the north in which Irish influence survived; he was in major orders, wrote chiefly in Latin and added devotional passages. This composite volume was soon after rebound, leaves were wrongly arranged and contributions confused, though they tended to adhere in groups. The rebound volume was copied shortly after 1000 by the scribe who produced the existing manuscript, who added some passages at the end (d). Some entries (x) have no decided character and are devoid of any clear association with strata a–d, and might have come into the collection at any time.

From the Teutonic and classical pagan strata, Grattan and Singer drew the conclusion that, as early as the 8th century in England, and 'even in the darkest part of the dark age, there was some literacy outside the monasteries' and that 'outside them too was a certain amount of professional or semi-professional leechcraft' (16). They pointed out, as Bonser, **517**, and Rubin, **527**, **531** and **562**, were later to point out, that illustrations of leeches in Anglo-Saxon medical manuscripts rarely show them as tonsured. Grattan and Singer, then, explicitly regarded *Lac* as a working textbook, a copy of cures that were applied in the actual practice of medicine. Its practical purpose and popular character were also touched on by Storms;

the compiler of *Lac*, unlike the compiler of *Lb*, 'did not aim at a scientific handbook' (17), and 'the Leechbook may be characterised as the handbook of the Anglo-Saxon medical man, the Lacnunga may be characterised as the handbook of the Anglo-Saxon medicine-man' (24). Cameron, **565**, makes a similar point in a rather different way: 'Even a casual comparison of *Bald's Leechbook* with *Lacnunga* will show that one was compiled by an expert physician (or under his supervision) and that the other was put together by someone with no obvious knowledge either of medicine or of order' (195).

The correspondences between some of the remedies in *Lac* and *Lb*, on which Storms remarked, are examined in detail in Meaney's recent study of the light cast on the compilation of *Lb*1&2 by other vernacular recipe collections (**393**). *Lac* is shown to be highly significant for the establishment of the textual history of *Lb*1&2. *Lac* could not have been copied from the version of *Lb*1&2 contained in the surviving manuscript (R), Meaney concludes; it represents the sole evidence of an intermediate stage between the exemplar of the Nowell recipe collection and the exemplar from which *Lb* was copied into R. Meaney also comments on the disintegration of the head-to-toe order of which there are traces in the early sections of *Lac*; she suggests that at least some of its disorder is probably the result of the confused state in which it was transmitted to the last copyist, but also observes that the 'compiler' gives the impression of incorporating whatever came to hand. In broad general outline, then, it still seems to hold true that *Lb* and *Lac* are independent developments from a common stock of material, and Singer's speculation (**327**) that at least some of this common stock derived from a version of the Herbarium somewhat different from the one translated into OE in Vitellius C.iii still seems to be regarded as viable. Cameron, **551**, outrules the claim made by Storms, following Cockayne, that the underlying classical sources were translated into OE from Greek, and some scholars would hold it inherently improbable that vernacular recipe collections were in circulation before the reign of Alfred (cf. Bately, **564**), but it is worth observing that Meaney's dating of the origins of the extant vernacular recipe collections to before the reign of Alfred is paralleled by de Vriend's dating of the translation of OE Herbarium to 8th century Mercia (**401**).

STUDY OF *Lac*: SURVEY

The developments by which *Lb*1&2 has replaced *Lac* as the work which typifies Anglo-Saxon medical practice are outlined above in 'Leechbook,' pp. 214–18. Evaluation of the nature and quality of *Lac* remains unchanged. Grattan and Singer, **326**, who, together with Bonser, **517**, were charged by Talbot, **369**, 156–7, with having misrepresented Anglo-Saxon medicine as 'a hotchpotch of incantations, charms, magic, and old wives' recipes' by concentrating on the 'relatively unimportant' *Lac*; by no means thought highly of it: *Lac*, in the opinion of Grattan and Singer, is 'on as low a cultural level as any [document] in the Anglo-Saxon language' (7). What has changed is the intention to regard the most rational, orderly, learned and classically-based OE medical writings as representative of their era.

Whereas Grattan and Singer (like Storms, **325**, and Grendon, **314**) discerned in *Lac* survivals of pre-Christian Germanic paganism, Talbot, **369**, disposed of its paganism as a historically irrelevant 10th century lapse triggered by the Danish invasions: 'In Bede's time the kind of nonsense that appears in the Lacnunga was not tolerated .... The *real* attitude of churchmen towards medicine can best be seen in the section devoted to medicine in Isidore's Etymologies .... In not one instance does he counsel recourse to religious, superstitious or magical means for the treatment of disease .... No amount of quotations from the lives of saints, where miraculous cures are described, can obscure the fact that in a society that produced writers like Ælfric ... Byrhtferth and others, superstition and magic would have little place. It is Byrhtferth, the foreign scholars from abroad and their successors from Lotharingia and Lorraine, who *rightly* represent the *true* attitude towards science (and with it, medicine) in England after the tenth-century revival. The Lacnunga may show the "final pathological disintegration of Greek medical thought" but it does not show that Anglo-Saxon scholars were involved in it' (**524**, 23, emphases added). Singer, **327**, in his revised edition of Cockayne, writing only five years earlier, had been equally adamant that the Anglo-Saxon scholars that Talbot named were *not* representative: 'The Anglo-Saxon leech had ... no understanding even of the rudiments of the science of classical antiquity ... and the demonstration of sources provides the chief interest of these volumes of Cockayne. The general level of this medicine will be found far lower, far more barbarous than the common accounts of Anglo-Saxon culture suggest' (xix–xx). The usual picture of Anglo-Saxon culture, Singer observed, is drawn from the writings of 'a select few like Bede and Alfred'; Cockayne's *Leechdoms* give 'a peep into a darker, a more barbarous, and a wholly imitative aspect of Anglo-Saxon society ... and this dark side has to be considered if the truth is to be told of the life of a people' (xlvi).

The larger issue at stake, then, in the disagreement concerning whether *Lac* or *Lb* (particularly *Lb*1&2, as well as the Herbarium) is to be regarded as typical of Anglo-Saxon medicine, is a fundamental difference of opinion over whether or not learned and orthodox individuals, notably Bede, Ælfric and Byrhtferth, typify the mainstream of Anglo-Saxon culture. The very preservation of *Lac*, with its putative combination of Germanic paganism and emotional Christian piety—particularly as Anglo-Saxon texts are generally thought to have been preserved by monastic copyists—raises doubts concerning the typicality of Ælfric and Byrhtferth which are not disposed of by Talbot's argument that *Lac*'s paganism is a Danish-inspired aberration from the orthodoxy that he believes to have prevailed universally in the age of Bede. Its preservation, in the same manuscript as a translation of the Herbarium, and even—as Ker and others opine—in the same script, also raises the question of whether the distinction between rational medicine

and superstitious practices that Talbot and others wish to enforce was one
that was recognized at the centre where the copy was made. Doubts concerning the typicality of Bede and Ælfric are certainly not dispelled by
Grattan and Singer's explanation of the combination of seemingly diverse
elements in *Lac*: 'Monastic stupidity, or the tolerance of monastic scholarship doubtless accepted elements of classical Paganism, but can hardly
have welcomed openly Pagan spells invoking the Northern gods and involving Northern mythology. Invocations of these must have been copied in the
monasteries, if they were copied there, with blank misunderstanding' (16).
We can, as they intimate, avoid imputing either mental vacuity or syncretistic religious beliefs to the members of an Anglo-Saxon monastic community
if we assume that Harley 585 was copied for/by a lay practitioner (and thus
indicative of a degree of lay literacy on a scale not usually contemplated
by literary historians of the period); but still the doubts remain concerning
the extent to which learned and orthodox scholars, such as Bede, Ælfric
and Byrhtferth, can be regarded as spokesmen of mainstream Anglo-Saxon
society.

The study of OE literature in the past few decades has, for the most
part, been dominated by learned orthodoxy (generally accompanied by
a demonstration that the bulk of OE writings derive from Latin ecclesiastical or classical sources): Stanley's determinedly unsuccessful *Search
for Anglo-Saxon Paganism*, 1975,[3] can be taken as representatively mainstream. Doubts concerning the typicality of Ælfric do not assail Jolly, **395**,
who, in 1985, urged readers of OE medical literature to regard the 'magical elements' as having been thoroughly neutralized and assimilated to the
orthodox Christian world view of late Anglo-Saxon society as evidenced in
the homilies of Ælfric (see also Hohler, **387**).[4] Meaney, **554**, on the other
hand, in her study of Ælfric's homilies, published in the same year (see also
Meaney, **392**), argues that Ælfric's condemnations of superstitious and pagan practices are addressed to customs that were actually current in late
Anglo-Saxon England, and Archbishop Wulfstan would also seem to have
been under the impression that, in the matter of Christian orthodoxy, the
world view of late Anglo-Saxon England left a good deal to be desired. The
frequency with which the recent publications refer a text under discussion
to Ælfric's condemnation of the erroneous and misleading books circulating
in his time is one of the signs that the tide is turning (the connection drawn
by Kobayashi, **148**, with the OE translation of Apollonius is particularly
unexpected; see e.g., Cross and Hill, **55**, Tristram, **80**, Healey, **394**). Hill,
1988, in a study of the prose paternoster dialogue of the poetic *SS*, which
intimates that the absence of a separate FC classification of the dialogue

---

[3] E.G. Stanley, *The Search for Anglo-Saxon Paganism* (Cambridge: Brewer, 1975).

[4] Among the recent articles on the metrical charms, outside the scope of this volume
of annotations, but of methodological significance for the study of magico-medical literature, is John D. Niles, 'The *Æcerbot* Ritual in Context,' *Old English Literature in
Context*, ed. John D. Niles (Woodbridge: Brewer–Boydell, 1980) 44–56, 163–4.

is symptomatic of its status as a repressed text, affirms: 'When the time comes, as it inevitably will, that a genuinely sophisticated and comprehensive history of OE literature is written, it will have to take into account this strange dialogue, for it, too, is part of the record of the development of the Anglo-Saxon peoples from their traditional, pagan, Germanic origins to that literate Christian nation which was the first English-speaking state' (175–6). In this projected rewriting of literary history there perhaps may be, not merely a resurrection of the old binary oppositions (Germanic noble savagery *versus* orthodox Christian piety, folklore as degenerate classical learning *versus* primitive beliefs reaching back to the dawn of time, etc.), but a recognition of the number of texts which are, as Hill describes the paternoster dialogue, 'virtually syncretistic in character' (174), and *Lac* may perhaps emerge as no less representative of its time than *Lb*1&2 is now held to be.

Flint, **575**, in a fine study, *The Rise of Magic in Early Medieval Europe*, too important to omit, even though it lies outside the chronological limits of this Annotated Bibliography, advances a much more sophisticated view than Jolly, arguing for 'a double process,' in which there was not merely a rejection of magic by orthodox intellectual churchmen but an 'active rescue, preservation and encouragement' of some ' "magical" survivals' (4). She is centrally concerned to suggest that churchmen's willingness to accommodate pagan customs did not come about because either they or the church were weak. Rather, the church deliberately found a place for certain magical practices 'for the best, not the worst, of reasons' (396): 'for the furtherance of a relationship between people and the supernatural that, it was fervently believed, would improve human life' (4). Whereas Jolly presents us with simple Christian cultural imperialism and the repressive tolerance of pagan beliefs, Flint accepts the necessity for negotiation between Christianity and the societies with which it came into contact; but, all the same, she regards the church as having been, wisely and wittingly, in full strategic control of the negotiation, with the result that what emerged triumphant was *Christian* magic: 'A culture engaged in becoming dominant, in this case the culture of the early European Christian Church, had both to make concessions and invent attractions if its aims were to be fulfilled' (407).

A medievalist who suspects that the Christian conversion of Europe consisted rather more of Christianity's conversion by secular society than of Christianity's conversion of the known world, is bound to feel doubtful about this. The accommodations, as Flint intimates, had the capacity for getting out of control: she finds, in OE sources, for instance, evidence of 'a greater willingness at a local level than at a central one to make compromises with older beliefs' (135) and compromises which 'might not have met with the fullest approval at the highest level of ecclesiastical politics' (193). It may well be that, at exceptionally learned centres of rigorous orthodoxy, a few intellectual churchmen were as able to distinguish between Christianity and pagan magic as a late 20th century scholar for whom that distinction is subtle and yet significant—whether any distinction at all existed in the minds of the compilers, practitioners and beneficiaries of the cures in *Lacnunga* is another matter. To put it another way, *Lacnunga* might be the expression of a New Age with a mystical apprehension of the one-ness of the supernatural; it might, on the other hand, be the product of an eclecticism made possible because the distinctness of different structures of belief were not clearly apprehended.

Magic, as Thorndike, 1905, argued, apropos of early medieval scientific writings, was 'a body of beliefs universally held'; 'everybody was a magician.' It is not an incidental element in the writings of the learned but 'characteristic of the whole mental attitude.'[5] Notwithstanding the dawning of an age of truly holistic medicine to which Sanborn draws our attention, modern scientific investigation into the healing properties of organic substances is unlikely to prove that all, or even the majority of OE remedies, particularly those in *Lac*, were rational and pragmatically efficacious, thereby enabling us to appreciate the wisdom of the ancients entirely on our own scientifically-derived terms; it is not the ingestion of organic substances, efficacious or otherwise, that constitutes the primary obstacle to regarding Anglo-Saxon magico-medical literature as rational. Although Cameron's rehabilitation of Anglo-Saxon medical literature has, to date, served to focus attention on the primarily rational medical cures of *Lb*1&2 (565), he offers a means by which *Lac* may be recovered from the outer darkness to which Talbot consigned it, in stating what earlier historians of medicine, either despite or because of their training in medical science, had no wish to acknowledge; namely, that the disposition of the patient's mind, as well as the treatment of the patient's body, is involved in the recovery of health: 'Today the physician imparts confidence in his healing powers by his white coat, his air of detachment ... they supply just as much a non-rational part of the treatment as the intoning of charms. One kind appeals in a society which boasts its belief in a world governed by "scientific" cause and effect; the other in a society where all things were believed to be at the whim of the gods .... The milieus are different and the rituals are different, but the effect is the same, a reassured patient; so presumably the results should be similar. This is a justification for magic treatments in a society which believes in magic as a ruling factor in the operation of the universe, and if it does not work in our society it is because we no longer believe in magic in that way' (212).

Cameron's analysis of the consulting-room interaction in terms of confidence inspired and reassurance imparted is perhaps unduly rooted in the realm of the socially mundane and pragmatically explicable, and sacerdotal absolution (as well as the mass, to which some general studies of magic refer) may be the closest available contemporary Western analogy to the co-operative construction of reality by a physician and sufferer who share a

---

[5]Lynn Thorndike, *Studies in the History of Magic*, Studies in History, Economics and Public Law 24 (New York: Columbia UP, 1905) 29.

belief in the intangible; but his analysis nevertheless makes it possible for us to read the remedies of *Lac* and other Anglo-Saxon recipe collections without seeking merely to find in them recognizable evidence of pragmatically efficacious and rational practices. *Lac* may never come to be regarded as 'a precious medical document' but, as popular culture and religious belief attract more attention, it too may become, as well as *Lb*1&2 'a precious social and cultural ... document, [which] deserves close study in all its aspects' (Cameron, **390**, 178).

RECIPE COLLECTIONS

I: LEECHBOOK-RELATED RECIPES

MANUSCRIPTS

London, British Library, Cotton Galba A.xiv, f. 118rv   FC B.21.2.2
Ker 157 (s. xi¹), art. IX

Nowell Transcript: FC B.21.2.3
London, British Library, Add. 43703, ff. 261–4v
(London, British Library, Cotton Otho B.xi)
Ker 180 (s. x med.–xi¹), art. 11

London, British Library, Harley 55, ff. 1–3   FC B.21.2.4
Ker 225, art. 1   s. xi¹

EDITIONS; MANUSCRIPT DESCRIPTION AND RELATIONSHIPS

Summary

Recent scholarship suggests that, from a very early date, there were a number of recipe collections circulating and being copied with variations. Meaney, **393**, considers that, even before the reign of Alfred, remedies were circulating independently and that small groups of them had begun to adhere. FC classify three recipe groups as variants of *Lb*. Two other collections which have connections with *Lb* are not included in FC, one recorded on the Omont Fragment, which was brought to light after the *Plan for the Dictionary of Old English* appeared, and the *De Beta* group, occurring at the end of *MedQuad* in O, which, until quite recently, was generally regarded as ME (see pp. 315–16, 'Herbarium Complex'). It now seems that (with the possible exception of the collection in Harley 55) these groups were not copied from *Lb*, but developed from a common or related exemplar.

The two recipes in Galba A.xiv closely resemble two in *Lb*2.65, and have recently been edited by Muir, **332**. The collection in Harley 55 was included by Cockayne, **297**, and Leonhardi, **310**, in their editions of *Lb*, because it answers to the description of material which is listed in *Lb*2's table of contents, but missing from the work itself. The most substantial of the three groups (and thus the most significant for the textual history of the transmission and development of *Lb*) is preserved only in a transcript by Nowell of a manuscript mostly lost in the Cottonian fire. All but seven of the recipes in Nowell are found in *Lb*; these seven have been edited by Braekman, **328**, and more recently by Torkar, **329**, who includes an incomplete recipe omitted by Braekman, which may, however, belong to one of the earlier recipes (Meaney, **393**, 248).

Many of the parallels between these three recipe groups and *Lb* were recorded by Ker. The relationship has been most fully studied by Meaney, **393**, who concludes that the Nowell and Galba recipes derive from an exemplar similar to that of *Lb*1&2, but that the Harley collection may have been copied from *Lb*2.59 before it was lost. The Nowell collection's relation to *Lb* is also examined by Torkar, and more briefly by Cameron, **390**. For a table of correspondences between Nowell and *Lb*, see Ker, 233. Parallels between *Lb*1&2, *Nowell*, *Lac* and the other two recipe collections (as well as the *De Beta* group, *Lb*3, and Omont) are tabled by Meaney, 238–9, and there is a more detailed comparative examination of *Lb*1&2 and Nowell in her Appendix, 265–8.

Galba A.xiv   FC B.21.2.2

Galba contains two herbal recipes for restoring the body to health, also found in *Lb*2.65 ('To gehealdene lichoman haelo mid drihtnes gyfe').

The manuscript consists chiefly of private devotions in Latin, and contains prayers and recipes in OE (one of the 'Miscellaneous Recipes' [FC B.21.5.6], as well as FC B.21.2.2); it also contains a prose charm (FC B.23.1.11). Ker reports that the manuscript was badly damaged by the 1731 fire, and his account is based on Wanley's. He states that the oldest parts are probably s. xi in., and may have been written for male use, but the manuscript was extensively added to in s. xi[1] for the use of a female member of a religious house, probably Nunnaminster. The manuscript has been described by Bishop, 1918,[1] and, more recently, by Muir, **332**, who edits it in full (where legible), and suggests refoliations. Muir find evidence that the manuscript was being added to 1029–47, and redefines its generic character.

Meaney, **393**, 241, states that the recipes on f. 118 are recorded in a hand that appears nowhere else in the manuscript, and she dates this hand not later than *c*. 1000. The remedies are not now completely legible, but where they can be compared with *Lb*, the relationship is extremely close; it is more probable that Galba and *Lb* had a common original than that Galba copies from *Lb*. Muir considers that the 'charm' for foot troubles on f. 72r originally followed the recipes.

Nowell Transcript   FC B.21.2.3

The collection consists of some 50 remedies, tending to group by topic, all of which duplicate remedies in *Lb*1&2, expect for five headed 'Wið utsyhte' and two headed 'Gyf utgong forseten sy' (discontinuously recorded, see below). As edited by Torkar, **329**, there is also an incomplete recipe beginning 'meng eal tosomne.'

---

[1]Edmund Bishop, *Liturgica Historica. Papers on the Liturgy and Religious Life of the Western Church*, ed. R.H. Connolly and K. Sisam (Oxford: Clarendon, 1918) 384–91.

Meaney, **393**, 246–50, explains that, at the end of Cotton Otho B.xi—
then containing the *OE Bede*, a copy of the Winchester contents of the
Parker manuscript (including *ASC* to 1001), and other material—a scribe,
probably early in the 11th century and certainly at Winchester, copied
some herbal recipes; these were already missing when the manuscript was
badly damaged in the Cottonian fire, and are preserved only in Nowell's
transcript. Ker (who also gives a Winchester provenance) shows that the
manuscript, as described by Smith and Wanley, was in disarray. In view of
the incomplete recipe, Ker suggested that there was a leaf missing in Otho
or its exemplar; Meaney (who finds evidence of considerable confusion on
the part of the Otho scribe or his exemplar) concludes that the remainder
of the recipe is to be found higher up the page (at lines 3–5), because a
leaf had been misplaced. In her examination of the relationship of the *De
Beta* recipes to *Lb*, Meaney finds evidence that irregular scraps of vellum
with recipes on them were used by the scribe when he first transcribed his
rearranged text, and that some that had been overlooked were inserted in
the manuscript at a later date; she suggests that the collection transcribed
by Nowell may likewise have used scraps of vellum for sorting. There is a
full bibliographical account of early manuscript descriptions and an examination of Nowell's 1562 transcript in Grant, **373**, with particular reference
to its fidelity to the original; there is also a note by Meaney, **396**.

The probable Winchester provenance of both Otho and *Lb* might lead
one to suppose a direct relationship, but Torkar and Meaney both favour
derivation from a common source, and so too does Cameron, **390**. Both
Lb and Nowell, Cameron observes, are at a distance from known Latin
sources, and he infers that the recipes 'had been copied sufficiently often
for not one but two corrupt forms to have developed' (**390**, 168). Torkar's
argument that Otho could not have been copied from *Lb* because it is is
more markedly Anglian in its language, and employs orthographical conventions that were obsolete by 900, rests upon acceptance of Nowell as an
exact copy of Otho. Torkar considers this issue, but, although Grant's article, arguing that Nowell assimilated Otho to 16th century orthographic
conventions, was published two years before Torkar's edition, he does not
address Grant's findings. (For doubts concerning early Anglian attributions
generally, see Bately, **564**.) Meaney is inclined to agree with Torkar, but
her conclusions rest on a comparative analysis of content. She shows that
the original compiler on whose work Nowell and *Lb* drew was better at collecting than discriminating, for there are some duplicated recipes, derived
from different sources, whose basic identity appears to have gone unnoticed
by the original compiler, as well as by subsequent compilers and copyists.

Harley 55   FC B.21.2.4

The extended account of treatment for 'the half dead disease' in Harley 55,
consisting of six groups of cures, interspersed with diagnostic observations,
corresponds to the description of *Lb*2.59 in the table of contents (Cockayne

297, 2: 172); the chapter itself is missing from the *Lb* manuscript owing to the loss of a gathering.

Ker describes Harley 55 as four half sheets, perhaps from the end of a manuscript (it also includes legal documents); the recipes are written in 'a rather large handsome hand.' Harley 55 is one of the manuscripts connected with Archbishop Wulfstan (d. 1023). Meaney, **393**, describes the language of the text as 'virtually identical' with that of *Lb*, 'even though it was copied some fifty years later' (240). She concludes that the relationship between Harley and *Lb* cannot be positively established, but thinks it possible that the Harley collection was copied from *Lb* before the gathering was lost.

II: OMONT FRAGMENT (*OFr*)

MANUSCRIPT

Louvain-la-Neuve, Université Catholique de Louvain,   Not listed FC
Centre Général de Documentation, Fragmenta H. Omont 3[2]

Ker, *Suppl.*, 417   s. x in.

EDITION, DESCRIPTION

A single leaf, containing 11 recipes (27 lines) on the recto, was brought to light in 1977 by Schauman and A. Cameron, **330**. Eight recipes are for feet, thighs and loins, and the last three are for paralysis. The fragment (beginning 'Wið yflum and miclum footsuilun') is described at length by the editors. Their study of physical characteristics, orthography and language (cf. Dresher, **391**) led them to date it second half of the 9th century, and both found evidence that it originated at a Mercian centre (cf. Bately, **564**). Ker, *Suppl.*, gives a 10th century dating, and observes that it is probably from the end of a manuscript; M.L. Cameron, **390**, conjectures that the leaf may have formed the conclusion to a complete medical text arranged in head-to-toe order. Nothing is recorded of the early history of the fragment (the remarks of Napier, **308**, on the Wellcome Library fragment, are suggestive.)

Textual relationships are most fully studied by Meaney, **393**, who states that six remedies are paralleled in *Lb*1&2, but there are differences in ingredients or in the ways in which they are described. The other five duplicated remedies are grouped in the same order in both *OFr* and *Lb*, forming the bulk of *Lb*1.23; only the first remedy in this chapter of *Lb* is without parallel in *OFr*, and *OFr* inserts two unique remedies using seal-skin. Meaney thinks it likely that *Lb* and *OFr* go back to a common, probably rather distant, ancestor; common vocabulary suggests that this ancestor might have been English. The one remedy *OFr* shares with *Lac* (85) cannot have been copied directly from *OFr*, because Schauman and Cameron were able to use

---

[2] So Meaney, **393**, 243 (formerly Louvain, Bibliothèque de l'Université, Section des Manuscrits, Fragmenta H. Omont 3).

Lac to correct an error by the *OFr* scribe. *OFr* has also two remedies (both concerned with foot problems) from *Herb*, probably not the same translation as that in Vitellius C.iii. 'All in all,' she concludes, 'Omont is an early witness to the tendency, epitomized in Bald's *Leechbook*, of gathering together remedies for a malady from whatever sources were available' (245). M.L. Cameron, **390**, 168–70, considers textual relationships more briefly. He deduces, on the basis of Schauman and A. Cameron's early dating, that *OFr*, being a copy, shows that OE medical texts were in existence quite some time before the compilation of *Lb*; *Lb*, in the shared recipes, seems to be copying from a damaged or corrupt manuscript, which suggests that the exemplar was old when *Lb* was made.

III: MISCELLANEOUS RECIPES, CHIEFLY COCKAYNE'S 'FLY LEAF LEECHDOMS' AND 'LEECHDOMS OMITTED IN THEIR PLACE'

MANUSCRIPTS

Cambridge, Corpus Christi College 41, p. 208   FC B.21.5.1
Ker 32, art. 8   s. xi¹ or xi med.

London, Wellcome Historical Medical Library, 75.46   FC B.21.5.2
Ker 98   s. x/xi

London, British Library, Cotton Domitian i, f. 55v   FC B.21.5.3
Ker 146, art. d   s. x²

London, British Library, Cotton Faustina A.x, ff. 115v, 116r FC B.21.5.4
Ker 154B (s. xii¹), arts. 2, 3

London, British Library, Cotton Galba A.ii, iii [burnt]   FC B.21.5.5
Ker 156

London, British Library, Cotton Galba A.xiv, ff. 139rv, 136r FC B.21.5.6
Ker 157 (s. xi¹), art. XII

London, British Library, Cotton Titus D.xxvi, ff. 16v–17   FC B.21.5.7
Ker 202 (1023–35), art. c   s. xi¹

London, British Library, Cotton Vitellius C.iii, f. 18v,   FC B.21.5.8
   ff. 82v–3
Ker 219 (s. xi¹), arts. 2, 3   s. xi² (art. 2), s. xi med.,
   xi/xii (art. 3)

London, British Library, Cotton Vitellius E.xviii, f. 15v   FC B.21.5.9
Ker 224, arts. n, o   s. xi med.

EDITIONS, MANUSCRIPT DESCRIPTION (following Ker)

Summary

In addition to the recipe groups whose relationship to *Lb* has been established (including *De Beta* and *OFr*) there are a number of other individual recipes and recipe groups; most of these are added in margins or on blank spaces. The Wellcome fragment (FC B.21.5.2), like Omont (see above, pp. 233–4) is a single sheet.

Nine items (some of them containing more than one distinct cluster of remedies) are listed by FC. Most were included among the recipes that Cockayne, **400**, 1: 374–82, printed as 'Fly Leaf Leechdoms,' i.e., FC B.21.5.1, B.21.5.3, B.21.5.7–8. FC B.21.5.9, from Vitellius E.xviii, is printed in the same volume, under 'Charms,' Cockayne, **400**, 1: 388. FC B.21.5.4, from Faustina A.x, was also printed by Cockayne, **298**, 3: 292, in the midst of 'Charms, continued' under the heading 'Leechdoms Omitted in their Place.' Cockayne's foliations differ from Ker's, and his handling of charms and recipes is characterized by general disorder. The difference between 'recipes' and 'charms' is, in many cases, a very fine one. Given the current concern to establish the rational efficacy of Anglo-Saxon cures, a comprehensive redefinition of medical charms as recipes is likely to occur in the near future, particularly as, in several manuscripts (Galba A.xiv, Faustina A.x, Vitellius E.xviii and CCCC 41) recipes and charms are contiguous (see Dietrich, **299**, and Muir, **332**).

Of the remaining recipes listed by FC, the Wellcome fragment has been printed by Napier, **308**, and Galba A.xiv has been transcribed (where legible) by Muir, **332**. FC B.21.5.5 is known only from Wanley's description of manuscripts destroyed in the Cottonian fire.

Ker, *Suppl.*, and emendations to Ker, Blockley, **45**, yield no other OE medical material (apart from *OFr*) not included in FC, whether classified as recipes or under some other heading. But the possibility that there are scribbled recipes in other manuscripts or on fragments that were unknown to Ker (and hence to the present writer) cannot be outruled. Fugitive or little-known recipes are particularly likely to exist in continental manuscripts containing Anglo-Saxon recipes, for which Ker (Appendix) chiefly relied on printed descriptions (see, for instance, Stuart, **384**). There are, doubtless, a number of Germanized OE recipes, but only one of these, 'uuidhar cancur,' found in Sudhoff, **458**, and other editions listed by Greenfield and Robinson, appears to have impinged on the English-speaking world. Sims-Williams, 1990, suggests that a charm to stop bleeding in the same manuscript may have been carried to the Continent by an Anglo-Saxon missionary nun.[3]

It can be stated with reasonable confidence, however, that the recipes listed in this section have not received much attention. Their relationship to one another and to the other major collections has not been studied, and it thus, perhaps, remains an open question whether the clusters of 'Miscellaneous Recipes' are excerpts from existing medical codices or medical codices in the making. One correspondence, between *Lac* and one of

---

[3] Patrick Sims-Williams, *Religion and Literature in Western England, 600–800* (Cambridge: Cambridge UP, 1990) 300.

the recipes in Vitellius C.iii (FC B.21.5.8), was noted by Ker. The eye remedies were fleetingly noticed by James, **485**; see also Rubin, **531**.

Two of the manuscripts containing OE recipes (Galba and Titus) are thought by Ker to have passed into the ownership of women. Some of the substances used in medical preparations were sent as gifts to the Anglo-Saxon monastic women with whom Boniface and his missionary associates were in correspondence in the 8th century.[4] Muir, **332**, seems to be intimating that Galba has been annotated by both men and women who were being taught at a monastic school at St Mary's Convent, Nunnaminster; Meaney, **393**, 241, is clearly willing to accept that recipes may have been added to Galba by a monastic woman. Female ownership of Titus, described by Birch, **274**, as a religious and scientific compendium, may suggest its use in a monastic women's school; education standards among monastic women are generally held to have declined in the late Anglo-Saxon period, but perhaps there is a case to be made that Galba A.xiv is testimony to the continuity of monastic women's engagement in the practice of medicine.

CCCC 41   FC B.21.5.1   Cockayne, **400**, 1: 382

A single, short, remedy for pain in the eye ('wið eahwærce') is one of a number of OE items which have been added on specially ruled lines in the margins, probably by the same early or mid-11th century scribe. The additions include the prose section of the metrical *SS* as well as homilies and charms. For manuscript description, see below, pp. 239–40, 'Prose Charms and Charm Headings.'

Wellcome Historical Medical Library, 75.46   FC B.21.5.2   Napier, **308**

This group of five recipes is written in three different hands, dated to the 11th century by Napier. Napier explained that the fragment (formerly known as Lanhydrock, Bodmin, Collection of Lord Clifden, B.12.16, f. 144) was found in the binding of a volume published in Antwerp, 1558, and he speculated that it may have been among the recipes to which Bishop Bale referred in the 1549 Preface to Leland's *New Yeares Gift to King Henry VIII*: 'Some they sold to the grossers and sopesellers, and some over see to the bokebynders, not in small nombre, but at tymes whole shyppes fulle, to the wonderynge of the foren nacyons.' Ker observes that it was 'probably originally a blank end-leaf of a (medical?) manuscript.'[5]

The *incipits* are as follows: 'Wiþ heortæce,' 'Wiþ lungenadle,' 'Hat wyrcean þe sylf wennsealfe,' 'Wiþ wennas sealf,' 'Wiþ liferadle.'

---

[4] Michael Tangl, ed., *Die Briefe des heiligen Bonifatius und Lullus*, MGH ES I (2nd edn. Berlin: Teubner, 1955) nos. 49, 79.

[5] Also described by S.A.J. Moorat, *Catalogue of Western Manuscripts on Medicine and Science in the Wellcome Historical Medical Library*, 2 vols. (London: Wellcome Historical Medical Library, 1962) vol. 1.

Domitian A.i   FC B.21.5.3   Cockayne, **400**, 1: 382

A single recipe, beginning 'Þas wyrta sceolon to wensealfe,' is contained in
a manuscript whose chief OE contents are glosses to Isidore and Bede and
a book-list. It is written in square Anglo-Saxon minuscule, s. x², and the
manuscript is from St Augustine's, Canterbury.

Faustina A.x   FC B.21.5.4   Cockayne, **298**, 3: 292

The recipes are on two different folios in two different hands, added to originally blank spaces. Part B, whose principle contents are an OE translation
of the Rule of Benedict, has been bound with Part A (see Introduction,
'Durham and Other Proverbs,' p. 34) since the 12th century. A hand similar to that of the Rule has added what Ker describes as 'two recipes for
eyesalve, a nonsense charm *wiþ utsiht*, with directions for use, two charms
in Latin *Contra frigora* and *Contra febres*.' On f. 116v are, in a later 12th
century hand, recipes *wið þa bleinna*, *wið hefdeca*, *wið ranca*, and *wið ner-
awað*, and a charm in Latin *Contra cotidianas febres*. (See further 'Prose
Charms and Charm Headings,' FC B.23.1.10, pp. 243–4.) Dietrich, **299**,
held that all these items were part of a medical codex, and argued that the
OE recipes and charm are early Northumbrian.

Galba A.ii, iii [burnt]   FC B.21.5.5

Galba A.ii and iii, a collection of sermons bound in two volumes, were
totally destroyed by fire, and knowledge of recipes in these manuscripts
depends on Wanley's report of 'Medicamenta contra varios morbos. Sax-
onicè.' He also lists 'Carmina quaedam et Medicamenta Normanno-Gallicè
et Latine, litteris Saxonicis' (231), runic alphabets and notes on computus.

Galba A.xiv   FC B.21.5.6   Muir, **332**

Galba A.xiv also contains some 'Leechbook-related Recipes' (FC B.21.2.2),
and is described above, p. 231, in connection with them. The foliation is
confused. Ker reports that the text of art. XII is 'still complete but badly
stained and blurred': f. 139r is illegible, ff. 139v and 136r are partly legible.
Relying on the description of Wanley, who also printed the *incipit* (f. 139v)
and *explicit* (f. 136), Ker states that f. 139v 'deals with the virtues of the
teeth (?) and the right foot,' and f. 136 'with the gall as a remedy for
sore eyes.' Muir does not include these folios in the body of his edition,
but offers a diplomatic transcript in an appendix. He has succeeded in
deciphering, in addition to the *incipit* and *explicit*, a few individual words,
and two consecutive lines of the recipe for sore eyes. The recipe for sore
eyes was, conceivably, one of a group of remedies. The *incipit* reads: 'Ðas
cræftas syndon be þam deore þe we on urum geðeode Broc hata ð.'

Titus D.xxvi   FC B.21.5.7   Cockayne, **400**, 1: 380

A single recipe, 'Wið þa blegene,' has been added to a blank space in an
early 11th century hand. Titus D.xxvi and xxvii, containing mainly Latin
prayers and private devotions as well as Ælfric's *De Temporibus* and other
short OE pieces, including computistica and prognostics, were originally
a single manuscript; Ker lists the OE contents in their present order, but
considers that D.xxvii was originally bound before D.xxvi. The manuscript
and its contents were described at length by Birch, **274**, who printed a
number of items in it, including the recipe. The recipe was also printed by
Wyatt, **320**. Ker agrees with Birch that the manuscript was written for
Ælfwine at the time when he was deacon of New Minster, with the possible
exception of some slightly later additions, which include the recipe. The
interlineation of feminine forms throughout suggests ownership by a woman
in the twelfth century; Birch was inclined to think that this owner was one
of the two abbesses of St Mary at Winchester mentioned in the Calendar
(Wulfthrytha or Heahfleda).

Vitellius C.iii   FC B.21.5.8   Cockayne, **400**, 1: 374–8

Recipe groups on two widely separated folios are added to Vitellius C.iii;
for manuscript description, see 'Herbarium Complex,' p. 312 below. The
first group (f. 18v) are headed 'Ad uertiginem' and 'Ad pectoris dolorem'
(Cockayne, **400**, 1: 378). Ker states that the first five lines are glossed in
a 14th century hand, and the words 'Wið innoþes astyrunge,' which Cockayne prints at the head of these, belong to the table of contents for *Herb*
(at Cockayne, 1: 68/14). The second group (ff. 82v–3), followed by recipes
in Latin and a tract on urine, consists of four recipes in three hands, mid-
to late 11th century, or perhaps early 12th. Ker points out that the first
recipe of this group is also in *Lac* (Cockayne, **298**, 3: 4/4–15.).

Vitellius E.xviii   FC B.21.5.9   Cockayne, **298**, 3: 388

Both of the remedies, one for lung disease in cattle and one for ailing sheep,
are fragmentary, especially the first. A number of OE texts, including 'explanations of secret writing,' are in the same hand; see further 'Prognostics'
and 'Prose Charms and Charm Headings,' pp. 244–5 and 260 below. Like
the charms and prognostics in this manuscript, the recipes suggest that
farming played a significant part in the lives of the users of the manuscript.
Ker thinks it likely that it is a Winchester manuscript.

PROSE CHARMS AND CHARM HEADINGS

A question mark against an item in square brackets indicates a possible anomaly in FC's classification.

I: MANUSCRIPTS, EDITIONS, STUDIES OF INDIVIDUAL PROSE CHARMS

Cattle-theft charm; Headings	FC B.23.1.1–3

Cambridge, Corpus Christi College 41, pp. 206, 272, 326
Ker 32 (s. xi¹) s. xi¹ or xi med.

art. 7	*Gif feoh sy undernumen*	Storms 12
art. 10	*Wið ealra feonda grimnessum*	Storms 48
art. 14	*Wið sarum eagum, Wið sarum earum,*	
	Wið magan seocnesse	[?Storms A4–6]

Storms 12 (beginning 'Gif feoh sy undernumen') consists of OE directions for use of a Latin charm (pp. 206–8 of the manuscript). Cockayne, **400**, 1: 392, and Storms print only the directions and a short OE–Latin incantation; a few lines of the Latin charm were printed by McBryde, **339**. The text is printed in full by James, *Descriptive Catalogue*, 1912, 1: 83, and more recently, by Grant, **378**, who analyses its structure. For its relation to other cattle-theft charms, see immediately below, on Storms 11AB.

Storms 48 is a Latin charm with an OE heading ('Wið ealra feonda grimnessum'), printed by Cockayne, **400**, 1: 386, and re-edited by Grant. Art. 14, three Latin charms with OE headings, was printed by Cockayne, **400**, 1: 387 ('Wið sarum eagum,' 'Wið sarum earum,' and 'Wið magan seocnesse'); the texts are the same as Storms A4–6 (listed by FC, following Ker), but Storms attributes the last two charms to Gonville and Caius College 397, f. 49v.

The prose charms and headings are among the items added in blank spaces, and in the margins on specially ruled lines, in a manuscript whose principal OE contents are *OE Bede*. These additions, described by Ker as 'probably all in one unusual angular hand of s. xi¹ or xi med.,' number eighteen in all, and include four metrical charms, which are 'For a Swarm of Bees,' the 'Journey Charm,' and two metrical charms for the recovery of lost cattle (Storms 15, 13). Also included in the marginalia are a Latin charm for childbirth (Storms 43), employing the *Sator* formula, the prose paternoster dialogue of the poetic *SS*, and a recipe (FC B.21.5.1). The manuscript, according to art. 19, was given to Exeter by Bishop Leofric (d. 1072), but is not recorded in his list of gifts.

Grant, who edits two of the charms containing OE, as well as the Latin *Sator* formula and the liturgical marginalia, argues for a close connection between this manuscript and CCCC 422, and assigns CCCC 41 to New Minster at Winchester. James, 1: 84, pointed out that Storms 12 derived in part from the hymn of St Secundius (Sechnall) on St Patrick; Grant, who examines the sources of Storms 12, 48, and the *Sator* formula, argues that all three are 'loricas,' and suggests that the marginalia of CCCC 41 are unified by an interest in Irish texts of an unorthodox nature (see also Vaughan-Sterling, **552**, Amies, **550**, Hill, **547**). Voigts, **388**, endorses Grant's argument for a Winchester provenance, but most aspects of Grant's study are criticized by Hohler, **387**, who points out Grant's misuse of the term 'lorica.' Hohler, who gives the liturgical sources for Storms 48 (parallels with *Lb* and *Lac* are noted by Grant), appears to incline to the view that 'charms,' at least in this manuscript, are in fact corrupt prayers for use by ecclesiastics, whose orthodoxy or otherwise depends on the intentions of their users, known only to God and possibly to Hohler.

Cattle-theft charms   FC B.23.1.4–6

'Gyf feoh sy underfangen'

Cambridge, Corpus Christi College 190, f. 130
Ker 45A, art. b   s. xi[1]   Storms 11A
London, British Library, Cotton Tiberius A.iii, f. 106
Ker 186, art. 28   s. xi med.

'Gyf feoh sy undernumen'

Cambridge, Corpus Christi College 383, p. 87
Ker 65, art. 20   s. xi/xii   [?Storms 11B]
Rochester, Cathedral Library, *Textus Roffensis*, f. 95r
Ker 373A, art. 31   s. xii[1]

What may be called the cattle-thief charm proper (a Latin–OE formula and OE directions on its use for the recovery of stolen cattle or household goods), appears in four manuscripts. Storms 11A and 11B represent a distinction between the version found in Tiberius A.iii and in CCCC 190 (the latter also preserved in a 17th century paper transcript, Harley 438), and the version found in *Textus Roffensis* (also preserved in a 17th century paper transcript, Julius C.2, f. 66v). As printed by Storms, the difference is too slight to warrant classification as two separate versions, as Grant, **378**, 114, n. 7, observes.

FC, who further distinguish between Tiberius A.iii and CCCC 190, thus classifying three separate versions, are somewhat misleading. *Textus Roffensis* and CCCC 383 are distinctive because in these two manuscripts the cattle-thief charm proper is followed by what appears to be an excerpt from a legal document pertaining to land ownership (beginning 'Hit becwaeð ₇ becwael se ðe hit ahte'). But Storms did not include the legal formula in Storms 11B, because he did not regard it as part of the text. Cockayne, **298**, 3: 286–8, on the other hand, conflated the Latin–OE charm from Tiberius A.iii with the legal fragment from *Textus Roffensis* (and Julius C.2). If, then, the legal formula is accepted as an integral part of the text in the manuscripts in which it appears, FC rightly distinguish between the version preserved in CCCC 190 and that recorded in *Textus Roffensis* and CCCC 383 (even though the distinction is not evident in the edition they cite), but it would have been more in keeping with their customary practice if, instead of tabling Tiberius A.iii as a third, distinct version (FC B.23.1.5), they had listed it with CCCC 190 in FC B.23.1.4. Confusion has possibly arisen from the fact that Cockayne's note to the effect that the legal formula does not appear in Tiberius A.iii is easily overlooked, and Ker, who implicitly rejects the view that the legal formula has any connection with the charm proper, equates the versions in *Textus Roffensis* and CCCC 383 (the latter manuscript unknown to Storms) with Storms 11B.

The *Textus Roffensis* version was first printed by Grimm, **430**, who culled it from Wanley, 114–15, and transcripts by Kemble. Cockayne, Ker states, derived his collation of *Textus Roffensis* and Julius C.2 from Hearne, 1720. Grendon A15 (**314**) is a conflation of all the available manuscripts and transcripts, since, like McBryde, **340**, but unlike Storms, he was aware that the resemblance between *Textus Roffensis* and CCCC 383 had been pointed out by early 19th century German scholars. A facsimile of *Textus Roffensis* was brought out by Sawyer, **295**; like Skemp, **344**, Storms, and, more recently, Grant (**378**, 114, n. 7), Sawyer considered that there was no intended connection between the Latin–OE charm and the legal formula, which, he pointed out, occurs on its own in some manuscripts. Arguments in favour of accepting the legal formula as an integral part of the charm are advanced by Grendon, **314**, 221–3, McBryde, **339**, and Stuart, **397**.

Storms 11AB is one of several cattle-thief charms which are sometimes considered as a group: that is, one other prose charm, Storms 12 (see above) and two metrical charms, Storms 13, 15, all from CCCC 41; and an extract from *Lac*, Storms 14, which is also regarded as a metrical charm (FC A.43.5). These five charms fall into three groups: (1) the two prose charms, which have much the same OE directions, although the Latin incantations differ (Storms 12 invokes saints whereas Storms 11AB alludes to the crucifixion); (2) Storms 13 and 14, which contain a similar incantation (beginning 'Bethlem hattæ seo burh ðe Crist on geboren wes') and similar directions for turning towards the four directions of the compass while invoking the cross; (3) Storms 15, whose unique features include an appeal to 'Garmund, Godes ðegen.' The most noticeable connection between the prose and metrical charms is that Storms 13 contains a short formula beginning 'Judeas Crist ahengon' which roughly echoes a few lines of Storms

11AB. Some preliminary remarks on textual distinctness and manuscript relationships were made by McBryde, **339**. Grant, who deals briefly with the manuscript relationship of Storms 11AB, 12, 13 and 14, offers a diagram which is 'in no way to be taken as an accurate stemma.' He deduces, however, that 11AB follow 'a different, more corrupt recension' of the text represented by Storms 12 (**378**, 9). The relationship of Storms 11AB to the metrical cattle-thief charms is also studied by Schneider, **367**, and Hill, **379**.

Textus Roffensis is a Rochester manuscript consisting of two parts, written in the same hand; Part A contains laws, genealogies etc., and Part B is a Rochester cartulary. Ker states that both parts were probably compiled in the time of Bishop Ernulf (1115–24), and that the laws are related to CCCC 383; special letter forms distinguish OE from the Latin throughout. CCCC 383, written in 'a neat, small, round hand,' is probably from St Paul's Cathedral, London; there is no break in the manuscript between the charm proper and the legal text that precedes it. For Tiberius A.iii, see 'Lapidary,' p. 200, and 'Prognostics,' p. 259; the charm would seem, from Ker's description, to be in the same hand as *Lap.*

Addresses to the cross   FC B.23.1.7

'*Gyf þe þynce þaet ðine fynd þe þwyrlice ymbe þe ðrydian*'

Cambridge, Corpus Christ College 391, pp. 617–18
Ker 67 (s. xi²), art. c   s. xi/xii
London, British Library, Cotton Tiberius A.iii., f. 59rv
Ker 186, art. 10d   s. xi med.
The charm (if such it is) consists of a series of OE instructions for addressing Latin prayers to the Cross. Zupitza, **306**, printed his version from the Corpus manuscript. Tiberius does not appear to have been edited and is presumably an inferior text; Ker's *incipit* reads: 'Gyf þe þince þaet ðine fynd þe hwirlice [*sic*] embe þridian.'

The charm is added to CCCC 391 in a blank space at the end of a quire; the hand is described as 'rough' by Ker, and dated early 12th century by Zupitza. For description of this manuscript see 'Prognostics,' p. 259. In Tiberius A.iii (see also 'Lapidary,' p. 200, and 'Prognostics,' p. 259), the charm is preceded and followed by Adorations to the Cross (Latin and OE), ff. 58–60.

Heading   FC B.23.1.8

he mæg alysan [...] gastas of helle wite

London, British Library, Add. 37517, f. 139
Ker 129 (s. xi in.) s. x/xi
Ker states that f. 139, originally blank, 'contains the rubric *he mæg alysan [...] gastas of helle wite*, in front of an alphabetical formula in Latin

(letters A–D only), added s. x/xi (Latin in caroline minuscule).' The OE in the manuscript, known as the Bosworth Psalter, consists chiefly of some interlinear glosses to psalms and canticles. The manuscript is of unknown provenance, but the calendar is 'probably a St Augustine's production.'

Heading(s); to obtain favours; celestial letter   FC B.23.1.9

London, British Library, Cotton Caligula A.xv, ff. 129r, 140r
Ker 139A   s. xi²

       art. d *Wið gedrif* [*wið poccas, wið geswell*]   Storms 68 [?A9–10]
       art. u *Gif þu wille gangan to þinum hlaforde*   Storms 69
       art. v *Se engel brohte þis gewrit of heofonum*   Storms 34

Art. d contains three OE headings to Latin prayers; the first of these, headed 'Wið gedrif,' is Storms 68. All three were printed by Cockayne, **298**, 3: 295. The last two ('wið poccas' and 'wið geswell') were included by Storms in his Appendix (A9–10); they appear to have been overlooked by FC. The text of A9 is also included by Dickins and Wilson, **352**, in their study of 'St Kasi.'

Storms 69 gives an inscription (partly unintelligible and partly in Latin) with instructions, in OE, that one should carry the inscription on one's person in order to gain the favour of a lord or king. The instruction is partly erased. Storms reads: 'Gif þu wille gangan to þinum hlaforde.' Storms 34 is a 'Letter from Heaven,' in Latin, with an OE explanation of its uses and powers, which, in this case, are extensive. Storms 35, from *Lac*, also employs a 'Letter from Heaven,' but the largely unintelligible mixture of Hebrew, Aramaic, Latin and Greek in this charm is a specific treatment for dysentery; see Braekman, **389**. Six types of heavenly letter were known to Förster, **337**.

OE prognostics and notes on computus are written in the same hand as the charms; for manuscript description, see 'Prognostics,' p. 259.

[Two Latin charms]; for dysentery   FC B.23.1.10

London, British Library, Cotton Faustina A.x, f. 116r
Ker 154B   s. xii¹

       art. 2. [*Contra febres, Contra frigora*]   [?Storms 39, 40]
         Þis man sceal singan nigon syþon wið utsiht   Storms 82

Storms 39 and 40 (listed by FC), are respectively headed *Contra febres* and *Contra frigora*, and contain no OE. Storms 82 (which resembles Storms 83, from *Lac*) contains OE directions for intoning an 'unintelligible' charm, 'wið utsiht,' and involves the use of a boiled egg ('hrerenbræden æg'): see Meroney, **358**. These three charms are printed by Cockayne, **298**, 3: 294 (not 292, as stated by Ker, or 292–4, as stated by FC). Immediately above them, Cockayne prints another exclusively Latin charm, also for fever, from the same manuscript, which is in a later 12th century hand; FC's inclusion of this (art. 3) is presumably a typographical error. For discussion, see Dietrich, **299**, and, for Storms 40, see Bonser, **355**.

The three charms printed by Storms, together with two recipes for eye-salve (FC B.21.5.4), are added in a blank space at the foot of two consecutive folios in a hand resembling the main hand. See further, 'Recipe Collections,' p. 237.

For foot troubles   FC B.23.1.11

London, British Library, Cotton Galba A.xiv, f. 72r
Ker 157 (s. xi¹)
    art. X *Wið fotcoþe*
As printed by Ker, the instruction, 'Wið fot[coþe singe man] þas fers ærest,' is followed by a Latin formula, invoking Edward, Grimbald, Bride and Cedd, which concludes '⁊ biddan drihten ⁊ þas halgan þæt him gescilde wið þan coþe.' The text was printed by Logeman, **303**, who was doubtful of the reliability of the transcript of Wanley, 231. Muir, **332**, who has recently edited the manuscript in full, thinks otherwise, and finds in Wanley reason to believe that the charm (which he calls a 'recipe') originally followed the two recipes on f. 118. For manuscript description, see 'Recipe Collections,' p. 231.

For charming bees; St Columkill's Circle; for theft   FC B.23.1.12
(with rectangle); for charming cattle; for charming crops

London, British Library, Cotton Vitellius E.xviii, ff. 15v, 16
Ker 224   s. xi med.
    art. k ... *e mædere cið on þinre hyfe*
        l *Þis is sancte columcille circul*   Storms 85
        m *Þonne þe man hwet forstele*   Storms 86
        p) *Þis is þinan yrfe to bote*   Storms 50
        q) *lange sticcan feðerecgede*
The opening to art. k, for protecting bees against theft, is damaged (printed by Cockayne, **400**, 1: 397). Storms 85 and 86 (also printed by Cockayne, **400**, 1: 395–6) are graphic. Storms 85 depicts 'Saint Columkill's Circle,' accompanied by OE directions for inscribing the circle on stone and wedging it into the ground. Storms 86 shows a rectangular design; OE instructions state that, in the event of theft, a copy should be made in silence and placed in the left shoe. Storms 50, following Cockayne, conflates an instruction for charming cattle by intoning 'Agios' (art. p) with an OE direction belonging to a charm for crops (art. q); both charms are damaged. The charm for crops (art. q) is printed in full by Ker. Cockayne, whose handling of the charms and recipes in this manuscript is highly erratic, also gives the full text of art. q, but prints it as four distinct fragments: Cockayne, **400**, 1: 386 (conflated with art. p); 3: 291 ('Fragment of a charm'); 1: 397 ('ibid, fol. 16a'—the order of the first two phrases is reversed); 3: 295 ('A blessing on fruit of the field'). This last fragment is printed as Storms A2.

Förster, **318**, suggested that 'Saint Columkill's Circle' was closely connected in origin with *Spera Apulei*, a circular diagram employed in prognostication, which, in Vitellius E.xviii, f. 16, is accompanied by a Latin
explanation with OE gloss. In Grendon's anthology the charm is entitled
'A field remedy' (Grendon D11), but Förster, pointing to the inscription
within the circle ('contra apes'), identified the inscribed stone circle as a
means of gaining protection against bees. Storms holds that the charm is
for bees and that *contra* 'may have been a mistaken translation of OE *wiþ*,
which has both meanings' (**325**, 311); cf. art. k and the metrical charm, 'For
a Swarm of Bees,' whose object is to persuade bees to settle (FC A.43.8).
The St Columkill's legend and its connection with Storms 85 is mentioned
in Singer, **470**. For bee charms generally, see Elsakkers, **560**, Fife, **519**.
For Storms 86, see Schneider, **367**.

A number of OE prose pieces in this manuscript are written in the same
hand as the charms; for manuscript description, see 'Recipe Collections,' p.
238, and 'Prognostics,' p. 260.

For bleeding (horses and men); against a dwarf   FC B.23.1.13

Oxford, Bodleian, Auct. F.3.6, ff. ii verso, iii
Ker 296 (s. xi¹–xi²)

> art. b *wið þone dworh*   Storms 78
>   *Gif men ierne blod of nebbe*   Storms 77

Storms 77 and 78 are 'unintelligible' inscriptions with OE directions for
their use. In Storms 78, the inscription is preceded by the statement that
it is to be written if someone has blood running from the nose, and followed
by 'Ge horse ge men blod seten.' In Storms 78, a fragment of gibberish is
followed by an OE instruction to write on three wafers, 'wið þone dworh,'
after which is written: 'Thebal gutta.' As Storms notes, wafers are also
employed in the metrical charm 'Against a Dwarf' (FC A.43.3). Both
charms were printed by Napier, **308**. Meroney, **358**, deciphers much of
Storms 77 and its *Lb* parallel (Storms 76).

The charms, together with a scribble, *scurfede hors*, are entered in blank
spaces, in 11th century hands, described by Ker as 'rough.' An inscription
below the charms (Latin and OE) records the gift of the manuscript to
Exeter by Bishop Leofric. Ker explains that the leaves on which these
appear are now foliated as flyleaves, but are, in actuality, the first two
leaves of the first quire.

Heading   FC B.23.1.14

Oxford, Bodleian, Barlow 35, f. 54v
Ker 298   s. xi in.

> art. b *Wið blodryne*

Ker states that a heading, 'Wið blodryne. writ ð,' followed by a Latin
charm, is added on specially ruled lines at the foot of the page. The Latin
charm does not appear to have been printed in full.

The charm, together with Latin–OE glossaries from Ælfric's Grammar and Glossary, is added in Anglo-Saxon minuscule to a manuscript containing Alcuin on Genesis and other texts written by continental scribes in the 10th century; it was in England by s. xi in. and probably earlier. A 12th century scribe has inserted caroline forms for some of the letters in the Latin lemmata.

To aid a pregnant woman; for unknown swelling;   FC B.23.1.15
for stitch; heading

Oxford, Bodleian, Junius 85 + 86, f. 17rv
Ker 336   s. xi med.
      art. 3 *Wið wif bearneacenu*   Storms 45
           Wið gestice   Storms 49
           Wið uncuðum swyle   Storms 41
           Wið toðece

Three charms in Latin with OE titles and directions for use and the incomplete fragment of a fourth are written, without break or change of hand, at the end of a homily; the writing on the verso is over erasure.

Storms 45, headed 'Wið wif bearn eacenu,' contains a Latin formula which alludes to the child-bearing of Mary and Elizabeth and invokes Longinus; the OE directions state that the inscription is to be written on wax and bound under the right foot. Storms 49, headed 'Wið gestice,' also contains a Latin formula invoking Longinus. Storms 41 has an OE heading, 'Wið uncuðum swyle,' and instructions for intoning a Latin couplet, 'on ðine laecefinger.' Cockayne, **400**, 1: 392, 393, 394, prints all four items; the fourth consists of a heading, 'wið toð ece,' and a fragment of Latin, which Cockayne relates to *Lac*, 100. All four items are printed with discussion, by Telting, **296**; for toothache charms, see Townend, **361**; for magico-medical literature pertaining to pregnancy, see Deegan, **559**. Discussed by Meaney, **573**.

Blood stanching cross   FC B.23.1.16

Oxford, St John's College 17, f. 175r
Ker 360   s. xii in.
      art. f *Wið blodrinu of nosu*   Storms 54

The instruction, which Ker gives as 'Wið blodrinu of nosu wriht on his forheafod on cristes mel,' is followed by words arranged in the form of a cross, transcribed from Greek, meaning 'Let us stand respectfully, let us stand in awe.' The Greek phrase is from the mass of St John Chrysostom, associated with the ritual of the eucharist; see Singer, **345**, Olivieri, **500**. The charm has been printed a number of times (it is found in Cockayne, **400**, 1: 394, as well as in Storms 54). Cameron, **565**, 213, suggests that the combined effect of the awesome procedure and the pressure of the finger on the forehead could have caused constriction of peripheral blood vessels:

'Thus, although the remedy was wholly magical in intent, it may actually have worked' (213).

The manuscript (J) is held to be a copy of material compiled by Byrht-ferth (see further pp. 150-1, 161-2, 'Byrhtferth'). Cameron, **551**, 150, however, considers that the Latin medical texts amongst which the charm is recorded (five folios in all, found at the beginning and end of the manuscript) are a later addition to Byrhtferth's material; Ker makes no distinction be-tween the hand of the charm and the OE found elsewhere in J, which was perhaps responsible for the Thorney annals and other additions throughout the manuscript. The five folios of medical texts, including the charm, were printed in full, with translation and discussion, by Singer, **236**.

Fever charm; for stanching blood (runic)   FC B.23.1.17

Vatican City, Reg. Lat. 338,[1] ff. 91, 111
Ker 390   s. xi[1]
    art. a *Þis mon sceal wið 'þaet' gedrif writan*
    art. b *Wið blodryne*

The charm against fever (art. a) lists seven names, those of the Sleepers of Ephesus, and instructs that these are to be written 'on þreom leac-bladan.' It was printed by Stokes, **305**, whence Holthausen, **307**. Ker prints the direction more exactly, but omits the names, 'Eugenius, Stephanus, Portar-ius, Dyonisius, Sambuius, Cecilius et Cyriacus.' For discussion, see Bonser, **355**, Flint, **575**. Ker reports that art. b has an OE heading, 'wið blodryne,' which is followed by letters of the Greek, Latin and runic alphabets. Stokes omits the OE heading, and prints only a 'list of Anglo-Saxon runes' (144). For a comparable use of runes for blood stanching, see Dickins, **351**. No complete text of art. b is known to the writer.

Ker states that arts. a and b are added in blank spaces in two different English hands, s. xi[1]; the 10th century Vatican manuscript is written in continental hands, and there is no evidence that it has ever been in England.

Fever charm   FC B.23.1.18

Worcester, Cathedral Library, Q.5, f. 85v
Ker 399   s. xi med.
    art. b *Ðis maeg wið gedrif.*

A Latin formula (invoking the Seven Sleepers, orders of angels, Mary, the four evangelists, etc.) is preceded by an OE heading ('Ðis maeg wið gedrif') and directions for writing on wafers which are to be fed to the patient: 'genim .ix. oflaetan 7 gewrit on ælcere on þas wisan: iesus christus, 7 sing þærofer .IX. pater noster 7 syle ætan ænne daeg .III. 7 oðerne .iii. 7 ðriddan .III. 7 cweðe æt alcon siðan þis ofer þone mann.'

---

[1] The error in Ker, *Catalogue*, 383 for 338, is corrected by Ker, *Suppl.*

The charm, first transcribed by Schenkl, **304**, and overlooked by Cockayne, was printed by Napier, **308** (quoted here), and subsequently by Liebermann (see **309, 336**); Liebermann prints only the OE. It is virtually identical to Storms 36, printed from a 17th century transcript, Harley 464. The Seven Sleepers are invoked in a number of fever charms; see Bonser, **355**, and the Vatican fever charm above (FC B.23.1.17).

The charm is added to a blank leaf at the end of the manuscript; Napier's dating of the hand (late 10th or early 11th century) is somewhat earlier than Ker's. Elsewhere, OE is found only in some glosses to Bede's *De arte metrica*.

II: ANTHOLOGIES, COVERAGE AND CLASSIFICATIONS, CONCORDANCES; SOME RELATED GENERAL STUDIES

Grendon's anthology of Anglo-Saxon charms (**314**) combined alphabetic and numerical classification, based on the five main categories he identified (see accompanying concordance to the three major editions, pp. 251–6). Storms, **325**, numbered consecutively the OE and Latin charms he printed, ordering them according to his analysis of their cultural constitution. Both anthologies carried a high proportion of identical material, and drew substantially on *Lb* and *Lac*; they also included charms from other manuscripts (both prose and metrical), some of which had previously been edited by Cockayne, **400** and **298**.

Magoun, **363**, reviewing Storms's edition, remarked that it was 'something of a life's work' to identify the charms in one edition in terms of another, and offered a partial concordance. Lendinara, **381**, classifies a total of 124 OE–Latin charms, with extensive cross-referencing between editions; she follows Storms in numbering them consecutively, but as she organizes them on different principles, the numbers do not coincide. FC list 18 items under 'Prose charms and charm headings'; some of these items comprise a single charm whose only OE element is the heading, others represent substantial vernacular groups. The recently published *Manual of Old English Prose* (1990) retains FC's groupings but adopts a different system of alphabetic and numerical classification. What is badly needed to facilitate discussion of the relatively neglected 'Prose charms and headings' is a system of descriptive titles; Storms's titles (which are adopted, with some modifications, in the present work) may not command general assent (and his translation of some of the OE titles is arguable), but they are much more helpful for all practical purposes than are the various numerical classifications. Attention is drawn to the Catalogue of *incipits* of medical and scientific writings in Old and Middle English being prepared by Voigts (announced Deegan, **559**).

For prose charms not included in any of the three major editions, see 'Explanatory Notes' to the accompanying concordance, p. 250. The charm printed by Priebsch, **440**, is also among those classified by Grendon (AA18),

but was regarded by him as linguistically too late to be accounted as OE.[2]
For a recent identification of a corrupt OE charm in a 13th century hand,
see Brown and Voigts, **544**. Just as the difference between recipes and
charms was by no means clear-cut, even to earlier scholars who considered it appropriate to make such discriminations, so too the distinction
between charms and prayers is, and surely was, extremely fluid. Bonser's
Anglo-Saxon and Celtic Bibliography, 1957, includes under 'Medicine' texts
edited by Fehr, **471**, from CCCC 422 and Laud 482, which FC classify as
'Liturgical.' Wordsworth, **448**, also draws the *Durham Ritual* and *Book of
Cerne* into the discussion of charms.[3] Of particular interest in this connection are Jolly, **395**, and Hohler, **387**. Given that the charms use (and
misuse) a number of languages, the isolated study of OE texts in this area,
as in all others, is a dubious practice.

The anthologies of Storms and Grendon are introduced by a study of
Anglo-Saxon magic; both editions are accompanied by translation, and each
of the charms Storms prints is accompanied by detailed analysis. Magoun's
reviews of these anthologies (**353** and **363**) are useful supplements. General studies of Anglo-Saxon charms and magic in the Anglo-Saxon period
usually refer only to *Lb*, *Lac* and/or the metrical charms. Prose charms
figure incidentally in broadly-based studies of Anglo-Saxon medicine (particularly Bonser, **517**); annotations in this volume do not attempt to identify discussion of prose charms in broadly-based studies of magico-medicine
(identification of prose charms among the many texts to which such studies
invariably refer, sometimes without accompanying documentation, is hazardous, and, given that individual texts rarely receive extended discussion
in such studies, the labour involved scarcely seemed warranted).

For studies in which the methodology of studying charms is a central
issue, see Brie, **452**, Barley, **528**, Nöth, **377**, and Cameron, **565**; Lendinara,
380, is also of interest to theoreticians. For ecclesiastical attitudes to the
use of charms and non-ecclesiastical practitioners of magic, see particularly
Brie, **452**, **457**, Stürzl, **366**, Crawford, **518**, Meaney, **573**, Flint, **575**.
Grendon, 140–59, discusses 'the attitude assumed by the medieval Church
and State towards magic in general and charms in particular,' and cites
'all extant Anglo-Saxon legislation, as well as penitentials and ecclesiastical
admonitions, pertaining to charms' (140–2). For philological studies of OE
terms for practitioners of prohibited magic, see Brie **452**, Mezger, **494**, and
Serjeantson, **495**.

---

[2] The charm (dated *c*. 1311–24) has been transcribed and edited by T.M. Smallwood,
' "God was born in Bethlehem ... ": The Tradition of a Middle English Charm,' *Medium
Ævum* 58 (1989): 206–23. The manuscript is now Paris, Bibl. nat., nouv. acq. lat. 693.
Smallwood notes that its most obvious forerunner is Storms 13.

[3] Sims-Williams, 1990, ch. 10, 'Prayer and Magic,' 273–327, includes an interesting
study of two early private prayer books, Royal 2 A.xx and Harley 7653 (formerly Add.
5004).

CHARMS: CONCORDANCE TO THE EDITIONS OF COCKAYNE, GRENDON AND STORMS

The accompanying chart (pp. 251–6) tables the passages printed as charms by Grendon, **314**, Storms, **325**, and Cockayne, **400** and **298**, and gives the corresponding FC classification. A few anomalies encountered in FC's classification, noted in the introductory description of charms and manuscripts, are indicated by question marks; anyone who has worked closely with the *Plan for the Dictionary of Old English* will have discovered that, relative to the size of the undertaking, such anomalies are rare. Wright, **294**, 15–16, collates *Lb* charms in Grendon and Storms; Magoun, **363** and **365**, tables correspondences between Grendon and Storms.

Explanatory Notes

Grendon's classification distinguishes five types: A, Exorcisms of Disease or Disease-spirits; B, Herbal Charms; C, Charms for transferring disease; D, Amulet charms; E, Charm remedies. Storms distinguishes the degree of foreign influence (numbering begins with charms 'of pure Germanic origin,' 129).

Storms's anthology contains 86 charms, and an Appendix of 16 Latin prayers. Storms, 37–40, 43, 52, 55–62, 64, 71–2, 80, are Latin only (and are not from *Lb* or *Lac*). Storms, Appendix (A1–16), includes some charms with OE headings.

Grendon prints 62 charms but gives a classified list of 87 others (162–4). His classified list includes two of the prose charms not included in any of the three major editions, which are as follows: FC B.23.1.7 (Zupitza, **306**); FC B.23.1.8 and FC B.23.1.14 (Ker 129, **298**); FC B.23.1.11 (Logeman, **303**, Muir, **332**); FC B.23.1.17 (Stokes, **305**; Grendon AA14); FC B.23.1.18 (Napier, **308**; Grendon AA15): Storms 36, edited from Harley 464 (17th century), closely resembles FC B.23.1.18.

Twelve Metrical charms, including five from *Lac* and one from *Lb*, are classified by FC as 'Poetry,' and are thus covered only incidentally by the annotations in this volume. A few articles with ambiguous titles, listed in bibliographies consulted, which deal only with metrical charms are included for the purposes of clarification. Metrical charms in FC's classification have an 'A' prefix.

The titles listed are those adopted by respective editors (occasionally abbreviated), except in the case of metrical charms, where FC titles are employed. Grendon's titles are editorial; Storms generally encloses editorial titles in square brackets.

CONCORDANCE TO THE EDITIONS OF COCKAYNE, GRENDON AND STORMS

A question mark against an item in square brackets indicates a possible anomaly in FC's classification.

STORMS		GRENDON	COCKAYNE	Lb	Lac	FC
1	For a Swarm of Bees	A4	1:384			A.43.8
2	For a Sudden Stitch	A1	3:52–4		75–6	A.43.4
3	*Wiþ cyrnel*	A9	3:62		95	
4	Against a Wen	A3				A.43.12
5	For the Water-Elf Disease	B5	2:350	3.63		A.43.7
6	*Wiþ blæce*	C1	2:76	1.32.2		
7	Against a Dwarf	A2	3:42		56	A.43.3
8	For Unfruitful Land	A13	1:398–404			A.43.1
9	The Nine Herbs Charm	B4	3:30–6		45–6	A.43.2
10	For Delayed Birth	E1	3:66–8		103	A.43.6
11A	[*Wiþ þeofþe*]		3:286			{B.23.1.4 {B.23.1.5
11B	[*Wiþ þeofþe*]					[B.23.1.6?]
12	[*Wiþ þeofþe*]		1:392			B.23.1.1
13	For Loss of Cattle	A21	1:390–2			A.43.10
14	For Loss of Cattle	A22	3:60		91	A.43.5
15	For Loss of Cattle	A16	1:384			A.43.9
16	A Journey charm	A14	1:388–90			A.43.11
17A	[*Wiþ ælfadle oppe ælfsogoþan*]					
17B	——	B3	2:346	3.62		
17C	——					

STORMS		GRENDON	COCKAYNE	Lb	Lac	FC
17D	[Wiþ ælfadle oþþe ælfsogoþan]	A24	2:348	3.62		
18	Se halga drænc		3:10–12		11	
19	[Seo halige sealf]		3:22–4		29	
20	[Sealf wiþ ælfcynne]	E8	2:344	3.61		
21	[Wiþ wennum]	E13	3:74		114	
22	[Wiþ ylfa gescotum]	E2	2:290	2.65		
23	[Wiþ lungenadle]		3:56		79	
24	Wiþ swine fær steorfan	E4	3:56		82	
25	Wiþ fleogendan attre	C3	3:52		74	
26	Wiþ utwærce		2:290–2	2.65		
27	Wiþ lenctenadle		2:134	1.62		
28	Wiþ deofle		2:352	3.64		
29	Wiþ wambe wærce	C2	2:318	3.18		
30	Wiþ nædran slite		2:110–12	1.45.3–4		
		('Lost Apocrypha' section of *Lac*; omitted by Cockayne)				
31	[Wiþ attre]					
32	[Wiþ leodrunan]	D8	2:138	1.64		
33	Wiþ lenctenadle (runic)	{A18 / D9}	2:140	1.65		**B.25.4.3**
34	[Gewrit of heofenum]	D10	3:280–2			**B.23.1.9**
35	Wiþ utsihte	(Harley 464)	3:66		102	
36	Wiþ gedrif					{Not listed FC / [B.23.1.18 ?]
37	*Septem dormientes* (Latin only)					

STORMS		GRENDON	COCKAYNE	Lb	Lac	FC
38	[Septem dormientes] (Latin only)					[B.23.1.10?]
[39]	Contra febres (Latin only)					[B.23.1.10?]
[40]	Contra frigora (Latin only)					B.23.1.15
41	Wiþ uncuþum swyle	A23	1:394			B.23.1.15
42	Wiþ liþwærce	A20	2:322	3.24		
43	[Sator formula] (Latin only)					
44	Wiþ Dweorh	E6	3:38–40		51	
45	Wiþ wif bearn eacenu		1:392			B.23.1.15
46	Gif hors biþ gewræht	A19	3:62		94	
47	Gif hors biþ gescoten		3:64		97	
48	Wiþ ealra feonda gerimnessum		1:386			B.23.1.2
49	Wiþ gestice		1:393			B.23.1.15
50	Þis is þinan yrfe to bote		1:386			B.23.1.12
51	Contra dolorum dentium		3:64		100	
52	Ad dentium dolorum (Latin only)					
53	Wiþ omum und blegnum		3:42		57	
54	Wiþ blodrinu of nosu	E7	1:394			B.23.1.16
55–60	[To stanch Bleeding] (Latin only)					
61	[Against demoniacal possession] (Latin only)					
62	[Contra felon] (Latin only)					
63	Gif wif ne mæge bearn beran		3:64		98	
64	Contra febres (Latin only)					

STORMS		GRENDON	COCKAYNE	Lb	Lac	FC
65	[Wiþ topece]	A10	3:8		8	
66	Wiþ oman	A12	3:70		110	
67	Wiþ horses oman and mannes	A11	3:70		109	
68	Wiþ gedrif		3:295			B.23.1.9
69	[To obtain favours]	D7	3:290			B.23.1.9
70	[Wiþ þa blacan blegene]	A17	3:8		9	
71	[Against black blains] (Latin only)					
72	Contra felon (Latin only)					
73	[Wiþ wyrme]	A5	3:10		10	
74	Wiþ þeofentum	A6	3:58		83	
75	[Wiþ corne]	A7	3:62		96	
76	Blodseten	D6	2:54	1.9.4		
77	[Blodseten]					B.23.1.13
78	[Wiþ dworh]					B.23.1.13
79	[Wiþ fleogendum atre]	B7	2:112–14	1.45.5		
80	Medicina contra febres (Latin only)					
81	[Wiþ nædran bite]		2:114	1.45.5		
82	[Wiþ utsiht]	A8	3:294			B.23.1.10
83	[Wiþ utsihte]	B6	3:68		105	
84	Wiþ cyrnla		3:68		106	
85	Þis is Sancte Columcille Circul	D11	1:395			B.23.1.12
86	[Wiþ þeofte]	D12	1:396			B.23.1.12

STORMS		GRENDON	COCKAYNE	Lb	Lac	FC
A1	*Tractatus Medici* (Latin only)					
A2	[*Æcres bletsung*] (incomplete)		3:295, 290 1:388, 397			**B.23.1.12** (incomplete)
A3	*Contra occulorum dolorum*		3:60–2		92	
A4	*Wiþ sarum eagum*		1:387			**B.23.1.3**
A5	*Wiþ sarum earum*		1:387			**[B.23.1.3?]**
A6	*Wiþ magan seocnesse*		1:387			**[B.23.1.3?]**
A7	[*Wiþ poccas*]		3:78		118	
A8	[Against smallpox] (Latin only)					
A9	*Wiþ poccas*		3:295			**[B.23.1.9]**
A10	*Wiþ geswell*		3:295			**[B.23.1.9]**
A11	[For a sore throat] (Latin only)					
A12	*Benedictio Herbarum*		3:79		118	
A13	*Alia*		3:79		118	
A14	*Benedictio Unguenti*		3:79		118	
A15	*Alia*		3:80		118	
A16	[Against all evils] (Latin only)					

Continued on next page

PROGNOSTICS; ALPHABET DIVINATION; TABLES OF LUCKY AND UNLUCKY DAYS; PROHIBITION AGAINST BLOODLETTING

MANUSCRIPTS

PROGNOSTICS

The prognostic texts classified by FC as 'Prose' are listed, together with the interlinear glosses to Tiberius A.iii [FC C.16]

Cambridge, Corpus Christi College 391, pp. 713–21   W   FC B.23.3.1
Ker 67, art. d(i–v), d(viii)   s. xi²
Sunshine (art. d(i)); Thunder (art. d(ii)); Nativity, by
weekdays (art. d(iii)); Nativity, lunar (art. d(iv)); Medical (art. d(v)); Dreams, lunar (art. d(viii))

London, British Library, Cotton Caligula A.xv,   C   FC B.23.3.2
    ff. 125v–6, 131v–2
Ker 139A, arts. a, p, q   s. xi²
Prognostics: Medical (art. a); Dreams, lunar (art. p);
Nativity, lunar (art. q)

London, British Library, Cotton Tiberius A.iii,   T   FC B.23.3.3
    ff. 37v–40v, 41–3
Ker 186, art. 7h–m, o–r   s. xi med.
Dreams, lunar (art. 7h); Dreambook (art. 7i); Propitious days, lunar (art. 7j); Medical (art. 7k); Thunder
(art. 7l); New moon (art. 7m); Nativity, lunar (art. 7o);
Harvest (art. 7p); Dreambook (art. 7q); Omens in pregnancy (art. 7r)

Interlinear Glosses, ff. 27v–37v   FC C.16
Dreambook, 'De somniorum diuersitate ... danielis
prophete' (art. 7a); 'De obseruacione lune' (art. 7b);
Dreams, lunar (art. 7c); Harvest (art. 7d); Nativity, lunar (art. 7e); Medical (art. 7f); Thunder (art. 7g)

London, British Library, Cotton Vespasian D.xiv,   V   FC B.23.3.5
    ff. 75v, 103v
Ker 209, arts. 26, 34   s. xii med.
Harvest (art. 26); Thunder (art. 34)

Oxford, Bodleian, Hatton 115 (formerly Junius 23),   H FC B.23.3.6
    ff. 148–53v
Ker 332 (s. xi², xii med.), arts. 35a–f, i–k   s. xii
Dreams, lunar (art. a); Nativity, lunar (art. b); Nativity,
by weekday (art. c.); Harvest (art. d.); Wind (art. e);
Sunshine (art. f); Thunder (art. i); Dreambook (art. j);
Propitious days, lunar (art. k)

ALPHABET DIVINATION

London, British Library, Cotton Titus D.xxvii,   FC B.23.3.4
    ff. 55v–6v
Ker 202 (1023–35), art. i   s. xi¹

TABLES OF LUCKY AND UNLUCKY DAYS

Cambridge, Corpus Christi College 391, pp. 718, 721   W FC B.23.2.1
Ker 67, arts. d(vi, vii), e   s. xi² and s. xiii in.
3 lucky birth-days (art. d(vi)); 3 unlucky days for bloodletting (arts. d(vii), e)

Cambridge, Corpus Christi College 422, p. 27   FC B.23.2.2
Ker 70B, art. a   s. xi med.
Lunar calendar, for bloodletting

London, British Library, Cotton Caligula A.xv,   C FC B.23.2.3
    ff. 130–1
Ker 139A, arts. e, h, i   s. xi²
24 unlucky days of the year (art. e); 24 unlucky days for
bloodletting (art. h); 3 lucky birth-days (art. i)

London, British Library, Cotton Vitellius C.viii, f. 22rv   FC B.23.2.4
Ker 221, art. 2   s. xi¹
3 unlucky days for bloodletting

London, British Library, Cotton Vitellius E.xviii,   Vi FC B.23.2.5
    ff. 9, 15rv
Ker 224, arts. d, h, i, j   s. xi med.
24 unlucky days of the year (art. d); 3 lucky birth-days
(art. h); 3 unlucky days for bloodletting (art. i); 24 unlucky days for bloodletting (art. j)

London, British Library, Harley 3271, ff. 90v–1   FC B.23.2.6
Ker 239, arts. 8, 9   s. xi¹
24 unlucky days for bloodletting

PROHIBITION AGAINST BLOODLETTING

London, British Library, Cotton Vitellius E.xviii, f. 13 Vi FC B.23.4
Ker 224, art. g   s. xi med.

MANUSCRIPT DESCRIPTION (following Ker)

CCCC 391 (W)

W, a Worcester manuscript once (incorrectly) known as 'Portiforium Oswaldi,' is 'a small thick book of 326 leaves.' The prognostics and tables at pp. 713–21 (art. d) are all in one hand; art. e, an incomplete copy of the 'Three unlucky days for blood-letting' which immediately precedes it (art. d(vii)), is a latter addition by the 'tremulous' Worcester hand. It contains prayers, one of which is classified as a prose charm.

Caligula A.xv (C)

C consists of two parts. Part A, which was written at Christ Church, Canterbury, contains prognostics, notes on computus and prose charms; Part B (containing Ælfric's *De temporibus anni*) may also have been written there. The three quires which make up Part A, with the exception of the annals 'are by one scribe who was writing soon after 1073,' and are considered at some length by Förster, **321**.

Tiberius A.iii (T)

T, whose principle OE contents are an interlinear gloss to the Rule of Benedict, also contains prose charms, some computus texts and *Lap.* It is probably a Christ Church manuscript (see further 'Lapidary,' p. 200). There are four sets of Latin prognostics at 65rv (art. 12); two of these duplicate texts with OE interlinear glosses in art. 7 (e, f). Ker, who identifies two distinct hands in Latin and three distinct hands in OE, distinguishes between the hand of the interlinear glosses at 27v–37v and that of the OE entries at 37v–42v. Förster, **313**, gives a bibliographical description of the codex.

Vespasian D.xiv (V)

V (studied by Förster, **94**, Handley, **96** and Richards, **95**), also contains the *OE Dicts* and *OE Elucidarium*; it is mainly in one hand. Three folios, including 75 and 103, are thought by Ker to be additions in originally blank spaces. V is described by Ker as a Rochester or Canterbury manuscript, which, judging from the grammatical forms of the prayer to Mary in art. r, was probably in female ownership s. xii ex.

Hatton 115 (H)

H was at Worcester in the first half of the 13th century; its collection of homilies and admonitions are closely related to those found in other Worcester manuscripts. The prognostic texts (art. 35), in a 12th century 'pointed' hand, are followed by two pages, blank except for scribbles and two notes (one in the 'tremulous' hand); they occupy the last two quires, and are of a later date. Art. 35 consists of 11 paragraphs, each introduced by a red initial letter.

Vitellius E.xviii (Vi)

Vi, thought by Ker to have been written at Winchester, has a continuous interlinear OE gloss to a psalter and canticles of the Gallican version. As well as tables of unlucky days and the prohibition against bloodletting, it contains OE notes on computus, recipes and a number of prose charms; all of these items, Ker states, 'seem to be in the same hand as the gloss.'

Titus D.xxvi and xxvii (originally a single manuscript), chiefly contain Latin prayers and devotions, and, like V and Galba A.xiv, show signs of having been owned (or perhaps used in a monastic school) by women in the 12th century; see further 'Recipe Collections,' p. 238. The manuscript, examined by Birch **274**, also contains notes on computus (in more than one hand) and part of Ælfric's version of *De temporibus*, and can be dated 1023–35. The alphabet prognostications and the recipe are among the early additions; both are added in blank spaces in a hand dated s. xi[1] by Ker.

Part B of *CCCC 422*, 'the Red Book of Darley,' contains a missal with OE headings; Part A contains the poetic *SS*. The table of lucky and unlucky days, and notes on computus, are on a preliminary quire containing the calendar. Most of Part B is 'in a round hand, datable probably soon after 1060.' See Grant, **378**, reviewed by Hohler, **387**.

Vitellius C.viii contains two computistic texts (perhaps in a later hand); the table of unlucky days (here described as the 'Egyptian Days') is in the same hand as an OE fragment of *De temporibus*.

Harley 3271 also contains Ælfric's *Grammar* and various types of notes in OE and Latin, including notes on computus, in a number of different, contemporary hands. The Latin entries include a table of lucky and unlucky days of the moon (added in a blank space, f. 102v, similar to one appearing in Titus D.xxvii) and short pieces on lucky and unlucky days, ff. 120–4v.

Further description of the chief manuscripts can be found throughout Förster's serial edition of the prognostics; for C, see particularly **321**.

PROGNOSTICS

EDITIONS

The principle manuscripts containing OE prognostics are CCCC 391 (W), Tiberius A.iii (T), and Hatton 115 (H); the last was known to Cockayne as Junius 23. Almost all of the prognostic material in W and T, as well as the three prognostics in Caligula A.xv (C), was edited by Förster, **311**, **312**, **315**, **316**, **317**, **318**, **319** and **321**. The exceptions are a brontology from T (printed by Cockayne, **298**, 3: 180–2) and the text concerning omens in pregnancy, also in T (Cockayne, **298**, 3: 144). A sentence at the end of a medical prognostic in W which was overlooked by Förster, **318**, 34, was printed by Ker. Cockayne, **298**, had previously printed a number of prognostics from T and C, as well as all the prognostics from H (Cockayne, **298**, 3: 158–68). Some of the prognostics in H were printed parallel by Förster, but Cockayne's edition of H is the only complete one. The two prognostics in V were printed by Assmann, **301** and **302**; they can also be found in Warner's EETS edition of V, **4**. Details of the texts printed by Cockayne and in Förster's various publications, which include interlinear glosses to Latin prognostic texts (FC C.16) to which some of the OE prognostic texts are closely related, can be found in the annotations.

Although Cockayne does not always identify clearly the manuscript(s) from which he has elected to print a given text, his edition has the great virtue of gathering together in one volume a substantial body of prognostic texts, and their omission in Singer's revised edition, **327**, is much to be regretted. Förster's edition of the prognostics, dispersed over a number of issues of *Archiv* (1908–16), extending into a volume of *Englische Studien* (1925–6), and still reverberating in the pages of *Anglia* in 1944, is not notable for its succinct clarity. Locating the few lines of OE not previously printed by Förster amidst the pages of apparatus, commentary, and texts printed for comparison is no easy feat; identifying the texts printed in a given article in terms of those printed by Cockayne, even with the invaluable assistance of FC and Ker, is a time-consuming business, and the writer does not claim to have pieced together Förster's *addenda, corrigenda*, second thoughts and duplications, with the comprehensive thoroughness to which Förster himself aspired. A new, complete, edition is badly needed.

SOURCES AND DERIVATION

Förster was essentially concerned to establish the Latin (ultimately Greek and/or Babylonian) textual tradition to which the OE texts belonged and to define their stemmatic relationships. Then, as now, opinions tended to divide sharply on the question of whether 'superstitious beliefs' in the Anglo-Saxon period represent pagan survivals or whether folklore is merely a popularized (and degenerate) version of classical learning. Förster, **337**, clearly aligned himself with the latter school of thought, particularly opposing Fischer, **436** (other early proponents of the 'pagan survival' school of thought who were particularly influential include Grimm, **430** and Kemble, **429**; see also Hampson, **272**). But although Förster cited a number of Latin parallels, as well as West European vernacular ones, it is worth observing that, in general, the Latin parallels he cites are not sources but analogues. Few of the Latin manuscripts on which Förster draws for comparisons are earlier than the 12th century, and many are a good deal later (the chief exceptions are the Latin texts in T and Titus D.xxvii, a few of which have OE glosses), and the Latin parallels he cites are sometimes not close enough to warrant the conclusion that the OE is directly translated from a Latin exemplar.

The existence of a Latin textual tradition widely disseminated through-out Europe probably must be accepted as evidence of the prior existence of the Latin tradition, although the possibility need not be outruled that Anglo-Saxons were instrumental in the development of that tradition (see, for instance, Talbot, **369**). But although it seems likely that most, if not all, of the various types of OE prognostics had classical models, it does not follow that the OE prognostic texts are wholly, or even substantially, derived from Latin sources. Förster rightly drew attention to the culturally alien nature of some of the dream images that were lodged in the popular psyche by the Dreambooks (the lions in a Dreambook glossed in T are a case in point), but, as Martin, **383**, points out, the Dreambooks vary con-siderably in the number of dream interpretations they offer, and, like the proverb collections and herbals, appear to have been regarded by scribes as texts that could be freely augmented. Although determination of the nature and extent of this augmentation necessarily depends on identifying the material derived from late classical sources, it is unfortunate that the attempt to identify sources has the effect of foregrounding the derivative nature of vernacular texts, when it is their independence which is, finally, of broad historical interest.

The prognostics may not shed much light on the survival of Germanic paganism, but, unless they are to be regarded as esoteric literary exercises, they represent an as yet unexplored body of information on the preoccu-pations of late Anglo-Saxon monks, who were, presumably, responsible for their compilation and transmission. The concerns evinced by the prog-nostics are, overwhelmingly, mundane and secular. Crops, livestock, and weather are matters one would expect to be of interest to monastic commu-nities; others, such as determining the sex of an unborn child and propitious days for weddings, are not. The range of matters on which the laity sought advice from monastics would seem to have been remarkably wide (see Flint, **575**); unless the explanation lies in the relative lateness with which clerical celibacy was enforced. See further pp. 267–9 below, 'Tables of Lucky and Unlucky Days.'

A majority of the prognostics involve the influence of the moon, and thus (for those who reject the view that interconnection of planetary move-ment and human affairs is a popular or pagan belief) is bound up with the question of whether the study of astrology was pursued by the Anglo-Saxons, it being generally concluded that Arabic astrology had not reached them in any form. See particularly Wendel, **347**, Henel, **222**, Thorndike, **487**; cf. Flint, **575**. More recent studies of the dissemination of Arabic astrology in Western Europe can be conveniently located through Kren's *Annotated Bibliography* of medieval science and technology (1985).

CLASSIFICATION

Förster classified the prognostics according to generic type, identifying versions within each type on the basis of manuscript relationships (the preliminary classification of prognostic types in Förster, **337**, was developed and modified in Förster, **311**, **312**, **315**, **316**, **317**, **318**, **319** and **321**. FC's classification according to manuscript, although inevitably obscuring the copying of the same texts into more than one manuscript, has the advantage of preserving the integrity of prognostic groups. Close connection with Latin texts found in the same manuscripts, particularly those with interlinear glosses in Tiberius A.iii, was established by Förster.

The possibilities for grouping and classification are numerous. The following outline of the varieties and textual relationships of the prognostic texts is an adaptation of Förster's classification of types, re-ordered to suggest the existence of four broad categories of prognostic: divination by natural phenomena (brontologies, harvest prognostics, sunshine, wind, and new moon prognostics); nativity prognostics and propitious days (see also 'Tables of Lucky and Unlucky days,' p. 268); dream interpretation; medical prognostics (see also 'Tables of Lucky and Unlucky Days,' pp. 268–9, and 'Prohibition against Bloodletting,' p. 269).

Brontologies

Förster, **311**, identified five types of OE brontology. W contains one based on compass directions and another on days of the week. Two other passages in W constitute a single brontology based on the canonical hours. The brontology in W based on days of the week is closely related to the brontologies in T and H (Cockayne, **298**, 3: 180, 166–8). V attributes significance to the month of the year in which thunder is first heard (Assmann, **301**, Warner, **4**). In T there is an interlinear gloss to a Latin brontology whose organizing principle is the hour of the day (or night) when thunder occurs; this is classified as a gloss (FC C.16, art. 7g), and was printed by Förster **311**, 50–2. Förster, **94**, lists two Latin analogues for the canonical brontology, for which Förster, **311**, had been unable to find a parallel.

Harvest/Weather Prognostics

Förster, **312**, identifies a group of prognostics concerning the nature of the seasons and the quality of the harvest, which he terms 'Bauernpraktiken.' In H the predictions for the year depend on the day of the week on which the midwinter mass is celebrated (Cockayne, **298**, 3: 162–4). In T predictions for the year depend on the weekday on which the calend of January falls; so also in V (Warner, **4**, Assmann, **302**), as well as in a Latin text with interlinear gloss in T (FC C.16, art. 7d).

Sunshine and Wind

One set of prognostics in H regards sunshine and wind as omens of prevailing conditions (war, peace, plague, good harvests, etc.); predictions are based on the occurrence of sunshine on the first twelve days after Christmas, and on the occurrence of wind during the night in the same period.

W contains an almost identical sunshine prognostic: the first three days
are missing. Wind on any of the 12 nights after Christmas has a dire significance; sunshine, in most cases, is auspicious. See Förster, **316**; for H,
see Cockayne, **298**, 3: 164–6.

New Moon

Found only in T, and printed only by Cockayne, **298**, 3: 180, are prognostics based on the day of the week on which the new moon appears. Like the
prognostics based on sunshine and wind, the new moon prognostications
are concerned with general conditions, including weather; medical considerations figure prominently.

Nativity Prognostics

(1) By day of the week

Förster, **317**, 297–300, studies a set of prognostics which predict the character and fortune of a child according to the night or day of the week on
which it is born: the entry for Saturday (the last day of the week) specifies
'whether male or female' ('swa wer swa wif'). Förster prints parallel nativity prognostics from W and H (H is found in Cockayne, **298**, 3: 162).

(2) Lunar Month

Another set of prognostics predicts the fortunes of a man, according to the
age of the moon at the time of his birth. Förster, **318**, distinguishes between the version represented by an interlinear gloss in T, f. 36v (FC C.16,
art. 7e), which he prints (**318**, 18–21) and the closely related lunar nativity
prognostics found in WCTH, which he prints parallel (for CT, see Cockayne, **298**, 3: 156–8; for H, see Cockayne, **298**, 3: 160–2). WCT has 30
days; H contains only 14.

Propitious Days (Lunar)

This type of prognostic (found in H and T) works its way through the lunar month, enumerating, for every day of the month, the specific activities
which will prosper if they are begun on that particular day (see Förster,
318). H begins with the promise that, when the moon is one night old,
any request put to the king will meet with success. Both OE versions are
fragmentary. H (see Cockayne, **298**, 3: 176–80) contains the first 17 days of
the month; T contains only the first three. Similar in kind is an interlinear
gloss in T, art. 7b, 'De obseruacione lune,' a full set of prognostics for the
30 days of the month (Cockayne, **298**, 3: 184–96); see Förster, **324**.

Dreambooks

Förster, **321**, argued that dream lore was not of popular origin but derived
from the learned tradition, particularly the Latin *Somniale Danielis*, which,
he considered, must already have been in existence by the 4th century,

although the earliest exact translation from the Latin known to him dated from the 12th century. Three different Dreambooks are found in T (all three interpret dream images as portents of future events). The first of these is an interlinear gloss (FC C.16, art. 7a). Its 302 dream interpretations are alphabetically organized, and the rubric claims the authority of the prophet Daniel: 'De somniorum diuersitate secundum ordinem abcharii danielis prophete' (printed Förster, **315**, 47–70; Cockayne, **298**, 3: 198–214). The second Dreambook in T has 97 dream interpretations and is closely related to the Dreambook in H. Cockayne, **298**, 3: 168–76, used H as a base text, collated with T; Förster considered that T was an earlier and better text than H, and printed the two versions parallel. Finally, T contains a short fragment, less consistent in its alphabetic organization, consisting of 25/36 items (**312**, 302–5; *corrigenda* in **313**, 37). There is also a short Latin Dreambook in Titus D.xxvi (without OE gloss). See also 'Alphabet Divination,' p. 266.

The Latin textual tradition has been more recently examined by Martin, **383**, who edits a 9th century Latin Dreambook of English provenance, and concludes that the Latin text glossed in T is a hybrid version, combining the version that he edits and the version that underlies ME Dreambooks (for which, see Förster, **343**). Martin also draws attention to a Latin fragment in a late 10th century manuscript, Sloane 475, ff. 217v–8r, which appears to be related to the glossed text in T.

Dream Prognostics (Lunar)

Whereas the Dreambooks regard dream images as self-sufficient portents of the future, another series of prognostics regards the influence of the moon as the critical factor in determining the outcome of dreams; dreams betoken good or ill, depending on the age of the moon at the time of their occurrence (e.g., 'On anre nihte ealdne monan, swa hwæt swa þe mæteð, þæt cymð to gefean'). Förster, **321**, identifies three different versions. One version consists of the closely related lunar dream calendars in CTW (Förster regarded W as furthest from the original). A broadly similar version is found in H. There is also an interlinear gloss in T, ff. 35v–6 (FC C.16, art. 7c). All versions cover a full cycle of 30 days, beginning with the one-day-old moon, but there are omissions and conflations: the interlinear gloss is the fullest, with 29 separate items; CTW contains 20 items and H has 19. Cockayne, **298**, 3: 158–60, prints H.

Medical Prognostics (Lunar)

For medical prognostics which predict the chances of recovery from an illness according to the time of the lunar month (or 'the age of the moon') when it was contracted, see Förster, **318**. Förster identified three OE types, the first of which is found in C, and also in a Latin text with OE gloss preserved in T, f. 36v–7 (FC C.16, art. 7f); Cockayne, **298**, 3: 150–1, reproduces the manuscript layout (Latin and OE tables for the lunar month occupy parallel columns) and the accompanying circular diagram. Förster, **318**, connects this diagram with the *Spera Apulei* and the prose charm 'St Columkill's Circle' (Storms 85). The lunar medical prognostics in T and W (not in tabular form) are comparable but not identical (Cockayne, **298**, 3: 182, prints T). The conclusion to W, overlooked by Förster, was printed by Ker, 67.

Omens in Pregnancy

Unique to T is a passage containing instructions on how to divine the sex of the unborn child from the bearing of an expectant mother; it also adds the information that eating nuts or fruit in the fourth or fifth month of pregnancy can have an adverse affect on the mental capacity of the unborn child, and that eating the flesh of male animals may result in severe deformity. It was printed by Cockayne, **298**, 3: 144, together with a passage in the same manuscript, 'On the Formation of the Foetus' (see below, p. 270). Talbot, **524**, suggests that both texts may derive ultimately from Hippocrates; see also Deegan, **559**.

ALPHABET DIVINATION

The sole OE prognostic contained in Titus D.xxvii (which begins, 'A he gangeð and biþ his siðfæt gesund') was first printed in 1877 by Sievers, **300**, who compared it with some Latin *sortes* from German manuscripts previously edited by him. Birch, **274**, in his study of the history of the manuscript, which appeared the following year, speculated that the text might have been a preparatory draft for a series of illuminated capitals. Skeat, **334**, printed the text and offered a translation, and suggested that the text was a form of riddle, to which he proposed solutions. Skeat also pointed out that the series concludes with a metrical doxology (also found in 'Gloria II' [FC A.27]). Bradley, **335**, identified the text as an alphabet divination, and, by comparing it with the Latin *sortes* printed by Sievers and others, offered a reconstructed Latin original. Bradley, then, like Förster (see above, pp. 261–2, 'Prognostics') establishes that the OE text belongs to a Latin genre, but cannot be regarded as having definitively proved that the specifics of the OE alphabet divination are derived from a Latin source; the possibility of a connection with the alphabetically organized Dreambooks does not seem to have been explored. Dieterich, **444**, covers the general topic of alphabet divination. Given the frequency with which runic alphabets appear in Anglo-Saxon manuscripts, and their occasional use in charms (see 'Prose Charms and Charm Headings,' p. 247), it would be interesting to know whether it, as well as the Roman alphabet, was employed as an organizing principle in prognostic texts.

TABLES OF LUCKY AND UNLUCKY DAYS

EDITIONS

Tables of lucky and unlucky days appear in six manuscripts, two of which also contain prognostics, i.e., CCCC 391 (W) and Caligula A.xv (C). Most of these were printed by Förster, **322**. The remaining tables, from CCCC 442 and Harley 3271, and a copy of the three unlucky days for bloodletting overlooked by Förster, in Vitellius E.xviii (Vi), were printed by Henel, **323**. A number of the tables had earlier been printed by Cockayne, **298**. Both Henel and Förster identify textual relationships of the OE versions as well as Latin sources/analogues; some Latin sources/analogues are found in the manuscripts in which the OE prognostics and tables occur. Henel is more informative concerning computistical elements. Like Förster, Henel, **222**, considers that the tables are not reflections of popular belief but derive from late classical learning.

CLASSIFICATIONS AND STUDY

Other groupings of the prognostic texts and tables, cutting across the division established by Förster and Henel (and adopted by FC), suggest themselves. The 3 lucky birth-days and 24 unlucky days of the year, which FC include under 'Tables of Lucky and Unlucky Days,' have more in common with the nativity prognostics and tables of propitious days (see 'Prognostics,' p. 264 above) than with the remainder of the tables, which have to do with bloodletting (see also 'Prohibition against Bloodletting,' p. 269). Phlebotomy is regarded by medical historians as having played an important part in OE medical practice; see particularly Bonser, **517**, and Rubin, **531**. Auspicious times for bloodletting were variously defined, and opinions also differed concerning the manner in which it was to be carried out and the conditions for which desanguination was appropriate; see Sanborn, **424**, Stuart, **384**, Meaney, **392**.

As Henel, **222**, Wendel, **347**, and others point out, Ælfric's Epiphany Homily regards the notion of 'unlucky days' as heterodox. Explicit Christian piety in the tables, and in the prognostics, too, sometimes anticipates charges of heterodoxy (as, for instance the conclusion to the table of 24 unlucky days for bloodletting, which states: 'nis þis nan wiglung, ac wise menn hit afunden þurh þone halgan wisdom swa heom god ælmihtig gedihte'). Although study of the OE charms has attended to their conjunction of ostensibly antagonistic forms of faith in the supernatural, no comparable study of the prognostics and tables has been encountered (Henel, **222**, is broadly illuminating). Some specific discussion of OE texts is, however, included in the recent study of magic by Flint, **575**. Meaney, **392**, in an examination of Ælfric's condemnations of various forms of divination, which includes incidental consideration of some prognostic texts (see also Meaney, **554**), argues, in contrast to Henel and Wendel, that Ælfric was addressing himself to actually existing practices.

Three Lucky Birth-days

It is part of the definition of the three lucky birth-days (one in the latter half of December, the other two in the early part of January) that they are days on which no woman is born; but whatever man is born on these three days will not rot until doomsday. Förster, **322**, printed virtually identical texts from C and W, and identified two Latin versions (one in Titus D.xxvi, f. 3v). Henel, **323**, printed a closely similar version from Vi, and mentioned two other Latin versions (one in CCCC 422, p. 49). Cockayne, **298**, 3: 154/8–14, prints C.

Twenty-four Unlucky Days of the Year

The table is found in both C and Vi (headed, in Vi only, 'De Diebus Malis Cuiusque Mensis'); both texts were printed by Förster, **322**. The C text was printed by Cockayne, **298**, 3: 224. The table is preceded by a rubric stating that there are two days in every month which are inauspicious for any enterprise (whatever is begun on these days, 'ne wurð hit næfre geendod'), and followed by a brief testimony to the truth of the prognostication (ending 'gyme se þe wille'). Unlike the table of 24 unpropitious days for bloodletting, this table runs from January to December.

Twenty-four Unlucky Days for Bloodletting (etc.)

Förster, **322**, prints parallel the text from C and Vi. The table is introduced by a rubric which explains that ancient leeches affirmed in Latin books that there are two days in every month on which it is dangerous to drink (presumably medical potions) or let blood; and a horse on which a leech tested this doctrine soon lay dead (see Smith, **346**). The conclusion to the table explains that March ('Hlyda') is its starting point because the world was created in that month, and the conclusion also warns that it is dangerous to let blood when the moon is four or five nights old, and on All Hallows day. Henel, **323**, prints a variant from Harley 3271, headed 'De Diebus Malis,' which differs chiefly in the addition of a warning against gooseflesh (unwholesome to the sick and not to be eaten on the last day of March and December). Cockayne, **298**, 3: 152–4, prints C. Förster gives the closest source as pseudo-Bede, *De minutione sanguinis sive de phlebotomia*. Henel disagrees, and adduces Latin texts found in Titus D.xxvii, ff. 22–3, and Harley 3271, ff. 120–1r; he also examines some connections with Ælfric's homilies.

Three Unlucky Days for Bloodletting (etc.); the 'Egyptian days'

Förster identified two versions. The first is contained in *Lac*, 117, and in Vitellius C.viii, the second in Vi and W. Only the first version identifies the three unlucky days as 'Egyptian days,' 'þæt is on ure geþeode "plihtlice dagas." ' Förster considered that the two versions derived from a common source, and referred them (as well as the 24 unlucky days for bloodletting, etc.) to pseudo-Bede, *De minutione sanguinis sive de phlebotomia*, and a Latin text in Titus D.xxvi, f. 3v. W duplicates a few lines from the beginning of this text; i.e., a fragment of the text which appears in full in art. d (vii) is found in art. e; the duplicated lines were printed by Förster, **321**, 77). For 'Egyptian days,' see Stuart, **384**, and Meaney, **392**.

Calendar for bloodletting (etc.); Latin–OE

Förster, **318**, prints a table, Latin only, found in T, f. 65r, and Titus D.xxvii, f. 6r; each of the 30 days of the month is briefly identified as either good or bad, presumed to be for bloodletting. The OE text in CCCC 422, is preceded by a Latin version (printed by Henel, **323**).

PROHIBITION AGAINST BLOODLETTING; THE 'DOG DAYS'

Henel, **323**, **331**, prints, with discussion, an OE passage from Vi concerning the dog days, together with a Latin parallel for the second half of the text found in Titus D.xxvi, f. 4v, and Harley 3271, ff. 123v–4r (headed 'De Flebotomatione Mensis Agusti' [*sic*]). The prohibited days for bloodletting are the 18 days before Lammas and the 35 which follow it, which, Henel explains, means 14th July (marked in most Anglo-Saxon calendars as 'Dies caniculares hic incipiunt') to 5th September (usually marked 'Dies caniculares finiuntur').

ON THE HUMAN FOETUS

MANUSCRIPT

London, British Library, Tiberius A.iii, ff. 40v–1   FC B.21.4
Ker 186, art. 7n   s. xi med.

Between *PD* and 'Prognostics' Cockayne, **298**, 3: 144–6, printed two pieces
from Tiberius A.iii relating to pregnancy, the first of which begins with
an account of the means of determining the sex of an unborn child from
the bearing of its mother; see *Omens in Pregnancy*, p. 266 above. The
second piece, in a more factual style, describes the development of the foetus month by month. 'On the Human Foetus' figures in general histories
of Anglo-Saxon medicine, particularly Bonser, **517**, and Rubin, **531**. Rubin, who states that both the pieces in Tiberius A.iii concerning pregnancy
are from Hippocrates, echoes Talbot, **524**, who observes that the headings for *Lb*'s (significantly?) missing chapter on gynaecology (*Lb*2.60, of
which there is a quite detailed description in the table of contents, Cockayne, **297**, 2: 173) suggest knowledge of an abridgement of Hippocrates,
De mulierum affectibus, as do fragments occurring in other Anglo-Saxon
manuscripts dealing with the formation of the foetus, signs of pregnancy,
prognostication of the sex of the child and other details of gynaecological
interest. Gynaecological texts figure in the more recent study of medical
works known in Anglo-Saxon England by Cameron, **551**. See also Deegan **559**, who foreshadows a detailed study of medicaments prescribed for
female complaints in Anglo-Saxon medical texts.[1]

---

[1] For a review of literature in this area, see Helen Rodnite Lemay, 'Antonius Guainar-
ius and Medieval Gynaecology,' *Women of the Medieval World*, ed. Julius Kirshner and
Suzanne F. Wemple (Oxford: Blackwell, 1985) 317–36. Kren's *Annotated Bibliography*,
1985, also lists many relevant publications.

LEECHBOOK, LACNUNGA, RECIPES, PROSE CHARMS AND PROGNOSTICS: ANNOTATIONS

SEE ALSO Warner, **4**; Förster, **94**; Henel, **222**; Hampson, **272**; Birch, **274**; Cockayne, **400**; Bierbaumer, **416**; 'General and Miscellaneous Magico-Medical,' pp. 341–83

FACSIMILES

LEECHBOOK

294 Wright, C.E. *Bald's Leechbook (British Museum Royal Manuscript 12. D.xvii).* With an appendix by Randolph Quirk. Early English Manuscripts in Facsimile 5. Copenhagen: Rosenkilde, 1955.

Facsimile of R (*Lb*1–3).

Introduction, 11–30. A short discussion of manuscripts containing OE medical material, 11–12, is followed by an examination of R: physical appearance and features, 12; contents, 13–18; the scribal hand, 18–23; marginalia and manuscript history, 23–7; survey of scholarship, 27–30. Quirk's 'Language of the Leechbook' (unnumbered page) instances some features 'consistent with West Saxon dialect and scribal practice of about 950 AD, with some forms ... possibly suggesting an archetype of perhaps fifty years earlier.'

Wright considers the implications of the Latin colophon to *Lb*2, and deduces from manuscript presentation that *Lb*3 was originally a separate work; analysis of the organization and different character of the three books confirms this. *Lb*1 and 2, closely related to Alfred by *Lb*2.64, may be one of the works inspired by Alfred as part of his attempt to effect an intellectual recovery. Close examination of the script shows that it is identical with Parker Chronicle annals for 925–55. Wright dates these and *Lb* to the 950s; that *Lb* was written at Old Minster (to which Ker, 1941, 112, attributes these two manuscripts, together with the Tollemache Orosius and Cotton Otho B.xi) is 'not susceptible of proof' (23). Wright's examination of the marginalia (23–6) reveals that Cockayne, **297**, wrongly interpreted musical notes as cypher writing. The only OE marginal addition ('Wið þa blacan blegene,' Cockayne, **297**, 2: 128) is in 'a hasty, uneven shaky hand' (24), which has features in common with Harley 585, and it possibly belongs to the same period (early 11th century). This addition possibly indicates that another manuscript of *Lb* was in existence in the early 11th century. The 'Nota' symbols (*c.* 1200), and the Latin memorandum inserted at a charm against demonic possession (*Lb*3.64), indicate that the text was being studied and used. Rochester ownership is possible, as a 'Medicinale Anglicum' appears in a Rochester catalogue of 1202 (as well as in the Glastonbury catalogue mentioned by Cockayne), and many Rochester manuscripts passed into the Royal collection.

295 Sawyer, Peter H. *Textus Roffensis.* Vol. 1. Early English Manuscripts in Facsimile 7. Copenhagen: Rosenkilde, 1962. 2 vols.

Facsimile of Rochester, Cathedral Library, *Textus Roffensis*; prose cattle-charm at f. 95v [FC B.23.1.6; the legal formula to which the charm is linked in *Textus Roffensis* is found in Cockayne, **298**, 3: 286–8; *not* Storms 11B]. Sawyer suggests that the legal formula was not intended to be part of the incantation belonging to the charm, because it appears separately in other manuscripts (19).

EDITIONS

LEECHBOOK, LACNUNGA, ETC.

296 Telting, A. 'Angel-Saksische bezwerigsformulieren.' *De Vrije Fries* 2 (1842): 1–9.

Prints three charms (and the beginning of a fourth) from Junius 85 (Storms 45, 49, 41), 2–3, with Dutch translation. Notes, textual and interpretive, 4–7, comment on the use of the names of Christ, John and Lazarus, as a form of sympathetic analogy in (i); the use of wax as an amulet and the allusion to the baptism of John as a narrative analogy in (ii); the frequency with which Longinus, mentioned in (iii), is named in blood-stanching charms. There is a discussion of the implications of *lœcefinger* ('healing finger'), which occurs in (i), 8–9.

297 Cockayne, Oswald. *Leechdoms, Wortcunning and Starcraft of Early England.* Vol. 2. Rolls Series 35. London: Longman, 1865. 3 vols. [Nendeln]: Kraus, 1965.

Prints from R, with translation, *Lb*1–3, 1–360. Also prints, 280–8, Recipes from Harley 55 [FC B.21.2.4], in place of missing leaves. Facsimile of R, f. 55v, frontispiece. Glossary, 361–415.

Preface, vii–xxxviii. Some brief remarks on the diet and 'tolerable degree of civilization' attained by the Anglo-Saxons is followed by an account of the sources and language of *Lb*, together with some remarks on the manuscript, its markings and its date (first half of the 10th century); Glastonbury provenance is suggested. Cockayne considers that *Lb*3 is 'of the same age; possibly by the same hand as the other two' (xxxiii), but recognizes that it differs from *Lb*1 and *Lb*2; it is characterized by 'the monkish habit of saying some good words over the sick' (xxxiii). References to Oxa and Dun and others bear out the existence of a school of medicine among the Anglo-Saxons. Cockayne accepts the authenticity of the report that Alfred had sent to Jerusalem. He defines the sources as a mixture of Hibernian, Scandinavian and Celtic, but considers that Anglo-Saxons must also have drawn on Greek writers, which were transmitted to them through the school established by Theodore. Cockayne also observes that some recipes in *Lb* also appear in *Lac*.

298 **Cockayne, Oswald.** *Leechdoms, Wortcunning and Starcraft in Early England.* Vol. 3. Rolls Series 35. London: Longman, 1866. 3 vols. [Nendeln]: Kraus, 1965.

Prints, with translation: *Lac* at 2–80; *PD* at 82–144. Durham Glossary of Names of Plants, 297–305; Saxon Names of Plants, 309–50. Glossary, 353–74; Index, 377–98.

Also prints the following, with translation (Ker's foliation is substituted throughout):

Medical Texts. 'On the Formation of the Foetus,' from Tiberius A.iii, ff. 40v–1 [FC B.21.4], 146. Recipes ('Leechdoms omitted in their place'), from Faustina A.x, ff. 115v–16r [FC B.21.5.4], 292. [See also Cockayne, 400, 1: 374–82, 388.]

Prognostics. From Tiberius A.iii [FC B.23.3.3], collated with Caligula A.xv [FC B.23.3.2] at 150–1, 154/15–158/19, as follows: ff. 42v–3, 'Omens in Pregnancy' (art. r), 144; ff. 37v–8, Lunar Dream Prognostic (art. h), 154/15–156/16; f. 41rv, Nativity Prognostic (art. o), 156/17–158/19; f. 40rv, Brontology (art. l), 180/9–18; f. 40v, Lunar Prognostic, '*New Moon*' (art. m) 180/19–182/4; f. 40, Medical Prognostic (art. k), 182/5–27. Also prints glosses from Tiberius A.iii [FC C.16], as follows: ff. 36v–7, Lunar Calendar (medical), Latin–OE (art. f), 150–1; ff. 32v–5v, 'De observacione luna et que cauenda sunt,' OE only (art. b), 184–96; ff. 27v–32v, Dreambook, 'De somniorum diversitate secundum ordinem abcharii danielis prophete,' OE only (art. a), 198–214. From Hatton 115, ff. 148–53v [FC B.23.3.6], 158–80, roughly collated with Tiberius A.iii [FC B.23.3.3, arts. i, j] at 168/8–176/24. [Includes two non-prognostic texts, on the number of masses and psalms equivalent to fasts of a certain length (arts. g, h), at 166/17–25; for itemization of Hatton's contents, see above, p. 258, 'Manuscripts'].

Computistica ('Starcraft'). From Tiberius A.iii, f. 179, On the Length of Shadow [FC B.20.12.2], 218–22. From Caligula A.xv, f. 126v, Table of Duration of Moonshine [FC B.20.9], 222–4; ff. 130–1v, Rules for Finding Movable Feasts [FC B.20.1.2], 226/1–21 (arts. f, g, j), 226/30–228/4 (art. l); f. 131r, Epacts and Concurrents [FC B.20.2.2]), 226/22–9 (art. k), 228/5–8 (art. m); f. 131v, Rules for Finding the Age of the Moon [FC B.20.6], 228/9–20; On the Three Fridays for Fasting [FC B.20.11.2], 228/21–5; f. 143rv, Epacts [FC B.20.2.3], 282. Also prints *De Temporibus*, 232–81 [FC B.1.9.4].

Table of Unlucky Days, from Cotton Caligula, A.xv [FC B.23.2.3]: f. 130v (art. h), 152/1–154/7; f. 131r (art. i), 154/8–14; f. 130r (art. e), 224.

Charms. From Tiberius A.iii, f. 106 [Storms 11A], with the legal fragment which follows this charm in *Textus Roffensis*, f. 95, and in CCCC 383, f. 66v [FC B.23.1.6], 286–8. From Caligula A.xv, f. 140rv [Storms 34, 69], 288–90. From Vitellius E.xviii, f. 16r [part of FC B.23.1.12, art. q, as two fragments, the second of which was printed as Storms A2; for the remainder of art. q, see Cockayne, **400**, 1: 388, 397], 290/24–6, 295/1–4; from Faustina A.x, ff. 115v–16r [a Latin charm, *Contra cotidianas febres* and Storms 39, 40, 82], 294; from Caligula A.xv, f. 129 [FC B.23.1.9, art. d; the first of these three items was printed as Storms 68, the other two as Storms A9–10], 295. [See also Cockayne, **400**, 1: 384–404.]

Preface, vii–xxx. A brief account of pagan gods and dream lore is followed by an account of the astrology of Trismegistos, together with a discussion of the identity of Ælfric and his works. Although some readers want 'something deep dyed in heathen lore, full of Thor and Woden and the goddess Hel' (vii), the Saxons assimilated classical learning too. On the one hand, 'even the heathenism of the Saxons, even their wild mythology had in it an element of truth' (viii); on the other, 'the Greeks read, copied, and transmitted to us such scientific doctrine, and the Saxons should not be blamed for doing the like' (xiv). Various pieces on the Computus have so ecclesiastical an aspect that they hardly seem to belong to the department of science, 'but since the Computus is essentially an endeavour to find a remedy for the incommensurability of two quantities, the periodic time of the earth's rotation upon its axis and of its revolution round the focal point of the solar system, it is in reality deeply involved in the intricacies of astronomical calculation' (xxix). However, no known treatise can be produced, with the possible exception of *ByrM*, 'of which Wanley gives a much less attractive account than the book deserves' (xxix).

299 Dietrich, Franz Eduard Christoph. 'Drei altheidnische Segenformeln: Nebst einigen Jüngeren, auf Runendenkmälern und in Hss. aufgefunden.' *Zeitschrift für deutsches Altertum und deutsche Litteratur* 14 (1867): 193–217.

Prints, from Cotton Faustina A.x, f. 115v, two recipes [FC B.21.5.4], with Mn. German translation, and a charm [Storms 82], 202–3. Dietrich suggests that these items, and the two Latin remedies for fever which follow [Storms 39 and 40], are the conclusion to a medical codex. Dietrich shows that the two recipes and the charm contain many early (8th century) Northumbrian forms, and he reconstructs the charm as a strophic apostrophe to *Erce*, with reference to a metrical charm in *Lac* [FC A.43.1] (203–14).

Also prints, 193–7, with discussion: 'Old Norse *Heilsegen*,' a runic inscription from Cotton Caligula A.xv, f. 122; Northumbrian runic inscriptions (magic spells against cramp) found on three rings, 197–202; Latin and vernacular charms from a 14th century German manuscript, 214–17.

300 **Sievers, E.** 'Bedeutung der Buchstaben.' *Zeitschrift für deutsches Altertum und deutsche Litteratur* 21 (1877): 189–90.

Prints, from Titus D.xxvii, f. 55v, an item missed by Cockayne [FC B.23.3.4], which Sievers identifies as an OE version of the German and Latin 'deutungen der buchstaben' already printed in *Zeitschrift für deutsches Altertum* (13: 368, 17: 84, 18: 297), and having particular interest on account of its age. [See Bradley, **335**.]

301 **Assmann, Bruno.** 'Eine Regel über den Donner.' *Anglia* 10 (1888): 185.

Prints, without comment, a brontology from Vespasian D.xiv, f. 103v [FC B.23.3.5, art. 34].

302 **Assmann, Bruno.** 'Prophezeiung aus dem 1.Januar für das Jahr.' *Anglia* 11 (1889): 369.

Prints a prognostic from Vespasian D.xiv, f. 75v [FC B.23.3.5, art. 26]. Comments only that the language is 12th century.

303 **Logeman, H.** 'Anglo-Saxonica Minora.' *Anglia* 11 (1889): 97–120.

Prints a charm from Cotton Galba A.xiv, f. 72 [FC B.23.1.11], 111; the manuscript was much damaged in the 1731 fire, and the transcript of Wanley, 231, cannot be relied on. For the name 'Ceadda' in this extract, Logeman refers to *Anglia* 10: 131. Also prints a number of other short texts, including 'Names of Winds' [FC B.24.5], 104; Arundel 60, f. 149r, 'On the Ages of the World' [FC B.24.25.3], 105.

304 **Schenkl, Heinrich.** *Die Bibliotheken der englischen Kathedralen. Bibliotheca Patrum Latinorum Britannica.* Vol. 3, pt. 2. Vienna: Gerold, 1889. 3 vols. 1891–1908.

Prints a charm against fever from Worcester, Cathedral Library, Q.5 [FC B.23.1.18], 67.

305 **Stokes, Whitley.** 'Glosses from Turin and Rome: IV. The Anglosaxon Prose and Glosses in Rome.' *Beiträge zur Kunde der indogermanischen Sprachen* 17 (1891): 144–5.

At 144 prints a charm against fever, from Regina 338, f. 88v [FC B.23.1.17], 'first published, with gross inaccuracy, in Greith's *Spicilegium Vaticanum*, 1838, p. 45.' Stokes suggests that the names of the Seven Sleepers are perhaps employed because sleep cures fever. [Also prints runes from the same manuscript, f. 90, and glosses to Bede's metrical Life of Cuthbert from Regina 204.]

306 Z[upitza], J. 'Kreuzzauber.' *Archiv für das Studium der neueren Sprachen und Literaturen* 88 (1892): 364–5.

Prints, without comment, a cross charm in an early 12th century hand, CCCC 391, pp. 617–8 [FC B.23.1.7].

307 Holthausen, F. 'Altenglische Kleinigkeiten.' *Archiv für das Studium der neueren Sprachen und Literaturen* 99 (1897): 424–5.

Reprints texts, and abbreviated commentary, from Stokes, **305**; includes a fever charm [FC B.23.1.17].

308 Napier, A. 'Altenglische Miscellen.' *Archiv für das Studium der neueren Sprachen und Literaturen* 84 (1890): 323–7.

Prints prose charms: (i) two charms (11th century), from Bodleian, Auct. F.3.6, ff. 1, 2v [FC B.23.1.13], 323; (2) a charm against fever from Worcester, Cathedral Library, Q.5 [FC B.23.1.18], 323–4. Napier notes that the second of the charms in Bodleian echoes *Lb*, Cockayne, **297**, 2: 54. The Worcester charm, discovered and transcribed by Schenkl, **304**, is in a late 10th or early 11th century hand. [See also Liebermann, **309**.]

Also prints, with textual notes, five recipes from a fragment in the possession of Lord Robartes, found in the binding of a copy of *Fabulae de schematibus et tropis*, ed. P. Mosellani, published in Antwerp, 1558 [FC B.21.5.2: now Wellcome Historical Medical Library 75.46]. Napier states that there are Latin pen trials on the verso, and that the recipes are in three distinct 11th century hands: (a) is in the first hand (characterized by Frankish forms of *f*, *g* and *r*); (b), (c) and (d) are in the second hand, and (e) is in the third hand.

309 Liebermann, F. 'Eine angelsächsische Fieberbeschwörung.' *Archiv für das Studium der neueren Sprachen und Literaturen* 104 (1900): 123.

Prints, without comment, the OE *incipit* of a charm that Schenkl, **304**, found on the last page of Worcester, Cathedral Library, Q.5, which was overlooked by Cockayne [FC B.23.1.18]. [See Napier, **308**, **336**.]

310 Leonhardi, Günther. *Kleinere angelsächsische Denkmäler I.* Bibliothek der angelsächsischen Prosa 6. Hamburg: Grand, 1905. 6 vols.

Edits, 1–109, *Lb*1–3 from R, collated with Cockayne, **297**. Includes recipes from Harley 55 [FC B.21.2.4] in place of missing leaves; omits the metrical charm 'For Water-Elf Disease' [FC A.43.7]. Manuscript description, 110–12; textual notes, 113–20.

Also edits, 121–55, *Lac* from H, collated with Cockayne, **298**. Notes, 156–9, include brief remarks on the dialect; a Northern origin is suggested. Phonology, 160–74. Omits the metrical charms and the *Lorica* [FC C.22], of which the OE only is separately printed, together with the Latin–OE gloss from Cambridge, University Library Ll.1.10 [FC C.83]; Latin variants from H and four other manuscripts, 175–93. Includes study of the Latin text of the *Lorica*, 194–205; the relationship of the two OE glosses to one another and to the Latin, 206–15; phonology and inflexions, 226–39.

311 Förster, Max. 'Beiträge zur mittelalterlichen Volkskunde I.' *Archiv für das Studium der neueren Sprachen und Literaturen* 120 (1908): 45–52.

Prints four brontologies ('Donnerbücher') from CCCC 391, pp. 713–4 [FC B.23.3.1, art. d(ii)], 46–8. Also prints a brontology from Tiberius A.iii, f. 37rv, Latin with OE interlinear gloss [FC C.16, art. g], 50–1.

Förster defines five types of OE brontology, according to their organizing element: the month (exemplified by Assmann, **301**); the day of the week; the hour of the night or day; the canonical hours; the direction. The Tiberius Latin–OE gloss printed by Förster is an example of the third type, covering only some of the 24 hours. He cites Latin analogues, from 15th century manuscripts, for the OE brontologies printed, and argues that two of them constitute a single brontology of the canonical hours variety. [See further Förster, **94**.]

312 Förster, Max. 'Beiträge zur mittelalterlichen Volkskunde II.' *Archiv für das Studium der neueren Sprachen und Literaturen* 120 (1908): 296–305.

Prints, from Tiberius A.iii, f. 41v, a type of prophecy for the year ('Bauernpraktik') [FC B.23.3.3, art. 7p], 297–8. Also prints, from the same manuscript, f. 36rv, a Latin and OE gloss of the same type [FC C.16, art. d], 296–7.

Förster observes that the Latin original is hard to locate because prognostics such as these are handled freely by copyists; he offers for comparison three 14th and 15th century versions from German manuscripts. Bibliography, **301**.

Also prints, from Tiberius A.iii, f. 42rv, a Dreambook [FC B.23.3.3, art. 7q], 302–5. Förster tables correspondences with two other OE Dreambooks (Hatton 115 and Tiberius A.iii), and a Latin version in a German manuscript; the underlying alphabetical ordering of the Dreambook printed is only sporadically discernible.

313 Förster, Max. 'Beiträge zur mittelalterlichen Volkskunde III.' *Archiv für das Studium der neueren Sprachen und Literaturen* 121 (1908): 30–46.

Förster analyses the composition of the Tiberius A.iii codex (six manuscripts) and scribal hands (10 in all), and gives a bibliographical description of contents: includes identification and generic classification of prognostics, and brief notes on sources and analogues. Prints a sentence of a text [FC B.23.3.3, art. 7q] omitted in Förster, **312**, at 37.

314 Grendon, Felix. 'The Anglo-Saxon Charms.' *Journal of American Folk-Lore* 22 (1909): 105–237. Separately printed, 1909. New York: Steckert, 1930.

Prints 62 extracts from *Lac*, *Lb*, *Herb* and other manuscripts, with translation facing, as tabled below, 164–213. Notes, 214–37. 'List of Charms not
included in the Text,' 162–4, classifies a further 87 charms [84 according to
Grendon, 110], to which reference is made in the introductory comments.

Extracts from *Lb*: A5, A18, A20, A24, B2–3, B5, B7, C1–2, C4–5, D1–6,
D8–9, E2–3, E8–10, E12, E14 [includes a metrical charm, B5].

Extracts from *Lac*: A1–2, A6–7, A9–12, A17, A19, A22, B4, B6, C3, D10,
E1, E4, E6, E13 [includes five metrical charms, A1–2, A22, B4, E1].

Extracts from *Herb* (V): B1, E5, E11.

Prose Charms and Headings, from: Faustina A.x, f. 116r (A8); Julius C.ii,
f. 66v and *Textus Roffensis*, f. 95 (A15); Junius 85, p. 17 (A23); Caligula
A.xv, f. 136v (D7); Vitellius E.xviii, f. 13v (D11–12); St John's College 17,
f. 175 (E7). Also prints metrical charms from: Royal 4 A.xiv, f. 106v (A3);
CCCC 41, pp. 182, 350–3, 206 (A4, A14, A16, A21), Caligula A.vii, f. 176r
and Junius 85, p. 103 (A13). [See further above, 'Concordance to Editions,'
pp. 251–6.]

'Manuscripts and Editions,' 105–10. 'General Characteristics of Spells,'
110–123, discusses narrative introductions in the heroic style, appeals to
a superior spirit, the use of potent names or letters, methods of dealing
with disease-demons, the exorcist's boast of power, ceremonial directions
to patient and exorcist, singing of incantations on parts of the body and
other objects, statement of time for the performance of rites, sympathy and
the association of ideas and minor superstitious practices. 'Classification
of Charms,' 123–40, defines five major groups (Exorcisms, Herbal charms,
Charms for transferring disease, Amulet charms, and Charm remedies) and
subdivisions within these. 'Christian Elements in the Charms,' 140–59, cites
legislation pertaining to charms and examines the extent to which Christian
elements were substituted for pagan ones. [For reviews see Magoun, **353**;
Binz, **462**.]

315 Förster, Max. 'Beiträge zur mittelalterlichen Volkskunde IV.' *Archiv für
das Studium der neueren Sprachen und Literaturen* 125 (1910): 39–70.

Prints Latin–OE Dreambook ('Pseudo-Danielsche') from Tiberius A.iii, ff.
27v–32v [FC C.16, art. a], 47–70; preliminary survey of alphabetically-
organized Dreambooks, remarks on manuscript dating and orthography
(11th century, South of England), the relationship of the Latin and OE
and the question of whether the scribe was glossing or copying an older,
pre-existing OE gloss.

316 Förster, Max. 'Beiträge zur mittelalterlichen Volkskunde VI.' *Archiv für
das Studium der neueren Sprachen und Literaturen* 128 (1912): 55–71.

Prints parallel a wind prophecy ('Windbuch') from Hatton 115, f. 149v [FC
B.23.3.6], ed. Cockayne, **298**, 3: 164, and a Latin version from Ashmole 345,
f. 69r (15th century), 56–8.

Förster concludes that the OE derives from a Latin text already existing by the 11th century. Other late medieval and early modern parallels, Latin and vernacular, are quoted. Ultimately, the entire genus derives from Babylonian *Sturmprognosen* (54-64).

Also prints a sunshine prophecy ('Sonnenscheinbuch') [FC B.23.3.1, art. d(i)], from CCCC 391, p. 713, with variants from Hatton 115, f.149v (ed. Cockayne, **298**, 3: 164-6), 65-6.

Förster dates this incomplete text (beginning *in medias res* with prophecies for the third day after Christmas) second half of the 11th century, provenance Worcester. It is thus the earliest version of a form of prophecy found in many languages; Förster prints 16th century German and 17th century Swedish versions for comparison. In his view, the OE sunshine prophecy demonstrates the existence of a Latin original in England *c*. 1000 (a number of later medieval Latin versions are cited); the Latin source probably derived from a much older Greek version, which in turn may have derived from a Babylonian version, since many Babylonian sun prophecies are known to have existed (64-71).

317 Förster, Max. 'Beiträge zur mittelalterlichen Volkskunde VII.' *Archiv für das Studium der neueren Sprachen und Literaturen* 128 (1912): 285-308.

Prints parallel two nativity prognostics ('Wochenstage-Geburtsprognoses') from CCCC 391, p. 715, [FC B.23.3.1, art. d(iii)], late 11th century, and from Hatton 115, f. 148v, ed. Cockayne, **298**, 3: 162 [FC B.23.3.6], 12th century, with textual notes, 297-300.

Three Latin versions are printed for comparison, 301-3: Group (C) Cambridge, University Library, Gg 1.1, f. 393v, 15th century, and Ashmole 342, ff. 9-25v, *c*. 1400; Group (D) Ashmole 342, p. 25, *c*. 1400; Group (E) Tiberius A.iii, f. 65r, mid-11th century [cf. Förster, **313**, 39], and Titus D.xxvi, f. 6v, *c*. 1050 (ed. Birch, **274**, 477-8, and **57**, 256). From a detailed comparison (303-5) Förster concludes that all these versions derive ultimately from a common original. The Latin version on which the OE versions were based most closely resembled (D), and must have been in existence by *c*. 1000. Several recent examples of this form of prophecy are printed, 305-8. (Other subsections deal with ME brontologies and 'Bauernpraktiken.')

318 Förster, Max. 'Beiträge zur mittelalterlichen Volkskunde VIII.' *Archiv für das Studium der neueren Sprachen und Literaturen* 129 (1912): 16-49.

Prints, with textual notes, lunar nativity calendars, two versions: (1) Latin and OE interlinear gloss from Tiberius A.iii, f. 36v [FC C.16, art. e], at 18-21; (2) Parallel edition of CCCC 391, p. 716 [FC B.23.3.1, art. d(iv)], Caligula A.xv, f. 132r [FC B.23.3.2, art. q], Tiberius A.iii, f. 41rv [FC B.23.3.3, art. o], and Hatton 115, f. 148v (reprinted from Cockayne, **298**, 3: 160-3), at 21-6.

The glossed Latin in version (1) belongs to the same text group as the Latin in Tiberius A.xv, f. 65r, Titus D.xxvi, ff. 7v–8r, and three Latin manuscripts dated 12th–16th century (listed at 16–17). The four OE texts in version (2) appear superficially to be very different from one another (although Caligula and Tiberius appear to have been copied from the same exemplar); nevertheless, Förster concludes that they ultimately derived from a single Latin recension, which was distinct from the recension represented by version (1). The verbal dissimilarity of the four OE texts in version (2) may suggest that their shared source was in OE, but their stiffness of style reveals that they must have originated as interlinear glosses. A comparable 18th century English lunar nativity calendar is printed at 26–30.

Also prints lunar medical prognostics, three versions: (1) Latin and OE interlinear gloss from Tiberius A.iii, ff. 36v–7r [FC C.16, art. f], with variations from Caligula A.xv, ff. 125v–6v [FC B.23.3.2, art. a], at 32–4; (2) CCCC 391, p. 717 [FC B.23.3.1, art. d(v)]; (3) Tiberius A.iii, f. 40r [FC B.23.3.3, art. k]. Versions (2) and (3) are printed parallel at 34–6.

Also prints, at 43–5, propitious days (lunar) from Tiberius A.iii, ff. 39v–40r [FC B.23.3.3, art. j], together with the full version of this text, found in Hatton 115, ff. 152v–3v, as printed by Cockayne, **298**, 3: 176–80.

Includes a Latin 'Alderlasslunare' from Tiberius A.iii, f. 65r, at 36–7, and 'Sphaera Apulei,' i.e., the Latin text from Caligula A.xv, f. 125v, which accompanies the circular diagram reproduced by Cockayne, **298**, 3: 150. A similar text, including four lines glossed in OE [FC C.37] is printed from Vitellius E.xviii, f. 16r (at 45–7). The text is of Greek origin; Latin parallels are found in two 9th century manuscripts, Paris, Cod. lat. 11411, f. 99r, and Petersburg, lat. Q.1.34, f. 88r. A similar 'Krankheitsorakel' is found in 'Sancte Columcille Circul' [Storms 85], and must derive from the same source, although the inscription within the circle shows that it was intended as a protection against bees ('*contra apes,*' etc.) *The Universal Fortuneteller* (early 19th century) is quoted to demonstrate the figure's enduring connection with the Wheel of Fortune.

319 Förster, Max. 'Beiträge zur mittelalterlichen Volkskunde IX.' *Archiv für das Studium der neueren Sprachen und Literaturen* 134 (1916): 264–93.

Prints 'the second OE Dreambook,' a parallel edition of Tiberius A.iii, ff. 38r–9v [FC B.23.3.3, art. i] and Hatton 115, ff. 150v–2v [FC B.23.3.6], designated 'TB' by Förster, at 270–93. Apparatus includes parallels with the first and third OE Dreambooks; i.e., TA, the Latin–OE in Tiberius A.iii, ff. 27v–32v [FC C.16, art. a], and TC, Tiberius A.iii, f. 42rv [FC B.23.3.3, art. q]. Also prints parallels from other Latin versions and from three Greek Dreambooks.

Tiberius is used as a base for TB because it is older and is a better text than Hatton, which was unfortunately used as a base text by Cockayne, **298**, 3: 168/8–176/15]. Hatton lacks 31 of the 97 dreams in Tiberius (items 44–53,

72–81, 87 and 97); Tiberius lacks only item 38. An exact source for TB is lacking, but it has 32 dreams in common with TA. The Latin Dreambooks doubtless derive from Greek (264–9).

320 Wyatt, Alfred J. *An Anglo-Saxon Reader*. Cambridge: Cambridge UP, 1919.

Prints six recipes from *Lb*, a recipe from Titus D.xxvi [FC B.21.5.7], and a recipe from *Lac*, 123–5; Notes, 525–6.

321 Förster, Max. 'Die altenglischen Traumlunare.' *Englische Studien* 60 (1925–6): 58–93.

Prints, with textual notes, lunar dream prognostics, three versions: (1) Latin and OE interlinear gloss, from Tiberius A.iii, ff. 35v–6r [FC C.16, art. c], at 67–74; (2) Parallel edition of Caligula A.xv, ff. 131v–2r [FC B.23.3.2, art. p], Tiberius A.iii, ff. 37v–8 [FC B.23.3.3., art. h], and CCCC 391, pp. 720–1 [FC B.23.3.1, art. d(viii)], at 79–86; (3) Hatton 115, f. 148r [FC B.23.3.6], at 90–2. Texts are accompanied by a catalogue of OE manuscript contents and examination of manuscript dating. Concerning version (2), Förster concludes (79) that Caligula and Tiberius have more in common with one another than with CCCC 391, and that Caligula is closer to the original.

Also prints a Table of Lucky and Unlucky Days, 'Three Unlucky Days,' from CCCC 391, p. 721 [FC B.23.2.1, art. e], at 77. These four lines, added *c.* 1200 at the end of the manuscript in the hand of the well-known Worcester glossator, are a copy, with linguistic variations, of the Table of Unlucky Days which appears on p. 718 of the same manuscript [FC B.23.2.1, art. d(vii)].

Also prints, without comment, a computistical text from Caligula A.xv, f. 127v, *De Bissexto* [FC B.20.5], at 75.

Introduction, 58–65, argues that the learned tradition is the basis of dream lore. All Western Dreambooks derive from the Latin *Somniale Danielis*, which is of Greek, ultimately Babylonian, origin (Slavonic Dreambooks derive directly from Greek); the oldest exact translation is a 12th/13th century Provençal interlinear gloss. Förster lists 12 divergent Latin versions, 10th–15th century, in which he discerns two groups, descended from two different Greek Dreambooks. The Latin archetype of the group into which three 11th century English versions fall (Tiberius A.iii, ff. 35v–6r, Titus D.xxvi, f. 9r, and CCCC 391, pp. 718–20), must have been in existence by the 8th/9th century. Förster argues that, although the three OE versions printed by him are formally and substantially different, versions (2) and (3), like the OE gloss to Tiberius, must have derived from Latin texts. The OE versions (2) and (3) have more in common with one another than with the Latin of Tiberius, and their lost Latin originals appear to have been closer to CCCC 391 and Vat. lat. 642 than to Tiberius and Titus. A Welsh Dreambook, *c.* 1910, printed at 92–3, illustrates the continuity of ancient and modern dream lore.

322 Förster, Max. 'Die altenglischen Verzeichnisse von Glücks- und Unglücks-
tagen.' *Studies in English Philology: A Miscellany in Honor of Frederick
Klaeber.* Ed. Kemp Malone and Martin B. Rudd. Minneapolis: Minnesota
UP, 1929. 258–77.

Classification and parallel editions of the following Tables of Lucky and Unlucky Days: (1) Lucky Nativity days [FC B.23.2.1, art. d(vi), and B.23.2.3,
art. i], 260; (2) 24 Unlucky days [FC B.23.2.5, art. d, and B.23.2.3, art.
e], 262–4; (3) 24 critical days for bloodletting [FC B.23.2.3, art. h, and
B.23.2.5, art. j], 266–9; (4) Three critical moondays, Version 1 [FC B.23.2.4,
and Harley 585, ff. 190rv, i.e. *Lac* 117], 271–3, Version 2 [FC B.23.2.5, art.
i, and B.23.2.1, art. d(vii)], 273–4. [See also Förster, **321**.]

A brief introduction stresses the Latin and Greek origins of the material; the
commentary throughout adduces numerous analogues, chiefly later medieval
Latin. Brief bibliography of the subject is incorporated in footnotes.

323 Henel, Heinrich. 'Altenglischer Mönchsaberglaube.' *Englische Studien* 69
(1934–5): 329–49.

Prints Prohibition against Bloodletting and Tables of Lucky and Unlucky
Days, as follows: (1) Prohibition against Bloodletting [FC B.23.4], 331; (2)
Bloodletting days [FC B.23.2.2], 334–5; (3) 24 critical bloodletting days [FC
B.23.2.6], 336–8; (4) Three lucky nativity days [FC B.23.2.5, art. h], 346–7.

Also prints a computistical text 'On the Length of Summer and Winter'
from Harley 3217 [FC B.20.16], derived from *OE Martyrology*, 347. Henel
compares it with *ByrM* (Crawford, **212**, 86, 92), and doubts whether the
astrological significance of the Pleiades (not named in Crawford, 210–12)
was known to Anglo-Saxons generally.

Henel's introduction (opposing Fischer, **436**) addresses the need to distinguish between pagan German beliefs and monastic superstitions developed
from learned sources (which were impossible to eradicate, despite the re-
forming efforts of Dunstan and Ælfric's opposition), and observes that many
superstitions and warnings attach to bloodletting. Commentary throughout
adduces later medieval Latin parallels; includes identification of days in FC
B.23.2.6, and examination of the process by which it came into existence;
discussion of orthodox censure of (un)lucky days.

324 Förster, Max. 'Vom Fortleben antiker Sammellunare im Englischen und
in anderen Volkssprachen.' *Anglia* 67 (1944): 1–171.

Prints Latin and OE interlinear gloss of a 30-day lunar prognostic, from
Tiberius A.iii, ff. 32v–5v, 'De obseruatione lune & que cauenda sunt' [FC
C.16, art. b], 79–129, with textual notes. Glossary, 166–70. Förster gives
an account of the manuscript and its Canterbury connections (41–9), dates
the copying of the glosses *c.* 1080 (50–4), argues that the original must date
back to the first half of the 8th century (54–7), remarks on the inexactness

of the translation (57–8), discusses orthodox attitudes to lunar prognoses (58–64), language and orthography (64–78).

Förster demonstrates the survival of originally Babylonian astrological beliefs in European vernaculars up to the 17th century and beyond. He discusses Greek and Latin 'Sammellunare' (prognostics for a number of questions, usually seven in number, related to the 30 days of the lunar month, as distinct from the 'Speziallunare,' which answer only one and the same question for all days), and defines four types (1–41). Medieval and early Modern parallels in English, German, Dutch, Icelandic, French, Provençal, and Welsh are tabled, 41–165.

325 Storms, G. *Anglo-Saxon Magic.* The Hague: Nijhoff, 1948.

Part 2, 132–311, prints 86 OE and Latin extracts from *Lac*, *Lb* and 21 other manuscripts, as tabled below, with item by item translation and commentary (numerical organization reflects the editor's analysis of component elements; higher numbers indicate a greater degree of Christian influence). Appendix, 312–18, contains 16 'prayers used as charm formulas' (viii) in Latin, some with OE headings. Glossary of Plant Names, 319–28; Bibliography, 329–33; Index, 334–6.

Extracts from *Lac*: nos. 2, 3, 7, 9–10, 14, 18–19, 21, 23–5, 31, 35, 44, 46–7, 51, 53, 63, 65–7, 70, 73–5, 83–4; A3, A7, A12–15. [Five of these (nos. 2, 7, 9, 10, 14), wholly or in part, are classified as metrical].

Extracts from *Lb*: nos. 5–6, 17, 20, 22, 26–30, 32–3, 42, 76, 79, 81. [One of these (no. 5) is classified as metrical.]

Prose Charms and Charm Headings: from CCCC 190, f. 130, collated with Harley 438, p. 128, and Tiberius A.iii, f. 106 (no. 11A); from *Textus Roffensis*, f. 95, collated with Julius C.2, f. 66v (no. 11B); from CCCC 41, pp. 206, 272, 326 (nos. 12, 48, A4); Caligula A.xv, ff. 140r, 129r, 140v, 129 (nos. 34, 68–9, A9–10); from Harley 464, f. 177 (no. 36; not listed FC); from Junius 85, p. 17 (nos. 41, 45, 49); Vitellius E.xviii, f. 13v (nos. 50, 85–6, A2); St John's College 17, f. 175r (no. 54); Bodley Auct. 7.3.6, ff. 2v, 1 (nos. 77–8); from Faustina A.x, f. 116r (no. 82); from Gonville and Caius College 379, f. 49r (nos. A5–6; erroneously (?) included in FC B.23.1.3). Also prints metrical charms: from CCCC 41, pp. 182, 206, 350–3 (nos. 1, 13, 15–16); Royal 4 A.xiv, f. 106v (no. 4); Caligula A.vii, ff. 176r–8r (no. 8).

Latin charms: from Faustina A.x, f. 116r (nos. 39–40; erroneously included in FC B.23.1.10); from CCCC 41, p. 329, 'The Sator Formula (for Childbirth)' (no. 43); from Royal 2 A.xx, ff. 16v, 49r, 45v, 52 (nos. 37–8, 55–61, A8, A11, A16); Gonville and Caius College 397, f. 49r (nos. 62, 72); Cambridge, Queens' College 7, f. 142v (no. 64); Junius 163, f. 227 (no. 71); CCCC 367, f. 52r (no. 80); from Harley 1585, pp. 24–6 (no. A1).

Part 1, 1–129. Ch. 1, 'Introduction,' 1–11, examines the characteristics of magic; ch. 2, 'The Manuscripts,' 12–26, lists manuscripts, describes *Lac* and

Lb; ch. 3, 'Of Magic and Magical Practices,' 27–48, is principally concerned with the definition of magic [incorporates Storms, **360**]; ch. 4, 'Structure and Atmosphere of the Ritual,' 49–106, examines ingredients and their use in the charms and practices employed; ch. 5, 'Borrowing or Tradition,' 107–29, includes discussion of the influence of classical sources, Indo-European parallels (esp. OI), Anglo-Saxon laws and the introduction of Christian elements.

Ch. 2, 'The Manuscripts,' 12–26, argues that the three books of *Lb* were originally separate, and identifies their distinguishing characteristics (the colophon shows that *Lb*3 is an addition to *Lb*1&2; although *Lb*1&2 at first sight present a greater unity, their contents point to an original independence). *Lb*1 deals with the exterior body and employs head-to-toe order. *Lb*2 deals with internal disorders and much of it derives from Alexander of Tralles; because it borrows from fewer writers than the first book, it gives a more orderly impression. *Lb*3 has little unity, its prescriptions are mostly short, and Christian elements (which may be additions, or may have replaced older pagan practices) are strongly marked. *Lac* is disorderly, drawing on many sources, showing no less Christian influence but far more magical elements. Close parallels between *Lb* and *Lac* (*Lb*1.1 and *Lac* 1; *Lb* 1.15 and *Lac* 112, 113), show that both derive from earlier OE translations of Alexander of Tralles (Bk. 7); other parallels are tabled. Anglian forms indicate that both manuscripts were based on northern originals, and the original translation of works such as Alexander of Tralles, Pliny the Elder, Marcellus, Galen and Apuleius, must have been made before the time of Alfred, when both Latin and Greek were understood. 'The Leechbook may be characterised as the handbook of the Anglo-Saxon medical man, the Lacnunga may be characterised as the handbook of the Anglo-Saxon medicine-man' (24). [For reviews see Jost, **362**; Magoun, **363**.]

326 Grattan, H.G., and Charles Singer. *Anglo-Saxon Magic and Medicine.* Publications of the Wellcome Historical Medical Museum NS 3. London: Oxford UP, 1952.

Part 2, edition of *Lac*, from H: ' "Lacnunga": An Anglo-Saxon Magico-Medical Commonplace Book' (includes *Lorica*). Text, 96–204, with translation facing. Collated with Cockayne, **298**, and Leonhardi, **310** (variants in apparatus). Editorial section numbers represent the assumed strata of compilation. The glossary mentioned on the title page was omitted, but plant names (largely normalized) are included in the Index, 229–34. Facsimile of ff. 130r, 141r, 156v, 160v, 183v.

Notes, 206–27, discuss: the manuscript, its scripts and date (*c.* 1000); editorial principles and manuscript versions of the *Lorica*. 'Brief Survey of Grammar,' 212–27, defines the language as late WS, with traces of Anglian (a few of which are Northumbrian) and of two SE dialects, Kentish and 'Sächsische Patois.' The editors accept Leonhardi's opinion that the first version of the whole work was Northern, and consider that the late Kentish forms were introduced either before or soon after the text 'acquired WS dress' (212). There is no certainty whether the language of the first transliteration into WS already contained traces of 'Sächsische Patois' or whether they were due to a later scribe. Some transitional forms, 'more like ME than AS,' are recorded, 226–7.

Part 1, 'A General Survey of Magico-Medical Practice in Anglo-Saxon England' contains: (1) 'Introduction,' 3–22 (Barbarian Magico-Medicine, Character of Anglo-Saxon Magico-Medicine, Analysis of *Lac*); (2) 'Sources of Anglo-Saxon Medico-Magic,' 23–79; (3) 'Semantics of Anglo-Saxon Plant-Names,' 80–91; (4) 'Rational Elements,' 92–4. [Substantially reproduced in Singer, **327**; refers to *Herb*, 71–91, *et passim*; to *ByrM*, 92–4.]

The analysis of *Lac* (15–22) distinguishes three main strata: classical pagan, teutonic pagan, and emotional Christian piety. A collection of recipes on the head-to-toe plan was put together in the 9th century from the leechcraft exemplified in *Herb*, perhaps by a monastic *medicus* (the core of this was i–xvii). The second leech, who added esp. lxxix–lxxxiii and clxix–clxxi, 'had had some monastic training, probably in one of the smaller Western houses where local superstitions were more influential, but he did not dwell in a monastery and had only a vestigial knowledge of Latin' (21). The third compiler, an inmate of a small monastery in the North in which Irish influence survived, was in major orders, wrote chiefly in Latin and added devotional passages (esp. lxiv–lxviii and clix–clxix). This composite volume (*a, b* and *c*) was rebound, leaves were wrongly arranged and contributions confused, though still tending to adhere in groups. The volume was then copied shortly after 1000 by a scribe who produced the existing manuscript and added some devotional passages at the end (*d*). In addition, there are scattered throughout a few entries of no decided character that might have come into the collection at any time (*x*). Palaeographical signs suggest that the scribe of H was 'vaguely conscious' (19) of dealing with two kinds of entry. [For reviews see Magoun, **365**.]

327 **Cockayne, Oswald.** *Leechdoms, Wortcunning and Starcraft in Early England.* Rev. edn., with a new introduction by Charles Singer. 3 vols. London: Holland, 1961.

Reprints Cockayne, **400, 297, 298**, omitting the glossaries from Vols. 2 and 3, as well as 'Durham Glossary of Plants,' 'Saxon Names of Plants' and 'Historical Fragments' from Vol. 3 (Cockayne, 2: 361–415; 3: 297–454). Also omits some prognostic texts (Cockayne, 3: 158–215); pagination of Vol. 3 only differs from Cockayne's. Singer's Introduction replaces Cockayne's three Prefaces; the *Lorica*, which Cockayne, 1: lxviii–lxxv, printed from *Lac* and Cambridge, University Library, Ll.1.10 [FC C.83], is thus also lacking, and so, too, are the additions and corrections included by Cockayne in each of his three volumes.

Introduction, ix–xlvii. Singer surveys the contents of the three volumes and discusses the main themes raised by the material: Recession of Greek medicine filtered through Latin; Latin formularies; Roman magic; Pythagorean devices; Pagan Latin liturgical elements; Byzantine astrology and theurgy; Pagan Teutonic incantations; Celtic magic; 'Hisperic' literature; South Italian classical survivals; Identification of plant names; the Leechdoms and rational medicine. Singer's thesis is that 'the Anglo-Saxon leech had no originality ... no understanding of even the rudiments of the science of classical antiquity ... and the demonstration of sources provides the chief interest of these volumes of Cockayne. The general level of this medicine will be found far lower, far more barbarous, than the common accounts of Anglo-Saxon culture suggest' (xix–xx). In sum 'Cockayne's *Leechdoms* provide good examples of the darkest and deliquescent stage of an outdated culture' (xlvii). [Substantially reproduces Grattan and Singer, **326**.]

328 Braekman, W. 'Some Minor Old English Texts.' *Archiv für das studium der neueren Sprachen und Literaturen* 202 (1965-6): 271-6.

Edits, from Nowell's transcript of Otho B.xi, ff. 261v–2r, the seven recipes not found in *Lb* (five for *utsihte*, 'dysentery,' and two for constipation), 275-6 [FC B.21.2.3]. [See Torkar, **329**.]

Introductory remarks, 275, state the bare facts concerning the destruction of the manuscript, Nowell's transcript, and the relation of the recipes to *Lb*. The textual commentary notes that an outbreak of dysentery in 987 is recorded by Simeon of Durham and that a type of bacillary dysentery was suffered by the Danish army in Kent, *c.* 1010. Braekman also comments on some of the ingredients: comfrey is mentioned as a remedy in Cockayne, **298**, 3: 44-6, 'no doubt because it was seen as a powerful plant'; rye is rarely mentioned in the Leechdoms, but is included in a salve for a worm-eaten and mortified body (Cockayne **297**, 2: 126); green dwarfelder and rue are employed in remedies for both diarrhoea and constipation; the purgative seeds (*lybcorna*) are the seeds of the castor oil plant; hen's egg and elder bark were both remedies for *utsihte*.

329 Torkar, Roland. 'Zu den ae. Medizinaltexten in Otho B. XI und Royal 12 D. XVII: Mit einer Edition der Unica (Ker, No. 180 art. 11a–d).' *Anglia* 94 (1976): 319-38.

Prints seven recipes from Nowell's transcript of Otho B.xi [FC B.21.2.3], 330. Textual notes, 331-8, take issue *inter alia* with Braekman, **328**, who omitted part of one recipe (art. 11c).

Torkar examines the relation of the Nowell transcript recipes (O) to *Lb* (R). He inclines finally towards the view that R and O had a common archetype (though the possibility cannot be outruled that the unique material that O contains was drawn from a different source) but his first concern is to explain that the particular circumstances of preservation frustrate the application of stemmatic criteria. That O includes recipes for diarrhoea and constipation which are not found in R does not outrule the possibility that O drew on R, since the missing chapters of R included recipes for these ailments. Torkar argues, however, that this possibility is outruled by the language and orthography of the transcript: Anglian characteristics are more strongly marked in O than in R, and certain of its orthographic features (*uu* for *w*, and *eburfean* for *eoforfearn*) belong, at the latest, to the very beginning of Alfred's reign. [See also Meaney, **393**; cf. Grant, **373**.]

330 **Schauman, Bella, and Angus Cameron.** 'A Newly-found Leaf of Old English from Louvain.' *Anglia* 95 (1977): 289–312.

Edited text of the Omont Fragment (Fragmenta H. Omont, 3), 291–3, with translation, 293–4. Photographic reproduction of recto and verso (between 296–7).

In the introductory remarks, the editors note parallels with *Lb*2.64, 65 and *Lac* 49, and state: 'If our dating of the Omont Fragment is correct, then the traditions of medical writing in English can be taken back by at least a century.' It 'seems to be one of the earliest pieces of OE to have survived' (288). The material description is by Schauman, 284–304. Despite the fact that the recto's particular ruling system is that common among Anglo-Saxon scribes of the 10th–12th centuries, certain letter forms suggest to her a date *c.* 850–900, and a centre under Mercian influence. She suggests that the ruling of the recto of Omont, and that of *Vespasian Psalter*, may be anomalous, thus indicating an early practice in a single English scribal area. Cameron examines the language, 304–12. On the basis of Omont's similarities with the Corpus Glossary and Bodleian, Tanner 10, and the additional evidence of the orthography, Cameron 'would date it between 850 and 900 AD, and place it at a scriptorium where Mercian conventions of writing were observed' (312).

331 **Olds, Barbara M.** 'The Anglo-Saxon Leechbook III: A Critical Edition and Translation.' Diss. U of Denver, 1984. Dir. Raymond R. Tripp, Jr. [*DAI* 45 (1984): 3127A.]

Edits *Lb*3 from R, 55–163, with translation facing, and explanatory notes. Appendix A, 'Glossary of Plant Names,' 168–204; Appendix B, 'Glossary of Diseases in Leechbook III,' 205.

Ch. 1, 'Anglo-Saxon Medical Texts and the Leechbook,' 1–11, summarizes manuscript history from Wright, **294**. *Lb*3 is 'perhaps the best example of the complexity and diversity of Anglo-Saxon medicine ... at once extremely practical and wildly fantastic .... It is a document that deserves study from many different perspectives—cultural, medical, botanical and histori-cal' (10). Ch. 2, 'Contents of *Lb*3,' 12–33, gives an account of ingredients, measurements, ceremonies and restrictions, diagnosis and prognostication, media for mixing prescriptions and types of prescriptions. Ch. 3, 'Scholar-ship about Anglo-Saxon Medicine: Sources Studies and Criticism,' 34–54, observes that the disagreement between Singer and Talbot (**369**) 'is more a matter of interpretation of the significance of the sources than a disagreement about the sources themselves' (39), and that much research on the language, vocabulary, sources, cultural influences and medical effectiveness of *Lb*3 remains to be done.

332 Muir, Bernard James. *A Pre-Conquest English Prayer-Book (BL MSS Cotton Galba A.xiv and Nero A.ii (ff. 3–13)).* Henry Bradshaw Society 103. Woodbridge: Boydell–Boydell, 1988.

Critical edition of the manuscript includes: prose charm, 'A Formula for Curing Ailments in the Foot,' f. 72r [FC B.23.1.11], 89, emended from Wanley, 231; recipes, f. 118rv, 'Two Medical Recipes for Restoring the Body to Health through Prayer' [FC B.21.2.2], 150. Diplomatic transcript of the near illegible recipes, ff. 136, 139 [FC B.21.5.6], 211–12. The three *incipits* given in the charm 'must be to hymns or prayers that were well known at the time, but which can no longer be identified. If Wanley was consistent in cataloguing the contents of *G*, as is my contention, then this recipe came after that of f. 118 below before the fire' (89).

Muir describes the manuscript, script and scribes, and discusses the language and analogues of the devotional texts. Foliation is examined (217–20). He deduces that it was in use at St Mary's, Nunnaminster (xiv); the computistical tables (for 1029–47) enable a more precise dating of the manuscript and suggest that the leaves from Nero were originally part of Galba (xv). The manuscript is 'not a *formal* liturgical book' (xvi); it began as a blank book and 'may have been used as an "exercise" book by those being taught in the monastery' (xvii).

COMMENTARY

333 Zimmer, H. 'Keltische studien: 13. Ein altirischer zauberspruch aus der Vikingerzeit.' *Zeitschrift für vergleichende Sprachforschung* 33 (1895): 141–53.

On the charm in *Lb*1.45.5, concerning which Cockayne, **297**, 2: 113, observes: 'The charm is said in the table of contents to be Scottish, that is Gaelic, but the words themselves seem to belong to no known language.' Zimmer argues that it is a corrupt Irish charm which shows Danish influence, and thus must be of originally Irish origin, dating from the time of the Viking invasions there. Much of the argument hinges on the derivation of OIrish *éile* 'incantation' from Germanic; about half of the charm is reconstructed.

334 Skeat, Walter W. 'An Anglo-Saxon Enigma.' *Athenæum* no. 3626 (1897): 543.

Skeat points out that the item printed by Sievers, **300**, and Birch, **274** [FC B.23.3.4], concludes with a doxology, and suggests that the text is a form of riddle: 'It is obvious that each letter denotes some word that begins with that letter; and my solution is that all the words are Latin. I do not understand all the English, and some of the answers are guesses, but I think I have the right idea, which scholars with more leisure and superior acumen can easily improve on.' There follows a MnE translation with Skeat's suggested Latin solutions (e.g., 'Avis(?). He goes and his path will be uninjured.')

335 **Bradley, Henry.** 'An Anglo-Saxon Enigma.' *Athenæum* no. 3630 (1897): 682–3.

The OE text that Skeat, **334**, designates an enigma [FC B.23.3.4] is 'a translation of an alphabetically arranged series of Latin sentences intended to be used as *sortes*.' The letters prefixed to the lines are those with which the Latin sentences began, except in the case of CFXYZ, 'where the compiler of the original *sortes* seems to have contented himself with stating the ominous significance conventionally attached to the letters, not having been able to embody it in a sentence with the right initial' (682), and the sentences which simply express devout sentiments may have been intended to signify a favourable omen or refusal of an answer. Bradley gives his reconstruction of the Latin original, drawing upon the 'Sortes Apostolorum' in Codex Canonum (Paris, 1687), 370–3, which are, however, not alphabetical. A set of alphabetic *sortes* was printed by Sievers (*Zeitschrift für deutsches Altertum* 18: 297), but only the first of these ('A significat prosperum iter et viam felicem') corresponds with the OE.

336 **Napier, A.** 'Die ags. Fieberbeschwörung.' *Archiv für das Studium der neueren Sprachen und Literaturen* 104 (1900): 361.

Napier points out that the charm to which Liebermann, **309**, draws attention [FC B.23.1.18] has already been printed by him (Napier, **308**.)

337 **Förster, Max.** 'Die Kleinliteratur des Aberglaubens im Altenglischen.' *Archiv für das Studium der neueren Sprachen und Literaturen* 110 (1903): 346–58.

Prolegomenon to Förster's serial edition of prognostic texts (**311–313**, **315–319**, **343**), which supersede this publication. Classification according to type foreshadows the categories adopted in the later publications: prophecies for the year ('Bauernpraktiken'); wind, sunshine and thunder prognostics; unlucky days of the month and Egyptian days; horoscopes and nativity prognostics; medical prognoses; the influence of the moon on dreams and Dreambooks. Förster offers some preliminary observations on manuscript relationships; in contrast to Fischer, **436**, he is concerned to demonstrate the Latin and learned origins of the beliefs embodied in this group of texts, and cites numerous Latin and vernacular analogues, mostly post-12th century, and a few from (pseudo-)Bede. A bibliography of studies of the six versions of the OE 'Letter from Heaven' is included.

338 Osthoff, H. 'Ags. Blǣce, Blǣcǒrūstfel.' *Englische Studien* 32 (1903): 181–5.

Osthoff shows that *blāc*, *blǣc* and *blæc* are easily confused, and that this affects the interpretation of *blǣce* and its compound *blǣcǒrūstfel* (glossed 'vitaglio'), which signify *lepra alba*, as opposed to *lepra maculata nigra*. (*Lb*, 'wið ðam yflan blǣce, wið blǣce'; all other references are to *BT*, vocabularies and glosses).

339 McBryde, J.M., Jr. 'Charms to Recover Stolen Cattle.' *Modern Language Notes* 21 (1906): 180–3.

McBryde concludes that the charm to recover stolen cattle in CCCC 190 [FC B.23.1.4] represents 'two independent charms loosely and carelessly tacked together' (181), and that the OE conclusion to the Latin formula must originally have been in Latin. This bi-partite charm is 'clearly ritualistic, developing out of priestly ceremonies based on the finding of the Cross by St. Helena' (181), and is virtually identical to Cockayne, **298**, 3: 286 [FC B.23.1.5/6], except that in Cockayne it is joined to a 'rhythmical recital of the legal right of the owner to the stolen property' (182), which is essentially the same as the oath administered in such cases (ed. Thorpe, *Ancient Laws*, 1: 184). Cockayne, 3: 286–8, thus represents a stringing together of charms by someone 'determined to omit no step for the restoration of his property' (183): heathen ceremony is followed by citation of the loss and recovery of the cross; the patriarchs are invoked to hamper the movements of the thief; finally, aid of the law is invoked by the recitation of an indisputable claim to possession. (Includes text of FC B.23.1.4, as well as German and ME versions.)

340 McBryde, J.M., Jr. 'Anglo-Saxon Charms.' *Modern Language Notes* 21 (1906): 264–5.

Further to McBryde, **339**. The legal formula attached to cattle-thief charms in Cockayne, **297**, 2: 286–8 [FC B.23.1.6], which is printed by Thorpe, 1: 184, had previously been printed, arranged as verse, by Leo (*Rectitudines*, 1842, 56–7). Leo took his text from Schmid (*Die Gesetze der Angelsachsen*, 1832, 216–17), who printed his text from CCCC 383, collated with *Textus Roffensis*. Textual variants in Schmid and Leo as compared with Cockayne are tabled. Whereas Leo calls the whole passage 'eidesformel,' Schmid (lvii) insists that it should be called a legal declaration of ownership in answer to the claims of another, and also points out that CCCC 383 must post-date the 10th century, since it contains the laws of Canute.

341 Schmitt, Lorenz. *Lautliche Untersuchung der Sprache des Læceboc.* Bonn: Hanstein, 1908.

Not sighted. According to Greenfield and Robinson, 6393, incorporates Schmitt, **456**.

342 **Schlutter, Otto B.** 'Oððæt seo ex sy gesoht.' *Anglia* 32 (1909): 257–8.

Cockayne, **298**, has incorrectly interpreted 'oððæt seo ex sy gesoht' (in *Lac* 1) as 'until the axis be reached.' 'Ex' here means 'cerebrum.' A similar recipe in *Lb*1.1.3, contains this instruction: 'þæt heafod hoh of dune þ se seaw mæge þ heafod geondyrnan.' The instruction in *Lac* ('ahoh þæt heafod nyþerweard, oððæt seo ex sy gesoht') thus means that the patient is to incline the head backwards so that the interior cavity is accessible; i.e., the cure is to be inhaled through the nostrils so it can run about the head.

343 **Förster, Max.** 'Beiträge zur mittelalterlichen Volkskunde V.' *Archiv für das Studium der neueren Sprachen und Literaturen* 127 (1911): 31–84.

Comparative study of 10 Latin Dreambooks, 10th–15th centuries; includes reference to the extended Latin–OE gloss in Tiberius A.iii [FC C.16, art. a]. Prints a ME Dreambook found in three 14th–15th century manuscripts.

344 **Skemp, A.R.** 'The Old English Charms.' *Modern Language Review* 6 (1911): 289–301.

Textual notes on Grendon, **314**, concerning some metrical charms [FC A.43.2, 3, 11, 4] and three prose charms, Grendon A10 [*Lac*], A24 [*Lb*] and A15. A24 is evidence that ceremonial directions are not always given in full, and the omission suggests that some obscurities in the charms might vanish if the accompanying ceremonial were fully known. *Contra* Grendon, **314**, 222, McBryde, **339**, and Cockayne, **298**, 3: 286–8, Skemp considers that there is no inner connection between the cattle-thief charm in Grendon A15 and the legal fragment which follows it in two manuscripts; the charm refers to stolen livestock, the legal fragment refers solely to land, and the personal pronoun *hine* in the legal fragment signifies he who bequeathed the land, not the protestor. Skemp also points out that, although Grendon prints the legal fragment as verse, it is highly irregular, and it would be better to regard the form as 'very rhetorical prose, borrowing verse rhythms and ornaments' (299). [Skemp's review of Grendon, **314**, 262–6 of the same vol., adds nothing to the study of the texts.]

345 **Singer, Charles.** 'On a Greek Charm used in England in the Twelfth Century.' *Annals of Medical History* 1 (1917): 258–60.

Identifies the Latin words inscribed in the form of a cross in the charm to stanch bleeding (St John's College 17) as a translation of a Greek formula [FC B.23.1.16].

346 **Smith, Major General Sir Frederick.** *The Early History of Veterinary Literature and its British Development.* Vol. 1. London: Baillière, 1919. 4 vols. 1919[1916]–33.

'The Veterinary Art of Anglo-Saxon England,' 61–71, distinguishes between the early period, when there must have been medical schools based on Greece and Rome (e.g. at Winchester, Malmesbury and Glastonbury), and the intense superstition of the 11th century, for which the church is to blame for having kept the masses at heel 'by the potent weapons of fear and superstition' (62). Anglo-Saxon medical literature presents superstition 'in all its horrible forms,' not, however, unmixed with close observation and acute professional instinct. 'For this the Greek school must be thanked, although, if evident in human practice, it does not appear in the veterinary practice of the late Anglo-Saxon period' (62). After a brief glance at the Laws of Ine and Æthelstan, with particular reference to horses, Smith delivers the opinion that vets may have been inferior in skill to 'the relatively cultured Anglo-Saxon medical man,' because they were probably Britons (64). Some dozen references to animal diseases in Cockayne are cited [chiefly from *Lac*]. Smith diagnoses the horse in *Lb*1.88 as suffering from erysipelas (cf. *Lac* 109). He reserves opinion on whether cattle lung-disease referred to in cures and charms was pleuro-pneumonia or TB, and mentions the use of a horse to demonstrate, evidently to someone on whom superstition had not taken its fearful hold, the ill effects of bloodletting on an unlucky day (Cockayne, **298** 3: 152).

347 Wendel, Theodore Otto. *The Medieval Attitude to Astrology, particularly in England.* Yale Studies in English 60. New Haven: Yale UP, 1920.

Ch. 3, 'Astrology in Old English Literature,' 42–8. All astrological science among Teutonic peoples was imported, although allusions to superstitions regarding the sun and moon in *Germania*, ch. 11, *De Bello Gallico*, 6.21, *Theodore's Penitential*, ch. 27 (ed. Thorpe), and Laws of Cnut (ed. Liebermann, 1: 312), suggest that there were points of contact. The nearest approach to astrology in Celtic lore was (un)lucky days, cloud divination and nativity predictions. The prognostic treatises in Cockayne, **298**, 3: 150–229, derived from Latin and Greek, embody learned superstitions which later became the common property of the uncultured. Ælfric's homilies show that even the belief in (un)lucky days was disapproved; his Epiphany homily is the sole extended OE reference to astrology, and shows how foreign the subject was to his hearers (ed. Thorpe, *HomCath*, 1: 110). 'Fischer [**436**], p. 21, is surely wrong when he takes this homily, as well as the texts printed by Cockayne, as evidence that astrology was "still" current among the English in the tenth century' (46, n. 2). The refusal to bury Archbishop Gerard of York (1100–8) because a copy of Firmicus Maternus was found under his pillow at death (*Gesta Pontificum Anglorum*, 3.18, ed. Hamilton) is an early indication of revived interest in astrology in England, and with the second quarter of the century we are in a new age of medieval science.

348 Schlutter, Otto Bernard. 'OE. *sárcréne* "so tender and sore to the touch as to make you cry with pain." ' *Neophilologus* 7 (1922): 211–12.

NED states incorrectly that there is no trace of *croon* in OE, and that it appears to be a Low German word that came into Scots in the early ME period. As Schlutter explained years ago, OE *sárcréne* (to which, *contra BT* and Cockayne, **297**, 2: 176, 9 (*Lb*), Schlutter attaches the meaning given in the title of this article) is a compound of *sar*, 'dolor' and *crén*, 'garrulus,' *crén* being an umlaut form of the adjective *crónan*, corresponding to, not borrowed from, MDu *krônen*.

349 **Bonser, Wilfrid.** 'The Dissimilarity of Ancient Irish Magic from that of the Anglo-Saxons.' *Folklore* 37 (1926): 271–88.

Bonser argues that Celtic and Anglo-Saxon magic were entirely different, and parallels represent a common source, not direct contact. In his view, Celtic influence on Anglo-Saxon magic is to be found only in corrupted charms, which may have been transmitted by Columba and Aidan. Druidical powers and practices, and their use by Celtic saints, are detailed, 272–80. Whereas 'widdershins' is associated with ill luck among the Celts, among the Anglo-Saxons it is merely regarded as contrary to nature (cf. 'sungonges,' *Lb*1.47.1; Cockayne, **400**, 1: 400). Although there are a great number of OE words that denote magic and sorcery, only *dry* (in *drycræft*) appears to derive from Celtic. Three Anglo-Saxon charms containing corrupt Irish are elucidated, 286–8. Cockayne, **298**, 3: 10, (cure for swallowing an insect); 'Gonomil orgomil marbumil,' means 'I wound the animal, I strike the animal, I kill the animal.' Cockayne, **297**, 2: 54 (a charm intended to stop blood); 'struth fola' suggests 'sruth fola,' 'a stream of blood'; other words in this charm (such as 'argreinn' and 'tart') might be Irish, but it is possibly an admixture of a number of languages, such as Hebrew. The beginning of the incantation in *Lb*1.45.5, might mean 'Christ healed [the blind man with his] spittle, which he put across his eyes so that they were entirely whole,' although the obvious difficulty remains that this is a charm against venom, not blindness. [See Banks, **479**.]

350 **Bonser, Wilfrid.** 'Magical Practices Against Elves.' *Folklore* 37 (1926): 350–63.

Elf-shot or flying venom represents the attribution of disease to erroneous superstitious causes and, before the coming of medicine, magic was employed against it. The notion is a native Teutonic one, and appears to have influenced Finnish beliefs. Anglo-Saxon elves were thought of as small beings, usually male, dwelling everywhere, and especially in wastelands. Mischief caused by elves took various forms. They shot at domestic animals (*Lac* 60, 97; *Lb*1.88.2, *Lb*2.65.1) and caused stitch (*Lb*2.64, *Lac* 76). There are charms against elves, elf-disease, water-elf-disease, and the influence of elves (*Lac* 2, *Lb*3.63, *Lb*3.41; *Lb*1.64). They were also credited with causing hiccups or heartburn (*ælfsogotha*). Christianity equated elf-shot and flying venom with demonic possession, and charms were modified accordingly (*Lb*3.62). Elves were a source of apparitions, especially at night (*Lb*3.61;

*Lb*2.65.5; *Lb*3.54). So too were dwarfs: their association with nightmare is illustrated by the description of asthma in *PD* 51: 'at times he writhes as if against a dwarf.' [Selected citations only.]

351 Dickins, Bruce. 'Runic Rings and Old English Charms.' *Archiv für das Studium der neueren Sprachen und Literaturen* 167 (1935): 252.

Dickins deciphers the runic inscriptions on three rings (gold, brass and agate). He reads the third and tenth letters in the runic inscriptions on the rings of gold and bronze (*British Museum Guide to Anglo-Saxon Antiquities*, 116–17) [?FC E.19, 25] as Northumbrian *k*, not *y*; this reading connects these runically inscribed rings with the OE charm for stanching blood, Cockayne, **297**, 2: 54 [*Lb*], which also has the collocation *ærcrio* (runic *ærkriu*) and ends with *leNo*. Cockayne, 2: 112 [*Lb*], is described in the table of contents as 'a second Gaelic sovereign charm.' Dickins comments that part of Cockayne, **298**, 3: 78 [*Lac*], is reasonably interpreted as Irish, but he does not think that either of the two mentioned has been read as Gaelic (Irish or Scots), or as any other language.

352 Dickins, Bruce, and R.M. Wilson. 'Sent Kasi.' *Leeds Studies in English* 6 (1937): 67–73.

'St Kasi,' in a ME charm against rats, Bodleian, Rawlinson C.288 (ed. Sisam, 1925), is identified with St Nicaise or Nicasius; a number of saints bore this name, but Nicasius of Rheims was associated with rodents in medieval France. He is invoked in charms against smallpox in three manuscripts: Caligula A.xv, f. 125 [FC B.23.1.9], Bodleian, James 27, p. 127 (transcript of Otho A.xiii), and Royal 2 A.xx, f. 52 [Storms A9]. The authors deduce that these three charms may derive from a common original; but their connection with the ME charm is difficult to establish. Nicasius was not well known in England (a few church dedications and Anglo-Saxon liturgical calendar entries are instanced); belief in his efficacy against rats may have been introduced by Lotharingian ecclesiastics such as Giso of Wells or Leofric of Exeter, or it may have spread from Calais in the late 14th or early 15th century.

353 Magoun, Francis Peabody, Jr. 'Zu den ae. Zaubersprüchen.' *Archiv für das Studium der neueren Sprachen und Literaturen* 171 (1937): 17–35.

Corrections, emendations and commentary to Grendon, **314**, A1–24, B1–6, C1–4, D1–12, E1–12.

354 Shook, L.K. 'Notes on the Old English Charms.' *Modern Language Notes* 55 (1940): 139–40.

Shook identifies some previously unnoticed Christian elements (liturgical and biblical) in Grendon A12 [*Lac*], A13 [FC A.43.11], A19 [*Lac*], B4 [FC A.43.2], and E2 [*Lb*].

355 Bonser, W. 'The Seven Sleepers of Ephesus in Anglo-Saxon and Later Recipes.' *Folklore* 56 (1945): 254–6.

The names of the Seven Sleepers of Ephesus, invoked in the (metrical) *Lac* charm against dwarf-induced nightmare [FC A.43.3] are frequently used to secure sleep, and also to allay fever. Worcester, Cathedral Library Q.5 [FC B.23.1.18] similarly instructs that the names of the Seven Sleepers are to be written on wafers. Latin charms containing the seven names also appear in the 11th century Royal 2 A.xx, f. 52r [Storms 37]; the (unprinted) Royal 12 E.xx, f. 162v; and Faustina A.x, f. 136/116 [Storms 39]. They also appear in two 14th century Latin charms, one found in an English manuscript in the Royal Library at Stockholm [Stephens, **426**], and the other in a manuscript dated 1361 in the University Library of Breslau, as well as in a Welsh charm of the *Physicians of Myddvai*. Appeal to the seven sleepers is evidently appropriate for cases of insomnia or any diseases for which sleep would be beneficial: 'The medieval mind, like that of the savage before it, worked on a logic of its own' (256). Anglo-Saxon knowledge of this legend, which is related by Ælfric (*HomCath*, 2: 424–6, ed. Thorpe), could derive from an oriental, classical or Teutonic source.

356 Fazakerley, Mary Eleanor. 'Studies in the Old English Lacnunga.' B.A. thesis. U of Liverpool, 1945.

Not sighted. According to Grattan and Singer, **326**, the thesis takes the form of 'a glossary which records every spelling-variant found in the main part of the text, supplemented by chapters which include (with references to Sievers's *Angelsächs. Gr.*) some account of inflexions as well as of stressed vowels' (213). Bonser, 1957, 7411, states that the typescript is available from the University of Liverpool Library.

357 Magoun, Francis Peabody, Jr. 'Noþðæs sweoster; "Need's" sisters.' *Archiv für Nordisk Filologi* 60 (1945): 98–106.

Contra Grendon, **314**, A9 [in *Lac*] is the only representative in OE of a type not uncommon in the Germanic world. This charm was not appropriate to lot casting ceremonies, and it is distinct from modern children's counting out games, which use *ascending* number sequences. It is a 'counting down and out charm' to rid a patient of glandular swelling or scrofula; as the numbers are recited backwards from nine to zero, disease-demons are supposed, analogically, to depart one by one from the source of infection. Magoun retracts his earlier suggestion (**353**) that *Noþðæs* is a masculine personal name, and proposes to identify it with the Scandinavian name for the N-rune, OW Norse *nauð(r)*, which in OE or Anglo-Danish would be *noþ* (and the earlier reading may well have been *Nope sweoster*): *nine* sisters, because the N-rune is tenth in ON and OE, and nine is a favourite magic number in Germanic antiquity. A9 is linguistically Anglian, and its origin in the Danelaw appears confirmed by the Old Danish loan word. The OE translator may not have recognized *Noð* as a doublet of *Nyd*; like many foreign words in OE charms it may have been taken on faith as having 'powerful though obscure significance.'

358 **Meroney, Howard.** 'Irish in the Old English Charms.' *Speculum* 20 (1945–6): 172–82.

Meroney, criticizing widespread neglect of Zimmer, **333**, and consequent underestimation of Irish influence, identifies Irish words in seven charms, in order to demonstrate that these 'supposedly senseless medical prescriptions' were not 'hocuspocus to their compilers, and that we must infer some kind of professional contact between the Anglo-Saxon *læce* and the Old Irish *lieig*' (182). Charms examined are *Lac*, f. 191r (Cockayne **298**, 3: 78); *Lb* [1.45.5], and its parallels in *Lac*; *Lac*[10]; *Lb*[1.9.4], and its parallel [FC B.23.1.13]; Cockayne, **298**, 3: 294 [Storms 82], and its parallel in *Lac*; *Lac*[83]; Cockayne, 3: 295 [Grendon A6]. About 90 Irish words are identified (some previously identified by Zimmer, **333**, and others), accounting, through repetition, for over half of the words in the charms examined; phrases and larger syntactical units are intelligible, including a roughly consecutive passage of 18 words [in *Lb*1.9.4 and FC B.23.1.13].

359 **Curtis, Jay Leumas.** 'The Vocabulary of Medical *Cræftas* in the Old English *Leechbook of Bald*.' Diss. U of North Carolina, Chapel Hill, 1946. Dir. E.E. Ericson.

Not sighted. According to Pulsiano, 1988, 111, studies the medical vocabulary with particular attention to 'habits of compounding and borrowing, native terms, learned loans, folk handling of foreign terms, development of folk-etymology and related phenomena.'

360 **Storms, Godfrid.** 'An Anglo-Saxon Prescription from the *Lacnunga*.' *English Studies* 28 (1947): 33–41.

The salve for the preparation of broken bones in *Lac* 12, serves to illustrate the close connection between magic and medicine. The salve is compounded of 35 herbs, their names arranged in alliterative groups, presumably as a mnemonic aid. The prescription requires bark to be cut from near the base of the trunk on the east side because this is where trees are strongest, and where the rays of the sun are absorbed; its healing power is thus added to that of the tree and transmitted to the sufferer. Doubtless the trees used would have had associations with power, and the power of the bark is increased by boiling it in holy water. The prescription specifies that the fat used must come from specified male animals; this is because they were regarded as the more powerful of the species. Bones, pounded with the back of an axe, are added; this represents the influence of like upon like, and the axe, a powerful weapon in its own right, has additional significance in that it would have caused broken bones in fighting. Old (rank, i.e., powerful) butter is added, and so is soap; Storms conjectures that it had associations with fighting off evil spirits. Storms prints the recipe, with translation (40–1), and sums up: 'All details, however odd and meaningless they may appear at first sight, prove to tend to one and the same object, the driving out of the disease spirit and the healing of the wound' (41). [Incorporated in Storms, **325**.]

361 Townend, B.R. 'The Narrative Charm with Reference to Tooth-ache.' *British Dental Journal* 85 (1948): 29–34, 86.

The narrative charm, widespread in time and space, is among the multitudinous superstitious devices that 'the misplaced energy of mankind has invented with the idea of preventing and curing disease' (29). The early leech put more faith in spells than drugs; the science of pharmacology originates in the realization that 'the spell was valueless and the drug was the thing' (31). At 31–4, Townend cites examples of narrative charms employed for toothache, mostly German and Danish, and observes that, according to Grendon's schema, the narrative themes employed are nos. 1, 3, 4, 5, 9, 11. The most favoured type is the meeting of Christ or Mary with a holy or human sufferer in which the toothache is commanded to leave or instructions are given (e.g., *Lac*, Cockayne, **298**, 3: 64). 'Holy' persons connected with toothache include Ahab and Job, and the saint most commonly invoked is Apollonia, whose martyrdom is often narrated as a charm. Folkloric anecdotes are adduced to illustrate the continuity of superstition to the present day: 'We are still fascinated by words of power ... and many of us use such words ["democracy," "fascism," "communism"] with no more meaning than our ancestors who recited a narrative charm' (34). At 86 is Townend's reply to a letter of objection to the foregoing article; it further illuminates his attitude to his patients, but contributes nothing to the understanding of narrative charms.

362 Jost, Karl. Rev. of *Anglo-Saxon Magic*, by G. Storms [**325**]. *English Studies* 31 (1950): 101–5.

Chiefly textual disagreements with Storms, **325**, concerning Storms 1 [FC A.43.8], 7 [FC A.43.3], 15 [FC A.43.9], 5 [FC A.43.7]. *Contra* Storms, Jost holds that Storms 31 [*Lac*] needs no additions to form an ideal charm against poison; he offers a restoration of the Latin, based on *Vita et Actus Beati Johannis Apostoli et Evangelistae* (the source for *HomCath* 1: 72/9 ff., ed. Thorpe), with which the charm agrees almost verbatim.

363 Magoun, Francis Peabody, Jr. Rev. of *Anglo-Saxon Magic*, by G. Storms [**325**]. *Speculum* 28 (1953): 203–12.

Concordance of the editions of Storms and Grendon (**314**), 206–7; extensive notes on individual charms, and bibliographical additions.

364 Derolez, R. *Runica Manuscripta: The English Tradition*. Bruges: Tempel, 1954.

Derolez gives his transcription of the runes in *Lb* (Storms 33) and agrees with Storms that Cockayne's interpretation ('thine hand vexeth, thine hand vexeth') is doubtful; despite the relative earliness of the manuscript, 'the runes are so poorly made that the scribe can have no notion of what he copied' (417).

365 **Magoun, F.P., Jr.** Rev. of *Anglo-Saxon Magic and Medicine*, by H.G. Grattan and Charles Singer [**326**]. *Speculum* 29 (1954): 564–9.

Notes on *Lac*, and a concordance to the editions of Grendon, **314**, and Storms, **325** (as in Magoun, **363**).

366 **Stürzl, Erwin.** 'Die christlichen Elemente in den altenglischen Zaubersegen.' *Die Sprache* 6 (1960): 75–93.

Addresses the issue of ecclesiastical attitudes to pagan beliefs and their reflection in a number of the prose and metrical charms in *Lb* and *Lac*. Taken as a whole, the Anglo-Saxon charms are living proof that religion and ('white') magic were not in opposition.

367 **Schneider, Karl.** 'Die strophischen Strukturen und heidnisch-religiösen Elemente der ae. Zauberspruchgruppe "wið þeofðe." ' *Festschrift zum 75. Geburtstag von Theodore Spira*. Ed. H. Viebrock and W. Erzgräber. Heidelberg: Winter, 1961. 38–56.

Schneider analyses the strophic structure of charms against theft (Storms 15, 13, 14, 11AB), and attempts to reconstruct the underlying pagan version of these charms, associating the four compass points with sun positions. He also explicates Storms 86 in terms of runic number magic (51–5). In his opinion, his analysis of the cattle-thief charms has not only illuminated strophic variations. It provides new evidence of Anglo-Saxon pagan beliefs, particularly in 'den Urwesengott und an die jugendlichen göttlichen Brüder' (Garmund): Schneider makes comparative reference to the Frank's casket (56).

368 **Peters, R.A.** 'OE *ælf, -ælf, ælfen, -ælfen.*' *Philological Quarterly* 42 (1963): 250–7.

Peters offers 'a systematic examination of the eleven "elf" words in OE' (250). 'In the OE charms and *Leechbook* the elves are always malign or disease spirits in contrast to their more gentle feminine counterparts who appear only in OE glosses (*feldælfen*, etc.)' (253).

369 **Talbot, C.H.** 'Some Notes on Anglo-Saxon Medicine.' *Bulletin of Medical History* 9 (1965): 156–69.

Talbot refutes 'the accepted view among all medical historians ... that the emergence of Salerno and Salernitan medicine brought a new and rational element to the hitherto debased practice of the West,' by arguing that 'the texts used and published by the earliest Salernitan writers of the 11th century were known and read in Anglo-Saxon England almost two centuries beforehand' (157). Singer and Bonser, following Payne, **449**, hold that the

12th century *PD* marks the introduction into England of superior Salernitan medical knowledge; but *Lb*1&2, which is a copy of a 9th century exemplar, also makes use of writings attributed to Gariopontus and Petrocellus. Talbot prints parallel a number of passages from *Lb*2, *Passionarius Galeni* and Petrocellus, demonstrating that, at points, the OE translator was working from a disordered source; he 'was not merely following one text blindly, but excerpting at will, and blending the elements according to his own knowledge and experience' (167). The same sources were available to the compiler of *Lb*1, though not used to the same extent. *Passionarius Galeni* is an 11th century compilation of Arelius, Priscianus and the so-called Aesculapius and, already by the 9th century, Arelius and Aesculapius were combined in many texts; but *Lb*1&2 has material from all three as well as material identical to Petrocellus. The explanation is that the so-called Petrocellus already existed as a separate work in the 9th century (the attribution to Petrocellus occurs only in the late manuscript that de Renzi, 1856, printed). The oldest manuscript (Sloane 2839, 11th century) was once owned by Echternach, the monastery founded by Willibrord, and some fragments in Germany may also have originated with Anglo-Saxon missionaries. 'It might be going too far at this stage to suggest that the Petrocellus text may have been an Anglo-Saxon compilation, but there is no denying that the Leechbook of Bald was based partly on it and is the earliest witness, apart from the Echternach manuscript, to its existence' (168).

370 Meritt, Herbert Dean. *Some of the Hardest Glosses in Old English.* Stanford: Stanford UP, 1968.

Includes consideration of several words in Cockayne, **400, 297, 298.** *Hunta* (several times used in *Lb* for remedies against its bite) = 'spider,' *musca venenosa* or *musca venenata* (12); *ofnete (Lb)* may be an adverb like *swiðe* and *longe* (23); *æpeningas*, in a remedy for stomach ache in *Lb*2.2.2 ('mænigfeald æppelcyn peran æpeningas') is associated by Cockayne, 2: 368, with *openærs* and defined by *BT* Supplement (under *æppelcynn*) as 'medlars,' but is interpreted by Meritt as 'unweighed amounts,' because 'the term *pening* is so frequent in stating the amount of the remedy to be taken' (115–16).

371 Thun, Nils. 'The Malignant Elves: Notes on Anglo-Saxon Magic and Germanic Myth.' *Studia Neophilologica* 41 (1969): 378–96.

Thun attributes the contrast between the Anglo-Saxon *ælf* ('thoroughly bad and harmful') and the ON *álfar*, 'sometimes benevolent and sometimes malevolent') to 'conversion experience.' The incorporation of pre-Christian elements into the Christian world view is further advanced in *Beowulf* than it is in Anglo-Saxon medical literature, in which elves are, nevertheless, conceived as bringing disease. Thun distinguishes between 'spirit intrusion' and 'disease-object intrusion' (shooting by elves and witches; shooting dwarfs, also part of this common Germanic belief, are not attested in OE). Shooting denotes disease in 'Wiþ Færstice' [FC A.43.4] and in six passages found in

Lb and *Lac*, all of which involve domestic animals; there is a difference of terminology (*Lb*, *ofscoten*; cf. *Lac*, *gesceotan*); the use of a broken needle for horse bloat may suggest the work of spirits was suspected. Thun remarks upon the *wæterælf* and the three recipes for curing *ælfadl* in *Lb*; he relates the cure employing the smoke of the plant *ælfþone* to Scandinavian popular tradition, which attributes skin eruptions to elves, and employs fumigation as a cure. Thun also remarks on the widespread belief in sucking elves (*ælf-sogoða*); the implication of sorcery in *Lb*2.65.2; and a possible allusion to sexual congress with demons (*Lb*3.61, *mannum* = 'people with whom the devil has sexual intercourse'). Three of the four occurrences of *ylfig* proba-bly mean 'epilepsy.' Personal names containing *Ælf-*, some of which may be of Scandinavian origin, are probably survivals from a time when elves were regarded favourably. The appearance of *ælfsciene* in *Judith* and *Genesis*, more unexpected than names containing this element, may be explained by lack of reflection over the exact meaning of poetical vocabulary.

372 Meaney, Audrey L. 'Alfred, the Patriarch and the White Stone.' *Parergon* 6 (1971): 22–3.

Abstract of Meaney, **382**.

373 Grant, Raymond J.S. 'Laurence Nowell's Transcript of BM Cotton Otho B. xi.' *Anglo-Saxon England* 3 (1974): 111–24.

Grant 'brings together the relevant information about the original contents of the manuscript, the surviving fragments, the transcript and modern sec-ondary sources' (113). The transcript's particular value is that it alone preserves Item 11, 'Herb recipes' [FC B.21.2.3]. The existence of this item is unremarked by later users of the manuscript, and it must be presumed lost well before the Cotton fire. Most of these recipes occur also in the R version of *Lb*; Ker lists the correspondences and describes four items contained in *Nowell* but not in R. Taking the Bede text in Otho as representative, Grant compares it with the corresponding passages in Add. 43703 to assess the ac-curacy and usefulness of the transcript. He demonstrates frequent confusion of *æsc* with *a*, and *e* with *ea*, misleading suggestions of non-WS (especially Mercian) forms, and confusions of the inflectional endings *-en*, *-an* and *-on*. He shows that Nowell was influenced by spelling conventions of his own time (e.g., *i* and *y* were interchangeable), and lists confusions arising from Eliza-bethan difficulties with the handwriting. 'Throughout there are changes in which Nowell seems to be trying to correct to what he thought was standard OE' (123). Thus, 'Nowell's transcript of the Bede text is of no use to the student of spellings, phonology or inflections and no dialect indications can be drawn from it' (124). But very few words are omitted, homeoteleuta are very rare, and changes of word order are few, so that the transcript can be used as evidence for contents and word order.

374 Bierbaumer, Peter. *Der botanische Wortschatz des Altenglischen.* 1. Teil. *Das Læcebōc.* Grazer Beiträge zur englischen Philologie. Bern: Lang, 1975. 3 vols. 1975–9. [See also **416, 542.**]

The complete botanical vocabulary of *Lb* is presented alphabetically, 1–152. Introduction, v–xv, sets forth principles and procedures. Each lemma is followed by a critical presentation of all instances of the term as found in Leonhardi, **310**, arranged according to the morphological case in which they occur. The meaning of each term is given in German and English; Latin botanical terms are also specified. 'Where the definition of the term is different from that given in the dictionaries, it is discussed briefly. Similarly the etymology of the respective term is discussed if new arguments can be given. The rationale behind the formation of compound plant names is explained by stating their literal meaning and the relevant botanical, pharmaceutical, and socio-historical facts' (168). A summary of contents (in English) enumerates the lemmata which, in the author's opinion, deserve special attention, 167–8. Appendices, 153–62, include an index of Latin botanical plant names and OE equivalents, 159–62. Bibliography, 162–6.

375 Meaney, Audrey. 'King Alfred and his Secretariat.' *Parergon* 11 (1975): 16–24.

Discussion of *Lb*1&2, 16–18. Meaney deduces that the Winchester scriptorium was significantly instrumental in the implementation of Alfred's vernacular education scheme (implicitly requiring the establishment of primary schools by bishops as well as translation into English of books 'necessary for all men to know'): in effect, Winchester served as a royal publishing house, with scribes being trained on the job. Asser records that he had seen gifts sent to Alfred by Elias (presumably by means of English pilgrims returning home), and *Lb*2.64's claim to report what Elias commanded to be told to Alfred, like the OE Orosius's inclusion of the journeys that Ohthere related to Alfred, is evidence that both works took their final form in the same circle. Meaney finds evidence for the provenance of *Lb* in other Winchester manuscripts which contain similar recipes; BL Add. 34652 [FC B.21.2.3] may be copied from the working papers from which *Lb* was compiled. She does not think there is enough evidence to conclude that Alfred would have considered that a medical text was one of the books necessary to know (despite Asser's implication that his health preoccupied him), and the colophon indicates that *Lb* was a private venture (perhaps by one of the court physicians who were unable to diagnose Alfred's affliction): 'Yet since it represents another branch of human knowledge, and appears to be an attempt at a compendium of all contemporary ideas and practice, it is not out of place in this scheme' (18). [See also Meaney, **382**; cf. Wright, **294**.]

376 Stuart, H. 'The Anglo-Saxon Elf.' *Studia Neophilologica* 48 (1976): 313–20.

Stuart examines the apparent incompatibility of conceptions of the elf in leechdoms, glosses, proper names, and poems, in order to demonstrate how and why the nature of the elf changed after Christianity was introduced (see Thun, **371**). Stuart hypothesizes a process of agglutination and concludes that 'the various descriptions of elves encountered in OE texts can be related,' and that 'many of the paradoxes they present are to be explained as part of a continual and ever more complicated process of cultural absorption' (320). Stuart discerns two elvish traditions: 'one, of free-ranging creatures of no fixed gender and allied with Thunor ... the other, a group of magically powerful women who ride over the land, have the same property of shooting disease-laden darts, and may be mountain-elves. It is also probable that the second group are followers of Woden, humble relations of the valkyries' (320).

377 Nöth, Winfried. 'Semiotics of the Old English Charm.' *Semiotica* 19 (1977): 59–83.

Literary approaches, though tending to ignore the prose charms, 'which constitute the great majority' of the available texts, have done much to clarify the cultural context of OE charms. Nöth examines 'the neglected dimensions' of OE charms, 'action and sign' (60). Analysis is restricted to charms against diseases in *Lac* (many examples from Grattan and Singer, **326**, some prose), and focuses on 'Features and Definition of the Old English Charm,' 60–4; 'The Semantic Dimension,' 65–8; 'The Syntactic Structure,' 68–71; 'The Pragmatic Framework,' 71–5. Observations on 'Magic Communication Today,' 75–6, conclude: 'As in the case of magic, the degree of success in advertising depends on the extent to which the consumer is unable to recognize the basis of this semiotic pathology' (76).

378 Grant, Raymond J.S. *Cambridge, Corpus Christi College 41: The Loricas and the Missal. Costerus* NS 17. Amsterdam: Rodopi, 1978.

Prints marginalia from CCCC 41: (1) from pp. 206–8, including a prose cattle-theft charm (Storms 12), at 5–6; (2) from p. 272, a Latin charm with OE heading (Storms 48), at 15–16; (3) from p. 329, a Latin charm with the 'Sator' palindrome (Storms 43), at 18–19.

Ch. 1, 'The Loricas of Corpus 41,' 1–26, argues that (1) is a single tri-partite lorica for 'protection of the soul during and after life' (14); the Latin portions are not concerned with cattle-theft, but are of Irish ancestry, and derive in part from a hymn later known as 'St. Patrick's Breastplate.' The manuscript relations of the 'cattle-theft charm' are inconclusively dealt with at 7–9: Grant's concern is to show that it is 'most fully represented in Corpus 41, and that the later texts in CCCC 190 [Storms 11A], the *Textus Roffensis* and CCCC 383 [Storms 11B] were copied after Corpus 41 and follow a different, more corrupt, recension of the text' (9). Grant also reclassifies as loricas the other two items he prints, as well as the paternoster dialogue of the poetic *SS*. The inclusion of the latter text confirms his thesis that the marginalia of CCCC 41 are not random; the selection is determined by an interest in texts with Irish connections which deal with 'ecclesiastical fiction'

(26), and that the charms are of three main types (against theft, against specific physical ills, and for the general protection of body and soul). Ch. 2, 'Corpus 41—An 11th-century Missal,' 27–50, examines the Latin liturgical marginalia (printed at 51–112), establishes a relationship with CCCC 422, and locates the manuscript at New Minster, Winchester. [For reviews see Hohler, **387**; Voigts, **388**.]

379 **Hill, Thomas D.** 'The Theme of the Cosmological Cross in Two Old English Cattle Theft Charms.' *Notes and Queries* NS 25 (1978): 488–90.

The cross, which figures in all but one of the cattle-theft charms in Storms 11–15, is linked in Storms 13 [FC A.43.10] and 14 [FC A.43.5] with instructions to pray towards all four corners of the earth. Hill identifies Eph. 3.18–19 as the origin of this cosmological cross motif, and demonstrates its currency in patristic and later writings, including Ælfric's Palm Sunday homily (ed. Thorpe, *HomCath* 2: 254–6). Christ on the cross draws all things to him, as the cattle are to be drawn. The allusion also recalls his creation of the world. OE charms invest the user with power implicit in a previous manifestation of God's will, and recovery of the cross is cited in cattle-theft charms in the hope that the cattle likewise will be recovered. The power implicit in the theme of the cosmological Cross is the power to fix and determine directions and to impose order; loss of cattle involves disorder and misplacing. Allusion to the cosmological cross thus provides appropriate symbolic ritual and is also proof that exegetical motifs were known to the unlearned.

380 **Lendinara, Patrizia.** 'Un incantesimo del *Lǣcebōc*.' *Annali, Istituto Universitario Orientale di Napoli, Filologia germanica* 21 (1978): 7–16.

In certain charms (e.g., Grendon D6, D8–D12, E7) writing is prescribed by itself, not as a supplement to spoken words. In such charms, the magic triad of action, object and speech is expressed in action, writing and silence.

381 **Lendinara, Patrizia.** 'Gli incantesimi del periodo Anglosassone: una ricerca bibliografica.' *Annali, Istituto Universitario Orientale di Napoli, Filologia germanica* 21 (1978): 299–362.

Lists, by manuscript, 124 metrical and prose charms, with incipits. For each charm gives, where appropriate, Ker and FC classification; Grendon (**314**) and Storms (**325**) number; page references for Cockayne, **297**, **298** and **400**, Grattan and Singer, **326**, and Dobbie, **27**. A briefly annotated bibliography of 208 publications identifies, in terms of the five major editions, the charms edited or studied. [Separately catalogues a number of items which are grouped together in other classificatory systems. Includes Latin-only charms edited by Storms and Grendon, and a ME charm, Grendon AA18 (see Priebsch, **440**); also includes (as Lendinara 31) a cure for lung-disease in cattle in Vitellius E.xvii, f. 15v (Ker 224, art. n), which is classified as a Recipe by FC (FC B.21.5.9).]

382 Meaney, Audrey L. 'Alfred, the Patriarch and the White Stone.' *AUMLA: Journal of the Australasian Universities Language and Literature Association* 49 (1978): 65–79.

'All this Dominus Elias, Patriarch in Jerusalem, ordered to be said to King Alfred' (*Lb*2.64) is reminiscent of the account of Ohthere's journey incorporated in the OE translation of Orosius's *History*; thus, both these passages might have been selected from Alfred's Commonplace Book for inclusion in works translated and compiled under his aegis. The Winchester provenance of the manuscript supports this, since *ASC*, OE Bede and OE Orosius were copied at Winchester between 890 and 960 (see Meaney, **375**). Meaney considers it significant that all the drugs specified in the passage preceding attribution to the Patriarch could have been products of Syria, though she recognizes that it is not always easy to determine the precise substance intended by *Lb* (discussion of these, 68–9). If it is accepted that the medicines were assembled by the Patriarch for sending to King Alfred, it must be accepted that 'the White Stone' was with them. There is evidence that some of the virtues, magical rather than medical, were already attached to it before it left Jerusalem, but she accepts that white stones had always been regarded in the British Isles as magical (71–7). She finds that the elements in *Lb*1&2 which we consider magical are of mixed origin—basically Mediterranean and learned, but often affected by native English belief: the virtues attributed to the White Stone may therefore be regarded as 'in some ways typifying the magical elements in the work as a whole' (77). [See also Meaney, **548**.]

383 Martin, Lawrence T. 'The Earliest Version of the Latin *Somniale Danielis*.' *Manuscripta* 23 (1979): 131–41.

Prints, for the first time, a damaged fragment of the Latin *Somniale Danielis* from BL Harley 3017, f. 1 (first half of the 9th century; originating at Fleury, but shown to have been in England in Anglo-Saxon times by the appearance of a runic alphabet on f. 61r). The Harley fragment (H) differs from the Anglo-Saxon version (T), represented by Tiberius A.iii (Latin–OE), Titus D.xxvi (Latin only) and a Latin fragment in Sloane 475 (10th century). It also differs from W, the version underlying two 14th century ME versions, which is found in a number of manuscripts, the earliest dated 10th century. Martin examines the relationships at some length (includes a brief analysis of the Tiberius A.iii Dreambook [FC C.16]) and concludes, provisionally, that T is a hybrid, compiled from both W and H versions. [Bibliographical information on editions of Welsh, OI, Irish, German, French and 16th century Greek; adds Latin versions in English manuscripts to those listed by Förster, **315**.]

384 Stuart, Heather. 'A Ninth Century Account of Diets and *Dies Aegyptiaci*.' *Scriptorium* 33 (1979): 237–44.

An examination of Leiden, Vossianus Lat. F.96a, a fragment containing three medical texts in two different hands; its insular script might point to Irish or Anglo-Saxon connection. Folio 1 contains a set of medical prescriptions, which have parallels in *MedQuad*, *Lb* and *Lac*, accompanied by OE and Irish glosses. Folio 2v, transcribed by Stuart, contains an account of Diets and *Dies Aegyptiaci*; its closest parallels are in manuscripts of French provenance, and it belongs to a tradition of dangerous days for bloodletting which differs from Cockayne, **298**, 3: 76, 152 [*Lac* 117 and FC B.23.2.3].

385 Voigts, Linda E. 'British Library, Royal 12 D. xvii, f. 30v.' *Old English Newsletter* 13.1 (1979): 12–13.

F. 30v (reproduced) illustrates the large hand and generous margins of R. A nota-sign in the left margin, added s. xii–xiii, should perhaps be read as 'tota,' signifying that the entire chapter should be referred to or re-copied; other marginal notations indicate later use of the codex (see Voigts, **543**). The appearance of the neumes here and on f. 89v has been regarded as accidental; but elsewhere in *Lb* instructions for preparation of a medicament involve singing the Gloria, the Miserere mei and the paternoster, so that the neumes on f. 30v may also 'represent the fact that, for the Anglo-Saxons, the natural and supernatural were not discrete but were rather complementary aspects of the healing process' (12).

386 Braekman, Willy L. 'Notes on Old English Charms.' *Neophilologus* 64 (1980): 461–9.

Notes on the herbs in the 'Nine-Herbs Charm' [FC A.43.2] and *Naborrede* in *Lac* 94 (Storms 46). *Naborrede* is a Germanic compound meaning 'a fever caused by voracity,' and fits the context of a charm to cure lameness in horses brought about by a sprain (the outward symptoms of sprain resemble those of laminitis, caused by over-eating). Braekman concludes that *Naborrede unde uenisti* is the opening line of a partially preserved Teutonic charm which, except for the personified demon *Naborrede* (who is held responsible for the fever), has been translated into Latin.

387 Hohler, Christopher. Rev. of *Cambridge, Corpus Christi College 41: The Loricas and the Missal*, by Raymond J.S. Grant [**378**]. *Medium Ævum* 49 (1980): 275–8.

One of Hohler's criticisms of Grant, **378**, is that he has treated the 'charms' he prints as ' "folklore," "literature," and "verse" ' (277). The *Sator-arepo* word-square (Storms 43) is made up of two prayers, the Blessing of Alms offered on behalf of the living (found in *York Missal* and the *Manuale Norvegicum*) and the ordinary 'German' prayer for a woman in childbirth (*Pontifical Romano-Germanique*). Storms 48 consists of three verses from Psalm 117, three verses from the First Canticle of Moses (taken from a 'Roman' Psalter), and the corrupt text of two exorcisms; one of these is unknown to Hohler, the other is widespread (it is also found in Storms 19

[*Lac*], which includes 'two blessings for fruit in the middle of a service for a sick man,' 278). 'All these things are prayers to be uttered by some officiant, and not loricas, which are personal prayers to God' (278). In Hohler's view the appearance of the *Sator-arepo* word-square has no significance, and he 'strongly suspects that the Curse on a thief will have been regarded as equally respectable before 1066, though not necessarily in its varying accompaniments' (277), it being his contention that 'charms' of the kind found in this manuscript represent degenerate copies of priests' Manuals: 'It is difficult, if a priest who does not in fact know Latin has to recite Latin prayers to an audience whose native language is German or Welsh, to ensure that what he says will be a [*sic*] in a form God is likely to understand or approve. But the intention will probably be good' (278).

388 **Voigts, Linda Ehrsam.** Rev. of *Cambridge, Corpus Christi College 41: The Loricas and the Missal*, by Raymond J.S. Grant [**378**]. *Speculum* 56 (1981): 927–8.

Voigts notes, as a minor addition to the connections between CCCC 41 and 422 pointed out by Grant (their shared material and Winchester provenance), that 'C.C.C.C. 41 and the *Læceboc* (Royal 12 D.xvii) have a charm in common (p. 17) and that Bald's Leechbook is likewise by a Winchester scribe' (928).

389 **Braekmann, Willy L.** 'Notes on Old English Charms II.' *Neophilologus* 67 (1983): 605–10.

Braekman reads the charm to cure a horse in *Lac* 106 (Storms 84), unsatisfactorily emended by Grattan and Singer, **326**, as the opening lines of a hymn of praise to Mary which foreshadows the defeat of evil ('Arcus super nos sedit, uirgo [Maria] natabit, lux et [h]ora sedebit'). *Arcus* is associated with Satan and the first horseman of Rev. 6.2. The *Arcus* passage is employed in later medieval charms for a woman's delivery, but is more likely to have originally been a horse charm. The celestial letter in *Lac* 102 (Storms 35) is closely paralleled by a Middle Dutch charm in BL Add. 39,638 (15th century), possibly from a lost ME version; it may preserve a few words which are closer to the original than the OE version. Another 15th century Dutch parallel is noted by Storms, **325**, 213. [See Olsan, **398A**.]

390 **Cameron, M.L.** 'Bald's *Leechbook*: Its Sources and their Use in its Compilation.' *Anglo-Saxon England* 12 (1983): 153–82.

Cameron's purpose here (see Cameron, **551**) is to clarify the problem of sources and their use in compiling *Lb*1&2, to assess the compiler's competence, and determine the social and economic conditions implied as prevailing in England. *Lb*1&2 shares several recipes with *Herb*, which was perhaps translated into OE as early as *Lb*1&2: but because *Herb* shares so many recipes with other collections, one cannot assume it was a primary source.

The close interrelation of one group of sources (*Passionarius Galeni*, *Petrocellus*, and others) makes it impossible to tell which of them may have been in the hands of the compiler. Problems with the relation of *Lb*1&2 to the Omont Fragment and the Nowell transcript [FC B.21.2.3] are also noted: Cameron regards *Lb*1&2 as a corrupt copy of much older exemplars. The compiler (seemingly a practising physician) appears to have been highly selective in the interests of practical utility; the selection of materials also seems to have been influenced by what was available in England. Cameron cautions that it is difficult to distinguish mistranslation from corruption, and the translator may have been no less competent than his Greek and Latin originals. Cameron regards the prevalence of certain types of cures as an index of social actuality; he instances cures for diseases of the eye, the liver, and the spleen and for dysentery and malaria: 'All in all, it was not a healthy community, resembling in this way most primitive communities in similar situations today' (177). Cameron's summary conclusion stresses the level of expertise and predominately rational approach of *Lb*1&2, which is, in sum, 'a precious social and cultural, as well as medical, document, and deserves close study in all its aspects' (178). Appendix, 178–82, gives text and sources of *Lb*1.4, with translation.

391 Dresher, Bezalel Elan. 'Second Fronting in the Old English Dialect of the Omont Leaf.' *Cahiers Linguistiques d'Ottawa* 12 (1984): 39–48.

Argues that the Omont Fragment 'provides new evidence that the controversial sound change known as the "Second Fronting" actually consisted of two separate changes: the addition of a raising rule and the loss of a backing rule' (39). The Fragment is in a dialect in which *a*-Restoration has been lost, although it has not added *æ*-Raising; it thus removes the last remaining argument for the unity of the changes traditionally grouped under the name of the Second Fronting. Cameron's failure to treat these two changes separately (**330**) results in 'a seemingly paradoxical situation' (45–6).

392 Meaney, Audrey L. 'Ælfric and Idolatry.' *Journal of Religious History* 13 (1984): 119–35.

Meaney argues that superstitious and magical practices condemned by Ælfric are ones he believed to be current in late Anglo-Saxon England, and that his purpose was political: 'A "white witch" would have been more dangerous than a black one, because her magic would seduce men away from Christianity' (135). In the discussion of practices such as (lunar) divination, lucky days and Egyptian days, Meaney concurs with Henel, **222**, that there is no evidence of native Germanic or Arabian influenced beliefs concerning the planets (128), but she regards the Epiphany Homily (*contra* Wendel, **347**, 46) as evidence of contemporary beliefs in planetary influence, and disagrees with Henel, **222**, 296 ff., that the *Pseudo-Egbert Penitential* is valueless as a source for English circumstances. OE prognostic texts are cited only at 124–5; Ælfric's conception of unlucky days for letting blood

from livestock differs from the 'Egyptian days' of FC B.23.2.4, and two
distinct traditions may have become confused. Ælfric's condemnations of
medical magic are discussed at 126–35: 'country people must be brought
to see how dangerous their devotion to these cunning men and women was;
they might obtain health from them in this life, but they would be damned
for it in the next' (135).

393 **Meaney, Audrey, L.** 'Variant Versions of Old English Medical Remedies
and the Compilation of Bald's *Leechbook.' Anglo-Saxon England* 13 (1984):
235–68.

Meaney examines the relationships of the 100 or so extant medical remedies preserved, usually in different manuscripts, in two or three versions,
which are obviously closely related, in order to draw conclusions about the
method of compilation of *Lb*1&2. She describes and compares *Lb*1&2 and
*Lb*3 (in which most of the repeated remedies appear at least once), and
then examines four recipe collections which have minor parallels with *Lb*
(FC B.21.2.4, FC B.21.2.2, the Omont Fragment, and the *De Beta* group in
Harley 6258B). She then discusses the important duplications in the Nowell
transcript [FC B.21.2.3] and in *Lac* (table of correspondences, 238–9, 259).
Meaney concludes that, even before Alfred's time, remedies were circulating
independently, and little groups must have started to adhere. *Lb*1&2, resulting from an Alfredian compilation, is 'the most comprehensive and best
organized of all the OE medical compilations.' She suggests, tentatively,
that the scribe of Otho B.xi [FC B.21.2.3] was copying from 'the last few
surviving sheets' of the Alfredian compilation (a suggestion based in part on
parallels between the arrangement of this and *Lb*1&2 (detailed in Appendix,
265–68). There must have been at least one intermediate stage between the
exemplar of Otho and *Lb*1&2 as it is found in Royal. *Lac* alone offers evidence of an intermediate stage: it 'could not have been directly copied from
Royal ... [it] must have been copied from a version midway between that
underlying Otho and our extant text in Royal' (263). But the relationship
of the remedies in *Lb*1&2 and *Lac* is highly complex and elusive—there may,
for instance, have been *two* intermediate stages between Otho's exemplar
and Royal; or the Alfredian version may have been partly destroyed after it
was copied into Royal and only fragments of it came into the hands of the
Lac compiler.

394 **Healey, Antoinette di Paolo.** 'Anglo-Saxon Use of the Apocryphal Gospel.' *The Anglo-Saxons: Synthesis and Achievement.* Ed. J. Douglas Woods
and David A.E. Pelteret. Waterloo, Ont.: Wilfrid Laurier UP, 1985. 93–104.

Healey demonstrates that, although apocryphal material was condemned
by Ælfric, the *Gospel of Nicodemus*, the *Gospel of Pseudo-Matthew* and
Vindicta Salvatoris (Legend of St Veronica) influenced poets, stone carvers
and medical charms; in a cure for malaria in *Lb*, Veronica is silently invoked

because her own cure was effected in silence when she touched the hem of Christ's robe [Storms 33].

395 Jolly, Karen Louise. 'Anglo-Saxon Charms in the Context of a Christian World View.' *Journal of Medieval History* 11 (1985): 279–93.

Jolly argues that the charms, 'far from being examples of the remnants of paganism, are evidence of the integration of popular material into a Christian view of the world' (279). She first outlines the Augustinian view of the world, as found in Ælfric's homilies, and then analyses the 'elf' charms, which are grouped together in *Lb*3.61–8; Jolly considers that Storms, **325**, and Grendon, **314**, have distorted the nature of the charms by decontextualizing them and that they have given insufficient attention to Christian ritual. She concludes that the charms are not magic because 'they fight the very evil by which magic is defined' (291); nor can they be classified as miracles in Augustinian terms, because they are not used to display a sign from God to humanity, but they are Christian in their exclusion of pagan elements and their inclusion of Christian elements, and by virtue of the fact that they 'occur in Christian texts for use by Christian priests to perform for a Christian people. Any who used these charms would have regarded them as consistent with a Christian world view, and we would be wise to do the same—setting them firmly within the Christian tradition of late Anglo-Saxon England' (291).

396 Meaney, Audrey L. 'London, British Library Additional Ms. 43703.' *Old English Newsletter* 19.1 (1985): 34–5.

A note on Nowell's 1562 transcript of herbal recipes, ff. 261–4 (reproduced).

397 Stuart, Heather. 'Utterance Instructions in Anglo-Saxon Charms.' *Parergon* NS 3 (1985): 31–7.

Stuart argues that the choice between *cweþan* and *singan* in the utterance instruction is determined by the type of incantation used. Examples are drawn from the metrical charms [FC A.43.11, 1, 7, 6, 2, 4], and from *Lac* [Storms 65], *Lb*1 (Cockayne, **297**, 2: 136, 116, 114 [Storms 81]) and *Herb* (Cockayne, **400**, 1: 120). *Contra* Sawyer, **295**, Stuart considers that the metrical legal formula attached to the cattle-thief charm in *Textus Roffensis* [FC B.23.1.6] must be part of the incantation, because the change from *cweþan* to *singan* in the utterance instruction is consistent with one of the general principles she discerns, that long poetic incantations are to be 'sung.'

398 Brown, George Hardin. 'Solving the "Solve" Riddle in B.L. MS Harley 585.' *Viator* 18 (1987): 45–51.

'Solue iubedster catenis,' in the charm entitled 'Gif wif ne mæge bearn beran' [*Lac* 98], is a truncated and slightly corrupted version of a verse directed to St Peter, commonly occurring in the liturgy and in anthologies (e.g., the 8th century epigrams of Mildred of Worcester); it occurs on f. 183,

and Brown considers that f. 179/10 to the end of *Lac* is more than usually
garbled, in a different hand, and thus a later addition by an author (whether
or not the scribe) who had a tenuous knowledge of Latin. *Contra* Grattan
and Singer, **326**, 186–7—who relocate the heading to serve as a title for three
charms on f. 185rv ('Pagan Rites for Miscarriage'), rearrange the words to
' "iube; solue, deus," ter, "catenis," ' and attach them to the end of the
preceding charm for an elf-shot horse—Brown argues that the heading has
not been misplaced, and that a verse that was addressed to the 'heavenly
key-bearing authority of binding and loosing' is 'apt as a Christian charm
against miscarriage or impeded birth' (49).

398A Olsan, Lea. 'The *Arcus* Charms and Christian Magic.' *Neophilologus* 73
(1989): 438–47.

Olsan interprets Storms 84 as a charm to induce a horse to give birth,
which combines and unifies thought, language and action. She argues
that *wið cyrnla*, which Braekman, **389**, (following Grattan and Singer,
326, and others) retained in his reconstruction, belongs (as Cockayne, **298**,
suggested) to the preceding charm in *Lac*. *Arcus*, interpreted as Satan by
Braekman, is the rainbow of Gen. 9.12–13. It symbolized divine power over
the waters and help in distress (Ælfric's *Interrogationes Sigewulf*), and had a
place in the humoral theory of correspondences (*PD*; Cockayne, **298**, 3: 82,
84); graphic representation of this theory in *ByrM* illuminates *virgo maria
natabit* and other phrases in the parallel charm (for childbirth) in Royal 17
A.viii (14th century). Storms 84, a 'rudimentary Anglo-Saxon variant,' is 'a
three part incantation to be spoken 3×3 times, with nine Pater Nosters to
insure the Christianity of the whole procedure' (444), which is unique in the
use of barley bread; it is an instance of belief in the magical power of words
(*bere*, 'barley,' resembles *beren*, 'to bear' and *berende*, 'fruitful'). 'In the
ritual of pronouncing the charm over the barley bread and then introducing
it into the body of the horse, the leech induces the birth, first because the
bread becomes a tangible vehicle of the incantation, and second because the
name of the remedy, *beren hlaf*, has homeopathic efficacy' (445).

THE HERBARIUM COMPLEX:
ENLARGED HERBARIUM AND MEDICINA DE QUADRUPEDIBUS

MANUSCRIPTS

THE ESTABLISHED OE CANON (BVH)   FC B.21.1.1

Oxford, Bodleian, Hatton 76, ff. 68r–73v (table of con-   B
    tents); 74r–124r (*Herb*); 124v–130r (*MedQuad*)
Ker 328B, art. 1   s. xi med.
(Transcript: Bodleian, Junius 58)

London, British Library, Harley 585, ff. 1r–101v (*Herb*);   H
    101v–14v (*MedQuad*); 115r–29v (table of contents)
Ker 231, art. 1   s. x/xi, xi[1]

London, British Library, Cotton Vitellius C.iii,   V
    ff. 12r–18v (table of contents); 19r–74v (*Herb*); 75r–
    82v (*MedQuad*)
Ker 219, art. 1   s. xi[1]

'PERI DIDAXEON VERSION'[1]   NOT LISTED FC

London, British Library, Harley 6258B, ff. 1r–44r   O
    (*Herb*); 44v–51r (*MedQuad*); f. 51r, 'Wið eafodece
    pollege'; f. 51v, *De Beta*
Ker, xix, and Ker, *Suppl.*, post s. xii

SUMMARY NOTE ON THE FOUR VERSIONS

H is incomplete, and more disordered than V. The table of contents in BVH refers only to *Herb*; in H it follows *MedQuad* instead of preceding *Herb* as it does in V (the only illustrated copy) as well as in B (which has a leather tag sewn in to mark the beginning of the table of contents). Generally, B and V are more closely related to one another than to H. O is later (and only residually OE), as well as shorter; it differs from the other three versions in being alphabetically organized, and it has no table of contents. The chronology of BVH is not firmly established; the most recent consideration of dating makes V significantly later than H.

---

[1] This title, used here to identify the manuscript copy whose language is not universally regarded as OE, does not have wider currency.

MANUSCRIPTS; DESCRIPTION (following Ker and de Vriend)

The manuscript presentation of the text is described by de Vriend, **401**, xi–xx, on whom the following summary draws, as well as on Ker. De Vriend also gives a full list of manuscript contents and of earlier manuscript descriptions. V, particularly its full page illustrations, has been studied by Voigts (see pp. 323–4 below, 'Illustrations'). Voigts, **414**, studies anew the codex as a whole and its history. Flom, **412**, may still be of interest.

Vitellius C.iii (V)

Herb and *MedQuad* occupy most of ff. 11–85; these folios constitute the second of three originally separate manuscripts now bound together. (The remaining texts in this manuscript are a collection of Latin and OE recipes in different 11th–13th century hands which begin on the last leaf of *MedQuad*; see 'Recipe Collections,' FC B.21.5.8, p. 238), and a 13th century Latin tract on urine.) *Herb*, *MedQuad* and the table of contents are mostly written in a single, very regular hand (also described by Flom, **412**). The exceptions (listed by de Vriend, xv–xvi) include the OE plant names in the titles of chapters in the text of *Herb* and the animal names belonging to some of the additional drawings in *Herb*; two recipes on f. 18v and a note on f. 17v; the numbering of the chapters in the table of contents and the text. Folios 62–74 are disarranged, having been bound in the wrong order. Five chapters are omitted from the table of contents (de Vriend, chs. XI, LXXI, XCI, XCIX and CLXXX), and the chapters are incorrectly numbered I–CLXXIX, in a hand which Ker dates s. xi med. The words 'Wið innoþes astyrunge' (f. 18v), which Cockayne includes under 'Fly Leaf Leechdoms' (1: 378), belong to the table of contents of *Herb* (cf. Cockayne, **400**, 1: 68/14).

The top lines of many folios are deformed as a result of shrinkage in the 1731 fire, and one of the green pigments used in the illustrations has greatly damaged several folios. James agreed with Wanley in identifying this manuscript with the 'Herbarius anglice depictus' in the Catalogue of Henry Eastry, Prior of Christchurch (d. 1331), but Ker doubts this identification.

Hatton 76 (B)

Two originally separate manuscripts are bound together; *Herb* and *Med-Quad* on ff. 68–130r comprise the bulk of Part B, and are mostly written in a single regular hand, which Ker dates s. xi med. The exceptions (listed by de Vriend, xxi–xxii), include the titles and the entire chs. CXX–CXXIII in the table of contents (in a different contemporary hand) and the titles in the text, which are in a later hand (probably 12th century).

Ker states that the table of contents is headed 'Incipiunt capitel (?) libri medicinalis' and numbered I–CLXXXIII, the entry 'saxifraga' being omitted between XCVII and XCVIII, as in V. Single leaves are missing after ff. 72, 114, 119, and 130, and part of f. 130 has been cut away. A leather tag sewn to f. 68 marks the beginning of the herbal. Both Parts A and B of the manuscript were at Worcester in s. xiii in.

The Junius transcript of Hatton 76 is described by de Vriend as 'very accurate.'

Harley 585 (H)

Herb is followed by the only surviving copy of *Lacnunga*; the table of contents (ff. 115r–29v) in this version follows *MedQuad*, which is incomplete. H lacks the illustrations found in V and for which spaces have been left in H. It is written in 'a rather rough and debased square Anglo-Saxon minuscule' (Ker).

Ker states that *Herb* begins imperfectly in ch. 4 (de Vriend, ch. IV.10), before which 10 or 12 leaves are missing, containing chs. 1–3, 6–8 and part of 9. *MedQuad* ends imperfectly at the bottom of f. 114v (de Vriend, ch. VI.6). Since ff. 114–21 are a regular quire of eight leaves, it is unlikely that the rest of the text of *MedQuad*, as edited by Cockayne (VB), was ever in this manuscript. The scribe copied the herbal from an exemplar in which the leaves were in disorder at two points. As a result, chs. 6–8 and part of 9 came here between chs. 1 and 11 and chs. 75–97, and part of ch. 98 came between ch. 5 and the second part of ch. 9. The numbering of chapters was altered to run consecutively and was adopted in the table of contents. The table of contents, added s. xi[1], headed 'Incipiunt capituli libri medicinalis,' ends imperfectly at the title for ch. 178. One leaf is missing after f. 129. More careful scrutiny of de Vriend's explanation of the disorder (xxiv) might reveal that he expresses the matter differently because he has a different conception of the process.

Harley 6258B (O)

O was not described by Wanley and is not listed in Ker's *Catalogue* because he regarded it as post-1200 (see Ker, xix). De Vriend, **401** and **405**, however, argues that O is OE, and the view has gained currency (see further below, '*Peri Didaxeon* Version,' pp. 315–16).

O is a poor copy and contains no illustrations; Cockayne, **400**, 1: lxxxiv, described it as 'a mean manuscript.' De Vriend states that the text of the codex is in one hand; the same hand or one similar is responsible for the chapter titles, the titles of cures added in the margin, and most glosses. It also contains *Peri Didaxeon*, in the same hand (see further below, pp. 327–8). Smaller sized leaves were inserted after the completion of the original; all but f. 22 are in the correct (alphabetical) position. The manuscript, especially ff. 11–19, is badly damaged and hard to read, probably through fire, and has been remounted. The script is irregular and untidy.

COMPOSITION OF THE TEXT; RELATIONSHIP OF
THE THREE OLDEST VERSIONS (BVH)

The Herbarium Complex is based on a number of treatises, originally distinct, but commonly associated in Latin manuscripts. Cockayne, **400**, printed the OE translation as a tripartite work ('Herbarium of Apuleius,' 'Herbarium continued from Dioskurides, etc.' and 'Medicina de Quadrupedibus'). It is now more usually regarded as consisting of two parts, the enlarged Herbarium and the *Medicina de Quadrupedibus*, although a few writers (Stuart, **536**, Lambert, **502**) distinguish 'the OE Dioscorides.' The title '*Herbarium*' appears on the title page of V (f. 19v) and in most Latin manuscripts, but the title '*Medicina de Quadrupedibus*,' first used by Junius in his transcript of B, was given currency by Cockayne. There is broad agreement concerning the general nature of the sources, except that the derivation of chs. 135–85, once thought to derive from *Materia Medica*, is still under discussion (see most recently, Cameron, **551**, Hofstetter, **423**, and Riddle, **422**). There is a recent summary outline of the composition of *Herb* in D'Aronco, **425**.

1. The Enlarged Herbarium

   (a) *De herba vetonnica liber* (ch. 1)

   (b) Herbarium pseudo-Apulei (chs. 2–132)

   (c) 'Dioscorides': *Materia medica/Liber medicinae ex herbis femininis/Curae Herbis* (chs. 133–85)

2. *Medicina de Quadrupedibus*

   (a) *Liber de taxone* (ch. 1)

   (b) Treatise on the mulberry (ch. 2)

   (c) 'Sextus Placitus': short or A-version of *Liber medicinae ex animalibus* (chs. 3–14)

Like the Latin versions, the enlarged Herbarium in the three oldest English versions, BVH, is accompanied by a table of contents (which, in H, follows *MedQuad*, instead of preceding *Herb*). The OE Herbarium, in its complete form, BV) consists of 185 chapters, each containing recipes for the medical use of a specific plant, often accompanied by a description of the plant and its habitat. The first chapter concerns the uses of betony. The chapters are numbered in the text but, particularly in B and H, there are discrepancies between the table of contents and the numbering in the text.

MedQuad is written in BVH, as well as in O, as a continuous text; as edited by de Vriend, **401** and **405**, *MedQuad* consists of 14 chapters. The first of these is what Singer described as 'a disgusting little treatise on the badger' (**327**, xxi) and takes the form of a letter from one Idpartus, King of the Egyptians, to the Emperor Octavius; then follow prescriptions which make use of mulberry (ch. 2). These two chapters were printed as one by Cockayne. Then follow 12 sections on the medical uses of various animals (one each on the hart, the fox, the hare, the ram, the boar, the wolf, the lion, the bull, the elephant, and the dog, and two chapters on the buck).

H's text is incomplete (chapters are missing at the beginning of *Herb* and from the Sextus Placitus section of *MedQuad*), and so is its table of contents. B and V are identical in their ordering of chapters: the organization of *Herb* in H is slightly different, but this is probably the accidental result of the disorderly state of the scribe's exemplar. De Vriend, **401**, shows that all of the three oldest versions have a common archetype, but B and V are more closely related to one another than to H, which belongs to a different branch.

DATE AND PROVENANCE OF THE THREE EARLIEST MANUSCRIPTS (BVH); LANGUAGE

The individual manuscripts are variously dated, and there is no agreement on the relative order of dating. On Ker's dating, H is the earliest (s. x/xi), V is s. xi¹, and B is the latest (s. xi med.). Beccaria, **514**, however, makes H the latest: he dates B and V first half of the 11th century, and H mid-11th century. He is thus roughly in agreement with Cockayne, **400**, who dated both B and V between 1000 and 1066, and H a little later. Voigts, **414** and **417**, agrees with Ker's mid-11th century dating of B; but she adopts an early date for H (late 10th century), and argues for the latest possible mid-11th century date for V. Wright, **294**, was in agreement with Ker on V (*c.* 1000); Flom's dating of V (1040–50) was uniquely narrow (**412**); Grattan and Singer's dating of V (*c.* 950) is egregious (**326**, 77; also Singer, **327**, xxi). De Vriend, **401**, records only the datings of previous scholars.

Cockayne, like Wanley, identified V with the codex referred to in a late medieval Christ Church catalogue, and a Christ Church provenance is fairly generally assumed. Flom, **412**, assigned it to either Canterbury or Rochester. Voigts, **414** and **417**, however, argues strongly for an East Anglian provenance for V. Neither B nor H appear to have been assigned. De Vriend argues, on linguistic grounds, that *MedQuad* is directly descended from an early Anglian original, probably 8th century, and that *Herb* is either a direct descendant from an early version which was adapted to late WS standard, or else a new translation; this is doubted by Bately, **564**.

'PERI DIDAXEON VERSION' (O); LANGUAGE, DATE AND DIALECT, TEXTUAL RELATIONSHIP; LEXICOGRAPHY

The vernacular version of the Herbarium Complex in O, regarded by Ker as post-12th century, was deliberately excluded from both his *Catalogue* and *Supplement*. It was so universally regarded as ME when the *Plan for the Dictionary of Old English* appeared in 1973 that, despite the intention to include in the new OE dictionary everything that *MED* includes as OE, the O version of *Herb* is not listed in FC. But de Vriend's edition of *MedQuad* (405) argued that the Herbarium Complex in O was an example of residual OE (i.e., late WS copied by a scribe able to understand and copy texts in late WS *Schriftsprache*, but so influenced by the linguistic changes of his own period that these are frequently reflected in texts copied by him). The argument (essentially depending on the interpretation of statistical distribution of forms) is repeated in his EETS edition of *Herb* and *MedQuad*, **401**. De Vriend, **401**, xxx, also addressed Ker's post-12th century dating, and pointed out that Berberich, **402**, the first to edit *Herb* from O, as well as Wright, **294**, and *MED*, date O mid-12th century, and Grattan and Singer, **326**, date it 1130; de Vriend dates it second half of the 12th century 'at the latest.' Delcourt, **404**, another early editor of O, also dated it mid-12th century, but as de Vriend also points out, both Delcourt and Berberich were at pains to establish the ME character of the language of O. Hallender, **421**, reviewing de Vriend, **405**, commended the edition but found his case for regarding O as OE unconvincing.

O is not only later but shorter than the other three versions and different in organization. There is no table of contents. *Herb* is arranged in rough alphabetical order ('*a*-order'), according to the Latin names, and marginal titles are prefixed to the cures they belong to, in round brackets. There are fewer cures, and some cures are shorter than their parallels in BVH. There are some close resemblances to B, but no close relationship can be established; de Vriend concludes, however, that O belongs to the same textual tradition as the other three versions. He considers that the translation underlying O was made in the reign of Alfred and that the translator was Anglian. Berberich described the language of *Herb* as late WS, but Delcourt concluded that *MedQuad* originated on the border of WS and Anglian or WS and Kentish territory.

Botanical terms are studied by D'Aronco, **425** (Enlarged Herbal only), and the Herbarium Complex is included in Vol. 2 of Bierbaumer's alphabetical lists of OE botanical terms, **416**. D'Aronco agrees with de Vriend that O should be regarded as OE. For botanical terms, see further 'Plant Names,' pp. 325–6.

DE BETA RECIPES

MedQuad is immediately followed in O by a single OE recipe ('Wið eafodece pollege') and a group of recipes (six OE and three Latin) headed 'De Beta,' which were printed as 'Fly Leaf Leechdoms' by Cockayne, **400**, 1: 380–2. The *De Beta* group was included by Berberich in his edition of *Herb* (**402**). 'Wið eafodece pollege,' which Berberich omitted, was printed by Delcourt, **404**. Meaney, **393**, includes discussion of *De Beta*. She finds that the last four recipes in *De Beta* duplicate four in Bald's Leechbook; two of these (for sinew problems), which both employ mugwort, are translated from the

Latin Herbarium; but whereas in most manuscripts of that work, Latin or OE, the two remedies belong to different species of mugwort, in *Lb* and O they follow each other immediately and no distinction of species is made. She thinks it likely that these two versions go back to a common ancestor in OE, and that this was different from the translation underlying the complete English Herbarium in V and its cognates (including O).

EDITIONS

Cockayne, in his edition of the Herbarium Complex (**400**), printed V with variants from B and H and occasionally O, remarking: 'The collation of this MS. [O] was not carried through, it was not desirable. For the history of our language it may some day be required that the whole should be printed for comparison with our earlier text' (1: lxxxv). Berberich, **402**, who edited *Herb* from O in 1902, and Delcourt, **404**, who edited *MedQuad* from the same manuscript in 1914, examined phonology and inflexions at length. Hilbelink's incomplete edition of *Herb* from V (chs. 1–132 only, without the table of contents) was also a dissertation exercise in the study of phonology (**403**).

De Vriend's edition of *MedQuad* (**405**) is a parallel edition of V (with variants from BH) and a Latin text which, he showed, belonged to the same family as the OE translations (Lucca 296, with textual variants from Harley 4968); he also printed parallel passages from the Latin text in Bodley 130. De Vriend's choice of manuscripts reflects the three significant arguments he advanced in this edition; the OE character of O, the family group to which the OE translations belong, and the direction of the translation of Bodley 130 (see 'Plant Names,' p. 325). De Vriend's EETS edition of both *Herb* and *MedQuad* (**401**) also prints parallel V and O; a different group of Latin manuscripts is drawn into relationship with *Herb*, and Bodley 130 is excluded from consideration. Otherwise the EETS edition incorporates, in a compressed form, most of the material in the earlier edition of *MedQuad*; only **405** carries a translation of V.

ORIGINS OF THE HERBAL AND THE LATIN TEXTUAL TRADITION

Establishment of the relationship of OE works translated from Latin necessarily depends on the prior elucidation of the Latin textual tradition; in the case of the Herbarium (Complex in more than one sense of the word) there are many studies, indispensable to the specialist scholar conducting independent research into the relationship of the OE to the Latin manuscripts, which make little or no reference to the OE translations (only a few are listed in this volume of annotations). For all other purposes, prior study of the Latin textual tradition is more than adequately mediated through the work of de Vriend, **401** and **405**, and Voigts, **414** and **420**, which supersede the accounts offered in Singer's various surveys of the classical sources of Anglo-Saxon medical literature (such as the introduction to Grattan and

Singer, **326**, and Singer's introduction to the revised edition of Cockayne, **327**). There are, in addition, three publications by Singer which trace the development of the Herbarium of pseudo-Apuleius, deriving it from a Greek tradition of illustrated herbals that reaches back to the 4th century BC, **410**, **483** and **484**, which need to be used with caution. The most comprehensive of these three studies, Singer, **410**, also contains some extended discussion of the OE Herbal, chiefly the illustrations in V. (Arber, **411**, deals only with botany as a scientific study from the classical period onwards, not the textual tradition.)

The general configurations of the Latin textual tradition were established by Howald and Sigerist, 1927 (this standard edition of the Latin text does not include pseudo-Dioscorides).[2] Articles by Sigerist are often mentioned as useful and/or having important bearing on the Latin textual tradition (**488**, **492** and **501**). Howald and Sigerist, xxvi, and subsequently Singer, produced charts illustrating the relationship of the extant manuscripts (see Grattan and Singer, **326**, 26, which places V in the South Italian Group, in a direct line of descent from Montecassino V.97; see below, 'Nearest Source Latin Manuscripts,' p. 321). Of these charts, Voigts, **414**, remarks: 'They are useful in showing the multitude of extant MSS. and in illustrating in a general way the complexities of the tradition. Hunger [**493**] contends that Howald and Sigerist's division of the tradition into three recensions ... has been helpful, but he suggests that their chart depicting lines of descent, like the charts of Charles Singer, is not of particular use. Without denigrating the magnitude of the efforts of these three men, I would reiterate that the differing pictorial and textual recensions may render meaningless a stem that does not differentiate between the two. Further, the stems omit some MSS. and are characterized by a number of small errors' (59).

De Vriend's two editions represent the only comprehensive study of the relationship of the OE to the Latin manuscripts. Scholarship to date is independently summarized by D'Aronco, in a study of the botanical lexicon of *Herb*, which also takes account of the work of Hofstetter, **423**. Voigts, **418** and **420**, is primarily concerned with the Latin tradition in so far as it has bearing on the author portrait in V, but is more broadly informative, and her dissertation, **414**, though pre-dating de Vriend, still serves as a valuable introduction to the area. The following summary is drawn from the work of these three scholars.

---

[2] *Antonii Musae de herba vettonica liber. Pseudoapulei herbarius. Anonymi de taxone liber. Sexti Placiti liber medicinae ex animalibus, etc.*, ed. E. Howald and H.E. Sigerist, Corpus Medicorum Latinorum 4 (Leipzig: Teubner, 1927). For editions of pseudo-Dioscorides see H.F. Kästner, 'Pseudo-Dioscoridis de Herbis Femininis,' *Hermes* 31 (1896): 578–636, and 32 (1897): 160; John M. Riddle, 'Dioscorides,' *Catalogus Translationum et Commentariorum: Medieval and Renaissance Latin Translations and Commentaries*, ed. F. Edward Cranz and Paul O. Kristeller (Washington: Catholic U of America P, 1980) 4: 1–143, 6 vols. to date, 1960–.

Herbarium

The Herbarium of pseudo-Apuleius is itself a compilation of many sources, and draws particularly on Pliny's *Naturalis Historia*. In its original form the Herbarium consisted of 130 chapters: a chapter on the mandrake was added at an early date. It is thought to have originated either in South Italy (particularly in Sicily)[3] or in North Africa (Hunger, **493**, xviii). Although Singer, **410**, argued that it was translated from Greek, both Sigerist, **488**, and Hunger, **493**, argued that there is no evidence of a Greek original, and most scholars accept that the Herbarium was composed in Latin in the 4th century AD. (For a full bibliography, see Voigts, **420**, 215, n. 8.) It was attributed to the second century Platonic philosopher, Apuleius. Various reasons have been suggested for this fictitious attribution. One view is that it was intended to give the work more authority (e.g., Sigerist, **492**, 33–4). Others have suggested that a confusion of names is involved: Apuleius may be a corruption of Peleus, the name of the father of Achilles, whose great-grandfather Chiron, the inventor of medical botany, was to instruct him in the art of healing,[4] or it could be a Christian surrogate for Apollo (Grattan and Singer, **326**, 78). Voigts, **420**, argues that Apuleius's association with the god of medicine was a significant factor in the attribution.

In older Latin manuscripts *De herba vetonica* is a separate work, but it merged with the Herbarium early on; de Vriend concludes that, although it is attributed to Antonius Musa, physician to the Emperor Augustine, it belongs to the same tradition as the Herbarium and is contemporaneous with it. *Liber medicinae ex herbis femininis* is usually (not invariably) found in combination with the Herbarium, but always appears as an independent text with its own *incipit* and *explicit*. It appears to have been in existence by the 6th century. The attribution to Dioscorides, the 1st century author of *De materia medica*, is fictitious, although the two works contain some comparable material. De Vriend considers that the *Liber medicinae* contains three categories of chapters: some are clearly from *De materia medica*, other chapters bear a loose relation to chapters in the Herbarium, and others are not found in any other extant text.

Medicina de Quadrupedibus

Liber de taxone and *Liber medicinae ex animalibus* were commonly associated with the Herbarium of pseudo-Apuleius: their composition is dated to the 5th century. *Liber de taxone* purports to be a letter addressed to Octavius from a fictitious Egyptian King, Idpartus; the real author has not been identified. Sextus Placitus, to whom *Liber medicinae ex animalibus* is attributed, cannot be identified either, and most scholars agree

---

[3] Ch. H. Talbot, 'Medico-Historical Introduction,' C.H. Talbot and F. Unterkircher, *Medicina Antiqua. Libri quattuor medicinae. Codex Vindobonensis 93 der österreichischen Nationalbibliothek*, Codices Selecti 27 (Graz: Akademische Drucke, 1972), *Kommentarband*, 11–35, at 35.

[4] Talbot 29.

with Cockayne, **400**, 1: lxxxix, that he was 'a nominis umbra.' Like the
Herbarium, *Liber medicinae ex animalibus* draws liberally on Pliny's *Natural History*, and it may have been compiled to supplement the Herbarium.
There are two versions of *Liber medicinae*: the B version is closer to the
archetype than the A-Version. The A-Version is not only shorter than the
B-Version; there are differences in substance, wording and organization,
and the cures derived from Pliny show less deviation from the original in
the B-Version. Only two early Latin manuscripts (Lucca 296 and Harley
4986) contain the A-Version of Sextus Placitus; and Lucca is the only early
Latin manuscript that contains the treatise on the mulberry.

PECULIARITIES OF THE OE IN RELATION TO
THE (EARLIEST) LATIN MSS

The OE translation, de Vriend establishes, is unusual in containing the A-
Version of Sextus Placitus. It also contains one of the two earliest extant
versions of the treatise on the mulberry. Although BVH give no indication that the treatise on the mulberry is distinct from *Liber de taxone* (O
contains an illegible marginal note at this point), the treatise contains no
mention of any four-footed animals and is evidently intrusive. The OE
Herbarium Complex is also peculiar in its organization. In most Latin
manuscripts *Medicina de Quadrupedibus* comes after the Herbarium and is
followed by *Liber medicinae ex herbis femininis*. The most striking oddi-
ties are in chs. 133–85, most recently studied by Hofstetter, **423**. D'Aronco,
425, explains: 'The OE Herbarium treats only 53 plants while the *Liber
medicinae ex herbis femininis* treats 71; there is no agreement in the order in which plants are treated; there are changes in the medical uses of
herbs; and some plants that appear in OE Herbarium derive directly from
Dioscorides, *De materia medica*, while for others there seems to be no direct
Latin source' (97). The influence of Dioscorides has recently been studied
in depth by Riddle, **422** and **556**, and the forthcoming second volume of
his full-length work will doubtless cast further light on this matter.

Another peculiar characteristic of *Herb* is the table of contents; in this,
names of herbs are given in Latin and OE and those of the cures in OE.
Two Latin recensions of the Herbarium contain an index, but this differs
from the OE translation. Whereas in the Latin manuscripts the index
lists ailments according to head-to-toe order and gives the chapter number
where the remedy can be found, the OE index gives names of plants with the
numbers of the relevant chapters, followed by a list of ailments or symptoms
for which the plant supplies remedies. As Voigts, **543**, points out, this is
less sophisticated, but shows that the herbals are not mindless copying, as
Singer claimed (**410**, **483** and **484**), but were for practical use.

Other additions and omissions have been noted; as, for instance, D'Aronco points out that the translator omitted some parts of *De herba vetonnica
liber* such as the greetings of Antonio Musa to M. Agrippa, and the

celebration of the virtues of the betony and the final prayer to the plant. Singer, **327**, remarks that there are additions of a superstitious character to all sections.

ENGLISH KNOWLEDGE OF THE HERBARIUM COMPLEX
(including Westphalia 192)

It is generally considered that the existence of three (or four) OE translations of the Herbarium Complex is evidence of the work's popularity in England. There are a number of English manuscripts of the Latin text, and at least one of these (British Library, Add. 8926) is *c.* 1000. Further, de Vriend, **405**, argues that Bodley 130 (see 'Plant Names,' p. 325) is a Latin translation from an OE version that belonged to the same textual tradition as the surviving OE works. De Vriend argues that *MedQuad* and probably *Herb* were originally translated in the 8th century; Cameron, **551**, takes a more conservative view. He states that it is not clear how long the complex had been known in England, but suggests that the Latin Herbarium may have been known in England in the 9th century since Herten, Westphalia 192, ff. 1–20, a 9th century manuscript containing an illustrated Herbarium, may have been of English origin. Westphalia 192 was destroyed during the 1939–45 war, but was described by Sudhoff, 1917.[5]

NEAREST SOURCE LATIN MANUSCRIPTS (including
Montecassino V.97; Lucca 296; Vossianus Q.9; Harley 4986)

Howald and Sigerist, 1927, listed 47 Latin manuscripts of the Herbarium, some of which are fragments; Beccaria, **514**, lists 25 which pre-date the 12th century. But there is no single Latin version that closely parallels the OE throughout. De Vriend's parallel edition of *Herb*, **401**, draws in turn on eight different Latin manuscripts; his selection of closest source manuscripts is based on early date, and on consideration of both the text and the illustrations.

Two of the eight Latin manuscripts which de Vriend regards as closely related to *Herb* are of particular interest, and commonly mentioned in connection with it. Leiden, Bibliothek der Rijksuniversiteit, Vossianus latinus Q.9 (Vo), is by far the oldest extant text (6th or 7th century). Montecassino, Archivio della Badia, V.97 (Ca), 9th/10th century, has close iconographical links with the Leiden manuscript as well as with V (a facsimile of Montecassino V.97 is found in Hunger, **493**).

In his EETS edition of *MedQuad*, **401**, de Vriend prints parallel Lucca 296 (L), with variants from Harley 4986 (Ha). These two alone contain the A-Version of *Liber Medicinae*, and L also contains the treatise on the mulberry; they also differ because both contain *Epistula de Marcellus*. De Vriend concluded that the OE version was based on a text that belonged to

---

[5] Karl Sudhoff, 'Codex Medicus Hertensis (Nr. 192),' *Archiv für Geschichte der Medizin* 10 (1917): 265–313.

the same family as Lucca, although there is no direct relationship between them. Ha is 10th–12th century, glossed in German, and probably written in Germany. L is 8th–10th century, and probably of North Italian origin.

ILLUSTRATIONS; STUDY OF THE HERBAL

Details of the illustrations are included in de Vriend's description of the manuscripts (**401**). V is handsomely illustrated throughout with coloured drawings. Like the illustrated Latin manuscripts, it has (with a few exceptions) one illustration to each chapter (plants in *Herb* and animals in *MedQuad*); there are also some additional drawings in both *Herb* and *MedQuad* (the additional drawings in *Herb* chiefly depict snakes and scorpions). There is a striking resemblance between the illustrations in V and Montecassino V.97. In B, spaces for illustrations have been left, which roughly correspond to the illustrations of V. There are also three faded stylus drawings, a stylized flower (f. 76r), a dog sitting up (f. 95r) and a dragon (f. 126v). H has 'rude marginal sketches,' mainly of serpents, and some zoomorphically elaborated initials (serpents or 'biting beasts'), and the opening capital of ch. 33 is decorated in a special way, perhaps to mark the beginning of the Dioscorides section. Some of the initials were originally coloured red, but have now faded.

Singer, in his studies of the origins and development of the illustrated herbal (**410**, **483** and **484**), pointed out that Mediterranean origin of the illustrations in V is shown by the fact that some of the plants depicted are native only to that area; the relatively accurate drawings of the scorpion also confirm that the illustrations are copies of southern originals. The continued copying of a series of plant illustrations which had, in the course of centuries of repeated copying, become so far removed from the originals that they were useless for the purposes of identification, and which, in any case, included plants which could not be cultivated in the climatic conditions of countries such as England, did nothing to enhance Singer's opinion of the human race: 'Man is an imitative animal, but we doubt if any better instance of his imitativeness could be found than this constant copying and re-copying for over a thousand years, with enormous labour and technical skill, of a futile work with its unrecognizable figures and its incomprehensible vocabulary' (**483**, 104–5). More recently, Kádár, **413**, has argued that degeneration of zoomorphic illustrations at the hands of copyists makes difficult the identification of pictorial archetypes. Voigts, **418**, regards fidelity to the representation and form of a late antique herbal as a distinctive feature of V. Among the studies of the tradition of illustration she mentions are those by Bethe, 1945, and Grape-Albers, 1977.[6]

---

[6] Erich Bethe, *Buch und Bild im Altertum* (Leipzig: Harrassowitz, 1945); Heide Grape-Albers, *Spätantike Bilder aus der Welt des Arztes: medizinische Bilderhandschriften der Spätantike und ihre mittelalterliche Überlieferung* (Wiesbaden: Pressler, 1977).

In addition to the chapter illustrations of plants and animals, V has full page drawings on ff. 11v, 19r, and a title page, f. 19v, which bears an inscription in green, red and blue capitals, surrounded by a broad ornamental fillet. The title is damaged; Voigts (differing only slightly from Ker) reads this inscription as: 'HERBARIVUM APVLEI PLATONICI QVOD ACCEPIT AB ESCOLAPIO ET ALCHIRONE CENTAVRO MAGISRO ACHILLIS.' The three figures in the author portrait are designated in the lower frame 'ESCOLAPIVS.PLATO.CENTAVRVS.' The full page illustrations, as well as a number of the plant illustrations, have been widely reproduced (the author portrait and title page are included in Voigts, **417, 418**).

Voigts, **420**, establishes that the author portrait represents Apuleius Platonicus receiving a book from the god of medicine, Aesculapius, and from Chiron the Centaur, mentor of Aesculapius (some earlier writers interpret Aesculapius as the recipient of the book), and her examination of the reasons for the attribution of the herbal to Apuleius demonstrates that the author portrait gives the work itself a close connection with the god of medicine. Voigts, **418**, examines the implications of late Anglo-Saxon monastic copying of a medical work that announces its association with a classical pagan divinity. Her conclusion suggests that the OE Herbal, and *Lac* and *Lb* also, are evidence that the hostility to non-Christian religions expressed by orthodox reformers like Ælfric and Wulfstan is in contrast with the attitudes of at least some of their contemporaries.

Voigts, **417**, dates V somewhat later than has been customary, partly on the basis of her examination of the colouring of the illustrations and plant titles; she also studies the dedication page, which she shows to have been original to the codex (it was not described by Wanley). The central figure, transfixing beasts underfoot, and flanked on either side by a soldier and a monk, was interpreted by Cockayne, **400**, 1: lxxvii, as a church dignitary for whom the work was copied, but Voigts thinks it more likely that the codex is dedicated to a bishop or abbot, a saint rather than a contemporary historical cleric. Her case for an East Anglian provenance, rather than the Christ Church provenance favoured earlier this century, involves the dedication page's stylistic connections with other Anglo-Saxon manuscript illuminations and with Franco-Flemish art. Voigts, **419**, establishes a connection between some of the *MedQuad* illustrations in V and other manuscripts.

Whereas *Lac* and *Lb* were apt to be poorly regarded by medical historians because of their non-rational cures and practices, *Herb*, though having much stronger claims to intellectual respectability by virtue of its origins in the learning of the ancient world, was liable to be dismissed as a degenerate fossil; as Singer remarked, more than once, 'the only thing English about these works is their language' (**483**, 106). Voigts, **414**, esp. 65–71, is concerned to argue against 'a tradition which views the herbal as a curious detritus of classical culture with no practical implications for the medieval culture which transmitted it' (65), and to establish in its place the view that medical codices like V were 'functional books of remedies' (67). Voigts, **418**, draws attention to a number of signs of continuing use of early medieval medical codices, particularly use by monastics, such as the addition of recipes, leather marking tabs and indexes. Voigts, **543**, further develops the argument, pointing out that the Anglo-Saxon pharmocopoeia cannot be assumed to have been limited merely to plants which are now capable of cultivation in England, both because of climatic changes which have occurred since the Anglo-Saxon period, and because there is considerable evidence of the importation of drugs from the continent, in the documentation of the Anglo-Saxon mission to the continent, as well as in *Lb*. Voigts's work on *Herb*, echoed in Sanborn's discussion of *PD* and Anglo-Saxon medical practices, **424**, and paralleled by Cameron's later work on *Lb*, **390** and **565**, thus represents a seminal movement towards the rehabilitation of Anglo-Saxon medical literature (see further '*Leechbook*,' pp. 215–18, and '*Peri Didaxeon*,' pp. 327–8). Rehabilitation remains selective, recognizably in tune with the orthodoxies of our era: who will venture to testify to the rational efficacy of remedies employing animal substances in *MedQuad*, including its 'disgusting little treatise on the badger' (Singer, **327**, xxi)?

PLANT NAMES

MANUSCRIPT

Oxford, Bodleian Library, Bodley 130   FC B.21.1.2
Ker 302, art. a   s. xi²

OE names are given for eight of the plants illustrated in the Latin text of
the Herbarium Complex in Bodley 130. These are listed as a separate item
by FC under 'Pseudo-Apuleius Herbarium,' and also under 'Glosses,' with
two other manuscripts (FC C.71). The plant names are printed by Ker:
f. 1 'Se mare curmelle,' f. 1v 'Se lesse curmelle,' f. 4v 'hoclef,' f. 44 'Foxes
gloue,' f. 44 'Megeþe,' f. 44v 'Wulfescamb,' f. 45 'Henep,' f. 55 'Ifig.' Ker
states that the plant names are nearly contemporary with the text (other
English names were added in the 13th century) and that the manuscript
bears the Bury St Edmunds *ex libris* mark on f. 1.

A facsimile of the manuscript was brought out by Gunther, **399**, in
1925. Gunther's dating of the manuscript, *c.* 1100, is generally current
(cf. Ker). Singer's chart of manuscript relationships (Grattan and Singer,
326, 26) distinguishes two main branches; Bodley 130 belongs to one of
these (related to the 'Anglo-Norman Group'), the OE pseudo-Apuleius to
the other. Both Singer (esp. **410**) and Voigts, **414** and **543**, compare the
illustrations of Bodley 130 with those of Vitellius C.iii; the illustrations,
as well as the text, appear to belong to different traditions. Gunther devoted some attention to plant identification and the illustrations, but was
primarily interested in the textual tradition; his examination includes comparative reference to V. De Vriend, **405**, gives a new interest to Bodley
130 by arguing that it is, for the greater part, a Latin translation of the OE
version found in V, made by a translator who did not know OE well; cf.
Riddle, **422**. De Vriend, **405**, prints parallel passages from Bodley 130, but
these parallels, and the associated argument, do not appear in his EETS
edition of *Herb* and *MedQuad*, **401**.

PLANT NAMES, GENERAL STUDY OF; GLOSSES
AND WORD-LISTS

This Annotated Bibliography covers only incidentally editions and scholarship pertaining to interlinear glosses and glossaries (FC Sections 'C' and
'D').

All botanical terms in the glosses and glossaries are covered by Bierbaumer, **542**; editions of the glosses are listed by him and, a little less
comprehensively, by D'Aronco, **425**. Of particular note are the *Durham
Plant Glossary* (FC D.6), and the closely related *Laud Herbal Glossary*
(FC D.26). The former was printed by Cockayne, **298**, 3: 299–305, and,

more recently, by von Lindheim, 1941,[1] who suggests that it may owe its origins to books brought over by Theodore. *The Laud Glossary* was used by Cockayne, **298**, 3: 311–50, in his compilation of 'Saxon Names of Worts and Trees,' and has been edited by Stracke, 1974.[2] Both were omitted in Singer's revised edition of Cockayne, **327**.

Among other glosses of related interest are the glosses to the Herbal of pseudo-Apuleius in Oxford, Bodleian, Ashmole 1431 (FC C.36), a 12th century manuscript from St Augustine's; the 57 glosses for plant names and diseases have been printed by Gough, **532** (see also Bierbaumer, **539**). Kitson, **567**, is among those who have studied its botanical lemmata. Glosses to a few of the titles of Macer's *De viribus herbarum* (a Latin poem discussing 77 plants) occur in the 12th century manuscript bound up with V (FC C.84) and are also printed by Gough. Bierbaumer, **374**, **416** and **542**, is the only comprehensive study of botanical terms; early studies of plant names include Hoops, **435** and **438**, Earle, **431**, Skeat, **441**, and von Erhard-Siebald, **497**.

---

[1] Durham Cathedral, Hunter 100, ed. Bogislav von Lindheim, *Das Durhamer Planzenglossar*, Beiträge zur englischen Philologie 35 (Bochum-Langendreer: Pöppinghaus, 1941; New York: Johnson, [1967]).

[2] Oxford, Bodleian, Laud Misc. 567, ed. J. Richard Stracke, *The Laud Herbal Glossary* (Amsterdam: Rodopi, 1974).

PERI DIDAXEON

MANUSCRIPT

London, British Library, Harley 6258B, ff. 51v–66v   O   NOT LISTED FC
Ker, *Catalogue*, xix, and *Suppl.*, 126, n. 1, post 1200

PERI DIDAXEON

The collection of recipes introduced in the manuscript as 'Incipit liber qui dicitur peri didaxeon' is incomplete; it breaks off at the heading to a chapter on internal bleeding (Cockayne, **298**, 3: ch. 67). It follows a version of the Herbarium Complex which de Vriend, **401** and **405**, claimed as residual OE and dated mid-12th century, whereas Ker, *Suppl.*, reiterated his judgement that the manuscript was 'a good deal later' (126, n. 1) than second half of the 12th century; for details of this and manuscript description, see 'Herbarium Complex,' pp. 313, 315–16. *Peri Didaxeon* ('Of the Schools') is in the same hand as the vernacular version of *Herb* and *MedQuad*. The existence of a single copy used to be taken to suggest that it was not a widely known text (e.g., Payne, **449**, Rubin, **531**).

De Vriend, **401**, xxix, n. 6, cites a 1905 study (Schiessl, **409**, not sighted) which demonstrates that the language of *PD* is further removed from late WS than that of *Herb* and *MedQuad* in Harley 6258B. De Vriend nevertheless considers that it is 'just possible' to regard *PD* as 'belonging to the OE linguistic tradition'; but, noting that Löweneck had shown that it belongs to a later textual tradition than the Herbarium Complex, he asserted that 'from the historical point of view it would certainly be wrong to include it among the major texts containing Anglo-Saxon medical lore.' De Vriend, however, would seem to have overlooked Talbot's rebuttal of Löweneck's view of the sources of *PD* (**369**), and in the last decade, *PD* has been accepted as an Anglo-Saxon medical text. (Study of its language is also included in Schlemilch, **93**.)

Löweneck's 1896 edition of *PD* (**406**) was highly critical of Cockayne's handling of the text. Löweneck printed parallel passages from a work edited by De Renzi, 1856,[1] from a 12th century manuscript, entitled *Practica Petrocelli Salernitani*, but regarded the English work as an abstract of the *Practica* rather than a translation of it. Löweneck remarked upon the decayed inflexions of *PD* as evidence of its relative lateness, but he did not study the language; he dated the text between 1035 and 1200 because the *Practica* was attributed to an 11th century Salernitan writer in De Renzi's edition (and because he also found some correspondences with Gariopontus).

---

[1] Salvatore De Renzi, ed., *Collectio Salernitana*, 5 vols. (Naples: Filiatre-Sebezio, 1852–9).

Early medical historians, such as Payne, **449**, Bonser **517**, and Singer, esp. **236**, thus regarded *PD* as representative of a more advanced form of knowledge than was available to Anglo-Saxon medical writers (but cf. Singer, **237**). It was favourably compared with *Lb*, *Lac* and the OE Herbarium Complex, and shown to be relatively free of superstition and more rational and systematic in its approach. In 1965, however, Talbot, **369**, showed that the *Practica* was not an 11th century Salernitan composition, but a compilation of earlier writings which was in circulation at least as early as the 9th century (see also Hoops, **408**). *PD*, Talbot demonstrated, does not represent a medical knowledge superior to that available to Anglo-Saxons; *Lb*1&2 draw on the same sources (see further 'Leechbook,' pp. 215–16). The *Practica*, Talbot tentatively suggested, far from representing the arrival in England of the superior medical knowledge of an 11th century Italian, might originally have been compiled in England and transmitted to the continent by 8th century Anglo-Saxon missionaries. Cameron, **390**, 164, entertains the same possibility.

Bierbaumer, who included *PD* in Vol. 2 of his list of OE botanical terms, is among those who accept it as, in some sense, linguistically OE (see esp. **416**, xi–xii). Voigts, **418**, 13, n. 14, observes that Cockayne, **298**, was wise to number it among the body of medical material. Sanborn, **424**, bases her claims for the enlightened quality of Anglo-Saxon medical literature as a whole on a demonstration of some of the strengths of *PD*. Talbot, **369**, was essentially concerned to show that the quality of Anglo-Saxon medical knowledge, as represented by *Lb*1&2, had been sorely underestimated by medical historians such as Bonser and Singer, and he establishes, though only by implication, a strong case for regarding *PD* as a mid or post 12th century copy of a text which took its final form in the Anglo-Saxon period (i.e., in its conservative sense, before or until shortly after the Norman Conquest). The matter is, conceivably, more fully argued out by Sanborn in her (untraced) dissertation, **407**.

HERBARIUM COMPLEX AND PERI DIDAXEON:
ANNOTATIONS

SEE ALSO Cockayne, **298**; Grendon, **314**; Grattan and Singer, **326**; 'General and Miscellaneous Magico-Medical,' pp. 341–83.

FACSIMILE

PLANT NAMES

399 Gunther, Robert T. *The Herbal of Apuleius Barbarus, From the Early Twelfth-Century Manuscript Formerly in the Abbey of Bury St. Edmunds (MS. Bodley 130)*. Oxford: Roxburghe Club, 1925.

Facsimile (with two black-and-white and five colour plates), of Bodley 130, 1–96; includes OE plant names [FC B.21.1.2]. Appendices, 99–141, contain botanical identification and notes on the herbs; tables of comparison (of the number and ordering of plants and animals in various versions of pseudo-Apuleius, Dioscorides and Sextus Placitus) include V. Description of Bodley 130 and its relation to the Latin manuscript tradition, xiii–xxxiv.

EDITIONS

HERBARIUM AND MEDICINA DE QUADRUPEDIBUS

400 Cockayne, Oswald. *Leechdoms, Wortcunning and Starcraft of Early England*. Vol. 1. Rolls Series 35. London: Longman, 1864. 3 vols. [Nendeln]: Kraus, 1965.

Prints Herbarium complex from V, with textual variants from B, H, and occasionally O, as: *Herbarium of Apuleius*, at 1–248; *Herbarium continued from Dioskorides*, at 248–324; *Medicina de Quadrupedibus*, at 326–72. With translation facing throughout. Facsimile of V, f. 45v.

Also prints the following, with translation (Ker's foliation is substituted throughout):

Recipes ('Fly Leaf Leechdoms'). From Vitellius C.iii, ff. 18v, 82v–3 [FC B.21.5.8], 378, 374, 376/1–9; f. 83rv, four Latin recipes, 376/10–25. [The words 'Wið innoþes astyrunge,' at 378/1, belong to the table of contents of *Herb*.] From Titus D.xxvi, ff. 16v–17 [FC B.21.5.7], 380. From Harley

6258B, f. 51rv [*Wiþ eafoð* and *De Beta*, not listed FC], 380–2. From Domitian i, f. 55v [FC B.21.5.3], 382. From CCCC 41, p. 208 [FC B.21.5.1], 382. Under 'Charms,' prints two Recipes from Vitellius E.xviii, f. 15v [FC B.21.5.9], 388/1–10. [See also Cockayne, **298**, 3: 292, for FC B.21.5.4.]

Charms. From CCCC 41, pp. 206, 182 [Storms 15, 1], 384; p. 272 [Storms 48], 386; p. 326 [Storms A4–6], 387; pp. 350–3, 206 [Storms 16, 13, 12], 388–92. From Junius 85, f. 17 [Storms 45, 49, 41, and *Wiþ toð ece*], 392/15–25, 393/18–21, 394/1–7. From St John's College 17, f. 175 [Storms 54], 394. From Vitellius E.xviii, ff. 15v, 16 [most of FC B.23.1.12, including Storms 50, Storms 85, 86], 386/1–7, 395–7. [For the remainder of FC B.23.1.12, art. q, see Cockayne, **298**, 3: 290, 295.] From Caligula A.vii, ff. 176–8 [Storms 8], 398–404. [See also Cockayne, **298**, 3: 286–90, 294–5.]

Preface, ix–cv. Cockayne surveys the medical knowledge and superstitions of antiquity: 'Saxons, Angles and all the Gothic races were wholly unable to accept, to use, to learn, the medical skill of Hellas and of its pupil Italy' (xxi); Anglo-Saxon surgery (as evidenced by Bede's account of the death of Æthelthryth) also compares unfavourably with Mediterranean expertise. There follows an account of magical practices, which are also present in late Latin works, and of popular beliefs (nightmare, dwarfs and demons; exorcism and prayer; the knot in OE, Latin and Greek; lovers' charms, abortions and storms), at xxvii–liii. Unable to root these out, the church threw over them the garb of religion. Cockayne is of the opinion that 'the Gothic people' had indigenous knowledge of herbal cures. Anglo-Saxon botany was not free of error, but learned scholars still disagree among themselves. The Colloquium of Ælfric Bata and the Lorica show that 'the Saxons, in their way, tried to learn languages' (lxxv). At lxviii–lxxv, Cockayne prints the Lorica, Latin–OE gloss from Cambridge, University Library, Ll.1.10 [FC C.83] and the OE gloss from *Lac* [FC C.22]. Cockayne then turns to *Herb* and *MedQuad*: V (dated 1000–1066) is described; the physical condition of the manuscript; its illustrations and their lack of naturalism (comparison with five Latin manuscripts of English provenance); brief description of B, H, and O. There is some discussion of the difficulties of identifying the plants referred to, lxxxv–lxxxviii; the sources, lxxxviii–xc; orthography and language, xc–cv.

401 De Vriend, Hubert Jan. *The Old English Herbarium and Medicina de Quadrupedibus.* EETS 286. London: Oxford UP, 1984.

Prints parallel V and O (with relevant variants from B and H recorded in the apparatus) and a composite Latin text from eight manuscripts: *Herb*, 1–233; *MedQuad*, 234–73. Textual Notes, 275–85; Explanatory Notes, 286–338; Bibliography, 339–44; Glossary, 345–88.

Appendices, 389–403: (1) Indexes of plant names (official botanical, non-English, OE, MnE); (2) List of parallel cures: *Lb*; *Lac*; Pliny (*MedQuad* only); Serenus's *Liber Medicinalis*; *Liber de Medicamentis*. Facsimiles of: V, f. 74r; B, f. 74r; H, f. 66v; O, f. 7r.

Introduction contains a detailed description of the OE and Latin manuscripts on which the edition is based, and their interrelationship (xi–lv). The editor argues for an early date of translation into OE, probably 8th century; *MedQuad* is closely connected with an early Anglian exemplar and *Herb* is either a direct descendant from an early version which was adapted to late WS standard, or else a new translation. VBH have a common ancestor; H belongs to a different branch. O is based on an earlier OE manuscript that belongs to the same tradition as VBH. The choice of Latin manuscripts is explained (Lucca 296 with variants from Harley 4986 is printed parallel to *MedQuad*; the OE is based on a version belonging to the same family as Lucca, but there is no direct relationship between the OE and Lucca). 'The Sources,' lv–lxviii, examines the Latin textual tradition; includes a list of printed editions of Latin manuscripts. 'The Language of the Old English Manuscripts,' lxviii–lxxix, offers substantiation for the argument that *MedQuad* is directly descended from an Anglian original and that O should be regarded as OE, not ME. Observations on identification of plants, lxxix–lxxxi, and weights and measures, lxxxi–lxxxiv; includes a table of equivalents compiled from Latin and OE (the Roman system having disintegrated, OE texts attach different values to the same terms).

HERBARIUM

402 Berberich, Hugo. *Das Herbarium Apuleii nach einer früh-mittelenglischen Fassung.* Anglistische Forschungen 5. Heidelberg: Winter, 1902. Amsterdam: Swets, 1966.

Prints *Herb* from O, with emendations from VBH in apparatus, 65–139. Marginal cross-references to corresponding chapters in Cockayne, **400**. Includes herb cures, f. 51r [*De Beta*, with one omission; see Delcourt, **404**].

Introduction contains general remarks on: manuscript, 1–4; relationship of O to VBH, 4–7; the script, abbreviations and accents, date and dialect of the translation (mid-12th century, WS origin), 7–13; and detailed description of phonology and inflexions, 14–64. No glossary.

403 Hilbelink, Aaltje Johanna Geertruida. *Cotton MS. Vitellius C.iii of the Herbarium Apuleii.* Diss. U of Amsterdam. Amsterdam: Swets, 1930.

Prints *Herb* from V, collated with B and H, 1–97; chs. 1–132 only, omits table of contents. O is not collated because it is late and textually dissimilar. Phonology and accidence, 98–104.

MEDICINA DE QUADRUPEDIBUS

404 Delcourt, Joseph. *Medicina de Quadrupedibus, an early ME. Version.*
Anglistische Forschungen 40. Heidelberg: Winter, 1914.

Prints *MedQuad* from O, 1–25, emendations from Cockayne, **400** (chiefly
V), with manuscript reading in apparatus. Translation facing, based on
Cockayne. Glossary, 26–40. Includes a herb cure from f. 51r, 'Wið eafodece
pollege' (omitted by Berberich, **402**).

Introduction, vii–li. Delcourt's edition is 'intended exclusively for a contribution to the study of early ME. grammar' (viii): phonology and accidence
are described at xx–li. Delcourt considers that, although the work preserves
many characteristics of OE, it can be 'safely ascribed' to *c.* 1150 (ME characteristics tabled at xv–xvi); certain features, neither characteristic of WS,
nor exclusively belonging to other dialects, lead him to conclude that the
borderland between WS and Anglian or Kentish territory is a more probable
place of origin than Wessex (xix–xx). O is a considerably shorter version of
the text and contains some strikingly different readings (xiii–xv); the scribe
was 'not very particular about the exactness and correctness of what he
wrote' (xii).

405 De Vriend, Hubert Jan. *The Old English Medicina de Quadrupedibus.*
Diss. U Groningen. Tilburg: Gionotten, 1972.

Prints parallel, 2–61: O and V, with textual variants from BH; Lucca 296,
with textual variants from Harley 4986; corresponding passages of Bodley
130. Textual Notes, 63–8; Commentary, 69–92; Index Verborum, 93–146.
Select Bibliography, 147–50. Translation of V, 153–62.

1: Description of OE and Latin manuscripts, xi–xxxvi. 2: 'Medicina de
Quadrupedibus,' xxxvii–lv, explains the textual tradition of the work and
manuscript relationships. Lucca 296 and Harley 4986 (which differ markedly
from each other) are the only two early manuscripts containing the A version of Sextus, and the OE translations were based on a text belonging to
the same family as Lucca. Bodley 130, a Latin version deviating from all
others, is for the greater part a Latin translation of the OE version found in
V and B; in many cases readings can only be accounted for if we assume an
OE exemplar, rendered by a translator who did not know OE well (table of
relations, xlvi–lii). B and V have a common archetype which is not the ancestor of H. O is a later copy of an OE text that belonged to the same group,
and its translation is 'an indication that the work was done in the period
anterior to the revival of learning under King Alfred, probably somewhere in
the ninth century' (liv). 3: 'Language of the Four OE Texts,' lvii–civ, claims
(*contra* Berberich, **402**, and Delcourt, **404**) that O is a typical example of
residual OE (i.e., late WS copied by a scribe able to understand and copy
texts in late WS *Schriftsprache*, but so influenced by linguistic changes of
his own period that these are frequently reflected in texts copied by him).

The editor's case rests on statistical evidence presented in an examination of vowels, consonants and accidence: 'O represents a much more advanced stage in the transitional levelling of inflexions but, in the great majority of cases, the regular late WS endings occur more frequently than all other endings taken together' (xcviii). Syntax 'offers little of interest' but gives reason to assume that the translator was Anglian, as does vocabulary (lists nine words indicating Anglian provenance, civ). [For reviews see Hallender, **421**.]

PERI DIDAXEON

406 Löweneck, Max. *Peri Didaxeon, eine sammlung von rezepten in englischer sprache aus dem 11./12. Jahrhundert.* Erlanger Beiträge zur Englischen Philologie und Vergleichenden Literaturgeschichte 12. Erlangen: Junge, 1896.

Prints *PD* from O, collated with Cockayne, **400**; parallel passages from Petrocellus's *Practica* (ed. Salvatore de Renzi, Naples, 1856, Vol. 4), on facing pages, 1–53. Marginal and interlinear glosses in the apparatus. Textual notes, 54–7.

Introduction, v–viii: Löweneck explains the shortcomings of Cockayne, **400** (misread rubrics; incorrect discrimination of *ʒ/g, a/æ, d/ð, m/n*; some unintelligible readings). As his own parallel edition immediately reveals, the source of *PD* is Petrocellus's *Practica*; a few passages derive from Gariopontus and the opening paragraph of ch. 1 is ultimately from Isidore 4, 3 f., but the OE translator may not have known Isidore directly. The English text is merely an abstract of the *Practica* and adheres only loosely to the original order of chapters. The translator himself may have assembled his material from Petrocellus and other sources, but was probably working from a ready-made Latin compilation [see Hoops, **408**]. The decayed inflexions speak for themselves; on the basis of current scholarly dating of *Practica* [see Talbot, **369**] Löweneck dates *PD* between *c.* 1035 and 1200 (viii). [For reviews see Hoops, **408**.]

407 Sanborn, Linda. 'An Edition of British Library MS. Harley 6258B: *Peri Didaxeon.*' Diss. U of Ottawa, 1983.

Cited Sanborn, **424**; not traceable in *DAI*.

COMMENTARY

408 Hoops, Johannes. Rev. of *Peri Didaxeon, eine sammlung von rezepten in englischer sprache aus dem 11./12. Jahrhundert*, by Max Löweneck [**406**]. *Literaturblatt für germanische und romanische Philologie* 20 (1899): 65–72.

Hoops considers two possibilities not raised by Löweneck (66–7). *PD* may not be based directly on Petrocellus. It might have derived from a compilation on which Petrocellus drew; but as it is probably not an 11th century translation, it is more likely to be derived from a work based on him (e.g., the Salernitan-derived poem, *Regimen sanitatis*, was influential in England from the 12th century on). More plausibly, it may have been based on a redaction of Petrocellus that differed from the version known to Löweneck, which may yet be discovered; in this connection, Hoops mentions work on the Salernitan compendium in a Breslau manuscript (Henschel, *Janus* 1, 1846, 40 ff., 300 ff.) and medical codices at Monte Cassino. Corrections and emendations to Löweneck, 68–72.

409 Schiessl, J. *Laut- und Flexionsverhältnisse der frühmittelenglischen Rezepten-sammlung Peri Didaxeon.* Diss. U Erlangen, 1905.

Not sighted. According to de Vriend, **401**, xxix, shows that, although *PD* is in the same hand as *Herb* and *MedQuad* in O, the language is further removed from late WS.

410 Singer, Charles. 'Greek Biology and Its Relation to the Rise of Modern Biology.' *Studies in the History and Method of Science.* Vol. 2. Ed. Charles Singer. Oxford: Oxford UP, 1921. 1–101. 2 vols. 1917–21.

Traces the Greek origins of herbals and examines their Latin development and dissemination (particularly pseudo-Apuleius). In discussing English herbal illustrations, 11th–13th century (69–72), Singer distinguishes between Naturalistic and Romanesque style; both traditions reached the West from Italy, by different routes. Comparison of manuscripts suggests that the naturalistic style may derive from the same place as Beneventan script; but the first herbals brought to England were probably prepared in the north of France (e.g., Betony in Vitellius C.iii). The artists' models, however, must have betrayed the fullest evidence of an origin from further south, for traces of a Mediterranean flora may still be discerned in the English copies (e.g., Henbane in V). The native English style of draftsmanship is less marked in herbals than in ecclesiastical documents, but is discernible in manuscripts such as Bodley 130; this style was replaced after the Conquest by the more formal Romanesque style, and had disappeared by the beginning of the 13th century. No English herbal illustrations show Celtic influence. Illustrations of Dioscorides occasionally group plants according to form and family, and in V there is 'a real grouping of Umbelliferous plants, and ... traces of a rudimentary attempt at a system of classification ... [which] cannot be placed to the credit of the Anglo-Saxon leech, but to the compiler of the work from which he was translating' (80). In line with the southern origin of certain herbal illustrations is the fact that *PD* was a translation of a known Salernitan document, and English leechcraft of the 11th and 12th centuries was influenced by Salerno. [See also Singer, **483, 484**.]

411 Arber, Agnes. *Herbals, Their Origins and Evolution. A Chapter in the History of Botany, 1470–1670.* 2nd rev. edn. Cambridge: Cambridge UP, 1938. [1st edn. 1912.]

This study of printed herbals approaches its subject primarily from a botanical, and secondarily from an artistic standpoint. Ch. 1, 1–12, gives an account of the early history of Botany, Aristotelian and medical Botany, and the philosophical approach to the study of plants. *Herb* is briefly mentioned in ch. 3, 'The Early History of the English Herbal,' at 38–41. Arber describes *Herb* as perhaps the first treatise which opened to the English the herbal medicine of southern Europe and thus connected Britain with the mainstream in the history of systematic botany. She observes that the work is mostly concerned with the virtues of herbs; it makes little attempt to discuss plants botanically, and many of the accounts of virtues of plants are more in the nature of charms than of medical recipes. Arber bestows an admiring glance on the description of how to uproot mandrake (Cockayne, **400**, 1: 244–6) which, she remarks, is still an object of horror in Palestine; cf. white-bryony in Britain.

412 Flom, George T. 'On the Old English Herbal of Apuleius Vitellius C III.' *JEGP* 40 (1941): 29–37.

Vitellius C.iii is a unique volume that claims attention because of its contents, and because it is a striking example of Insular script in late OE times. Flom notes the removal of ff. 2 and 142 to the Psalter to which they originally belonged. He refers the reader to Cockayne, **400**, for the early history and damaged state of the manuscript, and outlines its contents (30–2). From an examination of the script (33–7), he concludes: 'The manuscript must have been written at Canterbury (or Rochester). The script puts the date at *c.* 1040–1050' (37). (Black-and-white plate of f. 62r between 32 and 33.)

413 Kádár, Zoltán. 'Some Notes on the Common Archetypes of Pharmaco-Zoological Illustrations in the MSS. [*sic*] Cotton Vitellius C., III. and the Greek Theriaca.' *Communicationes de Historia Artis Medicinae. Orvostoteneti Kozlemenyek.* Supplement 6 (1972): 85–95.

Kádár concludes that the snake and serpent illustrations in V have a relatively old Hellenistic archetype because they are closer to the dynamic style of comparable illustrations in a 10th–11th century manuscript of Nicander's *Theriaca* (Paris, Bibliothèque Nationale, Suppl. gr. 247) than to the late classical style of the paraphrase of Eutecnios in Vienna Nationalbibliothek, Cod. med. gr. 1 (6th century) and New York, Pierpont Morgan Library, Cod. M, 652 (10th century), 'a remarkable phenomenon from the point of view of the development of pharmaco-zoological illustration, pharmacology and especially the history of toxicology' (91). The dog-like appearance of the unfamiliar ichneumon, more marked in V than in the 7th century pseudo-Apuleius codex of Leiden, Univ. Lid. Cod. Vossianus lat. Q.9, illustrates the point that degeneration at the hands of copyists makes it difficult to recognize original classical archetypes. Black-and-white illustrations from the manuscripts discussed.

414 **Voigts, Linda Ehrsam.** 'The Old English Herbal in Cotton MS. Vitellius C. iii: Studies.' Diss. U of Missouri, 1973. Dir. Milton McC. Gatch. [*DAI* 35 (1974): 1068A.]

Ch. 1, 5–33, contains a full examination of V and its history; detailed description of ff. 11–82v (enlarged Herbal) includes discussion of previously unnoted fragments and inscriptions; study of manuscript history casts doubts on the Christ Church, Canterbury ascription. Ch. 2, 34–64, first treats the tradition of the pseudo-Apuleius manuscripts, with particular attention to Vossianus lat. Q.9, Vienna 93, and the relationship of Cassino and V, and surveys OE versions and Latin versions preserved in English manuscripts. Voigts leans to the view that V did not derive from Casinensis 97, but does not rule out the possibility of a common (English?) prototype. 'Differences between the Monte Cassino and English codices may suggest that we have an instance of separate recensions of text and illustrations' (58); failure to take account of this may render meaningless the stemma of Howald and Sigerist, 1927, and of Singer, **326**. An examination of the use of the herbals (65–71) argues that, notwithstanding highly stylized illustrations, medical codices like V were functional and practical; Voigts points to the addition of synonyms for plant names and indexes, the monastic cultivation of herbs, the leather tab added to Bodley 76, the addition of recipes in later hands and the numerousness of extant copies. [See further Voigts, **418, 543**.] The style, genre and iconography of the author and title page (f. 19rv) and the dedication page (f. 11v) are separately examined in ch. 3, 72–126, and ch. 4, 127–86. [Voigts, **417, 420**, summarizes and further substantiates the argument of chs. 3 and 4.]

415 **Voigts, Linda Ehrsam.** 'A New Look at a MS of the Old English Translation of the *Herbarium Apuleii*.' *Manuscripta* 19 (1975): 84–5.

Abstract of Voigts, **417**.

416 **Bierbaumer, Peter.** *Der botanische Wortschatz des Altenglischen.* II. Teil. *Lacnunga, Herbarium Apuleii, Peri Didaxeon.* Grazer Beiträge zur englischen Philologie 2. Bern: Lang, 1976. 3 vols. 1975–9. [See also **374, 542**.]

The complete botanical vocabulary of *Lac*, *Herb*, and *PD* is presented in a single alphabetical list, 1–139. Introduction, iv–xv, describes the manuscripts, texts and language of each of the three works, and sets out the compiler's principles and procedures, which are the same as for Bierbaumer, **374**, except that, for *Herb* and *PD*, the Latin sources provide an additional means for identifying terms. The respective textual bases for the three works covered in this volume are the editions of Grattan and Singer, **326**, Cockayne, **400**, and Löweneck, **406**. A summary (in English), 158–68, details the results of Bierbaumer's study (additions and corrections to *BT*, including foreign words which should be deleted, and new semantic and etymological information). Appendices, 140–57, include an index of Latin botanical plant names and OE equivalents.

417 Voigts, Linda Ehrsam. 'A New Look at a Manuscript Containing the Old English Translation of the *Herbarium Apulei.*' *Manuscripta* 20 (1976): 40–60.

Voigts presents arguments for a late dating of Vitellius C.iii (1050 at the earliest) and for an East Anglian provenance. The artist who coloured the plant illustrations in V was also responsible for the OE plant names accompanying the illustrations (they use the same colour pigments). As the colourist's script is mid-11th century, the manuscript must have become a usable codex at that date. The dedication page (f. 11v) has stylistic and material connections with the author portrait (f. 19r), and must therefore be original to this manuscript. Both the dedication page and author portrait have close affinities with the Psalter in Tiberius C.vi, 2nd half of the 11th century, provenance Winchester or Thorney Abbey (e.g., it has the same virulent green pigment and tonsured figures with hair coloured blue). The dedication page also has affinities with tomb sculpture of the 12th and later centuries (and its central figure, who has no nimbus, suggests that the codex was dedicated to a saint). Both V and Tiberius have resemblances to 11th century Franco-Flemish illumination (e.g., the depiction of standing instead of sitting recipients and donors links the dedication page with those executed by or under Abbot Odbert of St-Bertin, 986–1007), and Voigts draws attention to the strong ties between monasteries such as St-Bertin and those of fenland East Anglia: she suggests Thorney, Peterborough, Croyland, Ramsey or Ely. (Eight black-and-white illustrations, 57–60, include V, ff. 19r and 11v, examples of dedication pages and tomb sculpture for comparison.) Corrigendum in *Manuscripta* 21 (1977): 62. Voigts amends the last sentence of **417** to read: 'It is necessary to date this codex as late as possible, at the very least, 1050, a century later than the date some historians of medicine would assign it.'

418 Voigts, Linda Ehrsam. 'One Anglo-Saxon View of the Classical Gods.' *Studies in Iconography* 3 (1977): 3–16.

The efficacy of many of the recipes in *Herb* is attested to by a pagan deity or hero associated with the healing arts; he/she is credited with discovery of the plant or with having given it to Man (e.g., *Herb* 23, 13, 36, 90, 175, 13, 23, 182, 73, 49). *Herb* does not evince the apprehension of pagan authorities that motivated the expurgator of Vienna 93 (13th century). In Vitellius C.iii, Graeco-Roman gods are cited on the title page as the authority from which the work as a whole derives, and Apuleius, Aesculapius and Chiron figure in the author portrait; Voigts discusses the author portrait and title page in V, emphasizing its fidelity to classical iconography. Features such as the monastic dedication page of V, f. 11v, and the prayers and marginal neumes, show that ecclesiastics were among those who made practical use of the medical codices; perhaps they understood these pagan references in Augustine's terms; *De Civitate Dei*, 8.23–6, emphasizes Aesculapius's mortality but praises his skill; so also Isidore, *Etymologiae*, Bk. 4.3–4; and a hymn once attributed to Fulbert of Chartres (*PL* 141: 340–1). 'The tendentiousness of Ælfric [*De Falsis Diis*, lines 286–91] should not blind us to the fact that the Anglo-Saxons who conveyed Germanic pagan lore in medical texts were as well the transmitters of a medical tradition that saw the Mediterranean gods of healing as moral physicians par excellence, worthy of respect and guarantors of the authority of their medical texts' (11). (Black-and-white reproduction of f. 19 at 6, 8.)

419 Voigts, Linda E. 'British Library, Cotton Vitellius C. iii, f. 82.' *Old English Newsletter* 12.1 (1978): 12–13.

Voigts points out similarities which show that the artist of V was familiar either with Harley 647 (a Carolingian manuscript of the *Aratea* held at St Augustine's from the year 1000) or with Anglo-Saxon manuscripts illustrated in this tradition, such as Harley 2506 or Cotton Tiberius B.v. Specifically, the dog on V, f. 82, resembles Anticanis and Syrius in Tiberius, B.v, ff. 44, 39v; the hare on V, f. 77v, resembles the illuminations of the constellation Lepus in Harley 647; the ram on V, f. 80, resembles the Aries illustration on Tiberius B.v, f. 32v. These affinities, linked with the connection Voigts, **418, 420**, has noted between the representation of Chiron in the author portrait on V, f. 19, and the Harley 647 illustrations of Centaurus, 'encourage us to see these medical MSS. in the larger tradition of A-S book production' (12). (Black-and-white reproduction of V, f. 82.)

420 Voigts, Linda Ehrsam. 'The Significance of the Name Apuleius to the *Herbarium Apulei*.' *Bulletin of the History of Medicine* 52 (1978): 214–27.

The confusion of Apuleius Platonicus and Plato is not unique to Vitellius C.iii; it occurs also in a 13th century copy of pseudo-Apuleius, Vienna Nationalbibliothek 93. Beyond this confusion is the question of the assignment of the name of a 2nd century orator and writer to a 4th century remedy book—for Voigts finds no evidence in the *Apologia* that the real Apuleius studied medicine or wrote about it. Apuleius was a priest of Aesculapius, the god of medicine (*Liber Floridarum*, ch. 18). Aesculapius was significant in the culture that spawned and transmitted pseudo-Apuleius, and is much cited and depicted in manuscript copies of the work. Voigts examines four representative manuscripts, including the title-page and author portrait of V, f. 19, which, in her view, shows Plato/Apuleius receiving the book from Aesculapius and Chiron. She concludes that 'a factor, or perhaps *the* factor, in the decision of the 4th century herbalist to appropriate the name of Apuleius of Maduara was the wish to declaim that the ultimate source of the herbarium was the god of medicine' (227). The titles, *incipits* and author portraits make the point most tellingly that 'if the authority for this herbal is Aesculapius (and Chiron, the mentor of Aesculapius), then the most likely recipient of the wisdom of the god would be one who had shown special devotion to him, his priest Apuleius' (227).

421 Hallender, Lars-Gunnar. Rev. of *The Old English Medicina de Quadru-pedibus*, by Hubert Jan de Vriend [**405**]. *English Studies* 62 (1981): 553–6.

Hallender finds de Vriend's case for the Old Englishness of MS O un-convincing; the table showing frequencies in percentages of the late WS graphemes 'might equally be used to prove the Middle English character of the manuscript' (555).

422 Riddle, John M. 'Pseudo-Dioscorides' *Ex herbis femininis* and Early Me-dieval Medical Botany.' *Journal of the History of Biology* 14 (1981): 43–81.

Riddle argues that *Ex herbis femininis* was compiled in the late 5th or early 6th century in southern Europe. Only a small proportion of its 71 chapters are taken from Dioscorides without modification and some 14 chapters are totally unrelated to Dioscorides or any other known source. Singer, **484**, and others consider that the new material was derived from Pliny and pseudo-Apuleius; but Riddle concludes that the compiler added new material from his own medical and botanical experience. Some consideration is given to the reason for the designation of the herbs as 'female' (probably the work of a copyist) and the illustrations (which Riddle regards as sufficient for identification by those already familiar with plants). The OE translation is 'still another example of the adaptiveness of the copyists/translators' (70). Riddle instances a few changes at 70–1; some may have been made 'to suit the botanical characteristics' of the region (56). Notwithstanding the conclusions of de Vriend, **405**, Riddle finds no evidence that the fragments of *Ex herbis femininis* in Bodley 130 were translated into Latin from OE (56, n. 34). Table of herbs, 73–81, collates the OE and Latin versions.

423 Hofstetter, Walter. 'Zur lateinischen Quelle des altenglischen Pseudo-Dioskurides.' *Anglia* 101 (1983): 315–60.

Addresses the question of the derivation of OE pseudo-Dioscorides, for which, unlike the other two parts of *Herb*, there is no single clearly de-fined source; detailed examination of textual relationships and tables of correspondences (the iconographic relationship requires separate analysis). Hofstetter establishes a close connection between the OE, *De herbis femi-ninis*, *Curae Herbarum* (in Uppsala 664, Lucca 296, Wellcome 573, Leiden 1283), and a botanical-medical compilation in Paris, BN 13955, ff. 145r–6r, and considers its possible implications. Bibliography, 358–60, includes list of Latin manuscripts.

424 Sanborn, Linda. 'Anglo-Saxon Medical Practices and the *Peri Didaxeon*.' *Revue de L'Université d'Ottawa* 55 (1985): 7–13.

'As attitudes towards medieval medicine become less prejudiced, renewed investigation of long-ignored texts like the Peri Didaxeon will yield substantial rewards' (13). Although Bonser, **510**, and Grattan and Singer, **326**, have ridiculed Anglo-Saxon medical literature, much of it had classical authority behind it. Continuing advances in medical technology are 'creating new respect for centuries old plant-medicines,' and 'many accepted notions concerning medicine must be drastically altered in favour of those of the ancients' (9). Recent scholarship (Voigts, **543**, and Talbot, **369**) has cautiously come to accept that Anglo-Saxon medical literature was pragmatic, empirical and efficacious. Pages 11–13 deal with *PD* ('a very remarkable work,' 11). Its exposition of the doctrine of the four humours is unique in OE; this theory underlies the practice of bloodletting. Sanborn details the medical conditions for which bloodletting was employed, the times and the manner of carrying it out, and notes that opinions differed concerning the correct anatomical locations for bloodletting. Herbal remedies were employed to restore the balance of the humours. Sanborn suggests practical reasons for the ingredients with which herbs were mixed (e.g., honey, vinegar and beer are antiseptic).

425 D'Aronco, Maria Amalia. 'The Botanical Lexicon of the Old English *Herbarium.*' *Anglo-Saxon England* 17 (1988): 15–33.

D'Aronco analyses the OE terminology created to render Latin terms for medicinal herbs (most of which were not indigenous to England), particularly with a view to determining the influence of the Latin sources. Analysis is limited to *Herb*, chs. 1–185 (which does not present the same difficulties as *Lb*1&2 and *PD*, because its sources are fully known and its translator aimed to provide information useful for the recognition of the herbs); the textual tradition of the Herbarium complex is outlined at 17–21. At 23–31 D'Aronco examines: terms that belong to the indigenous Germanic heritage; different types of direct and indirect linguistic borrowings; loan formations. 'The most relevant fact to emerge from this analysis is that the botanical terminology of the Old English *Herbarium*, as regards the names of plants, consists largely of loan words, loan translations and loan renditions, while the terminology related to the parts of plants, the fruits and seeds, is mostly Germanic.... Numerous plant names remain which designate both native and foreign plants and which are analysable as autonomous creations in Old English. These are compounds created according to a pattern based on taxonomic categories; in effect, they provide a summary description of the plant by reference to what are considered its salient features' (32). Although the coining of compounds is characteristically Germanic, new formulations seem likely to have been stimulated by Anglo-Saxon knowledge of Greek and Latin terminology derived from medical treatises.

GENERAL AND MISCELLANEOUS MAGICO-MEDICAL: ANNOTATIONS

SEE ALSO Anderson, **17**; Singer, **236**; Singer, **237**

426 **Stephens, George.** 'Extracts in Prose and Verse from an Old English Medical Manuscript, preserved in the Royal Library at Stockholm.' *Archaeologia* 30 (1844): 349–418.

Prints a long metrical item, 349–95, together with prose recipes, 395–99, and charms, 399–403. Glossary, 403–16. Brief observations on the (unnamed) manuscript [Stockholm, Kgl. Bibl., med. Misc. XIV] date it to the reign of Edward III, certainly not later than that of Richard II (416–18). The manuscript is paper, but said to contain two parchment pages (ff. 4 and 5), which are not printed.

427 **Thrupp, J.** 'British Superstitions as to Hares, Geese, and Poultry.' *Transactions of the Ethnological Society of London* NS 5 (1867): 162–6.

Superstitions regarding the three classes of animal which, according to Caesar, were bred but not eaten by the Ancient Britons, were prevalent throughout Europe, for 'the religion of savages is often nothing but a vague belief in the supernatural' (162); brief allusions to the Life of Cuthbert, the *Colloquy* and Theodore's Penitential.

428 **Akerman, John Yonge.** 'Notes on the *"hwiting treow"* of the Anglo-Saxons.' *Archaeologia* 42 (1869): 124–6.

Identifies (as rowan) the fruit-bearing tree whose twigs were employed by Germanic peoples for casting lots (*Germania*, ch. 10): the only OE text referred to is an Ælfric gloss, 'hwiting: variculus arbor.'

429 **Kemble, John Mitchell.** *The Saxons in England.* Vol. 1. 2nd rev. edn. by Walter de Gray Birch. London: Quaritch, 1876. 2 vols. [1st edn. London: Longman, 1849.]

Appendix, 523–35; prints charms, chiefly from Harley 585 (*Lac*), all of which were edited by Cockayne, **400, 298**, together with excerpts from OE Laws, and the penitential canons of Theodore and Ecbert pertaining to heathen practices. Ch. 12, 'Heathendom,' 327–432, deals with 'the acknowledged creed of the Saxons,' particularly the nature of the Northern pantheon. Minimal reference to OE texts; the real value of the study lies in its bearing on the history of Anglo-Saxon scholarship. The child, 'to whom this great creation is full of playmates, beings animate or inanimate ... knows more of

their peculiarities than the halting steps of scientific observation is always able to undertake. . . . Such as the child is has the child-nation been, before the busy hum of commerce, the crashing stroke of the pistons . . . necessarily banished more natural music from our ears' (433).

430 **Grimm, Jacob.** *Deutsche Mythologie.* 4th edn. Posthumously edited by Elard Hugo Meyer. Berlin: Guttersloh, 1875–8. 3 vols. [Previous edns. 1842, 1844, 1854.] Translated as *Teutonic Mythology* by James Stephen Stallybrass. London: Bell, 1880–8. 4 vols.

Vol. 1 covers gods and their cults (includes chapters on worship, temples and priests), heroes, wise women, wights and elves, giants, creation and the elements (chs. 1–20). Vol. 2 contains chapters on trees and animals, sky and stars, day and night, summer and winter, time and world, souls, death, destiny and well-being ('Schicksal und Heil'), personifications, poetry, spectres, translation ('Gespenster'), the devil, magic, superstition, sicknesses, herbs and stones, spells and charms (chs. 21–38). Vol. 3 consists of a Supplement (compiled from Grimm's notes by Meyer for the 4th edn.) and an Appendix (texts of Anglo-Saxon genealogies, medieval and modern examples of 'Aberglaube' and 'Beschwörungen,' included by Grimm in Vol. 1, 1st edn. only). Stallybrass's translation retains the chapter numbers of the 4th edn., but renders the first two volumes as three. Brief comparative references to OE texts occur throughout. Ch. 38, 'Sprüche und Segen' (2: 1023–44), examines words for 'saying' and 'singing' and the powers attributed to songs and runes, which yield information about heathen religious beliefs; includes text and discussion of metrical charms [FC A.43.1, 4, 7, 8]. Appendix (3: 492–3) includes text of the 'Journey Charm' [FC A.43.11], and (from Wanley, 114–15, and Kemble's transcripts) cattle-thief charms [FC A.43.9, 10, B.23.1.6].

431 **Earle, John.** *Plant Names from the Tenth to the Fifteenth Century.* Oxford: Clarendon, 1880.

Prints a number of ME word-lists, together with: three OE lists (from Wright, 30, 285, 66, 78); Durham Plant Gloss (from Cockayne, 298, 3: 299–305); names from the chapter headings of *Herb*, together with Junius's Greek annotations (Wanley, 72), 1–84. Notes, 85. Indexes (Latin, OE and French), 97–118. Introduction, ix–cxii, covers: the development of systematic nomenclature from Theophrastus to the present; Anglo-Saxon derivation of plant names and botanical knowledge from the Roman missionaries, and Anglo-Saxon missionary influence on German plant names; confusions created by Linnaeus's nomenclature; whether old plant names can be identified with the plant signified; the neglect of vernacular names. 'The fascination of Plant-names has its foundation in two instincts, love of Nature and curiosity about Language. . . . Could we penetrate to the original suggestive idea that called forth the name, it would bring valuable information about the first openings of the human mind towards Nature; and the merest dream of

such a discovery invests with a strange charm the words that could tell, if we could understand, so much of the forgotten infancy of the human race' (vi). Earle regrets that veneration of classical languages, in the 7th and 8th centuries as well as in the 17th and 18th, led to the adoption of foreign nomenclature, enforcing the severance of the popular and learned traditions, and concludes with an impassioned plea for the (re-)creation of a vernacular nomenclature.

432 Black, W.G. *Folkmedicine: A Chapter in the History of Culture.* Folklore Society Publication 12. London: Folklore Society, 1883.

A highly generalized excursus. Specific reference to OE consists chiefly of a citation of the wen charm [FC A.43.12]; Cockayne, **297**, 2: 51, illustrates the widespread belief in 'toothworms' as a cause of dental decay.

433 Zupitza, Julius. 'Ein Zauberspruch.' *Zeitschrift für deutsches Altertum und deutsche Litteratur* 31 (1887): 45–52.

Discussion of the metrical 'wen charm' [FC A.43.12]; text and Modern German translation.

434 Dyer, T. Thiselton. *The Folklore of Plants.* London: Chatto, 1889.

No index. In this eclectically generalized survey, no allusion to OE texts was sighted.

435 Hoops, Johannes. 'Über die altenglischen Pflanzennamen.' Diss. U Freiburg im Breisgau, 1889.

Hoops examines plants in OE poetry, 12–41, superstitions attaching to plants, 41–67, and OE plant names, 68–84. Some 500 names of plants are listed, 68–71; Hoops remarks briefly on etymology, loan-words and indigenous coinings, and concludes with a study of *þung*, 83–4.

436 Fischer, August. *Aberglaube unter den Angel-Sachsen.* Programme der Herzoglichen Realgymnasiums zu Meiningen. Meiningen: Keyssnerschen Hofbuchdruckerie, 1891.

'Reste des heidnischen Cultus,' 5–10, cites regulatory and homiletic texts as evidence of the endurance of heathen traditions. The discussion of 'Böse Geister und Ungeheuer,' 10–15, 'Zauber,' 16–21, and 'Weissagung,' 21–7, draws primarily on Ælfric's homilies and metrical texts, with occasional reference to *Lb* and *Lac*. The prognostic texts help to illustrate the survival of fatalistic beliefs and the currency of astrology; a brief account of their variety, 22–4, emphasizes the significance attached to the phases of the moon in Anglo-Saxon soothsaying and dream lore. A wide-ranging survey of 'Schutz-und Heilmittel,' 27–42, examines supernatural aids and enemies to health, and includes a section on plant lore, based chiefly on *Herb*. Fischer concludes that, among the Christianized Anglo-Saxons, many pagan beliefs lingered on for a long time as superstitions: 'Es ist nicht zu leugnen, dass

ihnen die Beweggründe ihrer Hoffnung und Furcht und die leitenden Motive ihrer Thaten zum grossen Teil von der bekämpften, aber immer noch lebendigen Tradition der Meinungen ihrer Voreltern an die Hand gegeben wurden' (42).

437 Berdoe, Edward. *The Origin and Growth of the Healing Art: A Popular History of Medicine in all Ages and Countries.* London: Swan, 1893.

'Medicine of the Druids, Teutons, Anglo-Saxons, and Welsh,' 269–86, states: 'The most ignorant persons practised the profession, and particularly old women, who were supposed to be the most expert and were in high repute amongst the Anglo-Saxons. After the establishment of Christianity the clergy succeeded to the business carried on by ancient dames, and it must be admitted that the superstitious element in their treatment of disease was not less prominent than in that of their venerable predecessors' (274). *Lb* is described, as one of the many medical books that Alfred had translated; the letter of Helias to Alfred implies that there were medical schools. *Lb*1.13 (for harelip) illustrates the existence of rational treatment; other examples serve to demonstrate that 'such medical learning as existed amongst the Angles, Saxons, and Goths was found only in a corrupted state in the monasteries. . . . Herbal remedies were, for the most, useless or worse, and the treatment was so intermingled with magic ceremonies and religious superstitious uses, that Greek science, so far as it related to the healing art, was all but smothered by absurdities' (279).

438 Hoops, Johannes. 'Pflanzenaberglaube bei den Angelsachsen.' *Globus* 63 (1893): 303, 324.

Not sighted; listed Bonser, 1957, 7392.

439 Schröder, Edward. 'Über das Spell.' *Zeitschrift fur deutsches Altertum* 37 (1893): 241–68.

A comparative philological study of *spell*.

440 Priebsch, R. 'An Old English Charm and the "Wiener Hundesegen." ' *Academy* 49 (1896): 428.

Concerning a charm in a manuscript dated by Priebsch 12th century (formerly Library of Lord Ashburnham, Appendix no. 120, f. 191v). The first four lines, when stripped of the redundancy common to charms, reduce to a core statement, 'God was iborin in bedlem . . . þer nes inemnedne wolf ne þef.' This corresponds to the first line of the Wiener Hundesegen (Imperial Library of Vienna, Codex 552), 'Christ uuart gaboren er uuolf ode diob.' Priebsch concludes that both charms had a common origin in pagan Saxony, and postulates an ur-form in which Woden held the place of Christ; thus, *'Wæs Woden geboren ær wulf oþþe þeof.' The meaning may have been that Woden existed before all evil in the world; whereas the OE [*sic*] is a general blessing, there are signs that the Wiener Hundesegen is a shepherds' charm

to protect herds. [Grendon, **314**, lists this charm as AA18, but does not include the text because of the lateness of the language.]

441 **Skeat, Walter W.** 'Anglo-Saxon Plant-Names.' *Notes and Queries* 8th ser., 9 (1896): 163–4.

Our ancestors had a curious habit of connecting the names of plants with those of well-known animals (such as 'fox-glove'). 'The names are simply childish, such as children would be pleased with' (163); ingenious attempts to find alternative explanations merely evade the evidence, and are 'not the way to understand the workings of the human mind, on which true etymology often throws much unexpected light' (163). Skeat gives a list of OE plant names with an animal component, drawn from the Glossary of Cockayne, **298**; there must have been many more such names, he surmises, which were not recorded.

442 **Stokes, Whitley.** 'A Celtic Leech Book.' *Zeitschrift für celtische Philologie* 1 (1897): 17–25.

'Transcript of 4 pages of a 9th c. ms. in the University Library, Leiden. With glossary' (Bonser, 1957, 7421), i.e., Vossianus Lat. F.96a. [See Stuart, **384**, who describes Stokes's transcript as 'nonsensical.']

443 **Weinhold, Karl.** 'Die mystische Neunzahl bei den Deutschen.' *Abhandlungen der königlichen Akademie der Wissenschaften, Berlin, phil.-hist.* 2 (1897): 1–61.

Listed Greenfield and Robinson, 3965. Examples of multiples of nine employed in magical healing include the instruction for singing a charm thrice times nine in *Lac* 119 (35); no reference to Leechdoms at 39.

444 **Dieterich, Albrecht.** 'ABC-Denkmäler.' *Reinisches Museum für Philologie* NS 56 (1901): 77–105.

Wide-ranging discussion of alphabet divination; no specific discussion of the OE text.

445 **March, H. Colley.** 'Customs Relating to Iron.' *Folklore* 12 (1901): 340–1.

In Cockayne, **297**, 2: 218 [*Lb*], iron is employed merely as an alternative to 'pot-boilers' (hot stones placed in liquid to raise the temperature). Cockayne, **400**, 1: 244 [*Herb*] is an example of the superstitious use of iron. *Bewrit* is an error for *bewrið* (possibly the OE translator took *circumscribunt* for *inscribunt*); thus the iron is to be used, not to inscribe the mandrake, but to draw a circle about it, as in Pliny's *Natural History*, 25.13.

446 **Ebermann, Oskar.** 'Blut- und Wundsegen in ihrer Entwicklung dargestellt.' *Palaestra* 24 (1903).

Chiefly a study of German charms; 24–35 deal with *Jordan-segen*, the 'Christ was born in Bethlehem' group. In his examination of metrical form,

52–64, Ebermann notes that, whereas Latin charms use rhyme, Germanic languages use alliteration, especially of verbs.

447 Jordan, Richard. *Die altenglichsen Säugetiername.* Anglistische Forschungen 12. Heidelberg: Winter, 1903.

Lists the forms and etymology of some 100 OE animal names, grouped according to biological class. Covers much of the OE corpus, including Cockayne, **400, 297, 298**, *Wond* and *Alex*.

448 Wordsworth, Christopher. 'Two Yorkshire Charms or Amulets: Exorcisms and Adjurations.' *Yorkshire Archaeological Journal* 17 (1903): 377–412.

Occasionally cites parallels in Cockayne, **297, 298**; principal reference is to the Durham Ritual, including OE glosses. Topics include amulets, elves, exorcisms, blessings and adjurations, prayers and charms; discussion has bearing on the relationship of Christian and heathen magic, and there is some examination of the penitential canons of Theodore and Ecbert which deal with heathen magic. Texts discussed include a prayer against the poison of venomous creatures, found in the Durham Ritual and also in the *Book of Nunnaminster*, edn. 1899, 90; cf. *Book of Cerne*, edn. 1902, 157. Listed Bonser, 1957, 7549.

449 Payne, Joseph Frank. *English Medicine in the Anglo-Saxon Times.* Oxford: Clarendon, 1904.

Lecture 1. Ch. 1, 'The History of Medicine,' 4–7; Payne's intention is 'to lay something like the first stone' (5) in the unwritten history of medicine in Britain. Ch. 2, 'The History of Anglo-Saxon Medicine,' 7–29. Tacitus's reference to women's treatment of wounds points to a popular, Germanic tradition of medicine, but Anglo-Saxon literary documentation refers only to ecclesiastics and laymen as leeches. Bede's *History* yields information on epidemics and the medical profession (15–22); its account of Æthelthryth is examined in detail (22–9). The presence of medical books prescribing Southern European herbs is revealed by the Boniface correspondence. Ch. 3, 'The Anglo-Saxon Medical Literature,' 29–62; *Lb*, which Payne relates to Alfred's education programme, is discussed on 39–62. *Lb* is primarily therapeutical, with no statement of principles whether of pathology or treatment. The remedies are chiefly herbal, often involving the union of a large number of herbs. The employment of elaborate compounds of herbs, contrasting with the simple infusions of Galen and the School of Salerno 'shows that the art of pharmacy was in a very low state' (49). Anglo-Saxon leeches achieved for themselves a herbal medicine founded on empirical knowledge of plants. But, especially in *Lb*2 (predominately concerned with internal diseases), knowledge derives from Greek medical writings, transmitted through Latin. 'There is nothing in this book which recalls any writer of the school of Salerno' (55). Anglo-Saxon medical literature took shape when European

medicine was at its lowest ebb: 'It is no discredit to Anglo-Saxon compilers that they failed to construct from [the available translations] a satisfactory body of medical science. But ... they were quite incapable, from want of experience or of a learned tradition, of supplying anything original from their own resources. There is hardly anything that suggests what we call clinical observation' (59). Ch. 4, 'The "Herbarium" of Apuleius,' 62–82; although the Herbarium is a poor work of natural history by modern standards, Anglo-Saxon scholars showed intelligence and good sense in taking the best work on the subject they could find in Europe and translating it. Anglo-Saxons could illustrate skilfully from nature, but earlier drawings were copied because the purpose was not to illustrate known objects but to identify the plants described by classical writers. Anglo-Saxon names are used for some 500 plants; this is evidence of an extensive knowledge of medicinal plants. The impetus derived from the monasteries, but 'there must also have been a popular and widespread love of flowers—a national characteristic which may still be recognized in the cottage gardens of the South of England' (82).

Lecture 2. Ch. 1, 'Surgery,' 83–94. Surgery can reach a considerable degree of excellence without possessing a literature; there is evidence of a wide range of empirical knowledge, but the complicated directions for surgery were probably copied from books. Ch. 2, 'Charms and Superstitious Medicine,' 94–142. 'What there was of the superstitious and magical in the Anglo-Saxon writers was not peculiar to them, but was in part derived from the literature of a much higher and older civilization than theirs' (94). Payne outlines the way in which magical elements, banished by the School of Hippocrates, came to mingle with and form so important a part of European medicine for many centuries. Teutonic and Celtic elements are hard to identify: 'A great deal of so called "folk-medicine" is old-fashioned regular medicine which has sunk down to the level of the unlearned and has sometimes put on a rustic dress' (108). Christianity opposed pagan charms with its own: 'In their condemnation of evil the clergy maintained an atmosphere which was pre-eminently favourable to superstition and credulity' (110). Payne's account of charms draws chiefly on *Lac*: he looks briefly at herb gathering charms, verbal formulas, exorcism, narrative charms, material magic and amulets, ways of transferring disease, and the nine herbs charm (114–42). Ch. 3, 'Peri Didaxeon,' 143–59. *PD* suggests that, had the OE school not been violently cut short by the Norman invasion, it might have entered on a new phase, tinctured by the medicine of Salerno; but *PD* may not have been widely known. Payne remarks on the absence of superstition in *PD*, the limitation of prescriptions to a small number of ingredients, and the preponderance of Southern European herbs. *Lb*, leaving aside its recourse to magic, compares favourably with *PD*. Anglo-Saxon leeches had a wider knowledge of herbs, but the Salernitans made a more intelligent selection; their formulae are clear and simple, whereas Anglo-Saxon compounds have no regular system and combine a large number of drugs. Under

Edward the Confessor, the Anglo-Saxon leech lost ground in court circles to Normans, who had little to teach them. The Anglo-Saxon tradition remained productive until the mid-12th century and survives in medieval popular vernacular works and the herbals of Culpepper and his followers: 'Even in our own day there exists a popular herbal medicine, strangely combined with the use of charms and magical ceremonies of very ancient origin, which still holds its place in popular belief. In this corrupt and undignified form we may still trace some features of the old Anglo-Saxon medicine' (162). (Twenty-three black-and-white plates.)

450 Leonhardi, Günther. *Die Lorica des Gildas.* Diss. U Leipzig. Hamburg, 1905.

Not sighted. Listed Greenfield and Robinson, 6252.

451 Randolph, Charles Brewster. 'The Mandragora of the Ancients in Folklore and Medicine.' *Proceedings of the American Academy of Arts and Sciences* 40 (1905): 487–537.

Folkloric tales of the mandrake (not grown north of the Alps) are a medieval development; Randolph's study focuses on Greek and Roman knowledge of the mandragora's anaesthetic properties, and concludes that anaesthetics, doubtless due to attendant dangers, were not generally used in medieval or antique times. In explaining why he thinks that the chapter on the mandrake in pseudo-Apuleius is a later interpolation, and demonstrating that it closely corresponds to Avicenna's account, he observes that, in the OE version [Cockayne, **400**, 1: 244], this chapter appears to have been further tampered with (520–2).

452 Brie, Maria. 'Der germanische, insbesondere der englische Zauberspruch.' *Mitteilungen der schlesischen Gesellschaft für Volkskunde* 8 (1906): 1–36.

Illustrates three theoretically distinct categories of verbal magic ('Gewalt des Wortes') which in practice merge ('die Beschwörung, den Hexenspruch und den Segen'). Many examples, English as well as German and Norwegian, are drawn from 16th–19th century sources; brief remarks on some metrical charms [FC B.43.3, 4, 8, 11, 12]; also cites Cockayne, 3: 62; 2: 350; 3: 294; 3: 64; 1: 393; 1: 390; 3: 60. Survey of legal prohibitions of magic practices in Anglo-Saxon and later medieval periods, 6–11.

453 Geldner, Johann. *Untersuchungen zu altenglischen Krankheitsnamen.* 1. Teil. Diss. U Würzburg, 1906. 2. und 3. Teil. Augsburg: Pfeiffer, 1907–8. Repr. (3 pts. in 1 vol.) Braunschweig: Westermann, 1908.

Geldner presents, without preliminary or concluding remarks, an alphabetically-organized study of well over 100 OE terms for sickness and disease. Editions on which the study is based include Cockayne, **400**, **297** and **298**.

454 McBryde, J.M., Jr. 'Charms for Thieves.' *Modern Language Notes* 22 (1907): 168–70.

Prints an undated Latin charm against thieves and some analogous English charms, 16th–17th century, with brief explanatory notes.

455 Schlutter, O.B. 'Anglo-Saxonica.' *Anglia* 30 (1907): 123–34, 394–400; 31 (1908): 51–71, 135–40, 521–42; 33 (1910): 137–42.

Includes numerous emendations to, and textual notes on, Cockayne, **400, 297, 298**, and Leonhardi, **310**.

456 Schmitt, Lorenz. *Die Akzente in ae Handschriften mit Berücksichtigung der Akzente im Lateinischen und Althochdeutschen.* Diss. U Bonn. Bonn: Eisele, 1907.

Not sighted. See Schmitt, **341**.

457 Brie, Maria. 'Über die ags. Bezeichnung des Wortes Zauberer.' *Englische Studien* 41 (1909): 20–7.

Enumerates, and briefly comments on, words pertaining to practitioners of magic not permitted by the church: *gealdor-*; *dry*; *wīgelere*; *wicce* and *wicca*; *-lǣca*; *hellerune*; *hægtesse*; *wælcyrge*. [Undocumented citations.]

458 Sudhoff, Karl. 'Die gedruckten mittelalterlichen medizinischen Texte in germanischen Sprachen.' *Archiv für Geschichte der Medizin* 3 (1909): 273–303.

A bibliographical catalogue of medieval medical material in Germany, Sweden, England and the Netherlands; includes 10 OE items (at 297–300), previously edited by Cockayne, **400, 297, 298**, Dietrich, **299**, and Napier, **308**. Prints a Germanized OE recipe, 'uuidhar cancur,' 274 [see Von Steinmeyer, **465**].

459 Schlutter, O.B. 'Anglo-Saxonica. Altenglisches aus Leidener Handschriften: neuntes (zehntes) Jahrhundert.' *Anglia* 33 (1910): 239–34.

Examines the OE glosses in Leiden, Vossianus Lat. F.96a. [See Stokes, **442**, Stuart, **384**.]

460 Thöne, Franz. *Die Namen der menschlichen Körperteile bei den Angelsachsen.* Diss. U Erlangen. Kiel: Fiencke, 1912.

Gives the forms and etymology of some 250 OE anatomical terms, listed alphabetically, 20-120; index, 127–32, includes compounds. Sources include Cockayne, **297, 298, 400**. Appendix, 121–6, lists some 50 poetical terms. Introduction surveys the linguistic resources of OE, 1–11, and classifies the terms on anatomical principles, 12–19.

461 Mercier, Charles Arthur. *Astrology in Medicine.* London: Macmillan, 1914.

Fitzpatrick Lectures for 1913. Lecture 1, 1–38, a general explanation of Astrology as a Science, beginning with the Chaldeans; the relation between

the heavens and the humours. Lecture 2, 39–75, an easily-grasped account of Lecture 1's application to medicine, from the 12th century onwards. Under all this lies 'the insatiable craving of the human mind for explanation.... Can we assume ourselves that we have outgrown and discarded the mental carapace that renders such beliefs as astrology possible.... And even in medicine itself, do we never take that for an explanation that is no explanation?' (75). Addendum on 'Saints and Signs,' delivered to the Casual Club, 79–89, ruminates quite interestingly on the invocation of saints to protect all parts of the body but does not offer specific reference: 'It used to be a point of honour with me, and I believe with other members of this Club, never to read up on the subject of the evening's discussion' (80).

462 Binz, Gustav. Rev. of 'The Anglo-Saxon Charms,' by Felix Grendon [**314**]. *Anglia Beiblatt* NS 27 (1916): 161–3.

Textual notes, and 'important additions' to the bibliography of Grendon, **314**; i.e., important to the comparative study of Germanic literature.

463 Bradley, Henry. 'Some Emendations in Old English Texts.' *Modern Language Review* 11 (1916): 212–15.

Includes a textual note on *Lb*1 6.7 (*þeforþorne* = 'bramblespine') and on 'Spider in Old English' [FC A.43.3].

464 Meissner, R. 'Die Zunge des grossen Mannes.' *Anglia* 40 (1916): 375–93.

Analysis of the metrical charm 'For a swarm of bees' [FC A.43.8].

465 Von Steinmeyer, Elias. *Die kleineren althochdeutschen Sprachdenkmäler.* Berlin: Weidmann, 1916.

Prints a 'Germanized OE recipe' (Greenfield and Robinson, 6382), 39; 'uuidhar cancur,' from Basel, Universitätsbibliothek, F. III. 15a, f. 17.

466 Singer, Charles. 'The Lorica of Gildas the Briton (?547). A Magicomedical Text containing an Anatomical Vocabulary.' *Proceedings of the Royal Society of Medicine* 12 (1918–19): Section of the History of Medicine 124–44.

Reprinted in Singer, **516**. [See Singer, **467**.]

467 Singer, Dorothea Waley. 'Survey of Medical Manuscripts in the British Isles dating from before the Sixteenth Century.' *Proceedings of the Royal Society of Medicine* 12 (1918–19): Section of the History of Medicine 96–107.

Singer lists the subject headings of a catalogue compiled by her, which contains some 30,000 manuscripts; about half 'fall in the medical or quasi-medical categories' (100). None of the (quasi-) medical manuscripts predates the 8th century, and most are dated 1200–1500; the manuscripts yield only a few thousand texts, since many are duplicates. Singer emphasizes the historical importance of medieval medical texts; her paper consists chiefly of

brief observations on 34 slides of medical manuscripts shown to her original audience, and it includes a numerical breakdown of medical texts according to subject, as well as three distribution graphs (chronology of 'All MSS. (Medical),' and 'English MSS. (Medical),' and 'No. of Medical MSS. in Western Languages'). [See Robbins, **525**. Many libraries which hold *Proceedings of the Royal Society of Medicine* did not receive the 'Section of the History of Medicine' for Vol. 12, which was issued as a Supplement; a copy is held by The Royal Society of Medicine Library, 1 Wimpole Street, London W1M 8AE.]

468 Holthausen, F. 'Zu altenglischen Dichtungen. 14. Zaubersegen.' *Anglia Beiblatt* 31 (1920): 30-2.

Textual notes on the metrical charms.

469 Holthausen, F. 'Zu den altenglischen Zaubersprüchen und Segen.' *Anglia Beiblatt* 31 (1920): 116–20.

Textual notes on the metrical charms [FC A.43.1–4, 6, 11].

470 Singer, Charles Joseph. 'Early English Magic and Medicine.' *Proceedings of the British Academy* 9 (1920): 341–74.

Singer emphasizes the close relation that existed in Anglo-Saxon thought between external and internal worlds, macrocosm and microcosm; Byrhtferth's diagram of 'the four fours' is illustrated and discussed. *Lac* is 'our best source of the primitive medicine of this country untouched by Christian influence' (342). Woden warring against the serpent in 'Lay of the Nine Herbs' [*Lac*, FC A.43.2] is a well-known Teutonic myth, and Woden was regarded as a bringer of good luck and good health. The custom of uttering a charm against disease is of Indo-European origin, and occurs over and over again in Anglo-Saxon literature; the charm against Flying Venom [*Lac* 74] illustrates the combination of pagan and Christian invocations which is frequently found in Anglo-Saxon charms. Much disease was attributed to supernatural beings; remedies for water-elf disease and elf-shot cattle [*Lb*] are examples of this tendency. Singer remarks that the doctrine of specific venoms, belief in the power of the number nine and in elf-shot, are not characteristic of Greek or Byzantine medicine; they are distinctively Teutonic, and all three are to be found in *Lac*. A description of Celtic magic is followed by some remarks on Anglo-Saxon plant lore and the tradition of plant illustration in herbals; Vitellius C.iii and Bodley 130 'attain a degree of realism and truth exhibited in no other department of medieval art' (367), even though the texts are merely bad copies of Latin works. [Abridged in Singer, **516**.]

471 Fehr, Bernhard. 'Altenglische Ritualtexte für Krankenbesuch, heilige Ölung und Begräbnis.' *Texte unde Forschungen zur englischen Kulturgeschichte. Festgabe für Felix Liebermann.* Ed. Max Förster and Karl Wildhagen. Halle: Niemeyer, 1921. 20–67.

Prints, with discussion, three *Ordines* for the visiting of the sick and the anointing and burial of the dead, from Laud 482 and CCCC 422 [FC B.12.5.3, 11]. Listed Bonser, 1957, 7412.

472 Thompson, Charles John Samuel. 'Chirurgie Anglo-Saxonne.' *1er Congrès de l'histoire de l'art guérir, 1920.* Liber Memorialis, 1921. 61-4.

Not sighted. Listed Bonser, 1957, 7479; unable to verify.

473 Rohde, Eleanour Sinclair. *The Old English Herbals.* New York: Longman, 1922.

Ch. 1, 'The Anglo-Saxon Herbals,' 1–41. 'In these manuscripts are embedded beliefs that carry us back to the dawn of time' (2). In them we find: 'what plant life meant to our ancestors' (2); 'the beliefs and customs of humble everyday people in Anglo-Saxon times' (12); 'traces not merely of the ancient religion, but of a religion older than that of Woden' (3). This is 'their strongest fascination,' and we should try to look at the world of nature as early Anglo-Saxons did, although 'one cannot help wondering how much the Saxons incorporated of the herb lore of the ancient Britons' (6). Rohde outlines the character of *Lb*, *PD*, *Herb* and *Lac* (5–12), and draws chiefly on *Lb* and *Lac* in remarking upon the following: beliefs concerning the origins of disease (elves, flying venom, worm and demonic possession); the almost exclusive use of herbs in healing recipes; the numerousness of recipes for broken heads, bleeding noses and mad dog bites; the picturesqueness of some cures; the use of herbs as amulets (Anglo-Saxons must have assimilated Druidic lore, but herbs held sacred by Druids are not prominent); the use of charms and incantations while administering and picking herbs; the transference of disease to inanimate objects; the prominence of nine and three as magic numbers; the intertwining of Nature worship with Christian rites and ceremonies (13–36). The chapter concludes with the author's transportation into a nameless dim past while contemplating 'the *Erce* charm' [FC A.43.1]. (Black-and-white plates include Vitellius C.iii, f. 19r.)

474 Sigerist, Henry E. *Studien und Texte zur frühmittalterlichen Rezeptliteratur.* Studien zur Geschichte der Medizin 13. Leipzig: Barth, 1923.

Edits *Antidotaria* from seven pre-Salernitan manuscripts (600–1000), 17–167, including Harley 5792 (7th/8th century), 17–21; Cambridge, University Library, Gg.5.35 (11th century), 160–7. Examines their contents and sources and compares them with the Salernitan *Antidotarium Nicolai*, in order to trace the development of this kind of literature from Greek sources through the early Middle Ages to Salerno, 1–16, 168–86. A comparison of these *Antidotaria* with the Salernitan pharmacopoeia, 187–95, makes evident that its chief sources were Arabic, and that de Renzi's claim that the Salernitan literature had not been influenced by the Arabs was incorrect.

475 Singer, Charles, and Henry E. Sigerist. *Essays on the History of Medicine: Presented to Karl Sudhoff on the Occasion of his Seventieth Birthday.* London: Oxford UP, 1924.

No OE reference. (Includes Charles and Dorothea Singer, 'The Origins of the Medical School of Salerno, the First European University: An Attempted Reconstruction,' 121–38.)

476 Diepgen, Paul. 'Zur Tradition des Pseudoapuleius.' *Janus* 29 (1925): 55–70, 140–60.

No OE reference apparent. Widely cited.

477 MacArthur, W.P. 'Some Notes on Old-time Leprosy in England and Ireland.' *Journal of the Royal Army Medical Corps* 45 (1925): 410–22.

MacArthur takes issue with the account of medieval leper laws in James Simpson's *Leprosy.* English legislation making leprosy a valid cause for divorce is found, if at all, in Edgar's laws; but OE terms for diseases are untrustworthy. *Seo mycle adl,* said by Simpson to signify leprosy, is not among the words for that disease in Ælfric's Grammar, and OE usually translates 'leprosy'—figurative and literal—by derivates or variants of *hreof,* whose meanings included scab, ulcerations and other morbid conditions (413, n. 1). MacArthur doubts that leprosy was prevalent in early England and Ireland; assessment of its incidence is hampered by biblical conceptions and linguistic imprecision. Irish sources claimed as the earliest references to leprosy actually refer to bubonic plague: *lobhar* also signifies a person with distempers or wretched appearance; *clam* also means scurvy, and, like English 'leprosy,' signified mange in animals; *samtrusg* cannot have been leprosy (416–17). Claims that there was a leper-hospital at Armagh in 869 are based on mistranslation (420–2). [No discussion of OE medical texts.]

478 MacArthur, W.P. 'Old-time Plague in Britain.' *Journal of the Royal Army Medical Corps* 47 (1926): 401–18.

MacArthur explains that bubonic plague is a disease of fleas, there being usually no evidence of its spread from one person to another; because its optimum temperature is *c.* 70 degrees F, it is dormant in winter in temperate climates. His account of epidemics in England up to the 17th century mentions the Anglo-Saxon period at 405. The Great Plague of Justinian (543) which swept Europe is mentioned by Irish chroniclers, and must have affected England; Irish records reveal that the plague of 664, described only in general terms by Bede, was also bubonic. Many epidemics, often attributed to hunger, are mentioned in Anglo-Saxon, Danish and Norman times ('Anglorum fames' became proverbial): 'It is likely that some of these old nameless and unrecognizable pestilences were bubonic plague, especially those recorded as causing a sudden high mortality, and accompanied by much panic' (405). [No discussion of OE medical texts.]

479 Banks, M.B. 'Widdershins; Irish Tuaithbheal, Tuathal.' *Folklore* 38 (1927): 86–8.

Takes issue with Bonser, **349**, 276, 283–5. Turning *deisal* was a widespread Aryan custom, not peculiar to the Celts, and its underlying motive was 'man's desire to move in harmony with the course of nature as observed by him through the centuries in the heavens' (86). Bonser says that *widdershins* was a custom not taken over, but Banks cites some examples of 13th–16th century practice in Ireland and Scotland. [No reference to OE texts.]

480 Bonser, Wilfrid. 'A Comparative Study of Magical Practices among the Anglo-Saxons.' Diss. U of London, 1927.

Not sighted. Listed Bonser, 1957, 7487.

481 Grattan, J.H.G. 'Three Anglo-Saxon Charms from the *Lacnunga*.' *Modern Language Review* 22 (1927): 1–6.

Discussion of metrical charms [FC A.43.2–4].

482 Ohrt, Ferdinand. 'Beitrage zur Segenforschung.' *Zeitschrift des Vereins für Volkskunde* 37 (1927): 1–9.

Suggests some Byzantine sources for Germanic and Nordic charms; includes discussion of Woden and the adder in the 'Nine Herbs Charm' [FC A.43.2].

483 Singer, Charles. 'Herbals.' *Edinburgh Review* 237 (1923): 95–112. Separately printed Bungay: Clay, 1927.

The thesis of Singer's survey of plant illustration from palaeolithic times to the Renaissance is that, in the development of naturalistic representation, plant illustration has always lagged behind. [Abridged account of the antique origins and development of herbals as in Singer, **410**.] 'Man is an imitative animal, but we doubt that any better instance of his imitativeness could be found than this constant copying and re-copying, for over a thousand years, with enormous labour and technical skill, of a futile work with its unrecognizable figures and its incomprehensible vocabulary' (104–5). The only thing English about OE herbals is their language: 'When they differ from their classical original it is usually due to an error of the translator or the scribe, to some misarrangement of the text, or to the introduction of some passage copied from another classical source. Even the figures can be shown to be taken from French or Italian documents' (106).

484 Singer, Charles. 'The Herbal in Antiquity and its Transmission to Later Ages.' *Journal of Hellenic Studies* 47 (1927): 1–52.

Singer traces the history of the illustrated herbal to modern times from its first appearance in the 4th century BC, with particular reference to the descent and transmission of Dioscorides, and the origins of pseudo-Apuleius. An abridged version of Singer, **410**, which mentions *Herb* (V) as an 'interesting branch' of the tradition (summary of conclusions at 50–2). In this

survey, Singer's thesis is the continuity of the classical tradition; contemporary English herb lore 'is not that of the ancient Anglo-Saxon, whose medical system was too primitive and debased to survive. It is rather the misinterpreted remains of Pliny and Apuleius, of Dioskurides and Galen, perverted at fortieth hand' (50).

485 James, R.R. 'Ophthalmic Leechdoms.' *British Journal of Ophthalmology.* 12 (1928): 401–10.

Abstracts some pertinent material from Cockayne, **400, 297, 298**: herbal cures for eye conditions in *Herb*, animal substances employed for ophthalmic treatment in *MedQuad* and Flyleaf Leechdoms; ophthalmic remedies in *Lb*. James contributes the observation that the Anglo-Saxon leech relied principally on extracts from roots or leaves, mixed in water, wine or honey.

486 Singer, Charles. 'Sketches in the History of English Medicine.' *Chemist and Druggist* 108 (1928): 823–32.

Late imperial medical practices are best preserved in Anglo-Saxon manuscripts because, between the 9th and 12th centuries, manuscripts suffered less destruction in southern England than elsewhere in Europe. To classical originals 'a certain amount of traditional pagan Teutonic magic has been added, and on top of all a Christian dressing has been put' (824). Although it is often assumed that these manuscripts were prepared in monasteries, Singer deduces, from illustrations of untonsured leeches and from cures specifying the ministrations of a priest, that some were prepared for laymen. Native Teutonic medicine may be distinguished from foreign elements by certain characteristic ideas; elfshot, the worm theory of disease, and arrangement of material in nines. Demonic possession represents a quite different conception of disease, but Anglo-Saxons swallowed anything, including many disagreeable substances to exorcise demons: 'an Anglo-Saxon remedy was sometimes worse than an Anglo-Saxon disease' (827). Plant lore is the most attractive aspect of Anglo-Saxon medicine, but is not native because many of the medicinal plants, non-naturalistically represented, are of southern origin. There are some attempts to measure quantities; pepper, aloes, zedoary and myrrh are frequently mentioned and may have been imported. Surgery, except for bloodletting, was practically unknown; branding, of Roman origin, was popular. Anglo-Saxon medical practices remained intact until the 13th century when new influences entered from the Arab world, although continental drugs were more accessible after the Conquest, and were given in smaller quantities. (Black-and-white illustrations from V, and from 12th and 13th century manuscripts, including Oxford, St John's College 17.)

487 Thorndike, Lynn. *A History of Magic and Experimental Science during the First Thirteen Centuries of our Era.* Vol. 1. New York: Columbia UP, 1929. 8 vols. 1923–58.

Ch. 29, 'Latin Astrology and Divination, Especially in the Ninth, Tenth and Eleventh Centuries,' 672–96, makes brief reference to Anglo-Saxon material; lists early medieval manuscripts containing *Spera Apuleii*, 692–6. Ch. 31, 'Anglo-Saxon, Salernitan, and other Latin Medicine in Manuscripts from the Ninth to the Twelfth Century,' 719–41, distinguishes early medieval medicine from post-classical medicine and later medieval medicine (which was influenced by Arab and oriental translations). A brief description of *Lb* concludes: 'The "modern" character of Bald's and Cild's book cannot be said to have any diminution of superstition as against the writings of antiquity. But we do find nature herbs introduced, also popular medicine and probably a considerable amount of Teutonic and perhaps also Celtic folklore, which, however, has been more or less Christianized. Indeed, the connection between medicine and religion is remarkably close' (722–3).

488 Sigerist, H.E. 'Zum Herbarius Pseudo-Apulei.' *Archiv für Geschichte der Medizin* 23 (1930): 197–204.

Concerns the circulation of the Latin text; examines illustrations, remedies and terms. Argues, against Singer, **410, 484**, that although pseudo-Apuleius doubtless drew on extant herbals, it was composed in Latin, not translated from Greek. Widely cited.

489 Strachan, L.R.M. 'Hernia among the Anglo-Saxons.' *Notes and Queries* 160 (1931): 192–3.

OE *bryce* ('breaking'), meaning 'hernia,' is not found, although its equivalent is found in late ME and many modern Germanic languages; nor is there an OE cognate of modern Icelandic *kvipslit*. The only OE term for hernia is *heala*, possibly related to 'hollow.' The sole example of its use cited by *BT* is Alfred's *Cura Pastoralis*, where it means hydrocele, not intestinal hernia (cf. Lev. 21.18, 20).

490 Baesecke, Georg. *Der Vocabularius Sti. Galli in der angelsächsischen Mission.* Halle: Niemeyer, 1933.

Not sighted; according to Greenfield and Robinson, 6384, 115, gives the text of the Germanized recipe printed by von Steinmeyer, **465**.

491 Mincoff, Marco K. 'Die Bedeutungsentwicklung der ags. Ausdrücke für "Kraft" und "Macht." ' *Palaestra* 188 (1933).

A study of the semantic development of *strang, stearc, swiþ, eofoþ, ellen, cræft, mægen, miht, wealdan* and *rice*.

492 Sigerist, Henry E. 'The Medical Literature of the Early Middle Ages.' *Bulletin of the Institute of the History of Medicine* 2 (1934): 26–52, 559–610.

This two-part autobiographical article projects, as the culmination of Sigerist's lifelong enquiry into the means by which Greek literature was transmitted to the West and how it survived there, a three-volume study of early

medieval medical literature. The projected study was to comprise: a geographically arranged catalogue of manuscripts; texts hitherto unpublished or unsatisfactorily edited; a history of the development and characteristics of early medieval medicine (including medical centres and the influence of the monasteries) together with an account of the transmission of the texts. Sigerist's sporadic observations on 43 manuscripts he examined during his summer holidays in Italy (38–50, 596–610), France and Belgium (560–93) and Switzerland (593–96) might still be of interest to scholars (includes Lucca 296, 36, 48). Catalogues of medieval medical manuscripts (esp. French) included in documentation.

493 Hunger, Friedrich W.T. *The Herbal of Pseudo-Apuleius from the Ninth Century MS. in the Abbey of Monte Cassino—Codex Casinensis 97— Together with the first printed Edition of Joh. Phil. de Lignamine—Editio Princeps Romae 1481—both in Facsimile.* Leiden: Brill, 1935.

Facsimile of the version identified by Howald and Sigerist, *Antonii Musae de Herba Vettonica Liber*, 1927, xxvi, as the closest relative of *Herb* in V, and depicted by Singer, **326**, 26–7, as the direct ancestor of V. The introduction examines the origins of the Herbal, which, unlike Singer, **484**, Hunger regards as Latin, not Greek (xvii–xviii), and the textual tradition. Whereas the stemma of Howald and Sigerist showed de Lignamine's *editio princeps* in a different line of descent from Casinensis 97, Hunger demonstrates that the *editio princeps* was based on Casinensis 97 (xxv–xxviii), and that two manuscripts which Howald and Sigerist show as antedating the *editio princeps* (British Library, Add. 17063 and 21115) cannot be sister manuscripts of the source of the *editio princeps* but must be copies of the first edition (xxxix).

494 Mezger, F. 'Der germanische Kult und die ae. Feminina auf -*icge* und -*estre*.' *Archiv für das Studium der neueren Sprachen und Literaturen* 168 (1935): 177–84.

Examines feminine suffixes relating to magic and witchcraft; -*icge*, 177–81, -*estre*, 181–4. [Extensive OE citations; undocumented.]

495 Serjeantson, Mary Sidney. 'The Vocabulary of Folk-lore in Old and Middle English.' *Folklore* (1936): 42–73.

Serjeantson does not examine our ancestors' beliefs (which have been over-elaborated on inadequate evidence by scholars such as Grimm, **430**, and Grendon, **314**) but OE *words* (and their ME developments) for 'magic, witchcraft and sorcery in general, together with the names for persons practising these; divination and augury; charms, spells and incantations; dreams, spectres and illusions; and supernatural beings' (43). Her demonstration of 'the variety and in some cases the picturesqueness' (73) of the vocabulary ranges widely (and fleetingly) over the OE corpus; relies heavily on Grendon, **314**.

496 Singer, Charles Joseph. 'Magic and Medicine in Early England.' *Nature* 137 (1936): 1081.

Fison Memorial lecture synopsis. The mass of pre-Anglo-Saxon magico-medical material in use in England has almost entirely disappeared; the only recognizable traces of it have been recovered by folklorists. English medical folklore is largely in line with, and probably derived from, the herb lore of Salerno. The Leechbooks, however, whether Latin or English, contain some material of distinctive character, some of pagan origin. In them, magical and simple herbal remedies are inextricably linked. Anglo-Saxon leeches were probably men of yeoman or farmer class who combined with their calling a hereditary knowledge of leechcraft. The actual remedies represent, on the whole, corrupted and misunderstood classical medicine of Greek origin. Ecclesiastical elements are strong. The Leechbooks provide evidence for some direct traffic in Anglo-Saxon times between Southern Italy and England. A certain amount of material consists of direct translation of Salernitan remedies, and there is evidence of direct copying of figures from that source. Pagan elements, whether classical, Anglo-Saxon, Celtic, or other, are very few and unimportant. The material and spirit of the Leechbooks are overwhelmingly Latin and Christian.

497 Von Erhardt-Siebold, Erika. 'The Hellebore in Anglo-Saxon Pharmacy.' *Englische Studien* 71 (1936–7): 161–70.

Aldhelm's Riddle 98 (*'Elleborus'*) shows that *Mezereum L.* (daphne) was a common substitute for genuine *hellebore* in Anglo-Saxon pharmacy (both are useful for purging and vomiting but can also cause vertigo and convulsions). Four of the OE synonyms for *hellebore* found in Leechdoms and glosses (*BT*) confirm this conclusion: *ceasterwyrt* and *ceasteræsc* ('daphne-mountain-ash') are related to Gk *cestron*, meaning 'bolt, hammer,' hence *hamorwyrt*; *wedeberge*, 'madberry,' 'refers to mental disorders which had been associated with the name *hellebore* since antiquity, while clearly pointing to a berry-bearing plant' (169). 'This result is particularly interesting, since the assumption heretofore was that the Mezereum had been used as a medicament in Northern Europe only at a comparatively late date' (169). Pliny, *Natural History*, 13.21.35, provided the medieval pharmacist with vindication of his equation *elleborus = daphne (Mezereum)*, and even in some classical texts *hellebore* may refer to substitutes other than the *veratrum* species (frequently termed *hellebore* in antiquity and in modern times).

498 Magoun, F.P., Jr. 'Strophische Überreste in den altenglischen Zaubersprüchen.' *Englische Studien* 72 (1937–8): 1–6.

Analysis of *Fafnismál*, st. 13, and metrical charms, Grendon A1 and A13, illustrates the triadic structure and metre characteristic of *galdrar* (a common-Germanic magic-ritual poetic form); Grendon A4 (5–6), A14 (2–3), A16 (7–9), E1 (4–6), B4 (5–6) [all metrical charms] are similar in form. Magoun remarks briefly on the relation of this metrical form to the *ljóðháttr*.

499 Gramm, Willi. *Die Körperpflege der Angelsachsen. Eine kulturegeschicht-lich-etymologische Untersuchung.* Anglistische Forschungen 86. Heidelberg: Winter, 1938.

1, 'Kulturgeschichtlicher Teil,' 1–38, surveys in turn 'Das Körperideal' and 'Die Bewertung der Körperschönheit,' the care of the face, hair, beard, teeth, hands and feet, bathing and bodily exercise; the etymological word-list in Part 2, 39–120, adopts the same classifications (prints relevant Latin passages, 121–6). Texts covered include Cockayne, **400, 297, 298**.

500 Olivieri, Alexander. 'Medicinalia magica.' *Philologische Wochenschrift* 59 (1939): 142–3.

Prints, with discussion, the Greek text from Vatican Palatino 199, f. 122r, which consists of three remedies for stanching blood from Aetius Amidenus. Two of these contain the incantatory formula, 'Let us stand respectfully, let us stand in awe.' [Storms, **325**, prints the second of these two remedies in his commentary on Storms 54, explaining that the Latin formula employed in the charm is a Latin transcription of a Greek formula commonly used to stop bleeding; the article itself has no OE reference.]

501 Sigerist, Henry E. 'Materia Medica in the Middle Ages: A Review.' *Bulletin of the History of Medicine* 7 (1939): 417–23.

In his review of Margaret Sinclair Ogden's *The 'Liber de Diversis Medicinis'* (EETS 27, 1938) Sigerist includes a summary of the descent of the *Materia Medica* of Dioscorides up to the *Dyascorides alphabeticus* (possibly a product of the pre-Constantinian period of the Salernitan School), and some account of the *Antidotaria* and *Receptaria* of the early Middle Ages. No mention of OE texts. Widely cited.

502 Lambert, Catherine. 'The Old English Medical Vocabulary.' *Proceedings of the Royal Society of Medicine* 33 (1939–40): 137–45.

Copious examples are drawn from *Herb*, *MedQuad*, *Lb*, and *Lac*. Lambert observes that the commonest words in OE for illness were *untrumness*, and compounds with *-trymness*. *Adl* was the most important word for disease, and its compounds were used for a variety of maladies. *Coðu* survived in literature until the 15th century, and still survives in dialect for a disease in cattle. Lambert discusses these words and their compounds (137–8), and goes on to discuss less common words for physical and mental disease and their remedies (138–54).

503 Helboek, Hans. 'Studies on Prehistoric and Anglo-Saxon Cultivated Plants in England.' *Proceedings of the Prehistoric Society* 6 (1940): 176–8.

The table of impressions of grain on Cambridgeshire pottery sherds, 176, includes Anglo-Saxon cemetery finds: naked barley (1); husked barley (34); oats (6); flax (2); woad (1); wild oat-grass (1). Impressions of emmer occur only on Bronze Age sherds; common wheat (identified only at an Early

Iron Age settlement) appears to have been rare. Barley, imported from the east, was an important cultivated plant in Stone-Age Europe; naked and husked barley occur with equal frequency in the Bronze Age, but the husked species predominated in Anglo-Saxon times. Oats were presumably introduced into Britain by the Romans. Flax was present in Central Europe from late Neolithic times and in Denmark from the Early Iron Age. Woad was already cultivated in Northern countries in the Iron Age. Knowledge of grain growing had reached the British Isles in the latter part of the Stone Age, but the relative paucity of pottery inhibits a comprehensive picture of its extent and nature. [No reference to OE texts.]

504 Bonser, Wilfrid. 'Epidemics during the Anglo-Saxon Period. With an Appendix by Lieut.-General Sir William MacArthur.' *Journal of the British Archaeological Association.* 3rd ser. 9 (1946 *for* 1944): 48–71.

Bonser remarks upon possible historical effects of plague (decline of Northumbria, Danish conquest), relative immunity of England before Danish incursions, terror inspired by religious attitudes, derivation from classical sources of both Anglo-Saxon theories of aetiology (supernatural arrows and corruption of the air), transmission by travelling monks and mobility in times of war, crowded and unhygienic conditions (48–52). He identifies four periods of epidemics (recorded outbreaks in Ireland and England, *c.* 526–1087, tabled at 52–3): 6th and 7th century (chiefly 'pestis flava,' yellow plague); Danish invasion period and reign of the Confessor (apparently resulting from famine). MacArthur's Appendix, 66–71, argues that the famine fevers recorded in *ASC* were, like those in 18th and 19th century Ireland, lice-transmitted typhus epidemics, usually beginning and ending with outbreaks of relapsing fever, aggravated by hunger, inclement weather, and consequent mobility in search of food (Rushworth Gospels, Matt. 8.15, shows that *drif, ASC* 1087 = 'fever,' not 'diarrhoea'). Whereas Justinian's plague and the 664 plague described by Bede were bubonic, 'the "mortalitas magna" of the 6th century, named at the time the Pestis Flava and the Buidhe Chonaill, was a severe form of *relapsing fever*, with jaundice common enough to dominate the general picture of the disease' (71). [No discussion of OE medical texts.]

505 Magoun, Francis Peabody, Jr. 'On Some Survivals of Pagan Belief in Anglo-Saxon England.' *Harvard Theological Review* 40 (1947): 33-46.

The concept of 'mana' as a power also possessed by the non-human creation is one that OE shares with ON; Magoun explores this proposition, chiefly with reference to *Beowulf.* Two charms in *Lb* are also mentioned; Grendon B5 (the metrical charm, 'For the Water-Elf Disease'), lines 14–15, invokes the mana of earth to overcome the disease-bearing water-elf; in Grendon D5, lines 1–2 [Cockayne, 2: 296], the eight-fold potency of the agate is equated with mana.

506 Storms, G. *Anglo-Saxon Magic.* Diss. 's-Gravenhage [The Hague], 1948.

Not sighted. Listed de Vriend, **401**.

507 Helm, Karl. 'Der angelsächsische Flursege.' *Hessische Blätter für Volkskunde* 41 (1950): 34–44.

Argues that the metrical charm for unfruitful land [FC A.43.1] is evidence of the survival of the Nerthus cult.

508 Holthausen, F. 'Zur Textkritik alt- und mittelenglischer Gedichte.' *Archiv für das Studium der neueren Sprachen und Literaturen* 187 (1950): 98–107.

'Zu den Zaubersprüchen,' 99–100, contains emendations to the metrical charms, based on Holthausen's analysis of metre. Also includes a note on the 'Proverb from Wynfrid's time,' 101; Holthausen takes *foreldit* as an intransitive verb, and translates: 'Often the lazy becomes too old for glory, for every lucky expedition.'

509 MacArthur, Sir William. 'A Brief Story of English Malaria.' *British Medical Bulletin* 8 (1951): 76–9.

Identifies *lenctenadl*, 'spring ill,' as malaria; in England parasites were dormant in winter, causing relapses in spring (78). At one point, *OE Bede* substitutes *lenctenadl* for *febris*.

510 Bonser, Wilfrid. 'Anglo-Saxon Medical Nomenclature.' *English and Germanic Studies* 4 (1951–2): 13–19.

Bonser's intention is to supplement Lambert, **502**, and to elucidate Anglo-Saxon usage and psychology; the Anglo-Saxon and late Latin period marks 'the lowest degradation to which medicine has fallen' (13), and the lack of precision both in diagnosis and terminology is especially marked. Words for the body (especially in *Lac* and the Lorica) show a considerable though superficial knowledge of anatomy; *lic + hama = 'living* body.' Words for disease in general are *adl*, *coðu*, *ece*, *wærc* and *seocness*; Bonser gives the meaning of some compounds in which these occur, particularly those mistranslated by Cockayne (examples include *fotadl* = 'septic foot' not 'gout'; *lipadl* = ?'rheumatoid arthritis'; *lenden-ece* = 'kidney disease' not 'lumbago'; *sweorcoðu* = ?'quinsy.') Internal diseases were a complete mystery, and therefore not taken in hand; but there are many words for the digestive tract and its diseases (examples include *heortcoðu* = 'disordered stomach'). The exterior of the body claimed most attention, and therefore many words relate to morbid skin conditions; these were prevalent, according to Bonser, because of lack of vitamins and hygiene, and are attributed by *Lb* to overeating (examples include *hreofl* and *blæco*, which may mean leprosy, although Bonser finds no evidence of its existence in the period). Pestilence was caused by Viking depredations and severe winters: pestilence of both Man and beast is usually termed *wol* in *OE Bede*, but *ASC* differentiates (*orfcwealm* or *mancwealm*). *Lenctenadl* = 'flu,' because typhus was unknown;

cynelic adl = 'jaundice,' not 'scrofula.' Some words used for surgical instruments and salves, together with compounds containing *læce*, are listed. [Many other OE terms cited; annotation mentions only those elucidated by the author.]

511 Bonser, Wilfrid. 'General Medical Practice in Anglo-Saxon England.' *Science, Medicine and History. Essays on the Evolution of Scientific Thought and Medical Practice written in Honour of Charles Singer.* Vol. 1. Ed. E. Ashworth Underwood. London: Oxford UP, 1953. 154–63. 2 vols. New York: Arno, 1975.

A brief survey of the available sources, adumbrating the direction of Bonser, **517**, into which the illustrative material here appearing was incorporated.

512 Grön, Fredrik. 'Remarks on the Earliest Medical Conditions in Norway and Iceland with Special Reference to British Influence.' *Science, Medicine and History. Essays on the Evolution of Scientific Thought and Medical Practice written in Honour of Charles Singer.* Vol 1. Ed. E. Ashworth Underwood. London: Oxford UP, 1953. 143–53. 2 vols. New York: Arno, 1975.

Cockayne, **297**, pointed out that active relations between Norway and the British Isles left a deep impression on the popular medicine of both countries. Grön gives miscellaneous examples, with particular emphasis on terminology. At 147 he compares *Hávamál* 137 (which Grön construes as an allusion to the use of earthworm against sickness from bites) with the use of crushed earthworm in Cockayne, **297**, 2: 328 [*Lb*]. At 151–2 he deals with some OE expressions in *Lb* derived from ON, mentioned by Cockayne, 2: xxxii. The first element of *torbegete* is found in combinations of words in ON, and the whole word means 'difficult to get.' *Rudniolin* means 'red hollow stalk,' called in Norwegian *vasspepper*, and thus English 'water pepper.' *Fornets palm* is *Orchis maculata*, and derives its name from 'an ON giant called Fornjotr.' Grön agrees with Cockayne, 2: 369, that behind *Anawyrm* ('Ons Worm') is the story of King Aun in *Ynglinga Saga* (ch. 29), which must have passed to Anglo-Saxon from Norwegian. Grön also suggests that dysentery and leprosy reached Norway from Anglo-Saxon England.

513 Forster, Leonard. ' "Rivos cruoris torridi" in Charms to Staunch Bleeding.' *English Studies* 36 (1955): 308–9.

The Latin charm in Storms 57–9 (from Royal 2 A.xx, 11th century), appearing in an uncorrupted form in Storms 57, is stanza 17 of Sedulius's *Hymnus de Vita Christi*, referring to the healing of the woman with an issue of blood; it takes the place of the *historiola*, providing the basis of analogy for the invocation. The Latin of the invocation in all three versions is corrupt but seems to point to Mark 5.29. Sedulius's hymn was popular in the Middle Ages, and other charms may prove to contain echoes of its miracle stanzas.

514 Beccaria, Augusto. *I Codici de Medicina del Periodo Presalernitano (Secoli IX, X e XI).* Storia e Letteratura, Raccolta di Studi e Testi 53. Rome: Edizioni di Storia e Letteratura, 1956.

Descriptive catalogue of pre-Salernitan medical manuscripts. Sixteen English manuscripts (OE and Latin) are described, at 237–75: Cambridge, University Library Gg.5.35 and St John's College D.4; Cheltenham, Library of Sir Thomas Phillipps 386; Glasgow, Hunter V.3.2.; British Library, Vitellius C.iii, Harley 585, Harley 3271, Harley 4986, Sloane 475, Sloane 1122, Royal 12 D.xvii, Arundel 166 and Add. 8928; Bodleian, Hatton 76 and Bodley 130.

515 Davidson, Thomas. 'Elfshot Cattle.' *Antiquity* 30 (1956): 149–55.

Davidson adduces 17th–19th century evidence of belief in elf-shot in Britain (especially Scotland and Ireland) and its relationship to neolithic flints. *Lac* (especially the cure for elf-shot horse) is cited as evidence of Anglo-Saxon attribution of human and animal diseases to elf-shot (153–4). Davidson explains that curved plough furrows in Scotland and the North were intended to protect plough oxen by confusing, or 'wandering,' fairy marksmen when they took aim. Davidson is struck by the survival into the late 19th century of 'passive acceptance of the supernatural, ... of the most primitive belief that all natural phenomena were the work of unseen spirits to whom was attributed all the ills that beset mankind' (155).

516 Singer, Charles Joseph. *From Magic to Science: Essays on the Scientific Twilight.* New York: Dover, 1958.

Ch. 1, 'Science under the Roman Empire,' 1–58. Ch. 2, 'The Dark Ages and the Dawn of Science,' 59–110. Surveys the limitations and content of medieval science, with some reference to Arabian infiltration and scholasticism, and the (re-)birth of the scientific idea in the Renaissance. Ch. 3, 'The Lorica of Gildas the Briton: A Magical Text of the Sixth Century,' 111–32. Prints text of Harley 2965 (Latin), with translation, 122–7. Introduction discusses title, author and date, 111–16; language, 117–22. Notes on vocabulary, with reference to the two OE glosses, i.e., in *Lac* [FC C.22] and the *Book of Cerne* [FC C.83], 127–31; Appendix, 132, lists six manuscript versions. Ch. 4, 'Early English Magic and Medicine,' 133–67 (abridgement of Singer, **470**). Ch. 5, 'Early Herbals,' 168–98 (abridgement of Singer, **483**). Ch. 6, 'The Visions of Hildegard of Bingen,' 199–239. Ch. 7, 'The School of Salerno and its Legends,' 240–8.

517 Bonser, Wilfrid. *The Medical Background of Anglo-Saxon England: A Study in History, Psychology and Folklore.* Publications of the Wellcome Historical Medical Library NS 3. London: Wellcome Historical Medical Library, 1963.

Bonser hopes to show 'that the medical background will throw new light on the social and economic conditions [and] some aspects of political history

which have not hitherto been fully explained' (vii). This broad survey of the topic is prolifically illustrated by translations from OE and Latin texts; commentary on the substance of the texts is minimal. There is no index of texts; manuscript sources, listed xvii–xix, are those edited by Cockayne, **400, 297, 298**, and some Latin manuscripts, including Oxford, St John's College 17. Contents: Part 1: General (Introduction; Documents and research material; Aetiology of disease and sources of Anglo-Saxon knowledge of medicine), 3–47. Part 2: Historical (Epidemics; Hospitals; Surgery; Medical histories of distinguished persons), 51–113. Part 3: The Pagan Background (Survivals of paganism; Elves, elf-shot and nightmare), 117–67. Part 4: The Church as Physician (Healing by holy men in person; Healing by means of relics), 171–210. Part 5: Magic As An Adjunct To Medicine (Things possessing magical properties which aid cures; Taboos; Protective measures; Sympathetic magic), 213–54. Part 6: Diseases and Conditions Treated by Magical Means (Mental diseases and devil-possession; Child-birth; 'King's Evil'; Poison; Prognostic measures), 257–89. Part 7: Remedial Measures (Remedies and applications; Herb remedies; Animal and mineral remedies), 293–346. Part 8: Food, Drink and Diet, 349–65. Part 9: Organic (And A Few Other) Diseases And Their Treatment (Skin diseases; The body from the head downwards; Other diseases), 369–418. Part 10: Veterinary and Agricultural Magic (Veterinary medicine and charms for livestock; The Earth, and charms for the fertility of the fields), 421–40.

518 Crawford, Jane. 'Evidence for Witchcraft in Anglo-Saxon England.' *Medium Ævum* 32 (1963): 99–116.

Crawford finds little evidence in the Anglo-Saxon period of 'ideas of witchcraft which so tortured Europe in later centuries' (115–16). Magico-medical literature figures, in general terms, in the wide variety of material drawn into the discussion: 'This body of material edited by Cockayne can scarcely be regarded as the spells and formulae of dreaded magicians, for any lingering traces of native medical lore they contain are embedded in a Graeco-Roman medical tradition. The men who used these recipes and charms were the accepted medical practitioners of their time, and it is highly likely that they received especial training' (101). A few metrical charms are considered [FC A.43.1, 2, 4, 8]. 'As yet the Anglo-Saxons were without the concept of especially evil woman magicians' (106): *wyrtgælstre*, in the horoscope warning against a woman born on the fifth day of the moon because she will be *yfeldæda 7 wyrtgælstre* [Cockayne, **298**, 3: 186], suggests that those who worked with herbs used incantations as an integral part of their cure (105). *Lb*3[.61] reflects belief in the power the devil may assume over both body and mind; 'It is tempting to suggest that originally the heading of this receipt may have read *wiþ ælfcynne* ... and that some scribe, thinking the salve meant to shield Christians from heathen foes, added to the title other enemies he thought it would prevail against' (110).

519 Fife, Austin E. 'Christian Swarm Charms from the Ninth to the Nineteenth Centuries.' *Journal of American Folklore* 77 (1964): 154–60.

Reference is made only to the metrical charm [FC A.43.8].

520 Wells, Calvin. *Bones, Bodies and Disease: Evidence of Disease and Abnormality in Early Man*. Ancient Peoples and Places 37. London: Thames, 1964.

This frequently cited and wide-ranging palaeopathological study (Stone Age to the 18th century) includes chapters on types of abnormalities (36–130) and trephination (141–8), but contains no specific study of the Anglo-Saxon period; a 'Saxon' jaw and thigh bone, and a trephined British skull, are included among the plates.

521 MacKinney, Loren Carey. *Medical Illustrations in Medieval Manuscripts*. London: Wellcome Historical Medical Library, 1965.

Illustrations from manuscripts (some 12th century, few earlier), showing the practice of medicine, surgery, dentistry, etc.; includes check-list of medieval miniatures in extant manuscripts.

522 Talbot, C.H., and E.A. Hammond. *The Medical Practitioners in Medieval England: A Biographical Register*. Publications of the Wellcome Historical Medical Library NS 8. London: Wellcome Historical Medical Library, 1965.

Problems of definition and documentation, v–x. The names of only a few Anglo-Saxons are recorded (Cynefrid, 31, is the earliest).

523 Lauer, Hans Hugo. 'Zur Beurteilung des Arabismus in der Medizin des mittelalterlichen England.' *Sudhoffs Archiv: Vierteljarhsschrift für Geschichte der Medizin und der Naturwissenschaften, der Pharmazie und der Mathematik* 51 (1967): 326–48.

Lauer surveys Arab influence in England up to the 14th century, arguing that it participated fully in the reception of Arab medicine in the 12th century; brief consideration of the Anglo-Saxon period postulates that familiarity with oriental drugs (*Lb*) shows that Anglo-Saxons had contact with the east.

524 Talbot, C.H. *Medicine in Medieval England*. London: Oldbourne, 1967.

Ch. 1, 'Anglo-Saxon Medicine,' 9–23, outlines Anglo-Saxon contact with, and creation of, centres of learning. Talbot surveys the transmission to the West of Galen and Hippocrates (via Oribasius), and of Pliny and Dioscorides (via Soranus of Ephesus), in order to indicate the extensive medical material to which Theodore could have had access when he established the Canterbury school. Contact with continental educational centres initiated by missionary activity, Alfred's importation of teachers, and the pedagogic activity of Abbo at Byrhtferth's Ramsey, receive notice. Then follows a

summary account of the Latin sources of *Lb*1&2, *PD*, *Herb*, and *MedQuad*, which echoes the discovery of Talbot, **369**, that *Lb*1&2 draws on the same sources as *PD*. Talbot observes that the headings for *Lb*'s missing chapter on gynaecology [*Lb*2.60] suggest knowledge of an abridgement of Hippocrates, *De mulierum affectibus*, as do fragments occurring in other Anglo-Saxon manuscripts dealing with the formation of the foetus, signs of pregnancy, prognostication of the sex of the child and other details of gynaecological interest. Codex Hertensis 192, of 9th century English origin, containing the work of Dioscorides, Antonius Musa and Sextus Placitus, is evidence that these texts were circulating in England well before the date assigned to the OE translations. Talbot emphasizes the atypicality of *Lac*, which he regards as a product of 10th century pagan decadence. 'No amount of quotations from the lives of saints, where miraculous cures are described, can obscure the fact that in a society that produced writers like Ælfric ... Byrhtferth and others, superstition and magic would have little place' (22). It is men such as these who are characteristically representative of (medical) science in England after the 10th century revival. *Lac* 'may show "the final, pathological disintegration of Greek medical thought," but it does not show that Anglo-Saxon scholars were involved in it' (23). [Subsequent chapters deal with Arab medicine, the Schools of Salerno and Montpellier, and aspects of later medieval medicine.]

525 Robbins, Rossell Hope. 'A Note on the Singer Survey of Medical Manuscripts in the British Isles.' *Chaucer Review* 4 (1969–70): 68–70.

Singer, **467**, is still the only published source of information on her catalogue of Latin and vernacular medical manuscripts in Great Britain, 8th–15th century (BM CUP D.65; available on microfilm in the US, in the Library of Congress, Olfin Library at Cornell, etc.). For the advanced scholar, the filing cards in these shoe-type boxes are of utmost value, but Robbins cautions (with particular reference to ME manuscripts) that her survey is incomplete, errs in the dating of manuscripts, confuses medical and non-medical texts and inflates the figures.

526 Schneider, Karl. 'Zu den altenglischen Zaubersprüchen.' *Anglia* 87 (1969): 282–302.

Analysis of two metrical charms [FC A.43.7, 12].

527 Rubin, Stanley. 'The Medical Practitioner in Anglo-Saxon England.' *Journal of the Royal College of General Practitioners* 20 (1970): 63–71.

Reproduced in abridged form, with some additions, in Rubin, **531**.

528 Barley, Nigel. 'Anglo-Saxon Magico-Medicine.' *Journal of the Anthropological Society of Oxford* 3 (1972): 67–76.

Barley considers that the basic mistake of previous studies of the OE magico-medical literature is that they deal with its ultimate historical origins, instead of looking at the synchronic system. Anglo-Saxons primarily regard

sickness as an invasion of the body (flying venoms, *wyrm* and evil spirits). Either the intrusive force can be removed or a transfusion of *hælu* into the body can be given. 'From this view of the world stems the leech's concern with ingestion and excretion ... with destructuring the present state and redefining boundaries' (70). Disease is also regarded as a disruption of the natural order of the body; in such cases, cure takes the form of reaffirming Man's place in the regular course of events. The more a disorder is localized, the more likely it is to be treated by a salve; more diffuse maladies are treated by drinks. 'The general principle is an association of symptoms and remedies with a subsequent destructuring to achieve identity of the two' (73). (Examples are: the reduction of ingredients to a destructured mass, the use of alcohol, the use of ingredients that have been broken down by fermentation and curdling). Often the link between ailment and cure seems mainly linguistic. 'Anglo-Saxon ethnomedicine is far from being the unstructured mass that some authors have implied, but a rich symbolic system in no way inferior to those treated by anthropologists in other parts of the world' (76). [Numerous examples, in translation; undocumented.]

529 Howe, G. Melvyn. *Man, Environment and Disease in Britain: A Medical Geography through the Ages.* New York: Barnes, 1972.

Ch. 6, 'Pre-Norman and Norman Times,' 73–92, gives a rudimentary account of settlements from prehistoric times to the Conquest, with occasional reference to the landscape (73–82). 'Palaeopathologists ... have indicated the presence of leprosy, syphilis, tuberculosis, osteo-arthritis, tumours and dental caries' (83). The frequency of leprosy cannot be gauged since what was called 'leprosy' was influenced by biblical usage; the term may apply to skin diseases, which may be inferred from poor diet and the lack of personal hygiene. The presence of syphilis is confirmed only by one skull (female); there is need for caution, since bone lesions are caused by yaws as well as by syphilis (both venereal and endemic). 'Plague' and 'pestilence' are generic terms for diseases with a high mortality; true plague (bubonic or pneumonic) might have been included in the range of meanings, but typhus or some other disease may have been meant. Howe summarizes MacArthur, 509, on malaria, and refers to the pestilence reported in *ASC* 1010 or 1011 (possibly dysentery, which prevails where standards of hygiene and sanitation are low). 'Pock disease' and 'pox' refer to smallpox (insignificant until the 16th century), not to syphilis. Howe does not consider treatment of disease, but observes that *Lb* 'embodies some of the best medical literature available in Britain and western Europe at that time and also provides an indication of the separation between spiritual and physical conceptions of disease healing' (92).

530 Riddle, John M. 'Theory and Practice in Medieval Medicine.' *Viator* 5 (1974): 147–84.

Riddle takes issue with early medical historians (Sudhoff, Sigerist and Singer), arguing that drug therapy and medical education of the late Roman and

early medieval period were not distinct and that the movement to re-establish
the pre-eminence of medical theory (from the 11th century onward), was
somewhat retrogressive, since 'it produced a gap between theory and practice which did little to aid the practicing physician because the new drug
theory was unworkable' (159). Cites Talbot, **524**, 18–19, on the purposeful
and rational modifications to earlier works made by *Lb*.

531 Rubin, Stanley. *Medieval English Medicine (AD 500–1300).* Newton Abbot: David; New York: Barnes, 1974.

Rubin intends 'as complete and accurate a picture as primary evidence per-
mits of disease, sickness and medical practice in their widest sense' and
purports to show 'how disease and its consequences were seen through contemporary eyes' (9). Ch. 2, 'Medical Sources,' 43–69, stresses the unique-
ness of the existence of a vernacular medical literature, and characterizes
in turn *Herb*, *MedQuad*, *Lb*, *Lac* and *PD*; there is also brief reference to
Miscellaneous Leechdoms and St John's College 17. Some additions to
Herb suggest first-hand knowledge, but many plant names are inaccurate.
MedQuad best reveals 'the primitive and distasteful side of English Dark
Age medicine' (50), although honey prescribed for earache may have been
beneficial (ch. 11), and the chapter on the dog includes rational treatment
for a fracture. *Lb* is based on traditional ideas rather than knowledge of
pathological processes, but the translator shows genuine understanding of
his material in the selection and organization of material. *Lac* is 'an inferior medical work' (62), providing many examples of pagan magic. The two
centuries that separate *PD* from *Lb* may account for the greater degree of
rational material, although many passages are common to both texts. Rubin
concludes that the effects of the cures described in all these treatises cannot
have been very beneficial by any standards: 'some of the herbal mixtures
and ointments may well have had ameliorating properties, but it cannot be
surprising that many turned to the help and comfort offered by the Church'
(69). Ch. 4, 'The Physician and his Treatment,' 97–128, describes magic and
superstition in medicine (109–18) and miscellaneous treatments (118–28),
drawing chiefly on *Lb* and *Lac*, and concludes that 'the Anglo-Saxon leech
did try to alleviate the sickness and distress from which his patients suffered
and carried out his work with some regard to the ethics and morality of his
calling' (128). Ch. 5, 'Surgery,' 129–49, draws chiefly on *Lb* and *Herb*, and
gives particular attention to fractures, dislocations and wounds, amputa-
tions (and the use of narcotics), suturing and bloodletting. The description
of the technique for amputation in *Lb*1.35 is remarkably accurate. Anglo-
Saxon surgeons are unlikely to have performed the operations described,
in view of the general standards of the time; suturing and operation inci-
sions were not beyond their competence. Legal attitudes to personal injury
are discussed at 144–9. Remaining chapters, containing little reference to
OE medical texts, are: ch. 1, 'Archaeological Evidence,' 19–42 (reviews the
types of diseases most commonly found in surviving bones); ch. 3, 'Religious

Sources,' 70–96 (includes discussion of Anglo-Saxon epidemics); ch. 6, 'The Problem of Leprosy,' 150–71; ch. 7, 'The Monastic Infirmary,' 172–88; ch. 8, 'Towards Enlightenment,' 189–208.

532 Gough, J.V. 'Some Old English Glosses.' *Anglia* 92 (1974): 273–90.

Prints, with commentary, previously unpublished glosses from four manuscripts, including the Anderson Pontifical [FC C.82.5]. The glosses in Ashmole 1431 [misnumbered as 1931; FC C.36], at 275–9, are names of herbs and the diseases for which they are remedies, written in a hand nearly contemporary with the manuscript, which Gough dates late 11th century. The glosses in St John's College 17 (once belonging to St Augustine's, but not produced there) are listed; Gough prints, 283–4, names of relationships [FC C.95.2], names of the months [FC B.24.4], and names of week days [FC B.24.3], the last inaccurately transcribed by Jones, *Bede Opera*, 1943, 340. Glosses to some of the titles of the chapters of the *De viribus herbarum* of 'Macer' [FC C.84], printed at 285–8, occur in the 6 folios, of 12th century date, which have been bound into Vitellius C.iii. [See also Bierbaumer, **539**.]

533 Chowdharay-Best, G. 'Notes on the Healing Properties of Saliva.' *Folklore* 86 (1975): 195–200.

The author asserts that the healing properties of saliva have been known since Pliny; the OE example cited (from *Lac*) conflates Storms 42 and 73.

534 Clarke, Basil. *Mental Disorder in Earlier Britain: Exploratory Studies.* Cardiff: Blackwell, 1975.

Ch. 2, 'Early Britain,' examines the Anglo-Saxon period with particular reference to hagiography, especially Guthlac's Life, 39–55. *Lb*2.27 is a rare example of theory of the humours touching on mental disorder. Discussion of 'Teutonic' ideas (46–9) identifies elf-shot as 'most related to psychiatric aetiology' (46). Of the recipes against elves, *Lb*3.41 is 'most closely related to overt mental disorder'; the conjunction of demons and elves here (and in *Lb*3.61), prepares the way for 'medieval versions of the possession hypothesis' (47). Epilepsy was partially distinguished (*Lb*2.59 merges it with 'the half-dead disease'), but there was 'no articulated system of elves which might be associated with different types of illness, in a connected prototheory of mental disorder' (47). One suggested reason for the absence of spirit-manipulators is that elves, like *moira* and luck, were 'a low-level concept for the passing explanation of the strange personal event about which little could be done' (48); ritual in some recipes suggests the role was discharged in etiolated form by ecclesiastical exorcists (i.e., capable of expelling, but not using, the spirit). Loose social bonds, evidenced by applications to healing places by individuals (not clans), 'led to sensible provisions under Anglo-Saxon law' (55) for the unbalanced and incapable (discussed 56–61, in ch. 3, 'Mental Disorder in its Setting').

535 Kylstra, H.E. 'Ale and Beer in Germanic.' *Iceland and the Medieval World: Studies in Honour of Ian Maxwell.* Ed. Gabriel Turville-Petre and John Stanley Martin. Melbourne: Organising Committee for Publishing a Volume in Honour of Professor Maxwell, 1975. 7–16.

In the glosses, *mulsum* is equated with both *beor* and *medu*, and in *Herb*, '*beor* translated *mulsum* wherever traceable in the Latin text' (9); Kylstra deduces that '*beer* in Anglo-Saxon England was a hydromel or aqueous mead, about the manner of fermentation, etc., of which, however, nothing whatsoever is known' (9). *Ealu*, on the other hand, 'was clearly much the same *ale* as that of a later age' (10); *alehoof* (*OED*) was probably the *hof* in *Lb* [Cockayne, **297**, 2: 34]. *Ale* is more frequently mentioned in *OE* than *beor*; disregarding *Herb*, where *beor* alone occurs, the ratio is approximately 8:1 (14, n. 8).

536 Stuart, Heather. 'Some Old English Medical Terms.' *Parergon* 13 (1975): 21–35.

An exhaustive study of two general terms, *lǽcecrǽft* and *lǽcedom*, as they occur in the major OE medical treatises. Stuart discusses in turn *Lb*1&2, *Lb*3, *Lac*, *Herb*, OE Dioscorides, *MedQuad*, *PD* and Cockayne's Flyleaf Leechdoms. She tables five significances of *lǽcecrǽft* and ten of *lǽcedom*, 32–3, and offers them for comparison with *BT* and *MED*. 'The main problem to emerge is the degree to which the Anglo-Saxon translators of the medical treatises were influenced by their sources in the choice and use of *lǽcecrǽft* and *lǽcedom*' (33). The conclusion summarizes points of interest: (1) 'Within each text the semantic relationship between the terms differs.' (2) 'The flexibility with which these terms are semantically extended to cover concepts similar to but not included by their dictionary definitions.' (3) 'Each term is normally used to cover a specific area of meaning: though not so precisely defined as modern medical terms, such usage may indicate a higher degree of precision among the Anglo-Saxon medical writers than has previously been thought' (33).

537 Fell, Christine E. 'Old English *beor.*' *Leeds Studies in English* 8 (1976 *for* 1975): 76–93.

Lb (especially Cockayne, **297**, 2: 298) and *Lac* (discussed 84–6) support the thesis that *beor* was not synonymous with *ealu*, and that it was sweeter and more rare (*beor* and *medu* are much less commonly recommended than *ealu*, and fewer qualifying adjectives are used for *beor* than for *ealu*; unlike *win* and *ealu*, beer requires no added sweetening). *Beor* must have been more potent; it is forbidden to sufferers from shingles [*Lb*1.36], and the warning that it should not be drunk by a pregnant woman [*Lb*?] casts light on ecclesiastical laws such as *Poenitentiale Ecgberti*, which imposes penalties on women who contrive an abortion *mid drynce oððe mid oðrum mislicum þingum*.

538 Müller, Gunter. 'Zur Heilkraft der Walküre: Sondersprachliches der Magie in kontinentalen und skandinavischen Zeugnissen.' *Frühmittelalterliche Studien* 10 (1976): 350–61.

Müller's study of valkyrie *Wundheilzauber* is based on the Edda (prose and poetic) and the Merseburg charms; philological comparisons with OE are few.

539 Bierbaumer, P. 'Zu J.V. Goughs Ausgabe einiger altenglischer Glossen.' *Anglia* 95 (1977): 115–21.

Corrections to Gough, **532**.

540 Page, R.I. 'Old English Liturgical Rubrics in Corpus Christi College, Cambridge, MS 422.' *Anglia* (1978): 149–58.

Prints some rubrics that Fehr, **471**, found unintelligible.

541 Nelson, Marie. 'Sound as Meaning in Old English Charms, Riddles, and Maxims.' *The Twenty-Seventh Annual Mountain Interstate Foreign Language Conference: Selected Proceedings*. Ed. E. Zayas-Bazán and M. Laurentino Suárez. Johnson City, TN: East Tennessee State U, 1977. 122–8.

Refers only to metrical charms [FC A.43.2, 4, 12].

542 Bierbaumer, Peter. *Der botanische Wortschatz des Altenglischen*. III. Teil. *Des botanische Wortschatz in altenglischen Glossen*. Grazer Beiträge zur englischen Philologie 3. Frankfurt am Main: Lang, 1979. 3 vols. 1975–9. [See also **374, 416**.]

The botanical vocabulary contained in the interlinear glosses and Latin–OE glossaries listed by FC (chs. C and D), is arranged alphabetically under some 950 headwords, 1–227. Introduction, v–xlvi, includes manuscript description in list of texts and editions, and outlines principles and procedures, as in Bierbaumer, **374, 416**. 'Main stress is laid on the interpretation of the degree of meaning-equivalence between lemma and gloss, especially in those cases where, in our opinion, the existing editions fail to give the necessary information' (337). A summary of contents (in English) details the most important results, 337–41. Appendices, 278–336, contain a matrix showing the distribution of the glosses in the major glossaries, table of relationships between the major glossaries (based on numerical data), index of the lemmata and Latin interpretamenta, and index of modern Latin botanical plant names and OE equivalents.

543 Voigts, Linda E. 'Anglo-Saxon Plant Remedies and the Anglo-Saxons.' *Isis* 70 (1979): 250–68.

Voigts examines the belief that Anglo-Saxon medical texts manifest an uncritical copying of classical texts with no understanding or thought to their practical use, and calls into question the view that the illustrations in Vitellius C.iii and Bodley 130 are inaccurate and stylized and include plants not

found north of the Alps. The survival of four OE translations of pseudo-Apuleius testify to its popularity. Changes to the original make it a more useful tool (e.g., the omission of directions inessential for obtaining the plant Betony; the addition of a simplified table of contents). *Lb* is 'the best instance of an Anglo-Saxon vernacular medical text that gives every indication of being intelligently compiled for practical use' (257). The compilation of herbal remedies and relatively sophisticated surgical procedures may indicate a long-standing tradition of vernacular medicine. Additions to Anglo-Saxon herbals appear to have been made by users, as do marginal notations to *Lb*, and the addition of recipes to V provides the strongest indications of a living remedy book. There is evidence (in the Boniface correspondence and other sources) that Mediterranean plants were available through trade and exchange between individuals and monastic houses. Temperatures in Northern Europe, 1000–1200, 'were at least $1°$ to $2°$ C higher' than now, and rainfall 'was 10 percent less' (262); it may have been possible to cultivate Mediterranean plants in England, since the Mediterranean peony is found naturalized at Steep Holm on the grounds of a 13th century priory, and was formerly found growing on the site of a Gloucestershire abbey. Monastic herb gardens (and the paucity of Anglo-Saxon records of these) are discussed at 263–6.

544 Brown, Jane Hetherington, and Linda Ehrsam Voigts. 'University of Glasgow, Hunter MS. U.3.2., f.210v.' *Old English Newsletter* 14.1 (1980): 12–13.

A 13th century inscription in the margin of a 12th century Psalter gives directions for the preparation and use of an amulet. The charm to be inscribed reads: 'usy+begete+agala+lentotan+domnes+cibu+glaes.' Brown and Voigts identify the charm as 'a corrupted form of OE,' and print normalized OE forms for all words but *cibu*, which they derive from Latin *cibus*.

545 Fell, C.E. 'A Note on Old English Wine Terminology: The Problem of *Cæren*.' *Nottingham Medieval Studies* 25 (1981): 1–12.

Examination of the terminology for three side-products of viticulture, *cæren*, *must*, and *eced* ('vinegar'), includes reference to *Lb* and *Lac* (Cockayne, **297**, 2: 46, 312, 24, 276; **298**, 3: 284) and the Omont Fragment (Schauman and Cameron, **330**, 293). Fell argues that these words probably entered OE as trade terms, but that their complete naturalization supports the view that viticulture was an aspect of the domestic economy. *BT*'s definitions of *must* ('must, new wine') and *cæren* ('a sort of wine, boiled wine') conceal the fact that these were 'primarily sweetening agents' whose 'value in an economy where sugar was unknown and the supply of honey unstable is self-evident' (9).

546 **Foley, John Miles.** '*Lǣcdom* and *Bajanje*: A Comparative Study of Old English and Serbo-Croatian Charms.' *Centrepoint: A Journal of Interdisciplinary Studies* (New York) 4.3 (1981): 33–40.

This comparison of some examples of verbal magic in OE and Serbo-Croatian charms, concentrating on the crucial importance of sound as the source of their power, refers briefly to three metrical charms ('Wiþ Dweorh' [FC A.43.3]; 'Wiþ feos nimunge' [FC A.43.9]; 'Æcerbot' [FC A.43.1]) and to Grendon B6 [*Lac*], an 'unintelligible charm,' in which the sounds are, nevertheless, 'ordered by a number of responsial or echoic functions' (34).

547 **Hill, Thomas D.** 'Invocation of the Trinity and the Tradition of the *Lorica* in Old English Poetry.' *Speculum* 56 (1981): 259–67.

Hill suggests that the convention of prayer to the Trinity in time of danger, attested by eight poems, including the 'Journey Charm' [FC A.43.11], has its origin in the early Irish *lorica* tradition. These poetic prayers represent a form of syncretism different from the forms found in *Beowulf* and OE charms, because the language and content of the poetic prayers is unequivocally Christian, 'but the folk belief which underlies this motif reflects the habits of thought of an archaic people accustomed to the power of the word and of the sacred name in incantation and magic' (267).

548 **Meaney, Audrey L.** *Anglo-Saxon Amulets and Curing Stones.* British Archeological Reports, British Series 96. Oxford: British Archeological Reports, 1981.

'Introduction,' 3–37, contains a section on Anglo-Saxon written charms using amulets (15–24), which discusses material in *Lac* and *Lb*. Ch. 2, 'Vegetable Amulets,' 38–65, includes discussion of herbal amulets in OE medical texts (38–59), and makes reference to *Herb*, the paintings in Vitellius C.iii, and *Lb*. Ch. 3, 'Mineral Amulets,' 66–105, includes a translation of *Lap*, (103–4), which follows Evans and Serjeantson, **284**. There is also a discussion of *gagates* in *Lb*2.64, which Meaney identifies (*contra* Cockayne, **297**, 2: 297, and Evans, **288**, 52) as jet, not agate (71–3), and the 'white stone' in *Lb*, which (*contra* Cockayne, **297**, 2: xxiv, and Wright, **294**, 18) she identifies as rock-crystal, not alabaster (92–3). [See also Meaney, **382**.] Ch. 4, 'Animal Amulets,' 106–47, has a subsection entitled 'Animal amulets in OE writings' (103–13), which discusses material in *MedQuad*, *Lb* and *Lac*. Sketches throughout the chapter are primarily from Cotton Vitellius C.iii. Ch. 5, 'Manufactured Amulets,' 148–71, includes discussion of the magical qualities of 'godwebbe,' a high quality cloth used for healing in *MedQuad*, *Lac* and *Lb* (187–8). Ch. 6, 'Found Amulets,' 192–238, analyses grave-goods, etc.

549 **Nelson, Marie.** 'An Old English Charm Against Nightmare.' *Germanic Notes* 13 (1982): 17–18.

Examination of the metrical charm 'Wið dweorh' [FC A.43.3].

550 Amies, Marion. 'The *Journey Charm*: A Lorica for Life's Journey.' *Neophilologus* 67 (1983): 448–62.

Amies argues that 'ambiguity of diction and the similarity of ideas expressed to those in homiletic and lorical traditions' (448) suggest that the Journey Charm may have been seen as a protection against spiritual dangers on the journey through life and the soul's journey after death. Parallels with the OE glosses to the Lorica of Gildas in *Lac* and in Cambridge, University Library, Ll.1.10 [FC C.22, 83] are examined at 451–3.

551 Cameron, M.L. 'The Sources of Medical Knowledge in Anglo-Saxon England.' *Anglo-Saxon England* 11 (1983): 135–55.

Cameron examines the chief surviving medical records of England prior to 1100 (OE and Latin) with a view to determining their sources, in order to show what books and records were available to the Anglo-Saxon physician and to compare him adequately with his continental contemporaries (only works that can be shown to have been composed or copied in England are admitted as evidence). He finds evidence for knowledge of the following: 'Oribasius, the *Synopsis* and *Euporistes* in the "new" translation; Vindicianus, *Epistula ad Pentadium Nepotem* and *Epitome Altera*; Theodorus Priscianus and pseudo-Theodore; pseudo-Apuleius, the Herbarium complex; Marcellus, *De Medicamentis*; Cassius Felix, *De Medicina*; Alexander of Tralles, the *Latin Alexander*, containing the fragments of Philumenus and Philagrius of Epirus; *Passionarius Galeni* (Gariopontus); "Petrocellus"; and collections similar to those in Sloane 475 and St Gallen 751, containing recipes and various short tracts and epistles. The *Aurelius de acutis Passionibus* and *Esculapius de chronicis Passionibus* may have been used too, but, because of the free borrowing from them by the *Passionarius Galeni*, it is difficult to be certain' (151–2). He concludes: 'at each period examined, English physicians were using the same texts as were available elsewhere in Europe. If their medicine was debased and superstition-ridden, it was no more so than that of other countries and in most respects was borrowed directly from the Classical Greek and Latin background which was later to be the source of the Salernitan School.... If English medicine had any national character, it was that perhaps less emphasis was placed on bleeding and more on diet and medicines, though even in that it was seldom acting to the patient's advantage' (152). Appendix, 153–5, tables medical items in Oxford, St John's College 17 and Cambridge, University Library Gg.5.35. [Specific discussion of *Lb* and *Herb*, 145–50; refers to Byrhtferth and *J*, 150–1.]

552 Vaughan-Sterling, Judith A. 'Anglo-Saxon *Metrical Charms*: Poetry as Ritual.' *JEGP* 82 (1983): 186–200.

The author argues that the metrical charms should be viewed in close relation to Anglo-Saxon poems, because they are set off from everyday speech by similar techniques and share certain cultural factors. Manuscript pointing in *Lac* (Storms 2) is evidence that the Anglo-Saxons took the same view, and the fact that, in CCCC 41, the same scribe recorded charms and the poetic *SS* as marginalia [FC A.43.8–11] suggests that 'this scribe may have seen some direct affinity between the poetry and the ritual texts' (188).

553 **Horsley, G.H.R., and E.R. Waterhouse.** 'The Greek *nomen sacrum* XP- in Some Latin and Old English Manuscripts.' *Scriptorium* 38 (1984): 211–30.

'The hypothesis that the combination XP̄S is a symbol-equivalent for *Christus* in Latin texts, unrecognized as Greek, receives considerable support from two observations, one relating to Latin MSS, the other to OE glosses in Latin MSS' (215). Examination of OE glosses, 218–27; no reference to OE magico-medical texts.

554 **Meaney, Audrey L.** 'Ælfric's Use of his Sources in his Homily on Auguries.' *English Studies* 66 (1985): 477–95.

From a study of Ælfric's handling of his sources, Meaney concludes (as in Meaney, **392**) that 'we must accept what he has to say about idolatrous practices as referring to things current in the society he knew' (495). For *De Auguriis*, line 103a (ed. Skeat), *oððe on brywlæce*, which has no known source, Meaney refers to a charm remedy for a spoiled brew in *Lb*1.67; 'brewing is traditionally regarded as vulnerable to witchcraft' (483).

555 **Nelson, Marie.** 'A Woman's Charm.' *Studia Neophilologica* 57 (1985): 3–8.

Nelson argues that the metrical charm 'For delayed birth' [FC A.43.6] serves the purpose of preparing its speaker for the experience of giving birth.

556 **Riddle, John M.** *Dioscorides on Pharmacy and Medicine.* Austin: Texas UP, 1985.

A study of *De Materia Medica.* Riddle examines the life of Dioscorides and the contemporary state of the medical arts, and the two organizational schemes of the work (plants and medical usages), and postulates that the animal and mineral drugs have the same theoretical affinities as did his plant products. Ch. 5, 'Done and Undone,' 168–218, on the Greco-Roman acceptance of Dioscorides, discusses the tradition of manuscript illustration up to the 6th century. The influence of Dioscorides on later centuries is the subject of a projected second volume (xx).

557 **Riddle, John M.** 'Ancient and Medieval Chemotherapy for Cancer.' *Isis* 76 (1985): 319–30.

Riddle argues that examination of pharmaceutical and medical authorities of the Graeco-Roman, classical Islamic and medieval periods reveals that many of the natural substances they recommend contain compounds discovered in the 1960s and 70s which are currently utilized in cancer treatments; he suggests that modern scientists might employ the history of a drug as the

starting point for conducting animal and clinical tests: 'For too long we
have believed that the past was filled more with superstition and stupidities
than with experienced judgements about medicine' (330). Among Riddle's
examples is birthwort (328), recommended for nasal carcinoma by pseudo-
Apuleius, and containing aristolochic acid, which, in 1969, was found to
have antitumoral qualities; no OE reference.

558 Weston, L.M.C. 'The Language of Magic in Two Old English Metrical
Charms.' *Neuphilologische Mitteilungen* 86 (1985): 176–86.

An analysis of the interaction of poetic form and magical force in 'Wið
Færstice' [FC A.43.4] and the 'Nine Herbs Charm' [FC A.43.2].

559 Deegan, Marilyn. 'Pregnancy and Childbirth in the Anglo-Saxon Med-
ical Texts: A Preliminary Survey.' *Medicine in Early Medieval England*.
Ed. Marilyn Deegan and D.G. Scragg. Manchester: Manchester Centre for
Anglo-Saxon Studies, 1987. 17–26.

Even though there is archeological evidence that childbirth was hazardous,
relatively little OE material deals with obstetrics and gynaecology: 'While
it fell to women to minister to each other in pregnancy and childbirth, it
was men, and probably celibate monks at that, who had control over the
production of texts' (18). 'It is still possible to put together a picture of the
problems encountered by Anglo-Saxon women in the course of their repro-
ductive life, and of the medical and spiritual means available to alleviate
them' (24). Extant medical writings cover most of the categories listed in
the index to the missing *Lb*2.60. Deegan offers the following examples, di-
agnosing the complaint, analysing the active principles of the constituents
of the remedy, and assessing their physiological effects: herbal remedies
(*Herb* 60.1, 104.2, 143.2, *Lb*3.38); an animal product remedy (*MedQuad*,
4.1); a charm (*Lac* 171); prognostications of the sex of the unborn child [FC
B.23.3.3], which evinces the still current but anatomically unfounded belief
that the sex of a child can be determined from whether or not the woman is
carrying the foetus high; 'On the Human Foetus' [FC B.21.4], which shows
that 'the Anglo-Saxons, like the classical medical writers before them, attempted to understand the creation of life in a schematic and philosophical
way' (24).

560 Elsakkers, Marianne. 'The Beekeeper's Magic: Taking a Closer Look at
the Old Germanic Bee Charms.' *Mankind Quarterly* 27 (1987): 447–61.

Elsakkers analyses only the Lorscher Bienensegen and the OE metrical
charm [FC A.43.8]; she relates them to the practices of beekeeping, and
argues that they have so many characteristics of oral poetry that they must
have belonged originally to an oral tradition.

561 Jolly, Karen Louise. 'Anglo-Saxon Charms in the Context of Popular
Religion.' *DAI* 48 (1988): 2426A. [Diss. U of California, Santa Barbara,
1987. Co-Chairs: C. Warren Hollister; Jeffrey B. Russell.]

Dissertation not sighted. According to *DAI*, Jolly adopts 'a multi-discip-linary, yet essentially historical approach,' and draws upon homilies, laws, canons, medical manuscripts, Domesday Book, and archaeological and archi-tectural remains. The early chapters are concerned with definitional prob-lems, and ch. 3 investigates the social context in which popular Christian practices developed; Jolly, **395**, appears to represent a summary of the re-maining chapters.

562 **Rubin, Stanley.** 'The Anglo-Saxon Physician.' *Medicine in Early Medieval England*. Ed. Marilyn Deegan and D.G. Scragg. Manchester: Manchester Centre for Anglo-Saxon Studies, 1987. 7–15.

To a greater extent than his continental counterpart, the Anglo-Saxon physi-cian was 'not regarded as a person with any particular claim to be noticed and recorded' (7), and 'did not acquire the dignity afforded to contemporary Welsh and Irish healers' (9). Rubin distinguishes lay and monastic practi-tioners, arguing from *Lb* ('leeches *teach*') that education, chiefly consisting of uncritical memorization of texts, was available to the lay leech; marginal additions to remedies show a modicum of enterprise. Legal compensation for injuries confirms that there was no perceived shortage of medical atten-tion; midwives and 'wise-women,' village healers and hermits, must have been among the many unnamed practitioners. The emerging professionals (OE *'leechfee'*) were 'given a fairly good press' (10); 12th century criticisms suggest that formation of professional lay bodies was accompanied by in-creased interest in money and a concomitant decline in ethics (although Anglo-Saxon patients may have been more fatalistic about illness). The monastery physician may in many cases have been no more than a nurse, as there are records of lay physicians being called in; 'monasteries were begin-ning to train their own physicians' from the 11th century on (11). Evidence of empirical knowledge and skill, chiefly shown in surgical practices in *Lb*, 'should not be exaggerated' (14). Many herbs were unobtainable; the need for varying treatment as a disease progressed is unrecognized; despite the emergence of primitive notions of internal physiology in the 11th century, the leech 'had little appreciation of internal disease' (13). But 'the Anglo-Saxon physician and his immediate successors did try to alleviate the sickness and distress from which their patients suffered and carried out their work with at least some regard to the ethics and morality of their calling' (15).

563 **Norri, Juhani.** 'Notes on the Study of English Medical Vocabulary from the Historical Point of View.' *Neophilologica Fennica*. Ed. Leena Kahlas-Tarkka. Mémoires de la Société Néophilogique de Helsinki 45. Helsinki: Société Néophilogique, 1987. 335–50.

The author offers a general indication of problems encountered in creating a systematic approach to the study of early medical vocabulary. Norri raises the question of the extent to which vernacular translations of Latin medi-cal literature constitute a 'special' language (335–8), and dilates upon the importance of extra-linguistic factors in the interpretation of terms (338–43); in practice, the effect of theories of disease (e.g., the doctrine of the humours) cannot be distinguished from that of popular beliefs (e.g., in elf-shot). Two matters connected with linguistic analysis of the material are considered: delimitation of the scope of the terms to be inventoried (their categorization and grammatical structure); the usefulness of parallel recipe collections in the interpretation of a corrupt text. There is no specific discussion of OE material: 'The following questions are worth studying: the number of Anglo-Saxon terms as compared to loan-words, differences in the distribution of native and borrowed words (are certain concepts more often expressed by Anglo-Saxon terms than by loan-words?), wordpairs (the Anglo-Saxon word and the loan-word occurring side by side), the occurrence of synonymy and polysemy, general expressions versus specific expressions' (347).

564 Bately, Janet M. 'Old English Prose before and during the Reign of Alfred.' *Anglo-Saxon England* 17 (1988): 93–138.

In recent years, scholars have sought to extend the list of works originally composed in Mercian (or Anglian) dialect before 900, and, in some cases, have dated works 'before Alfred.' A high proportion of these works are medical (discussed 98–103). De Vriend's case for the 8th century origins of *Herb* and *MedQuad* (**401**) rests on the weight value of the *penig*; Bately argues (citing a private communication from Grierson) that the evidence will not bear the interpretation de Vriend places on it. Orthographical evidence appears to indicate an early or possibly pre-10th century date of composition for some of the medical remedies in *Lac*, *Lb*, the Nowell transcript [FC B.21.2.3], and the Omont Fragment (e.g., Meaney, **393**, Schauman and Cameron, **330**), but 'any attempt to use other types of linguistic evidence, particularly that of vocabulary, to determine the date—and indeed the dialect—of medical material is necessarily bound up with a consideration of other allegedly "Mercian" or "Anglian" texts' (103). Bately is not convinced that 'all the so-called Mercian words must originally have been peculiar to the territory called Mercia, or even to territory controlled by Mercians. They could have been current also in a large area of Wessex and used by writers of West Saxon origin' (109). She concludes that, by the 890s, 'there was already a tradition of prose writing with well-developed mannerisms, co-existing with the plainer and more workman-like style of the *Chronicle* and laws' (138), but that it was not the exclusive property of Mercia.

565 Cameron, M.L. 'Anglo-Saxon Medicine and Magic.' *Anglo-Saxon England* 17 (1988): 191–215.

Cameron surveys approaches to Anglo-Saxon medical literature, and argues that 'editors and commentators have been prone to assume the non-rationality of any remedy for which they could adduce a magic feature, on

the premise that Anglo-Saxon medicine was primarily non-rational' (195).
He examines a number of the remedies classified as magical by Storms, **325**,
in order to demonstrate that if one looks for rationality it may be found
more often than would once have been admitted. The majority of Anglo-
Saxon remedies use plant material and many of the plants supplying drugs
today were used in ancient times; some must have had a beneficial effect.
Examples of plant and other remedies which may be rationally explained
are discussed at 195–210 (most examples are drawn from *Lb*; some from *Lac*
and *Herb*). Cameron does not deny that magic remedies were used, particularly to treat intractable ailments that do not today readily yield to rational
procedure. The rituals of the modern medical profession cater to our belief
in a 'scientific' world. Given that the world was 'more incomprehensible to
the medieval mind ... there was a legitimate place in medicine for what
we call magic' (215). Cameron endorses the 'kindly advice' of Payne, **449**,
38–9, that 'the only way to understand these old writers is to try to put
ourselves as far as possible in their place.'

565A Cameron, M.L. 'On *Þeor* and *Þeoradl.*' *Anglia* 106 (1988): 124–9.

Cameron advances 'Wiþ þeoradle on eagum þe mon gefigo hæt on læden
hatte cimosis' [*Lb*1.2.23] as a clue to the meaning of *þeor*. He argues that
'*gefigo* is the same as *ficitas* which is related to *trachoma*, a roughness of
the inside of the eyelid,' and that 'a comparison of recipes from different
sources [Cassius Felix, *Liber Teropetici* and Marcellus] shows that similar
ingredients were used to treat this roughness' (125). From a study of the
other OE remedies, Cameron concludes that *þeor* and *þeoradl* 'were terms
used to describe a dry roughness externally of epithelial tissues, particularly
of the skin, such as might result from a vitamin deficiency or a reaction to
an allergen and, by extension, a similar dryness and roughness of internal
tissues' (129). Cockayne thus appears to have been right in translating *þeor*
as 'the dry disease.'

566 Deegan, Marilyn, and Stanley Rubin. 'Written in Bones: Palaeopathology and Anglo-Saxon Remedies.' *Archaeology Today* 9 (1988): 40–5.

The authors' intention is to suggest that the combination of palaeopathological and literary evidence can extend knowledge of Anglo-Saxon health
and medical practices. The 13 accompanying illustrations include specimens of untreated fractures, although treatments are recorded in OE texts.
Discussion of head injuries refers to *Lb*; methods of trepanning, not mentioned in OE medical texts, but successfully practised, are described. The
three commonest dental conditions were periodontal disease, abscesses and
caries (the latter less rife than in Modern Britain, possibly because beet
and cane sugars were absent); some cures for caries are described. Bags of
teeth suspended from the necks of some skeletons found in one cemetery
may suggest that the wearers were tribal dentists, but it is more probable
(in view of compensation for lost teeth in the Laws of Alfred) that canine

teeth had magical significance. *PD*'s 'perceptive and thoughtful' chapter on teeth is contrasted with a charm for toothache in *Lac*. Osteoarthritis, one of the commonest diseases found in Anglo-Saxon skeletons, is attributed to hard physical work and poor roadways. Joint pains, frequently mentioned in the literature, probably resulted from arthritis; some cures for this and for synovitis are enumerated. [Unreferenced citations].

567 Kitson, Peter. 'Two Old English Plant-Names and Related Matters.' *English Studies* 69 (1988): 97–112.

Kitson concludes that *cex*, in Ashmole 1431, f. 21v [FC C.36] is an OE plant name, adopted by Anglo-Saxons from Cornish in the 11th century, and derived ultimately from classical Latin *cicuta*, which denoted hemlock, ground elder, masterwort and wild angelica, and had the secondary sense of the hollow stems of these umbellifers and things made from them. This word was borrowed into Brittonic in connection with the medical use of ground elder and masterwort; whatever the form in which it was borrowed (probably *cicita/cicitum*), it was reshaped by analogy with the etymon of Welsh *ceg* 'mouth, gullet.' Concerning *æðelferðingwyrt*, Kitson concludes that Cockayne's implicit identification with stitchwort still holds (**298**, 3: 312; **297**, 2: 369), and that Bierbaumer was right to return to it in his second thoughts (**416**, 7; **542**, 5; cf. **374**, 14.)

568 Davies, Anthony. 'Witches in Anglo-Saxon History: Five Case Histories.' *Superstition and Popular Medicine in Anglo-Saxon England*. Ed. D.G. Scragg. Manchester: Manchester Centre for Anglo-Saxon Studies, 1989. 41–56.

Anglo-Saxon witches described by Norman historians are shown to have little in common with the witch of Ailsworth, whose death is recorded in a 948 charter. [No reference to OE magico-medical literature.]

569 Hill, Arnoldus. 'Old English *līcþrōwere* "a leper" and Old Norse *líkþrá* "leprosy."' *Essays on English Language in Honour of Bertil Sundby*. Ed. Leiv Egil Breivik et al. Oslo, 1989. 131–44.

Not sighted. Listed *Anglo-Saxon England* 19, Bibliography for 1989, 252.

570 Kitson, Peter. 'From Eastern Learning to Western Folklore: The Transmission of some Medico-magical Ideas.' *Superstition and Popular Medicine in Anglo-Saxon England*. Ed. D.G. Scragg. Manchester: Manchester Centre for Anglo-Saxon Studies, 1989. 57–71.

Kitson argues that seven of the eight virtues attributed to *gagates* in *Lb*2.66 (i.e., jet, the only gemstone produced in early Britain) derived from a conflation of jet and agate entries in the Latin Damigeron. Attribution of power against lightning, ascribed in classical texts only to *ceraunius* or *ceraunia* 'thunder stone,' and identified with flints and belemnites in Germanic folklore, must rest on 'equation of jet with varieties of fossil including thunderstones native to Anglo-Saxon England.' OE characteristically classifies stones by colour; both jet and ammonites (likewise considered efficacious against snakes) would have been 'black stones from Whitby,' and, as they vary in shape, 'it would have been easy to include with them the more widely-occurring belemnites' (64). Further, whetstones such as the Sutton Hoo sceptre, similar in size and shape to two Low German staves of jet, were associated with lightning and thunder. *Lb*2.66 (probably composed by an Englishman, in either Latin or OE) thus represents 'fusion of Latin-derived ultimately eastern learning with traditional native lore typical in the literature and culture of the Anglo-Saxons' (65). In *Lb*2.55.5, 'the wine, myrrh and frankincense surely bespeak ultimate foreign influence for all that the "elf" may imply assimilation to native tradition' (61); interpretation of *seið* as 'magically induced enfeeblement' links this prescription of jet more closely to the fourth virtue attributed to it in *Lb*2.66 (68, n. 28).

571 Manchester, Keith, and Charlotte Roberts. 'The Palaeopathology of Leprosy in Britain: A Review.' *World Archaeology* 21 (1989): 265–72.

Leprosy, known from 600 BC in India, had arrived in Britain by the 5th century AD; the afflicted person whose skeleton is found in a Romano-British cemetery in Dorset probably came from 'the Mediterranean littoral where, it is known, leprosy existed from earlier times. There is not, as yet, evidence of leprosy from such early times in the remainder of western Europe' (266). It became a 'disease of significant prevalence and social importance' in the post-Norman Conquest era. It was rare in Anglo-Saxon Britain; the evidence 'is solely palaeopathological.... There is, as yet, no irrefutable literary or artform evidence from this period' (267). 'Close correlation exists between the small numbers of leprous skeletons identified prior to the Norman Conquest and the small number of leprosy hospitals' (268). Later medieval treatment and diagnosis are examined.

572 McIntosh, Angus. 'English Compounds Containing OE -*lāc*, -*lǣcan*, ON -*leik* and Some Related Matters.' *Essays on English Language in Honour of Bertil Sundby.* Ed. Leiv Egil Breivik et al. Oslo, 1989. 221–36.

Not sighted. Listed *Anglo-Saxon England* 19, Bibliography for 1989, 253.

573 Meaney, Audrey L. 'Women, Witchcraft and Magic in Anglo-Saxon England.' *Superstition and Popular Medicine in Anglo-Saxon England.* Ed. D.G. Scragg. Manchester: Manchester Centre for Anglo-Saxon Studies, 1989. 9–40.

Meaney assesses archaeological and documentary evidence connecting Anglo-Saxon women with supernatural *practices* (only the statement that a girl born on the fifth day of the moon will be *yfeldæda and wyrtgælstre* [FC B.23.3.3] suggests that a woman could become a witch involuntarily, and even this implies deliberate action); Meaney finds neither covens nor diabolic compacts, only 'woman in her basic feminine roles' (29) attempting to manipulate her environment in ecclesiastically unacceptable ways, and she attributes the greater frequency with which women were accused of working magic to the fact that, in the pagan past, they had had 'a more responsible position within both sacred and secular society' (30). Re-examination of the meanings of *wælcyrige, burgrune, leodrune, hel(le)rune, hægtesse,* and *wicce,* is followed by consideration of penitentials, glosses and homilies; charms confirming a connection between women and white magic are described (23–7): *Herb* 104.2 (also in *Lb*3.37); the Sator formula; Storms 45; Storms 10 [*Lac*]; *MedQuad* 2; *Lac* 152. Two charms 'have been interpreted as showing that female witches were feared for more sinister reasons' (26), but *Viþ wif gemædlan* [*Lb*3.57] might refer to 'malicious gossip, backbiting' (cf. the power of an eloquent woman to negate a charm for making land fruitful [FC A.43.8]), and *wiþ þam mannum þe deofol midhæmð* [*Lb*3.61] need not have been a defence against females only.

574 Parker, S.J. 'Skulls, Symbols and Surgery: A Review of the Evidence for Trepanation in Anglo-Saxon England and a Consideration of the Motives behind the Practice.' *Superstition and Popular Medicine in Anglo-Saxon England.* Ed. D.G. Scragg. Manchester: Manchester Centre for Anglo-Saxon Studies, 1989. 73–84.

Parker tables 30 cases of trepanation in Britain, including 13 Anglo-Saxon, describes techniques for carrying out this hazardous operation and difficulties of diagnosis, and argues that 'only in the widest context of both Magic and Medicine can we hope to achieve a plausible explanation of the incidence of trepanation in Anglo-Saxon England.' It 'could be seen as a powerful aid to exorcism because it removes the physical barrier of the cranium allowing the [disease] spirit an easy exit from the body' (83). [No reference to OE magico-medical literature.]

575 Flint, Valerie I.J. *The Rise of Magic in Early Medieval Europe.* Princeton: Princeton UP, 1991.

OE (and Anglo-Latin) writings, touched upon throughout the analysis of Christian condemnation and encouragement of magic in Part II, 'The Magic of the Heavens,' 87–201, and Part III, 'The Magic of the Earth,' 203–330, receive extended consideration under 'Christian Medical Magic,' 301–30. Late 10th and 11th century English codices (e.g., *Lac, Lb,* Titus D.xxvi and xxvii, Caligula A.xv, Vitellius C.iii, Tiberius A.iii, Vitellius E.xviii, and CCCC 41) are especially rich in instances of Christian adaptations of healing magic, reflecting the resurgence of non-Christian practices (312–20); monastic communities, having assumed significant pastoral responsibilities, were 'determined to confront the problem ... and the more closely they could emulate the methods of the opposition, of course, the better' (325). Examples discussed include charms and incantations in *Lac* [10, 11]; *Lb*2.65; use of names of the Seven Sleepers and verses from John's Gospel, which appear in several codices, including Titus D.xxvi and xxvii ('excellent examples of the kind of little pocket book a Christian pastor and healer might have about him,' 314). 'Neutral' practices (neither Christian nor non-Christian), include tables of (un)lucky days (322–3); Caligula A.xv (Cockayne, **298**, 3: 155) 'shows that its writer was both aware of the presence of witchcraft and conscious of how close the two forms of activity had drawn' (323). English sources are rich in thunder prognostics (191–2), and belief in the power of the moon, one of the reasons for encouragement of the study of astrology, is particularly marked (133–5); the fact that collections of medical and other prognostics based on the moon, such as Tiberius A.iii, f. 38r, were copied in monastic scriptoria, yet condemned in ecclesiastical councils, is 'evidence of a greater willingness at a local level than at a central one to make compromises with older beliefs' (135). Part I, 'Introduction,' includes consideration of early medieval sources, 36–58; Part IV, 'The Magus,' 331–92.

INDEX OF AUTHORS OF STUDIES ANNOTATED

References are to entry numbers.

SUBJECT INDEX TO ANNOTATIONS

References (in bold) are to entry numbers.